The Middle Kingdom

This work by S. Wells Williams is a complete look at the Chinese Empire during the mid-nineteenth century. Subjects include the divisions of the Empire, geographical descriptions, religion and art, literature, the second war between Great Britain and China and social life among the Chinese.

The Kegan Paul China Library

Wanderings in China
Robert Fortune

Village Life in China
Arthur H. Smith

China
Mortimer Menpes and Henry Arthur Blake

Social Life of the Chinese
Justus Doolittle

Rulers of China
A. C. Moule

Beyond the Golden Lotus
Ko Lien Hua Ying

Jade
Berthold Laufer

The Golden Peaches of Samarkand
Edward H. Schafer

Old Buddha
Der Ling

Sun Tzu on the Art of War
Lionel Giles

Things Chinese
J. Ball Dyer

Two Years in the Forbidden City
Der Ling

The Middle Kingdom, Vol. 1 & 2
S. Wells Williams

SIGNING OF THE TREATY OF PEKING BY LORD ELGIN AND PRINCE KUNG.

FROM A CHINESE PAINTING.

THE MIDDLE KINGDOM

A SURVEY OF THE GEOGRAPHY, GOVERNMENT, LITERATURE, SOCIAL LIFE, ARTS AND HISTORY OF THE CHINESE EMPIRE AND ITS INHABITANTS

VOLUME II

BY

S. WELLS WILLIAMS

Routledge
Taylor & Francis Group
LONDON AND NEW YORK

First published 2005 by Kegan Paul Limited

Published 2019 by Routledge
2 Park Square, Milton Park, Abingdon, Oxon OX14 4RN
52 Vanderbilt Avenue, New York, NY 10017

Routledge is an imprint of the Taylor & Francis Group, an informa business

British Library Cataloguing in Publication Data

Library of Congress Cataloging-in-Publication Data
Applied for.

ISBN 13: 978-0-415-49927-9 (hbk) (VolumeII)

CONTENTS OF VOLUME II.

CHAPTER XV.

CHAPTER XVI.

CHAPTER XXIII.

CHAPTER XXIV.

LIST OF ILLUSTRATIONS IN VOLUME II.

THE

MIDDLE KINGDOM.

CHAPTER XV.

INDUSTRIAL ARTS OF THE CHINESE.

THE superiority of the Chinese over their immediate neighbors in the enjoyments of life and in the degree of security for which individuals can look under the protection of law have their bases chiefly in the industry of the people. Agriculture holds the first place among the branches of labor, and the honors paid to it by the annual ploughing ceremony are given from a deep sense of its importance to the public welfare; not alone to provide a regular supply of food and labor for the population, but also to meet the wants of government by moderate taxes, and long experience of the greater ease of governing an agricultural than a mercantile or warlike community. Notwithstanding the encouragement given to tillage, many tracts of land still lie waste, some of it the most fertile in the country; partly because the people have not the skill and capital to drain and render it productive, partly because they have not sufficient prospect of remuneration to encourage them to make the necessary outlay, and sometimes from the outrages of local banditti making it unsafe to live in secluded districts.

Landed property is held in clans or families as much as possible, and is not entailed, nor are overgrown estates frequent. The land is all held directly from the crown, no allodial property being acknowledged; if mesne lords existed in feudal times they are now unknown. The conditions of common tenure are the payment of an annual tax, the fee for alienation, with a money composition for personal service to the government, a charge generally incorporated into the direct tax as a kind of scutage. The proprietors of land record their names in the district and take out a *hung ki*, or 'red deed,' which secures them in possession as long as the ground tax is paid. This sum varies according to the fertility, location, and use of the land, from $1.50 per acre for the best, down to twenty or thirty cents for unproductive or hilly fields. As the exactions for alienation or sale of lands are high, amounting to as much as one-third of the sale price sometimes, the people accept white deeds from each other as proofs of ownership and responsibility for taxes. As many as twenty or thirty such deeds of sale occasionally accompany the original *hung ki*, without which they are suspicious if not valueless. In order to keep the knowledge of the alienations of land in government offices, so that the taxes can be assured, it is customary to furnish a *ki-wei*, or 'deed-end,' containing a note of the terms of sale and amount of tax liable on the property. There is no other proof of ownership required; and the simplicity and efficiency of this mode of transfer offer a striking contrast to the cumbrous rules enforced in western kingdoms. Revised codes of land laws are issued by the provincial authorities when necessary, as was done in 1846 at Canton.[1]

The paternal estate and houses thereon descend to the eldest son, but his brothers can remain upon it with their families, and devise their portion *in perpetuo* to their children, or an amicable composition can be made; daughters never inherit, nor can an adopted son of another clan succeed. A mortgagee must enter into possession of the property and make himself responsible for the payment of the taxes; unless explicitly stated, the land can be redeemed any time within thirty years on payment of the original sum. Sections XC. to C. of the Code contain the laws relating to this subject, some of which bear a resemblance to those established among the Hebrews, and intended to secure a similar result of retaining the land in the same clan or tribe.

---

[1] T. T. Meadows in *N. C. Br. R. A. S. Transactions*, Hongkong, 1848, Vol. I.

The enclosure of recent alluvial deposits cannot be made without the cognizance of the authorities, but the terms are not onerous; for waste hillsides and poor spots ample time is allowed for a return of the capital expended in reclaiming them before assessment is made.

The Chinese are rather gardeners than farmers, if regard be had to the small size of their grounds. They are ignorant, too, of many of those operations whereby soils naturally unfruitful are made fertile and the natural fertility sustained at the cheapest rate by proper manuring and rotation of crops; but they make up for the disadvantages of poor implements by hard work. Their agricultural utensils are few and simple, and are probably now made similar to those used centuries ago. The broad hoe is used in soft land more than any other tool; the weight of its large wooden blade, which is edged with iron, adds impetus to the blow. Spades, rakes, and mattocks are employed in kitchen gardening, and the plough and harrow in rice cultivation. The plough is made of wood, except the iron-edged share, which lies flat and penetrates the soil about five inches. The whole implement is so simple and rude that one would think the inventor of it was a laborer, who, tired of the toil of spading, called the ox to his aid and tied his shovel to a rail;—fastening the animal at one end and guiding the other, he was so pleased with the relief that he never thought of improving it much further than to sharpen the spade to a coulter and bend the rail to a beam and handle. The harrow is a heavy stick armed with a single row of stout wooden teeth, and furnished with a framework to guide it; or a triangular machine, with rows of iron teeth, on which the driver rides to sink it in the ooze.

The buffalo is used in rice cultivation, and the ox and ass in dry ploughing; horses, mules, cows, and goats likewise render service to the farmer in various ways, and are often yoked in most ludicrous combinations. The team which Nieuhoff depicts of a man driving his wife and his ass yoked to the same plough is too bad for China often to present, though it has been so frequently repeated and used to point a comparison that one almost expects on landing to see half the women in the harness. It may be doubted, however, if this country can vie with some portions of Germany and Holland in the matter of mongrel teams employed on farms.

The arrangements of farriers' shops in China are very similar to those of European countries, saving that the tools are of the simplest character. The manner of trussing up the poor beast

Manner of Shoeing Horses.

which is to be shod would seem, however, an unnecessary exercise of caution in the case of a majority of the over-worked horses and mules. The animal is fastened to a frame and lifted almost entirely off the ground, while a rope twisted about his nose and tightened at will with a turn-stick controls the least attempt at unruliness. Iron shoes are employed in the north; in the south, where horses are little used, they are usually left unshod, though the fore feet are often covered with leather shoes which fit the hoof.

An early rain is necessary to the preparation of rice-fields, except where water can be turned upon them. The grain is first soaked, and when it begins to swell is sown very thickly in a small plat containing liquid manure. When about six inches high the shoots are planted into the fields, which, from being an unsightly marsh, are in a few days transformed to fields clothed with living green. Holding the seedlings in one hand, the laborer wades through the mud, at every step sticking into it five or six sprouts, which take root without further care; six men can transplant two acres a day, one or two of whom are engaged in supplying the others with shoots. The amount of grain required to sow a Chinese *mao* in this way is thirty-seven and one-half catties, or three hundred and thirty pounds—about two and one-half bushels to an English acre. The produce is on an average tenfold. Rent of land is usually paid according to the amount of the crop, the landlord paying the taxes and the tenant stocking the farm; leases are for three, four, or seven years; the terms vary according to the position and goodness of the soil.[1]

Grain is not sown broadcast, and this facilitates hoeing and weeding the fields as they require. Two crops are planted, one of which ripens after the other; maize and pulse, millet and sesamum, or sorghum and squash are thus grown together. The plough is an efficient tool in soft soil, but a wide hoe, the blade set almost at a right angle, is the common implement in the north. Barrow describes a drill-plough in common use in the north which remarkably economizes time and seed. "It consisted of two parallel poles of wood shod at the lower extremity

---

[1] The amount of tribute rice sent to Peking from

Kiangsu Province	is.......696,000	tons of	640 catties,	or	974,400	peculs
Chehkiang	"	445,000	"	"	"	633,000	"
Kiangsí	"	80,000	"	"	"	112,000	"
Hupeh	"	50,000	"	"	"	70,000	"
						1,789,400	"
Of this the Chinese Company carried in 1875 to Tientsin..						626,900	"
Went by junks						1,162,500	"

with iron to open the furrows; these poles were placed upon wheels; a small hopper was attached to each pole to drop the seeds into the furrow, which were covered with earth by a transverse piece of wood fixed behind, that just swept the face of the ground."[1]

The extent to which terrace cultivation has been described as common is a good instance of the way in which erroneous impressions concerning China obtain currency from accounts not exactly incorrect, perhaps, but made to convey wrong notions by the mode of their description. The hills are terraced chiefly for rice cultivation or to retain soil which would otherwise be washed away; and this restricts their gradation, generally speaking, to the southern and eastern provinces. Most of the hills in Kwangtung and Fuhkien are unfit for the plough except near their bases, while in the north it is unnecessary to go to great expense in terracing for a crop of cotton, wheat, or millet. Much labor has been expended in terracing, and many hillsides otherwise useless are thus rendered productive; but this does not mean that every hill is cut into plats, nor that the entire face of the country is one vast garden. Terracing was probably a more important feature of agriculture in Palestine in former days than it is in China. The natural terraces of the loess districts, and their extraordinary convenience as well as fertility, have already been noticed in a former chapter. These, it should however be remembered, do not occur south of the Yangtsz' River.

The ingenuity of the farmer is well exhibited in the various modes he employs to insure a supply of water for his rice. In some places pools are made in level fields as reservoirs of rain, from which the water is lifted as occasion requires by well-sweeps. It is also expeditiously raised by two men holding a pail between them by ropes, and with a swinging motion rapidly dipping the water out of the tank into little furrows. A favorite plan is to use a natural brooklet and conduct it from one plat to another till it has irrigated the whole hillside. It is where such water privileges offer that the terrace cultivation is best

---

[1] *Travels in China*, London, 1804.

developed, especially in the neighborhood of large cities, where the demand for provisions promises the cultivator a sure reward for his labor. The appearance of the slopes thus graduated into small ledges is beautiful; each plat is divided by a bank serving the triple purpose of fence, path, and dyke, and near which the rills glide with refreshing lapse, turning whithersoever the master willeth. This primitive method of upland irrigation is carried out far more perfectly in China than in Switzerland, where it is better known to the generality of travellers. Water is not often wasted upon grass meadows in the former country. The food these marshy plats furnish to insects, mollusks, snakes, and birds is surprising to one who examines them for the first time. Wheels of various sorts are also contrived to assist in this labor, some worked by cattle, some by human toil, and others carried round by the stream whose waters they elevate. The last are very common on the banks of the rivers Siang, Kan, Min, and their affluents, wherever the banks are convenient for this purpose. High wheels of bamboo, firmly fixed on an axle in the bank, or on pillars driven into the bed, and furnished with buckets, pursue their stately round, and pour their earnings of two hundred and fifty or three hundred tons a day into troughs fixed at an elevation of twenty or thirty feet above the stream. The box-trough, containing an axle to be turned by two men treading the pedals, is rather a more clumsy contrivance, used for slight elevations; the chain of paddles runs around two axles and in the trough as closely as possible, and raises the water ten or twelve feet in an equable current.

Few carts or wagons are used with animals in the southern and eastern provinces where boats are at all available, human strength supplying the means of transportation; the implements of husbandry and the grain taken from the fields both being carried on the back of the laborer. It is not an uncommon sight about Canton to see a ploughman, when he has done his work, turn his buffalo loose and shoulder his plough, harrow, and hoe, with the harness, and carry them all home. It is when one crosses the Yangtsz' on his way north that pack animals are met transporting goods and food in great droves; here, too, people on carts and wheelbarrows fill the roads. On the Great

Plain a sail is raised on the latter when a fair wind will help the man to trundle it over a level way.

The Chinese manure the plant rather than the ground, both in the seed and growing grain. The preparation of manure from night soil, by mixing it with earth and drying it into cakes, furnishes employment to multitudes who transport at all hours their noisome loads through the narrow city streets. Tanks

Pedler's Barrow.

are dug by the wayside, pails are placed in the streets and retiring stalls opened among the dwellings, whose contents are carried away in boats and buckets; but it is a small compensation for this constant pollution of the sweet breath of heaven to know that the avails are to be by and by brought to market. Science may yet ascertain how the benefits of this necessary work can be obtained without its disgusting exposure among the Chinese. Besides this principal ingredient of manure vats, other substances are diligently collected, as hair from the barber's shop, exploded fire-crackers and sweepings from the streets, lime and plaster from kitchens and old buildings, soot, bones, fish and animal remains, the mud from the bottom of canals and tanks, and dung of every kind. In Kiangsu a small leaf clover (*Medicago sativa*) is grown through the winter upon ridges raised in the rice-fields, and the plants pulled up in the spring and scattered over the fields to be ploughed and harrowed into the wet soil with the stubble, their decomposition furnishing large quantities of ammonia to the seedlings. Vegetable rubbish is also collected and covered with turf, and then slowly burned; the residue is a rich black earth, which is laid upon the seeds themselves when planted. The refuse left after expressing the oil from ground-nuts, beans, vegetable tallow, tea, and cabbage seeds, etc., is mixed with earth and made into cakes, to be sold to farmers. The bean-cake made in Liautung thus aids the cotton and sugar planter in Swatow with a rich compost.

The ripe grain is cut with bill-hooks and sickles, or pulled up by the roots; scythes, mowing-machines, and cradles are unknown where human arms are so plenty. Rice-straw is made into brooms and besoms; the rice is thrashed out against the side of a tub having a curtain on one side, or bound into sheaves and carried away to be stacked. The thrashing-floors about Canton are made of a mixture of sand and lime, well pounded upon an inclined surface enclosed by a curb; a little cement added in the last coat makes it impervious to the rain; with proper care it lasts many years, and is used by all the villagers for thrashing rice, peas, mustard, turnips, and other seeds, either with unshod oxen or flails. Where frost and snow come the ground requires to be repaired every season; and each farmer usually has his own.

The cultivation of food plants forms so large a proportion of those demanding the attention of the Chinese, that excepting hemp, indigo, cotton, silk, and tea, those raised for manufacture are quite unimportant. The great cotton region is the basin of the Yangtsz' kiang, where the white and yellow varieties grow side by side. The manure used is mud taken from the canals and spread with ashes over the ploughed fields, in which seeds are sown about the 20th of April. The seeds are planted, after sprouting, five or six in a hole, being rubbed with ashes as they are put in, and weeded out if necessary. After the winter crops have been gathered cotton-fields are easily made ready for the shoots, which, while growing, are carefully tended, thinned, hoed, and weeded, until the flowers begin to appear about August. As the pods begin to ripen and burst the cultivator collects them before they fall, to clean the cotton of seeds and husks. The weather is carefully watched, for a dry summer or a wet autumn are alike unpropitious, and as the pods are ripening from August to October, it is not uncommon for the crop to be partially lost. The seeds are separated by a wheel turning two rollers, and the cotton sold by each farmer to merchants in the towns. Some he keeps for weaving at home; spinning-wheels and looms being common articles of furniture in the houses of the peasantry. Cotton is cultivated in every province, and most of it is used where it grows. Around Peking the plant is hardly a foot high; the bolls are cleaned for wadding to a great extent, while the woody stalks supply fuel to the poor. Minute directions are given in Sü's *Encyclopædia of Agriculture* respecting the cultivation of this plant, whose total crop clothes the millions of the Empire without depending on any other land.[1]

Hemp is largely cultivated north of the Mei ling, and also grows in Fuhkien; grass-cloth made from the *Dolichos bulbosus* is used for summer dresses. There are four plants which produce a fibre made into cloth known under this name, viz.: the *Cannabis sativa*, or common hemp, at Canton; the *Bœhmeria nivea*, a species of nettle; the *Sida tiliæfolia*, or abutilon hemp, in Chihlí; and the *Hibiscus cannabinus*. The coloring matter used for dyeing blue is derived from two plants, the *Polygonum tinctorium* at the south, and the *tien tsing* (*Isatis indigotica*), cultivated at Shanghai and Chusan. The mulberry is raised as a shade and fruit tree in the northern provinces, where it forms a beautiful plant fifty feet high; elsewhere the consumption of the leaves renders its culture an important branch of labor in

[1] Fortune's *Wanderings*, Chap. XIV.; *Chinese Repository*, Vol. XVIII., pp. 449–469.

the silk-producing provinces. Some growers allow it to attain its natural height, others cut it down to increase the branches and the produce of leaves. In Chehkiang it is cut in January and deprived of its useless branches, leaving only the outer ones, which are trimmed into two or three points in order to force the plant to extend itself. The trees are set out in rows twelve feet or more apart, each tree being half that distance from its neighbor and opposite the intervals in the parallel rows; the interspaces are occupied with legumes or greens. The trees are propagated by seed and by suckers, but soon losing their vigor from being constantly stripped of leaves, are then rooted up and replaced by fresh nurslings.

Sugar is only a southern and southeastern crop. The name *ché*, by which it is known, is an original character, which favors the opinion that the plant is indigenous in China, and the same argument is applicable to wheat, hemp, mulberry, tea, and some of the common fruits, as the plum, pear, and orange. The canes are pressed in machines, and the juice boiled to sugar or boiled and hawked about the streets for consumption by the people. The sugar-mill consists merely of two upright cylinders, between which the cane is introduced as they turn, and the juice received into reservoirs; it is then boiled down and sent to the refiners to undergo the necessary processes to fit it for market; much is lost by this slovenly manufacture.

Many plants are cultivated for their oil, used in the arts or in cooking. The seeds of two or three species of *Eleococea* belonging to the Euphorbiaceous family, and the *Curcas purgans*, are gathered, and by pressure furnish an oil to mix with lacker and paints, or to smear boats as a preservative against teredoes and other insects. It is deleterious when taken into the system, but does not appear to injure those who use or express it. The tallow-tree (*Stillingia sebifera*) grows over the eastern provinces; it is a beautiful tree, resembling the aspen in its shape and foliage, and would form a valuable addition to the list of shade-trees in any country. Mr. Denny, the United States Consul at Shanghai, has recently sent a quantity of these seeds to California, where efforts are being made to grow them. The tree has been introduced into India for its timber. The seeds grow in clusters like ivy berries, and are collected in November; when ripe the capsule divides, and falling off discovers two or three kernels covered with the pure, hard white tallow. When the tallow is to be prepared, these are picked from the stalks and put into an open wooden cylinder with a perforated bottom, in which they are well steamed over boiling water. In ten or fifteen minutes the tallow covering the seeds becomes soft, and they are thrown into a stone mortar and gently beaten with mallets to detach it. The whole is then sifted on a hot sieve, by which the tallow is separated from the kernels, though containing the brown skin which envelops the latter and presenting a dirty appearance. The tallow in this state is enclosed in a straw cylinder, or laid upon layers of straw held together by iron hoops, and subjected to pressure in a rude press, from which it runs clear in a semifluid state and soon hardens into cakes. The candles made from it become soft in hot weather, and are sometimes coated by dipping them in colored wax.[1] From one hundred and thirty-three pounds of nuts is obtained some forty or fifty pounds of tallow.

The departments of floriculture and arboriculture have received great attention, but the efforts of their promoters are directed to producing something curious or bizarre, rather than improving the quality of their fruits or enlarging the number of their flowers. A common mode of multiplying specimens is to slit the stem and insert half of it in damp earth tied around the stalk until it has rooted, and then cutting off the whole. Dwarfing trees or forcing them to grow in grotesque shapes employs much time and patience. The juniper, cypress, pine, elm, bamboo, peach, plum, and flowering-almond are selected for this purpose; the former is trained into the shapes of deer or other animals, pagodas, etc., with extraordinary fidelity, the eyes, tongue, or other parts being added to complete the resemblance. The principle of the operation depends upon retarding the circulation of the sap by stinting the supply of water, confining the roots, and bending the branches into the desired form when young and pliable, afterwards retaining them in

---

[1] Fortune's *Wanderings*, p. 78.

their forced position in pots, and clipping off all the vigorous shoots, until, as is the case of the cramped feet of women, nature gives up the contest and yields to art. These, like the similar exhibitions in sculpture and painting, indicate the uncultivated taste of the people, who admire the fantastic and monstrous more than the natural. Some of the clumps placed in large earthen vases, consisting of bamboos, flowers, and dwarf trees growing closely together upon a piece of rock-work, and overshadowing the water in the vase, in which gold-fish swim through the crevices of the stone, are beautiful specimens of Chinese art. Without understanding the principles of an aquarium, the people have succeeded in combining animal and vegetable life in these elegant ornaments of their houses.

The annual ceremony of ploughing is of very ancient origin. At Peking it consists in ploughing the sacred field in the Temple of Agriculture with a highly ornamented plough kept for the purpose, the Emperor holding it while turning over three furrows, the princes five, and the high ministers nine. These furrows were, however, so short that the monarchs of the present dynasty altered the ancient rule, ploughing four furrows and returning again over the ground. The ceremony finished, the Emperor and his ministers repair to the terrace adjoining the plat, and remain till it has all been ploughed. The crop of wheat is used in idolatrous services. The rank of the actors renders the ceremony more imposing at Peking, but the people of the capital only know that such a performance takes place, as they are not admitted inside of the enclosure when it is observed by the Emperor and his suite. This ceremony is also required of all high officers throughout the Empire, and is attended with more or less parade in April.

In the provinces its celebration varies, and as there are two festivals coming near together connected with agriculture, one or the other of them is apt to predominate. The annual ploughing ritual is one, and the *lih chun*, or 'First day of spring,' is the other and prior in date. The prefect of every city and his subordinates on that day repair to the appointed spot outside of the walls, accompanied by music and a great procession of the citizens, carrying through the streets a paper image of the buffalo or ox, which, with the idol image worshipped at the same time, are at some places taken into his *yamun*. Here the whole is placed on an altar, and the officials present walk around and whip the effigy with rods before it is set on fire and scrambled for by the people present. Besides the paper ox, a clay one is also made and taken beyond the eastern gate, sometimes accompanied by or holding hundreds of little images inside; after the ceremonies are over it is broken up, and the pieces and small images are carried off by the crowd to scatter the powder on their own fields, in the hope of thereby insuring a good crop.

In Ningpo the principal features of the ceremony consist of a solemn worship by all the local officers of a clay image of a buffalo and an idol of a cow-herd. The prefect then ploughs a small piece of ground, and he and his associates disperse till the morrow, when they come together in another temple at dawn. Here a series of prostrations and recitals of prayers are performed by the "fathers of the people" in their presence, some of whom have no respect for the worship, while others, perhaps, evince deep reverence. As soon as it is over the clay ox is brought out, and a procession consisting of all the officers pass around it repeatedly, striking the body at a given signal, and concluding the ceremony by a heavy blow on the head. The crowd then rush in and tear the effigy to pieces, each one carrying off a portion to strew on his fields.[1]

The various modes of catching and rearing fish exhibit the contrivance and skill of the Chinese quite as much as their agricultural operations. Some persons reckon that at least one-tenth of the population in the prefecture of Kwangchau derive their food from the water, and necessity leads them to invent and try many ingenious ways of securing the finny tribes.

---

[1] Père Cibot in *Mém. conc. les Chinois*, Tome III., p. 499. *Penal Code*, pp. 94–106, 526. *Chinese Repository*, Vol. II., p. 350; Vol. III., pp. 121, 231; Vol. V., p. 485. *La Chine Ouverte*, p. 346. *Foreign Missionary Chronicle*, Vol. XIII., p. 296. Gray's *China*, Vol. II., pp. 115–117. Doolittle's *Social Life*, Vol. II., pp. 18–23. *Revue de l'Orient*, Tome V. (1844), p. 297. Baron d'Hervey Saint-Denys, *Recherches sur l'Agriculture et l'Horticulture des Chinois*, Paris, 1850. *Journal N. C. Br. R. A. Soc.*, No. IV., pp. 209 ff.

Nets woven of hempen thread are boiled in a solution of gambier to preserve them from rotting. The smacks which swarm along the coast go out in pairs, partly that the crews may afford mutual relief and protection, but chiefly to join in dragging the net. In the shallows of rivers rows of heavy posts are driven down and nets secured to them, which are examined and changed at every tide. Those who attend these nets, more-

Group and Residence of Fishermen near Canton.

over, attach scoops or drag-nets to their boats, so loaded that they will sink and gather the sole, ray, and other fish feeding near the bottom. Lifting-nets, twenty feet square, are suspended from poles elevated and depressed by a hawser worked by a windlass on shore; the nets are baited with the whites of eggs spread on the meshes.

The fishermen along the coast form an industrious, though rather turbulent community, by no means confining their enterprises to their professed business when piracy, dakoity, or marauding on shore hold out greater prospects of gain. When their boats become unseaworthy they are still considered landworthy, and are transformed into houses by setting them bodily upon a stone foundation above the reach of the tide, or breaking them up to construct rude huts.

Cormorants are trained in great numbers to capture fish in the rivers and lakes; they will disperse at a given signal and return with their prey, but not often without the precaution of a neck-ring. A single boatman can easily oversee twelve or fifteen of these birds, and although hundreds may be out upon the

The Fishing Cormorant.

water each one knows its own master. If one seize a fish too heavy for him alone, another comes to his assistance, and the two carry it aboard; but such cases are very rare compared with others where the weak or young bird is unceremoniously robbed of its capture. When several hundreds of them fish together the scene becomes animated and noisy in the extreme. The birds themselves are fed on bean-curd and eels or fish. They lay eggs when three years old, which are often hatched under barnyard hens, and the chickens fed with eel's blood and hash. They do not fish during the summer months. The price of a pair varies from five to eight dollars.

Mussels are caught in cylindrical basket-traps attached to a single rope and drifted with the tide near the bottom. Similar traps for catching land-crabs are laid along the edges of rice-fields, baited with dried fish. When the receding tide leaves the river banks dry the boat people get overboard and wade in the mud, or push themselves along on a board with one foot, in search of such things as harbor in the ooze.

In moonlight nights low, narrow shallops, provided with a wide white board fastened to the wale and floating upon the water, are anchored in still water; as the moon shines on the board the deceived fish leap out upon it or into the boat; twenty or thirty of these decoy boats can be seen near Macao engaged in this fishery on moonlight evenings. Sometimes a boat furnished with a treadle goes up and down near the shores striking boards against its bottom and sides; the startled fish are caught in the net dragging astern. The crews of many small boats combine to drive the fish into their nets by splashing and striking the water, or into a pool on the margin of the river at high tide, in which they are easily retained by wattles, and scooped out when the water has fallen. Divers clap sticks together under water to drive their prey into the nets set for them, or catch them with their toes when, terrified at the noise, they hide in the mud. Neither fly-fishing nor angling with hook and line is much practised; its tedium and small returns would be poor amends to a Chinese for the elegance of the tackle or the science displayed in adapting the fly to the fish's taste.

By these and other contrivances the Chinese capture the finny tribes, and it is no surprise to hear that China contains as many millions of people as there are days in the year when one sees upon what a large proportion of them feed and how they live. Their expenditure of human labor appears enormous to those who are accustomed to the manufactories and engines of western lands, but perhaps nothing would cause so much distress in China as the premature and inconsiderate introduction of labor-saving machines. Population is so close upon the means of production, not seldom overpassing them, that those who would be thrown out of employment would, owing to their ignorance as to the best resources and want of means to do anything by themselves, suffer and cause incalculable distress before relief and labor could be furnished them. There are, for instance, six or seven yards near Canton where logs are sawed by hand, but all of them together hardly turn out as many feet of boards as one water-wheel turning three or four saws would do. Yet the two hundred men employed in these yards would perhaps be half-starved if turned off in their present condition, even if they did not destroy their competitor; though there is every reason for believing that improvements will be introduced as soon as those who see their superiority are assured they can be made profitable.

The mechanical arts and implements of the Chinese partake of the same simplicity which has been remarked in their agricultural,—as if the faculty of invention or the notion of altering a thing had died with the discoverer, and he had had the best guarantee for the patent of his contrivance in the deprivation of all desire in his successors to alter it. This servility of imitation marks them in many things, but in machinery and metallurgy is chiefly owing to ignorance of the real nature of the materials they use, a knowledge which has only recently become familiar to ourselves. In the absence of superior models, it produces a degree of apathy to all improvement which strangely contrasts with their general industry and literary tastes. Simplicity of design pervades all operations, and when a machine directs in the best known manner the power of the hand which wields it, or aids in executing tiresome operations, its purpose is considered to be fully answered, for it was intended to assist and not to supplant human labor. Yet with all their simplicity some of them are both effectual and ingenious, and not a few are made to answer two or three ends. For example, the bellows, an oblong box divided into two compartments, and worked by a piston and two valves in the upper, which forces the wind into the lower part and out of the nozzle, is used by the travelling tinker as a seat when at work and a chest for his tools when his work is done; though it does not, indeed, serve all these purposes with efficiency.

In the arts of metallurgy the Chinese have attained only to mediocrity, and on the whole do not equal the Japanese. To this deficiency may perhaps be ascribed their little progress in some other branches which could not be executed without tools of peculiar size or nicety. Mines of iron, lead, copper, and zinc are worked, though the modes employed in digging the ore, preparing and smelting it, and purifying the metals have not yet been fully examined. Gold is used sparingly for ornaments, but is consumed in vast quantities for gilding; gold thread is commonly imported, and the ingots are known only as bullion. Mr. Gordon found the people in the country parts of Fuhkien quite ignorant of its value, for he could only pass doubloons for a dollar apiece, the natives having never seen them before.

The Chinese workmanship in chased, repoussé, and carved work of gold and silver—baskets, card-cases, teapots, combs, etc.—is almost unequalled. Their jewelry, too, admirably exhibits the delicate filigree work which agrees so well with their genius. Flower-baskets with chased flowers and figures of various sorts enamelled on the outside of the open work of wire, and set with precious stones, may perhaps be regarded as the masterpiece of native art in the working of metals.

Steel is everywhere manufactured in a rude way, but the foreign importation is gradually supplying a better article. The quality of this metal made is best shown by the carvings in the hardest stones for ornaments, which have never been exceeded elsewhere. Iron is cast into thin plates and various machines of considerable size, but the largest pieces they make, viz., bells and cannon, are small compared with the shafts and steam-hammers turned out abroad. Wrought iron is chiefly worked up into nails, screws, hinges, and small articles needed in daily life, though its quality is remarkably good. The *peh tung*, argentan or 'white copper' of the Chinese, is an alloy of copper 40.4, zinc 25.4, nickel 31.6, and iron 2.6, and occasionally a little silver; these proportions are nearly the same as German-silver. "When in a state of ore, it is said to be powdered, mixed with charcoal dust, and placed in jars over a slow fire, the metal rising in the form of vapor in a distilling apparatus, and afterward condensed in water."[1] When new, this alloy ap-

---

[1] Davis' *Chinese*, Vol. II., p. 235. *Penny Cyclopædia*, Art. COPPER. Natalis Rondot, *Commerce de la Chine*, 1849, p. 142.

pears as lustrous as silver, and is manufactured into incense-jars, flower-stands for temple service, boxes, a vast variety of fancy articles, and a few household utensils not intended to be used near the fire. Puzzling specimens of work are made of it, such as teapots enclosed in chinaware and ornamented with a handle and a spout of stone, and having characters on the sides. The white copper varies a good deal in its appearance and malleability, owing probably to mixtures added after distillation.

Copper is less used than iron for culinary vessels, but will probably increase as rapid importation diminishes the cost, for iron rusts quickly in the southern parts. The manufactures of gongs, cymbals and trumpets, lamps, brass-leaf for working into the *kin hwa*, or tinsel-flowers used in worship, and the copper coin of the country, consume probably four-fifths of all the copper used. The gong is employed on all occasions, and its piercing clamor can be heard at any time of day and night, especially if one lives near the water. It is an alloy of twenty parts of tin with eighty of copper, and is made by melting one hundred catties of *hung tung*, or 'red copper,' with twenty-five catties of tin. The alloy is run into thin plates, and the gongs are made by long and expert hammering until the requisite sonorousness is obtained.

Bells and tripods are frequently cast of a large size. The bells at Peking (mentioned in Volume I., p. 79) are peculiarly rich in quality of tone; they are almost invariably made without tongues, being sounded with a mallet. The tripods for receiving the ashes of papers consumed in worship also bear inscriptions of a religious character; the priests of temples containing them take great pride in showing their ancient bells, tripods, and other like rarities. The pieces of bronze formerly produced under the patronage of the Emperor Kienlung, as incense tripods, lions, astronomical instruments, and the infinite variety of ornaments, probably represent their highest attainments in this branch of metallurgy for beauty and excellence. The metallic mirrors, once the only reflectors the Chinese manufactured, are now nearly superseded by glass; the alloy is like that of gongs with a little silver added. These mirrors have long been remarkable for a singular property which some of them possess of reflecting the raised characters or device on the back when held in the sun; this is caused by their outline being traced upon the polished surface in very shallow lines, the whole plate being afterward rubbed until the lines are equally bright with the other parts, and only rendered visible by the strongest sunlight.[1] Besides the metallic articles already mentioned, the ornamental and antique bronze and copper figures, noticeable for their curious forms and fine polishing and tracery, afford the best specimens of Chinese art in imitating the human figure. They are mostly statuettes, representing men, gods, birds, monsters, etc., in grotesque shapes and attitudes; some of them are beautifully ornamented with delicate scrolls and flowers in niello work of silver or gold wire inserted into grooves cut in the metal.

The manufacture of glass is carried on chiefly at Canton, and its increasing use for windows, tumblers, lamps, mirrors, and other articles of household furniture, shows that the Chinese are quite ready to adopt such things from foreign countries as they find to be advantageous. The importation of broken glass for remelting has entirely ceased, but flints are carried from England for the use of glass-blowers. The furnaces are small, and from the ignorance, on the part of the workmen, of the constituents of good glass, their products are not uniform. Foreign window-glass is now brought so cheaply that the native inferior article, which distorts objects seen through it, is disappearing; colored articles and chandeliers are still made. The most finished articles which the Chinese have yet produced are ground shades for Argand lamps. Beautiful ornaments are made of the *liao-li*, the old native name for a vitreous composition like strass, between glass and porcelain. Ear-rings, wristlets, snuff-bottles, jars, cups, etc., are made of it, plain, colored, and variegated, in vast variety. Some of these articles exhibit different tints in layers, each layer being ground away where it is not wanted, as in cameo carving; blue, red, and yel-

[1] Other and perhaps more correct explanations of this peculiarity have been given.

low are the prevailing colors. The art of producing it has been known longer than glass-making, but was invented later than that of porcelain.

The cutting and setting of hard and precious stones is carried on to some extent. Spectacles are cut and ground in lathes from crystal, smoky quartz, and a variety of rose quartz resembling the cairngorm-stone, which the Chinese call *cha-tsing*, or 'tea-stone,' from its color. Their spectacles are not always true, and the wearer is obliged to have them ground away until his eyes are suited. The pebble is cut in a lathe, by a wire-saw working in its own dust, into a round shape with plane edges. When worn, the rim rests upon the cheek-bones; the frame has a hinge between the glasses, and the machine is sometimes kept on the ears by loops or weights. Foreign-shaped spectacles are supplanting these primitive optics, but the prejudice is still in favor of crystal. The cutting of diamonds is sometimes attempted, but it is not a favorite gem among the Chinese. Diamonds and corundums are both employed to drill holes in clamping and mending broken glass and porcelain; tumblers, jars, etc., are joined so securely in this way without cement as to hold fluids. Both these gems are used to cut glass, but another mode, not uncommon, is to grease the place to be fractured, and slowly follow the line along by a lighted joss-stick until it breaks.

Sir John Davis condensed all the important information known half a century ago concerning the materials and manufacture of porcelain in his valuable work, but great advance has since been made in a better understanding of this branch of Chinese industry. The word *porcelain* is derived from *porcellana*, which was given to the ware by the Portuguese under the belief that it was made from the fusion of egg-shells and fish's glue and scales to resemble the nacre of sea-shells (Cypræa) or porcellana. This instance of off-hand nomenclature is like that of the Chinese calling caoutchouc *elephant's skin* from its appearance.

M. Julien's translation of the *King-teh chin Tau Luh* (Paris, 1856) furnishes the native accounts of the porcelain manufactures at Kingteh chin, in Kiangsí, and adds so much from other sources that his work is a veritable classic in its special branch. He places the invention of porcelain between B.C. 185 and A.D. 85, and opening the first kiln, at Sinping (not far from the present centre of Honan province), under the reign of Changtí of the Eastern Han dynasty. From this the manufacture gradually extended as raw materials were found in other localities, especially in Fauliang, on the eastern shores of the Poyang Lake, where the best ware is still made. A second preface to this work, written by M. Salvétat, of the manufactory at Sèvres, gives the details of the introduction of the art into Europe about 1722, and the subsequent improvement to the time when European wares far exceeded the Chinese or Japanese for beauty. During the dreadful ravages of the Taiping rebellion the manufactories at Kingteh were all stopped.

A very brief epitome of M. Salvétat's paper will indicate the ingredients of porcelain and their manipulation: Two substances enter into all kinds of this ware; one a strong, infusible material which endures great heat, and the other, fusible at a low temperature, which communicates its transparency to the other as they together pass through the furnace. The first of these is called *kaolin*, from the name of a range of hills east of Kingteh chin, known as *Kao Ling* or 'High Ridge,' a word that has been adopted in Europe as a term for all varieties of the argillaceous or feldspathic components of porcelain. The other is known as *peh-tun-tsz'*, a Chinese term properly applied to the bricks of prepared silex, called *tun*, but now generally adopted to denote the fusible element. The discovery near Taochau fu of both of these in great purity led to the establishment of the kilns there in A.D. 583; and Chinese artists discriminate many varieties of each. It is apparently only since A.D. 1000, or thereabouts, that these kilns have produced the choice pieces now so highly prized.

The kaolin comes from decomposed granite, and is reduced by trituration and several washings to an impalpable powder; this last precipitate is put on cloths, one above another, and dried under slight pressure to a uniform paste ready for the furnace. The cakes of *peh-tun-tsz'* are prepared in a similar manner; other workmen mix the clay and the quartz—the bones and the flesh, as they are aptly called by the Chinese—in such proportions as the ware requires. In general, Chinese porcelain is more silicious than European, containing 70 parts of silex, 22 of alumine, 6 of potash and soda, with traces of lime, manganese, magnesia, and iron. Sèvres ware has 58 silex, 34½ alumine, 3 alkali, and 4½ lime; as the feldspar decreases the beauty of the ware diminishes, but its durability and usefulness increase.

To make ready the paste for the furnace, the bricks of both ingredients are trodden in a large basin by buffaloes or men till they are well mixed into a watery mass, which is then worked and kneaded again on slate slabs in small pieces till it is delivered into the hands of workmen to be fashioned on lathes and frames into the desired forms and sizes. These craftsmen work with very simple machinery, as is apparent from the rude drawings of their operations. M. Salvétat gives high praise to their skill in producing large jars without the aid of the machinery used in Europe, and indicates the great use they make of their feet in these operations—a feature of all Asiatic artisans which attracts the traveller's notice wherever he goes. Some of their procedures are inferior and ruder than the Japanese potters exhibit, but space does not allow them to be described in this sketch.

The glazing on Chinese ware contains silex mixed with lime and the ashes of burnt ferns, in such proportions as are found suitable for the different varieties. During the mixing of these ingredients the ashes are mostly eliminated, and the glazing really consists of quartz flexed by carbonate of lime. The liquid glaze is applied to the biscuit by dipping, by aspersion, and by washing, according to the nature of the ware; sometimes it is blown through a tube in a dewy shower oft repeated.

When ready for the furnace, the pieces are carried to workmen specially skilled in properly firing them, where the different sizes are placed in ovens particularly fitted to bake each kind. Large jars require a separate oven so as to adapt the fire to their size and thickness, continuing it at a uniform blast for several days. Cups and small pieces are baked one on top of another in smaller ovens, some of which are open and others closed. Coal and wood are both used for fuel. The pieces are taken from the furnaces when successfully baked, to be decorated and colored in all the various hues and pictures which have made Chinese porcelain so much sought after. Some of their ground colors of red, yellow, and green have not been equalled elsewhere; a careful analysis indicates the presence of the oxides of copper, cobalt, iron, lead, antimony, and manganese. Some of the rarest and most beautiful tints seem to have been the result of happy experiment, the knowledge of which died with its manufacture. It is not often that the Chinese artist adorns his plaque or jar with mythological or religious characters, preferring to let his fancy run riot in grotesque combinations of natural scenes, amid which, however, the unerring instinct or the accumulated experience of many successive generations seldom permit him to wander from a truly artistic conception. The amount of labor devoted to some minute treasure of porcelain decoration is little short of fabulous. Mr. Matthew Arnold's picture of the "cunning workman" who

> Pricks with vermilion some clear porcelain vase,
> An emperor's gift—at early morn he paints,
> And all day long, and when night comes, the lamp
> Lights up his studious forehead and thin hands,

could probably be seen scores of times in the humbler quarters of great cities in China.

Their ignorance of analytical chemistry compels them to follow a rule of thumb in the composition of their colors; but generally they use oxide of copper for green and bluish greens, gold for reds, oxide of cobalt for blues, of antimony for yellows, and of arsenic and tin for whites. The preparation and application of these materials admit of less scope and beauty than are found on the finest European ware, and their result is more like enamelling than painting. M. Salvétat admits that the Chinese potter has excelled in producing craquele ware, and certain hues, as sea-green, deep rosedon reds, and brilliant blues, which have not been equalled in Europe.

One elegant mode of ornament peculiar to them is seen in the *tao-ming tsz'-kí, lit.*, 'clear, bright porcelain,' called eyelet-hole ware or grains of rice, made in the reign Kienlung. The paste is cut through by a kind of stamp which takes out enough to form the figure, in which the glaze is inserted before the piece is finally joined and ready for the kiln. When fired the glaze becomes transparent; different patterns are frequently painted on the two surfaces, in which advantage is taken of the eyelet-holes to adapt them to two sets of figures. An instance of mechanical skill is occasionally seen in their articulated vases, in which one jar is baked inside of another, the outer one being perforated so as to show off the object within; the baking of such pieces must be very difficult and uncertain.

The ware sold at Canton for foreign use is painted in that city to suit the caprice of purchasers, and during the present century has become identified abroad with Chinese art, while it is really a combination of two or three styles. Its peculiarity consists in covering the dish with medallions and vignettes in bright colors, containing figures of heroes, arms, birds, etc.,.or scenes on a colored or white ground. Such ware is not commonly used by the Chinese, but its manufacture is unhappily beginning to affect their national taste. This style is quite different from the well-known blue willow pattern which has long been regarded as the *real Celestial ware.* This color does mark the common pottery and stoneware used all over the Empire by the poor, but the pattern is not so common.

It is not possible to enter here into all the niceties of this subject, which is now attracting great attention, and has been examined by Jacquemart, Prime, Young, and many others. Further researches into native and foreign books and collections will bring out new facts, legends, and specimens, while we may look for rare old pieces, as has been the case with the discovery of the small perfume bottles in Egypt, as soon as full liberty is given over all Asia to seek and dig.

Besides table furniture, porcelain statuettes and idols are common, and vases often bring extravagant prices, owing to some quality of fineness, coloring, antiquity, or shape, which native connoisseurs can only appreciate. The god of porcelain himself is usually made of this material. D'Entrecolles, in his account of the manufacture of the ware, says that this deity owes his divinity to his self-immolation in one of the furnaces in utter despair at being able to accomplish the Emperor's orders for the production of some vases of peculiar fineness; the pieces which came out of the furnace after the wretch was burned pleased his Majesty so much that he deified him. Cheap stoneware is made at Shauking, in Kwangtung, and many other places, some of it very pure and white.

The exportation of porcelain has formed a very ancient branch of commerce westward, and it is not strange that specimens should occasionally be met with even at a great distance from China. The discovery of Chinese bottles in Egypt and Asia Minor, containing quotations from Chinese poets, shows that intercourse existed between the extremes of Asia in the tenth or eleventh centuries. Rosellini seems to have been the earliest to notice these relics of an ancient trade, during his researches in Egypt in 1828, when he obtained two or three. In a letter written in reply to one from Sir J. F. Davis, he states that he found one of these little bottles in a "petit panier tissu de feuilles de palmier," with other objects of Egyptian manufacture, in a tomb, whose date he places between B.C. 1800 and 1100. His words are, "Ayant penétré dans un de ces trois tombeaux j'y ai trouvé," etc., which is as explicit as possible. He also adds, that many fragments of similar bottles had been offered to him by the peasants, which he had looked upon as quite modern till this discovery showed that they were real antiques.

Since then, several more have been picked up; Dr. Abbott's Egyptian collection in New York contains seventeen, all of which came from Egypt, but none, besides Rosellini's, out of a tomb directly into the hands of an Egyptologist. Layard and Cesnola bought similar bottles in Cyprus and Arban. However, one well-authenticated fact, like that of Rosellini's discovery, gives some evidence of a similar ancient origin to others precisely like it in shape, coloring, and inscriptions, for the trade between Arabia and Egypt to China has long since ceased; but as fifty years have passed without another bottle occurring in any of the numerous tombs opened by careful and competent persons, one is inclined to think that Rosellini's tomb may have been twice used to bury mummies in, or that he mistook its age.

The inscriptions and style of writing of five different kinds have been engraved, and Sir Walter H. Medhurst gives a translation of each, tracing the lines to their original authors. One of them is from Wang Wai (A.D. 702–745), and reads, *Ming yueh sung chung chao*, 'The bright moon shines amidst the firs.' A second reads, *Chih tsai tsz' shan chung*, 'Only in the midst of these mountains,' and it dates A.D. 831–837. A third is contracted from a line by Wei Ying-wuh (A.D. 702–795), being part of a stanza of eight lines, as follows: *Hwo kai yiu yih nien*, 'The flowers open, and lo, another year!' A fourth dates from A.D. 1068–1085, and is from the famous poet Su Tung-po: *Hăng hwa hung shih lí*, 'The apricot flowers bloom for miles around;' this is abridged from a distich in pentameter as follows:

> One mass of color, the apricot flowers bloom for miles around;
> The successful graduate urges on his steed as if flying.

Sir John Davis ascribes this inscription to a Chinese song written prior to the Christian era, but gives no proof of so early a date, and he is probably in error. The fifth inscription is of the same date as the last; it forms part of a quatrain by Chao Yung, and reads, *Liao teh shao jin chí*, 'Which few, I ween, can comprehend.' In Prime's work on pottery he has given fac-similes of five bottles whose inscriptions are the same as those explained by Medhurst; his No. 142 and No. 146 is the second in this list; his No. 143 is the first; his 144 is the third; and his 145 is the fifth and is different in shape from the others. The characters on the one found at Arban by Layard are written in a very cursive style.[1]

The age and origin of these bottles has excited much inquiry, but the weight of evidence points to their having been taken to Egypt and Arabia by the Arabs who traded at Canton and Hangchau down to the end of the Sung dynasty in 1278. They were, as Wilkinson suggests in his *Ancient Egyptians*, probably used by the purchasers to hold *kohl* to paint the eyes and

[1] Davis' *Sketches*, Vol. II., pp. 72–84. Medhurst's *China*, p. 135. Julien's *Histoire de la Porcelain Chinoise*, pp. xi–xxii. Prime's *Pottery and Porcelain*, p. 232. *N. C. Br. R. A. S. Transactions*, 1852, pp. 34–40; 1854, p. 93.

eyelids of women; their original use was probably to hold peppermint and other oils, bandoline and tooth-powders, though snuff is now generally carried in them, as glass bottles contain the essences and oils seen in shops. The uniformity in size, shape, coloring, and decoration in these bottles indicates that the trade was rather confined to one port in China, for at present a vast variety in all these particulars would be seen, as I ascertained some years ago at Canton when unsuccessfully looking in the shops for some having inscriptions like those discovered in Egypt. Mr. Fortune found one having the same inscription as No. 2, and Sir Harry Parkes came across three others, but their rarity now proves the change; and these were probably real antiques. The latter found two other inscriptions on similar bottles in China, whose authors lived A.D. 584 and later; and argues against their high antiquity from the metre having been introduced in later times. The strongest proof of their modern origin is the material and the date of the style of writing, neither of which could have been prior to the Han dynasty if Chinese records are worth anything; such simple lines as these five could indeed have been handed down and adopted by later poets from lost authors, but this possibility weighs nothing against the others. The more antiquarian researches extend in Asia, however, the more shall we find that the books and inscriptions now extant do not contain the earliest dates of inventions and travels.

The cheap pottery of the Chinese resembles the Egyptian ware in color and brittleness, but is less porous when unglazed. Tea-kettles, pans, plates, teapots, and articles of household use, bathing-tubs, immense jars, comparable to hogsheads, for holding water, fancy images, statuettes, figurines, toys, flower-pots, and a thousand other articles are everywhere burned from clay and sold at extremely low prices. The jars are used in shops to contain liquids, powders, etc.; in gardens to keep fish, collect rain, and receive manure and offal; and in boats and houses for the same purposes that barrels, pails, and pans are put to elsewhere. Water will boil sooner and a dish of vegetables be cooked more expeditiously in one of these earthen pots than in metal; the caloric seems to permeate the clay almost as soon as it is over the fire. Drum-shaped stools and garden seats, vitruvian ornaments for balustrades, fanciful flower-pots in the shape of buffaloes, representing the animal feeding under the shade of a tree growing out of its body, fishes, dragons, phœnixes, and other objects for decorating the ridges and for gargoyles are manufactured of this ware. Flat figures of the human form are set into frames to represent groups of persons, or elegantly shaped characters are arranged into sentences, both of them to put on the walls of rooms, making altogether a great variety of purposes to which this material is applied.

The lacquered-ware peculiar to China and Japan owes its lustre to the prepared sap of a kind of sumach (*Rhus vernicifera*) cultivated in both countries for this purpose. Wood oils are obtained from other plants, such as the *Curcas*, *Augia*, *Eleococcus*, and *Rhus semi-alatus*, and the different qualities of lacquered-ware are owing to the use of these inferior ingredients. The real varnish-tree is described by De Guignes as resembling the ash in its foliage and bark; it is about fifteen feet in height, and when seven years old furnishes the sap, which is carefully collected in the summer nights from incisions cut in the trunk. It comes to market in tubs holding the cakes, and those who collect it are careful to cover their faces and hands from contact with this irritating juice as they prepare it for market. A good yield of a thousand trees in one night would be twenty pounds avoirdupois weight of sap. The best sort is tawny rather than white in its inspissated state, and is kept well protected from the air by tarred paper. The body of lacquered-ware is usually seasoned pine, well smoothed, and the grooves covered with hempen lint or paper. A sizing of pig's gall, often mixed with very fine sand, makes a priming. The prepared lacquer is composed of the sap dissolved in spring-water, adding ground-nut oil, pig's gall, and rice vinegar in the sunshine with broad flat brushes till it is thoroughly mixed.

The principal object in preparing the wood is to cover it with a priming that will receive the lacquer and remain impervious to changes in temperature. This preparation varies a good deal according to the quality of the ware; it is laid on evenly, coat after coat, allowing each to dry before the next is spread.

The last coating is rubbed with pumice or the finest sandstone, finishing this priming with a smooth piece of slate. When ready the piece is taken into a close room having paper lattices and shut out from any air, where it receives a coating of clear lacquer. It is then put into a dark room to dry. The operation is repeated ten or fifteen times for the best kinds. Some workmen are so sensitive to the liquid lacquer that they cannot safely do this part of the manufacture; others go through all the processes without annoyance. Coloring matter to give the lacquer a brown hue, or to make an imitation of *venturina* (or *aventurine*, a brownish glass spangled throughout with copper filings) by mixing gold leaf, is added during these operations.

The gilding is performed by another set of workmen in a large workshop. The figures of the design are drawn on thick paper, which is then pricked all over to allow the powdered chalk to fall on the table and form the outline. Another workman completes the picture by cutting the lines with a burin or needle, and filling them with vermilion mixed in lacquer, as thick as needed. This afterward is covered by means of a hair-pencil with gold in leaf, or in powder laid on with a dossil; the gold is often mixed with fine lampblack. The proper lacquer is seldom used otherwise than in making this ware. The Chinese term for *tsih* includes this and all kinds of oils and paints, so that some confusion arises in describing their materials.[1] A beautiful fabric of lacquered-ware is made by inlaying the nacre of fresh and salt-water shells in a rough mosaic of flowers, animals, etc., into the composition, and then varnishing it. Another highly prized kind is made by covering the wood with a coating of fine powdered cinnabar and varnish three or four lines in thickness, and then carving figures upon it in relief. The great labor necessary to produce this ware renders it expensive, and it is not now produced.

The oils obtained from the nuts of other trees by simple pressure and by refining them afterward are quite numerous.

---

[1] N. Rondot, *Commerce de la Chine*, p. 120; *Journal Asiatique*, IV. Series, Tome XI., 1848, pp. 34–65; *Chinese Commercial Guide*, 5th Ed., p. 124.

The details of their manufacture and application may yet furnish many new hints and processes to western arts. The oil of the Eleococcus, after pressing (according to De Guignes), is boiled with Spanish white in the proportion of one ounce to half a pound of oil; as it begins to thicken it is taken off and poured into close vessels. It dissolves in turpentine and is used as a varnish, either clear or mixed with different colors; it defends woodwork from injury for a long time, and forms a good painter's oil. Boiled with iron rust it forms a reddish brown varnish. In order to prevent its penetrating into the wood when used clear, and to increase the lustre, a priming of lime and hog's blood simmered together into a paste is previously laid on.

The manufacture of silk is original among the Chinese, as well as those of porcelain and lacquered-ware, and in none of these have foreigners yet succeeded in fully equalling the native products. The notices of the cultivation of the mulberry and the rearing of silk-worms found in Chinese works have been industriously collected and published by M. Julien by order of the French government—another instance of the intelligent care of this nation to aid one of its great industries. The introduction by M. Beauvais indicates certain points worthy of the notice of cultivators; it has been remarked that the hints thus obtained from Julien's translation have been of more value to the people employed in silk culture in France than all that has been paid by the government for the promotion of Chinese literature from their first outlay in the last century.

The earliest notice in the *Shu King* of silk culture occurs in the *Yu Kung*. It is said the mulberry grounds were made fit for silk-worms, when speaking of the draining of Yen Chau (parts of Shantung and Chihlí), as if it was an usual culture; other references to silk in the same book show it to have been a well-known fabric at that date (B.C. 2204). The allusion, therefore, in the *Book of Odes* to silks of many sorts also strengthen the notice in the *Wei Kí*, which says:

> Síling shí, the Empress of Hwangtí, began to rear silk-worms:
> At this period Hwangtí invented the art of making clothing.

This legend carries the art back to B.C. 2600, or perhaps five centuries after the Deluge. Síling is said to have been her birthplace, and Lui Tsu her right name; she was deified and is still worshipped as the goddess of silk under the name of Yuenfí. In this act, as De Guignes observes, the Chinese resemble other ancient nations in ascribing the invention of spinning to women, and deifying them; thus the Egyptian Isis, the Lydian Arachne, and the Grecian Athene also handled the distaff. A temple called the *Sien-tsan Tao* exists in the palace grounds dedicated to Yuenfí, wherein she is worshipped annually in April by the Empress. The altar, grounds, sacrifices, ritual, and buildings are all in imitation of those in the Temple of Agriculture, of which they are a counterpart. The *Book of Rites* contains a notice of the festival held in honor of weaving, which corresponds to that of ploughing by the Emperor. "In the last month of spring the young Empress purified herself and offered a sacrifice to the goddess of silk-worms. She went into the eastern fields and collected mulberry leaves. She forbade noble dames and the ladies of statesmen adorning themselves, and excused her attendants from their sewing and embroidery, in order that they might give all their care to the rearing of silk-worms." The present enclosure was put up by Yungching in 1742, but its buildings are now much dilapidated.

The attention of the Chinese government to this important branch of industry has been unremitted, and at this day it supplies perhaps one-half of all the garments worn by the people. In the paraphrase to the fourth maxim of the *Shing Yu*, it is remarked: "In ancient times emperors ploughed the lands and empresses cultivated the mulberry. Though the most honorable, they did not disdain to toil and labor, as examples to the whole Empire, in order to induce all the people to seek these essential supports." One-half of the *Illustrations of Agriculture and Weaving* are devoted to delineating the various processes attending this manufacture; and Julien quotes more than twenty works and authors on this subject. Among other uses to which this material is put, may be remembered, in the second chapter of this work, the burning of many thousand pieces of plain, coarse silk as part of the offerings to the gods at Peking, and in the annual sacrifices before the tablets of Confucius.[1]

While the worms are growing, care is taken to keep them undisturbed by either noise or bright light; they are often changed from one hurdle to another that they may have roomy and cleanly places; the utmost attention is paid to their condition and feeding, and noting the right time for preparing them for spinning cocoons. Three days are required for this, and in six it is time to stifle the larvæ and reel the silk from the cocoons; but this being usually done by other workmen, those who rear the worms enclose the cocoons in a jar buried in the ground and lined with mats and leaves, interlaying them with salt, which kills the pupæ but keeps the silk supple, strong, and lustrous; preserved in this manner, they can be transported to any distance, or the reeling of the silk can be delayed until convenient. Another mode of destroying the cocoons is to spread them on trays and expose them by twos to the steam of boiling water, putting the upper in the place of the lower one according to the degree of heat they are in, taking care that the chrysalides are killed and the silk not injured. After exposure to steam the silk can be reeled off immediately, but if placed in the jars they must be put into warm water to dissolve the glue before the floss can be unwound.

The commission sent from France to China in 1844 to make inquiries into its industries consisted of skilled men, and their reports embody a great amount of details nowhere else to be found. The digested catalogue of the exhibits of M. Hedde at St. Etienne in 1848 contains four hundred and fifty-three articles relating to silk and mulberry alone. The amount of silk goods exported has never regained its value previous to 1854, in consequence of the destruction of skilled workmen and manufactories during the Tai-ping rebellion, and raw silk still forms the bulk of the export. The finest silk comes from Chehkiang province, and is known as *tsatli*, *tay-saam*, and *yuenhwa* in com-

---

[1] Julien, *Culturer des Muriers*, 1837; Pauthier, *Chine Moderne*, p. 21; Hedde, *Catalogue des Produits Sérigènes*, 1848, pp. 106–287; *Chinese Repository*, Vol. XVIII., pp. 303–314; *Commercial Guide*, 5th Ed., p. 136; Mailla, *Histoire de la Chine*, Tome I., p. 24; Biot, *Tcheou-li*, passim, 1851.

merce; the centre of the culture is at Hū-chau, a prefecture in the northwest of that province. The mulberry grows everywhere, and none of the provinces are without some silk, but Kwangtung, Sz'chuen, and Chehkiang furnish the best and most.

Great attention is paid in Shantung, Sz'chuen, and Kweichau to collecting wild silk from the cocoons of worms which feed on the ailantus, oak, and xanthoxylum. The insect is the *Attacus cynthia*, and its food the tender leaves of the ailantus and *Quercus mongholica* in Shantung, where great quantities of durable silk is woven. It is not so lustrous as that produced by the bombyx-worm, which feeds on the mulberry leaf, and comparatively little is exported. The proportion of manufactured silks sent abroad is less now than it was fifty years ago, but the home consumption is so enormous that an annual export to the value of nearly ninety millions of dollars has little effect on the prices. In 1854 the price of the best raw silk was about $330 a bale, and the export over fifty-one thousand bales; in 1860, the same sort was $550, and the export nearly eighty thousand bales; this increase in price was owing chiefly to disease in the trees in Europe, though the ravages of war in both Chehkiang and Kwangtung had destroyed much property in this branch.

The loom in China is worked by two hands, one of whom sits on the top of the frame, where he pulls the treadles and assists in changing the various parts of the machine. The workmen imitate almost any pattern, excelling particularly in crapes, and flowered satins and damasks for official dresses. The common people wear pongee and senshaw, which they frequently dye in gambier to a dust or black color; these fabrics constitute most durable garments. Many of the delicate silk tissues known in Europe are not manufactured by the Chinese, most of their fabrics being heavy. The *lo*, or law, is a beautiful article like grenadine and seldom sent abroad; it is used for summer robes, musquito curtains, festoons, and other purposes. The English words *satin*, *senshaw*, and *silk* are probably derived from the Chinese terms *sz'-twan*, *sien-sha*, and *sz'*, intermediately through other languages.

The skill of the Chinese in embroidery is well known, and the demand for such work to adorn the dresses of officers and ladies of every rank, for ornamenting purses, shoes, caps, fans, and other appendages of the dress of both sexes, and in working shawls, table covers, etc., for exportation, furnishes employment to myriads of men and women. The frame is placed on pivots and the pattern marked out upon the plain surface. There are many styles, with thread, braid, or floss, and an infinite variety in the quality, pattern, and beauty of the work; it is the art of Chinese women, and every young lady is expected to know how to do it. On fire screens the design appears the same on both sides, the ends of the threads being neatly concealed. This mode of embroidery seems also to have been known among the Hebrews, from the expression in Deborah's song (Judges v. 30), "Of divers colors of needle-work on both sides," which Sisera's mother vainly looked for him to bring home as spoil for her. Books are prepared for embroiderers containing patterns for their imitation or combination. The silk used is of the finest kind and color, gold and silver thread being introduced to impart a lustre to the figures on caps, purses, and shoes. Tassels and twisted cords for sedans or lanterns, knobs or buttons worn on the winter caps, and elegant fan and pipe-cases, purses or fobs, constitute only a few of the products of their needles. Spangles are made from brass leaves by cutting out a small ring by means of a double-edged stamp, which at one drive detaches from the sheet a wheel-shaped circle; these are flattened by a single stroke of the hammer upon an anvil, leaving a minute hole in the centre. Another way of making them is to bend a copper wire into a circle and flatten it. Their own needles are very slender, and are rapidly giving way to the foreign article; in sewing the tailor holds it between the forefinger and thumb, pressing against the thimble on the thumb as he pushes it into the cloth.

Our ascertaining the date of the introduction of cotton as a textile plant into China depends very much on the meaning of certain words rendered *cotton* by some annotators in the *Shu King*. The weight of proof is, however, strongly adverse to this view; but a historical notice dated about A.D. 500 plainly refers to cotton robes; in A.D. 670 it was called by a foreign name *kih-pei*, a contracted form of the Sanscrit name *karpasi*. The present name of *mien-hwa*, or 'cotton flower,' was naturally given to it from the resemblance of its seed envelope to the silky covering of the seeds of the *muh-mien shu*, or tree cotton (*Bombax*), common in Southern China. It was, however, one thing to admire cotton cloth brought as tribute, and quite another to introduce cotton-growing into China, which does not seem to have been attempted until the Sung dynasty. Early in the eleventh century the plant was brought over and cultivated in the northwestern provinces by persons from Khoten, where it was grown. If this tardy adoption seems difficult to explain, the still slower introduction of silk-growing (in A.D. 550) into Asia Minor from China, twelve centuries after her fabrics had been seen there, is more surprising. The opposition to cotton cultivation on the part of silk and hemp growers was so persistent that the plant had not fairly won its way into favor until the Yuen dynasty; and this was owing to a public-spirited woman, Lady Hwang, who distributed seeds throughout Kiangnan, now the great cotton region.

The durable cotton cloth made in the central provinces, called *nankeen* by foreigners, because Nanking is famous for its manufacture, is the chief produce of Chinese looms. It is now seldom sent out of the country, and the natives are even taking to the foreign fabric in its stead. Cotton seed in that part of China is sown early in June, about eighty pounds to an acre; in a good year the produce is about two thousand pounds, diminishing to one-half in poor seasons. It is manured with liquid bean-cake, often hoed, and the bolls gathered in October, usually by each family in its own plot. The seeds are separated by passing the pods between an iron and wooden roller on a frame, which presses out the seeds and does not break them. The cleaned cotton is then bowed ready for spinning, and the cloth is woven in simple looms by the people who are to wear it after it is dyed blue. The looms used in weaving cotton vary from twelve to sixteen inches in width; they are simple in their construction; no figures are woven in cotton fabrics, nor have the Chinese learned to print them as chintz or calico.

Whether the varied articles from the west now brought into close competition with this primitive Chinese manufacture will finally captivate the consumer's choice, and neutralize its production, depends chiefly on what can be substituted therefor. At present, such is the extent of the native crop that prices would not probably advance ten per cent. if the whole foreign importation of raw and manufactured cotton should suddenly stop. The only attempt to estimate the product has been in Kiangnan, at

The Cobbler and his Movable Workshop.

twenty-eight thousand five hundred tons, a figure below rather than above the truth.[1]

Leather is used to protect the felt soles of shoes and make saddles, bridles, quivers, harness, etc., but the entire consumption is small, and the leather extremely poor. Buffalo and horse-hides are tanned for sole leather, and calf-skin for upper leather to supply shoes for foreigners at the ports. Alum, saltpetre, gambier, and urine are the tanning materials employed, and the rapid manner in which the process is completed renders the leather both porous and tender.

Cobblers go about the streets plying their trade, provided

[1] *Journal N. C. Br. R. A. S.* (1859); *Chinese Repository*, XVIII., pp. 449–469; N. Rondot, *Commerce de la Chine*, 1849, p. 72; Fortune, *Wanderings*, Chap. XIV. (1847); Grosier, *Histoire de la Chine*, Tome III., pp. 193–204.

with a few bits of nankeen, silk, and yellowish sole leather with which to patch their customers' shoes. It is no small convenience to a man, as he passes along the street, to give his old shoe to a cobbler and his ragged jacket to a seamstress, while he calls the barber to shave him as he waits for them; and such a trio at work for a man is not an uncommon sight.

The chief woollen fabrics produced are felts of different qualities and rugs or carpets woven from coarse camel's-hair yarn. Tanned sheep-skins furnish the laboring poor in the northern provinces with clothing, and elsewhere felt supplies them with material for shoes, hats, and carpets. The fulling process is not very thoroughly done, and the fabric soon disintegrates unless protected by matting or cotton. The consumption of the good qualities for hats is large among out-door workmen, who prefer the doubled kind made in the shape of a hollow cycloid, so that it can be turned inside out. Camel's-hair rugs supply a durable and cheap covering for the brick divans and tiled floors in the colder districts, but the thick soles of Chinese shoes obviate the need of additional protection to the feet. Some of these rugs are fine specimens of art in their arrangement of patterns and figures in colored woollen yarns, though far inferior to the Persian. Pretty rugs are also made of dog, deer, and fox-skins sewed together in a kind of mosaic. Knitting and ornamental works in wool are unknown, since the far more elegant and durable embroidery in silk takes the place of these as fancy work among dames of high and low degree.

The subject of tea culture and the preparation of its leaf have engaged the attention of writers among the Chinese and Japanese; while its effects on the human system as a beverage have been discussed most carefully by eminent western chemists and pathologists. Its virtue in restoring the energies of the body and furnishing a drink of the gentlest and most salubrious nature has been fully tested in its native land for many centuries, and is rapidly becoming known the world over. The following are some of the leading facts relating to the plant and the preparation and nature of the leaf, derived from personal observation in the country or from the writings of competent observers.

Tea does not grow in the northern provinces of China and Japan; its range lies between the twenty-third and thirty-fifth degrees of latitude, and reaching in longitude from Yedo to Assam. No accounts have come to us of the tea shrub being cultivated for its infusion till A.D. 350. The people in different parts of China gave different names to the successive pickings of the leaves, which have now become disused. Our word *tea* is derived from the common sound of the character for the plant at the city of Amoy, where it is *tay;* at Canton and Peking it is *cha*, at Shanghai *dzo*, at Fuhchau *ta*. The Russians and Portuguese have retained the word *cha*, the Spanish is *te* or *tay*, and the Italians have both *te* and *cha*. Tea is so nearly akin to the various species of camellia that the Chinese have only one name for all. The principal difference to the common observer is in the thin leaf of the tea and the leathery glabrous leaf of the beautiful Camellia Japonica. When allowed to grow they both become high trees. The tea flower is small, single, and white, has no smell, and soon falls; its petals are less erect than the camellia. The seeds are three small nuts, like filberts in color, enclosed in a triangular shell which splits open when ripe, with valves between the seeds. Its taste is oily and bitter. Two species of camellia are cultivated for their oily seeds, the oil being known as tea-oil among the natives; it is used for lamps and cooking. There is probably only one species of the tea plant, and all the varieties have resulted from culture; but the *Thea viridis* is most cultivated. The nuts are ripe in October. They are put in a mixture of sand and earth, dampened to keep them fresh till spring; they generate heat and spoil if not thus separated. In March they are sown in a nursery, and the thrifty shoots transplanted the next year in rows about four feet apart. Leaves are collected when the plant is three years old, and this process is continued annually to a greater or less extent, according to the demand and strength, until the whole bush becomes so weak and diseased that it is pulled up for firewood to give place to a new shoot. On the average this is about the eighth year. The plants seldom exceed three feet; most of them are half that height, straggling and full of twigs, often covered with lichens, but well hoed and clean around their roots.

All tea plantations are merely patches of the shrubs cared for by small farmers, who cultivate the plants and sell the leaves to middle-men, or more often pick the crop themselves if they can afford to do so. The great plantation or farm, with its landlord and the needy laborer, each class trying to get as much as possible out of the other, are unknown in China; the farmer has not there learned to employ skill, machinery, and capital all for his own advantage, but each farmstead is worked by the family, who rather emulate each other in the reputation of their tea. Tea is cultivated on the slopes or bases of hills, where the drainage is quick and the moisture unfailing. This is of more consequence than the ingredients of the soil, but plants so continually depauperated and stripped require rich manure to supply their waste. In Japan the tea shrubs are sometimes grown as a hedge around a garden lot, but such plants are not stripped in this way. In gathering the earliest leaves, the pickers are careful to leave enough foliage at the end of the twigs; and the spring rains are depended on to stimulate the second and full crop of leaves. When these are scant or fail the tea harvest diminishes, and the regularity of the rains is so essential to a profitable cultivation that it will be one of the causes of failure where everything else in soil, climate, manuring, and manufacture may be favorable.

The first gathering is the most carefully done, for it goes to make the best sorts of black and green tea; and as the greatest part of the leaves are still undeveloped, the price must necessarily be very much higher. Such tea has a whitish down, like that on young birch leaves, and is called *pecoe*, or 'white hair,' and is most of it sent to England and Russia. In the last century, the green tea known as Young Hyson was made of these half-opened leaves picked in April and named from two words meaning 'rains before.' The second gathering varies somewhat according to the latitude—May 15th to June, when the foliage is fullest. This season is looked forward to by women and children in the tea districts as their working time; they run in crowds to the middle-men, who have bargained for the leaves on the plants, or apply to farmers who have not hands. The average produce is from sixteen to twenty-two ounces of green leaves for the healthiest plants, down to ten and eight ounces. The tea when cured is about one-fifth of its first weight, and one thousand square yards will contain about three hundred and fifty plants, each two feet across. They strip the twigs in the most summary manner, and fill their baskets with healthy leaves as they pick out the sticks and yellow leaves, for they are paid in this manner. Fifteen pounds is a good day's work, and six to eight cents is a day's wages. The time for picking lasts only ten or twelve days. There are curing houses, where families who grow and pick their own leaves bring them for sale at the market rate. The sorting employs many hands, for it is an important point in connection with the purity of the various descriptions, and much care is taken by dealers, in maintaining the quality of their lots, to have them cured carefully as well as sorted properly.

The management of this great branch of industry exhibits some of the best features of Chinese country life. It is only over a portion of each farm that the plant is grown, and its cultivation requires but little attention compared with rice and vegetables. The most delicate kinds are looked after and cured by priests in their secluded temples among the hills; these often have many acolytes who aid in preparing small lots to be sold at a high price.

When the leaves are brought in to the curers they are thinly spread on shallow trays to dry off all moisture by two or three hours' exposure. Meanwhile the roasting pans are heating, and when properly warmed some handfuls of leaves are thrown on them, and rapidly moved and shaken up for four or five minutes. The leaves make a slight crackling noise, become moist and flaccid as the juice is expelled, and give off even a sensible vapor. The whole is then poured out upon the rolling table, where each workman takes up a handful and makes it into a manageable ball, which he rolls back and forth on the rattan table to get rid of the sap and moisture as the leaves are twisted. This operation chafes the hands even with great precaution. The balls are opened and shaken out and then passed on to other workmen, who go through the same operation till they reach the headman, who examines the leaves to see if they have become curled. When properly done, and cooled, they are returned to the iron pans, under which a low charcoal fire is burning in the brickwork which supports them, and there kept in motion by the hand. If they need another rolling on the table it is now given them; an hour or more is spent in this manipu-

Mode of Firing Tea.

lation, when they are dried to a dull green color, and can be put away for sifting and sorting. This color becomes brighter after the exposure in sifting the cured leaves through sieves of various sizes; they are also winnowed to separate the dust, and afterward sorted into the various descriptions of green tea. Finally, the finer kinds are again fired three or four times, and the coarse kinds, as Twankay, Hyson, and Hyson Skin, once. The others furnish the Young Hyson, Gunpowder, Imperial, etc. Tea cured in this way is called *luh cha*, or 'green tea,' by the Chinese, while the other, or black tea, is termed *hung cha*, or 'red tea,' each name being taken from the tint of the infusion.

After the fresh leaves are allowed to lie exposed to the air on the bamboo trays over night or several hours, they are thrown into the air and tossed about and patted till they become soft; a heap is made of these wilted leaves and left to lie for an hour or more, when they have become moist and dark in color. They are then thrown on the hot pans for five minutes and rolled on the rattan table, previous to exposure out-of-doors for three or four hours on sieves, during which time they are turned over and opened out. After this they get a second roasting and rolling to give them their final curl. When the charcoal fire is ready, a basket shaped something like an hour-glass is placed endwise over it, having a sieve in the middle on which the leaves are thinly spread. When dried five minutes in this way they undergo another rolling, and are then thrown into a heap, until all the lot has passed over the fire. When this firing is finished, the leaves are opened out and are again thinly spread on the sieve in the basket for a few minutes, which finishes the drying and rolling for most of the heap, and makes the leaves a uniform black. They are now replaced in the basket in greater mass, and pushed against its sides by the hands in order to allow the heat to come up through the sieve and the vapor to escape; a basket over all retains the heat, but the contents are turned over until perfectly dry and the leaves become uniformly dark.

It will be seen from this that green tea retains far more of the peculiar oil and sap in the leaves than the black, which undergo a partial fermentation and emit a sensibly warm vapor as they lie in heaps after the first roasting. They thus become oxidized by longer contact in a warm moist state with the atmosphere, and a delicate analysis will detect a greater amount of oxidized insoluble extract in an infusion of black than green tea. The same difference has been observed in drying medicinal plants, as hemlock, belladonna, etc., for the apothecary's shop.

Green teas are mostly produced in the region south of the Yangtsz' River and west of Ningpo among the hills as one goes toward the Poyang Lake in Chehkiang and Nganhwui. The black tea comes from Fuhkien in the southeast and Hupeh and Hunan in the central region; Kwangtung and Sz'chuen provinces produce black, green, and brick teas. While the leaves of each species of the shrub can be cured into either green or black tea, the workmen in one district are able, by practice, to produce one kind in a superior style and quality; those in another region will do better with another kind. Soil, too, has a great influence, as it has in grape culture, in modifying the produce. Though the natives distinguish only these three kinds, their varieties are far too numerous to remember, and the names are mostly unknown in commerce.

Of black teas, the great mass is called *Congou*, or the 'well-worked,' a name which took the place of the *Bohea* of one hundred and fifty years ago, and is now itself giving way to the term English Breakfast tea. The finest sorts are either named from the place of their growth, or more frequently have fancy appellations in allusion to their color or form. Orange Pekoe is named "superior perfume;" pure Pekoe is "Lau-tsz' eyebrows;" "carnation hair," "red plum blossom," "lotus kernel," "sparrow's tongue," "dragon's pellet," "dragon's whiskers," "autumn dew," "pearl flower," or *Chu-lan*, are other names; *Souchong* and *Powchong* refer to the modes of packing.

In the trade, teas are more commonly classified by their locality than their names, as it is found that well-marked differences in the style of the produce continue year after year, all equally well-cured tea. These arise from diversities in soil, climate, age, and manufacturing, and furnish materials for still further multiplying the sorts by skilfully mixing them. Thus in black teas we have Hunan and Hupeh from two provinces, just as Georgia uplands and Sea Island indicate two sorts of cotton; Ningyong, Kai-sau, Ho-hau, Sing-chune-kí, etc., and many others, which are unknown out of China, are all names of places. One gentleman has given a list of localities, each furnishing its quota and peculiar product, amounting in all to forty-five for black and nine for green. The area of these regions is about four hundred and seventy thousand square miles.

It will have been seen already that the color of green tea, as well as its quality, depends very much on rapid and expert drying. When this kind is intended for home consumption soon after it is made, the color is of little consequence; but when the hue influences the sale, then it is not to be overlooked by the manufacturer or the broker. The first tea brought to Europe was from Fuhkien and all black; but as the trade extended probably some of the delicate Hyson sorts were now and then seen at Canton, and their appearance in England and Holland appreciated as more and more was sent. It was found, however, to be very difficult to maintain a uniform tint. If cured too slightly, the leaf was liable to fermentation during the voyage; if cured too much, it was unmarketable, which for the manufacturer was worse yet. Chinese ingenuity was equal to the call. Though no patent office was at hand to register the date when coloring green tea commenced, it is probably more than one hundred years since. The three hundred and forty-two chests and half chests which were so summarily opened on board the Dartmouth, the Eleanor, and the Beaver, when their contents were thrown overboard in Boston harbor, on December 16, 1773, furnishes probably no index of the consumption of tea in New England at that time. It was all called Bohea by John Adams, who speaks of three cargoes, as if the vessels had nothing else of note in their holds.

Dr. Holmes, in his ballad on the Boston Tea Party at its centennial celebration, says in the last verse:

> The waters in the rebel bay
>   Have kept the tea-leaf savor—
> Our old North Enders in their spray
>   Still taste a Hyson flavor;
> And Freedom's teacup still o'erflows
>   With ever fresh libations,
> To cheat of slumber all her foes
>   And cheer the wakening nations.

It has been noticed that emigrants to Australia, who had seldom tasted green tea before leaving England, usually prefer it in their new homes, as new settlers do in this country. The prevailing notion that green tea is cured on copper arose, no doubt, from the conclusion that real verdigris was the only source of a verdigris color, and the astringent taste confirmed the wrong idea. A more difficult question to answer is the inquiry, Why is it still believed ?

The operation of giving green tea its color is a simple one. A quantity of Prussian blue is pulverized to a very fine powder, and kept ready at the last roasting. Pure gypsum is burned in the charcoal fire till it is soft and fit for easily triturating. Four parts are then thoroughly mixed with three parts of Prussian blue, making a light blue powder. About five minutes before finally taking off the dried leaves this powder is sprinkled on them, and instantly the whole panful of two or three pounds is turned over by the workman's hands till a uniform color is obtained. His hands come out quite blue, but the compound gives the green leaves a brighter green hue. The quantity is not great, say about half a pound in a hundred of tea ; and as gypsum is not a dangerous or irritating substance, being constantly eaten by the Chinese, the other ingredient remains in an almost infinitesimal degree. If foreigners preferred yellow teas no doubt they could be favored, for the Chinese are much perplexed to account for this strange predilection, as they never drink this colored or faced tea. Turmeric root has been detected, too, in a very few analyses, but probably these were lots that needed to be refined at Canton to cover up mildew or supply a demand. The reasons for not drinking this tea are, however, owing more to the nature than the color of the leaf. The kinds of green tea are fewer than the black, and the regions producing it are less in area. Gunpowder and Imperial are foreign-made terms ; the teas are known as *siau chu* and *ta chu* by native dealers. The first is rolled to resemble shot or coarse gunpowder ; the other is named "sore crab's eyes," "sesamum seeds," and "pearls." Hyson is a corruption of *yu-tsien*, 'before the rains,' and of *Hi-chun*, meaning 'flourishing spring.' The last is alleged to be the name of a maiden who suggested to her father as long ago as 1700, or thereabouts, a better mode of sorting tea, and his business increased so much as his fine Hyson became known that he gave it her name. Members of this same family are still engaged in making this same tea, and the chop, known as the *Lí Yih-hing*, or 'Li's Extra Perfume,' is now in market, and has maintained its reputation for nearly two hundred years. Oolong is obtained in Fuhkien—a black tea with a green tea flavor, named Black Dragon from a story that Su was struck with the fragrance of the leaf from a plant where a black snake was found coiled. The great mart for green tea is Twankay, in Chehkiang province.

A *chop* is a well-known term in the tea trade; it is derived from the Chinese word *chop*, or 'stamp', such as an official uses, and in the tea trade denotes a certain number of packages from the same place, and all of the same quality. In the course of years the uniform excellence of a certain chop, like that of a certain vineyard, gives it a marketable value. A lawsuit arose in 1873 between two American houses at Canton in regard to the right to a certain chop of tea, among two brokers, each of whom claimed to sell the genuine lot. Such chops range from fifty to one thousand two hundred chests, averaging six hundred. English tea-tasters have learned that an admixture of scented teas in common sorts of Congou adds much to the flavor and sale. This is not often done for native-drank tea, and is chiefly practised at Canton. The flowers used are roses, Olea fragrans, tuberose, orange, jasmine, gardenia, and azalea. The stems, calyx, and other parts are carefully sorted out, so that only the petals remain. When the tea is ready for packing, dry and warm, the fresh flowers are mixed with it (forty pounds to one hundred pounds for the orange), and left thus in a mass for twenty-four hours; it is then sifted and winnowed in a fanning mill till the petals are separated. If the odor is insufficient, the operation may be repeated with the jasmine or orange. The proportion of jasmine is a little more than orange; of the azalea, nearly half and half. The length of time required to obtain the proper smell from these flowers differs, and among them all tea scented with the azalea is said to keep its perfume the longest.

The mode of scenting tea differs somewhat according to the flower itself, for the small blossom of the Olea cannot be separated by sifting as rose or jasmine leaves can. Tea thus perfumed is sent to England as Orange Pekoe and Scented Caper. It is mixed with fine teas; and there is much to commend in thus increasing the aroma and taste of this healthy beverage. The Scented Caper comes in the form of round pellets, which are made of black tea softened by sprinkling water on it until it is pliable; it is then tied in canvas bags and rolled with the feet by treading on it for a good while till most of the quantity takes this form; as soon as perfumed it is packed for shipment. When rolled and dried, such tea needs only a facing to make it into Imperial and Gunpowder among the green teas.

The Chinese have been charged with adulterating their tea by mixing in other leaves with the true tea-leaf, and adding other ingredients far worse than rose, jujube, and fern leaves, and the cases which have been proved of *lie-tea* being sent off have been applied to the entire export. The stimulus for some of this adulteration has come from the foreigner, who desires to get good pure tea at half its cost of manufacture. The foregoing details will plainly show that an article which has to go through so many hands before its infusion is poured out of the teapot on the other side of the world, and where the only machinery used is a fanning mill and a roasting pan, cannot be furnished at much under twenty-five cents a pound for the common sorts. The villanous mixture known at Shanghai as *ma-lu cha*, or 'race-course tea,' was the answer on the part of the native manufacturer to the demand for cheap tea, until the consumers in Great Britain protested at the deception put on them, and its importation was prohibited. Which of the parties was most blameworthy may be left for them to settle, but in our own papers, of course, most of the blame rested on the tempted party. It is not to be inferred, however, that all cheap tea is adulterated. The process of manufacture leaves a large percentage of broken material, which can be worked into passable tea; the produce of many regions has not the flavor of the finest sorts, and, as it is with wines, will not bear so much cost in curing. The tea brokers know this, and things equalize themselves. The dust, the leaf ribs, and the siftings are all consumed by the poor natives, who mix other leaves, too, with the real leaf. Tea can perhaps bear comparison with any other great staple of food in this respect; and when we can fairly estimate the consumption of tea sent out of China and Japan at more than three hundred millions of pounds, it must be conceded that it is a very pure article—not as much, probably, as even five per cent. of false leaf.

One mode of using tea known among Tibetans and Mongols remains to be noticed. The rich province of Sz'chuen, in the western part of China, furnishes an abundance of good tea; much of which is exported to Russia by way of Sí-ngan fu and Kansuh, to supply the inhabitants of Siberia. This brick tea is cured by pressing the damp leaves into the form of a brick or tile, varying in size and weight, eight to twelve inches long and one thick; in this form it is far more easily carried than in the leaf. In Tibet, as we have seen, it appears more as a soup than an infusion. The brick tea is composed of coarse leaves, or of stalks moistened by steaming over boiling water, and then pressed till dry and hard. When used, a piece is broken off and simmered with milk and butter and water, with a touch of vinegar or pepper. The dish is not inviting at first, but Abbé Huc endorses its refreshing qualities in restoring the failing energies. The pressing and drying is assisted by sprinkling the mass with rice-water as it is forced into the moulds. The Chinese mix other leaves with real tea to eke it out, in districts where it is not commonly grown, but they do not regard this as adulteration. Willow leaves are common in such mixtures. Large caravans cross the plateau laden with brick tea.

Packing tea is mostly done in the interior, where it is cured. The large dry leaves frequently found inside are usually furnished by a peculiar species of bamboo; the lead is made into thin sheets by pouring the melted metal on to a large square brick, covered with several thicknesses of paper, and letting another brick drop down instantly on it. In order to test the honesty of the packing, the foreign merchant often walks over the three hundred to six hundred chests which make a chop, and selects any four or five he may choose for examination. If they stand the inspection the whole is taken on their guaranty, and are then weighed, papered, labelled, and mottoed ready for shipping. In all these matters the Chinese are very expert. It is impossible to calculate the number of persons to whom the tea trade furnishes employment; nor could machinery well come into use to displace human labor.

The introduction of tea among western nations was slow at first. Marco Polo has no notice of its use. The Dutch brought it to Europe in 1591 according to some accounts; but a sample or two did not make a trade, and there would have been reference to it if it had been used. In 1660 Samuel Pepys writes, September 28th: "I did send for a cup of tea (a China drink), of which I had never drank before." Nearly seven years after he says: "Home, and there find my wife making of tea, a drink which Mr. Pellin, the pothicary, tells her is good for her cold and defluxions." In 1670 the importation into England was 79 pounds; in 1685 it was 12,070 pounds; most of it came from Batavia and sold for a long time between £10 and £5 a pound weight. In 1657 Mr. Garney opened a shop in London to sell the infusion, and paid an excise of 8d. per gallon; the present duty is 2s. 1d. per pound, or 4½ pounds to each person in a year, nearly all of which, as it is in Europe and elsewhere, is black tea. In 1725 only 375,000 pounds were consumed in Great Britain. The actual quantity now in the United Kingdom is 126,000,000 pounds, besides much on the way. The importation into the United States is worth $18,000,000 to $19,000,000, say 60,000,000 pounds. Russia takes more good tea than any other nation and pays more for it, because the former overland trade to Siberia could not afford to transport poor tea. The export from Assam is now 20,000,000 pounds, but those sorts are too strong for the public taste when used alone, and are consumed in mixtures. Tea is a native of Assam, but its discovery only dates from 1836 or thereabouts. It is cultivated in Java and Brazil, but there is not much to encourage the manufacturer in any country where coffee supplies a similar beverage, and the price of labor makes it equal to the imported article.

The remarkable work on agriculture of Paul Sü, a convert to Christianity in 1620, contains a brief account and directions for cultivating tea. In concluding the chapter he urges the greater use of tea as against spirits. "Tea is of a cooling nature, and if drunk too freely will produce exhaustion and lassitude. Country people before drinking it add ginger and salt to counteract this cooling property. It is an exceedingly useful plant; cultivate it and the benefit will be widely spread; drink it and the animal spirits will be lively and clear. The chief rulers, lords, and great men esteem it; the lower people, the poor and beggarly, will not be destitute of it; all use it daily and like it."

The chemical analyses which have made known to us the components of the four or five substances used as warm beverages, viz., tea, coffee, maté, cocoa, guarana, and kola, indicate three constituents found in them, to which, no doubt, their virtues are owing.

A volatile oil is observed when tea is distilled with water; about one pound comes from one hundred pounds of dried tea, possessing its peculiar aroma and flavor to a high degree. Much of it is pressed from the leaves when rolled and cured, but little as still remains, its effects upon the human system are noticeable and sometimes powerful. Tea-tasters who continually taste the quality of the various lots submitted by sample for their approval, do so by breathing upon a handful of leaves and instantly covering the nose, so as to get this volatile aroma as one important test. They also examine the infusion in several different ways, by its taste, color, and strength. Long practice in this business is alleged to have deleterious influence upon their nervous systems. The other beverages we drink, as well as tea, derive their peculiar and esteemed flavor and aroma from chemical substances produced in them during the process of drying and roasting; at least nothing of them can be perceived in their natural state. Another substance in tea regarded as the chief inducement and reward in its effect on the system is the peculiar principle called theine. If a few finely powdered leaves are placed on a watch-glass, covered with a paper cap and placed on a hot plate, a white vapor slowly rises and condenses in the cap in the form of colorless crystals. They exist in different proportions in the different kinds of tea, from one and one-half to five or six per cent. in green tea. Theine has no smell and a slightly bitter taste, and does not therefore attract us to drink the infusion; but the chemists tell us that it contains nearly thirty per cent. of nitrogen. The salts in other beverages, as coffee and cocoa, likewise contain much nitrogen, and all tend to repair the waste going on in the human system, reduce the amount of solid food necessary, diminish too the wear and tear of the body and consequent lassitude of the mind, and maintain the vigor of both upon a smaller amount of food. Tea does this more pleasantly, perhaps, than any of the others; but it does more than they do for old people in supplementing the impaired powers of digestion, and helping them to maintain their flesh and uphold the system in health longer than they otherwise would. It is no wonder, therefore, that tea has become one of the necessaries of life; and the sexagenarian invalid, too poor to buy a bit of meat for her meal, takes her pot of tea with what she has, and knows that she feels lighter, happier, and better fitted for her toil, and enjoys life more than if she had no tea. Unconsciously she echoes what the Chinese said centuries ago, "Drink it, and the animal spirits will be lively and clear."

The third substance (which is contained in tea more than in the other beverages mentioned) forms also an important ingredient in betel-nut and gambier, so extensively chewed in Southern Asia, viz., tannin or tannic acid. This gives the astringent taste to tea-leaves and their infusion, and is found to amount to seventeen per cent. in well-dried black tea, and much more than that in green tea, especially the Japan leaf. The effects of tannin are not clearly ascertained as apart from the oil and the theine, but Johnston considers them as conducing to the exhilarating, satisfying, and narcotic action of the beverage.

A remaining ingredient worthy of notice in tea, in common with other food-plants, is gluten. This forms one-fourth of the weight of the leaves, but in order to derive the greatest good from it which proper methods of cooking might bring out, we must contrive a mode of eating the leaves. The nutritious property of the gluten accounts for the general use of brick tea throughout the Asiatic plateau. Huc says he drank the dish in default of something better, for he was unaccustomed to it, but his cameleers would often take twenty to forty cups a day.

If the sanitary effects of tea upon the system are so great and wholesome, its influence since its general introduction among occidentals cannot be overlooked. The domestic, quiet life and habits of the Chinese owe much of their strength to the constant use of this beverage, for the weak infusion which they sip allows them to spend all the time they choose at the tea-table. If they were in the habit of sipping even their weak whiskey in the same way, misery, poverty, quarrels, and sickness would take the place of thrift, quiet, and industry. The general temperance seen among them is owing to the tea much more than any other cause. It has, moreover, won its way with us, till in the present generation the associations that cluster around the tea-table form an integral part of the social life among English-speaking peoples. One of the most likely means to restrict the use of spirits among them is to substitute the use of warm beverages of all kinds by those whose system has not become vitiated. Tea is one of the greatest benefits to the Chinese, Japanese, and Mongols, and its universal use, for at least fifteen centuries, throughout their territories has proven its satisfaction as a nervine, a stimulant, and a beverage. If one passing through the streets of Peking, Canton, or Ohosaka, and seeing the good-natured hilarity of the groups of laborers and loiterers around the *cha-kwan* and the *cha-ya* of those cities, doubts the value of tea as a harmonizer and satisfier of human wants and passions, it must be taken as a proof of his own unsatisfied cravings.

It is a necessary of life to all classes of natives, and that its use is not injurious is abundantly evident from its general acceptance and increasing adoption; the prejudice against the beverage out of China may be attributed chiefly to the use of strong green tea, which is no doubt prejudicial. If those who have given it up on this account will adopt a weaker infusion of black tea, general experience is proof that it will do them no harm, and they may be sure that they will not be so likely to be deceived by a colored article. Neither the Chinese nor Japanese use milk or sugar in their tea, and the peculiar taste and aroma of the infusion is much better perceived without those additions. Tea, when clear, cannot be drunk so strong without tasting an unpleasant bitterness, which these diluents partly hide.[1]

Among other vegetable productions whose preparation affords employment are cassia and camphor. The cassia tree (*Cinnamomum cassia*) grows commonly in Kwangsí, Yunnan, and further south; the leading mart for all the varieties of this spice in China is Ping-nan, in the former of these provinces. The kind known as *kwei-pí*, or 'skinny cassia,' affords the principal part of that spice used at the west. The bark is stripped from the twigs by running a knife along the branch and gradually loosening it; after it is taken off it lies a day in the sun, when the epidermis is easily scraped off, and it is dried into the quilled shape in which it comes to market. The immature flowers of this and two other species of Cinnamomum are also collected and dried under the name of *cassia buds*, and often packed with the bark; they require little or no other preparation than simple drying. The leaves and bark of the tree are also distilled, and furnish oil of cassia, a powerful and pleasant oil employed by perfumers and cooks. Few genera of plants are more useful to man than those included under the old name of Laurus, to which these fragrant spices of cassia and cinnamon belong; their wood, bark, buds, seeds, flowers, leaves, and oil are all used by the Chinese in carpentry, medicine, perfumery, and cookery. The confusion arising from using the term *cassia* for the spice instead of confining it to the medicine (*Cassia senna*) has been a constant source of error.

The camphor tree (*Camphora officinarum*) is another species of Laurus, found along the southern maritime regions and Formosa, and affords both timber and gum for exportation and domestic use. The tree itself is large, and furnishes excellent planks, beams, and boards. The gum is procured from the branches, roots, leaves, and chips by soaking them in water until the liquid becomes saturated; a gentle heat is then applied to this solution, and the sublimed camphor received in inverted cones made of rice-straw, from which it is detached in impure

[1] Fortune's *Tea Districts* (1852); *Chinese Repository*, Vol. VIII., pp. 132–164, Vol. XVIII., pp. 13–18; Davis' *Chinese*, Vol. II., pp. 336–449; *Chinese Commercial Guide* (1863), pp. 141–148; Ball's *Tea Culture and Manufacture*.

grains, resembling unrefined sugar in color. Grosier describes another mode of getting it by taking out the coagulum inspissated from the solution into an iron dish and covering with powdered earth; two or three layers are thus placed in the dish, when a cover is luted on, and by a slow heat the camphor sublimes into it in a cake. It comes to market in a crude state, and is refined after reaching Europe. The preparation of the gum, sawing the timber for trunks, articles of furniture, and vessels in whole or in part, occupies great numbers of carpenters, shipwrights, and boat-builders. The increasing demand for the gum and boards has caused the rapid destruction of so many trees in Formosa that there is some ground for fear lest they ere long be all cut off.

Many of the common manipulations of Chinese workmen afford good examples of their ingenious modes of attaining the same end which is elsewhere reached by complex machinery. For instance, the baker places his fire on a large iron plate worked by a crane, and swings it over a shallow pan embedded in masonry, in which the cakes and pastry are laid and soon baked. The price of fuel compels its economical use wherever it is employed; in the forge, the kitchen, the kiln, or the dwelling, no waste of wood or coal is seen. As an instance in point, the mode of burning shells to lime affords a good example. A low wall encloses a space ten or twelve feet across, in the middle of which a hole communicates underneath the wall through a passage to the pit, where the fire is urged by a fan turned by the feet. The wood is loosely laid over the bottom of the area, and the fire kindled at the orifice in the centre and fanned into a blaze as the shells are rapidly thrown in until the wall is filled up; in twelve hours the shells are calcined. Toward evening scores of villagers collect around the burning pile, bringing their kettles of rice or vegetables to cook. The good-humor manifested by these groups of old and young is a pleasing instance of the sociability and equality witnessed among the lower classes of Chinese. The lime is taken out next morning and sifted for the mason.

Handicraftsmen of every name are content with coarse-looking tools compared with those turned out at Sheffield, but the work produced by some of them is far from contemptible. The bench of a carpenter is a low, narrow, inclined form, like a drawing-knife frame, upon which he sits to plane, groove, and work his boards, using his feet and toes to steady them. His augurs, bits, and gimlets are worked with a bow, but most of the edge-tools employed by him and the blacksmith, though similar in shape, are less convenient than our own. They are sharpened with hones or grindstones, and also with a cold steel like a spoke-shave, with which the edge is scraped thin. The aptitude of Chinese workmen has often been noticed, and

Travelling Blacksmith and Equipment.

among them all the travelling blacksmith takes the palm for his compendious establishment. "I saw a blacksmith a few days since," writes one observer, "mending a pan, the arrangement of whose tools was singularly compact. His fire was held in an iron basin not unlike a coal-scuttle in shape, in the back corner of which the mouthpiece of the bellows entered. The anvil was a small square mass of iron, not very unlike our own, placed on a block, and a partition basket close by held the charcoal and tools, with the old iron and other rubbish he carried. The water to temper his iron was in an earthen pot, which just at this time was most usefully employed in boiling his dinner over the forge fire After he had done the job he took off his dinner, threw the water on the fire, picked out the coals and put them back into the basket, threw away the ashes, set the anvil astride of the bellows, and laying the fire-pan on the basket, slung the bellows on one end of his pole and the basket on the other, and walked off."[1] The mode of mending holes in cast-iron pans here noticed is a peculiar operation. The smith first files the lips of the hole clean, and after heating the dish firmly

Itinerant Dish-mender.

places it on a tile covered with wet felt. He then pours the liquid iron, fused in a crucible by the assistance of a flux, upon the hole, and immediately patters it down with a dossil of felt until it covers the edges of the pan above and below, and is then, while cooling, hammered until firmly fixed in its place.

Another ingenious and effectual method of mending porcelain and all manner of crockery ware is performed by itinerant workmen, who travel about with their workshop on their

[1] *Chinese Repository*, Vol. X., p. 473.

shoulders, as seen in the cut. By means of minute copper clamps, even the most delicate article of China-ware may be repaired and made to answer the purpose of a new piece; since no cement is used in this style of mending, it has the additional advantage of standing immersion in water.

The great number of craftsmen who ply their vocations in the street, as well as the more numerous class of hucksters who supply food as they go from house to house, furnish much to amuse and interest. Each of them has a peculiar call. The barber twangs a sort of tweezers like a long tuning-fork, the peddler twirls a hand-drum with clappers strung on each side, the refuse-buyer strikes a little gong, the fruiterer claps two bamboo sticks, and the fortune-teller tinkles a gong-bell; these, with the varied calls and cries of beggars, cadgers, chapmen, etc., fill the streets with a concert of strange sounds.

The delicate carving of Chinese workmen has often been described; many specimens of it are annually sent abroad. Few products of their skill are more remarkable than the balls containing ten or twelve separate spheres one within another. The manner of cutting them is ingenious. A piece of ivory or wood is first made perfectly globular, and then several conical holes are bored into it in such a manner that their apices all meet at the centre, which becomes hollow as the holes are bored into it. The sides of each having been marked with lines to indicate the number of globes to be cut out, the workman inserts a chisel or burin with a semicircular blade, bent so that the edge cuts the ivory, as the shaft is worked on the pivot, at the same depth in each hole. By successively cutting a little on the inside of each conical hole, the incisures meet, and a sphericle is at last detached, which is now turned over and its faces one after another brought opposite the largest hole, and firmly secured by wedges in the other apertures, while its surfaces are smoothed and carved. When the central sphere is done, a similar tool, somewhat larger, is again introduced into the holes, and another sphere detached and smoothed in the same way, and then another, until the whole is completed, each being polished and carved before the next outer one is commenced. It takes three or four months to complete a ball with fifteen inner globes, the price of which ranges from twenty to thirty dollars, according to the delicacy of the carving. Some writers have asserted that these curious toys were made of semispheres nicely luted together, and they have been boiled in oil for hours in order to separate them and solve the mystery of their construction.

Fans and card-cases are carved of wood, ivory, and mother-of-pearl in alto-relievo, with an elaborateness which shows the great skill and patience of the workman, and at the same time his crude conception of drawing, the figures, houses, trees, and other objects being grouped in violation of all propriety and perspective. Beautiful ornaments are made by carving roots of plants, branches, gnarled knots, etc., into fantastic groups of birds or animals, the artist taking advantage of the natural form of his material in the arrangement of his figures. Models of pagodas, boats, and houses are entirely constructed of ivory, even to representing the ornamental roofs, the men working at the oar, and women looking from the balconies. Baskets of elegant shape are woven from ivory splinths; and the shopmen at Canton exhibit a variety of seals, paper-knives, chessmen, counters, combs, etc., exceeding in finish and delicacy the same kind of work found anywhere else in the world. The most elaborate coat of arms, or complicated cypher, will also be imitated by these skilful carvers. The national taste prefers this style of carving on plane surfaces; it is seen on the walls of houses and granite slabs of fences, the woodwork of boats and shops, and on articles of furniture. Most of it is pretty, but the disproportion and cramped position of the figures detract from its beauty when judged by strict rules of western art.

The manufacture of enamels and cloisonné wares has lately received a great stimulus from their foreign demand. A copper vase is formed of the desired shape by hammering and soldering, on whose clean surface the figures to be enamelled are etched to show where the strips of copper are to be soldered before their interspaces are enamelled. This solder is made of borax and silver, and melts at a higher temperature than the enamel, which is reduced to a paste and filled into each cell of the pattern by brushes and styles, until the whole design is gone over. The various colored *liao*, or ingredients, are prepared in cakes by artists who keep their composition secret, but all the substances occur in China. The quality of the ware depends on the skill in mixing these cakes and fusing the colors in a charcoal fire, into which the piece is placed; imperfections and holes are covered and filled up when it is cooled, and the piece is again and again exposed to the fire. After the third ordeal it is ground smooth and polished on a lathe, and the brass work gilt. The specimens now made show very fine work, but their coloring hardly equals those of Kienlung's reign or still earlier in the Ming dynasty. Much inferior work has also been palmed off for that of the golden period of this art.

Fancy Carved Work.

The manufacture of mats for sails of junks and boats, floors, bedding, etc., employs thousands. A sail containing nearly four hundred square feet can be obtained for ten dollars. The rolls are largely exported, and still more extensively used in the country for covering packages for shipment. A stouter kind made of bamboo splinths serves as a material for huts, and fulfils many other purposes that are elsewhere attained by boards or canvas. Rattans are largely worked into mats, chairs, baskets, and other articles of domestic service. Several branches of manufacture have entirely grown up, or been much encouraged by the foreign trade, among which the preparation of vermilion, beating gold-leaf, cutting pearl buttons, dyeing and trimming pith-paper for artificial flowers, weaving and painting fancy window-blinds, and the preparation of sweetmeats are the principal.

The beautiful vermilion exported from Canton is prepared by triturating one part of quicksilver with two of sulphur until they form a blackish powder, which is put into a crucible having an iron lid closely luted down. When the fire acts on the mixture the lid is cooled to effect the sublimation; the deposit on the top is cinnabar and that on the sides is vermilion, according to the Chinese; all of them are powdered, levigated, decanted, and dried on tiles for use in painting and pharmacy, coloring candles and paper, and making red ink. The excellence of Chinese vermilion depends on the thoroughness of the grinding.[1]

It has often been said that the Chinese are so averse to change and improvement that they will obstinately adhere to their own modes, but, though slow to alter well-tried methods, such is not the case. Three new manufactures have been introduced during the present century, viz., that of glass, bronze-work, and Prussian blue. A Chinese sailor brought home the manufacture of the latter, which he had learned thoroughly in London, and the people now supply themselves. Works in bronze and brass have of late been set up, and watches and clocks are both extensively manufactured, with the exception of the springs. Fire-engines in imitation of foreign hand-engines are gradually coming into use. Brass cannon were made during the war with England in imitation of pieces taken from a wreck, and the frames of one or two vessels to be worked with wheels by men at a crank, in imitation of steamers, were found on the stocks at Ningpo when the English took the place. Since then the establishment of government arsenals at Fuhchau, Shanghai, Nanking, and Tientsin has stimulated and suggested as well as taught the people many applications of machinery. Yet until they can see their way clear to be remunerated for their outlay, it is unwise to urge or start doubtful experiments. This was shown at Canton ten years ago when a native company was formed to spin cotton yarn by steam machinery, and when the apparatus was all ready for work the cotton growers were quite unwilling to trust their raw cotton out of their hands. Moreover, it should be observed that few have taken the trouble to

---

[1] Compare an article by Julien in the *Nouv. Journ. Asiatique*, Tome V., 1830, pp. 208 ff.

explain or show them the improvements they are supposed to be so disinclined to adopt. Ploughs have been given the farmers near Shanghai, but they would not use them, which, however, may have been as much owing to the want of a proper harness, or a little instruction regarding their use, as to a dislike to take a new article.

The general aspect of Chinese society, in an industrial point of view, is one of its most pleasing features. The great body of the people are obliged to engage in manual labor in order to subsist, yet only a trifling proportion of them can be called beggars, while still fewer possess such a degree of wealth that they can live on its income. Property is safe enough to afford assurance to honest toil that it shall generally reap the reward of its labors, but if that toil prosper beyond the usual limits, the avarice of officials and the envy of neighbors easily find a multitude of contrivances to harass and impoverish the fortunate man, and the laws are not executed with such strictness as to deter them. The mechanical arts supply their wants, but having no better models before them, nor any scientific acquaintance with elementary principles and powers applicable to a great number of purposes, these arts have remained stationary. The abundance of labor must be employed, and its cheapness obviates the necessity of finding substitutes in machinery. The adoption of even a few things from abroad might involve so many changes, that even those intelligent natives who saw their advantages would hesitate in view of the momentous contingencies of a failure. The conflict between capital and labor in its various phases and struggles is becoming more and more marked the world over as civilization advances, and the Chinese polity is destined to endure its greatest strain in adjusting their forces among its industrious millions.

Imitation is a remarkable trait in the Chinese mind, though invention is not altogether wanting; the former leads the people to rest content with what they can get along with, even at some expense of time and waste of labor, where, too, an exhibition of ingenuity and science would perhaps be accompanied with suspicion, expense, or hindrances from both neighbors and rulers. The existence of the germ of arts and discoveries, whose development would have brought with them so many advantages and pointed to still further discoveries, leads one to inquire the reason why they were not carried out. Setting aside the view, which may properly be taken, that the wonderful discoveries now made in the arts by Europeans form part of God's great plan for the redemption of the race, the want of mutual confidence, insecurity of property, and debasing effects of heathenism upon the intellect will explain much of the apathy shown toward improvement. Invention among them has rather lacked encouragement than ceased to exist:—more than that, it has been checked by a suspicious, despotic sway, while no stimulus of necessity has existed to counterbalance and urge it forward, and has been stunted by the mode and materials of education. It was not till religious liberty and discussion arose in Europe that the inhabitants began to improve in science and arts as well as morals and good government; and when the ennobling and expanding principles of an enlarged civilization find their way into Chinese society and mind, it may reasonably be expected that rapid advances will be made in the comforts of this life, as well as in adopting the principles and exhibiting the conduct which prove a fitness for the enjoyments of the next.

CHAPTER XVI.

SCIENCE AMONG THE CHINESE.

THAT enlargement of the mind which results from the collection and investigation of facts, or from extensive reading of books on whose statements reliance can be placed, and which leads to the cultivation of knowledge for its own sake, has no existence in China. Sir John Davis justly observes that the Chinese "set no value on abstract science, apart from some obvious and immediate end of utility;" and he properly compares the actual state of the sciences among them with their condition in Europe previous to the adoption of the inductive mode of investigation. Even their few theories in explanation of the mysteries of nature are devoid of all fancy to make amends for want of fact and experiment, so that in reading them we are neither amused by their imagination nor instructed by their research. Perhaps the rapid advances made by Europeans, during the two past centuries, in the investigation of nature in all her departments and powers, has made us somewhat impatient of such a parade of nonsense as Chinese books exhibit. In addition to the general inferiority of Chinese mind to European in genius and imagination, it has moreover been hampered by a language the most tedious and meagre of all tongues, and wearied with a literature abounding in tiresome repetitions and unsatisfactory theories. Under these conditions, science, whether mathematical, physical, or natural, has made few advances during the last few centuries, and is now awaiting a new impulse from abroad in all its departments.

Murray's *China* (Vol. III., Chap. IV.) contains a fair account of the attainments of the Chinese in mathematics and astronomy. The notation of the Chinese is based on the decimal principle, but as their figures are not changed in value by position, it is difficult to write out clearly the several steps in solving a problem. Experiments have shown that it is easy enough to perform them with Chinese figures used in our way, omitting the characters for 100, 1,000, and 10,000 (*peh*, *tsien*, and *wan*); but it will be long before the change will become general, even if it be desirable. Arithmetical calculations are performed with the assistance of an abacus, called a *swanpan*, or 'counting board,' which is simply a shallow case divided longitudinally by a bar and crossed by several wires; on one side of this bar the wires bear five balls, on the other two. The five balls stand for units, the two balls being each worth five units. When the balls on any wire are taken for units, those next to the right stand for tens, the third for hundreds, and so on; while those on the left denote tenths, hundredths, etc. Simple calculations are done on this machine with accuracy and rapidity, but as it is only a convenient index for the progress and result of a calculation performed in the head, if an error be made the whole must be performed again, since the result only appears when the sum is finished. There are three sorts of figures, partly answering to the English, Roman, and Arabic forms—as *Seven*, VII., and 7—the most common of which are given on page 619 of Vol. I.; the complicated form is used for security in drafts and bills, and the abbreviated in common operations, accounts, etc., and in setting down large amounts in a more compact form than can be done by the other characters. This mode of notation is employed by the Japanese and Cochinchinese, and possesses some advantages over the method of using letters practised by the Greeks and Romans, as well as over the counters once employed in England, but falls far behind the Arabic system now in general use in the west.

Treatises on arithmetic are common, in which the simple rules are explained and illustrated by examples and questions. One of the best is the *Swan-fah Tung Tsung*, or 'General Comprehensive Arithmetic,' in five volumes, octavo, the author of which, Ching Yu-sz', lived in the Ming dynasty. The *Tsu-wei-shan Fang Sho Hioh*, or 'Mathematics of the Lagerstræmia Hill Institution,' in thirty-eight books, octavo, 1828, contains a complete course of mathematical instruction in geometry, trigonometry, mensuration, etc., together with a table of natural sines and tangents, and one of logarithmic sines, tangents, secants, etc., for every degree and minute. Both these compilations derive most of their value from the mathematical writings of the Roman Catholic missionaries; it is stated in the latter work that "the western scholar, John Napier, made logarithms."

The study of arithmetic has attracted attention among the Chinese from very early times, and the notices found in historical works indicate some treatises even extant in the Han dynasty, followed by a great number of general and particular works down to the Sung dynasty. One author of the Tang dynasty, in his problems on solid mensuration, offered one thousand taels of silver to whoever found a single word of error in the book. The Hindu processes in algebra were known to Chinese mathematicians, and are still studied, though all intellectual intercourse between the countries has long ceased. Down to the end of the Ming dynasty, these branches made slow progress. Since foreigners have begun to apply western science, the development has been rapid. Mr. Wylie has given, in his *Notes on Chinese Literature* (pp. 86–104), a digested account of the most valuable native works on astronomy and mathematics. One very comprehensive work on them is the *Thesaurus of Mathematics and Chronology*, published by imperial order about 1750.

The knowledge of mathematics, even among learned men, is very small, and the common people study it only as far as their business requires; the cumbersome notation and the little aid such studies give in the examinations doubtless discourage men from pursuing what they seem to have no taste for as a people.[1] A curious fact regarding the existence of six errors in these tables, discovered by Babbage to have been perpetuated in most of the European logarithmic tables since the publication of the *Trigonometria Artificialis* of Vlacq in 1633, proves the source whence the Chinese derived them, and their imitative fidelity in copying them. Chinese authors readily acknowledge the

[1] See *Notes and Queries on C. and J.*, Vol. I., p. 166, and Vol. III., p. 153.

superiority of western mathematicians, and generally ascribe their advances in the exact sciences to them.

The attainments made by the ancient Chinese in astronomy are not easily understood from their scanty records, for the mere notice of an eclipse is a very different thing from its calculation or description. They have been examined recently with renewed interest and care in view of the discoveries at Nineveh, which have furnished so many reliable notices in Western Asia of early days, and may lend some rays of light to illustrate the history and condition of Eastern Asia when more fully studied. The *Book of Records* contains some notices of instructions given by Yao to his astronomers Hí and Ho to ascertain the solstices and equinoxes, to employ intercalary months, and to fix the four seasons, in order that the husbandman might know when to commit his seed to the ground. If the time of the deluge be reckoned, according to Hales, at B.C. 3155, there will be an interval of about eight centuries to the days of Yao, B.C. 2357; this would be ample time for the observation that the primitive sacred year of three hundred and sixty days in Noah's time was wrong; also that the lunar year of about three hundred and fifty-four days was quite as incorrect, and required additional correction, which this ancient monarch is said to have made by an intercalation of seven lunar months in nineteen years. It is remarkable, too, that the time given as the date of the commencement of the astronomical observations sent to Aristotle from Babylon by command of Alexander should be B.C. 2233, or only a few years after the death of Yao; at that time the five additional days to complete the solar year were intercalated by the Chaldeans, and celebrated as days of festivity. Dr. Hales, who mentions this, says that many ancient nations, and also the Mexicans, had the same custom, but there are no traces of any particular observance of them by the Chinese, who, indeed, could not notice them in a lunar year.

The intercalation made by Yao has continued with little variation to this day. The Romish missionaries rectified the calendar during the reign of Kanghí, and have continued its preparation since that time. The adoption of the Julian solar year of three hundred and sixty-five and one-fourth days at this remote period is far from certain, though the fact of its existence among nations in the west is mentioned by the commentator upon the *Book of Records*, who flourished A.D. 1200. The attention the Chinese paid to the lunar year, and the very small difference their seven intercalations left between the true harmonizing of the lunar and solar years (only 1h. 27m. 32s.), would not derange the calculations to a degree to attract their notice. The period of the adoption of the cycle of sixty years, called *luh-shih hwa kiah-tsz'*, cannot be ascertained even with any close approach to probability. Though negative evidence is always the poorest basis on which to found a theory in any branch of knowledge, it still bears great influence in early Chinese history and science, and in no department more than astronomy. This sexagenary cycle, the Chinese assert, was contrived nearly three centuries before the time of Yao (B.C. 2637), and seems to have been perfectly arbitrary, for no explanation now exists of the reasons which induced its inventor, Hwangtí, or his minister, Nao the Great, to select this number. The years have each of them a separate name, formed by taking ten characters, called *shih kan*, or 'ten stems,' and joining to them twelve other characters, called the *shih-'rh chí*, or 'twelve branches,' five times repeated.

These two sets of horary characters are also applied to minutes and seconds, hours, days, and months, signs of the zodiac, points of the compass, etc. By giving the twelve branches the names of as many animals and apportioning the ten stems in couplets among the five elements, they are also made to play an important part in divination and astrology. The present year (1882) is the eighteenth year of the seventy-sixth cycle, or the four thousand five hundred and eighteenth since its institution; but no trace of a serial numbering of the sexagenary periods has yet been found in Chinese writings. The application of the characters to hours and days dates from about B.C. 1752, according to the *Shu King*, perhaps even before they were combined in a cyclic arrangement. This sexagenary division existed in India in early times, too, and is still followed there, where it is named the Cycle of Jupiter, "because the length of its years is measured by the passage of that planet, by its mean motion, through one sign of the zodiac." Rev. E. Burgess, in his translation of the *Surya Siddhanta*, says that the length of Jupiter's years is reckoned in that book at 361d. 0h. 38m., and adds: "It was doubtless on account of the near coincidence of this period with the true solar year that it was adopted as a measure of time; but it has not been satisfactorily ascertained, as far as we are aware, where the cycle originated, or what is its age, or why it was made to consist of sixty years, including five whole revolutions of the planet." It is not improbable, therefore, that the cycle, the two sets of characters, the twenty-four solar terms, with the twelve and twenty-eight lunar mansions or zodiacal asterisms, all of which play such an important part in Chinese astrology and astronomy, will be found to have been derived from the Chaldeans, and not from the Hindus, as has been confidently asserted. Though confessedly ancient in both India and China, their adoption was slow in its growth, while some striking similarities indicate a common origin, and so remote that its genesis is all a mystery.

The year is lunar, but its commencement is regulated by the sun. New Year falls on the first new moon after the sun enters Aquarius, which makes it come not before January 21st nor after February 19th. Besides the division into lunar months, the year is apportioned into twenty-four *tsieh*, or 'terms,' of about fifteen days each, depending upon the position of the sun; these are continued on from year to year, irrespective of the intercalations, the first one commencing about February 6th, when the sun is 15° in Aquarius. Their names have reference to the season of the year and obvious changes in nature at the time they come round, as *rain-water*, *vernal-equinox*, *spiked-grain*, *little-heat*, etc.

The Chinese divide the zodiac (*hwang tao*, or 'yellow road') into twenty-eight *siu* or *kung*, 'constellations' or 'lunar mansions,' but instead of an equable allotment, the signs occupy from 1° up to 31°; the Hindus arrange them nearly in spaces of 13° each. Their names and corresponding animals, with the principal stars answering to each asterism, are given in the table.

	Chin siu.	Corresponding Animal.	Constellation.		*Chin siu.*	Corresponding Animal.	Constellation.
1	*Kioh.*	Earth Dragon.	Spica, ζ Virgo.	15	*Kwei.*	Wolf.	Mirac.
2	*Kang.*	Sky Dragon.	ι κ λ μ Virgo.	16	*Leu.*	Dog.	αβ Aries.
3	*Ti.*	Badger.	α β γ δ Libra.	17	*Wei.*	Pheasant.	Musca.
4	*Fang.*	Hare.	β δ Scorpio.	18	*Mao.*	Cock.	Pleiades.
5	*Sin.*	Fox.	Antares.	19	*Pih.*	Raven.	Hyades.
6	*Wei.*	Tiger.	ε μ Scorpio.	20	*Tsui.*	Monkey.	λ Orion.
7	*Ki.*	Leopard.	γ δ Sagittarius.	21	*Tsan.*	Ape.	Rigel, Orion.
8	*Teu.*	Griffon.	ξ λ Sagittarius.	22	*Tsing.*	Tapir.	Gemini.
9	*Niu.*	Ox.	α β Sagittarius.	23	*Kwei.*	Sheep.	γ δ θ Cancer.
10	*Nü.*	Bat.	ε μ γ Aquarius.	24	*Liu.*	Muntjak.	δ ε ζ Hydra.
11	*Hü.*	Rat.	β Aquarius.	25	*Sing.*	Horse.	Alphard.
12	*Wei.*	Swallow.	α Aquarius &	26	*Chang.*	Deer.	κ λ μ Hydra.
			ε Pegasus.	27	*Yih.*	Snake.	α Crater.
13	*Shih.*	Boar.	Markab.	28	*Chăn.*	Worm.	γ ε Corvus.
14	*Pih.*	Porcupine.	Algenib.				

Instead of being equally divided in the four seasons, they are apportioned very empirically. Those numbered 7 to 14 belong to Aquarius and the north, and measure 98¼°; those from 1 to 7 belong to Scorpio and the east, and measure 75°; those from 15 to 21 belong to Taurus and the west, and measure 80°; and the last 7 belong to Leo and the south, and measure 112°. All these things show very crude knowledge of the heavenly bodies.

The zodiac is further divided into twelve signs or palaces, varying from 25° to 38° in length, named after the twelve branches or animals representing them, commencing with Aquarius or the rat, followed by the ox, tiger, hâre, dragon, snake, horse, sheep, monkey, cock, dog, and bear. These animals also occur among the twenty-eight asterisms, but they are used to denote the twelve branches in all astrological calculations, and not often referred to the zodiac. They are in constant use among the nations of Eastern Asia, so that the common people of Mongolia, Siam, and Japan are really more conversant with them, through their application to times of various length, than they are with the technical characters. The Hindus and Arabians, on the other hand, do not associate these or any other animals with the twelve signs, hours, and months, nor with the twenty-eight mansions; and this fact tends to show that the Chinese obtained them from a more ancient source. The name of one of the twenty-eight lunar mansions is given to every day in the year in perpetual rotation, consequently the same day of our week in every fourth week has the same character applied to it. The days are numbered from the first to the last day of the month, and the months from one to twelve through the year, except the intercalary month, called *jun yueh;* and there is also a trine division of the month into decades.[1]

The astronomical ideas of the common Chinese are vague and inaccurate. The knowledge contained in their own scientific books has not been taught, and they still believe the earth to be a plain surface, measuring each way about one thousand five hundred miles; around it the sun, moon, and stars revolve, the first at a distance of four thousand miles. This figure comes so near the earth's radius that it is reasonable to infer, with Chalmers, that it was calculated from the different elevation of the sun in different latitudes. The distance of the heavens from the earth was ascertained by one observer to be 81,394 *lí*, and by another subsequent to him to be 216,781½ *lí*, or about 73,000 miles; all of which indicates the lack of careful observation. The constellation of the *Peh Tao*, or Dipper, plays an important part in popular astronomy; the common saying is: 'When the handle of the *Northern Peck* points east at nightfall, it is spring over the land; when it points south, it is summer; and when west or north, it is respectively autumn and winter.' The Dipper has become a kind of natural clock from this circumstance, and as its handle always points to the bright stars in Scorpio, these two constellations are among the most familiar. These popular notions must not, however, be taken as a test of what was known in early times; it is quite as just to their scientific attainments in this branch to give them credit (as Wylie does) for having known more than has come down to our days; as to deny belief in the little that remains, because it presents some insoluble difficulties, as Chalmers is disposed to do.

---

[1] *Chinese Repository*, Vol. IX., pp. 573–584. De Guignes' *Voyages*, Vol. II., p. 414. *Chinese Chrestomathy.* Legge's *Shoo King*, passim. Chalmers, *On the Astronomy of the Ancient Chinese. Journal of the Am. Oriental Society*, Vol. VI., Art. III., and Vol. VIII., Arts. I. and VII. Whitney's *Oriental and Linguistic Studies*, Art. XII. *North China Br. R. A. S. Journal*, Nos. III. and IV.

Astronomy has been studied by the Chinese for astrological and state purposes, and their recorded observations of eclipses, comets, etc., have no small value to European astronomers and chronologists. Mailla has collected the notices of 460 solar eclipses, extending from B.C. 2159 to A.D. 1699, and Wylie furnishes a careful list of 925 solar and 574 lunar eclipses, extracted from Chinese works, observed between 2150 and A.D. 1785. Comets have been carefully noted whenever their brilliancy has enabled them to be seen, for they are regarded as portents by the people, and their course among the stars somewhat determines their influence. A list of 373 comets mentioned in Chinese records has been published by John Williams,[1] mostly extracted from Ma Twan-lin's *Antiquarian Researches*, and the *Shí Ki*. They extend from B.C. 611 to A.D. 1621; the general value of these records is estimated by the learned author as entitling them to credence. The curious and intimate connection between geomancy, horoscopy, and astrology, which the Chinese suppose exists, has a powerful influence in maintaining their errors, because of its bearing on every man's luck. Even with all the aid they have derived from Europeans, the Chinese seem to be unable to advance in the science of astronomy, when left to themselves, and to cling to their superstitions against every evidence. Some clouds having on one occasion covered the sky, so that an eclipse could not be seen, the courtiers joyfully repaired to the Emperor to felicitate him, that Heaven, touched by his virtues, had spared him the pain of witnessing the "eating of the sun." A native writer on astronomy, called Tsinglai, who published several works under the patronage of Yuen Yuen, the liberal-minded governor of Kwangtung in 1820, even at that late day, "makes the heavens to consist of ten concentric hollow spheres or envelopes: the first contains the moon's orbit; the second that of Mercury; those of Venus, the Sun, Mars, Jupiter, Saturn, and the twenty-eight constellations, follow; the ninth envelops and binds together the eight interior ones, and revolves daily; while the tenth is the abode of the

---

[1] *Observations of Comets, from* B.C. 611 *to* A.D. 1640. *Extracted from the Chinese Annals*. London, 1871.

Celestial Sovereign, the Great Ruler, with all the gods and sages, where they enjoy eternal tranquillity." He further says, "there are two north and two south poles, those of the equator and those of the ecliptic. The poles of the ecliptic regulate the varied machinery of the heavenly revolutions, and turn round unceasingly. The poles of the equator are the pivots of the primitive celestial body, and remain permanently unmoved. What are called the two poles, therefore, are really not stars, but two immovable points in the north and in the south."[1] The author of this astute cosmogony studied under Europeans, and published these remarks as the fruit of his researches.

The action and reaction of the elements furnish a satisfactory explanation to Chinese philosophers of the changes going on in the visible universe, for no possible contingency can arise which they are not prepared to solve by their analysis of the evolution of its powers. Through their speculations by this curious system they have been led away from carefully recording facts and processes, and have gone on, like a squirrel in a cage, making no progress toward the real knowledge of the elements they treat of. The following table contains the leading elementary correspondences which they use, but a full explanation would be out of place here.

This fanciful system is more or less received by their most intelligent men; and forms a sort of abracadabra in the hands of geomancers and fortune-tellers, by which, with a show of great learning, they impose on the people. The sun, moon, and planets influence sublunary events, especially the life and death of human beings, and changes in their color menace approaching calamities. Alterations in the appearance of the sun announce misfortunes to the state or its head, as revolts, famines, or the death of the Emperor; when the moon waxes red, or turns pale, men should be in awe at the unlucky times thus foreomened.

The sun is symbolized by the figure of a raven in a circle, and the moon by a rabbit on his hind legs pounding rice in a mortar, or by a three-legged toad. The last refers to the

---

[1] *Chinese Chrestomathy*, p. 397.

POWERS AND FUNCTIONS OF ELEMENTARY NATURE—PRINCIPLES WHICH ACT AND REACT ON EACH OTHER IN PRODUCING ALL THINGS.

Five *Hing*, or Elemental Powers.	Qualities of the Five *Hing* given in the *Shu King*.	Five Tastes produced by the Five *Hing*.	Five Points of Compass.	Dualities of the Ten Stems influenced by the Five *Hing*.	Activities of the Five *Hing*.	Five Corresponding Planets.	Five Colors.	Five Viscera.	Five Musical Notes.	Five Early Emperors.	Four Seasons.	Four Quarters of Lunar Zodiac.
水 Water.	Imbuing and Descending.	Salt.	North.	Jin-kwei.	Strengthening.	Mercury	Black.	Kidneys.	Yu.	Chuen-hüh, B.C. 2513.	Winter.	Sable Warrior.
火 Fire.	Blazing and Ascending.	Bitter.	South.	Ping-ting.	Penetrating.	Mars.	Carnation.	Heart.	Wei.	Yentí, (Shinnung) B.C. 2737.	Summer.	Vermilion Sparrow.
木 Wood.	Bending, Straightening.	Sour.	East.	Kiah-yih.	Nourishing.	Jupiter.	Azure.	Liver.	Kioh.	Tai-hao, (Fuh-hí) B.C. 2852.	Spring.	Azure Dragon.
金 Metal.	Obeying, Resisting.	Acid.	West.	Kăng-sin.	Destroying.	Venus.	White.	Lungs.	Shang.	Shao-hao, B.C. 2597.	Autumn.	White Tiger.
土 Earth.	Sowing, Reaping.	Sweet.	Centre.	Wu-kí.	Harmonizing.	Saturn.	Yellow.	Stomach.	Kung.	Hwangtí, B.C. 2697.		

legend of an ancient beauty, Chang-ngo, who drank the liquor of immortality and straightway ascended to the moon, where she was transformed into a toad, still to be traced in its face. It is a special object of worship in autumn, and moon-cakes dedicated to it are sold at this season. All the stars are ranged into constellations, and an emperor is installed over them, who resides at the north pole; five monarchs, also, live in the five stars in Leo, where is a palace, called *Wu Ti tso*, or 'Throne of the Five Emperors.' In this celestial government there is also an heir-apparent, empresses, sons and daughters, tribunals, and the constellations receive the names of men, animals, and other terrestrial objects. The Dipper is worshipped as the residence of the fates, where the duration of life, and other events relating to mankind, are measured and meted out. Doolittle's *Social Life* contains other popular notions connected with the stars, showing the ignorance still existing, and the fears excited by unusual phenomena among the heavenly bodies. Both heaven and the sun are worshipped by the government in appropriate temples on the west and east sides of Peking. The rainbow is the product of the impure vapors ascending from the earth meeting those descending from the sun.

If their knowledge of astronomy can be criticised as being anything but an exact science, the Chinese should not be denied credit for a certain amount of beauty in what may be called the romantic side of this study. In the myths and legends which have clustered about and doubtless in many cases perverted their observations of the stars, there are the sources of fêtes and subjects for pictorial illustration without number. One of these stories, forming the motive of a bowl decoration given upon the opposite page, is the fable of Aquila (*niu*) and Vega, known in Chinese and Japanese mythology as the Herdsman and Weaver-girl. The latter, the daughter of the sun-god, was so continually busied with her loom that her father became worried at her close habits and thought that by marrying her to a neighbor, who herded cattle on the banks of the Silver Stream of Heaven (the Milky Way), she might awake to a brighter manner of living.

"No sooner did the maiden become wife than her habits

and character utterly changed for the worse. She became not only very merry and lively, but quite forsook loom and needle, giving up her nights and days to play and idleness; no silly lover could have been more foolish than she. The sun-king, in great wrath at all this, concluded that the husband was the cause of it and determined to separate the couple. So he ordered him to remove to the other side of the river of stars, and told him that hereafter they should meet only once a year, on the seventh night of the seventh month. To make a bridge over the flood of stars, the sun-king called myriads of magpies, which thereupon flew together, and, making a bridge, supported the poor lover on their wings and backs as if it were a roadway of solid land. So bidding his weeping wife farewell, the lover-husband sorrowfully crossed the River of Heaven, and all the magpies instantly flew away. But the two were separated, the one to lead his ox, the other to ply her shuttle during the long hours of the day with diligent toil, and the sun-king again rejoiced in his daughter's industry.

"At last the time for their reunion drew near, and only one fear possessed the loving wife. What if it should rain? For the River of Heaven is always full to the brim, and one extra drop causes a flood which sweeps away even the bird bridge. But not a drop fell; all the heavens were clear. The magpies flew joyfully in myriads, making a way for the tiny feet of the little lady. Trembling with joy, and with heart fluttering more than the bridge of wings, she crossed the River of Heaven and was in the arms of her husband. This she did every year. The husband staid on his side of the river, and the wife came to him on the magpie bridge, save on the sad occasion when it rained. So every year the people hope for clear weather, and the happy festival is celebrated alike by old and young." [1]

These two constellations are worshipped principally by women, that they may gain cunning in the arts of needlework and making of fancy flowers. Watermelons, fruits, vegetables, cakes, etc., are placed with incense in the reception-room, and

---

[1] Somewhat abridged from Mr. W. E. Griffis' *Japanese Fairy World*, a book which has given us the cream of a great variety of stories from Eastern wonder-lore.

before these offerings are performed the kneelings and knockings in the usual way.

The entire day is divided into twelve two-hour periods called *shin*, commencing at eleven o'clock, P.M.; each hour is further subdivided into *kih*, or eighths, equal to fifteen of our minutes, and receives the same characters. There are various means employed to measure time, but the people are rapidly learning to reckon its progress by watches and clocks, and follow our divisions in preference to their own. A common substitute for watches are *time-sticks*, long round pieces of a composition of clay and sawdust, well mixed and wound in a spiral manner; the lapse of time is indicated by its equable slow combustion from one hour mark to another, until the whole is consumed, which in the longest is not less than a week. Dials are in common use, and frequently attached to the mariner's compass, by making the string which retains the cover in its place cast a shadow on the face of it. This lesson in dialing, Davis supposes they learned from the Jesuits. Clepsydras of various forms were anciently employed, some of which, from their description, were so disproportionately elegant and costly for such a clumsy mode of noting time, that their beauty more than their use was perhaps the principal object in preparing them.

The almanac holds an important place, its preparation having been early taken under the special care of the government, which looks upon a present of this important publication as one of the highest favors which it can confer on tributary vassals or friendly nations. It is annually prepared at Peking, under the direction of a bureau attached to the Board of Rites, and, by making it a penal offence to issue a counterfeit or pirated edition the governmental astrologers have monopolized the management of the superstitions of the people in regard to the fortunate or unlucky conjunctions of each day and hour. Besides the cabalistic part of it, the ephemeris also contains tables of the rising of the sun according to the latitudes of the principal places, times of the new and full moon, the beginning and length of the twenty-four terms, eclipses, application of the horary characters, conjunction of the planets, etc. Two or three editions are published for the convenience of the people, the prices of which vary from three to ten cents a copy. No one ventures to be without an almanac, lest he be liable to the greatest misfortunes, and run the imminent hazard of undertaking important events on black-balled days. The Europeans who were employed for many years in compiling the calendar were not allowed to interfere in the astrological part; it is to the discredit of the Chinese to aid thus in perpetuating folly and ignorance among the people, when they know that the whole system is false and absurd. Such governments as that of China, however, deem it necessary to uphold ancient superstitions, if they can thereby influence their security, or strengthen the reverence due them.

If their astronomical notions are vague, their geographical knowledge is ridiculous. The maps of their own territories are tolerably good, being originally drawn from actual surveys by nine of the Jesuits, between the years 1708–1718, and since that time have been filled up and changed to conform to the alterations and divisions. Their full surveys were engraved on copper at Paris, by order of Louis XIV., on sheets, measuring in all over a hundred square feet, and have formed the basis of all subsequent maps. The Chinese do not teach geography in their schools, even of their own empire. The common people have no knowledge, therefore, of the form and divisions of the globe, and the size and position of the kingdoms of the earth. Their common maps delineate them very erroneously, not even excepting their own possessions in Mongolia and Ílí—scattering islands, kingdoms, and continents, as they have heard of their existence, at haphazard in various corners beyond the frontiers. The two Americas and Africa are entirely omitted on most of them, and England, Holland, Portugal, Goa, Luçonia, Bokhara, Germany, France, and India, are arranged along the western side, from north to south, in a series of islands and headlands. The southern and eastern sides are similarly garnished by islands, as Japan, Lewchew, Formosa, Siam, Birmah, Java, the Sulu Islands, and others, while Russia occupies the whole of the northern frontier of their Middle Kingdom.

The geographical works of Tsinglai are not quite so erroneous as his astronomical, but the uneducated people, notwithstanding his efforts to teach them better, still generally suppose the earth to be an immense extended stationary plain. Their notions of its inhabitants are equally whimsical, and would grace the pages of Sir John Mandeville. In some parts of its surface they imagine the inhabitants to be all dwarfs, who tie themselves together in bunches for fear of being carried away by the eagles; in others they are all women, who conceive by looking at their shadows; and in a third kingdom, all the people have holes in their breasts, through which they thrust a pole, when carrying one another from place to place. Charts for the guidance of the navigator, or instruments to aid him in determining his position at sea, the Chinese are nearly or quite destitute of; they have retrograded rather than advanced in navigation, judging from the accounts of Fa-hian, Ibn Batuta, and other travellers, when their vessels frequented the ports in the Persian Gulf and on the Malabar coast, and carried on a large trade with the Archipelago. Itineraries are published, containing the distances between places on the principal thoroughfares throughout the provinces, and also lists of the ports, harbors, and islands on the coast, but nothing like sailing directions accompany the latter, nor do maps of the routes illustrate the former. Such knowledge as they have on these points is hidden away in their libraries, as the Latin and Greek classics were in European convents and castles a thousand years ago.

In the various branches of mensuration and formulæ used to describe the dimensions and weight of bodies, they have reached only a practical mediocrity. With a partial knowledge of trigonometry, and no instruments for ascertaining the heights of objects or their distances from the observer, still their lands are well measured, and the area of lots in towns and cities accurately ascertained. The *chih* or foot is the integer of length, but its standard value cannot be easily ascertained. In the *Chinese Commercial Guide*, p. 285, is a table of eighty-four observations on this point, taken at different times and places in China, whose extremes differ more than six inches. It is fixed by the Board of Works at 13⅛ in. English, but tradesmen at Canton employ foot measures varying from 14.625 to 14.81 in.; according to the tariff, it is reckoned at 14.1 in. English, and the *chang* of ten *chih* at $3\frac{1}{12}$ yds. During the past thirty years, the tariff weights and measures have gradually obtained acceptance as the standards, and this will probably result in securing uniformity in course of time. The *chih* is subdivided into ten *tsun* or puntos, and each *tsun* into ten *făn*. The *lí* is used for distances, and is usually reckoned at 1,825.55 ft. English, which gives 2.89 *lí* to an English mile; this is based on the estimate of 200 *lí* to a degree, but there were only 180 *lí* to a degree before Europeans came, which increases its length to 2,028.39 ft. or 2.6 *lí* to a mile, which is nearer the common estimate. The French missionaries divided the degree into 250 *lí* (each being then exactly 1,460.44 ft. English, or one-tenth of a French astronomical league), and also into sixty minutes and sixty seconds, to make it correspond to western notation; this measure has not been adopted in common use. The present rulers have established post-houses very generally, at intervals of ten *lí*, or about a league. The land measures are the *mao* and *king;* the former measures 6,000 square *chih*, or 808.6 square yards, and a hundred of them make a *king*. Taxes are collected, land is leased, and crops are estimated by the *mao* and its decimal parts; but examination has shown that the actual area of a *mao* grows less as one goes north; in Canton, it is about 4.76 *mao* to an acre, and at Peking it is six, and even smaller.

The weights and measures of the Chinese are twenty-four in all, and vary in their value even more than those of long measure. The common weights are called *tael*, *catty*, and *pecul* by foreigners; their values are respectively $1\frac{1}{3}$ oz. av., $1\frac{1}{3}$ lb. av., and $133\frac{1}{3}$ lbs. av., and thus roughly correspond to the English ounce, pound, and hundredweight. The Chinese deal in many articles by weight which among western nations are sold according to their quality—such as wood, silk, oil, whiskey, cloth, grain, poultry, etc.—so that it has been humorously observed that the Chinese sell everything by weight, except eggs and children. Their common measures correspond nearly to our gill, half-pint, pint, and peck, and are used to retail rice, beans, etc. The smaller ones are not very accurately constructed from bamboo-joints, but the peck measure, or *tao*, shaped like the frustum of a pyramid, must be officially examined and sealed before it can be used; at Canton it contains 6½ catties weight, or about 1.13 gallon. The decimals of the tael, called *mace*, *candareen*, and *cash* (*tsien*, *făn*, and *lí*), are employed in reckoning bullion, pearls, gems, drugs, etc.; ten cash making one candareen, ten candareens one mace, etc. The proportions between the Chinese and American moneys and weights is such that so many taels per pecul, or candareens per catty, is the same as so many dollars per hundredweight, or cents per pound.[1]

The monetary system is arranged on the principle of weight, and the divisions have the same names, *tael*, *mace*, *candareen*, and *cash*. The only native coin is a copper piece called *tsien*, because it originally weighed a mace; it is thin and circular, rather more than an inch in diameter, with a square hole in the middle for the convenience of stringing. The obverse bears the word *pao*, or 'current,' and the name of the province in Manchu, on each side of the square hole; the reverse has four words, *Taukwang*, *tung*, *pao*, *i.e.*, 'money current [during the reign of] Taukwang.' Mints for casting cash are established in each provincial capital under the direction of the Board of Revenue. The coin should consist of an alloy of copper, 50; zinc, 41½; lead, 6½; and tin, 2; or of equal parts of copper and zinc; but it has been so debased by iron and reduced in size during the last fifty years that it does not pay to counterfeit it. Each piece should weigh 58 grains troy, or 3.78 grammes, but most of those now in circulation are under 30 grains, and the rate of exchange varies in different parts of the land from 900 to 1,800 for a silver dollar.

The workmen in the mint are required to remain within the building except when leave of absence is obtained, but in spite of all the efforts of government, private coinage is issued to a great amount, and sometimes with the connivance of the mint-master. Neither silver nor gold has ever been coined to any extent in China. In seeking for the cause of this difference from all other Asiatic nations, it seems to lie in the commercial freedom which has done so much to elevate them. The gov-

---

[1] *Chinese Repository*, Vol. X., p. 650; *Chinese Chrestomathy; Chinese Commercial Guide*, Fifth Ed., pp. 265–288; Rondot, *Commerce de la Chine*, 1819.

ernment on the one hand is not strong enough to restrain counterfeiters, and not honest enough, on the other hand, to issue pieces of uniform standard for a series of years till it has obtained the confidence of its subjects. It will not receive base metal for taxes, and cannot force merchants to accept adulterated coins. As its foreign relations extend it will no doubt be obliged to issue a better national currency in the three metals. Attempts have been made to introduce a silver piece of the size of a tael, and specimens were made at Shanghai in 1856. A large coinage of native dollars was attempted in Fuhkien and Formosa, about 1835, to pay the troops on that island. One of them indicated that the piece was "pure silver for current use from the Chang-chau Commissariat; [weight] seven *mace* two *candareens*." The other was of the same weight and purity (417.4 grains troy), and besides the inscription in Chinese on the obverse, and in Manchu on the reverse, it had an effigy of the god of Longevity on the head and a tripod on the tail, to authenticate its official origin. These pieces were either melted or counterfeited to such an extent on their appearance, that they soon disappeared.

Foreign dollars are imported in great quantities from Mexico and San Francisco, and form the medium of trade at the open ports. They are often stamped by the person who pays them out, which soon destroys them as a coin, and they are then melted and refined to be cast into ingots of bullion, called *shoes of sycee*, from *sí-sz'* or 'fine floss'; these weigh from five mace to fifty taels, the larger pieces being stamped with the district magistrate's title and the date, to verify them. They are from ninety-seven to ninety-nine per cent. pure silver, but small ingots of ten or fifteen taels weight are less pure than the large *shoes*, as they are called from their shape. Gold bullion is cast into bars like cakes of India-ink in shape, weighing about ten taels, or hammered into thick leaves which can be examined but not separated by driving a punch through a pile of a hundred or more—a precaution against cheating. Large quantities are sent abroad in this shape.

Taxes and duties are paid in sycee of ninety-eight per cent. fineness, and licensed bankers are connected with the revenue department to whom the proceeds are paid, and who are allowed a small percentage for refining and becoming responsible for its purity. Dollars and ingots are counterfeited, and all classes have them inspected by *shroffs*, who, by practice, are able to decide by the sight alone upon the degree of alloy in a piece of silver, though usually they employ touchstone needles to assist them, different degrees of fineness imparting a different color to the needle. Books are prepared as aids to the detection of counterfeit dollars; in these the process of manufacture is carefully described; some of the pieces are marvels of skill in forgery.

Chartered banking companies are unknown, for a government warrant or charter would carry no weight with it, but private bankers are found in all large towns. Paper money was issued in immense quantities under the Mongol dynasty, and its convenience is highly praised by Marco Polo, who looked upon its emission by the Grand Khan as the highest secret of alchemy. Polo's ideas of this operation would please the "greenbackers" in the United States. He says, when describing Kublai's purchases: "So he buys such a quantity of those precious things every year that his treasure is endless, while all the while the money he pays away costs him nothing at all. If any of those pieces of paper are spoilt the owner carries them to the mint, and by paying three per cent. on the value he gets new pieces in exchange." The total issues of this highest secret of alchemy during Kublai's reign of thirty-four years are reckoned by Pauthier, the *Yuen Annals*, at equal to $624,135,500. The Khan's successors, however, overdid the manufacture, and when the people found out that they had nothing but paper to show for all the valuables they had parted with to the Mongols, it added strength to the rebellion of Hung-wu (A.D. 1359), which ended in their expulsion nine years afterward. The new dynasty was, nevertheless, obliged to issue its notes at first, but the mercantile instincts of the people soon asserted their power, and as industry revived they were superseded about 1455. The Manchus did not issue any Governmental paper till 1858, during the Tai-ping rebellion, and its circulation was limited to the capital from the first; seeing that even then it was known to have no basis of credit or funds.

A bank can be opened by any person or company, subject to certain laws and payments to Government, on reporting its organization. The number of these offices of deposit and emission is large in proportion to the business of a town, but their capital averages only two or three thousand taels; the number in Tientsin is stated at three hundred, at Peking it is less than four hundred, of which scores in each are mere branches. The check on over-issue of notes lies in the control exercised by the clearing-house of every city, where the standing of each bank is known by its operations. The circulation of the notes is limited in some cases to the street or neighborhood wherein the establishment is situated; often the payee has a claim on the payer of a bill for a full day if it be found to be counterfeit or worthless—a custom which involves a good deal of scribbling on the back of the bill to certify the names. Proportionally few counterfeit notes are met with, owing more to the limited range of the bills, making it easy to ask the bank, which recognizes its own paper by the check-tallies, of which the register contains two or three halves printed across the check-book. When silver is presented for exchange, the bills are usually, in Peking, filled up and dated as the customer wishes while he waits for them. Their face value ranges from one to a hundred *tiao*, or strings of cash, but their worth depends on the exchange between silver and cash, and as this fluctuates daily, the bills soon find their way home. These notes are unknown in the southern provinces, where dollars have long circulated; but their convenience is so great that people are willing to run slight risks on this account. Hongkong bills circulate on the mainland to very remote districts.

Banks issue circular letters of credit to travel through the Empire, and the system of remittance by drafts is as complete as in Europe; the rates charged are high, however, and vast sums of silver are constantly on the move. The habit of pawning goods is very general, and carries its disastrous results among all classes. There are three kinds of pawnshops, and the laws regulating them are strict and equitable; the chief evil arising from their number is the facility they give to thieves. Pawn tickets are exposed for sale in the streets, and form a curious branch of traffic. These establishments are generally very extensive, and the vast amount of goods stored in them, especially garments and jewelry, shows their universal patronage. One pawnbroker's warehouse at Tinghai was used by the English forces as a hospital, and accommodated between two and three hundred patients. The insecurity of commercial operations involves, of course, a high rate of interest, sometimes up to three per cent. a month, lowering according to circumstances to twelve or ten per cent. per annum. The legal pawnshops (*tang pu*) are allowed three years to redeem, and give three years' notice of dissolution. The restrictions on selling pawned articles works injuriously to the shops, in consequence of rapid depreciation or risks to the articles. If a fire occurs on the premises the pawner claims the full amount of his pledge; only one-half is paid if it communicates from a neighbor's house.[1]

One characteristic feature of Chinese society cannot be omitted in this connection, namely, its tendency to associate. It is a fertile principle applied to every branch of life, but especially conspicuous in all industrial operations. The people crystallize into associations; in the town and in the country, in buying and in selling, in studies, in fights, and in politics, everybody must co-operate with somebody else—women as well as men. To belong to one or more *hwui*, and be identified with its fortunes, and enlisted in its struggles, seems to be the stimulus to activity, resulting from the democratic element in the Chinese polity, to which we are to refer the continuity as well as many singular features of the national character. In trade capitalists associate to found great banks, to sell favorite medicines, or engross leading staples; little farmers club together to buy an ox, pedlers to get the custom of a street, porters to monopolize the loads in a ward, or chair-bearers to furnish all the sedans for a town. Beggars are allotted to one or

---

[1] Ed. Biot in *Journal Asiatique*, 1837, Tome III., p. 422, and Tome IV., pp. 97, 209; *Chinese Commercial Guide*, 1863, pp. 264–275; *N. C. As. Journal*, No. VI., pp. 52–71; Yule's *Marco Polo*, 1871, Vol. I., p. 378–385; Pauthier *Le Livre de M. Polo*, Cap. XCV., p. 319; Vissering *On Chinese Currency*, 1877; *Chinese Repository*, Vol. XX., p. 289; Doolittle's *Social Life*, Vol. II., pp. 138–247; *Notes and Queries on C. and J.*, Vol. II., p. 108.

two streets by their *hwui*, and driven off another's beat if they encroach. Each guild of carpenters, silkmen, masons, or even of physicians and teachers, works to advance its own interests, keep its own members in order, and defend itself against its opponents. Villagers form themselves into organizations against the wiles of powerful clans; and unscrupulous officials are met and balked by popular unions when they least expect it. Women and mothers get up a company to procure a trousseau, to buy an article of dress or furniture, to pay for a son's wedding. Associations are limited to a year, to a month, to a decade, according to their design. These various forms of co-operation teach the people to know each other, while they also furnish agencies for unscrupulous men to oppress and crush out their enemies, gratify their revenge, and intimidate enterprise. Nevertheless, until the people learn higher principles of morality, these habits of combining themselves bring more benefits to the whole body than evils, at the same time quickening the vitality of the mass, without which it would die out in brigandage and despair.[1]

The theory of war has received more attention among the Chinese than its practice, and their reputation as an unwarlike people is as ancient and general among their neighbors as that of their seclusion and ingenuity. The Mongols and Manchus, Huns and Tartars, all despised the effeminate braggadocio of Chinese troops, and easily overcame them in war, but were themselves in turn conquered in times of peace. Minute directions are given in books with regard to the drilling of troops, which are seldom reduced to practice. The puerile nature of the examinations which candidates for promotion in the army pass through, proves the remains of the ancient hand-to-hand encounter, and evinces the low standard still entertained of what an officer should be. Personal courage and brawn are highly esteemed, and the prowess of ancient heroes in the battle-field is lauded in songs, and embellished in novels.

The arms of the Chinese still consist of bows and arrows,

[1] For an account of the money *hwui* and details of their system, see M. Eug. Simon, Les Petites Sociétés d'Argent en Chine, *N. C. Br. R. As. Soc. Journal*, No. V., Art. I. (1868).

spears, matchlocks, swords, and cannon of various sizes and lengths. The bow is used more for show in the military examinations, than for service in battle. Rattan shields, painted with tigers' heads, are used on board the revenue cutters to turn the thrust of spears, and on ceremonial occasions, when the companies are paraded in full uniforms and equipments. The uniform of the different regiments of the *luh-ying* or 'native army,' consists of a jacket of brown, yellow, or blue, bordered with a wide edging of another color; the trowsers are usually blue. The cuirass is made of quilted and doubled cotton cloth, and covered with iron plates or brass knobs connected by copper bands; the helmet is iron or polished steel, sometimes inlaid, weighing two and one-fourth pounds, and has neck and ear lappets to protect those parts. The back of the jacket bears the word *yung*, 'courage,' and on the breast is painted the service to which the corps is attached, whether to the governor, commandant, or Emperor. The exhibition of courage among Chinese troops is not, however, always deferred to the time when they run away, spite of the disparaging reputation they have obtained in this respect from their British conquerors—who have, nevertheless, on more than one occasion, been led to admire the cool pluck of the same men when led by competent officers.

The matchlock is of wrought iron and plain bore; it has a longer barrel than a musket, so long that a rest is sometimes attached to the stock for greater ease in firing; the match is a cord of hemp or coir, and the pan must be uncovered with the hand before it can be fired, which necessarily interferes with, and almosts prevents its use in wet or windy weather. The cannon are cast, and although not of very uniform calibre from the mode of manufacture, are serviceable for salutes. The ginjal is a kind of swivel from six to fourteen feet long, resting on a tripod; being less liable to burst than the cannon, it is the most effective gun the Chinese possess.

Gunpowder was probably known to the Chinese in the latter part of the Han dynasty (A.D. 250), but its application in firearms at that time is not so plain. The exploits of Kung-ming in that period owe their interest to his use of gunpowder in modes like the Greek fire of the Byzantines, though the animated narratives of Lo Kwan-chung (A.D. 1300) in his *History of the Three States*, are not reliable history in this particular. Grosier (Vol. VII., pp. 176–200) has adduced the evidences proving the use of powder at or before the Christian era. The inferences that Europe obtained it from India rather than China have, however, a good deal of weight. Early Arab historians refer to it as Chinese snow and Chinese salt—a fact which only shows its eastern origin—while the Chinese compound term of *hwo-yioh*, or 'fire drug,' rather indicates a foreign source than otherwise.

Mr. W. F. Mayers has searched out and collated a considerable mass of evidence from Chinese sources bearing upon the introduction of explosives in native warfare and ordinary life. The conclusions of this writer point both to a foreign origin of gunpowder in China, and a much later use of the compound among their warriors than has generally been supposed. Coming, probably, from India or Central Asia about the fifth century A.D. the invention, he says, "perhaps found its way into China in connection with the manufacture of fireworks for purposes of diversion; and supplanting at some unascertained period the practice of producing a crepitating noise by burning bamboos as a charm against evil spirits." No evidence exists of the use of gunpowder as an agent of warfare until the middle of the twelfth century, nor did a knowledge of its propulsive effects come to the Chinese until the reign of Yungloh, in the fifteenth century—a thousand years after its first employment in fire-crackers.[1]

Fire-arms of large size were introduced toward the end of the Ming dynasty by foreign instructors; ginjals and matchlocks were known four centuries earlier in all the eastern and central regions of Asia, but none of those people could forge or cast large artillery, owing to their imperfect machinery. The gunpowder is badly mixed and triturated, though the proportions are nearly the same as our own. The native arms are now

---

[1] *North China Br. Royal Asiatic Soc. Journal*, 1870, No. VI., Art. V. Compare *Notes and Queries on C. and J.*

rapidly giving place to foreign in the imperial army, and the establishment of four or five arsenals under the management of competent instructors, where implements of warfare of every kind are manufactured, will, ere long, make an entire change in Chinese weapons and tactics. Some of their brass guns were of enormous size and great strength, but were of little use for practical warfare, owing to the bad carriages and rude means of working them.

The uniforms of Chinese troops are not even calculated to give them a fine appearance when drawn up for parade, and no one, looking at them, can believe that men dressed in loose jackets and trousers, with heavy shoes and bamboo caps, could be trained to cope with western soldiers. Fans or umbrellas are often made use of on parade to assuage the heat or protect from the rain, while the chief object of these reviews is to salute and knock head before some high officer. In order to repress insurrection, the government has been frequently compelled to buy off turbulent leaders with office and rewards, and thus disorganize and scatter the enemy it could not vanquish.

But however ridiculous the army and navy of the Chinese were half a century ago, in the isolation and ignorance which then held them, it cannot be alleged of what has been attempted within twenty years, and the promise of what may be done in as many more. The following *résumé* of the qualities of the Chinese soldier, from experience with Col. Gordon's "Ever Victorious Force" during the Tai-ping insurrection will be *à propos* of this subject to which this work cannot devote further space. "The old notion is pretty well got rid of, that they are at all a cowardly people when properly paid and efficiently led; while the regularity and order of their habits, which dispose them to peace in ordinary times, give place to a daring bordering upon recklessness in time of war. Their intelligence and capacity for remembering facts make them well fitted for use in modern warfare, as do also the coolness and calmness of their disposition. Physically they are on the average not so strong as Europeans, but considerably more so than most of the other races of the East; and on a cheap diet of rice, vegetables, salt fish, and pork, they can go through a vast amount of fatigue, whether in a temperate climate or a tropical one, where Europeans are ill-fitted for exertion. Their wants are few; they have no caste prejudices, and hardly any appetite for intoxicating liquors. Being of a lymphatic or lymphatic-bilious temperament, they enjoy a remarkable immunity from inflammatory disease, and the tubercular diathesis is little known amongst them."[1]

Their progress in real civilization is not to be fairly measured by their attainments in war, although it has been said that the two best general criteria of civilization among any people are superior skill in destroying their fellow men, and the degree of respect they pay to women. China falls far behind her place among the nations if judged by these tests alone, and in reality owes her present advance in numbers, industry, and wealth mainly to her peaceful character and policy. She would have probably presented a spectacle similar to the disunited hordes of Central Asia, had her people been actuated by a warlike spirit, for when divided into fifty or more feudal states, as was the case in the days of Confucius, she made no progress in the arts of life. The Manchu Emperors have endeavored to conquer their neighbors, the Birmans and Coreans, but in both cases had to be satisfied with the outward homage of a *kotow*, and a few articles of tribute, when a formal embassy presented itself in Peking. The Siamese, Cochinchinese, Coreans, Tibetans, Lewchewans, and some of the tribes of Turkestan, are nominally vassals of the Son of Heaven, and their names remain on the roll of feifs. The first two have ceased to *tsin kung*, or send tribute, since about 1860; and the Lewchewans are not likely to revisit their old quarters at Peking in any capacity; while the others derive advantage from the facilities of traffic which they are unwilling to give up.

The precepts of Confucius taught the rulers of China to conquer their neighbors by showing the excellence of a good government, for then their enemies would come and voluntarily range themselves under their sway; and although the kindness

---

[1] Andrew Wilson, *The "Ever Victorious Army." A History of the Chinese Campaign under Lieut.-Col. Gordon.* London, 1868, p. 269.

of the rulers of China to those fully in their power is as hypocritical as their rule is unjust, those nations who pay them this homage do it voluntarily, and experience no interference in their internal affairs. The maxims of Confucian polity, aided by the temper of the people, have had some effect, in the lapse of years, upon the nature of this quasi feudality. The weaker nations looked up to China, since they could look no higher, and their advances in just government, industry, and arts, is not a little owing to their political intercourse during past centuries. The Chinese Empire is a notable example of the admirable results of a peaceful policy; and the sincere desire of every well-wisher of his race doubtless is that this mighty mass of human beings may be Christianized and elevated from their present ignorance and weakness by a like peaceful infusion of the true principles of good order and liberty.

Many treatises upon the art and practice of war exist, one of which, called the *Soldier's Manual*,[1] in eighteen chapters, contains some good directions. The first chapter treats of the mode of marching, necessity of having plans of the country through which the army is to pass, and cautions the troops against harassing the people unnecessarily—not a useless admonition, for a body of Chinese soldiers is too often like a swarm of locusts upon the land. The second chapter teaches the mode of building bridges, the need there is of cautious explorations in marching, and of sending out scouts; this subject is also continued in the next section, and directions given about castrametation, placing sentries, and keeping the troops on the alert, as well as under strict discipline in camp. The rest of the book is chiefly devoted to directions for the management of an actual battle, sending out spies beforehand, choosing positions, and bringing the various parts of the army into action at the best time. The hope of reward is held out to induce the soldier to be brave, and the threats of punishment and death if he desert or turn his back in time of battle.

The utility of music in encouraging the soldiers and exciting them to the charge is fully appreciated, but to our notions it

---

[1] *Chinese Repository*, Vol. XI., p. 487.

no more deserves the name of music than the collection of half-drilled louts in petticoats does that of an army, when compared with a European force. Still, its antiquity, if nothing else, renders it a subject of great interest to the musical student, while its power over the people seems to be none the less because it is unscientific. However small their attainments in the theory and practice of music, no nation gives to this art a higher place. It was regarded by Confucius as an essential part in the government of a state, harmonizing and softening the relations between the different ranks of society, and causing them all to move on in consentaneous accord. It is remarked of the sage himself that having heard a tune in one of his ramblings, he did not know the taste of food for three weeks after—but, with all deference to the feelings of so distinguished a man, we cannot help thinking his food might have been quite as palatable without music, if it was no better then than it is at the present day. The Chinese never had anything like the musical contests among the Greeks, and their efforts have been directed to develop instrumental rather than vocal music.

The names and characters used for notes in vocal music are here given, though their real tone cannot be accurately represented by our staff. The second octave is denoted by affixing the sign *jin*, 'a man,' to the simple notes, or as shown in the second *ché*, by a peculiar hooked bottom.

If the first note in this scale be taken as the tonic, then they form a diatonic octave, with a supernumerary note, which is an octave above the second one *sz'*, the first one, *ho*, being an octave below *liu*, the eighth. But the semitones *i* and *fan* are very little used, and it loses in some degree its diatonic character. No chromatic scale exists among them, at least none of their instruments are made to express flat and sharp notes.

Barrow says that the Chinese learned this mode of writing music from Pereira, a Roman Catholic missionary, in 1670, but its existence in Japan and Corea invalidates this statement.

There are two kinds of music, known as the Southern and Northern, which differ in their character, and are readily recognized by the people. The octave in the former seems to have had only six notes, and the songs of the Miaotsz' and rural people in that portion of China are referable to such a gamut, while the eight-tone scale generally prevails in all theatres and more cultivated circles. Further examination by competent observers who can jot down on such a gamut the airs they hear in various regions of China, is necessary to ascertain these interesting points, which now seem to carry us back to remote antiquity, and have been noticed in other countries than China.

In writing instrumental music, marks, meaning to *push*, *fillip*, *hook*, etc., are added to denote the mode of playing the string; the two are united into very complicated combinations. For instance, in writing a tune for the lute or *kin*, "each note is a cluster of characters; one denotes the string, another the stud, a third informs you in what manner the fingers of the right hand are to be used, a fourth does the same in reference to the left, a fifth tells the performer in what way he must slide the hand before or after the appropriate sound has been given, and a sixth says, perhaps, that two notes are to be struck at the same time." These complex notes are difficult to learn and remember, therefore the Chinese usually play by the ear. This mode of notation, in addition to its complexity, must be varied by nearly every kind of instrument, inasmuch as the combinations fitted for one instrument are inapplicable to another; but music is written for only a few instruments, such as the lute and the guitar.

These notes, when simply written without directions combined with them as described above, indicate only their pitch in a certain scale, and do not denote either the length or the absolute pitch; they are written perpendicularly, and various marks of direction are given on the side of the column regarding the proportionate length of time in which certain notes are to be played, others to be trilled or repeated once, twice, or more times, and when the performer is to pause. Beats occur at regular intervals in some of the written tunes; all music is in common time and no triple measures are used, yet time is pretty well observed in orchestras. Of harmony and counterpoint they know nothing; the swell, diminish, flat, sharp, appogiatura, tie, and other marks which assist in giving expression to our written music, are for the most part unknown, nor are tunes set to any key. The neatness and adaptation of the European notation is better appreciated after studying the clumsy, imperfect mode which is here briefly described.[1]

No description can convey a true idea of Chinese vocal music, and few persons are able to imitate it when they have heard it. De Guignes says, "It is possible to sing a Chinese song, but I think it would be very difficult to give it the proper tone without having heard it by a native, and I rather believe that no one can perfectly imitate their notes." They seem, in some cases, to issue from the larynx and nose, the tongue, teeth, and lips having little to do with them, the modulation being made mostly with the muscles of the bronchia; at other times, the enunciation of the words requires a little more use of the lips and teeth. Singing is generally on a falsetto key; and this feature prevails throughout. Whether in the theatre or in the street, about the house or holding the guitar or lute, both men and women sing in this artificial tone somewhere between a squeal and a scream, and which no western musical instrument is able to imitate. Its character is plaintive and soft, not full or exhibiting much compass, though when two or three females sing together in recitative, not destitute of sweetness. Bass and tenor are not sung by men, nor a second treble by females, and the two performers are seldom heard together among the thousands of street musicians who get a precarious living by their skill in this line, as they accompany the guitar or rebeck. The chanting in Buddhist services resembles the Ambrosian and early Gregorian tones, and is accompanied only by striking a block

[1] Compare Dr. Jenkins in the *Journal N. C. Br. R. A. S.*, Vol. V., 1868, pp. 30 ff., and Rev. E. W. Syle in *ib.* Vol. II., 1859, p. 176; Père Amiot in *Mém. conc. les Chinois*, Vol. VI., pp. 1 ff.; *Notes and Queries on C. and J.*, Vol. IV., Arts. 2 and 3. Perny *Dict.*, app. No. XIV., p. 443.

and marking the time; the tenor voices of boys make a strong contrast to the gruff bass voices of the men in this service; some of the latter will carry their part as low as an octave below C or D in the bass, sounding most sepulchrally, like a trombone.

Three of the tunes inserted in Barrow's *Travels* are here quoted as specimens of Chinese airs The first is the most popular, the second, common at Shanghai, is called *Luh pan*, or 'Six Boards,' it has a strain at the beginning and end additional to the usual form.

MOH-LÍ HWA; OR, THE JASMINE FLOWER.

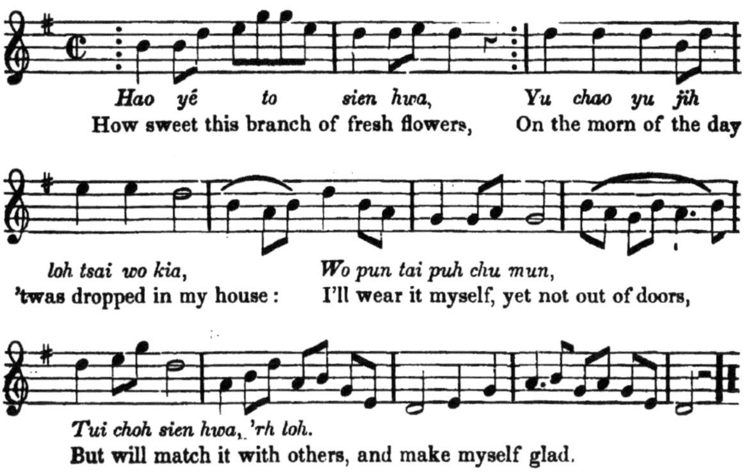

Hao yê to Moh-lí hwa,
Mwan yuen hwa kai sho puh kwei ta,
Wo pun tai tsz' yê ta,
Tai yu kung kan hwa jin ma.

How sweet this sprig of the jasmine flower!
Through the whole plat there's none to equal it;
I myself will wear this new plucked sprig,
Though I fear all who see it will envy me.

LUH PAN; OR, THE SIX BOARDS.

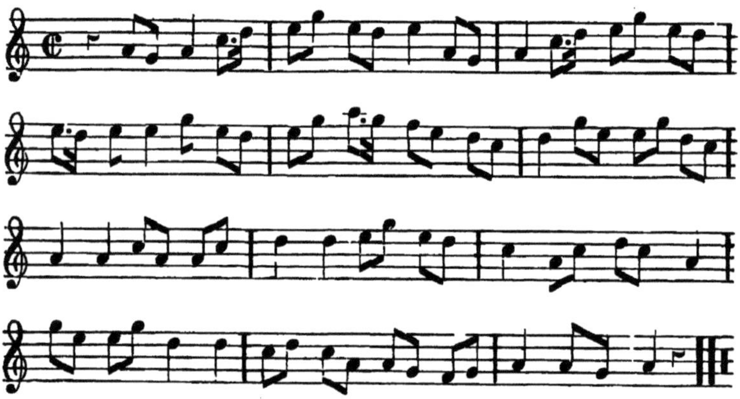

The literature on the art of music is large. One treatise on beating drums scientifically dates from about the year 860 A.D., and contains a list of about one hundred and twenty-nine symphonies, many of which are of Indian origin. Among the seventy-two instruments briefly described in the *Chinese Chrestomathy*, there are seventeen kinds of drums, from the large ones suspended in temples to assist in worship to others of lesser size and diverse shape used in war, in theatres, and in bands. Gongs, cymbals, tambourines, and musical vases are also described in considerable variety; the last consisting of a curious arrangement of twelve cups, more or less filled with water, and struck with rods. The Chinese are fond of the tinkling of small pieces of sonorous glass, caused by the wind striking them against each other as they are suspended from a frame or lamp. The simple succession of sounds arising from striking upon a harmonicon, jingling these glasses together, or touching different sized cymbals suspended in a frame, is a favorite species of music.

The stringed instruments to be played by thrumming are not as numerous as those of percussion, but they display more science. Nothing resembling the harp or Apollo's lyre has been observed among them. The *kin*, or 'scholar's lute,' is considered as the most finished, and has received more attention than any other orchestral implement; to excel in playing it is regarded as a scholarly accomplishment. A work entitled *The Lute-Player's Easy Lessons*, in two volumes, contains explanations of one hundred and nine terms and is illustrated by twenty-nine pictures of the position of the hands to aid in a full understanding of the twenty-three sets of tunes given in the second volume. This lute, it may be added, is of very ancient origin and derives its name from the word *kin*, 'to prohibit,' "because it restrains and checks evil passions and corrects the human heart." It is a board about four feet in length and eighteen inches wide, convex above and flat beneath, where are two holes opening into hollows. There are seven strings of silk, which pass over a bridge near the wide end through the board, and are tightened by nuts beneath; they are secured on two pegs at the smaller end. The sounding-board is divided by thirteen studs, "so placed that the length of the strings is divided first into two equal parts, then into three, etc., up to eight, with the omission of the seventh. The seven strings inclose the compass of a ninth or two-fifths, the middle one being treated like A upon the violin, viz., as a middle string, and each of the outer ones is tuned a fifth from it. This interval is treated like our octave in the violin, for the compass of the *kin* is made up of fifths. Each of the outer strings is tuned a fourth from the alternate string within the system, so that there is a major tone, an interval tone less than a minor third, and a major tone in the fifth. The Chinese leave the interval entire, and skip the half tone, while we divide it into two unequal parts. It will therefore readily appear that the mood or character of the music of the *kin* must be very different from that of western instruments, so that none of them can exactly do justice to the Chinese airs. One of the peculiarities in performing on the lute is sliding the left hand fingers along the string, and the trilling and other evolutions they are made to execute."

There are other instruments similar to the *kin*, one with thirty, and another with thirteen strings, played with plectrums. The number of instruments resembling the guitar, lute, cithern, spinet, etc., is considerable, some with silken, others with wire strings, but none of catgut. The balloon-shaped guitar, or *pípa*, has four strings arranged and secured like those of a violin; it is about three feet long, and the unvarnished upper table has twelve frets to guide the performer. The strings are tuned at the intervals of a fourth, a major tone, and a fourth, so that the outer strings are octaves to each other; but the player generally avoids the semitones. The *pípa* frequently accompanies the songs of strolling musicians and ballad singers. The *san hien*, or 'three-stringed guitar,' resembles a rebeck in its contour, but the neck and head is three feet long, and the body is cylindrical and hollow, usually covered with snake's skin, upon which the bridge is set. The strings are tuned as fourths to each other, and in this respect it seems to be the counterpart of the Grecian mercurian; their sound is low and dull, and the instrument is sometimes played in company with the *pípa*. Another kind of guitar, called *yueh kin*, or 'full moon guitar,' has a large round belly and short neck, resembling the theorbo or arch lute of Europe, but with only four strings, while that had ten or more. These four strings stand in pairs that are unisons with each other, having an interval of a fifth interposed between the pairs. The sound is smarter than that from the *pípa* or *kin*, and it is used in lively tunes, the strings being struck briskly with the nail or a plectrum. Similar in its construction to the *san hien* is the rebeck, or two-stringed fiddle, the rude appearance of which corresponds to the thin grating sounds which issue from it. This instrument is merely a bamboo stick thrust into a cylinder of the same material, and having two strings fastened at one end of the stick on pegs, and passing over a bridge on the cylinder to the other end; they are tuned at intervals of a fifth. The bow passes between the two strings, and as they are near each other, much of the skill required to play it is exhibited in wielding the bow so as not to make discord by scraping it against the wrong string while trying to produce a given sound. Europeans wonder how the Chinese can be delighted with the harsh gratings of this wretched machine, but none of their musical instruments are more popular, and the skill they exhibit in playing it deserves a better reward in the melody of the notes. A modification of it, called *tí kin*, or 'crowing lute,' is made by employing a cocoanut for the belly; its sounds are, if anything, more dissonant.

The *yang kin* is a kind of dulcimer, consisting of a greater or less number of brass wires of different lengths, tuned at proper intervals, and fastened upon a sounding-board; it is played with light hammers, and forms a rudimentary piano-forte, but the sounds are very attenuated. The *săng* is in like manner the embryo of the organ; it is a hollow conical-shaped box, which corresponds to a wind-chest, having a mouthpiece on one side, and communicating with thirteen reeds of different lengths inserted in the top; some of the tubes are provided with valves, part of them opening upward and part downward, so that some of them sound when the breath fills the wind-box, and others are only heard when it is sucked out and the air rushes down the tubes to refill it. The tubes stand in groups of four, four, three, two, around the top, and those having ventiges are placed so that the performer can open or close them at pleasure as he holds it. By covering the first set of holes and gently breathing in the mouthpiece, a sweet concert of sounds is produced, augmented to the octave and twelfth as the force of the breath is increased. By stopping certain groups, other notes, shriller and louder, are emitted; and any single tube can be sounded by inhaling the wind from the wind-box and stopping the other holes. It is a simple thing and no doubt among the most ancient of musical instruments, but it possesses no scope nor means of varying the tone of the tubes. Mr. Lay thinks it to be identical in principle and form with the organ invented by Jubal; the Chinese regard it more as a curious instrument than one possessing claims to admiration or attention.

Their wind instruments are numerous, but most of them are remarkable rather for clamor than sweetness or compass. The *hwang tih*, or flute, is about twice the length of our fife, and made of a bamboo tube neatly prepared and pierced with ten holes, two of which are placed near the end and unused, and one midway between the embouchure and the six equidistant ones for the fingers. This additional hole is covered with a thin film; the mouth-hole is bored about one-third of the way from the top. There are no keys, and the performers generally blow upon the embouchure so violently that the sounds are shrill and harsh, but when several of them play together the concert is more agreeable. The congener of the flute is the *shu tih*, or clarinet, which takes the lead in all musical performances, as it does in western bands. It has seven effective holes, one of which is stopped by the thumb, but no keys; the bell is of copper and sits loose upon the end, and the copper mouthpiece is ornamented with rings, and blown through a reed. The tones produced by it are shrill and deafening, and none of their instruments better characterize Chinese musical taste. A smaller one, of a sweeter tone, like a flageolet, is sometimes fitted with a singular shaped reed, so that it can be played upon by the nose. Street musicians sometimes endeavor to transform themselves into a travelling orchestra. One of these peripatetic Orpheuses will fit a flageolet to his nose, sling a small drum under one shoulder, and suspend a framework of four small cymbals upon the breast; the man, thus accoutred, aided by a couple of monkeys running after him, or sitting on his head and shoulders, goes from street to street singing a plaintive ditty, and accompanying his voice with his instruments, and drawing a crowd with his monkeys.

The horn resembles a trombone in principle, for the shaft is retractible within the cylindrical copper bell, and can be lengthened at pleasure. The sound is very grave, and in processions its hollow booming forms a great contrast to the shrill clarinets and cymbals. Another kind of horn, less grave, is made of a crooked stem expanding into a small bell at the end; the shaft is of two parts, one drawing into the other, so that the depth of tone can be modified. A long straight horn, resembling the funeral pipe of the Jews, is sometimes heard on funeral occasions, but this and the clarion, trumpet, and other kinds of pipes of ancient and modern make are not common.

The *lo*, or gong, is the type of Chinese music: a crashing harangue of rapid blows upon this sonorous plate, with a rattling accompaniment on small drums, and a crackling symphony of shrill notes from the clarinet and cymbal, constitute the chief features of their musical performances. The Emperor Kanghí endeavored to introduce foreign tunes and instruments among his courtiers, and the natives at Macao have heard good music from the Portuguese bands and choirs in that city from childhood, but not an instrument or a tune has been adopted by them. It seems to be a rule in Chinese music that the gong should only vary in rapidity of strokes, while the alternations of time into agreeable intervals are left to the drums. "This want of perception as to what is pleasing in rhythmical succession of sounds," Lay well observes, "is connected with another fact—the total absence of metrical effect in national poetry. The verses contain a particular number of words and set pauses in each line, but there is nothing like an interchange of long and short sounds. Among the Greeks the fall of the smith's hammer, the stroke of the oar, and the tread of the soldier in armor suggested some poetic measure, and their music exhibits a world of curious metres. But nothing of the sort can be heard in China, amid all the sounds and noises that salute the ear in a noisy country." It is probable that the impracticable, monosyllabic nature of the language has contributed to this result; though the genius and temperament of the people are the chief reasons.

A Chinese orchestra or band, when in full note, strikes upon the ear of a European as a collection of the most discordant sounds, and he immediately thinks of Hogarth's picture of the

Enraged Musician, as the best likeness of its dissonance. It seems, when hearing them, as if each performer had his own tune, and was trying to distinguish himself above his competitors by his zeal and force; but on listening carefully he will observe, amid the clangor, that they keep good time, one taking the octave, and the different instruments striking in with some regard to parts, only, however, to confound the confusion still more because they are not tuned on the same key. Bands and orchestras are employed on occasions of marriages and funerals, theatrical exhibitions, religious or civic processions, and reception of officers, but not to a very great extent in temples or ancestral worship; no nation makes more use of such music as they have than the Chinese. The people have an ear for music, and young men form clubs to learn and practise on various instruments and fit themselves for playing at weddings or birthday festivals. In respect to adopting foreign harmonies, which youths soon learn to appreciate when taught in mission schools, there is likely to be no competition, owing to the great differences between them. [1]

From this account of Chinese music, it may be readily inferred that it is not of such a character as to start the hearers off in a lively dance. A sort of mummer or posture-making is practised by persons attached to theatrical companies, and pantomimic art seems to have been understood in ancient times, but the exhibitions of it were probably as jejune as the caperings of puppets. As acrobats the Chinese are equal to any nation, and companies have performed in many western capitals within a few years past. Some of their performances are highly exciting, as throwing sharp cleavers at a man fastened to a post, till he cannot stir without cutting himself against their blades, is a common exhibition. To go through the tragedy of trying, con-

---

[1] *Chinese as They Are*, Chap. VIII. *Chinese Repository*, Vol. VIII., pp. 30–54. *Chinese Chrestomathy*, pp. 356–365. *Journal N. C. Br. R. A. Soc.*, No. II., 1859, p. 176; No. V., 1868, p. 30. *Journal of the Asiatic Soc. of Japan*, 1877, Vol. V., pp. 170–179. *German Asiatic Soc. of Japan*, 1876. Grosier, *Description générale de la Chine*, Tome VI., p. 258. Doolittle, *Social Life*, Vol. II., p. 216. Barrow's *Travels*, pp. 313–323. *Mémoires conc. les Chinois*, Tomes I., III., VI., etc.; for ancient musical knowledge, the last still furnishes the best analysis yet made.

demning, and killing a boy by stabbing him in the belly is not so common; the imitation of the gasping chest and pallid death hue are wonderfully natural. Ventriloquism, writing answers to questions asked of the spirits by means of rods moving over a dusted table, and other black art or magical tricks have long been known. In dancing and other forms of graceful motion they are entirely wanting, and one would almost as soon think of associating music and medicine as that Chinese music should be accompanied by quadrilles and cotillons, or that men with shoes like pattens could lead off women with feet like hoofs through the turns and mazes of a waltz or fandango.

Their deficiencies in music will not lead us to expect much from them in painting or sculpture, for all flow so much from the same general perception of the beautiful in sound, form, and color, that where one is deficient all are likely to be unappreciated. This want in Chinese mind (for we are hardly at liberty to call it a defect) is, to a greater or less degree, observable in all the races of Eastern Asia, none of whom exhibit a high appreciation of the beautiful or sublime in nature or art, or have produced much which proves that their true principles were ever understood. Painting is rather behind sculpture, but neither can be said to have advanced beyond rude imitations of nature.

Even the best painters have no proper idea of perspective or of blending light and shade, but the objects are exhibited as much as possible on a flat surface, as if the painter drew his picture from a balloon, and looked at the country with a vertical sun shining above him. As might be inferred from their deficiencies in linear drawing and landscapes, they eminently fail in delineating the human figure in its right proportions, position, and expressions, and of grouping the persons introduced into a piece in natural attitudes. The study of the human figure in all its proportions has not been attended to by painters any more than its anatomy has by surgeons. Shadows upon portraits are considered a great defect, and in order to avoid them a front view is usually taken. Landscapes are also painted without shading, the remote objects being as minutely depicted as those in the foreground, and the point of view in pieces of any size is changed for the nearer and remote parts. There is no vanishing point to their pictures, as might be inferred from their ignorance of perspective and the true elements of art.

Outline drawing is a favorite style of the art, and the wealthy adorn their houses with rough sketches in ink of figures and landscapes; but the humblest of such compositions as are common in the galleries and studios of western countries have never been produced by Chinese artists. Some of their

Representation of a Man Dreaming.

representations of abstract ideas are at least singular to us, and, like many other things brought from their country, attract notice from their oddity.

Their coloring is executed with great skill and accuracy—too much, indeed, in many cases, so that the painting loses something of the effect it would otherwise have from the scrupulous minuteness of the detail, though it looks well in paintings of flowers, animals, costumes, ornaments, and other single objects where this filling up is necessary to a true idea of the original. The tints of the human countenance are no better done, however, than its lineaments, and the lifeless opacity suggests the idea that the artist was not called in until his patron was about to be entombed from the sight of his sorrowing family. The paintings obtained at Canton may, some of them, seem to disprove these opinions of the mediocrity attained by the artists in that country, but the productions of the copyists in that city are not the proper criteria of native uneducated art. Some of them have had so much practice in copying foreign productions that it has begun to correct their own notions of designing. These constitute, however, a very small proportion of the whole, and have had no effect on national taste. The designs to be seen on plates and bowls are, although not the best, fairer specimens of art than the pieces sometimes procured at Canton. The beautiful fidelity with which engravings are copied at Canton is well seen in the paintings on ivory, especially miniatures and figures, some of which fully equal similar productions made elsewhere.[1]

As samples of Chinese illustrative art, the two adjoining wood-cuts may be considered as quite up to the average of their fairest achievements. The story of the first in brief is as follows: In the district of Tsung-ngan lived a crafty plebeian, who, envying the good fortune of all about him, became especially covetous of the burial ground of his district magistrate Chu. Hoping to gain a surreptitious benefit from the felicitous luck of the plat, he secretly buried his own tombstone there, and at the end of several years brought suit for its recovery. Unable to comprehend the affair, Chu repaired to the burial spot, where indeed the geomancy of the grave was found to be entirely in accord with the rules, but upon removing the earth the stone of his enemy's remote ancestry was disclosed. The suit was in consequence declared against him, Chu removed his residence to the black tea country, and his envious neighbor entered in triumph upon possession of the graveyard.

Not so readily, however, did the powers above condone this iniquity. One night there arose a tempest of unheard-of vio-

[1] Compare Owen Jones, *Grammar of Ornament*, Chap. XIV., and *Examples of Chinese Ornament* (London, 1867). *Gazette des Beaux-Arts* for October and November, 1873, and January, 1874.

The Vengeance of Heaven upon the False Grave.

lence, when the thunder and lightning were indescribable, the hideous roar and flash of which terrified the country far and near, boding no good to its wretched inhabitants. The following morning the grave was discovered in ruins, stone and epitaph uprooted, even the corpse and coffin missing. The vengeance of Heaven had repaired the injustice of man.

The illustration which depicts the tempest personified in its full terror shows us the *Lui Kung*, or God of Thunder, almost the only Chinese mythological deity who is drawn with wings. The cock's head and claws, the hammer and chisel, representing the splitting peal attending a flash, the circlet of fire encompassing a number of drums to typify the reverberating thunder and the ravages of the irresistible lightning, present a grotesque ensemble which is quite unique even among the *bizarrerie* of oriental figures; the somewhat juvenile attempts of the artist to sketch the destruction and rifling of the grave are much less notable.

Concerning the subject of the second illustration (taken, with the other, from the *Sacred Edict* of Kanghí), we are told that one Yuen, having conceived a violent hatred against an acquaintance, set out one morning, knife in hand, with the purpose of killing him. A venerable man sitting in a convent saw him pass, and was amazed to observe several scores of spirits closely following him, some of whom clutched his weapon, while others seemed endeavoring to delay his progress. "About the space of a meal-time" the patriarch noticed Yuen's return, accompanied this time by more than a hundred spirits wearing golden caps and bearing banners raised on high. Yuen himself appeared with so happy a face, in place of his gloomy countenance of the early morning, that the old man sadly concluded that his enemy must be dead and his revenge gratified. "When you passed this way at daybreak," he asked, "where were you going, and how do you return so soon?" "It was owing to my quarrel with Miu," said Yuen, "that made me wish to kill him. But in passing this convent door better thoughts came to me as I pondered upon the stress his wife and children would come to, and of his aged mother, none of whom had done me wrong. I determined then not to kill him, and return thus promptly

A would-be Assassin followed by Spirits.

from my evil purpose." It hardly needed the sage's commendations to increase the reformed murderer's inner contentment, imparted by the train of ghostly helpers; he continued on his way rejoicing. The reader may notice a pictorial idea as well as a moral not unlike those of more western countries.

The symbolism of the Chinese has not attracted the notice of foreign writers as much as it deserves. It meets us everywhere—on plates and crockery, on carpets, rugs, vases, wall pictures, shop signs, and visiting cards. Certain animals stand for well-understood characters in the language, and convey their sense to the native without any confusion. Owing to the similarity of sound, *fuh* denotes *bat* and *happiness*, and *luh* stands for *deer* and *official emolument*. The character *shao*, meaning 'longevity,' is represented in many ways—an old man leaning on his staff; a pine tree cut into the form of the character; a tortoise, which is among the longest-lived reptiles; a stork, supposed to be a bird which attains a great age, and a fabulous peach which is a thousand years ripening. A dragon and a phœnix, or *fung-whang*, are emblems of a newly wedded pair, and various modes of combination are adopted to represent marriage relations.

A rug will sometimes tell a story very neatly to the eye. In the centre is the *swastica*, or 'hammer of Thor,' which denotes *all*, and symbolizes all happiness that humanity desires. On the right is the *luh*, or 'deer,' which denotes honor and success in study, carrying the *yü-i*, or Buddhist sceptre, in its mouth, meaning success in literary labors. On the left is pictured a goose, indicating domestic felicity, and two bats complete the rug, with its good wishes.

In the plate represented in the picture the central figure is clad in the ancient costume of officials bearing the insignia or baton of a minister of State. The old man, with his gourd and peach, indicates an extreme and happy old age; and the figure with the basket corresponds to the cornucopia of western emblems. The five *bats* symbolize the *wu fuh*, or 'five happinesses,' which all mankind desires—riches, longevity, sound body, love of virtue, and a peaceful end.

The visiting card and note paper often indicate in their

adornments a good wish and a motto which does credit to the taste and heart of the designer. A most graceful and not uncommon way of wishing a guest good luck is to depict some happy emblem or a sentence of the language with a fortunate meaning on the bottom of his tea-cup. The characters "May your happiness know no bounds" frequently occur in this posi-

Symbols of Happiness and Old Age. (From a plaque.)

tion, and the oft-recurring five bats or three peaches can be employed with like signification. The mandarin duck is a well-understood emblem for conjugal affection; again, a cock and hen standing on an artificial rock-work symbolize the pleasures of a country life. Sometimes the eight symbols peculiar to the Buddhist sect, or the *pah sien* ('eight genii') indicative of their protection, are seen in the border of a plaque amid a device of running arabesques. The favorite dragon, in an infinite diversity of shapes, adorns the finer qualities of cups, plates, bowls, and vases, to represent imperial grandeur, but common people are not wont to use such patterns.

The brilliant paintings on pith-paper, or *rice-paper*, as it is commonly but incorrectly called, deserve special mention for their singular delicacy and spirit. This substance, whose velvety surface contrasts so admirably with bright colors, is a delicate vegetable film, consisting of long hexagonal cells, whose length is parallel to the surface of the film, and which are filled with air when the film is in its usual state; the peculiar softness which so well adapts it for receiving colors is owing to this structure. It is obtained from the pith of a species of Fatsia, a plant allied to the Aralia, growing in Formosa and Yunnan, in marshy districts. It is cultivated to some extent, but mostly gathered by cutting the branches of the wild plants, which resemble the elder. This pith forms a large item in the internal trade of China, and is worked up into toys as well as cut into sheets. The fragments are used to stuff pillows or fill up the soles of shoes, or wherever a light, dry material is needed. The largest and best sheets (ten by fifteen inches) are selected for the painters at Hongkong and Canton, where many hundreds of workmen are employed in making them. Under the direction of foreign ladies at Amoy and elsewhere, most accurate imitations of flowers and bouquets are now made by natives out of pith-paper. The pieces are cut nearly a foot long, and the pith is forced out by driving a stick into one end; it is then wet and put into bamboos, where it swells and dries straight. If too short to furnish the required breadth, several bits are pressed together until they adhere and make one long straight piece. The paring knife resembles a butcher's cleaver, a thin and sharp blade, which is touched up on a block of iron-wood at the last moment. The pith is pared on a square tile, having its ends guarded by a thin strip of brass, on which the knife rests. The pith is rolled over against its edge with the left hand; the right firmly holds it, slowly moving it leftward, as the workman pulls and rolls the pith in the same direction, as far as the tile allows. The pared sheet runs under the knife, and the paring goes on until only a centre three or four lines thick is left; and this remnant the thrifty workmen use or sell for an aperient. The paring resembles the operation of cutting out corks, and produces a smooth sheet about four feet long, the first half foot being too much grooved to be of use. The fresh sheets are pressed in a pile, smoothed by ironing and their fractures mended with mica. Most of the paper is trimmed into square sheets for the makers of artificial flowers, and sold in Formosa at about eight cents for five hundred sheets. An India-ink outline is first transferred by dampening and pressing it upon the paper, when the ink strikes off sufficiently to enable the workman to fill up the sketch; one outline will serve for limning several copies, and in large establishments the separate colors are laid on by different workmen. The manufacture of these paintings at Canton employs between two and three thousand hands.

Another tissue sometimes used by the Chinese for painting, more remarkable for its singularity than elegance, is the reticulated nerve-work of leaves, the parenchyma of the leaf having been removed by maceration, and the membrane filled with isinglass. The appearance of a painting on this transparent substance is pretty, but the colors do not retain their brilliancy. The Chinese admire paintings on glass, and some of the moonlight scenes or thunderstorms are good specimens of their art. The clouds and dark parts are done with India-ink, and a dark shade well befitting the subject is imparted to the whole scene by underlaying it with a piece of blackish paper. Portraits and other subjects are also done on glass, but the indifferent execution is rendered still more conspicuous by the transparency of the ground; the Hindus purchase large quantities of such glass pictures of their gods and goddesses. Looking-glasses are also painted on the back with singular effect by removing the quicksilver with a steel point according to a design previously sketched, and then painting the denuded portion.

Statuary is confined chiefly to molding idols out of clay or cutting them from wood, and carving animals to adorn balustrades and temples. Idols are generally made in a sitting posture and dressed, the face and hands being the only parts of the body seen, so that no opportunity is afforded for imitating the muscles and contour of the figure. The hideous monsters which guard the entrance of temples often exhibit more artistic skill than the unmeaning images enshrined within, and some even display much knowledge of character and proportion. Among their best performances in statuettes are the accurate baked and painted models of different classes of people; Canton and Tien-tsin artists excel in this branch.

Animals are sculptured in granite and cast in bronze, showing great skill and patience in the detail work; deformity in the model has resulted in the production of such animals, indeed, as were probably never beheld in any world. Images of lions, tigers, tortoises, elephants, rams, and other animals ornament bridges, temples, and tombs. The elephants in the long avenue of warriors, horses, lions, etc., leading up to the tomb of the Emperor Hungwu at Nanking are the only tolerable representations of their originals; the gigantic images guarding the tomb of Yungloh, his son, at Changping, near Peking, are noticeable for size alone. The united effect of the elaborate carving and grotesque ornaments seen upon the roofs, woodwork, and pillars of buildings is not devoid of beauty, though in their details there is a great violation of the true principles of art, just as the expression of a face may please which still has not a handsome feature in it. Short columns of stone or wood, surmounted by a lion, and a dragon twining around the shaft, the whole cut out of one block; or a lion sejant with half a dozen cubs crawling over his body, are among the ornaments of temples and graves which show the taste of the people.

The Chinese have a sense of the ridiculous, and exhibit it both in their sculpture and drawing in many ways. Lampoons, pasquinades, and caricatures are common, nor is any person below the dragon's throne spared by their pens or pencils, though they prefer subjects not likely to involve the authors—as in the one here selected from the many elicited during the war of 1840.

By far the best specimens of sculpture are their imitations of fruits, flowers, animals, etc., cut out of many kinds of stone, from gnarled roots of bamboo, wood, and other materials; but in these we admire the unwearied patience and cunning of the workmen in making grotesque combinations and figures out of apparently intractable materials, and do not seek for any indications of a pure taste or embodiment of an exalted conception. Inscriptions of a religious or geomantic character are often cut upon the faces of rocks, as was the case in India and Arabia,[1] and the picturesque characters of the language make a pretty appearance in such situations.

The small advances made in architecture have already been noticed in Chapter XIII.—a deficiency exhibited in the Huns and other nations of the Mongolian stock long after they had

Caricature of an English Foraging Party.

settled in Europe and Western Asia; nor was it until their amalgamation with the imaginative nations of Southern Europe had changed their original character that grand performances in architecture appeared among the latter. If the Chinese had a model of the Parthenon or the Pantheon in their own country, belike they would measurably imitate it in every part, but they would erect dozens in the same fashion. Perhaps an infusion of elegance and taste would have been imparted to them if the people had had frequent intercourse with more im-

[1] Compare Job XXX., 24.

aginative nations, but when there were no models of this superior kind to follow there was no likelihood of their originating them. In lighter edifices, as pavilions, rest-houses, kiosks, and arbors, there is, however, a degree of taste and adaptation that is unusual in other buildings, and quite in keeping with their fondness for tinsel and gilding rather than solidity and grandeur. On this point Lay's remark on the characteristics of the Attic, Egyptian, Gothic, and Chinese styles is apposite. "If we would see beauty, size, and proportion in all their excellence, we should look for it among the models of Greece; if we desire something that was wild and stupendous, we should find it in Egypt; if grandeur with a never-sated minuteness of decoration please us, we need look no further than to a cathedral; and lastly, if the romantic and the old-fashioned attract our fancy, the Chinese can point us to an exhaustless store in the recesses of their vast Empire. A lack of science and of conception is seen in all their buildings, but fancy seems to have had free license to gambol at pleasure; and what the architect wanted in developing a scheme he made up in a redundancy of imagination."

The Chinese have made but little progress in investigating the principles and forces of mechanics, but have practically understood most of the common powers in the various applications of which they are capable. The lever, wheel and axle, wedge and pinion, are all known in some form or other, but the modification of the wedge in the screw is not frequent. The sheave-blocks on board their vessels have only one pulley, but they understand the advantages of the windlass, and have adopted the capstain in working vessels, driving piles, raising timber, etc. They have long understood the mode of raising weights by a hooked pulley running on a rope, attached at each end to a cylinder of unequal diameters; by this contrivance, as the rope wound around the larger diameter it ran off the smaller one, raising the weight to the amount of the difference between the circumference of the two cylinders at a very small expense of strength. The graduations of the weighing-beam indicate their acquaintance with the relations between the balance and the weight on the long and short arm of the lever, and this mode of weighing is preferred for gold, pearls, and other valuable things. The overshot water-wheel is used to turn stones for grinding wheat and set in motion pestles to hull rice and press oil from seeds, and the undershot power for raising water. There is a great expenditure of human strength in most of their contrivances; in many, indeed, the object seems to have been rather to give a direction to this strength than to abridge it. For instance, they put a number of slings under a heavy stone and carry it off bodily on poles, in preference to making a low car to roll it away at half the expense of human power.

In other departments of science the attainments of the people are few and imperfect. Chemistry and metallurgy are unknown as sciences, but many operations in them are performed with a considerable degree of success. Sir J. Davis gives the detail of some experiments in oxidizing quicksilver and preparation of mercurial medicines which were performed by a native in the presence and at the request of Dr. Pearson at Canton, and "afforded a curious proof of similar results obtained by the most different and distant nations possessing very unequal scientific attainments, and bore no unfavorable testimony to Chinese shrewdness and ingenuity in the existing state of their knowledge."[1] The same opinion might be safely predicated of their metallurgic manipulations; the character of the work is the only index of the efficacy of the process. In bronzes they take a high place, and the delicacy of their niello work in gold and silver, upon wood as well as metal, cannot be surpassed.

This compendious review of the science of the Chinese can be brought to a close by a brief account of their theory and practice of medicine and surgery. Although they are almost as superstitious as the Hindus or North American Indians, they do not depend upon incantations and charms for relief in case of sickness, but resort to the prescriptions of the physician as the most reasonable and likely way to recover; mixed up, indeed, with many strange practices to assist the efficacy of the doses. These vary in every part of the Empire, and show the power of ignorance to perpetuate and strengthen the strangest supersti-

[1] *The Chinese*, Vol. II., pp. 266–270, 286.

tions where health and life are involved. Doolittle has collected many instances, and the experience of medical missionaries is uniform in this matter.

The dissection of the human body is never attempted, though some notions of its internal structure are taught in medical works, which are published in many forms. Mr. Wylie notices fifty-nine treatises of a medical and physiological character in his *Notes on Chinese Literature*. They contain references to a far greater number of authors, some of whom flourished in the earliest days of China, and many of whose writings exhibit good sense and sound advice amid the strangest theories. Dr. Harland has described the Chinese ideas of the organization of the body and the functions of the chief viscera in a lucid manner, and the diagram shown on p. 120 presents the popular opinions on this subject, for whatever foreigners may have imparted to them has not yet become generally known.

The Chinese seem to have no idea of the distinction between venous and arterial blood, nor between muscles and nerves, applying the word *kin* to both tendons and nerves. According to these physiologists, the brain (A) is the abode of the *yin* principle in its perfection, and at its base (B), where there is a reservoir of the marrow, communicates through the spine with the whole body. The larynx (C) goes through the lungs directly to the heart, expanding a little in its course, while the pharynx (D) passes over them to the stomach. The lungs (*a*, *a*, *a*, *a*, *a*, *a*) are white, and placed in the thorax; they consist of six lobes or leaves suspended from the spine, four on one side and two on the other; sound proceeds from holes in them, and they rule the various parts of the body. The centre of the thorax (or pit of the stomach) is the seat of the breath; joy and delight emanate from it, and it cannot be injured without danger. The heart (*b*) lies underneath the lungs, and is the prince of the body; thoughts proceed from it. The pericardium (*c*) comes from and envelops the heart and extends to the kidneys. There are three tubes communicating from the heart to the spleen, liver, and kidneys, but no clear ideas are held as to their office. Like the pharynx, they pass through the diaphragm, which is itself connected with the spine, ribs, and bowels. The

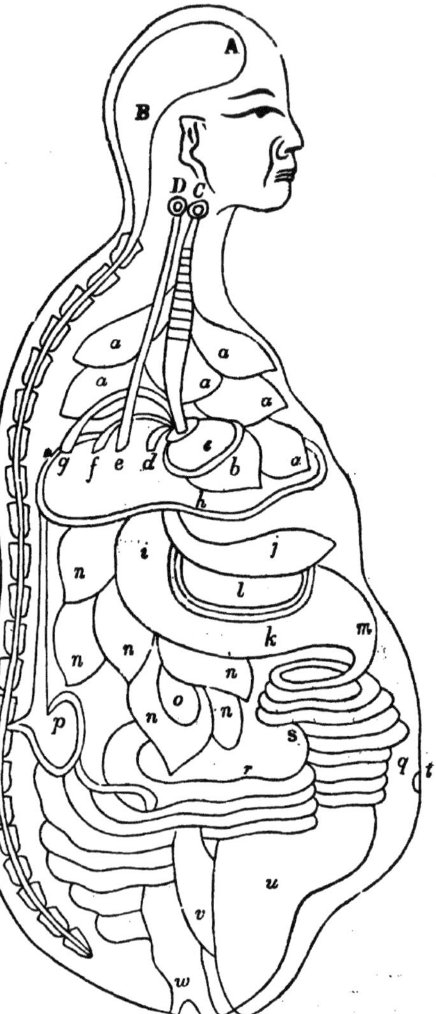

Chinese Notions of the Internal Structure of the Human Body.

A, *B*—The brain. *C*—Larynx. *D*—Pharynx. *a*,*a*,*a*,*a*,*a*, *a*—Lungs. *b*—Heart. *c*—Pericardium. *d*—Bond of connection with the spleen. *e*—The œsophagus. *f*—Bond of connection with the liver. *g*—Bond of connection with the kidneys. *h*—The diaphragm. *i*—Cardiac extremity. *j*—The spleen. *k*—The stomach. *l*—Omentum. *m*—The pylorus. *n*,*n*,*n*,*n*,*n*,*n*—The liver. *o*—The gall-bladder. *p*—The kidneys. *q*—The small intestines. *r*—The large intestines. *s*—Caput coli. *t*—The navel. *u*—The bladder. *v*—The "gate of life," sometimes placed in the right kidney. *w*—The rectum. *x*, *y*—The urinal and fœcal passages.

liver (*n*, *n*, *n*, *n*, *n*, *n*) is on the right side and has seven lobes; the soul resides in it, and schemes emanate from it; the gall-bladder (*o*) is below and projects upward into it, and when the person is angry it ascends; courage dwells in it; hence the Chinese sometimes procure the gall-bladder of animals, as tigers and bears, and even of men, especially notorious bandits executed for their crimes, and eat the bile contained in them, under the idea that it will impart courage. The spleen (*j*) lies between the stomach and diaphragm and assists in digestion, and the food passes from it into the stomach (*k*), and hence through the pylorus (*m*) into the large intestines. The omentum (*l*) overlies the stomach, but its office is unknown, and the mesentery and pancreas are entirely omitted.

The small intestines (*q*) are connected with the heart, and the urine passes through them into the bladder, separating from the food or fæces at the caput coli (*s*), where they divide from the larger intestines. The large intestines (*r*) are connected with the lungs and lie in the loins, having sixteen convolutions. The kidneys (*p*) are attached to the spinal marrow, and resemble an egg in shape, and the subtle generative fluid is eliminated by them above to the brain and below to the spermatic cord and sacral extremity; the testes, called *wai shin*, or 'outside kidneys,' communicate with them. The right kidney, or the passage from it (*v*), is called the "gate of life," and sends forth the subtle fluid to the spermatic vessels. The bladder (*u*) lies below the kidneys, and receives the urine from the small intestines at the iliac valve.

The osteology of the frame is briefly despatched: the pelvis, skull, forearm, and leg are considered as single bones, the processes of the joints being quite dispensed with, and the whole considered merely as a kind of internal framework, on and in which the necessary fleshy parts are upheld, but with which they have not much more connection by muscles and ligaments than the post has with the pile of mud it upholds. The *Tai-i Yuen*, or Medical College at Peking, contains a copper model of a man, about six feet high, on which are given the names of the pulses in different places; it is pierced with many small holes. In A.D. 1027 the Emperor had two anatomical figures made to illustrate the art of acupuncture, which is still practised. The irrigation of the body with blood is rather complicated, and authors vary greatly as to the manner in which it is accomplished. Some pictures represent tubes issuing from the fingers and toes, and running up the limbs into the trunk, where they are lost, or reach the heart, lungs, or some other organ as well as they can, wandering over most parts of the body in their course.

Theories are furnished in great variety to account for the nourishment of the body and the functions of the viscera, and upon their harmonious connection with each other and the five metals, colors, tastes, and planets is founded the well-being of the system; with all they hold an intimate relation, and their actions are alike built on the all-pervading functions of the *yin* and *yang*—those universal solvents in Chinese philosophy. The pulse is very carefully studied, and its condition regarded as the index of every condition of the body, even to determining the sex of an unborn infant; great parade is usually made by every practitioner in examining this important symptom.

Dr. Harland has made a table showing the sympathy supposed to exist between the different points of the pulses and the internal organs.[1] In each wrist the pulses are named *Inch*, *Bar*, and *Cubit* (the first being nearest the hand); a change in degree of pressure doubles the range of viscera thus indexed:

LEFT WRIST.

Inch,	when	lightly	pressed,	indicates	the state	of the	small intestines.
"	"	heavily	"	"	"	"	heart.
Bar,	"	lightly	"	"	"	"	gall-bladder.
"	"	heavily	"	"	"	"	liver.
Cubit,	"	lightly	"	"	"	"	urinary bladder.
"	"	heavily	"	"	"	"	kidneys.

RIGHT WRIST.

Inch,	when	lightly	pressed,	indicates	the state	of the	large intestines.
"	"	heavily	"	"	"	"	lungs.
Bar,	"	lightly	"	"	"	"	stomach.
"	"	heavily	"	"	"	"	spleen.
Cubit,	"	lightly	"	"	"	"	*san tseaou.*
"	"	heavily	"	"	"	"	*ming măn.*

The two latter meaning respectively 'Three Passages' and 'Gate of Life,' being purely imaginary organs, are difficult to describe.

A diseased state of an organ is supposed to be owing to a disagreement of the *yin* and *yang*, the presence of bad humors, or the more powerful agency of evil spirits, and until these agencies are corrected medicines cannot exercise their full efficacy. The surface of the body receives the closest attention, for there is not a square inch without its appropriate name. Plasters and lotions are applied to these places according to the diagnosis of the disease, predicated on the dual theory; and the strolling quacks and regular practitioners both administer the rationale and the dose together—considering, probably, that the medicine would lose half its efficacy upon the organs it was intended to affect if it was not mixed with faith to operate upon the sentient principle lodged there.

[1] *Transactions of the China Br. of Royal Asiatic Society*, Hongkong, Part I, 1847, p. 43.

The practice of the Chinese is far in advance of their theory, and some of their treatises on dietetics and medical practice contain good advice, the result of experience. Dr. W. Lockhart has translated a native treatise on midwifery, in which the author, confining himself principally to the best modes of treatment in all the stages of parturition, and dwelling briefly on the reasons of things, has greatly improved upon the physiologists. This branch of the profession is almost entirely in the hands of women. Surgical operations are chiefly confined to removing a tooth, puncturing sores and tumors with needles, or trying to reduce dislocations and reunite fractures by pressure or bandaging. Sometimes they successfully execute more difficult cases, as the amputation of a finger, operation for a harelip, and insertion of false teeth. In one case of dentistry four incisor teeth made of ivory were strung upon a piece of catgut and secured in their place by tying the string to the eye-teeth; they were renewed quarterly, and served their purpose tolerably well. The practice of acupuncture has some good results among the bad ones.[1] That of applying cauteries and caustics of various degrees of power is more general, and sometimes entails shocking distress upon the patient. Cases have presented themselves at the hospitals, where small sores, by the application of escharotics, have extended until a large part of the tissue, and even important organs, have been destroyed, the charlatan amusing his suffering patient by promises of ultimate cure. The moxa, or burning the flowers of the amaranthus upon the skin, is attended with less injury.

Turning in of the eyelashes is a common ailment, and native practitioners attempt to cure it by everting the lid and fastening it in its place by two slips of bamboo tightly bound on, or by a pair of tweezers, until the loose fold on the edge sloughs off; the eye is, however, more frequently disfigured by this clumsy process than is the trouble remedied. Poultices made of many strange or disgusting substances are applied to injured parts.

[1] Compare Rémusat (*Nouveaux Mélanges Asiatiques*, Tome I., pp. 358–380), who says that the first notion of acupuncture as practised in China was brought into Europe by one Ten-Rhyne, a Dutch surgeon, at the end of the seventeenth century.

Dr. Parker mentions the case of a man who, having injured the iris by a fall, was ordered by his native physician to cut a chicken in halves, laying one portion on the eye as a cataplasm and eating the other as an internal cure. Venesection is rarely attempted, but leeches and cupping are employed to remove the blood from a particular spot. Blood-letting is disapproved in fevers, "for," says the Chinese reasoner, "a fever is like a pot boiling; it is requisite to reduce the fire and not diminish the liquid in the vessel if we wish to cure the patient."

Many of the operations in cases of fracture present a strange mixture of folly and sense, proceeding from their ideas of the internal structure of the human body conflicting with those which common sense and experience teach. Père Ripa's description of the treatment he underwent to prevent the ill effects of a fall will serve as an illustration. Having been thrown from his horse and left fainting in the street, he was carried into a house, where a surgeon soon visited him. "He made me sit up in bed, placing near me a large basin filled with water, in which he put a thick piece of ice to reduce it to a freezing point. Then stripping me to the waist, he made me stretch my neck over the basin, while he continued for a good while to pour the water on my neck with a cup. The pain caused by this operation upon those nerves which take their rise from the pia mater was so great and insufferable that it seemed to me unequalled, but he said it would stanch the blood and restore me to my senses, which was actually the case, for in a short time my sight became clear and my mind resumed its powers. He next bound my head with a band drawn tight by two men who held the ends, while he struck the intermediate parts vigorously with a piece of wood, which shook my head violently, and gave me dreadful pain. This, he said, was to set the brain, which he supposed had been displaced, and it is true that after the second operation my head felt more free. A third operation was now performed, during which he made me, still stripped to the waist, walk in the open air supported by two persons; and while thus walking he unexpectedly threw a basin of freezing cold water over my breast. As this caused me to draw my breath with great vehemence, and as my chest had been injured by the fall, it may easily be imagined what were my sufferings under this infliction; but I was consoled by the information that if any rib had been dislocated, this sudden and hard breathing would restore it to its natural position. The next proceeding was not less painful and extravagant. The operator made me sit on the ground, and, assisted by two men, held a cloth upon my mouth and nose till I was almost suffocated. 'This,' said the Chinese Esculapius, 'by causing a violent heaving of the chest, will force back any rib that may have been dislocated.' The wound in my head not being deep, he healed it by stuffing it with burnt cotton. He then ordered that I should continue to walk much, supported by two persons; that I should not sit long, nor be allowed to sleep till ten o'clock at night, at which time I should eat a little thin rice soup. He assured me that these walks in the open air while fasting would prevent the blood from settling upon the chest, where it might corrupt. These remedies, though barbarous and excruciating, cured me so completely that in seven days I was able to resume my journey."[1]

The active daily practice of a popular Chinese doctor may be very well illustrated from Dr. Hobson's description of one Ta wang siensăng, or 'Dr. Rhubarb,' a medical practitioner in Canton. This man, after prescribing for the sick at his office until the hour of ten in the morning, would commence his rounds "in the sedan chair carried in great haste by three or four men. Those patients were visited first who had their names and residences first placed in the entry book, and as the streets were narrow and crowded, to avoid trouble in finding the house, a copy of the doctor's sign-board would be posted up outside the patient's door, so that the chairmen should be able at once to recognize the house without delay."

The doctor being ushered into the hall, or principal room, is met with bows and salutations by the father or elder brother of the family. Tea and pipes are offered in due form, and he is requested to feel his patient's pulse; if a male, he sits opposite

---

[1] Père Ripa, *Memoirs and Residence at Peking*, translated by F. Prandi, London, 1844, p. 67.

to him; if a female, a screen of bamboo intervenes, which is only removed in case it is requisite to see the tongue. The right hand is placed upon a book to steady it, and the doctor, with much gravity and a learned look, places his three fingers upon the pulsating vessel, pressing it alternately with each finger on the inner and outer side, and then making with three fingers a steady pressure for several minutes, not with watch in hand, to note the frequency of its beats, but with a thoughtful and calculating mind, to diagnose the disease and prognosticate its issue. The fingers being removed the patient immediately stretches out the other hand, which is felt in the same manner. Perhaps certain questions are asked of the father or mother concerning the sick person, but these are usually few, as it is presumed the pulse reveals everything needful to know. Ink and paper are produced and a prescription is written out, which consists of numerous ingredients, but there are one or two of only prime importance—the rest are servants or adjuvants. They are all taken from the vegetable kingdom, and are mostly simples of little efficacy. The prescription is taken to a druggist to be dispensed; the prescriber seldom makes up the medicine himself, and as large doses are popular (a *quid pro quo*), so the decoction made from the whole amounts to pints or even quarts, which are swallowed in large portions with the greatest ease; powders, boluses, pills, and electuaries are also used. If the patient is an officer of the government or a wealthy person, the nature of the disease, prognosis, and treatment are written down for the inspection of the family; for this the doctor's fee is a dollar. But generally speaking, both the doctor and the patient's friends are quite satisfied with a verbal communication; and if the man has a gift for speaking and has brass enough to use it to his advantage (both of which are seldom wanting in time-serving men), he will describe with a learned, self-satisfied air the ailment of the patient, and the number of days it will take to cure him. The fee is wrapped up in red paper, and called "golden thanks," varying in amount from fifteen to seventy cents or more, according to the means of the patient; the chair-bearers being paid extra. The doctor returns to make another visit if invited, but not otherwise. It is more common, if the patient is not at once benefited by the prescription, to call in another, then a third, then a fourth, and even more, until tired of physicians (for the Chinese patience is soon exhausted, and their faith by no means strong in all their doctors' asseverations) they have, as a last resort, application made to one of the genii, or a god possessing wonderful healing powers. The result is that the patient dies or lives, not according to the treatment received, for that must be generally inefficacious, but according as his natural strength is equal to surmount the difficulties by which he is surrounded.[1]

Dr. Hobson has given an analysis of 442 medicinal agents enumerated in one of the popular dispensatories; of the whole number, 314 are vegetable, 50 mineral, and 78 animal. The author gives the name of each one, the organ it affects, its properties, and lastly the mode of its exhibition. Medicines are arranged under six heads—tonics, astringents, resolvents, purgatives, alteratives of poisonous humors, and of the blood. Among the agents employed are many strange and repulsive substances, as snake-skins, fossil bones, rhinoceros or hart's horn shavings, silk-worm and human secretions, asbestos, moths, oyster-shells, etc. Calomel, vermilion, red precipitate, minium, arsenic, plumbago, and sulphate of copper are among the metallic medicines used by physicians; Dr. Henderson enumerates thirty-three distinct mineral medicines. The number of apothecary shops in towns indicates the great consumption of medicine; their arrangement is like the druggist shops in the west, though instead of huge glass jars at the windows filled with bright colored liquids, and long rows of vials and decanters in glass cases, three or four branching deer's horns are suspended from the walls, and lines of white and black gallipots cover the shelves. Hartshorn is reduced to a dust by filing, for exhibition in consumption. Many roots, as rhubarb, gentian, etc., are prepared by paring them into thin laminæ; others are powdered in a mortar with a pestle, or triturated in a narrow iron trough in which a close-fitting wheel is worked. The use of acids

[1] Dr. James Henderson in *Journal of the N. C. Br. of Royal Asiatic Society*, 1864, No. I., p. 54.

and reagents is unknown, for they imply more knowledge of chemistry than the Chinese possess. Vegetable substances, as camphor, myrrh, ginseng, rhubarb, gentian, and a great variety of roots, leaves, seeds, and barks, are generally taken as pills or decoctions. Many valuable recipes will probably be discovered in their books as soon as the terms used are accurately ascertained, and a better acquaintance with the botany and mineralogy enables the foreign student to test them intelligently.

The people sometimes cast lots as to which one of a dozen doctors they shall employ, and then scrupulously follow his directions, whatever they may be, as a departure therefrom would vitiate the sortilege. Sometimes an invalid will go to a doctor and ask for how much he will cure him, and how soon the cure can be performed. He states the diagnosis of his case, the pulse is examined, and every other symptom investigated, when the bargain is struck and a portion of the price paid. The patient then receives the suitable medicines, in quantity and variety better fitted for a horse than a man, for the doctor reasons that out of a great number it is more likely that some will prove efficacious, and the more he gets paid for the more he ought to administer. A decoction of a kettleful of simples is drunk down by the sick man, and he gives up both working and eating; if, however, at the expiration of the time specified he is not cured, he scolds his physician for an ignorant charlatan who cheats him out of his money, and seeks another, with whom he makes a similar bargain, and probably with similar results. Sagacious observance of cause and effect, symptoms and pains, gradually give a shrewd physician great power over his ignorant patients, and some of them become both rich and influential; a skilful physician is termed the "nation's hand."

A regular system of fees exists among the profession, but the remuneration is as often left to the generosity of the patient. New medicines, pills, powders, and salves are advertised and puffed by flaunting placards on the walls of the streets, some of them most disgustingly obscene; but the Chinese do not puff new nostrums by publishing a long list of recommendations from patients. The various ways devised by persons to dispose of their medicines exhibit much ingenuity. Sometimes a man, having spread a mat at the side of the street, and marshalled his gallipots and salves, will commence a harangue upon the goodness and efficacy of his preparations in loud and eloquent tones, until he has collected a crowd of hearers, some of whom he manages to persuade will be the better for taking some of his potions. He will exhibit their efficacy by first pounding his naked breast with a brick till it is livid, and then immediately healing the contusion by a lotion, having previously fortified the inner parts with a remedy; or he will cut open his flesh and heal the wound in a few moments by a wonderful elixir, which he alone can sell. Others, more learned or more professional, erect a pavilion or awning, fluttering with signs and streamers, and quietly seat themselves under it to wait for customers; or content themselves with a flag perched on a pole setting forth the potency of their pills. Dentists make a necklace of the rotten teeth they have obtained from the jaws of their customers, and perambulate the streets with these trophies of their skill hanging around their necks like a rosary. In general, however, the Chinese enjoy good health, and when ill from colds or fevers, lie abed and suspend working and eating, which in most cases allows nature to work her own cure, whatever doses they may take. They are perhaps as long-lived as most nations, though sanatory statistics are wanting to enable us to form any indisputable conclusions on this head.

The classes of diseases which most prevail in China are ophthalmic, cutaneous, and digestive; intermittent fevers are also common. The great disproportion of affections of the eye has often attracted observation. Dr. Lockhart ascribes it partly to the inflammation which often comes on at the commencement of winter, and which is allowed to run its course, leaving the organ in an unhealthy condition and very obnoxious to other diseases. This inflammation is beyond the skill of the native practitioners, and sometimes destroys the sight in a few days. Another fruitful source of disease is the practice of the barbers of turning the lids over and clearing their surfaces of the mucus which may be lodged there. He adds: "If the person's eyes be examined after this process, they will be found to be very red and irritated, and in process of time chronic conjunctivitis supervenes, which being considered proof of insufficient cleansing, the practice is persisted in, and the inner surface of the lid becomes covered with granulations. In other cases it becomes indurated like thin parchment, and the tarsal cartilages contract and induce entropium." Dense opacity of the cornea itself is frequently caused by this *barberous* practice, or constant pain and weeping ensues, both of which materially injure the sight, if the patient does not lose it. The practice of cleansing the ears in a similar way frequently results in their serious injury, and sometimes destruction. When the ill effects of such treatment of these delicate organs must be plain to every observing person in his own case, it is strange that he should still allow the operation to be repeated.

The physicians in charge of the missionary hospitals successfully established at so many cities in Eastern China have attended more to tumors, dislocations, wounds, and surgical cases, ophthalmic and cutaneous diseases, than to common clinical ailments. The hospitals here spoken of are little more than dispensaries, with a room or two for extreme or peculiarly interesting cases; there is little visiting the natives at their own houses.

Asthma, even in boys, is common at Amoy, and consumption at Canton and Chusan. Intermittent fevers prevail more or less wherever the cultivation of rice is carried on near villages and towns. Elephantiasis is known between Shanghai and Canton, but in the southern provinces leprosy seems to exist as its equivalent. This loathsome disease is regarded by the Chinese as incurable and contagious. Lazar-houses are provided for the residence of the infected, but as the allowance of poor patients is insufficient for their support, they go from street to street soliciting alms, to the great annoyance of every one. As soon as it appears in an individual, he is immediately separated from his family and driven forth an outcast, to herd with others similarly affected, and get his living from precarious charity. The institution of lazarettoes is praiseworthy, but they fail of affording relief on account of the mismanagement and peculation of those who have their supervision; and those who cannot get in are obliged to live in a village set apart for them north of the city. Lepers can intermarry among themselves, but on account of poverty and other causes they do not often do so, and the hardships of their lot soon end their days. This disease will probably exist among the Chinese until houses are built more above the ground, better ventilation of cities and improvement in diet are adopted, when it will disappear as it has in Southern Europe.

Diseases of an inflammatory nature are not so fatal or rapid among the Chinese as Europeans, nor do consumptions carry off so large a proportion of the inhabitants as in the United States. Dyspepsia has been frequently treated; it is ascribed by Dr. Hepburn to the abundant use of salt provisions, pickled vegetables, and fish, irregularity in eating, opium smoking, and immoderate use of tea; though it may be questioned whether the two last reasons are more general and powerful at Amoy than Canton, where dyspepsia is comparatively rare. The surgeons at the latter place have successfully treated hundreds of cases of stone, losing less than fifteen per cent. of all. Some of the patients were under ten years, and a few of the calculi weighed nearly half a pound. This malady is almost unknown in Northern China. The diseases which result from intemperate and licentious habits are not as violent in their effects as in countries where a greater use of animal food and higher living render the system more susceptible to the noxious consequences of the virus.

The existence of tumors and unnatural growths in great abundance and variety is satisfactorily accounted for by the inability of the native practitioners to remove them. Those which had a healthy growth increased until a morbid action supervened, and consequently sometimes grew to an enormous size. A peasant named Hu Lu went to England in 1831 to have an abdominal tumor extirpated weighing about seventy pounds; he died under the operation. No patients bear operations with more fortitude than the Chinese, and, owing to their lymphatic temperament, they are followed with less inflammation than is usual in European practice. Goitre is very common in the mountainous regions of the northern provinces; Dr. Gillan estimated that nearly one-sixth of the inhabitants met in the villages on the high land between Peking and Jeh ho were afflicted with this deformity, which, however, is said not to be so considered by the villagers themselves.

The Asiatic cholera has been a great scourge in China, but does not often become an epidemic anywhere, though sporadic cases constantly occur. It raged at Ningpo in May, 1820, and an intelligent native doctor informed Mr. Milne[1] that it was computed that ten thousand persons were carried off by it in the city and department of Ningpo during the summers of 1820–23. In 1842 it prevailed at Amoy and Changchau and their vicinity; more than a hundred deaths daily occurred at the former place for six or seven weeks. It raged violently at Hangchau in Chehkiang during the years 1821 and 1822, persons dropping down dead in the streets, or dying within an hour or two after the attack; many myriads were computed to have fallen victims, and the native doctors, finding their remedies useless, gave up all treatment. It carried off multitudes in Shantung and Kiangsu during the same years, and was as fitful in its progress in China as in Europe, going from one city to another, passing by towns apparently as obnoxious as those visited. The plague is said to have existed in Southern China about the beginning of the sixteenth century, but it has not been heard of lately.

Small-pox is a terrible scath, and although the practice and utility of vaccination have been known for fifty years past at Canton, its adoption is still limited even in that city. It was introduced in 1820 by Dr. Pearson, of the East India Company's establishment, and native assistants were fully instructed by him in the practice. Vaccination has now extended over all the Eighteen Provinces, and the government has given its sanction and assistance; it is chiefly owing to the heedlessness of the people in not availing themselves of it in time that it has done no more to lessen the ravages of the disease. Where children were gratuitously vaccinated it was found almost impossible to induce parents to bring them; and when the chil-

---

[1] *Chinese Repository*, Vol. XII., p. 487.

dren had been vaccinated it was increasingly difficult to get them to return to allow the physician to see the result of the operation. Inoculation has long been practised by inserting a pledget in the nostrils containing the virus; this mode is occasionally adopted in vaccination. The slovenly habits of the people, as well as insufficient protection and unwholesome food, give rise to many diseases of the skin, some of them incurable.

The science of medicine attracted very early attention, and there are numerous treatises on its various branches. But the search for the liquor of immortality and the philosopher's stone, with careful observations on the pulse as the leading tests of diseases, have led them astray from accurate diagnosis age after age. The common classification of diseases is under nine heads, viz., those which affect the pulse violently or feebly, those arising from cold, female and cutaneous diseases, those needing acupuncture, and diseases of the eyes, the mouth and its parts, and the bones. A professor of each of these classes is attached to the imperial family, who is taken from the Medical College at Peking; but he has no greater advantages there than he could get in his own reading and practice. No museums of morbid or comparative anatomy exist in the country, nor are there any lectures or dissections; and the routine which old custom has sanctioned will go on until modern practice, now rapidly taking its place, wins its way. Section CCXCVII. of the code orders that "whenever an unskilful practitioner, in administering medicine or using the puncturing needle, proceeds contrary to the established forms, and thereby causes the death of a patient, the magistrate shall call in other practitioners to examine the medicine or the wound, and if it appear that the injury done was unintentional, the practitioner shall then be treated according to the statute for accidental homicides, and shall not be any longer allowed to practise medicine. But if designedly he depart from the established forms, and deceives in his attempt to cure the malady in order to obtain property, then, according to its amount, he shall be treated as a thief; and if death ensue from his malpractice, then, for having thus used medicine with intent to kill, he shall be beheaded."[1] This statute is seldom carried into execution, however, and the doctors are allowed to kill and cure, *secundum artem*, as their patients give them the opportunity.

Natural history, in its various branches of geology, botany, zoölogy, etc., has received some attention, because the objects which come under it could not escape the notice of all the writers in Chinese literature. As sciences, however, none of them have an existence, and they are studied chiefly for their assistance in furnishing articles for the materia medica of the native physician. To these persons nothing comes amiss, and, like the ingredients of the hubbling, bubbling caldron of Macbeth's witches, the stranger it is the more potent they think a dose will be; in this particular they now act very much as the faculty did in England two centuries ago. It is to be regretted that their investigation should have taken such a direction, but the man of commanding influence has not yet arisen to direct their researches into nature and divert them from the marvellous and theoretical. On the whole, it may be said that in all departments of learning the Chinese are unscientific; and that while they have collected a great variety of facts, invented many arts, and brought a few to a high degree of excellence, they have never pursued a single subject in a way calculated to lead them to a right understanding of it, or reached a proper classification of the information they possessed relating to it.

---

[1] *Chinese Chrestomathy*, Chap. XVI., pp. 497–532. *Asiatic Soc. Transactions*, Hongkong, Art. III., 1847; No. III., 1852, Art. III. *Jour. N. C. Br. R. A. Soc.*, No. I., 1864, and No. VI., 1869. W. Lockhart, *Medical Missionary in China*, 1861. *Chinese Repository*, *passim*. Porter Smith's *Contributions to Chinese Materia Medica*, Shanghai, 1871. Flückiger & Hanbury, *Pharmacographia*, London, 1874. *China Review*, Vol. I., p. 176; Vol. III., p. 224. J. Dudgeon, *The Diseases of China*, Glasgow, 1877; *id.* in the *Chinese Recorder*, Vols. II., III., and IV., *passim*.

CHAPTER XVII.

HISTORY AND CHRONOLOGY OF CHINA.

THE history of the Chinese people has excited less attention among western scholars than it deserves, though in some respects no nation offers more claims to have its chronicles carefully and fairly examined. The belief is generally entertained that their pretensions to antiquity are extravagant and ridiculous, and incompatible with the Mosaic chronology; that they not only make the world to have existed myriads of years, but reckon the succession of their monarchs far beyond the creation, and ascribe to them a longevity that carries its own confutation on its face. In consequence of this opinion, some have denied the credibility of native historians altogether, and the whole subject of the settlement and early progress of this ancient race has been considered beyond the reach, and almost unworthy the attempt, of sober investigation. This erroneous and hasty conclusion is gradually giving way to a careful inquiry into those histories which show that the early records of the sons of Han contain much which is worthy of credence, and much more that is highly probable. A wide field is here opened for the researches of a Gibbon or a Niebuhr; for as long as we are destitute of a good history of China and its connections with other Asiatic nations, we shall not only be unable to form a correct opinion respecting the people, but shall lack many important data for a full illustration of the early history of the human race. It is easy to laud the early records of the Chinese to the skies, as French writers have done; and it is quite as easy to cry them down as worthless—manufactured in after-ages to please the variety of their writers. The reputation both people and records have received is owing, in some measure, to this undue laudation and depreciation, as well as to the intrinsic merits and defects of their histories. These, however, still mostly remain in their originals, and will require the united labors of many scholars to be fully brought to light and made a part of the world's library.

The enormous difficulties arising from the extent and tedious minuteness of native historians, coupled with the scarcity of translators competent or willing to undertake the labor of even such a *résumé* of these works as will satisfy rational curiosity, are now being slowly overcome, both by Chinese and foreign students. These researches, it is to be earnestly hoped, will be rewarded by promoting a juster estimate in the minds of both classes of their relative positions among the nations of the earth.

China, like other countries, has her mythological history, and it should be separated from the more recent and received, as her own historians regard it, as the fabrication of subsequent times. She also has her ancient history, whose earliest dates and events blend confusedly with the mythological, but gradually grow more credible and distinct as they come down the stream of time to the beginning of modern history. The early accounts of every nation whose founding was anterior to the practice of making and preserving authentic records must necessarily be obscure and doubtful. What is applicable to the Chinese has been true of other ancient people: "national vanity and a love of the marvellous have influenced them all, and furnished materials for many tales, as soon as the spirit of investigation has supplanted that appetite for wonders which marks the infancy of nations as well as of individuals." The ignorance of the "art preservative of all arts" will greatly explain the subsequent record of the wonderful, without supposing that the infancy of nations partook of the same traits of weakness and credulity as that of individuals. There is neither space nor time in this work to give the details concerning the history and succession of dynasties that have swayed the Middle Kingdom, for to one not specially engaged in their examination their recital is proverbially dry; the array of uncouth names destitute of lasting interest, and the absence of the charm of association with western nations render them uninviting to the general reader. Some account of the leading events and changes is all that is necessary to explain what has been elsewhere incidentally referred to.[1]

Chinese historians have endeavored to explain the creation and origin of the world around them; but, ignorant of the sublime fact that there is one Creator who upholds his works by the word of his power, they have invented various modes to account for it, and wearied themselves in theorizing and disputing with each other. One of them, Yangtsz', remarks, in view of these conflicting suppositions: "Who knows the affairs of remote antiquity, since no authentic records have come down to us? He who examines these stories will find it difficult to believe them, and careful scrutiny will convince him that they are without foundation. In the primeval ages no historical records were kept. Why then, since the ancient books that described those times were burnt by Tsin, should we misrepresent those remote ages, and satisfy ourselves with vague fables? However, as everything except heaven and earth must have a cause, it is clear that they have always existed, and that cause produced all sorts of men and beings, and endowed them with their various qualities. But it must have been man who in the beginning produced all things on earth, and who may therefore be viewed as the lord, and from whom rulers derive their dignities."

This extract is not a bad example of Chinese writers and historians; a mixture of sense and nonsense, partially laying the foundation of a just argument, and ending with a tremendous non-sequitur, apparently satisfactory to themselves, but showing pretty conclusively how little pains they take to gather facts and discuss their bearings. Some of these writers imagine that the world owes its existence to the retroactive agency of the dual powers *yin* and *yang*, which first formed the outline of the universe, and were themselves influenced by

---

[1] Among the works which will repay perusal on this topic are Mailla's *Histoire de la Chine* and Pauthier's *Chine*, in French, and Du Halde's *History*, translated into English; besides the briefer compilations of Murray, Grosier, Gutzlaff, Davis, and more recently of Boulger and Richthofen, Band I.

their own creations. One of the most sensible of their authors says:

> Heaven was formless, an utter chaos; the whole mass was nothing but confusion. Order was first produced in the pure ether, and out of it the universe came forth; the universe produced air, and air the milky-way. When the pure male principle *yang* had been diluted, it formed the heavens; the heavy and thick parts coagulated, and formed the earth. The refined particles united very soon, but the union of the thick and heavy went on slowly; therefore the heavens came into existence first, and the earth afterward. From the subtle essence of heaven and earth, the dual principles *yin* and *yang* were formed; from their joint operation came the four seasons, and these putting forth their energies gave birth to all the products of the earth. The warm effluence of the *yang* being condensed, produced fire; and the finest parts of fire formed the sun. The cold exhalations of the *yin* being likewise condensed, produced water; and the finest parts of the watery substance formed the moon. By the seminal influence of the sun and moon, came the stars. Thus heaven was adorned with the sun, moon, and stars; the earth also received rain, rivers, and dust.[1]

But this acute explanation, like the notions of Hesiod among the Greeks, was too subtle for the common people; they also wanted to personify and deify these powers and operations, but lacking the imaginative genius and fine taste of the Greeks, their divine personages are outrageous and their ideal beings shapeless monsters. No creator is known or imagined who, like Brahm, lives in space, ineffable, formless; but the first being, Pwanku, had the herculean task to mould the chaos which produced him and chisel out the earth that was to contain him. One legend is that "the dual powers were fixed when the primeval chaos separated. Chaos is bubbling turbid water, which enclosed and mingled with the dual powers, like a chick *in ovo*, but when their offspring Pwanku appeared their distinctiveness and operations were apparent. *Pwan* means a 'basin,' referring to the shell of the egg; *ku* means 'solid,' 'to secure,' intending to show how the first man Pwanku was hatched from the chaos by the dual powers, and then settled and exhibited the arrangement of the causes which produced him."

The Rationalists have penetrated furthest into the Dædalian

---

[1] *Chinese Repository*, Vol. III., p. 55.

mystery of this cosmogony,[1] and they go on to show what Pwanku did and how he did it. They picture him holding a chisel and mallet in his hands, splitting and fashioning vast

Pwanku Chiselling Out the Universe.

masses of granite floating confusedly in space. Behind the openings his powerful hand has made are seen the sun, moon, and stars, monuments of his stupendous labors; at his right

[1] For the Buddhist notions of cosmography and creation, see Rémusat, *Mélanges Posthumes*, pp. 65–131.

hand, inseparable companions of his toils, but whose generation is left in obscurity, stand the dragon, the phœnix, and the tortoise, and sometimes the unicorn, divine types and progenitors with himself of the animal creation. His efforts were continued eighteen thousand years, and by small degrees he and his work increased; the heavens rose, the earth spread out and thickened, and Pwanku grew in stature, six feet every day, till, his labors done, he died for the benefit of his handiwork. His head became mountains, his breath wind and clouds, and his voice thunder; his limbs were changed into the four poles, his veins into rivers, his sinews into the undulations of the earth's surface, and his flesh into fields; his beard, like Berenice's hair, was turned into stars, his skin and hair into herbs and trees, and his teeth, bones, and marrow into metals, rocks, and precious stones; his dropping sweat increased to rain, and lastly (*nascitur ridiculus mus*) the insects which stuck to his body were transformed into people!

Such was Pwanku, and these were his works. But these grotesque myths afford none of the pleasing images and personifications of Greek fable or Egyptian symbols; they fatigue without entertaining, and only illustrate the childish imagination of their authors. Pwanku was succeeded by three rulers of monstrous forms called the Celestial, Terrestrial, and Human sovereigns, impersonations of a trinity of powers, whose traces and influences run through Chinese philosophy, religion, and politics; their acts and characters are detailed with the utmost gravity, and more than Methusalean longevity allowed them to complete their plans. Their reigns continued eighteen thousand years (more or less according to the author quoted), during which time good government commenced, men learned to eat and drink, the sexes united, sleep was invented, and other improvements adopted. One would think, if the subjects of these wonderful beings were as long-lived, great perfection might have been attained in these and other useful arts; but the mysterious tortoise, companion of Pwanku, on whose carapace was written, in tadpole-headed characters, the history of the anterior world, did not survive, and their record has not come down. After them flourished two other monarchs, one of them called

Yu-chau, which means 'having a nest,' and the other Sui-jin, or 'match-man.' Whether the former invented nests for the abodes of his subjects, such as the Indians on the Orinoco have, is not stated; but the latter brought down fire from heaven for them to cook with, and became a second, or rather the first, Prometheus.

These fancies are gathered from a popular summary of knowledge, called the *Coral Forest of Ancient Matters*, and from the opening chapters of *History Made Easy*. A higher style of philosophizing is found in Chu Hí's disquisition, from which an extract has been given in Chapter XII. Another on Cosmogony will show that he comes no nearer to the great fact of creation than ancient western writers.

In the beginning heaven and earth were just the light and dark air. This one air revolved, grinding round and round. When it ground quickly much sediment was compressed, which, having no means of exit, coagulated and formed the earth in the centre. The subtle portion of the air then became heaven and the sun, moon, and stars, which unceasingly revolve on the outside. The earth is in the centre and motionless; it is not below the centre.

Heaven revolving without ceasing, day and night also revolve, and hence the earth is exactly in the centre. If heaven should stand still for one moment, then the earth must fall down; but heaven revolves quickly, and hence much sediment is coagulated in the centre. The earth is the sediment of the air; and hence it is said, the light, pure air became heaven, the heavy, muddy air became earth. . . .

At the beginning of heaven and earth, before chaos was divided, I think there were only two things—fire and water; and the sediment of the water formed the earth. When one ascends a height and looks down, the crowd of hills resemble the waves of the sea in appearance: the water just flowed like this. I know not at what period it coagulated. At first it was very soft, but afterward it coagulated and became hard. One asked whether it resembled sand thrown up by the tide? He replied, Just so; the coarsest sediment of the water became earth, and the purest portion of the fire became wind, thunder, lightning, sun, and stars. . . .

Before chaos was divided, the *yin-yang*, or light-dark air, was mixed up and dark, and when it divided the centre formed an enormous and most brilliant opening, and the two *i* or principles were established. Shao Kang-tsieh considers one hundred and twenty-nine thousand six hundred years to be a *yuen*, or kalpa; then, before this period of one hundred and twenty-nine thousand six hundred years there was another opening and spreading out of the world; and before that again, there was another like the present; so that motion and rest, light and darkness, have no beginning. As little things shadow forth great things, this may be illustrated by the revolutions of day and night. . . .

Kang-tsieh says, Heaven rests upon form, and earth reclines upon air. The reason why he repeats this frequently, and does not deviate from the idea, is lest people should seek some other place beyond heaven and earth. There is nothing outside heaven and earth, and hence their form has limits, while their air has no limit. Because the air is extremely condensed, therefore it can support the earth; if it were not so the earth would fall down.[1]

A third belief respecting the position of the earth in the centre of the universe derives great strength in the opinion of intelligent natives from these speculations of Chu Hí. His theory considers the world to be a plane surface, straight, square, and large, measuring each way about 1,500 miles (5,600 *lí*), and bounded on the four sides by the four seas. The sun is estimated to be about 4,000 miles from the earth. Another calculation made it 81,394 *lí*, and a third 216,781½ *lí*.

One thing is observable in these fictions, characteristic of the Chinese at the present day: there is no hierarchy of gods brought in to rule and inhabit the world they made, no conclave on Mt. Olympus, nor judgment of the mortal soul by Osiris; no transfer of human love and hate, passions and hopes, to the powers above; all here is ascribed to disembodied agencies or principles, and their works are represented as moving on in quiet order. There is no religion, no imagination; all is impassible, passionless, uninteresting. It may, perhaps, be considered of itself as sensible as the Greek or Egyptian mythology, if one looks for *sense* in such figments; but it has not, as in the latter countries, been explained in sublime poetry, shadowed forth in gorgeous ritual and magnificent festivals, represented in exquisite sculptures, nor preserved in faultless, imposing fanes and temples, filled with ideal creations. For this reason it appears more in its true colors, and, when compared with theirs, "loses discountenanced and like folly shows"—at least to us, who can examine both and compare them with the truth.

Their pure mythological history ends with the appearance of Fuh-hí, and their chronology has nothing to do with the long periods antecedent, varying from forty-five to five hundred

---

[1] Canon McClatchie's *Confucian Cosmogony*, pp. 53–59.

thousand years. These periods are, however, a mere twinkling compared with the kulpas of the Hindus, whose highest era, called the Unspeakably Inexpressible, requires four million four hundred and fifty-six thousand four hundred and forty-eight cyphers following a unit to represent it. If the epoch of Fuh-hí could be ascertained with any probability by comparison with the history of other nations, or with existing remains, it would tend not a little to settle some disputed chronological points in other countries; but the isolation of the Chinese throughout their whole existence makes it nearly impossible to weave in the events of their history with those of other nations, by comparing and verifying them with biblical, Egyptian, or Persian annals. Perhaps further investigations in the vast regions of Eastern and Central Asia may bring to light corroborative testimony as striking and unexpected as the explorations in Mosul, Persepolis, and Thebes.

The accession of Fuh-hí is placed in the Chinese annals B.C. 2852,[1] and with him commences the period known among them as the "highest antiquity." The weight of evidence which the later chronological examinations of Hales and Jackson have brought to bear against the common period of four thousand and four years prior to the Advent, is such as to cast great doubt over its authenticity, and lead to the adoption of a longer period in order to afford time for many occurrences, which otherwise would be crowded into too narrow a space. Chinese chronology, if it be allowed the least credit, strongly corroborates the results of Dr. Hales' researches, and particularly so in the date of Fuh-hí's accession. This is not the place to discuss the respective claims of the two eras, but by reckoning, as he does, the creation to be five thousand four hundred and eleven years, and the deluge three thousand one hundred and fifty-five years, before the Advent, we bring the commencement of ancient Chinese history three hundred and three years subsequent to the deluge, forty-seven before the death of Noah, and about three centuries before the confusion of tongues. If we suppose that the ante-

[1] Or 3322, according to Dr. Legge, whose date has been used elsewhere in this work, and has probably quite as much authority as the one above.

diluvians possessed a knowledge of the geography of the world, and that Noah, regarding himself as the monarch of the whole, divided it among his descendants before his death, there is nothing improbable in the further supposition that the progenitors of the black-haired race, and others of the house and lineage of Shem, found their way from the valley of the Euphrates across the defiles and steppes of Central Asia, to the fertile plains of China before the end of the third diluvian century. Whether the surface of the world was the same after the cataclysm as before does not affect this point; there was ample time for the multiplication of the species with the blessing promised by God, sufficient to form colonies, if there was time enough to increase to such a multitude as conspired to build the tower of Babel.

The views of Dr. Legge, that the present Chinese descend from settlers who came through Central Asia along the Tarim Valley and across the Desert into Kansuh, about B.C. 2200, and settled around the elbow of the Yellow River, under the leadership of Yao, Shun, Yu, and others, are very reasonable. These settlers found the land at that time occupied with tribes, whom they partly merged with themselves or drove into mountain recesses in Kweichau, where some of their descendants perhaps still remain. These earlier tribes may have furnished the names and reigns prior to Yao, and the later Chinese annalists incorporated them into their own histories, taking everything in early times as of course belonging to the *lí min*, or 'black-haired race.' The lapse of a millennium between the Deluge and Yao allows plenty of time for several successive emigrations from Western and Central Asia into the inviting plains of China, which, through the want of a written language or the destruction of records, have come down to us in misty, doubtful legends.

Fuh-hí and his seven successors are stated to have reigned seven hundred and forty-seven years, averaging ninety-three each. Those who follow Usher consider these monarchs to be Chinese travesties of the eight antediluvian patriarchs; and Marquis d'Urban has gone so far as to write what he calls the *Antediluvian History of China*, collecting all the notices history affords of their acts. The common chronology brings the deluge about thirteen years after the accession of Yao and the death of Shun (the last of the eight), B.C. 2205, or twenty-five years after the confusion of tongues. According to Hales, the last epoch is one hundred and twelve years before the call of Abraham, and these eight Chinese monarchs are therefore contemporaries of the patriarchs who lived between Shem and Abraham, commencing with Salah and ending with Nahor. The duration of their reigns, moreover, is such as would bear the same proportion to ages of five hundred years, which their contemporaries lived, as the present average of twenty and twenty-five years does to a life of sixty. The Assyrian tablets, deciphered by George Smith, contain a reference to the twenty-eighth century B.C., as the founding of that monarchy; which is a notice of more value as a chronological epoch than anything in Chinese annals, indeed, and may help to countenance a date that had before been regarded as mythological.

Supposing that the descendants of Shem, Ham, and Japheth, knowing from their fathers and grandfather, that the void world was before them, began to colonize almost as soon as they began to form families, three centuries would not be too long a time for some of them to settle in China, perhaps offsetting from Elam and Asshur, and other descendants of Shem in Persia. The capital of Fuh-hí slightly indicates, it may be thought, their route through Central Asia across the Desert to Kiayü kwan in Kansuh, and then down the Yellow River to the Great Plain near Kaifung. But these suppositions are only by the way, as is also the suggestion that teaching of fishing and grazing, the regulation of times and seasons, cultivation of music, and establishment of government, etc., compare well enough with the duties that might reasonably be supposed to belong to the founder of a colony and his successors, and subsequently ascribed to them as their own inventions. The long period allotted to human life at that date would allow these arts and sciences to take root and their memory to remain in popular legends until subsequent historians incorporated them into their writings. The Chinese annalists fill up the reigns of these chiefs, down to the time of Yao, with a series of inventions and improvements in the arts of life and good government, sufficient to bring society to that degree of comfort and order they suppose consonant with the character of the monarchs. The earliest records of the Chinese correspond much too closely with their present character to receive full belief; but they present an appearance of probability and naturalness not possessed by the early annals of Greece. No one contends for their credibility as history, but they are better than the Arabian Nights.

The commencement of the sexagenary cycle[1] in the sixty-first year of Hwangtí's reign (or B.C. 2637), five hundred and eighteen years after the deluge, eighty-two years after the death of Arphaxad, and about that time before the confusion of tongues, is worthy of notice. The use of the ten horary characters applied to days in order to denote their chronological sequence dates from the reign of Yu in the twentieth century B.C., and there are other passages in the *Shu King* showing similar application. Sz'ma Tsien's history now contains the first attempt to arrange the years in cycles of sixty; but he cannot fairly be claimed as the inventor of this system. He might almost as well be regarded as the inventor of his whole *annals*, for all the materials out of which he compiled them have now perished except the canonical books. The mention of the individual Nao the Great, who invented it, and the odd date of its adoption in the middle of a reign, do not weaken the alleged date of its origin in the minds of those who are inclined to take a statement of this kind on its own basis.

Three reigns, averaging eighty years' duration, intervened between that of Hwangtí and Yao, whose occupants were elected by the people, much as were Shemgar, Jephthah, and other judges in Israel, and probably exercised a similar sway. The reigns and characters of Yao and Shun have been immortalized by Confucius and Mencius; whatever was their real history, those sages showed great sagacity in going back to those remote times for models and fixing upon a period neither fabulous nor certain, one which prevented alike the cavils of scepticism and the appearance of complete fabrication.

---

[1] *Journal Asiatique*, Avril, 1836, p. 394.

A tremendous deluge occurred during the reign of Yao, B.C. 2293, caused, it is said, by the overflowing of the rivers in the north of China. Those who place the Noachic deluge B.C. 2348 regard this as only a different version of that event; Klaproth, who favors the Septuagint chronology, says that it is nearly synchronous with the deluge of Xisuthrus, B.C. 2297, a name derived, as is reasonably inferred by George Smith, from the Assyrian name Hasisadra, the ancient hero who survived the deluge. The record of this catastrophe in the *Shu King* is hardly applicable to an overwhelming flood: "The Emperor said, Oh! chief of the four mountains, destructive in their overthrow are the waters of the inundation. In their vast extent they embrace the mountains and overtop the hills, threatening the heavens with their floods, so that the inferior people groan and murmur. Is there a capable man to whom I can assign the correction of this calamity?"[1] They presented Kwăn as a proper man, but he showed his inefficiency in laboring nine years without success to drain off the waters. Yao was then advised to employ Shun, who called in Yu, a son of Kwăn, to his aid, and the floods were assuaged by deepening the beds of the rivers and opening new channels. These slight notices hardly comport with a flood like the Noachic deluge, and are with much greater probability referred to an overflow or a change in the bed of the Yellow River from its present course into the Gulf of Pechele through Chihlí northeast, to its recent one along the lowlands of Kiangsu. The weight of topographical evidence, combined with the strong chronological argument, the discussions in council said to have taken place regarding the disaster, and the time which elapsed before the region was drained, all pre-suppose and indicate a partial inundation, and strengthen the assumption that no traces of the Deluge exist in the histories of the Chinese. In our view of the chronology of the Bible, as compared with the Chinese, it requires a far greater constraint upon these records to bring them to refer to that event, than to suppose they allude to a local disaster not beyond the power of remedy.

---

[1] Legge's *Shu King*, p. 24, Hongkong, 1867.

The series of chieftains down to the accession of Yu may here be recapitulated. The entirely fabulous period ends with Sui-jin, and legendary history commences with Fuh-hí, who with four of his successors (Nos. 2, 3, 7, and 8) are commonly known as the Five Sovereigns. Their names and reigns are as follows:

	Names.	Years reigned.	Began B.C.	Other Events.
1	Fuh-hí	115	2852	The Deluge, B.C. 3155.
2	Shinnung	140	2737	Death of Noah, B.C. 2805.
3	Hwangtí	100	2697	
4	Shauhau	84	2597	Death of Arphaxad, 2715.
5	Chwenhüh	78	2513	Death of Shem, 2555.
6	Kuh	78	2435	Rise of Egyptian monarchy, 2450.
7	Yao	102	2357	Rise of Babylonian " 2300.
8	Shun	50	2255	Abraham's birth, 2153.

The records in the *Shu King* of Yao, Shun, and Yu the Great (B.C. 2205) are longer than those of any other persons who lived prior to Abraham. The chronicle represents the merits of Yu to have been first exhibited in reducing the waters and dividing the country into nine regions, and as he had assisted Shun in his government during his lifetime, he was unanimously called to the vacant dignity, and became the founder of the Hia dynasty. Allowing that the records of these times and people are brief and disjointed, and many things in them impossible to reconcile, still they are superior to the absurd tales describing the formation of some other ancient States, and should not be ridiculed as trivial or rejected as fabulous. The great advances made in settling obscure points in early history, by the success in deciphering records brought to light in Western Asia, lead to more respect for what we possess in Eastern Asia, rather than to reject the fragmentary records remaining. No one regards them as trustworthy, like the clay tablets exhumed at Nineveh, but if Abraham found the Egyptians to be living under a regular government not one hundred and fifty years after this, and Damascus, Babylon, Erech, and other cities were then old, no one need be unwilling to give the Chinese a line of monarchs, and a population quite sufficient to have deepened the channel of a river or raised dikes to restrain it. The glorious reigns and spotless characters of these three sovereigns are looked upon by the Chinese with much the same feelings of veneration that the Jews regard their three patriarchs; and to have had, or to have imagined, such progenitors and heroes is, to say the least, as much to their credit as the Achilles, Ulysses, and Romulus of the Greeks and Romans. A curious analogy can also be traced between the scheming Ulysses, warlike Romulus, and methodical Yao, and the subsequent character of the three great nations they represent.

Chinese historians supply many details regarding the conduct of Yu and Kieh Kwei, the first and last princes of the house of Hia, all the credible particulars of which are taken from the *Book of Records* and the *Bamboo Annals*. Dr. Legge candidly weighs the arguments in respect to the eclipse mentioned in the *Yuh Ching*, and gives his opinion as to its authenticity, even if it cannot yet be certainly referred to the year B.C. 2154. One such authentic notice lends strength to the reception of many vague statements, which are more likely to be the relics of fuller documents long since lost than the fabrications of later writers, such as were the Decretals of Isidore in the Middle Ages. In giving a full translation of the *Bamboo Books* in the prolegomena of the *Shu King*, Dr. Legge has shown one of the sources of ancient Chinese history outside of that work. There were many other works accessible to Sz'ma Tsien, nearly four centuries before they were discovered (A.D. 279), when he wrote his *Annals*. Pan Ku gives a list of the various books recovered after the death of Tsin Chí Hwangtí, amounting in all to thirteen thousand two hundred and nineteen volumes or chapters contained in six hundred and twenty different works. Well does Pauthier speak of the inestimable value which a similar catalogue of the extant literature of Greece and Rome at that epoch (B.C. 100) would now be.

One of the alleged records of the reign of Yu is an inscription traced on the rocks of Kau-lau shan, one of the peaks of Mount Hăng in Hunan, relating to the inundation. It contains seventy-seven characters only, and Amiot, who regarded it as genuine, has given its sense as follows:

The venerable Emperor said, Oh! aid and councillor! Who will help me in administering my affairs? The great and little islets (the inhabited places) even to their summits, the abodes of the beasts and birds, and all beings are widely inundated. Advise, send back the waters, and raise the dikes. For a long time, I have quite forgotten my family; I repose on the top of the mountain Yoh-lu. By prudence and my labors, I have moved the spirits; I know not the hours, but repose myself only in my incessant labors. The mountains Hwa, Yoh, Tai, and Hăng, have been the beginning and end of my enterprise; when my labors were completed, I offered a thanksgiving sacrifice at the solstice. My affliction has ceased; the confusion in nature has disappeared; the deep currents coming from the south flow into the sea; clothes can now be made, food can be prepared, all kingdoms will be at peace, and we can give ourselves to continual joy.[1]

Since Amiot's time, however, further opportunities have offered for more thorough inquiry into this relic by foreigners, and the results of their researches throw much doubt upon its authenticity, though they do not altogether destroy it. In the Introduction to the *Shu King*, Dr. Legge discusses the value of this tablet among other early records of that reign, and comes to the conclusion that it is a fabrication of the Han dynasty, if not later. The poet Han Yu (A.D. 800) gave it wide notoriety by his verses about its location and nature; but when he was there he could not find it on the peak, and cited only a Taoist priest as having seen it. More than three centuries afterward Chu Hí was equally unsuccessful, and his opinion that it was made by the priests of that sect has had much weight with his countrymen. It was not till one Ho Chí went to Mount Hăng, about A.D. 1210, and took a copy of the inscription from the stone then in a Taoist temple, that it was actually seen; and not till about 1510, that Chang Kí-wăn, another antiquary of Hunan province, published his copy in the form now generally accepted. In 1666 one Mao Tsăng-kien again found the tablet on the summit of Kau-lau, but reached it with much difficulty by the help of ladders and hooks, and found it so broken that the inscription could not be made out. A reduced *fac-simile* of Mao's copy is given by

---

[1] Pauthier, *La Chine*, p. 53; J. Hager's *Inscription of Yu*, Paris, 1802; Legge's *Shu King*, pp. 67–74; *Transactions of the N. C. Br. R. A. Soc.*, No. V., 1869, pp. 78–84; *Journal Asiatique*, 1867, Tome X., pp. 197–337.

Dr. Legge, whose translation differs from Amiot's in some particulars.

I received *the words of* the Emperor, saying, "Ah! Associate helper, aiding noble! The islands and islets may now be ascended, *that were* doors for the birds and beasts. *You* devoted your person to the great overflowings, and with the daybreak you rose up. Long were *you* abroad, forgetting your family; *you* lodged at the mountain's foot as in a hall; *your* wisdom schemed; *your* body was broken; *your* heart was all in a tremble. *You* went and sought to produce order and settlement. At Hwa, Yoh, Tai, and Hăng, by adopting the principle of dividing *the waters*, *your* undertakings were completed. With the remains of a taper, *you* offered your pure sacrifice. There were entanglement and obstruction, being swamped, and removals. The southern river flows on its course; for ever is the provision of food made sure; the myriad States enjoy repose; the beasts and birds are for ever fled away."

The characters in which this tablet is written are of an ancient tadpole form, and so difficult to read that grave doubts exist as to their proper meaning—and even as to which of two or three forms is the correct one. Since the copy of Mao was taken, the Manchu scholar Kwan-wăn, when Governor-General of Liang Hu in 1868, erected a stone tablet at Wu-chang, in the Pavilion of the Yellow Stork, upon the eminence overlooking the Yangtsz'. This he regarded as a true copy of the authentic *Yu Pai*, or 'Tablet of Yu.' A *fac-simile* of this tablet, and of another rubbing from a stone now existing at the foot of Mount Hăng (which is alleged to be an exact reproduction of the original on its top), was published by W. H. Medhurst in the *N. C. Asiatic Society Journal* for 1869. A comparison of these three will give the reader an idea of the difficulties and doubts attending the settlement of the credibility of this inscription. A living native writer quoted by Mr. Medhurst says that the earliest notice of the tablet is by Tsin Yung of the Tăng dynasty, about A.D. 700, from which he infers that the people of the time of Tăng must have seen the rock and its inscription. He regards the latter as consisting of fairy characters, utterly unreadable, and therefore all attempts to decipher them as valueless and misleading.

Amid so many conflicting opinions among native scholars, the verdict of foreigners may safely await further discoveries, and the day when competent observers can examine these localities and tablets for themselves. Without exaggerating the importance and credibility of the *Shu King* and other ancient Chinese records, they can be received as the writings of a very remote period; and while their claims to trustworthiness would be fortified if more intimations had been given of the manner in which they were kept during the long period antecedent to the era of Confucius, they still deserve a more respectful consideration than some modern writers are disposed to allow them. For instance, Davis remarks: "Yu is described as nine cubits in height, and it is stated that the skies rained gold in those days, which certainly (as Dr. Morrison observes) lessens the credit of the history of this period." Now, without laying too much stress upon the record, or the objections against it, this height is but little more than that of Og of Bashan, even if we adopt the present length of the cubit fourteen and one-tenth inches, English; and if *kin*, here called *gold*, be translated *metal* (which it can just as well be), it may be a notice of a meteoric shower of extraordinary duration. Let these venerable writings be investigated in a candid, cautious manner, weighing their internal evidence, and comparing their notices of those remote periods as much as they can be with those of other nations, and they will illustrate ancient history and customs in no slight degree. Mr. Murray has given a synopsis from Mailla of what is recorded of the Hia dynasty, which will fairly exhibit the matter of Chinese history. It is here introduced somewhat abridged, with dates inserted.

The accession of Yu (B.C. 2205) forms a remarkable era in Chinese history. The throne, which hitherto had been more or less elective, became from this period hereditary in the eldest son, with only those occasional and violent interruptions to which every despotic government is liable. The national annals, too, assume a more regular and authentic shape, the reigns of the sovereigns being at the same time reduced to a probable duration.

Yu justly acquired a lasting veneration, but it was chiefly by his labors under his two predecessors. When he himself ascended the throne, age had already overtaken him; still the lustre of his government was supported by able councillors, till it closed with his life at the end of seven years. Many of the grandees wished, according to former practice, to raise to the throne Pí-yih, his first minister, and a person of distinguished merit; but regard for the father, in this case, was strengthened by the excellent qualities of his son

Kí, or Tí Kí (*i.e.*, the Emperor Kí), and even Pí-yih insisted that the prince should be preferred (2197). His reign of nine years was only disturbed by the rebellion of a turbulent subject, and he was succeeded (2188) by his son, Tai Kang. But this youth was devoted to pleasure; music, wine, and hunting entirely engrossed his attention. The Chinese, after enduring him for twenty-nine years, dethroned him (2159), and his brother, Chung Kang, was nominated to succeed, and held the reins of government for thirteen years with a vigorous hand. He was followed by his son, Siang (2146), who, destitute of the energy his situation required, gave himself up to the advice of his minister Yeh, and was by him, in connection with his accomplice, Hantsu, declared incapable of reigning. The usurper ruled for seven years, when he was killed; and the rightful monarch collected his adherents and gave battle to Hantsu and the son of Yeh in the endeavor to regain his throne. Siang was completely defeated, and lost both his crown and life; the victors immediately marched to the capital, and made so general a massacre of the family that they believed the name and race of Yu to be for ever extinguished.

The Empress Min, however, managed to escape, and fled to a remote city, where she brought forth a son, called Shau Kang; and the better to conceal his origin, she employed him as a shepherd boy to tend flocks. Reports of the existence of such a youth, and his occupation, at length reached the ears of Hantsu, who sent orders to bring him, dead or alive. The royal widow then placed her son as under-cook in the household of a neighboring governor, where the lad soon distinguished himself by a spirit and temper so superior to this humble station, that the master's suspicions were roused, and obliged him to disclose his name and birth. The officer, being devotedly attached to the house of Yu, not only kept the secret, but watched for an opportunity to reinstate him, and meanwhile gave him a small government in a secluded situation, which he prudently administered. Yet he was more than thirty years old before the governor, by engaging other chiefs in his interest, could assemble such a force as might justify the attempt to make head against the usurper. The latter hastily assembled his troops and led them to the attack, but was defeated and taken prisoner by the young prince Chu himself; and Shau Kang, with his mother, returned with acclamations to the capital. His reign is reckoned to have been sixty-one years' duration in the chronology of the time, which includes the usurpation of forty years of Hantsu.

The country was ably governed by Shau Kang, and also by his son, Chu (2057), who ruled for seventeen years; but the succeeding sovereigns, in many instances, abandoned themselves to indolence and pleasure, and brought the kingly name into contempt. From Hwai to Kieh Kwei, a space of two hundred and twenty-two years, between B.C. 2040 and 1818, few records remain of the nine sovereigns, whose bare names succeed each other in the annals. At length the throne was occupied by Kieh Kwei (1818), a prince who is represented as having, in connexion with his consort, Mei-hí, practised every kind of violence and extortion, in order to accumulate treasure, which they spent in unbridled voluptuousness. They formed a large pond of wine, deep enough to float a boat, at which three thousand men drank at once. It was surrounded, too, by pyramids of delicate viands, which no one, however, was allowed to taste, till he had first intoxicated himself out of the lake. The drunken quarrels which ensued were their favorite amusement. In the interior of the palace the vilest orgies were celebrated, and the venerable ministers, who attempted to remonstrate against these excesses, were either put to death or exiled. The people were at once indignant and grieved at such crimes, which threatened the downfall of the dynasty; and the discarded statesmen put themselves under the direction of the wise Í Yin, and advised Chingtang, the ablest of their number, and a descendant of Hwangtí, to assume the reins of government, assuring him of their support. He with reluctance yielded to their solicitations, and assembling a force marched against Kieh Kwei, who came out to meet him at the head of a numerous army, but fled from the contest on seeing the defection of his troops, and ended his days in despicable obscurity, after occupying the throne fifty-two years.[1]

Chinese annals are generally occupied in this way; the Emperor and his ministers fill the whole field of historic vision; little is recorded of the condition, habits, arts, or occupations of the people, who are merely considered as attendants of the monarch, which is, in truth, a feature of the ancient records of nearly all countries and people. Monarchs controlled the chronicles of their reigns, and their own vanity, as well as their ideas of government and authority led them to represent the people as a mere background to their own stately dignity and acts.

The Shang dynasty began B.C. 1766, or about one hundred and twenty years before the Exodus, and maintained an unequal sway over the feudal States composing the Empire for a period of six hundred and forty-four years. Its first monarch, Chingtang, or Tang the Successful, is described as having paid religious worship to Shangtí, under which name, perhaps, the true God was intended. On account of a severe drought of seven years' duration, this monarch is reported to have prayed, saying, "I the child Lí presume to use a dark colored victim, and announce to thee, O Shang-tien Hao ('High Heaven's Ruler'). Now there is a great drought, and it is right I should be held responsible for it. I do not know but that I have offended the powers above and below." With regard to his own conduct, he blamed himself in six particulars, and his words were not ended when the rain descended copiously.

The fragmentary records of this dynasty contained in the *Shu King* are not so valuable to the student who wishes merely

[1] Hugh Murray, *China*, Vol. I., pp. 51–55 (edition of 1843).

to learn the succession of monarchs in those days, as to one who inquires what were the principles on which they ruled, what were the polity, the religion, the jurisdiction, and the checks of the Chinese government in those remote times. The regular records of those days will never be recovered, but the preservation of the last two parts of the *Shu King* indicates their existence by fair inference, and encourages those who try to reconstruct the early annals of China to give full value even to slight fragments. But these parts have been of great service to the people since they were written, in teaching them by precept and example on what the prosperity of a State was founded, and how their rulers could bring it to ruin. In these respects there are no ancient works outside of the Bible with which they can at all be compared. The later system of examination has given them an unparalleled influence in molding the national character of the Chinese. Of the eleven chapters now remaining all are occupied more or less with the relative duties of the prince and rulers, enforcing on each that the welfare of all was bound up with their faithfulness. One quotation will give an idea of their instructions. "Order your affairs by righteousness, order your heart by propriety, so shall you transmit a grand example to posterity. I have heard the saying, He who finds instructors for himself comes to the supreme dominion; he who says that others are not equal to himself comes to ruin. He who likes to ask becomes enlarged; he who uses *only* himself becomes small. Oh! he who would take care for his end must be attentive to his beginning. There is establishment for the observers of propriety, and overthrow for the blinded and wantonly indifferent. To revere and honor the way of Heaven is the way ever to preserve the favoring regard of Heaven."[1]

The chronicles of the Shang dynasty, as gathered from the *Bamboo Books* and other later records, resemble those of the Hia in being little more than a mere succession of the names of the sovereigns, interspersed here and there with notices of some remarkable events in the natural and political world. Luxurious and despised princes alternate with vigorous and warlike ones

[1] Part IV., Book II., Chap. IV., 8–9.

who commanded respect, and the condition of the State measurably corresponds with the character of the monarchs, the feudal barons sometimes increasing in power and territory by encroaching on their neighbors, and then suffering a reduction from some new State. The names of twenty-eight princes are given, the accounts of whose reigns are indeed fuller than those of the dukes of Edom in Genesis, but their slight notices would be more interesting if the same confidence could be reposed in them.

The bad sovereigns occupy more room in these *fasti* than the good ones, the palm of wickedness being given to Chau-sin, with whom the dynasty ended. The wars which broke out during this dynasty were numerous, but other events also find a place, though hardly anything which throws light on society or civilization. Droughts, famines, and other calamities were frequent and attended by dreadful omens and fearful sights; this fancied correlation between natural casualties and political convulsions is a feature running through Chinese history, and grows out of the peculiar position of the monarch as the vicegerent of heaven. The people seem to have looked for control and protection more to their local masters than to their lord paramount, ranging themselves under their separate banners as they were bidden. The *History Made Easy* speaks of the twenty-fifth monarch, Wu-yih (B.C. 1198), as the most wicked of them all. "Having made his images of clay in the shape of human beings, dignified them with the name of gods, overcome them at gambling, and set them aside in disgrace, he then, in order to complete his folly, made leathern bags and filled them with blood, and sent them up into the air, exclaiming, when his arrows hit them and the blood poured down, 'I have shot heaven,' meaning, I have killed the gods."

The names of Chau-sin and Tan-kí are coupled with those of Kieh and Mí-hí of the Hia dynasty, all of them synonymous in the Chinese annals for the acme of cruelty and licentiousness —as are those of Nero and Messalina in Roman history. Chau-sin is said one winter's morning to have seen a few women walking barelegged on the banks of a stream collecting shell-fish, and ordered their legs to be cut off, that he might see the marrow of persons who could resist cold so fearlessly. The heart of one of his reprovers was also brought him, in order to see wherein it differed from that of cowardly ministers. The last *Book of Shang* contains the vain remonstrance of another of them, who tells his sovereign that his dynasty is in the condition of one crossing a large stream who can find neither ford nor bank. Many acts of this nature alienated the hearts of the people, until Wăn wang, the leader of a State in the northwest of China, united the principal men against his misrule; but dying, bequeathed his crown and power to his son, Wu wang. He gradually gathered his forces and met Chau-sin at the head of a great army at Muh, near the junction of the rivers Kí and Wei, north of the Yellow River in Honan, where the defeat of the tyrant was complete. Feeling the contempt he was held in, and the hopeless struggle before him, he fled to his palace and burned himself with all his treasures, like another Sardanapalus, though his immolation (in B.C. 1122) preceded the Assyrian's by five centuries.

Wu wang, the martial king, the founder of the Chau dynasty, his father, Wăn wang, and his brother, Duke Chau, are among the most distinguished men of antiquity for their erudition, integrity, patriotism, and inventions. Wăn wang, Prince of Chau, was prime minister to Tai-ting, the grandfather of Chau-sin, but was imprisoned for his fidelity. His son obtained his liberation, and the sayings and acts of both occupy about twenty books in Part V. of the *Shu King*. Duke Chau survived his brother to become the director and support of his nephew; his counsels, occupying a large part of the history, are full of wisdom and equity. Book X. contains his warning advice about drunkenness, which has been remarkably influential among his countrymen ever since. No period of ancient Chinese history is more celebrated than that of the founding of this dynasty, chiefly because of the high character of its leading men, who were regarded by Confucius as the impersonations of everything wise and noble. Wu wang is represented as having invoked the assistance of Shangtí in his designs, and, when he was successful, returned thanks and offered prayers and sacrifices. He removed the capital from the province of Honan to the present

Sí-ngan, in Shensí, where it remained for a long period. This prince committed a great political blunder in dividing the Empire into petty states, thus destroying the ancient pure monarchy, and leaving himself only a small portion of territory and power, which were quite insufficient, in the hands of a weak prince, to maintain either the state or authority due the ruling sovereign. The number of States at one time was one hundred and twenty-five, at another forty-one, and, in the time of Confucius, about six hundred years after the establishment of the dynasty, fifty-two, some of them large kingdoms. From about B.C. 700 the imperial name and power lost the allegiance and respect of the feudal princes, and gradually became contemptible. Its nominal sway extended over the country lying north of the Yangtsz' kiang, the regions on the south being occupied by tribes of whom no intelligible record has been preserved.

The duration of the three dynasties, the Hia, Shang, and Chau, comprises a long and obscure period in the history of the world, extending from B.C. 2205 to 249, from the time when Terah dwelt in Charran, and the sixteenth dynasty of Theban kings ruled in Egypt, down to the reigns of Antiochus Soter and Ptolemy Philadelphus and the translation of the Septuagint.

I.—The HIA dynasty, founded by Yu the Great, existed four hundred and thirty-nine years, down to B.C. 1766, under seventeen monarchs, the records of whose reigns are very brief. Among contemporary events of importance are the call of Abraham, in the year B.C. 2093, Jacob's flight to Mesopotamia in 1916, Joseph's elevation in Egypt in 1885, and his father's arrival in 1863.

II.—The SHANG dynasty began with Tang the Successful, and continued six hundred and forty-four years, under twenty-eight sovereigns, down to B.C. 1122. This period was characterized by wars among rival princes, and the power of the sovereign depended chiefly upon his personal character. The principal contemporary events were the Exodus of the Israelites in 1648, their settlement in Palestine in 1608, judgeship of Othniel, 1564; of Deborah, 1406; of Gideon, 1359; of Samson, 1202; and death of Samuel in 1122.

III.—The CHAU dynasty began with Wu wang, and continued for eight hundred and seventy-three years, under thirty-five monarchs, down to B.C. 249, the longest of any recorded in history. The sway of many of these was little more than nominal, and the feudal States increased or diminished, according to the vigor of the monarch or the ambition of the princes. In B.C. 770 the capital was removed from Kao, near the River Wei in Shensí, to Lohyang, in the western part of Honan; this divides the house into the Western and Eastern Chau. The contemporary events of these eight centuries are too numerous to particularize. The accession of Saul in 1110; of David, 1070; of Rehoboam, 990; taking of Troy, 1084; of Samaria, 719; of Jerusalem, 586; death of Nebuchadnezzar, 561; accession of Cyrus and return of the Jews, 551; battle of Marathon, 490; accession of Alexander, 235; etc. The conquest of Egypt by Alexander in 322 brought the thirty-first and last dynasty of her native kings to an end, the first of which had begun under Menes about B.C. 2715, or twenty-two years after the supposed accession of Shinnung.

The absence of any great remains of human labor or art previous to the Great Wall, like the Pyramids, the Temple of Solomon, or the ruins and mounds in Syria, has led many to doubt the credibility of these early Chinese records. They ascribe them to the invention of the historians of the Han dynasty, working up the scattered relics of their ancient books into a readable narrative, and therefore try to bring every statement to a critical test for which there are few facts. The analogies between the records in the *Shu King* and the Aryan myths are skilfully explained by Mr. Kingsmill by reference to the meanings of the names of persons and places and titles, and a connection shown which has the merit at least of ingenuity and beauty. Almost the only actual known relic of these three dynasties is the series of ten stone drums (*shih ku*) now in the Confucian temple at Peking. They were discovered about A.D. 600, in the environs of the ancient capital of the Chau dynasty, and have been kept in Peking since the year 1126. They are irregularly shaped pillars, from eighteen to thirty-five inches high and about twenty-eight inches across; the inscriptions are much worn, but enough remains to show that they commemorate a great hunt of Süen wang (B.C. 827) in the region where they were found.[1]

Among the feudal States under the house of Chau, that of Tsin, on the northwest, had long been the most powerful, occupying nearly a fifth of the country, and its inhabitants forming a tenth of the whole population. One of the princes, called Chausiang wang, carried his encroachments into the acknowledged imperial possessions, and compelled its master, Tungchau kiun, the last monarch, to humble himself at his feet. Although, in fact, master of the whole Empire, he did not take the title, but left it to his son, Chwangsiang wang, who exterminated the blood royal and ended the Chau dynasty, yet lived only three years in possession of the supreme power.

The son carried on his father's successes until he had reduced all the petty States to his sway. He then took the name of Chí Hwangtí ('Emperor First') of the Tsin dynasty, and set himself to regulate his conquests and establish his authority by securing to his subjects a better government than had been experienced during the feudal times. He divided the country into thirty-six provinces, over which he placed governors, and went throughout them all to see that no injustice was practised.

This monarch, who has been called the Napoleon of China, was one of those extraordinary men who turn the course of events and give an impress to subsequent ages; Klaproth gives him a high character as a prince of energy and skill, but native historians detest his name and acts. It is recorded that at his new capital, Hienyang, on the banks of the Hwai, he constructed a palace exactly like those of all the kings who had submitted to him, and ordered that all the precious furniture of each and those persons who had inhabited them should be transported to it, and everything rearranged. The whole occupied an immense space, and the various parts communicated with each other by a magnificent colonnade and gallery. He made progresses through his dominions with a splendor hitherto unknown, accompanied by officials and troops from all parts, thus making

[1] *Journal of the N. C. Branch of R. A. Society*, Vols. VII., p. 137; VIII., pp. 23, 133. In the last paper, by Dr. Bushell, translations and fac-similes of the inscriptions are given, with many historical notices.

the people interested in each other and consenting to his sway. He also built public edifices, opened roads and canals to facilitate intercourse and trade between the various provinces, and repressed the incursions of the Huns, driving them into the wilds of Mongolia. In order to keep them out effectually, he conceived the idea of extending and uniting the short walls which the princes of some of the Northern States had erected on their frontier into one grand wall, stretching across the Empire from the sea to the Desert. This gigantic undertaking was completed in ten years (B.C. 204), at a vast expense in men and material, and not until the family of its builder had been destroyed. This mode of protecting the country, when once well begun, probably commended itself to the nation. It is impossible, indeed, to imagine otherwise how it could have been done, for the people were required to supply a quota of men from each place, feed and clothe them while at work, and continue this expense until their portion was built. No monarch could have maintained an army which could force his subjects against their will to do such a work or carry it on to completion after his death. It is one of the incidental proofs of a great population that so many laborers were found. However ineffectual it was to preserve his frontiers, it has made his name celebrated throughout the world, and his dynasty *Tsin* has given its name to China for all ages and nations.[1]

The vanity of the new monarch led him to endeavor to destroy all records written anterior to his own reign, that he might be by posterity regarded as the first Emperor of the Chinese race. Orders were issued that every book should be burned, and especially the writings of Confucius and Mencius, explanatory of the *Shu King* upon the feudal States of Chau, whose remembrance he wished to blot out. This strange command was executed to such an extent that many of the Chinese literati believe that not a perfect copy of the classical works escaped destruction, and the texts were only recovered by rewriting them from the memories of old scholars, a mode of reproduction

---

[1] Pauthier, *La Chine*, pp. 30, 221 ; *Mém. conc. les Chinois*, Tome III., p. 183.

that does not appear so singular to a Chinese as it does to us. If the same literary tragedy should be re-enacted to-day, thousands of persons might easily be found in China who could rewrite from memory the text and commentary of their nine classical works. "Nevertheless," as Klaproth remarks, "they were not in fact all lost; for in a country where writing is so common it was almost impossible that all the copies of works universally respected should be destroyed, especially at a time when the material on which they were written was very durable, being engraved with a stylet on bamboo tablets, or traced upon them with dark-colored varnish." The destruction was no doubt as nearly complete as possible, and not only were many works entirely destroyed, but a shade of doubt thereby thrown over the accuracy of others, and the records of the ancient dynasties rendered suspicious as well as incomplete. Not only were books sought after to be destroyed, but nearly five hundred literati were buried alive, in order that no one might remain to reproach, in their writings, the Emperor First with having committed so barbarous and insane an act.

The dynasty of Tsin, set up in such cruelty and blood, did not long survive the death of its founder; his son was unable to maintain his rule over the half-subdued feudal chieftains, and after a nominal reign of seven years he was overcome by Liu Pang, a soldier of fortune, who, having been employed by one of the chiefs as commander of his forces, used them to support his own authority when he had taken possession of the capital. Under the name of Kautsu he became the founder of the Han dynasty, and his accession is regarded as the commencement of modern Chinese history. The number and character of its heroes and literati are superior to most other periods, and to this day the term *Han-tsz'*, or 'Sons of Han,' is one of the favorite names by which the Chinese call themselves.

The first fourteen princes of this dynasty reigned in Shensí, but Kwangwu removed the capital from Chang-an to Lohyang, as was done in the Chau dynasty seven centuries before, the old one being ruined. During the reign of Ping Tí (or the 'Emperor Peace') the Prince of Peace, our Lord Jesus Christ, was born in Judea, a remarkable coincidence which has often attracted notice. During the reign of Ming tí, A.D. 65, a deputation was sent to India to obtain the sacred books and authorized teachers of Buddhism, which the Emperor intended to publicly introduce into China. This faith had already widely spread among his subjects, but henceforth it became the popular belief of the Chinese and extended eastward into Japan. This monarch and his successor, Chang tí, penetrated with their armies as far westward as the Caspian Sea, dividing and overcoming the various tribes on the confines of the Desert and at the foot of the Tien shan, and extending the limits of the monarchy in that direction farther than they are at present. The Chinese sway was maintained with varied success until toward the third century, and seems to have had a mollifying effect upon the nomads of those regions. In these distant expeditions the Chinese heard of the Romans, of whom their authors speak in the highest terms: "Everything precious and admirable in all other countries," say they, "comes from this land. Gold and silver money is coined there; ten of silver are worth one of gold. Their merchants trade by sea with Persia and India, and gain ten for one in their traffic. They are simple and upright, and never have two prices for their goods; grain is sold among them very cheap, and large sums are embarked in trade. Whenever ambassadors come to the frontiers they are provided with carriages to travel to the capital, and after their arrival a certain number of pieces of gold are furnished them for their expenses." This description, so characteristic of the shop-keeping Chinese, may be compared to many accounts given of the Chinese themselves by western authors.

Continuing the *résumé* of dynasties in order—

IV.—The Tsin dynasty is computed to end with Chwangsiang by the authors of the *History Made Easy*, and to have existed only three years, from B.C. 249 to 246.

V.—The After Tsin dynasty is sometimes joined to the preceding, but Chí Hwangtí regarded himself as the first monarch, and began a new house, which, however, lasted only forty-four years, from B.C. 246 to 202. The commotions in the farthest East during this period were not less destructive of life than the wars in Europe between the Carthaginians and Romans, and the Syrians, Greeks, and Egyptians.

VI., VII. The HAN and EASTERN HAN dynasties.—Liu Pang took the title of Han for his dynasty, after the name of his principality, and his family swayed the Middle Kingdom from B.C. 202 to A.D. 221, under twenty-six monarchs. The Han dynasty was the formative period of Chinese polity and institutions, and an instructive parallel can be drawn between the character and acts of the Emperors who reigned four hundred years in China, and the numerous consuls, dictators, and emperors who governed the Roman Empire for the same period from the time of Scipio Africanus to Heliogabalus. The founder of the Han is honored for having begun the system of competitive examinations for office, and his successors, Wăn tí, Wu tí, and Kwang-wu, developed literature, commerce, arts, and good government to a degree unknown before anywhere in Asia. In the West the Romans became the great world power, and the advent of Christ and establishment of His church within its borders only, render this period the turning epoch of progress among mankind.

The period between the overthrow of the Han dynasty, A.D. 190, and the establishment of the Eastern Tsin, A.D. 317, is one of the most interesting in Chinese history, from the variety of characters which the troubles of the times developed. The distractions of this period are described in the *History of the Three States*, but this entertaining work cannot be regarded as much better than a historical novel. It has, however, like Scott's stories, impressed the events and actors of those days upon the popular mind more than any history in the language.

VIII.—The AFTER HAN dynasty began A.D. 211, and continued forty-four years, under two princes, to A.D. 265. The country was divided into three principalities, called Wei, Wu, and Shuh. The first, under the son of Tsao Tsao, ruled the whole northern country at Lohyang, and was the most powerful of them for about forty years. The second, under Siun Kien, occupied the eastern provinces, from Shantung and the Yellow River down to the mountains of Fuhkien, holding his court at Nanking. The third, under Liu Pí, is regarded as the legitimate dynasty from his affinity with the Han; he had his capital at Chingtu fu, in Sz'chuen.

IX.—The TSIN dynasty was founded by Sz'ma Chao, a general in the employ of Hau of the last house, who seated himself on the throne of his master A.D. 265, the year of the latter's death. His son, Sz'ma Yen, took his place and extended his power over the whole Empire by 280. The inroads of the Huns and internal commotions were fast reducing the people to barbarism. Four Emperors of this house held their sway at Lohyang during fifty-two years, till A.D. 317. The Huns maintained their sway in Shensí until A.D. 352, under the designations of the Han and Chau dynasties. It is related of Liu Tsung, one of this barbaric race, that he built a great palace at Chang-an, where he gathered a myriad of the first subjects of his kingdom and lived in luxury and magnificence quite unknown before in China. Among his attendants was a body-guard of elegantly dressed women, many of whom were good musicians, which accompanied him on his progresses.

X.—The EASTERN TSIN is the same house as the last, but Yuen tí having moved his capital in 317 from Lohyang to Nanking, his successors are distinguished as the Eastern Tsin. Eleven princes reigned during a period of one hundred and three years, down to A.D. 420. Buddhism was the chief religion at this time, and the doctrines of Confucius were highly esteemed; "children of concubines, priests, old women, and nurses administered the government," says the indignant annalist. At this period twelve independent and opposing kings struggled for the ascendency in China, and held their ephemeral courts in the north and west. It was at this time that Constantine moved the capital of the Roman Empire in 328, and the nations of northern Europe under Attila invaded Italy in 410.

XI.—The SUNG, or Northern Sung dynasty, as it is often called to distinguish it from the XXIId dynasty (A.D. 970), is the first of the four dynasties known as the *Nan-peh Chao*, or 'South-north dynasties,' which preceded the Sui. It was founded by Liu Yu, who commanded the armies of Tsin, and gradually subdued all the opposing States. Displeased at the weakness of his master, Ngan tí, he caused him to be strangled, and placed his brother, Kung tí, upon the throne, who, fearing a like fate, abdicated the empty crown, and Liu Yu became monarch under the name of Kautsu, A.D. 420. Eight princes held the throne till A.D. 479, many of them monsters of cruelty, and soon cut off, when Siau Tau-ching, Duke of Tsí, the prime minister, recompensed them as their ancestor had those of Tsin.

XII. Tsí dynasty.—The new monarch took the name of Kau tí, or 'High Emperor,' but enjoyed his dignity only four years. Four princes succeeded him at Nanking, the last of whom, Ho tí, was besieged in his capital by a faithless minister, assisted by the prince of Liang, who overthrew the dynasty A.D. 502, after a duration of twenty-three years.

XIII. Liang dynasty.—The first Emperor, Wu tí, reigned forty-eight years, and reduced most of his opponents; his dominions are described as being mostly south of the Yangtsz' River, the Wei ruling the regions north of it. Wu tí did much to restore literature and the study of Confucius; envoys from India and Persia also came to his court, and his just sway allowed the land to recruit. In his latter days he was so great a devotee of Buddhism that he retired to a monastery, like Charles V., but being persuaded to resume his crown, employed his time in teaching those doctrines to his assembled courtiers. Three successors occupied the throne, the last of whom, King tí, was killed A.D. 557, after surrendering himself, by the general of the troops, who then seized the crown.

XIV. Chin dynasty.—Three brothers reigned most of the time this house held its sway. During this period and that of the three preceding families, the Hunnish kingdom of Wei ruled the northern parts of China from A.D. 386 to 534, under eleven monarchs, when it was violently separated into the Eastern and Western Wei, and a third one called Chau, which ere long destroyed the last Wei at Chang-an and occupied northwest China. It is probable that the intercourse between China and other parts of Asia was more extensive and complete during the Wei dynasty than at any other period. Its sovereigns had preserved peaceful relations with their ancestral seats, and with the tribes beyond Lake Baikal and the Obi River to the North Sea. Trade seems to have flourished throughout the regions lying between the Caspian Sea and Corea, and the records of this period present accounts of the State in this vast tract to be found nowhere else. One of these works referred to by Rémusat is the report of officers sent by Tai-wu during his reign to travel through his dominions (424–451) and give full accounts of them.

One of the sovereigns of Chau, Wu tí (A.D. 561–572), had given his daughter in marriage to Yang Kien, the Prince of Sui, one of his ministers, who, gradually extending his influence, took possession of the throne of his master Tsing tí in 580. In a few years he restored order to a distracted land by bringing the several States under his sway and reuniting all China under his hand A.D. 589, after it had been divided nearly four centuries.

XV. Sui dynasty.—The founder of this house has left an enduring name in Chinese annals by a survey of his dominions and division of them into interdependent *chau*, *kiun*, and *hien*, with corresponding officers, an arrangement which has ever since existed. He patronized letters and commerce, and tried to introduce the system of caste from India. After a vigorous reign of twenty-four years he was killed by his son Yang tí, who carried on his father's plans, and during the fourteen years of his reign extended the frontiers through the Tarim Valley and down to the Southern Ocean. His murder by one of his generals was the signal for several ambitious men to rise, but the Prince of Tang aided the son to rule for a year or two till he was removed, thus bringing the Sui dynasty to an end after thirty-nine years, but not before its two sovereigns had taught their subjects the benefits of an undivided sway.

XVI. Tang dynasty.—This celebrated line of princes began its sway in peace, and during the two hundred and eighty-seven years (618 to 908) they held the throne China was probably the most civilized country on earth ; the darkest days of the West, when Europe was wrapped in the ignorance and degradation of the Middle Ages, formed the brightest era of the East. They exercised a humanizing effect on all the surrounding countries, and led their inhabitants to see the benefits and understand the management of a government where the laws were above the officers. The people along the southern coast were completely civilized and incorporated into the Chinese race, and mark the change by always calling themselves *Tang Jin*, or 'Men of Tang.' An interesting work on the trade and condition of China at this time is the *Akhbar-al-Syn oual-Hind*, or 'Observations on China and India,' by two Arab travellers to those lands in the years 851 and 878, compiled by Abu Zaid and translated by Reinaud in 1845.[1] Lí Shí-min, the son of Lí Yuen the founder of this dynasty, may be regarded as the most accomplished monarch in the Chinese annals—famed alike for his wisdom and nobleness, his conquests and good government, his temperance, cultivated tastes, and patronage of literary men. While still Prince of Tang he contributed greatly to his father's elevation and to the extension of his sway over the regions of Central Asia. When the house of Tang was fully acknowledged, and the eleven rival States which had started up on the close of the house of Sui had been overcome, the capital was removed from Lohyang back to Chang-an, and everything done to compose the disordered country and reunite the distracted State under a regular and vigorous administration. Feeling himself unequal to all the cares of his great office, Lí Yuen, known as Kau-tsu Shin Yao tí (lit. 'High Progenitor, the Divine Yao Emperor'), resigned the yellow in favor of his son, who took the style of *Ching kwan* ('Pure Observer') for his reign, though his posthumous title is Tai-tsung Wăn-wu tí ('Our Exalted Ancestor, the Literary-Martial Emperor'), A.D. 627, and still further extended his victorious arms. One of his first acts was to establish schools and institute a system of literary examinations; he ordered a complete and accurate edition of all the classics to be published under the supervision of the most learned men in the Empire, and honored the memory of Confucius with special ceremonies of respect. Extraordinary pains were taken to prepare and preserve the historical records of former days and draw up full annals of the recent dynasties; these still await the examination of western scholars.

He constructed a code of laws for the direction of his high officers in their judicial functions, and made progresses through

---

[1] *Chinese Repository*, Vol. I., p. 6; Reinaud, *Relations des Voyages*, 2 Vols., Paris, 1845. Yule, *Cathay and the Way Thither*, Introd., p. cii.

his dominions to inspect the condition of the people. During his reign the limits of the Empire were extended over all the Turkish tribes lying west of Kansuh and south of the Tien shan as far as the Caspian Sea, which were placed under four satrapies or residences, those of Kuché, Pisha or Khoten, Harashar, and Kashgar, as their names are at present. West of the last many smaller tribes submitted and rendered a partial subjection to the Emperor, who arranged them into sixteen governments under the management of a governor-general over their own chieftains. His frontiers reached from the borders of Persia, the Caspian Sea, and the Altai of the Kirghís steppe, along those mountains to the north side of Gobi eastward to the Inner Hing-an. Sogdiana and part of Khorassan, and the regions around the Hindu-kush, also obeyed him. The rulers of Nipal and Magadha or Bahar in India sent their salutations by their ambassadors, and the Greek Emperor Theodosius sent an envoy to Sí-ngan in 643 carrying presents of rubies and emeralds, as did also the Persians. The Nestorian missionaries also presented themselves at court. Tai-tsung received them with respect, and heard them rehearse the leading tenets of their doctrine; he ordered a temple to be erected at his capital, and had some of their sacred books translated for his examination, though there is no evidence now remaining that any portion of the Bible was done into Chinese at this time.

Near the close of his life Tai-tsung undertook an expedition against Corea, but the conquest of that country was completed by his son after his death. A sentiment has been preserved at this time of his life which he uttered to his sons while sailing on the River Wei: "See, my children, the waves which float our fragile bark are able to submerge it in an instant; know assuredly that the people are like the waves, and the Emperor like this fragile bark." During his reign his life was attempted several times, once by his own son, but he was preserved from these attacks, and died after a reign of twenty-three years, deeply lamented by a grateful people. The Chinese accounts state that the foreign envoys resident at his court cut off their hair, some of them disfigured their faces, bled themselves, and sprinkled the blood around the bier in testimony of their grief.

Whatever may have been the truth in this respect, many proofs exist of the distinguished character of this monarch, and that the high reputation he enjoyed during his lifetime was a just tribute to his excellences. He will favorably compare with Akbar, Marcus Aurelius, and Kanghí, or with Charlemagne and Harun Al Raschid, who came to their thrones in the next century.

Tai-tsung was succeeded by his son Kau-tsung, whose indolent imbecility appeared the more despicable after his father's vigor, but his reign fills a large place in Chinese history, from the extraordinary career of his Empress, Wu Tsih-tien, or Wu hao ('Empress Wu') as she is called, who by her blandishments obtained entire control over him. The character of this woman has, no doubt, suffered much from the bad reputation native historians have given her, but enough can be gathered from their accounts to show that with all her cruelty she understood how to maintain the authority of the crown, repress foreign invasions, quell domestic sedition, and provide for the wants of the people. Introduced to the harem of Tai-tsung at the age of fourteen, she was sent at his death to the retreat where all his women were condemned for the rest of their days to honorable imprisonment. While a member of the palace Kau-tsung had been charmed with her appearance, and, having seen her at one of the state ceremonies connected with the ancestral worship, brought her back to the palace. His queen, Wang-shí, also favored his attentions in order to draw them off from another rival, but Wu Tsih-tien soon obtaining entire sway over the monarch, united both women against her; she managed to fill the principal offices with her friends, and by a series of manœuvres supplanted each in turn and became Empress. One means she took to excite suspicion against Wang-shí was, on occasion of the birth of her first child, after the Empress had visited it and before Kau-tsung came in to see his offspring, to strangle it and charge the crime upon her Majesty, which led to her trial, degradation, and imprisonment, and ere long to her death.

As soon as she became Empress (in 655), Wu began gradually to assume more and more authority, until, long before the Emperor's death in 684, she engrossed the whole management of affairs, and at his demise openly assumed the reins of government, which she wielded for twenty-one years with no weak hand. Her generals extended the limits of the Empire, and her officers carried into effect her orders to alleviate the miseries of the people. Her cruelty vented itself in the murder of all who opposed her will, even to her own sons and relatives; and her pride was rather exhibited than gratified by her assuming the titles of Queen of Heaven, Holy and Divine Ruler, Holy Mother, and Divine Sovereign. When she was disabled by age her son, Chung-sung, supported by some of the first men of the land, asserted his claim to the throne, and by a palace conspiracy succeeded in removing her to her own apartments, where she died aged eighty-one years. Her character has been blackened in native histories and popular tales, and her conduct held up as an additional evidence of the evil of allowing women to meddle with governments.[1]

A race of twenty monarchs swayed the sceptre of the house of Tang, but after the demise of the Empress Wu Tsih-tien none of them equalled Tai-tsung, and the Tang dynasty at last succumbed to ambitious ministers lording over its imbecile sovereigns. In the reign of Hiuen-tsung, about the year 722, the population of the Fifteen Provinces is said to have been 52,884,818. The last three or four Emperors exhibited the usual marks of a declining house—eunuchs or favorites promoted by them swayed the realm and dissipated its resources. At last, Lí Tsüen-chung, a general of Chau-tsung, whom he had aided in quelling the eunuchs in 904, rose against his master, destroyed him, and compelled his son, Chau-siuen tí, to abdicate, A.D. 907.

XVII. AFTER LIANG dynasty.—The destruction of the famous dynasty loosened the bonds of all government, and nine separate kings struggled for its provinces, some of whom, as Apkí over the Kítan in the north-east, succeeded in founding kingdoms. The Prince of Liang, the new Emperor, was unable to extend his sway beyond the provinces of Honan and Shantung. After

---

[1] *Chinese Repository*, Vol. III., p. 543; *Canton Miscellany*, No. 4, 1831, pp. 246 ff.

a short reign of six years he was killed by his brother, Liang Chu-tien, who, on his part, fell under the attack of a Turkish general, and ended this dynasty, A.D. 923, after a duration of sixteen years.

XVIII. AFTER TANG dynasty.—The conqueror called himself Chwang-tsung, and his dynasty Tang, as if in continuation of that line of princes, but this mode of securing popularity was unsuccessful. Like Pertinax, Aurelian, and others of the Roman emperors, he was killed by his troops, who chose a successor, and his grandson, unable to resist his enemies, burned himself in his palace, A.D. 936, thus ending the weak dynasty after thirteen years of struggle.

XIX. AFTER TSIN dynasty.—The Kítan or Tartars of Liautung, who had assisted in the overthrow of the last dynasty, compelled the new monarch to subsidize them at his accession, A.D. 936, by ceding to them sixteen cities in Chihlí, and promising an annual tribute of three hundred thousand pieces of silk. This disgraceful submission has ever since stigmatized Tien-fuh ('Heavenly Happiness') in the eyes of native historians. His nephew who succeeded him is known as Chuh tí (the 'Carried-away Emperor'), and was removed in 947 by those who put him on the throne, thus ending the meanest house which ever swayed the black-haired people.

XX. AFTER HAN dynasty.—The Tartars now endeavored to subdue the whole country, but were repulsed by Liu Chí-yuen, a loyal general who assumed the yellow in 947, and called his dynasty after the renowned house of Han; he and his son held sway four years, till A.D. 951, and then were cut off.

XXI. AFTER CHAU dynasty.—Ko Wei, the successful aspirant to the throne, maintained his seat, but died in three years, leaving his power to an adopted son, Shí-tsung, whose vigorous rule consolidated his still unsettled sway. His early death and the youth of his son decided his generals to bestow the sceptre upon the lately appointed tutor to the monarch, which closed the After Chau dynasty A.D. 960, after a brief duration of nine years. He was honored with a title, and, like Richard Cromwell, allowed to live in quiet till his death in 973, a fact creditable to the new monarch. These short-lived houses between A.D. 907-

960 are known in Chinese history as the *Wu tai*, or 'Five Dynasties.' While they struggled for supremacy in the valley of the Yellow River, the regions south and west were portioned among seven houses, who ruled them in a good degree of security. Fuhkien was held by the King of Min, and Kiangnan by the King of Wu; the regions of Sz'chuen, Nganhwui, and Kansuh were held by generals of note in the service of Tang; another general held Kwangtung at Canton through two or three reigns; and another exercised sway at Kingchau on the Yangtsz' River. It is needless to mention them all. During this period Europe was distracted by the wars of the Normans and Saracens, and learning there was at a low ebb.

XXII.—SUNG dynasty began A.D. 970, and maintained its power over the whole Empire for one hundred and fifty-seven years, till A.D. 1127. The mode in which its founder, Chau Kwang-yun, was made head of the State, reminds one of the way in which the Prætorian guards sometimes elevated their chiefs to the throne of the Cæsars. After the military leaders had decided upon their future sovereign they sent messengers to announce to him his new honor, who found him drunk, and "before he had time to reply the yellow robe was already thrown over his person." At the close of his reign of seventeen years the provinces had mostly submitted to his power at Kaifung, but the two Tartar kingdoms of Liau and Hia remained independent. This return to a centralized government proves the unity of the Chinese people at this time in their own limits, as well as their inability to induce their neighbors to adopt the same system of government. The successors of Tai-tsu of Sung had a constant struggle for existence with their adversaries on the north and west, the Liau and Hia, whose recent taste of power under the last two dynasties had shown them their opportunity. On the return of prosperity under his brother's reign of twenty-two years, the former institutions and political divisions were restored throughout the southern half of the Empire; good government was secured, aided by able generals and loyal ministers, and the rebels everywhere quelled. Chin-tsung was the third sovereign, and his reign of forty-one years is the brightest portion of the house of Sung. The kings of Hia in Kansuh acknowledged themselves to be his tributaries, but he bought a cowardly peace with the Liau on the north-east. During his reign and that of his son, Tin-tsung, a violent controversy arose among the literati and officials as to the best mode of conducting the government. Some of them, as Sz'ma Kwang the historian, contended for the maintenance of the old principles of the sages. Others, of whom Wang Ngan-shí was the distinguished leader, advocated reform and change to the entire overthrow of existing institutions. For the first time in the history of China, two political parties peacefully struggled for supremacy, each content to depend on argument and truth for the victory. The contest soon grew too bitter, however, and the accession of a new monarch, Shin-tsung, enabled Wang to dispossess his opponents and manage State affairs as he pleased. After a trial of eight or ten years the voice of the nation restored the conservatives to power, and the radicals were banished beyond the frontier. A discussion like this, involving all the cherished ideas of the Chinese, brought out deep and acute inquiry into the nature and uses of things generally, and the writers of this dynasty, at the head of whom was Chu Hí, made a lasting impression on the national mind.

The two sons of Shin-tsung were unable to oppose the northern hordes of Liau and Hia, except by setting a third aspirant against both. These were the Niu-chih or Kin,[1] the ancestors of the present Manchus, who carried away Hwui-tsung as a captive in 1125, and his son too the next year, pillaging Lohyang and possessing themselves of the region north of the Yellow River. This closed the Northern Sung. The Kin established themselves at Peking in 1118, whence they were driven in 1235 by Genghis Khan, and fled back to the ancestral haunts on the Songari and Liau Rivers.

XXIII.—SOUTHERN SUNG dynasty forms part of the preceding, for Kao-tsung, the brother of the last and ninth monarch of the weakened house of Northern Sung, seeing his capital in ruins, fled to Nanking, and soon after to the beautiful city of Hangchau on the eastern coast at the mouth of the Tsientang River.

---

[1] Two graves of the Kin monarchs exist on a hill west of Fangshan hien, fifty miles south-west of Peking; they were repaired by Kanghí. Dr. Bushell visited them in 1870.

Nanking was pillaged by the Kin, but Hangchau was too far for them. It gradually grew in size and strength, and became a famous capital. Kao-tsung resigned in 1162, after a reign of thirty-six years, and survived his abdication twenty-four years. The next Emperor was Hiao-tsung, who also resigned the yellow to Kwang-tsung, his son, and he again yielded it to his son Ning-tsung. This last, in his distress, called the rising Mongols into his service in 1228 to help against the Kin. The distance from the northern frontier, where the Mongols were flushed with their successes over the Tangouth of Hia at Ninghia in 1226, was too far for them to aid Ning-tsung at this time. He was, however, relieved from danger to himself, and the Mongols deferred their intentions for a few years. From this date for about fifty years the Sung grew weaker and weaker under the next five sovereigns, until the last scion, Tí Ping, was drowned with some of his courtiers, one of whom, clasping him in his arms, jumped from the vessel, and ended their life, dignity, and dynasty together. It had lasted one hundred and fifty-two years under nine monarchs, who showed less ability than those of Northern Sung, and were all much inferior as a whole to the house of Tang. Their patronage of letters and the arts of peace was unaccompanied by the vigor of their predecessors, for they were unwilling to leave the capital and risk all at the head of their troops. It is the genius and philosophy of its scholars that has made the Sung one of the great dynasties of the Middle Kingdom.

XXIV.—The Yuen dynasty was the first foreign sway to which the Sons of Han had submitted; their resistance to the army, which gradually overran the country, was weakened, however, by treachery and desultory tactics until the national spirit was frittered away. During the interval between the capture of Peking by Genghis and the final extinction of the Sung dynasty, the whole population had become somewhat accustomed to Mongol rule. Having no organized government of their own, these khans were content to allow the Chinese the full exercise of their own laws, if peace and taxation were duly upheld. Kublai had had ample opportunity to learn the character of his new subjects, and after the death of Màngu khan in 1260 and his own establishment at Peking in 1264, he in fifteen years brought his vast dominions under a methodical sway and developed their resources more than ever. Though failing in his attempt to conquer Japan, he enlarged elsewhere his vanishing frontiers during his life till they could neither be defined nor governed. His patronage of merit and scholarship proves the good results of his tutelage in China, while the short-lived glory of his administration in other hands chiefly proved what good material he had to work with in China in comparison with his own race.[1] He was a vigorous and magnificent prince, and had, moreover, the advantage of having his acts and splendor related by Marco Polo—a chronicler worthy of his subject. The Grand Canal, which was deepened and lengthened during his reign, is a lasting token of his sagacity and enlightened policy. An interesting monument of this dynasty, erected in 1345, is the gateway in the Kü-yung kwan (pass) of the Great Wall north of Peking. Upon the interior of this arch is cut a Buddhist charm in six different kinds of character—Mongolian, Chinese, Oigour, antique Devanagari, Niu-chih, and Tibetan.[2]

After the Grand Khan's death the Mongols retained their power under the reign of Ching-tsung, or Timur khan, a grandson of Kublai, and Wu-tsung, or Genesek khan,[3] a nephew of the former, but their successors met with opposition, or were destroyed by treachery. The offices were also filled with Mongols, without any regard to the former mode of conferring rank according to literary qualifications, and the native Chinese began to be thoroughly dissatisfied with a sway in which they had no part. The last and eleventh, named Ching-tsung, or Tohan-Timur, came to the throne at the age of thirteen, and gave himself up to pleasure, his eunuchs and ministers dividing the possessions and offices of the Chinese among themselves and their adherents. This conduct aroused his subjects, and Chu Yuen-chang, a plebeian by birth, and formerly a priest, raised the standard of

---

[1] See Rémusat, *Nouveaux Mélanges*, Tomes I., p. 427; II., pp. 64, 88, and 89–97, for a series of notices concerning the Mongol generals and history.

[2] Compare Wylie in the *R. A. Soc. Jour.*, Vol. V. (N.S.), p. 14; Fergusson, *Hist. Ind. and East. Architecture*, p. 708; Yule's *Polo*, I., pp. 28, 409.

[3] This should be Kaishau-kulluk khan, called *Kai-sang* in Chinese. Rémusat, *Nouveaux Mélanges*, Tome II., pp. 1–4.

GATEWAY OF THE YUEN DYNASTY, KŪ-YUNG KWAN, GREAT WALL.

revolt, and finally expelled the Mongols, A.D. 1368, after a duration of eighty-nine years.[1]

Like most of the preceding dynasties, the new one established itself on the misrule, luxury, and weakness of its predecessors; the people submitted to a vigorous rule, as one which exhibited the true exposition of the decrees of Heaven, and upheld its laws and the harmony of the universe; while a weak sovereign plainly evinced his usurpation of the "divine utensil" and unfitness for the post by the disorders, famines, piracies, and insurrections which afflicted the mismanaged State, and which were all taken by ambitious leaders as evidences of a change in the choice of Heaven, and reasons for their carrying out the new selection which had fallen on them. Amid all the revolutions in China, none have been founded on principle; they were mere mutations of masters, attended with more or less destruction of life, and no better appreciation of the rights of the subject or the powers of the rulers. Nor without some knowledge of the high obligations man owes his Maker and himself is it easy to see whence the sustaining motive of free religious and political institutions can be derived.

XXV. The MING, *i.e.*, 'BRIGHT dynasty.'—The character of Hungwu, as Chu Yuen-chang called his reign on his accession, has been well drawn by Rémusat, who accords him a high rank for the vigor and talents manifested in overcoming his enemies and cementing his power. He established his capital at Nanking, or the 'Southern Capital,' and after a reign of thirty years transmitted the sceptre to his grandson, Kienwăn, a youth of sixteen. Yungloh, his son, dissatisfied with this arrangement, overcame his nephew and seized the crown after five years, and moved the capital back to Peking in 1403. This prince is distinguished for the code of laws framed under his auspices, which has, with some modifications and additions, ever since remained as the basis of the administration. During the reign of Kiahtsing the Portuguese came to China, and in that of Wanleih, about 1580, the Jesuits gained an entrance into the

[1] One of the causes of their easy overthrow is stated to have been the enormous robbery of the people by the lavish issue of paper money, which at last became worthless.

country. In his time, too, the Niu-chih, or Kin, whom Genghis had driven away in 1235, again became numerous and troublesome, and took possession of the northern frontiers. The first chieftain of the Manchus who attained celebrity was Tienming, who in 1618 published a manifesto of his designs against the house of Ming, in which he announced to Heaven the seven things he was bound to revenge. These consisted of petty oppressions upon persons passing the frontiers, assisting his enemies, violating the oath and treaty of peace entered into between the two rulers, and killing his envoys. The fierce nomad had already assumed the title of Emperor, and "vowed to celebrate the funeral of his father with the slaughter of two hundred thousand Chinese." Tienming overran the north-eastern parts of China, and committed unsparing cruelties upon the people of Liautung, but died in 1627, before he had satisfied his revenge, leaving it and his army to his son Tientsung.

The Chinese army fought bravely, though unsuccessfully, against the warlike Manchus, whose chief not only strove to subdue, but endeavored, by promises and largesses, to win the troops from their allegiance. The apparently audacious attempt of this small force to subdue the Chinese was assisted by numerous bodies of rebels, who, like wasps, sprung up in various parts of the country, the leaders of each asserting his claims to the throne, and all of them rendering their common country an easier prey to the invader. One of them, called Lí Tsz'-ching, attacked Peking, and the last Emperor Hwai-tsung, feeling that he had little to hope for after the loss of his capital, and had already estranged the affections of his subjects by his ill conduct, first stabbed his daughter and then hung himself, in 1643, and ended the house of Ming, after two hundred and seventy-six years. The usurper received the submission of most of the eastern provinces, but the Chinese general, Wu San-kwei, in command of the army on the north, refused to acknowledge him, and, making peace with the Manchus, invoked the aid of Tsungteh in asserting the cause of the rightful claimant to the throne. This was willingly agreed to, and the united army marched to Peking and speedily entered the capital, which the rebel chief had left a heap of ruins when he took away his booty. The

Manchus now declared themselves the rulers of the Empire, but their chief dying, his son Shunchí, who at the age of six succeeded his father in 1644, is regarded as the first Emperor; his uncle, Aina-wang, ruled and reorganized the administration in his name.

XXVI. The TSING,[1] *i.e.*, 'PURE dynasty.'—During the eighteen years he sat upon the throne Shunchí and his officers subdued most of the northern and central provinces, but the maritime regions of the south held out against the invaders, and one of the leaders, by means of his fleets, carried devastation along the whole coast. The spirit of resistance was in some parts crushed, and in others exasperated by an order for all Chinese to adopt as a sign of submission the Tartar mode of shaving the front of the head and braiding the hair in a long queue. Those who gave this order, as Davis remarks, must have felt themselves very strong before venturing so far upon the spirit of the conquered, and imposing an outward universal badge of surrender upon all classes of the people. "Many are the changes which may be made in despotic countries, without the notice or even the knowledge of the larger portion of the community; but an entire alteration in the national costume affects every individual equally, from the highest to the lowest, and is perhaps of all others the most open and degrading mark of conquest." This order was resisted by many, who chose to lose their heads rather than part with their hair, but the mandate was gradually enforced, and has now for about two centuries been one of the distinguishing marks of a Chinese, though to this day the natives of Fuhkien near the seaboard wear a kerchief around their head to conceal it. The inhabitants of this province and of Kwangtung held out the longest against the invaders, and a vivid account of their capture of Canton, November 26, 1650, where the adherents of the late dynasty had intrenched themselves, has been left us by Martini, an eyewitness. Some time after its subjugation a brave man, Ching Chí-lung, harassed them by his fleet; and his son, Ching

[1] For the origin of the Manchus see Klaproth, *Mémoires sur l'Asie*, Tome I., p. 441.

Ching-kung, or Koxinga, molested the coast to such a degree that the Emperor Kanghí, in 1665, ordered all the people to retire three leagues inland, in order to prevent this heroic man from reaching them. This command was generally obeyed, and affords an instance of the singular mixture of power and weakness seen in many parts of Chinese legislation; for it might be supposed that a government which could compel its maritime subjects to leave their houses and towns and go into the country at great loss, might have easily armed and equipped a fleet to have defended those towns and homes. Koxinga, finding himself unable to make any serious impression upon the stability of the new government, went to Formosa, drove the Dutch out of Zealandia, and made himself master of the island.[1]

Shunchí died in 1661 and was succeeded by his son Kanghí,[2] who was eight years old at his accession, and remained under guardians till he was fourteen, when he assumed the reins of government, and swayed the power vested in his hands with a prudence, vigor, and success that have rendered him more celebrated than almost any other Asiatic monarch. It was in 1661 that Louis XIV. had assumed the sovereignty of France at about the same age, and for fifty-four years the reigns of these two monarchs ran parallel. During Kanghí's unusually long reign of sixty-one years (the longest in Chinese annals, except Taimao of the Shang dynasty, B.C. 1637–1562), he extended his dominions to the borders of Kokand and Badakshan on the west, and to the confines of Tibet on the south-west, simplifying the administration and consolidating his power in every part of his vast dominions. To his regulations, perhaps, are mainly owing the unity and peace which the Empire has exhibited for more than a century, and which has produced the impression abroad of the unchangeableness of Chinese institutions and character. This may be ascribed, chiefly, to his indefatigable applica-

[1] Compare the interesting translation from a Chinese record of the capture of Fort Zealandia, by H. E. Hobson, *Journal of N. C. Br. R. A. Society*, No. XI., Art. I., 1876.

[2] Rémusat, *Nouveaux Mélanges*, Tome II., pp. 21–44; Bouvet, *Life of Kanghí;* Gutzlaff, *Life of Kanghí*.

tion to all affairs of State, to his judgment and penetration in the choice of officers, his economy in regard to himself and liberal magnificence in everything that tended to the good of his dominions, and his sincere desire to promote the happiness of his people by a steady and vigorous execution of the laws and a continual watchfulness over the conduct of his high officers. These qualities have perhaps been unduly extolled by his foreign friends and biographers, the Romish missionaries, and if their expressions are taken in their strictest sense, as we understand them, they do elevate him too high. He is to be compared not with Alfred or William III. of England, Louis IX. or Henry IV. of France, and other European kings, but with other Chinese and Asiatic princes, few of whom equal him. The principal events of his long reign are the conquest of the Eleuths, and subjugation of several tribes lying on the north and south of the Tien shan ; an embassy across the Russian Possessions in 1713 to the khan of the Tourgouth Tartars, preparatory to their return to the Chinese territory; the settlement of the northern frontier between himself and the czar, of which Gerbillon has given a full account ; the survey of the Empire by the Romish missionaries ; and the publication of a great thesaurus of the language. In many things he showed himself liberal toward foreigners, and the country was thrown open to their commerce for many years.

His son Yungching succeeded in 1722, and is regarded by many natives as superior to his father. He endeavored to suppress Christianity and restore the ancient usages, which had somewhat fallen into desuetude during his father's sway, and generally seems to have held the sceptre to the benefit of his subjects. Yungching is regarded as an usurper, and is said to have changed the figure four to fourteen on the billet of nomination, himself being the fourteenth son, and the fourth being absent in Mongolia, where he was soon after arrested and imprisoned, and subsequently died in a palace near Peking; whether he was put to death or not is uncertain. Kienlung succeeded Yungching in 1736, and proved himself no unworthy descendant of his grandfather Kanghí; like him he had the singular fortune to reign sixty years, and for most of that period in peace.[1] Some local insurrections disturbed the general tranquillity, principally among the aborigines in Formosa and Kweichau, and in an unprovoked attack upon Birmah his armies sustained a signal defeat and were obliged to retreat. The incursions of the Nipalese into Tibet induced the Dalai Lama to apply to him for assistance, and in doing so he contrived to establish a guardianship over the whole country, and place bodies of troops in all the important positions, so that in effect he annexed that vast region to his Empire, but continued the lamas in the internal administration.

During his long reign Kienlung exhausted the resources of his Empire by building useless edifices and keeping up large armies. He received embassies from the Russians, Dutch, and English, by which the character of the Chinese and the nature of their country became better known to western nations. These embassies greatly strengthened the impression on the side of the Chinese of their superiority to all other nations, for they looked upon them as acknowledgments on the part of the governments who sent them of their allegiance to the court of Peking. The presents were regarded as tribute, the ambassadors as deputies from their masters to acknowledge the supremacy of the Emperor, and the requests they made for trade as rather another form of receiving presents in return than a mutual arrangement for a trade equally beneficial to both. Kienlung abdicated the throne in favor of his fifth son and retired with the title of *Supreme Emperor*, while his son, Kiaking, had that of Emperor.

The character of this prince was dissolute and superstitious, and his reign of twenty-five years was much disturbed by secret combinations against the government and by insurrections[2] and

---

[1] His character and enthusiasm for literary pursuits merit, on the whole, the lines inscribed by the Roman Catholic missionaries beneath his portrait in the *Mémoires conc. les Chinois:*

> Occupé sans relâche à touts les soins divers
> D'un gouvernement qu'on admire,
> Le plus grand potentat qui soit dans l'univers
> Et le meilleur lettré qui soit dans son Empire.

[2] Among the most serious of these was the revolt of the Peh lien kiao. *Lettres Édifiantes*, Tome III., pp. 291–298, 353, 379, etc. In 1789 the ladrones infested the southern coasts. *Ib.*, Tome II., p. 492.

pirates in and about the Empire. A conspiracy against him broke out in the palace in 1813, where he was for a time in some danger, but was rescued by the courage of his guard and family; one of his sons, Mien-ning, was designated as his successor for his bravery on this occasion. A fleet of about six hundred piratical junks, under Ching Yih and Chang Pau, infested the coasts of Kwangtung for several years, and were at last put down in 1810 by the provincial government taking advantage of internal dissensions between the leaders. The principal scene of the exploits of this fleet was the estuary of the Pearl River, whose numerous harbors and channels afforded shelter and escape to their vessels when pursued by the imperialists, while the towns upon the islands were plundered and the inhabitants killed if they resisted. The internal government of this audacious band was ascertained by two Englishmen, Mr. Turner and Mr. Glasspoole, who at different times fell into their hands and were obliged to accompany them in their marauding expeditions. To so great a height did they proceed that the governor of Canton went to Macao to reside, and entered into some arrangements with the Portuguese for assistance in suppressing them. The piratical fleet was attacked and blockaded for ten days by the combined forces, but without much damage; there was little prospect of overcoming them had not rivalry between the two leaders gone so far as to result in a severe engagement and loss on both sides. The conquered pirate soon after made his peace with the government, and the victor shortly afterward followed the same course. The story of those disturbed times to this day affords a frequent subject for the tales of old people in that region, and the same waters are still infested by the "foam of the sea," as the Chinese term these freebooters.

The reign of Kiaking ended in 1820; by the Emperor's will his second son was appointed to succeed him, and took the style Taukwang. He exhibited more energy and justice than his father, and his efforts purified the administration by the personal supervision taken of their leading members. His reign was marked by many local insurrections and disasters in one quarter or another of his vast dominions. A rebellion in Turkestan in 1828 was attended with great cruelty and treachery on the part of the Chinese, and its leader, Jehangír, was murdered, in violation of the most solemn promises. An insurrection in Formosa and a rising among the mountaineers of Kwangtung, in 1830–32, were put down more by money than by force, but as peace is both the end and evidence of good government in China, the authorities are not very particular how it is brought about.

The rapid increase of opium-smoking among his people led to many efforts to restrain this vice by prohibitions, penalties, executions, and other means, but all in vain. The Emperor's earnestness was stimulated by the death of his three eldest sons from its use, and the falling off of the revenue by smuggling the pernicious drug. In 1837–38 the collective opinion of the highest officials was taken after hearing their arguments for legalizing its importation; it was resolved to seize the dealers in it. The acts of Commissioner Lin resulted in the war with Great Britain and the opening of China to an extended intercourse with other nations. Defeated in his honest efforts to protect his people against their bane, the Emperor still fulfilled his treaty obligations, and died in 1850, just as the Tai-ping rebellion broke out.

His fourth son succeeded him under the style of Hienfung, but without his father's earnestness or vigor when the State required the highest qualities in its leader. The devastations of the rebels laid waste the southern half of the Empire, and their approach to Peking in 1853 was paralyzed by floods and want of supplies more than by the imperial troops. A second war with Great Britain, in 1858–60, completely broke down the seclusion of China, and at its conclusion an inglorious reign of eleven years ended at Jeh-ho in August, 1860. His only son succeeded to the throne at the age of five years, under the style of Tungchí; the government being under the control of two Empress-regents and Prince Kung, his uncle. During his reign of twelve years the vigor of the new authorities succeeded in completely quelling the Tai-ping rebellion, destroying the Mohammedan rising in Yunnan and Kansuh, and opening up diplomatic intercourse with the Treaty Powers. Just as the

Emperor began to exercise his authority, he died in January, 1875, without issue. The vacant "utensil" has been filled by the appointment of his cousin, a boy of four years, whose reign was styled Kwangsü. Affairs continue to be conducted by the same regency as before, now still more conversant with the new relations opening up with other lands. The real Empress-dowager, or *Tung Kung*, died April 18, 1881.

So far as can be judged from the imperfect data of native historians of former days, compared with the observations of foreigners at present, there is little doubt that this enormous population has been better governed by the Manchus than under the princes of the Ming dynasty; there has been more vigor in the administration of government and less palace favoritism and intrigue in the appointment of officers, more security of life and property from the exactions of local authorities, bands of robbers, or processes of law; in a word, the Manchu sway has well developed the industry and resources of the country, of which the population, loyalty, and content of the people are the best evidences.

The sovereigns of the Ming and Tsing dynasties, being more frequently mentioned in history than those of former princes, are here given, with the length of their reigns. For convenience of reference a table of the dynasties is appended, taken from the author's *Syllabic Dictionary of the Chinese Language*. In this list, compiled from a Chinese work (the *Digest of the Reigns of Emperors and Kings*), the Tsin and After Tsin dynasties are joined in one (No. 4), making a total of twenty-six dynasties.[1]

The whole number of acknowledged sovereigns in the twenty-six dynasties, according to the received Chinese chronology, from Yu the Great to Kwangsü, is 238, or 246 commencing with Fuh-hí; by including the names of some ursurpers and moribund claimants, the first number is increased to 250. From Yu the Great to the accession of Kwangsü (B.C. 2205 to A.D. 1875) is 4,080 years, which gives to each dynasty a duration of 157

[1] Compare the Chinese Chronological Tables by W. F. Mayers in *N. C. Br. R. A. S. Journal*, No. IV., Art. VIII., 1867.

Kwoh Hiao, or Reigning Title.	Miao Hiao, or Temple Title.	Began to Reign.	Length of Reign.	Contemporary Monarchs.
1. Hungwu....	Taitsu.........	1368	30	Tamerlane, Richard II., Robert II.
2. Kienwan....	Kienwan tí	1398	5	Manuel-Paleologus, Henry IV. of Eng.
3. Yungloh....	Taitsung.......	1403	22	James I., Henry V., Martin V.
4. Hunghi.....	Jintsung.......	1425	1	Amurath II., Henry VI., Charles VII.
5. Siuentih	Siuentsung.....	1426	10	Albert II., Cosmo de Medicis.
6. Chingtung ..	Yingtsung	1436	21	James II., Fred. III. of Aus., Nich. V.
7. Kingtai.....	Kingtí.........	1457	8	Mahomet II., Edward IV., Sixtus IV.
8. Chinghwa...	Hientsung	1465	23	James III., Ferd. and Isabella, Louis XI.
9. Hungchí....	Hiautsung	1488	18	Bajazet II., James IV., Henry VII.
10. Chingtih....	Wutsung.......	1506	16	James V., Henry VIII., Charles V.
11. Kiahtsing...	Shítsung.......	1522	45	Solyman II., Mary, Philip II., Henry II.
12. Lungking...	Muhtsung......	1567	6	Selim II., Elizabeth, Gregory III.
13. Wanleih	Shintsung......	1573	47	James I., Henry IV., Louis XIII.
14. Taichang ...	Kwangtsung ...	1620	1	Othman II., Philip IV., Gregory XV.
15. Tienkí......	Hítsung	1621	7	Amurath IV., Charles I., Urban VIII.
16. Tsungching.	Hwaitsung.....	1628	16	Innocent X., Frederick the Great.
1. Shunchí[1] ...	Chang hwangtí.	1644	18	Mahomet IV., Cromwell, Louis XIV.
2. Kanghí	Jin hwangtí ...	1662	61	Charles II., Clement IX., Sobieskv.
3. Yungching..	Hien hwangtí..	1723	13	Mahomet V., George II., Louis XV.
4. Kienlung ...	Shun hwangtí..	1736	60	Osman III., George III., Clement XIV
5. Kiaking	Jui hwangtí	1796	25	Selim III., Napoleon, Fred. Wm. II.
6. Taukwang ..	Ching hwangtí .	1821	30	Mahmoud, George IV., Louis XVIII.
7. Hienfung ...	Hien hwangtí ..	1851	11	Mahmoud, Victoria, Louis XVIII.
8. Tungchí	....	1862	12	Napoleon III., Alexander II.
9. Kwangsü[2] ..	....	1875		

Dynasty.	Number of Sovereigns.	Began.	Ended.	Duration.
1. Hia	Seventeen, averaging 26 years to each monarch's reign	B.C. 2205	B.C. 1766	439
2. Shang	Twenty-eight, averaging 23 years............	1766	1122	644
3. Chau	Thirty-four, averaging 25½ years	1122	255	867
4. Tsin........	Two, one reigning 37 years, the second 3 years.	255	206	40
5. Han........	Fourteen, averaging 16½ years	206	A.D. 25	231
6. East Han...	Twelve, averaging 16½ years...............	A.D. 25	221	196
7. After Han..	Two, one reigning 2, the other 41 years......	221	264	43
8. Tsin........	Four, averaging 14¼ years	265	322	57
9. East Tsin ..	Eleven, averaging about 9½ years	323	419	106
10. Sung	Eight, averaging 7¼ years	420	478	58
11. Tsí.........	Five, averaging 4⅜ years	479	502	23
12. Liang.......	Four, one 48 years, and three together 7 years.	502	556	54
13. Chin	Five, averaging about 6½ years	557	589	32
14. Sui.........	Three, one reigning 16, another 12, and another 2 years..............	589	619	30
15. Tang	Twenty, averaging 14⅛ years	620	907	287
16. After Liang.	Two, one 8 and one 7 years	907	923	16
17. After Tang .	Four, averaging 3¼ years.................	923	936	13
18. After Tsin..	Two, one 7 and one 3 years	936	946	10
19. After Han..	Two, one 3 years, another 1 year	947	951	4
20. After Chau .	Three, averaging 3 years.................	951	960	9
21. Sung	Nine, averaging 18½ years................	960	1127	167
22. South Sung.	Nine, averaging 17 years	1127	1280	153
23. Yuen.......	Nine, averaging 9⅝ years	1280	1368	88
24. Ming	Sixteen, averaging 17 years..............	1368	1644	276
25. Tsing	Eight up to 1875, averaging nearly 30 years..	1644		

[1] Shunchí and the four following monarchs are named in Manchu, Chidzueldimbukhé, Elkhe taifin, Khowaligasoun tob, Abkai wekhiyekhe, and Saichunga fengchen, respectively.

[2] Kwangsü was born August 14, 1871.

years, and to each monarch an average of 17 1/7 years. From Wu wang's accession to Kwangsü is 2,997 years, giving an average of 125 years to a dynasty and 15 1/2 to each sovereign. From the days of Menes in Egypt, B.C. 2719 to 331, Manetho reckons 31 dynasties and 378 kings, which is about 77 years to each family and 6 1/3 to each reign. In England the 34 sovereigns from William I. to Victoria (A.D. 1066 to 1837) averaged 22 2/3 years each; in Israel, the 23 kings from Saul to Zedekiah averaged 22 years during a monarchy of 507 years.

CHAPTER XVIII.

RELIGION OF THE CHINESE.

As results must have their proportionate causes, one wishes to know what are the reasons for the remarkable duration of the Chinese people. Why have not their institutions fallen into decrepitude, and this race given place to others during the forty centuries it claims to have existed? Is it owing to the geographical isolation of the land, which has prevented other nations easily reaching it? Or have the language and literature unified and upheld the people whom they have taught? Or, lastly, is it a religious belief and the power of a ruling class working together which has brought about the security and freedom now seen in this thrifty, industrious, and practical people? Probably all these causes have conduced to this end, and our present object is to outline what seems to have been their mode of operation.

The position of their country has tended to separate them from other Asiatic races, even from very early times. It compelled them to work out their own institutions without any hints or modifying interference from abroad. They seem, in fact, to have had no neighbors of any importance until about the Christian era, up to which time they occupied chiefly the basin of the Yellow River, or the nine northern provinces as the Empire is now divided. Till about B.C. 220 feudal States covered this region, and their quarrels only ended by their subjection to Tsin Chí Hwangtí, or the 'Emperor First,' whose strong hand molded the people as he led them to value security and yield to just laws. He thus prepared the way for the Emperors Wăn tí (B.C. 179–156) and Wu tí (B.C. 140–86), of the Han dynasty, to consolidate, during their long reigns of twenty-nine and fifty-four years, their schemes of good government.

The four northern provinces all lie on the south-eastern slope of the vast plateau of Central Asia, the ascent to which is confined to a few passes, leading up five or six thousand feet through mountain defiles to the sterile, bleak plains of Gobi. This desolate region has always given subsistence to wandering nomads, and enough to enable traders to cross its grassy wastes. When their numbers increased they burst their borders in periodical raids, ravaging and weakening those whom they were too few to conquer and too ignorant to govern. The Chinese were too unwarlike to keep these tribes in subjection for long, and never themselves colonized the region, though the attempt to ward off its perpetual menace to their safety, by building the Great Wall to bar out their enemies, proves how they had learned to dread them. Yet this desert waste has proved a better defense for China against armies coming from the basin of the Tarim River than the lofty mountains on its west did to ancient Persia and modern Russia. It was easier and more inviting for the Scythians, Huns, Mongols, and Turks successively to push their arms westward, and China thereby remained intact, even when driven within her own borders.

The western frontiers, between the Kiayü Pass in Kansuh, at the extreme end of the Great Wall, leading across the country south to the island of Hainan, are too wild and rough to be densely inhabited or easily crossed, so that the Chinese have always been unmolested in that direction. To invade the eastern sides, now so exposed, the ancients had no fleets powerful enough to attack the Middle Kingdom; and it is only within the present century that armies carried by steam have threatened her seaboard.

The Chinese have, therefore, been shut out by their natural defenses from both the assaults and the trade of the dwellers in India, Tibet, and Central Asia, to that degree which would have materially modified their civilization. The external influences which have molded them have been wholly religious, acting through the persistent labors of Buddhist missionaries from India. These zealous men came and went in a ceaseless stream for ten centuries, joining the caravans entering the northwestern marts and ships trading at southern ports.

In addition to this geographical isolation, the language of the Chinese has tended still more to separate them intellectually from their fellow-men. It is not strange, indeed, that a symbolic form of writing should have arisen among them, for the Egyptians and Mexicans exhibit other fashions of ideographic writing, as well as its caprices and the difficulty of extending it. But its long-continued use by the Chinese is hardly less remarkable than the proof it gives of their independence of other people in mental and political relations. Outside nations did not care to study Chinese books through such a medium, and its possessors had, without intending it, shut themselves out of easy interchange of thought. This shows that they could not have had much acquaintance in early times with any alphabetic writing like Sanscrit or Assyrian, for it is almost certain that, in that case, they would soon have begun to alter their ideographs into syllables and letters as the Egyptians did; while the manifest advantages of the phonetic over the symbolic principle would have gradually insured its triumph. In that case, however, the rivalries of feudal States would have resulted, as in Europe, in the formation of different languages, and perhaps prevented the growth of a great Chinese race. In Japan and Corea the struggle between symbols and sounds has long existed, and two written languages, the Chinese and a derived demotic, are now used side by side in each of those kingdoms.

This isolation has had its disadvantageous effects on the people thus cut off from their fellows, but the results now seen could not otherwise have been attained. Their literary tendencies could never have attained the strength of an institution if they had been surrounded by more intelligent nations; nor would they have filled the land to such a degree if they had been forced to constantly defend themselves, or had imbibed the lust of conquest. Either of these conditions would probably have brought their own national life to a premature close.

Isolation, however, is merely a potential factor in this question. It does not by itself account for that life nor furnish the reasons for its uniformity and endurance. These must be sought for in the moral and social teachings of their sages and great rulers, who have been leaders and counsellors, and in the character of the political institutions which have grown out of those teachings. A comparison of their national characteristics with those of other ancient and modern people shows four striking contrasts and deductions. The Chinese may be regarded as the only pagan nation which has maintained democratic habits under a purely despotic theory of government. This government has respected the rights of its subjects by placing them under the protection of law, with its sanctions and tribunals, and making the sovereign amenable in the popular mind for the continuance of his sway to the approval of a higher Power able to punish him. Lastly, it has prevented the domination of all feudal, hereditary, and priestly classes and interests by making the tenure of officers of government below the throne chiefly depend on their literary attainments. Not a trace of Judaistic, Assyrian, or Persian customs or dogmas appears in Chinese books in such definite form as to suggest a western origin. All is the indigenous outcome of native ideas and habits.

The real religious belief and practices of a heathen people are hard to describe intelligibly to those who have not lived among them. Men naturally exercise much freedom of thought in such matters, and feel the authority of their fellow-men over their minds irksome to bear; and though it is comparatively easy to depict their religious ceremonies and festivals, their real belief—that which constitutes their religion, their trust in danger and guide in doubt, their support in sorrow and hope for future reward—is not quickly examined nor easily described. The want of a well understood and acknowledged standard of doctrine, and the degree of latitude each one allows himself in his observance of rites or belief in dogmas, tends to confuse the inquirer; while his own diverse views, his imperfect knowledge, and misapprehension of the effect which this tenet or that ceremony has upon the heart of the worshipper, contribute still further to embarrass the subject. This, at least, is the case with the Chinese, and notwithstanding what has been written upon their religion, no one has very satisfactorily elucidated the true nature of their belief and the intent of their ritual. The reason is owing partly to the indefinite ideas of the people themselves upon the character of their ceremonies, and their consequent inability to give a clear notion of them; partly also to the variety of observances found in distant parts of the country, and the discordant opinions entertained by those belonging to the same sect; so that what is seen in one district is sometimes utterly unknown in the next province, and the opinions of one man are laughed at by another.

Before proceeding with the present outline two negative features of Chinese religion deserve to be noticed, which distinguish it from the faith of most other heathen nations. These are the absence of human sacrifices and the non-deification of vice. The prevalence of human offerings in almost all ages of the world, and among nations of different degrees of civilization, not only widely separated in respect of situation and power, but flourishing in ages remote from each other, and having little or no mutual influence, has often been noticed. Human sacrifices are offered to this day in some parts of Asia, Africa, and Polynesia, which the extension of Christian instruction and power has, it is to be hoped, greatly reduced and almost accomplished the extinction of; but no clear record of the sacrificial immolation of man by his fellow, "offering the fruit of his body for the sin of his soul," has been found in Chinese annals in such a shape as to carry the conviction that it formed part of the belief or practice of the people—although the Scythian custom of burying the servants and horses of a deceased prince or chieftain with him was perhaps observed before the days of Confucius, and may have been occasionally done since his time. This feature, negative though it be, stands in strong contrast with the appalling destruction of human life for religious reasons, still existing among the tribes of Western and Central Africa, and recorded as having been sanctioned among Aztecs and Egyptians, Hindus and Carthaginians, and other ancient nations, not excepting Syrians and Jews, Greeks and Romans.

The other, and still more remarkable trait of Chinese idolatry, is that there is no deification of sensuality, which, in the name of religion, could shield and countenance those licentious rites and orgies that enervated the minds of worshippers and polluted their hearts in so many other pagan countries. No Aphrodite or Lakshmi occurs in the list of Chinese goddesses; no weeping for Thammuz, no exposure in the temple of Mylitta or obscene rites of the Durga-puja, have ever been required or sanctioned by Chinese priests; no nautch girls as in Indian temples, or courtesans as at Corinth, are kept in their sacred buildings. Their speculations upon the dual powers of the *yin* and *yang* have never degenerated into the vile worship of the *linga* and *yoni* of the Hindus, or of Amun-kem, as pictured on the ruins of Thebes. Although they are a licentious people in word and deed, the Chinese have not endeavored to lead the votaries of pleasure, falsely so called, further down the road of ruin, by making its path lie through a temple and trying to sanctify its acts by putting them under the protection of a goddess. Nor does their mythology teem with disgusting relations of the amours of their deities; on the contrary, like the Romanists, they exalt and deify chastity and seclusion as a means of bringing the soul and body nearer to the highest excellence. Vice is, in a great degree, kept out of sight, as well as out of religion, and it may be safely said that no such significant sign as has been uncovered at Pompeii, with the inscription *Hic habitat felicitas*, was ever exhibited in a Chinese city.

To these traits of Chinese character may be added the preservative features of their regard for parents and superiors and their general peaceful industry. If there be any connection between the former of these virtues and the promise attached to the fifth commandment, "That thy days may be long in the land which the Lord thy God giveth thee," then the long duration of the Chinese people and Empire is a stupendous monument of the good effects of even a partial obedience to the law of God, by those who only had it inscribed on their hearts and not written in their hands.

The last point in the Chinese polity which has had great influence in preserving it is the religious beliefs recognized by the people and rulers. There are three sects (*san kiao*), which are usually called Confucianism, Buddhism, and Taoism, or Rationalism; the first is a foreign term, and vaguely denotes the belief of the literati generally, including the State religion. These three sects do not interfere with each other, however, and a man may worship at a Buddhist shrine or join in a Taoist festival while he accepts all the tenets of Confucius and worships him on State occasions; much as a lawyer in England may attend a Quaker meeting or the Governor of a State in America may be a Methodist minister. In China there is no generic term for religion in its usual sense. The word *kiao*, which means 'to teach,' or 'doctrines taught,' is applied to all sects and associations having a creed or ritual; the ancestral worship is never called a *kiao*, for everybody observes that at home just as much as he obeys his parents; it is a duty, not a sect.

No religious system has been found among the Chinese which taught the doctrine of atonement by the shedding of blood; an argument in favor of their antiquity. The State religion of China has had a remarkable history and antiquity, and, though modified somewhat during successive dynasties, has retained its main features during the past three thousand years. The simplicity and purity of this worship have attracted the notice of many foreigners, who have disagreed on various points as to its nature and origin. Their discussions have brought out sundry most interesting details respecting it; and whoever has visited the great Altar and Temple of Heaven at Peking, where the Emperor and his courtiers worship, must have been impressed with its simple grandeur. What was the precise idea connected with the words *tien*, 'heaven,' and *hwang tien*, 'imperial heaven,' as they were used in ancient times, is a very difficult point to determine; the worship rendered to them was probably of a mixed sort, the material heavens being taken as the most sublime manifestation of the power of their Maker, whose character was then less obscured and unknown than in after times, when it degenerated to Sabianism.

These discussions are not material to the present subject, and it is only needful to indicate the main results. The prime idea in this worship is that the Emperor is *Tien-tsz'*, or 'Son of Heaven,' the coördinate with Heaven and Earth, from whom he directly derives his right and power to rule on earth among mankind, the One Man who is their vicegerent and the third of the trinity (*san tsai*) of Heaven, Earth, and Man. With these ideas of his exalted position, he claims the homage of all his fellow-men. He cannot properly devolve on any other mortal his functions of their high priest to offer the oblations on the altars of Heaven and Earth at Peking at the two solstices. He is not, therefore, a despot by mere power, as other rulers are, but is so in the ordinance of nature, and the basis of his authority is divine. He is accountable personally to his two superordinate powers for its record and result. If the people suffer from pestilence or famine he is at fault, and must atone by prayer, sacrifice, and reformation as a disobedient son. One defect in all human governments—a sense of responsibility on the part of rulers to the God who ordains the powers that be—has thus been partly met and supplied in China. It has really been a check, too, on their tyranny and extortion; for the very books which contain this State ritual intimate the amenability of the sovereign to the Powers who appointed him to rule, and hint that the people will rise to vindicate themselves. The officials, too, all springing from the people, and knowing their feelings, hesitate to provoke a wrath which has swept away thousands of their number.

The objects of State worship are chiefly things, although persons are also included. There are three grades of sacrifices, the *great*, *medium*, and *inferior*, the last collectively called *kiun sz'*, or 'the crowd of sacrifices.' The objects to which the great sacrifices are offered are only four, viz.: *tien*, the heavens or sky, called the imperial concave expanse; *tí*, the earth, likewise dignified with the appellation imperial; *tai miao*, or the great temple of ancestors, wherein the tablets of deceased monarchs of this dynasty are placed; and, lastly, the *shié tsih*, or gods of the land and grain, the special patrons of each dynasty. The tablets representing these four great objects are placed on an equality by the present monarchs, which is strong presumptive proof that by *tien* is now meant the material heavens.

The medium sacrifices are offered to nine objects: The sun, or "great light," the moon, or "night light," the manes of the emperors and kings of former dynasties, Confucius, the ancient patrons of agriculture and silk, the gods of heaven, earth, and the cyclic year. The first six have separate temples erected for their worship in Peking. The inferior herd of sacrifices are offered to the ancient patron of the healing art and the innumerable spirits of deceased philanthropists, eminent statesmen, martyrs to virtue, etc.; clouds, rain, wind, and thunder; the five celebrated mountains, four seas, and four rivers; famous hills, great watercourses, flags, triviæ, gods of cannon, gates, queen goddess of earth, the north pole, and many other things. The State religion has been so far corrupted from its ancient simplicity, as given in the *Shu King* and *Lí Kí*, as to include gods terrestrial and stellar, ghosts infernal, flags, and cannon, as well as idols and tablets, the effigies and mementoes of deified persons.

The personages who assist the Emperor in his worship of the four superior objects, and perform most of the ceremonies, belong to the Imperial Clan and the Board of Rites; but while they go through with the ceremony, he, as pontifex maximus, refuses to pay the same homage that he demands of all who approach him, and puts off these superior Powers with three kneelings and nine profound bows. When he is ill, or in his minority, these services are all forborne, for they cannot properly be done by a substitute. When he worships Heaven he wears robes of a blue color, in allusion to the sky; and when he worships earth he puts on yellow to represent the clay of this earthly clod; so, likewise, he wears red for the sun and pale white for the moon. The princes, nobles, and officers who assist are clad in their usual court dresses, but no priests or women are admitted. The worship of Yuenfí, the goddess of silk, is alone, as we have seen, conducted by the Empress and her court. The temple of the sun is east, and that of the moon west of the city, and at the equinoxes a regulus, or prince of the Imperial Clan, is commissioned to perform the requisite ceremonies and offer the appointed sacrifices.

The winter solstice is the great day of this State worship. The Emperor goes from his palace the evening before, drawn by an elephant in his state car and escorted by about two thousand grandees, princes, musicians, and attendants, down to the Temple of Heaven. The cortége passes out by the southern road, reaching the Ching Yang Gate, opened only for his Majesty's use, and through it goes on two miles to the *Tien Tan.* He first repairs to the *Chai Kung,* or 'Palace of Fasting,' where he prepares himself by lonely meditation for his duty; "for the idea is that if there be not pious thoughts in his mind the spirits of the unseen will not come to the sacrifice." To assist him he looks at a copper statue, arrayed like a Taoist priest, whose mouth is covered by three fingers, denoting silence, while the other hand bears a tablet inscribed with 'Fast three days.' When the worship commences, and all the officiating attendants are in their places, the animals are killed, and as the odor of their burning flesh ascends to convey the sacrifice to the gods, the Emperor begins the rite, and is directed at every step by the masters of ceremonies. The worship to Heaven is at midnight, and the numerous poles around the great altar, and the fires in the furnaces shedding their glare over the marble terraces and richly dressed assembly, render this solemnity most striking.[1]

The hierophants in this worship of nature, so lauded by some infidels, are required to prepare themselves for the occasion by fasting, ablutions, change of garments, separation from their wives and pleasurable scenes, and from the dead; "for sickness and death defile, while banqueting dissipates the mind and unfits it for holding communion with the gods." The sacrifices consist of calves, hares, deer, sheep, or pigs, and the offerings of silks, grain, jade, etc. No garlands are placed on the victim when its life is taken, nor is the blood sprinkled on any particular spot or article. "The idea is that of a banquet; and when a sacrifice is performed to the supreme spirit of Heaven, the honor paid is believed by the Chinese to be increased by inviting other guests. The Emperors invite their ancestors to sit at the banquet with *Shangtí*. A father is to be honored as heaven, and a mother as earth. In no way could more perfect reverence be shown than in placing a father's tablet on the altar with that of Shangtí." To these remarks of Dr. Edkins explanatory of this union of the objects worshipped, it may be added that the Emperors regard their predecessors of every dynasty as still invested with power in Hades, and therefore invoke their blessing and presence by sacrifice and prayers.

[1] Compare the frontispiece of Volume I.; also *ibid.*, p. 76.

The statutes annex penalties of fines or blows in various degrees of punishment in case of informality or neglect, but "in these penalties there is not the least allusion to any displeasure of the things or beings worshipped; there is nothing to be feared but man's wrath—nothing but a forfeiture or a fine." Heavier chastisement, however, awaits any of the common people or the unauthorized who should presume to state their wants to high Heaven or worship these objects of imperial adoration; strangulation or banishment, according to the demerits of the case, would be their retribution. The *ignobile vulgus* may worship stocks and stones in almost any form they please, but death awaits them if they attempt to join the Son of Heaven, the Vicegerent of Heaven and Earth, in his adorations to the supposed sources of his power.[1]

In his capacity of Vicegerent, High Priest, and Mediator between his subjects and the higher Powers, there are many points of similarity between the assumptions of the Emperor and of the Pope at Rome. The idea the Chinese have of heaven seems to be pantheistic, and in worshipping heaven, earth, and terrestrial gods they mean to include and propitiate all superior powers. If, as seems probable, the original idea of *Shangtí*, as it can be imperfectly gleaned from early records, was that of a supreme Intelligence, it has since been lost. Of this worship, the effects in China upon the nation have been both positive and negative. One of the negative influences has been to dwarf the State hierarchy to a complete nullity—to prevent the growth of a class which could or did use the power of the monarchy to strengthen its own hold upon the people as their religious advisers, and on the government as a necessary aid to its efficiency.

The High Priests of China love power and adulation too well to share this worship with their subjects, and in engrossing it entirely they have escaped the political evils of a powerful hierarchy and the people the combined oppressions of a church

---

[1] *Chinese Repository*, Vol. III., pp. 49–53. Dr. J. Edkins, *Religions of China*, Chap. II.; this chapter, on Imperial Worship, gives a good account of these ceremonies. Legge's *Notions of the Chinese concerning God and Spirits*, pp. 23–36, 41–43, for the forms of prayer used.

and State. We have seen that the popular rights which are so plainly taught in the classics have been inculcated and perpetuated by the common school education; we shall soon see, moreover, that the ancestral worship could not admit the interference of priest, altar, or sacrifice outside of the door-posts. Yet it is probable that all combined would have been too weak to resist the seductive influence of a hierarchy in some form, if it had not been that the Emperor himself would yield his own unapproachable grandeur to no man. Being everything in his own person, it is too much to expect that he is going to vacate or reduce his prerogative, surrender his right to make or degrade gods of every kind for his subjects to worship, weaken his own prestige, or mortify the pride of his fellow-worshippers, the high ministers of State. The chains of caste woven in India, the fetters of the Inquisition forged in Spain, the silly rites practised by the augurs in old Rome, or the horrid cruelties and vile worship once seen in Egypt and Syria—in each case done under the sanction of the State—have all been wanting along the Yellow River, and spread none of their evils to hamper the rule of law in China.

This State religion is, therefore, a splendid and wonderful pageant; but it can no more be called the religion of the Chinese than the teachings of Socrates could be termed the faith of the Greeks. It is, however, intimately connected with the *Ju kiao*, or 'Sect of the Learned,' commonly called Confucianists by foreigners, because all its members and priests are learned men who venerate the classical writings. It is somewhat inappropriate to designate the *Ju kiao* a religious sect, or regard it otherwise than as a comprehensive term for those who adopt the writings of Confucius and Chu Hí and their disciples. The word *ju* denotes one of the literati, and was first adopted A.D. 1150, as an appellation for those who followed the speculations of Chu Hí regarding the *tai kih*, or 'Great Extreme.' This author's comments on the classics and his metaphysical writings have had greater influence on his countrymen than those of any other person except Confucius and Mencius; whose works, indeed, are received according to his explanations.

The remarks of Confucius upon religious subjects were very

few; he never taught the duty of man to any higher power than the head of the State or family, though he supposed himself commissioned by heaven to restore the doctrine and usages of the ancient kings. He admitted that he did not understand much about the gods; that they were beyond and above the comprehension of man; and that the obligations of man lay rather in doing his duty to his relatives and society than in worshipping spirits unknown. "Not knowing even life," said he, "how can we know death?" and when his disciples asked him in his last illness whom he would sacrifice to, he said he had already worshipped. Chu Hí resolved the few and obscure references to Shangtí in the *Shu King* into pure materialism; making nature to begin with the *tai kih*, called *premier principe matériel* by the French, which operating upon itself resolved itself into the dual powers, the *yin* and *yang*.

Sir John Davis compares this production of the *yin* and *yang* to the masculo-femininine principle in the development of the mundane egg in the Egyptian cosmogony, and quotes an extract showing that the idea was entertained among the Hindus, and that the androgyn of Plato was only another form of this myth. The Chinese have also the notion of an egg, and that the *tai kih* was evolved from it, or acted like the process of hatching going on in it, though it may be that with them the introduction of the egg is more for the sake of illustration than as the form of the cause. Some of Chu Hí's philosophical notions have already been quoted in Volume I.[1] His system of materialism captivates his countrymen, for it is far more thoroughly worked out than any other, and allows scope for the vagaries of every individual who thinks he understands and can apply it to explain whatever phenomena come in his way. Heat and cold, light and darkness, fire and water, mind and matter, every agent, power, and substance, known or supposed, are regarded as endued with these principles, which thus form a simple solution for every question. The infinite changes in the universe, the multiform actions and reactions in nature, and all the varied consequences seen and

---

[1] Pp. 683 ff. Canon McClatchie has made a careful translation of Chapter XLIX. of his works, giving his views on cosmogony.

unseen are alike easily explained by this form of cause and effect, this ingenious theory of evolution. With regard to the existence of gods and spirits, Chu Hí affirmed that sufficient knowledge was not possessed to say positively that they existed, and he saw no difficulty in omitting the subject altogether—a species of agnosticism or indifferentism, therefore, which has become the creed of nearly the entire body of educated men in the Empire. His system is also silent respecting the immortality of the soul, as well as future rewards and punishments. Virtue is rewarded and vice is punished in the individual or in his posterity on earth; but of a separate state of existence he or his disciples do not speak.

In thus disposing of the existence of superior powers, the philosophers do not shut out all intelligent agencies, but have instituted a class of sages or pure-minded men of exalted intellects and simple hearts, who have been raised up from time to time by Heaven, Shangtí, or some other power, as instructors and examples to mankind, and who therefore deserve the reverence of their fellows. The office of these *shing jin*, 'perfect men' or saints, is to expound the will of heaven and earth; they did not so much speak their own thoughts as illustrate and settle the principles on which the world should be governed; they were men intuitively wise without instruction, while common people must learn to be wise. Of all the saints in the calendar of the *Ju kiao* Confucius is the chief; with him are reckoned the early kings, Yao and Shun, with King Wăn and his two sons King Wu and Duke Chau; but China has produced no one since the "most holy teacher of ancient times" whom his proud disciples are willing to regard his equal—Mencius being only a "number two saint." The deceased Emperors of the reigning dynasty are canonized as its efficient and divine patrons, but a new line of monarchs would serve them as they did their predecessors, by reducing them to mere spirits. The demonolatry of the learned has gradually become so incorporated with popular superstitions that there is now little practical distinction; every one is willing to worship whatever can promise relief or afford assistance. A student of the classical works naturally adopts their views on these points, without supposing that they militate against worshipping his ancestors, joining the villagers in adoring the goddess of Mercy or any other Buddhistic idol, or calling in a Rationalist to write a charm. He also, on coming into office, expects to perform all the ex-officio religious ceremonies required of him, and add the worship of the Emperor to the rest.

Every magistrate is officially required to perform various idolatrous ceremonies at the temples. The objects of worship are numerous, including many others besides those forming the "herd of inferior sacrifices," and new deities are frequently made by the Emperor, on the same principle that new saints are canonized by the Pope. The worship of certain hills and rivers, and of spirits supposed to preside over particular cities and districts, has prevailed among the Chinese from ancient times, long before the rise of Rationalism or introduction of Buddhism, and is no doubt the origin of this official worship. In every city the *Ching-hwang miao, i.e.*, 'City and Moat Temple,' contains the tutelar divinity of the city called *Ching-hwang*, with other gods, and here on the solstices, equinoxes, new and full moons, etc., officers repair to sacrifice to it and to the gods of the land and grain. Over the door of the one in Canton is written, "Right and wrong, truth and falsehood are blended on earth, but all are most clearly distinguished in heaven."[1] Capt. Loch thus describes the Ching-hwang miao at Shanghai, as it stood in 1842:

In the centre of a serpentine sheet of water there is a rocky island, and on it a large temple of two stories, fitted up for the accommodation of the wealthy public. Pillars of carved wood support the roof, fretted groups of uncouth figures fill up the narrow spaces, while movable lattices screen the occupants from the warmth of the noonday sun. Nothing can surpass the beauty and truth to nature of the most minutely carved flowers and insects prodigally scattered over every screen and cornice. This is the central and largest temple. A number of other light aerial-looking structures of the same form are perched upon the corners of artificial rocky precipices and upon odd little islands. Light and fanciful wooden bridges connect most of these islands, and are thrown across the arms of the serpentine water, so that each sequestered spot can be visited in turn. At a certain passage of the sun the main temple is shaded in front by a rocky eminence, the large masses of which are connected with great art and propriety of taste, but in shape and adjustment most studiously grotesque. Trees and flowers and tufts of grass are planted where art must have been taxed to the utmost to procure them a lodgment. In another part of the garden there is a miniature wood of dwarf trees, with a dell and waterfall; the leaves, fruit, and blossoms of the trees are proportionate to their size. Tortuous pathways lead to the top of the artificial mountain, each turn formed with studied art to surprise and charm by offering at every point fresh views and objects. Flowers and creepers sprout out from crevices, trees hang over the jutting crags, small pavilions are seen from almost every vista, while grottoes and rocky recesses, shady bowers and labyrinths, are placed to entrap the unwary, each with an appropriate motto, one inviting the wanderer to repose, another offering a secluded retreat to the philosopher.[1]

Official Chinese records enumerate 1,560 temples dedicated to Confucius attached to the examination halls, the offerings presented in which are all eaten or used by the worshippers; there are, it is said, 62,606 pigs, rabbits, sheep, and deer, and 27,000 pieces of silk, annually offered upon their altars.[2] The municipal temple is not the only one where officers worship, but, like the common people, they bow before whatever they think can aid them in their business or estates. It has already been stated that the duty of Chinese officers extends to the securing of genial seasons by their good administration, and consequently if bad harvests ensue or epidemics rage the fault and removal of the calamity belong to them. The expedients they resort to are both ludicrous and melancholy. In 1835 the prefect of Canton, on occasion of a distressing drought of eight months, issued the following invitation, which would have better befitted a chieftain of the Sechuanas:

Pan, acting prefect of Kwangchau, issues this inviting summons. Since for a long time there has been no rain, and the prospects of drought continue, and supplications are unanswered, my heart is scorched with grief. In the whole province of Kwangtung, are there no extraordinary persons who can force the dragon to send rain? Be it known to you, all ye soldiers and people, that if there be any one, whether of this or any other province, priest or such like, who can by any craft or arts bring down abundance of rain, I respectfully request him to ascend the altar [of the dragon], and sincerely and reverently pray. And after the rain has fallen, I will liberally reward him with money and tablets to make known his merits.

This invitation called forth a Buddhist priest as a "rain maker," and the prefect erected an altar for him before his own office, upon which the man, armed with cymbal and wand, for three

---

[1] *Events in China*, p. 47. London, 1843.

[2] During the Han dynasty (A.D. 59) wine was drunk and sacrifices made to Confucius in the study halls. The victim offered was a dog. Biot, *Essai sur l'Instruction en Chine*, p. 168.

days vainly repeated his incantations from morning to night, exposed bareheaded to the hot sun, the butt of the jeering crowd. The prefect himself was lampooned by the people for his folly, the following quatrain being pasted under a copy of his invitation:

> **Kwangchau's great protector, the magnate Pan,**
> **Always acting without regard to reason;**
> **Now prays for rain, and getting no reply,**
> **Forthwith seeks for aid to force the dragon.**

The unsuccessful efforts of the priest did not render the calamity less grievous, and their urgent necessities led the people to resort to every expedient to force their gods to send rain. The authorities forbade the slaughter of animals, or in other words a fast was proclaimed, to keep the hot winds out of the city, the southern gate was shut, and all classes flocked to the temples. It was estimated that on one day twenty thousand persons went to a celebrated shrine of the goddess of Mercy, among whom were the Governor and Prefect and their suites, who all left their sedans and walked with the multitude. The Governor, as a last expedient, the day before rain came, intimated his intention of liberating all prisoners not charged with capital offences. As soon as the rain fell the people presented thank-offerings, and the southern gate of the city was opened, accompanied by an odd ceremony of burning off the tail of a live sow while the animal was held in a basket.

The officers and literati, though acknowledging the folly of these observances, and even ridiculing the worship of senseless blocks, still join in it. As an example of this: In 1867 a severe drought near Peking called forth a suggestion from a censor that if a white tiger were sacrificed by the Emperor to the dragon the rain would be liberated; for "it was his powerful enemies which kept the rain-god from acting." Wănsiang was deputed to perform the rite; rain came not many days later. The officer laughed, indeed, at the fancy, yet could not disenthrall himself from some degree of belief in its efficacy. Devotees sometimes become irritated against their gods, and resort to summary means to force them to hear their petitions.

It is said that the Governor in Canton, having repeatedly ascended in a time of drought to the temple of the god of Rain, dressed in his burdensome robes, through the heat of a tropical sun, on one of his visits said: "The god supposes I am lying when I beseech his aid; for how can he know, seated in his cool niche in the temple, that the ground is parched and the sky hot?" Whereupon he ordered his attendants to put a rope around his neck and haul his godship out of doors, that he might see and feel the state of the weather for himself. After his excellency had become cooled in the temple the idol was reinstated in its shrine, and the good effects of this treatment were deemed to be fully proved by the copious showers which soon after fell. The Emperor himself on such occasions resorts to unusual sacrifices, and sends his relatives and courtiers almost daily to various temples to pray and burn incense. Imperial patronage of the popular superstitions is sought after by the officers in one way and another to please the people, but it does not involve much outlay of funds.[1] One common mode is to solicit his Majesty for an inscription to be placed over the doorway of a temple, or memorialize him to confer a higher title upon the god. On occasion of a victory over the rebels in Kwangtung in 1822, the shrine of a neighboring deity, supposed to have assisted in obtaining it, received a new title commemorative of the event, and a temple was built for him at the expense of government.

The combined effect of the State religion and classical writings, notwithstanding their atheism and coldness, has had some effect in keeping the people out of the swinish ditch of pollution. It is one of their prime tenets that human nature is originally virtuous, and becomes corrupt entirely by bad precept and example. This is taught children from their earliest years, and officers refer repeatedly to it in their exhortations to obedience; its necessary results of happiness, if carried out, are illustrated by trite comparisons drawn from common life and general ex-

[1] Klaproth cites (among many) an instance of the manner in which favorable auguries are regarded and made use of by officials. *Mémoires sur l'Asie*, Tome I., p. 459.

perience. The Chinese seldom refer to the vengeance of the gods or future punishment as motives for reform, but to the well-being of individuals and good order of society in this world. Examples of this type of human perfection, fully developed, are constantly set before the people in Confucius and the ancient kings he delineates. The classical tenets require duties that carry their own arguments in their obedience, as well as afford matter of thought, while the standard books of Buddhists and Rationalists, where they do not reiterate the same obligations, are mostly filled with unprofitable speculations or solemn nonsense. Consequently the priests of those sects had only the superstitious fear of the people to work upon where reason was at fault, and so could not take the whole man captive; for his reason accorded with the teaching of the classics as far as they went, and only took up with divination and supplication of higher powers where their instructions ceased. The government, therefore, being composed chiefly of such people, educated to venerate pure reason, could not be induced to take the initiatory step of patronizing a religion of such an uncertain character, and confessedly inferior in its moral sanctions to what they already possessed. The current has, more or less, always set this way, and the two other sects have been tolerated when they did not interfere with government. It is too true that the instructions of Confucius and his school are imperfect and erroneous when measured by the standard of revelation. and the people can never emerge from selfish atheism and silly superstition as long as they have nothing better; but the vagaries of the Buddhists neither satisfy the reason nor reprove vice, nor does their celibate idleness benefit society. If the former be bad, the latter is worse.

The sect of the Rationalists, or *Tao kia*, is derived from Lau-tsz', or Lau-kiun. According to the legends he was born B.C. 604, in Ku, a hamlet in the kingdom of Tsu, supposed to lie in Luh-yeh hien, in the province of Honan. His birth was fifty-four years before Confucius. The story is that he had white hair and eyebrows at his birth, and was carried in the womb eighty years, whence he was called Lau-tsz', the 'old boy,' and Lau-kiun, the 'venerable prince.' Nothing reliable about his early life has come down to us, but, as was the case with Hesiod, his disciples have enveloped his actions and character in a nimbus of wonders. M. Julien has given a translation of their history, dated about A.D. 350, in his version of the *Tao Teh King*. Pauthier says he was appointed librarian by the Emperor, and diligently applied himself to the study of the ancient books, becoming acquainted with all the rites and histories of former times. During his life he is reported to have journeyed westward, but the extent and duration of his travel are not recorded, and even its occurrence is reasonably doubted. De Guignes says he went to Ta Tsin, a country under the rule of the Romans, but he forgets that the Romans had not then even conquered Italy; some suppose Ta Tsin to be Judea. His only extant work, the *Tao Teh King*, or 'Canons of Reason and Virtue,'[1] was written in Ling-pao, in Honan, before his travels, but whether the teachings contained in it are entirely his own or were derived from hints imported from India or Persia cannot be decided. It contains only five thousand three hundred and twenty characters, divided into eighty-one short chapters; the text of one edition is said to have been found in a tomb A.D. 574. It has been translated by Julien, Chalmers, and von Strauss. A parallel has been suggested between the sects of the Rationalists of China, the Zoroastrians of Persia, Essenes of Judea, Gnostics of the primitive church, and the eremites of the Thebaid, but a common source for their similarity—the desire of their members, after the sect had become recognized, to live without labor on the credulity of their fellowmen—explains most of the likeness, without supposing that their tenets were derived from each other.

The teachings of Lau-tsz' are not unlike those of Zeno; both recommend retirement and contemplation as the most effectual means of purifying the spiritual part of our nature, annihilating the passions, and finally returning to the bosom of *Tao*. His teachings on the highest subjects of human thought have furnished his countrymen ample materials for the most diverse

---

[1] Perhaps this may be rendered as the *Logos* of Plato, as near as any dogma can be compared to it.

views on these same themes according to their various fancies. In his striving after the infinite he can only describe *Tao* by what it is not and delineate *Teh* as an ideal virtue which no man can attain to. In Chapter XXI. they are thus blended: "The visible forms of the highest *Teh* only proceed from *Tao*; and *Tao* is a thing impalpable, indefinite. How indefinite! How impalpable! And [yet] therein are forms indefinite, impalpable! and [yet] therein are things (or entities). Profound and indistinct too, and [yet] therein are essences. These essences are profoundly real, and therein faith is found. From of old till now its name has never passed away. It gives issue to all existences at their beginnings. How [then] can I know the manner of the beginning of all existences? I know it by this [*Tao*]."

Such teachings are susceptible of almost any explanation, and Julien's extracts from the commentaries give one some idea of their diversity, though probably much well worth reading still lies buried in their pages. The names of sixty-four commentators are known, of whom three were reigning emperors; and their explanations have given their countrymen very doubtful guidance through this mystic book. To those who can compare its aspirations and dogmas with the speculations of Greek and Roman writers, the teachings of the Zendavesta, and the declarations of the Bible, the work of Lau-tsz' becomes of immense interest. His countrymen, however, to whom these great writers were all unknown, have looked upon this system of philosophy rather as the reveries of a wise man than the instructions of a practical thinker.

In Chapter I. he tries to define *tao*. It is reaching after the unknown. "The *tao* which can be expressed is not the eternal *tao*; the name which can be named is not the eternal name. The Nameless [being] is before heaven and earth; when named it is the mother of all things. Therefore, to be constantly passionless is to be able to see its spiritual essence; and to be constantly passionate is to see the forms (or limits) [of *tao*]. These two conditions are alike but have different names; they can both be called a mystery. The more it is examined into the more mysterious it is seen to be. It is the gate of all spiritual things." By the phrases "constantly passionless" and "constantly passionate" are denoted *non-existence* and *existence*, according to the commentators.

In Chapter LXV. there is a similar striving to describe *teh.* "In olden times those who practised *tao* did not do so to enlighten the people, but rather to render them simple-minded. When the people have too much worldly wisdom it makes them hard to govern. He who encourages this worldly wisdom in the government of a State is its misfortune; as he who governs without it is its blessing. To know aright these two things is to have a model State; and the constant exhibition of this ideal is what I call sublime *teh.* This sublime virtue [*teh*] is profound, is incommensurable, is opposed to time-serving plans. If followed it will bring about a state of general accord."

In Chapter XX. the lonely cynic seems to utter his sad cry at the little progress of his teachings. "All men are full of ambitious desires, like those greedy for the stalled ox, or the high delights of spring time. I alone am calm; my affections have not yet germinated; I am as a new-born babe which has not yet smiled on its mother. I am forlorn as one who has no home. All others have and to spare, I alone am like one who has lost all. In mind I am like a fool; I am all in a maze. Common people are bright enough; I am enveloped in darkness. Common people are sagacious enough; I am in gloom and confusion. I toss about as if on the sea; I float to and fro as if I was never to rest. Others have something they can do; I alone am good for nothing, and just like a lout. I am entirely solitary, differing from other men in that I glory in my Mother who nurses [all beings]."

The main object kept in view throughout this work is the inculcation of personal virtue, and Lau-tsz' founds his argument for its practice in the fitness of things, as he tries to prove by referring all the manifestations and laws of mind and matter to the unknown factor *tao.* In Chapter IV. he attempts to embody his struggling thoughts in these few words describing *tao:* "*Tao* is a void; still if one uses it, it seems to be inexhaustible. How profound it is! It seems like the patriarch of all things.

It softens sharp things, loosens tangled things, harmonizes brilliant things, and assimilates itself to worldly things of the dust. How tranquil it is! It seems to endure perpetually. I know not whose son it is. It seems so have existed before *Tí* [or Shangtí]."

Such utterances as these carry neither comfort nor repentance to the sorrowing, sinful heart of man; he cannot go to such an abnegation for guidance or relief in his troubles, and therefore the maxims of Lau-tsz' have fallen on callous hearts. Another extract, Chapter XLIX., is, however, more practical; it is not the only one which furnishes instruction of the highest character. "The perfect man [*shing jin*] has no immutable sentiments of his own, [for] he makes the mind of mankind his own. He who is good, I would meet with goodness; and he who is not good, I would still also meet with goodness; [for] *teh* is goodness. He who is sincere I would meet with sincerity; and he who is insincere, I would still also meet with sincerity; [for] *teh* is sincerity. The perfect man dwells in the world calm and reserved, his soul preserving the same regard for all mankind. The people all turn their eyes and ears toward him, and he regards them alike as his children."

In order to better understand these aphorisms, they need to be read with the help of the various commentaries; these furnish us with a better estimate of their value than any other guides. Foreign writers necessarily judge such a work by their own higher standard; as does M. Pauthier when he remarks upon the last extract: "La sagesse humaine ne peut être jamais exprimé des paroles plus saintes et plus profondes." He compares Lau-tsz' to his own countryman Rousseau—and these two had a good deal in common in their sad reflections upon the evils of the times. In another place the French author goes even farther, and regards the vague expressions in Chapter XLII., which show their derivation from the *Yih King*—viz.: "Tao produced one, one produced two, two produced three, and three produced all things"—as the Asiatic form of the doctrine and procession of the Holy Trinity and the biblical idea of the reunion of good men with their Maker!

One more extract from the *Tao-teh King* will fill the space at command; but sententious apothegms like these in Chapter XXXIII. are scattered throughout the book: "He who knows men is wise; [while] he who knows himself is perspicacious. He who conquers men is strong; [while] he who conquers himself is mighty. He who knows when he has enough is rich. He who acts energetically has a fixed purpose in view. He who does not miss his nature endures; [while] he who deceases and still is not extinct has immortality"—referring, as the commentators agree, to the life of the soul after it leaves the body.

Such a work can hardly be accurately translated into a European language; a perusal of all the translations enables one to appreciate this point. Some translators have missed the point of Lau-tsz's teachings by not attending to the parallelisms running through them, where one limb of the couplet illustrates and defines the other. In conclusion, it is still true that the absence of clear exposition on the duties of men in their marital, parental, and fraternal relations; the want of all instruction upon their obligations and rights as members of the family, the village, and the State; and lastly, his silence upon the voice of conscience and the effects of sin upon the soul of man, show that Lau-tsz' was more an ascetic than a philanthropist, more of a metaphysician than a humanitarian.

Mr. Samuel Johnson has indicated the high position this ancient relic holds in his examination of its tenets. "Nothing like this book exists in Chinese literature; nothing, so far as yet known, so lofty, so vital, so restful at the roots of strength; in structure as wonderful as in spirit; the fixed syllabic characters, formed for visible and definite meaning, here compacted into terse aphorisms of a mystical and universal wisdom, so subtly translated out of their ordinary spheres to meet a demand for spiritual expression that it is confessedly almost impossible to render them with certainty into another tongue. . . . It is a book of wonderful ethical and spiritual simplicity, and deals neither in speculative cosmogony nor in popular superstitions. It is not the speculations of an old philosopher, as Chalmers calls it. It is in practical earnest, and speaks from the heart and to the heart. Its religion resembles that of Fenelon or

Thomas à Kempis, combined with a perceptive rationalism of which they were not masters."[1]

The historian Sz'ma Tsien relates an interview which Confucius had with Lau-tsz' when, at the age of thirty-four (B.C. 517), he visited the capital to study the ritual of State worship, at which time the latter would be eighty-seven years old. Dr. Legge gives an account of this meeting, which it is to be wished could be better known, for the account is not very certain. The legendary history amplifies it largely, but in no extravagant style, and quite consonant to their different characters. Sz'ma Tsien makes the elder lecture the younger philosopher in the following style: "Those whom you talk about are dead, and their bones mouldered to dust; only their words remain. When the superior man gets his time, he mounts aloft; but when the time is against him, he moves as if his feet were entangled. I have heard that a good merchant, though he has rich treasures deeply stored, appears as if he were poor; and that the superior man whose virtue is complete is yet to outward seeming stupid. Put away your proud air and many desires, your insinuating habit and wild will. They are of no advantage to you. This is all which I have to tell you." To the reply of Confucius, that he had sought to get *tao* for twenty years, and had sought in vain, Lau-tsz' rejoined in a strain worthy of Diogenes, which Chwang-tsz' thus reports: "If tao could be offered to men, there is no one who would not willingly offer it to his prince; if it could be presented to men, everybody would like to present it to his parents; if it could be announced to men, each man would gladly announce it to his brothers; if it could be handed down to men, who would not wish to transmit it to his chil-

---

[1] Johnson, *Oriental Religions: China*, pp. 862–865. Pauthier, *La Chine*, pp. 110–120. Chalmers, *Speculations of the Old Philosopher*. Julien, *La Livre de la Voie et de la Vertu*, Paris, 1859; this last is the most scholarly work on this classic which has yet appeared. R. von Reinhold, *Der Weg zur Tugend*, Leipzig, 1870. Victor von Strauss, *Laò-Tsì's Taò Tè King, Aus dem Chinesischen ins Deutsche übersetzt*, Leipzig, 1870. See also Doolittle's *Vocabulary*, Vol. II., Part III. T. Watters, *Lao-Tzû, A Study in Chinese Philosophy*, Hongkong, 1870. Dr. Edkins in *Transactions of N. C. Br. R. A. S.* for 1855, Art. IV. F. H. Balfour, *Chuang Tsze's Divine Classic of Nan-hua*, Shanghai, 1881.

dren? Why then can you not obtain it? This is the reason. You are incapable of giving it an asylum in your heart."[1]

Such speculative teachings and waiting till the times were good were not adapted to entertain or benefit, and Confucius understood his countrymen and his own duty much better than Lau-tsz', in doing all he could by precept and practice to show them the excellence of what he believed to be right. The divergence of these two great men sprung from the differences in human minds in all climes and ages. The teachings of the *Tao-teh King*, however, are no more responsible for the subsequent organization and vagaries of the sect of Taoists down to the present time than the New Testament is for the legends of monkery or the absurdities of mystics. M. Bazin has endeavored to show that in China there has been, from early times, a progression from magic to mythology, from mythology to philosophy; and when philosophy began to crystallize into parties and take on an organized discipline of sects, during and after the Han dynasty down to the Tang, they took up the old native mythology against the newly arrived Buddhists, and imitated them by adopting Lau-tsz' as their god and his book as the foundation of their tenets. Previous to this period he was one among the philosophers of the Flowery Land; in time he has been taken as the founder of a system of religion. If the Gnostics had deified Lucretius and taken his poem as their text-book the cases would have been similar.

The earliest writers on Taoism are Chwang-tsz' and Lih-tsz' in the fourth century, who have been amplified by their followers. It is, as Wylie well observes, difficult to educe a well-ordered system out of the motley chaos of modern Taoism, where the pursuit of immortality, the conquest of the passions, a search after the philosopher's stone, the use of amulets, and the observance of fasts and sacrifices before gods, are mixed with the profound speculations of recluses upon abstruse questions of theology and philosophy. Some of the later writers of the Taoists discourse upon Reason in a way that would please Brownson and befit the pages of the *Dial*. The teachings of

[1] Legge, *Chinese Classics*, I. Proleg., p. 65. Julien, *Tao-te King*, Int., p. xxvii.

the ancient and modern transcendentalists are alike destitute of common sense and unproductive of good to their fellow-men. Dr. Medhurst quotes one of the Chinese Rationalists, who praises reason in a marvellous rhapsody:

What is there superior to heaven, and from which heaven and earth sprang? Nay, what is there superior to space and which moves in space? The great Tao is the parent of space, and space is the parent of heaven and earth, and heaven and earth produced men and things. . . . The venerable prince (Reason) arose prior to the great original, standing at the commencement of the mighty wonderful, and floating in the ocean of deep obscurity. He is spontaneous and self-existing, produced before the beginning of emptiness, commencing prior to uncaused existences, pervading all heaven and earth, whose beginning and end no years can circumscribe.

The sectarians suppose their founder was merely an impersonation of this power, and that he whom they call "the venerable prince, the origin of primary matter, the root of heaven and earth, the occupier of infinite space, the commencement of all things, farther back than the utmost stretch of numbers can reach," created the universe. They notice three incarnations of him during the present epoch, one during the Shang dynasty, B.C. 1407, one at the time of Confucius, and a third about A.D. 623, when a man of Shansí reported having seen an old man who called himself Lau-kiun. Only the priests of this sect are regarded as its members; they live in temples and small communities with their families, cultivating the ground attached to the establishment, and thus perpetuate their body; many lead a wandering life, and derive a precarious livelihood from the sale of charms and medical nostrums. They shave the sides of the head and coil the rest of the hair in a tuft upon the crown, thrusting a pin through it, and are readily recognized by their slate-colored robes. They study astrology and profess to have dealings with spirits, their books containing a great variety of stories of priests who have done wonderful acts by their help. The *Pastimes of the Study*, already noticed, is one of these books, and Davis introduces a pleasant story of Chwang and his wife from another work.[1] They long endeavored to find a beverage

[1] *The Chinese*, Vol. II., pp. 113–128. Wylie, *Notes on Chinese Literature*, p. 173. Giles, *Strange Stories from a Chinese Studio*, 1880.

which would insure immortality, and during the Tang dynasty the Emperor and highest officers were carried away with their delusions. The title of 'Heavenly Doctors' was conferred on them, and a superb temple erected to Lau-tsz' in Chang-an, containing his statue; examinations were ordered in A.D. 674, to be held in the *Tao-teh King*, and some of the priests reached the highest honors in the State. Since that time they have degenerated, and are now looked upon as ignorant cheats and designing jugglers, who are quite as willing to use their magical powers to injure their enemies as to help those who seek their aid.

In some places the votaries of Tao, on the third day of the third month, go barefoot over ignited charcoal; and on the anniversary of the birthday of the High Emperor of the Sombre Heavens, "they assemble together before the temple of this imaginary being, and having made a great fire, about fifteen or twenty feet in diameter, go over it barefoot, preceded by the priests, and bearing the gods in their arms. The previous ceremonies consist in chanting prayers, ringing bells, sprinkling holy water, blowing horns, and brandishing swords in and over the flames in order to subdue the demon, after which they dart through the devouring element. They firmly assert that if they possess a sincere mind they will not be injured by the fire, but both priests and people get miserably burnt on these occasions.[1] Yet such is the delusion, and the idea the people entertain of the benefit of these services, that they willingly contribute large sums to provide the sacrifices and pay the performers."[2]

This ceremony is practised in Fuhkien and at Batavia, but is not very general, for the Chinese are the antipodes of the Hindus in their endurance and relish for sufferings and austerities in the hope of obtaining future happiness. The Rationalists worship a great variety of idols, among which *Yuh-hwang Shangtí* is one of the highest; their pantheon also includes genii, devils, inferior spirits, and numberless other objects of

[1] Compare Escayrac de Lauture, *Mémoire sur la Chine, Religion*, pp. 87, 102. Yule's *Marco Polo*, Vol. I., p. 286. Also Bode's *Bokhara*, p. 271, for a similar practice among the Moslems.

[2] Medhurst's *China, its State and Prospects*, p. 168.

worship. The *Siu Shin Ki*, or 'Records of Researches concerning the Gods,' contains an account of the birth of the deity whose anniversary is celebrated as above described.

There was once a childless emperor called Tsingtih ('Pure Virtue'), who summoned a large company of Tao priests to perform their rites in his behalf, and continued their worship half a year. The Empress Pao Yueh-kwang ('Gemmeous Moonlight') on a night dreamed that she saw the great and eminent Lau-kiun, together with a large number of superior deities, riding in parti-colored carriages with vast resplendent banners and shaded by bright variegated umbrellas. Here was the great founder Lau-kiun sitting in a dragon carriage, and holding in his arms a young infant, whose body was entirely covered with pores, from which unbounded splendors issued, illuminating the hall of the palace with every precious color. Banners and canopies preceded Lau-kiun as he came floating along. Then was the heart of the Empress elated with joy, and reverently kneeling before him, said: "At present our monarch has no male descendants, and I wishfully beseech you for this child that he may become the sovereign of our hearts and altars. Prostrate I look up to your merciful kindness, earnestly imploring thee to commiserate and grant my request." He at once answered, "It is my special desire to present the boy to you;" whereupon she thankfully received him, and immediately returned from the pursuit of the dream, and found herself advanced a year in pregnancy. When the birth took place a resplendent light poured forth from the child's body, which filled the whole country with brilliant glare. His entire countenance was super-eminently beautiful, so that none became weary in beholding him. When in childhood he possessed the clearest intelligence and compassion, and taking the possessions of the country and the funds of the treasury, he distributed them to the poor and afflicted, the widowers and widows, orphans and childless, the houseless and sick, halt, deaf, blind, and lame.

Not long after this the demise of his father took place, and he succeeded to the government; but reflecting on the instability of life, he resigned his throne and its cares to his ministers, and repaired to the hills of Puming, where he gave himself up to meditation, and being perfected in merit ascended to heaven to enjoy eternal life. He however descended to earth again eight hundred times, and became the companion of the common people to instruct them in his doctrines. After that he made eight hundred more journeys, engaging in medical practice and successfully curing the people; and then another similar series, in which he exercised universal benevolence in hades and earth, expounded all abstract doctrines, elucidated the spiritual literature, magnanimously promulged the renovating ethics, gave glory to the widely spread merits of the gods, assisted the nation, and saved the people. During another eight hundred descents he exhibited patient suffering; though men took his life, yet he parted with his flesh and blood. After this he became the first of the verified golden genii, and was denominated the pure and immaculate one, self-existing, of highest intelligence.[1]

[1] *Chinese Repository*, Vol. X., p. 306.

These figments are evidently a reproduction of the vagaries of Hindu theosophists, and not the teachings of Lau-tsz', but they amuse his followers, to whom his own abstruse utterances are quite unintelligible. The learned Confucianists laugh at their fables, but are still so much the prey of fears as to be often duped by them, and follow even when sure of being deceived.

The organization of the Rationalists is a regular hierarchy. It is under the supervision of the government, which holds the chiefs responsible for the general conduct and teachings of the members. The head resides at Lung-hu Shan in Kiangsí, where is a large establishment, resorted to by many votaries, and gathering in a large revenue from their offerings. When he dies a piece of iron is cast into a well near by, and when it floats the name of his successor is found to be written on it. By their extravagant professions and pretences the priests of this sect maintain their influence over a laity as ignorant and credulous as themselves; their power to delude will only wane with the progress of truth and Christianity. The full history of the authors, divinities, vagaries, and varied fortunes of the Rationalists has yet to be written; when this is done it will illustrate the question King David asked six centuries before Lau-tsz' lived: Who will show us any good? And when his followers are able to say, Lord, lift thou up the light of thy countenance upon us, they will know why he failed to find *La Voie et la Vertu.*[1]

The most popular religious sect is that of the followers of Fuh, Fo, Făt, Hwut, or Fuh-tu, as it is called in different dialects in imitation of the Hindu word *Bodh*, or Truth;[2] this name is sometimes confounded with that of Fuh-hi, one of the early rulers in Chinese history. Their tenets had been promulged in Central Asia for centuries, and were known in Western China, but during the long period of disorders previous to the Han dy-

---

[1] Douglas, *Taouism*, London, 1879; this is by far the most readable account of it. Edkins, *Journal of Shanghai Scien. and Lit. Soc.*, No. III., 1859, pp. 309–314. Mayers, *No. Ch. Br. Roy. As. Soc.*, Vol. VI., 1870, pp. 31–44. Bazin, *Recherches sur l'origine, l'histoire, et la constitution des ordres religieux dans l'empire Chinois*, Paris, 1856, p. 70. Johnson, *Oriental Religions: China*, Part V., pp. 859–904. Nevius, *China and the Chinese*, Chap. IX., New York, 1869. Dr. W. A. P. Martin, *The Chinese*, p. 97, etc.

[2] Hardy enumerates fifty-six modes of writing the name. *Manual*, p. 354.

nasty they found little favor. In A.D. 65 the Emperor Ming ti sent an embassy to India, in consequence—as the Chinese historians say—of having dreamed that he saw the image of a foreign god. The embassy returned in A.D. 67, bringing with it some teachers of the faith to Lohyang. One cannot tell whether it was sent at first at the suggestion of the Rationalists, to seek for a wise man said to have appeared there, or whether, according to others, it arose from the remarkable expression of Confucius, already quoted, "The people of the west have sages [or a sage]." It may have been that this mission was excited by some indistinct tidings of the advent and death of Christ, though there is no trace of such a rumor having reached the land of Sinim. At that epoch they might have heard of or met the Apostles in their first tours through the Roman Empire and Syria.

The incidents in the life of Buddha have been enveloped in so much legendary narrative by his followers in India that the Chinese have placed his birth much too early—B.C. 1027—while the true date is B.C. 623 according to the best authorities; but when his actual mortal life is regarded as one in a series of incarnations, no surprise need be felt at these discrepancies. He was the son of Suddhodana, king of Kapilavastu, a city and country near Nipal, subject to the king of Magadha, now a part of Bahar. His mother, Maya, or Maha-maya déva, died ten days after his birth, which, according to the legends, was accomplished without pain and accompanied by amazing wonders. His name was Siddharta, or the 'Establisher,' until he became a Buddha, *i.e.*, him by whom truth is known. The name Gotama, or Samona-Godam, is a patronymic better known in Siam than China, where another family or clan name, Sakya-muni, is more common. At the age of fifteen he was made heir-apparent; at seventeen he was married to Yashodara, a Brahmin maiden of the Sakya clan, and his son Rahula was born the next year. At twenty-five he determined to become a recluse, and left his prospects and his father's court for an abode in the forest beyond Kapilavastu, in solitary spots "trying various methods to attain mental satisfaction, but in vain." After five years of this ascetic life "he came to the perception of the true condition and wants of mankind," and began his ministry of forty-nine years. He was now a *Buddha*, which is described as "entering into a state of reverie, emitting a bright light and reflecting on the four modes of truth."

He began his preaching at Benares by discourses on the four truths, which was termed the revolving of the wheel of the law. He formed his first disciples into a community, to whom he gave their rules, and when the number increased to fifty-six he sent them over the land to give instruction in the *four miseries*, and carry out the system by which all his disciples were taught they could attain final happiness in nirvana. This system, which exists in full strength to this day, is founded on monastic vows for the individual, living in spiritual communities for the disciples, voluntary poverty and universal preaching. Sakya-muni infused such energy into his followers that in a few years India was covered with their communities; and he developed rules for instruction, employment, punishment, and promotion, which have served ever since. His own life, after his visit to his father in the year 586, when thirty-seven years old, was passed mostly in delivering the *sutras*, or laws, thirty-five discourses in all; these are reverenced by all Buddhists, and copies are held to have moral and hygienic effects on those who do so, and bring good luck to the family and the State. As Sakya-muni lived long enough to see and correct the dangers of his system, at his death, in the year 543, he was able to confer much of his authority on his two chief disciples, Ananda and Kashiapa, and thus hand down the organization to posterity.

The few facts here stated respecting this remarkable man are selected from Hardy's *Manual of Buddhism*, where is given a good digest of the Hindu writers respecting their sage. One thing impresses the reader of this work as a peculiarity of Sakya-muni's teaching, and standing in strong contrast to the Brahminic system that followed it: it is the manner in which he has weakened and almost destroyed the power of the unseen world and of spiritual beings as agencies of restraint upon the heart of man, and of assistance in seeking after good. By his system of good works and self-denials, his followers are brought into such close relationship with the whole creation of invisible beings, into whose presence and fellowship they can enter by their own efforts and mediation, that the moral sanctions of a Supreme Ruler and God over all are neutralized, and the sense of sin in the human conscience done away with. Its removal is put under the control of the soul, and the degree of happiness and power attained in the future world depends on the individual—so many prayers, alms, austerities, and obediences result in so much honor, power, and enjoyment in the coming infinite. The past infinite is also made part of the conscious present, and moral fate worked like physical attraction, innumerable causes producing retributive results for rewards or for punishments. In such a theology, salvation by faith is rendered impossible, and sacrifice for sin by way of atonement useless. In this feature the ancient worship of China and the teachings of Confucius rise superior to Buddhism, and leave the soul of man more open to moral law.

The personal life and character of Buddha presents a wonderful exhibition of virtues, and one is not disposed to weigh the testimony of their reality as drawn out in Hardy's *Manual* so carefully as to neutralize the effect; but the glowing picture of his good actions for his fellow-men given in the fervid lines of Arnold's *Light of Asia*, takes one quite into the realm of fable, engendering the wish that the Confucian Analects and their matter-of-fact details could have been imitated by the disciples of Siddharta. In regard to both these great teachers, Confucius and Buddha, however, one may gladly adopt Dean Stanley's remark, "that it is difficult for those who believe the permanent elements of the Jewish and Christian religion to be universal and divine, not to hail these corresponding forms of truth or goodness elsewhere, or to recognize that the mere appearance of such saintlike or godlike characters in other parts of the earth, if not preparing the way for a greater manifestation, illustrates that manifestation by showing how mighty has been the witness borne to it even under circumstances of such discouragement, and even with effects inadequate to their grandeur."

Buddhist priests are more numerous in China than the Tao sz', and they obtained influence more rapidly over the people. Their demonolatry allows the incorporation of the deities and spirits of other religions, and goes even further, in permitting the priests to worship the gods of other pantheons, so that they could adapt themselves to the popular superstitions of the countries they went to, and ingraft all the foreign divinities into their calendar they saw fit. The Emperors at various times have, moreover, shown great devotion to their ceremonies and doctrines, and have built costly temples, and supported more priests than ever Jezebel did; but the teachings of Confucius and Mencius were too well understood among the people to be uprooted or overridden. The complete separation of the State religion from the worship of the common people accounts for the remarkable freedom of belief on religious topics. Mohammedanism and Buddhism, Taoist ceremonies and Lama temples, are all tolerated in a certain way, but none of them have in the least interfered with the State religion and the autocracy of the monarch as the Son of Heaven. They are, as every one knows, all essentially idolatrous, and the coming struggle between these various manifestations of error and the revealed truths and requirements of the Bible has only begun to cast its shadow over the land. The more subtile conflict, too, between the preaching of the Cross and faith alone in its sacrifice for salvation, and reliance on good works, and priestly interference in every form, has not yet begun at all.

The power of Buddhism in China has been owing chiefly to its ability and offer to supply the lack of certainty in the popular notions respecting a future state, and the nature of the gods who govern man and creation. Confucius uttered no speculations about those unseen things, and ancestral worship confined itself to a belief in the presence of the loved ones, who were ready to accept the homage of their children. That longing of the soul to know something of the life beyond the grave was measurably supplied by the teachings of Sakya-muni and his disciples, and, as was the case with Confucius, was illustrated and enforced by the earnest, virtuous life of their founder. Though the sect did not receive the imperial sanction till about A.D. 65, these teachings must have gradually grown familiar during the previous age. The conflict of opinions which ere long arose between the definite practical maxims of the Confucian moralists, and the vague speculations, well-defined good works and hopeful though unproved promises of future well-being, set forth by the Hindu missionaries, has continued ever since. It is an instructive chapter in human experience, and affords another illustration of the impossibility of man's answering Job's great question, "But how shall man be just with God?" The early sages opened no outlook into the blank future, offered no hopes of life, love, happiness, or reunion of the friends gone before, and their disciples necessarily fell back into helpless fatalism. Buddhism said, Keep my ten commandments, live a life of celibacy and contemplation, pray, fast, and give alms, and according to your works you will become pure, and be rewarded in the serene nirvana to which all life tends. But the Buddhist priesthood had no system of schools to teach their peculiar tenets, and, as there is only one set of books taught in the common schools, the elevating precepts of the sages brought forth their proper fruit in the tender mind. Poverty, idleness, and vows made by parents in the day of adversity to dedicate a son or a daughter to the life-long service of Buddha, still supply that priesthood with most of its members. The majority are unable to understand their own theological literature, and far more is known about its peculiar tenets in Europe than among the mass of the Chinese. The Confucianist, in his pride of office and learning, may ridicule their mummeries, but in his hour of weakness, pain, and death he turns to them for help, for he has nowhere else to go. Both are ignorant of the life and light revealed in the gospels, and cry out, "Who will show us any good?"

If the mythology of Buddhism was trivial and jejune, as we judge it after comparing it with the beautiful imagery and art of Greece and Egypt, it brought in nothing that was licentious in its rites or cruel in its sacrifices. Coming from India, where worship of the gods involved the prostitution of women, the adoration of the lingam, and the sacrifice of human beings, Buddhism was remarkably free from all revolting features. If it had nothing to offer the Chinese higher in morals or more exalted or true in its conception of the universe or its Maker, it did not sanction impurity or murder, or elevate such atrocities above the reach of law by making them sacred to the gods.

This last outrage of the Prince of Darkness on the soul of man, so common in Western Asia, has never been known or accepted to any great extent in the Middle Kingdom.

But, while it is true that Buddhism gave them a system of precepts and observances that set before them just laws and high motives for right actions, and proportionate rewards for the good works it enjoined, it could not furnish the highest standards, sanctions, and inducements for holy living. On becoming a part of the people, the Buddhists soon entered into their religious life as acknowledged teachers. They adapted their own tenets to the national mythology, took its gods and gave it theirs, acted as mediators and interpreters between men and gods, the living and the dead, and shaped popular belief on all these mysteries. The well-organized hierarchy numbered its members by myriads, and yet history records no successful attempts on its part to usurp political power, or place the priest above the laws. This tendency was always checked by the literati, who really had in the classics a higher standard of ethical philosophy than the Buddhists, and would not be driven from their position by imperial orders, nor coaxed by specious arguments to yield their ground. Constant discussions on these points have served to keep alive a spirit of inquiry and rivalry, and preserve both from stagnation. Though Buddhism, in its vagaries and will-worship, gave them nothing better than husks, put hypocrisy in place of devotion, taught its own dogmas instead of truth, and left its devotees with no sense of sin against any law, yet its salutary influence on the national life of China cannot be denied.

The worship of ancestors and of good and bad spirits supposed to pervade and rule this world was perfectly compatible with the reception of Buddhism; thus its priests gradually became the high priests of the popular superstition, and have since remained so. They first ingratiated themselves by making their services useful in the indigenous ritual, and were afterwards looked upon as necessary for its execution. They propagated their doctrines principally by books and tracts, rather than by collecting schools or disciples in their temples; the quiet, indolent life they led, apparently absorbed in books and worship, and yet not altogether estranged from the world, likewise held out charms to some people. China is full of temples, in most of which Buddhist priests are found, but it is not quite the true inference to suppose that all the buildings were erected or the priests hired, because the people wish to do reverence to Buddha. It is impossible to state the proportion in which Buddhist temples are found; there are one hundred and twenty-four in Canton alone, containing idols of every name and attribute, in most of which they live and act as the assistants of whoever comes to worship.

The tenets of Buddhism require a renunciation of the world and the observance of austerities to overcome evil passions and fit its disciples for future happiness.[1] A vow of celibacy is taken, the priests dwelling together for mutual assistance in attaining perfection by worship of Buddha and calling upon his name. They shave the entire head as a token of purity, but not the whole body, as the ancient Egyptian priests did; they profess to eat no animal food, wear no skin or woollen garments, and get their living by begging, by the alms of worshippers, and the cultivation of the grounds of the temple. Much of their support is derived from the sale of incense sticks, gilt paper, and candles, and from fees for services at funerals. In the great monasteries, like the Hai-chwang sz' at Canton, the priests perform the whole service; but in other temples they contrive to gain a livelihood, and many of those better situated derive a large portion of their income from entertaining strangers of wealth and distinction. The sale of charms, the profits of theatrical exhibitions, the fees paid by neighborhoods for feeding hungry ghosts on All-Souls' day, and other incidental services performed for the living or the dead, also furnish resources. Their largest monasteries contain extensive libraries, and a portion of the fraternity are well acquainted with letters, though most of them are ignorant even of their own books. Their moral character, as a class, is on a par with their countrymen, and many of them are respectable, intelligent, and sober-minded persons, who seem

[1] Rémusat terms these tenets not inaptly "a mixture of pantheism, rationalism, and idolatry." In Hardy (*Manual*, p. 212) we find that the *Wá-ling sz'* to five hundred Lo-hán is to honor five hundred rahats. In India this number seems to stand for *all*.

to be sincerely desirous of making themselves better, if possible, by their religious observances.

The liturgy is in Sanscrit transliterated in Chinese characters, with which priest and people are alike unacquainted, nor are there now any bilingual glossaries or dictionaries to explain the words. Dr. Milne, speaking of the use of unknown tongues in liturgies, remarks: "There is something to be said in favor of those Christians who believe in the magic powers of foreign words, and who think a prayer either more acceptable to the Deity, or more suited to common edification, because the people do not generally understand it. They are not singular in this belief. Some of the Jews had the same opinion; the followers of Buddha and Mohammed all cherish the same sentiment. From the chair of his holiness at Rome, and eastward through all Asia to the mountain retreats of the Yama-bus in Japan, this opinion is espoused. The bloody Druids of ancient Europe, the gymnosophists of India, the Mohammedan hatib, the Buddhists of China, the talapoins of Siam, and the bonzes of Japan, the Romish clergy, the vartabeds of the Armenian church, and the priests of the Abyssinian and Greek communions, all entertain the notion that the mysteries of religion will be the more revered the less they are understood, and the devotions of the people (performed by proxy) the more welcome in heaven for being dressed in the garb of a foreign tongue. Thus the synagogue and mosque, the pagan temple and Christian church, seem all to agree in ascribing marvellous efficacy to the sounds of an unknown language; and, as they have Jews and Mohammedans, Abyssinians and pagans, on their side, those Christians who plead for the use of an unknown tongue in the services of religion have certainly the majority. That Scripture, reason, and common sense should happen to be on the other side is indeed a misfortune for them, but there is no help for it."[1]

The following canon for exterminating misfortune is extracted from the Buddhist liturgy, but it is as unintelligible to the Chinese as it will be to the English reader. While repeating it

[1] *Encyclopædia Britannica*, Art. BUDDHISM. *Indochinese Gleaner*, Vol. III., p. 141. *Chinese Repository*, Vol. IX., p. 640. Yule's *Marco Polo*, Vol. II., p 260, and passim.

the priest strikes upon a sounding board called *muh yü*, or 'wooden fish,' shaped somewhat like a skull, in order to mark the time of his monotonous chant:

Nan-mo O-mí-to po-yé, to-ta-kia to-yé, to-tí-yé-ta O-mí-lí-to po-kwăn, O-mí-lí-to, sieh-tan-po-kwăn, O-mí-lí-to, kwăn-kia-lan-tí O-mí-lí-to, kwăn-kia-lan-tí; kia-mí-ní kia-kia-na, chih-to-kia-lí po-po-ho.

Similar invocations, with the name *O-mí-to*[1] *Fuh* (Amida Buddha), are repeated thousands and myriads of times to attain perfection, affording a good illustration of the propriety of our Saviour's direction, "When ye pray, use not vain repetitions as the heathen do; for they think they shall be heard for their much speaking." A plate in one Buddhistic work contains five thousand and forty-eight open dots, arranged in the shape of a pear; each dot to be filled up when the name of Buddha has been repeated a hundred or a thousand times, and then the paper to be burned to pass into the other world to the credit of the devotee. The Buddhists have a system of merits and demerits, of which Sir John Davis remarks that "this method of *keeping a score* with heaven is as foolish and dangerous a system of morality as that of penances and indulgences in the Romish church." In this Buddhist scale of actions, to repair a road, make a bridge, or dig a well, ranks as ten; to cure a disease, or give enough ground for a grave, as thirty; to set on foot some useful scheme ranks still higher. On the other hand, to reprove another unjustly counts as three on the debtor side; to level a tomb, as fifty; to dig up a corpse, as one hundred; to cut off a man's male heirs, as two hundred, and so on. This notion of keeping accounts with heaven prevails among all classes of the Chinese, and the score is usually settled about the end of the year by fasting and doing charitable acts, such as making a piece of road, repairing a temple, or distributing food, to prove their repentance and benefit the world. Festival days are chosen by devout people to distribute alms to the poor, and on such occasions troops of beggars cluster about their doors, holding clap-dishes in their outstretched hands, while the donor stands

[1] *O-mi-to* is derived from *amirta*, or 'deathless.' Hardy, *Manual*, p. 355.

behind the half-opened door dealing out rice to the clamorous crowd which he dares not trust inside.

Considering how few restraints this religion imposes on the evil propensities of the human heart, and how easily it provides for the expiation of crimes, it is surprising that it has not had as great success among the Chinese as among the Tibetans, Birmese, and Siamese. The thorough education in the reasonable teachings of the classics, and the want of filial duty shown by celibates to their parents in leaving them to take care of themselves, have had their effects in maintaining the purer but heartless moralities of the Confucianists. The priests have always had the better judgment of the people against them, and being shut out by their profession from entering into society as companions or equals, and regarded as servants to be sent for when their services were wanted, they can neither get nor maintain that influence over their countrymen which would enable them to form a party or a powerful sect. One of the officers in the reign of Chingtih of the Ming dynasty, Wang Yang-ning, who addressed a remonstrance to his sovereign against sending an embassy to India to fetch thence Buddhist books and priests, relies for his chief argument on a comparison between the precepts and tendency of that faith and the higher doctrines of the classics, proving to his own satisfaction that the latter contained all the good there was in the former, without its nonsense and evil. The opposition to Buddhism on the part of the literati has been in fact a controversy between common sense (imperfectly enlightened indeed) and superstitious fear; the first inclines the person to look at the subject with reference to the principles and practical results of the system, as exhibited in the writings and lives of its followers, while, not having themselves anything to look forward to beyond the grave, they are still led to entertain some of its dogmas, because there may be something in them after all, and they have themselves nothing better. The result is, as Dr. Morrison has observed, "Buddhism in China is decried by the learned, laughed at by the profligate, yet followed by all."

The paraphrase and commentary on the seventh of Kanghí's maxims against strange religions present a singular anomaly;

for while the Emperor Yungching in the paraphrase decries Buddhism and Rationalism, and exalts the "orthodox doctrine," as he terms the teachings of the classics, he was himself a daily worshipper of Buddhist idols served by the lamas. He inveighs against selling poor children to the priests in no measured terms, and shows the inutility and folly of repeating the books or reciting the unintelligible charms written by the priests, where the person never thought of performing what was good. He speaks against the promiscuous assemblage of men and women at the temples, which leads to unseemly acts, and joins in with another of his own class, who remarked, in reference to a festival, that "most of the worshippers are women, who like these worshipping days, because it gives them an opportunity to see and be seen in their fine clothes; and most of the men who go there, go to amuse themselves and look at the women." "The sum of the whole is, these dissolute priests of Buddha are lazy; they will neither labor in the fields nor traffic in the markets, and being without food and clothing, they set to work and invent means of deceiving people." But though this upholder of the good old way well exhibits the follies of these idolatrous sects, he has nothing better to present his countrymen than "the two living divinities placed in the family," nothing to lead their thoughts beyond this world. His best advice and consolation for their troubled and wearied souls is, "Seek not for happiness beyond your own sphere; perform not an action beyond the bounds of reason; attend solely to your own duty; then you will receive the protection of the gods." [1]

The instructions of Sakya-muni himself have now become so interwoven in the additions, ritualism, and errors of his followers during the ages since he died, that he is charged with many things which he probably never taught. Unlike the founders of Islamism and Zoroastrianism, his personal influence and identity have been lost amid the fables which have enveloped his acts, and the diversities of worship and doctrine baffle all explanation. When the patriarchs and missionaries of the sect

---

[1] Milne's *Sacred Edict*, pp. 133–143. *Chinese Repository*, Vol. I., p. 207; Vol. II., p. 265.

began to increase in Central Asia and China after the embassy of Ming tí, they were obliged to defend, explain, and develop their tenets against the Chinese literati, and also commend them to the observance of the people. In the former region their conquests were complete, and the Mongols still hold to the Buddhist faith as completely as the European nations did to popery until the Reformation. The history of Chinese Buddhism down to the present day has not yet been fully examined, but much has been done within the past few years by Julien, Beal, Edkins, Watters, Neumann, Kœppen, and others to make it known. Translations from Chinese Buddhistic travellers and moralists have brought out many obscure opinions and unexpected events in this branch of religious thought and missionary work, during a period of the world's history hitherto quite unknown to Europeans.[1]

The mutual forbearance exhibited by the different sects in China is owing a good deal to apathy, for where there is nothing to reach there is little to stimulate to effort. The government tolerates no denomination suspected of interfering with its own influence, and as none of the sects have any State patronage, none of them hold any power to wield for persecution, and the people soon tire of petty annoyances and unavailing invectives. The Buddhist priesthood is perpetuated mostly by the children given by parents who have vowed to do so in their distress, and by others purchased for serving in large monasteries. Persons occasionally enter late in life, weary with the vexations of the world; Mr. Milne was acquainted with one who had two sons when he took the vows upon him, but gave himself no care as to what had become of them. The only education which most of the acolytes receive consists in memorizing the prayers in the liturgy and reading the canonical works. A few fraternities have tutors from whom they receive instruction.

Nunneries also exist, most of them under the patronage of

---

[1] See Alabaster's *Wheel of the Law*, pp. 228–241, for a well-digested Life of Buddha, from the Siamese. Beal's *Romantic History of Buddha*, and *Catena of Buddhist Scriptures*. Edkins, *Chinese Buddhism*, Chaps. I to VI., gives a good *résumé* of the early progress of the faith. G. Bühler, *Three New Edicts of Asoka*, London (Trübner).

the Holy Mother, Queen of Heaven. The priests advocate their establishment as a good means of working upon the feelings of the more susceptible part of society, to whom they themselves cannot get admittance. The succession among the "sisters" is kept up by purchase and by self-consecration; the feet of children bought young are not bandaged. The novice is not admitted to full orders till she is sixteen, though previous to this she adopts the garb of the sisterhood; the only difference consists in the front part of the head being shaved and the hair plaited in a queue, while nuns shave the whole. It is not easy to distinguish monks from nuns as they walk the streets, for both have natural feet, wear clumsy shoes, long stockings drawn over full trousers, short jackets, and bald pates. Like her sister in Romish countries, the Chinese nun, when her head has been shaved—the opposite of taking the veil, though the hair of both is sacrificed—is required to live a life of devotion and mortification, eat vegetables, care nothing for the world, and think only of her eternal canonization, keeping herself busy with the service of the temple. "Daily exercises are to be conducted by her; the furniture of the small sanctuary that forms a part of the convent must be looked after and kept clean and orderly; those women or men who come to worship at the altars, and seek guidance and comfort, must be cared for and assisted. When there is leisure the sick and the poor are to be visited; and all who have placed themselves under her special direction and spiritual instruction have a strong claim upon her regard. That she may live the life of seclusion and self-denial, she must vow perpetual virginity. The thought of marriage should never enter her head, and the society of men must be shunned. On her death she will be swallowed up in nihility!" In Fuhchau the nunneries were all summarily abolished nearly fifty years ago by an officer who learned the dissolute lives of their inmates. They have not since been reopened for their residence, though this official provided husbands for most of their nuns. Such a proceeding would have been impossible in almost any other country, and shows the functions of Chinese officials for the welfare of society.

Most of them are taught to read the classics as well as their own liturgies, and a few of the sisterhood are said to be well read in the lore of the country. Each nun has her own disciples among the laity, and cultivates and extends her acquaintances as much as she can, inasmuch as upon them her support principally depends. Each of her patrons, whether male or female, receives a new name from her, as she herself also did when her head was shaven. Contributors' names are written or engraved in conspicuous places in the building; casual fees or donations go to the general expenses. Each nun also receives ten cents when public masses are recited for those who have engaged them. Their moral character is uniformly represented as dissolute, but while despised for their profligacy they are dreaded for the supposed power they can exert by means of their connection with spirits. The number of nunneries in the department of Ningpo is stated to be thirty, and the sisterhood in them all to amount to upward of three hundred persons.[1]

The numerous points of similarity between the rites of the Buddhists and those of the Romish church early attracted attention. Abbé Huc enumerates many of them: "The cross, the mitre, the dalmatica, the cope which the lamas wear on their journeys, or when performing some ceremony out of the temple; the service with double choirs, the psalmody, the exorcisms, the censer suspended from five chains, which you can open or close at pleasure; the benedictions given by extending the right hand over the heads of the faithful; the rosary, ecclesiastical celibacy, spiritual retirement, worship of the saints; the fasts, processions, litanies, and holy water—all these are analogies between ourselves and the Buddhists." In addition to these, the institution of nuns, worship of relics, masses for the dead, and burning of candles and incense, with ringing of bells during worship, are prominent usages common to both. Their priests alike teach a purgatory from which the soul can be released by their prayers; they also conduct service in a dead language, and pretend to miracles. Lastly, the doctrine of the perpetual virginity of Maya, the mother of Sakya-muni, is an article taught

[1] *Chinese Repository*, Vol. XIII., pp. 93–98. Doolittle's *Social Life*, I., p. 253. Milne's *Life in China*, pp. 134–146. Gray's *China*, I., pp. 105, 131–135.

by the Mongol Buddhists, who also practise a form of infant baptism, in which the lama dips the child three times under the water as he pronounces its name and gives it a blessing.

These numerous and striking resemblances led the Roman Catholic missionaries to conclude that some of them had been derived from the papal or Syrian priests who entered China before Kublai khan. M. Huc brings forward his hypothesis that Tsong Kaba, the teacher of the Buddhist reformer in Mongolia about that time, had adopted them from some of the Europeans who taught him the Christian doctrines.[1] Others refer them to St. Thomas, but Prémare ascribes them to the devil, who had thus imitated holy mother church in order to scandalize and oppose its rites. But as Davis observes, "To those who admit that most of the Romish ceremonies are borrowed directly from paganism, there is less difficulty in accounting for the resemblance." On this point it will be impossible to reach certainty. There have probably been some things borrowed by each from the other at various ages, without either knowing from whence they came or what were their tendencies. Fergusson shows the great probability that the monastic system, celibacy, and ascetic good works were adopted in the Eastern church from India; but the want of reliable records on either side hitherto has left much to inference and conjecture.

The worship is similar and equally imposing. One eye-witness describes the scene he saw in a Buddhist temple: "There stood fourteen priests, seven on each side of the altar, erect, motionless, with clasped hands and downcast eyes, their shaven heads and flowing gray robes adding to their solemn appearance. The low and measured tones of the slowly moving chant they

---

[1] Huc's *Travels in Tartary*, II., p. 50. Hardy's *Manual*, p. 142. *Missionary Recorder*, III., pp. 142, 181. Eitel, *Lectures on Buddhism*, and *Handbook for the Student of Chinese Buddhism*, Hongkong, 1870. James Fergusson, *Hist. Indian and Eastern Architecture*, Introduction. Rémusat, *Mélanges Posthumes*, p. 44. Klaproth in *Journal Asiatique*, Tome VII. (1831), p. 190; also Tome XI. (IVe Sér.), 1848, p. 535. Prof. E. E. Salisbury in *Journal Am. Or. Soc.*, Vol. I., No. II., 1844. *Jour. of the R. As. Soc.*, passim. Yule's *Marco Polo*, Vol. I., p. 406; also *Cathay and the Way Thither*, II., p. 551. W. Wordsworth, *The Church of Thibet and the Historical Analogies of Buddhism and Christianity*, London, 1877.

were singing might have awakened solemn emotions, too, and called away the thoughts from worldly objects. Three priests kept time with the music, one beating an immense drum, another a large iron vessel, and a third a wooden ball. After chanting, they kneeled upon low stools and bowed before the colossal image of Buddha, at the same time striking their heads upon the ground. Then rising and facing each other, they began slowly chanting some sentences, and rapidly increasing the music and their utterance until both were at the climax of rapidity, they diminished in the same way until they had returned to the original measure. In the meantime, some of the number could not restrain their curiosity, and, even while chanting and counting their beads, left their places to ask for books. The whole service forcibly reminded me of scenes in Romish chapels; the shaven heads of the priests, their long robes, mock solemnity, frequent prostrations, chantings, beads—yea, and their idol, too, all suggested their types, or their antitypes, in the apostate church."[1]

The expulsion of Buddhism from India, after its triumphs in the reign of Asoka, King of Majadha, was so complete that it henceforth divided into the northern and southern schools, the first taking Sanscrit and the other Pali as its sacred language. In the course of time the divergencies became fixed, and thus, without any actual schism, the Buddhists of Ceylon and Ultra Ganges have come to differ from those of Central Asia and China. The form of Buddhism prevailing among the Mongols and Tibetans differs more in its state and power than in its doctrines; it is called Shamanism, or *Hwang kiao* ('Yellow Sect') in Chinese, from the color of the priestly robes—a *Shaman* being one who has overcome all his passions; it is a Hindu word. The Dalai-Lama at H'lassa, in the great monastery of the Putala, is the pope of the religion, the abode of deity.[2] Mongolia swarms with lamas, and the government at Peking aids in sup-

---

[1] *Foreign Missionary Chronicle*, Vol. XIV., p. 300.

[2] For his origin see Klaproth, *Mémoires sur l'Asie*, Tome II., p. 90. Also Rémusat, *Mélanges Posthumes*, pp. 1–64, for some observations on this faith in a review of De Guignes' *Huns*. E. Schlagintweit, *Buddhism in Tibet*, with folio atlas of plates, Leipzig, 1863. J. Summers in *The Phœnix*, I., 1870, pp. 9–11.

porting them in order to maintain its sway more easily over the tribes, though the Manchus have endeavored to supplant the civil authority of the Dalai-Lama and banchin-erdeni, by partially aiding and gradually subdividing their power. The ritual of the Shamans, in which the leading tenets taught by the lamas are exhibited, contains their ten principal precepts, or decalogue, viz.: 1. Do not kill. 2. Do not steal. 3. Do not commit fornication. 4. Speak not falsely. 5. Drink no wine nor eat flesh. 6. Look not on gay silks or necklaces, use no perfumed ointment, and paint not the body. 7. Neither sing nor dance, and do no sleight of hand tricks or gymnastic acts, and go not to see or hear them. 8. Sit not on a high large couch. 9. Do not eat out of time. 10. Do not grasp hold of living images, gold, silver, money, or any valuable thing.[1] The book contains also twenty-four sections of directions as to the conduct to be observed in various places, and before different persons. When using the sacred books the devotee must consider himself to be in the presence of Buddha, and he is forbidden to study books of divination, physiognomy, medicine, drawing lots, astronomy, geography, alchemy, charms, magic, or poetry. No wonder the priests are ignorant when almost every source of instruction is thus debarred them. The number of temples scattered over Mongolia and Tibet and the proportion of priests are far greater than in China, and the literature is not less enormous for bulk than are the contents of the volumes tedious and uninstructive.[2] A good device for a religion of formality to economize time and accommodate ignorance is adopted by the lamas, which is to write the prayers on a piece of paper and fasten them to a wheel carried round by the wind or twirled by the hand; chests are also set up in temples having prayers engraved on the outside

---

[1] *Annales de la Foi*, Tome IX., p. 460.

[2] "The dreariest literature, perhaps," says Professor Whitney, "that was ever painfully scored down, and patiently studied, and religiously preserved" (*Oriental and Linguistic Studies*, Second Series, p. 98). For foreign bibliographies of Buddhism the reader may be referred to *L'Histoire de Çakya-Mouni*, par Foucaux (ad fin.), and Otto Kistner, *Buddha and his Doctrines: A Bibliographical Essay*, London, 1869. See also Trübner's *Record* for 1869, p. 513.

in large letters, and the prayer is repeated as often as the wind or the hand revolves the wheel or chest.

The Buddhist temples present much uniformity in their arrangement, and some of the monastic establishments are among the finest buildings in China. No cave temples are known, but caves have been turned into temples in many places, and miserable places they are for worship. On entering a Buddhist temple, one sees four colossal statues of the Four Great Kings who are supposed to govern the continents on each side of Mount Sumeru and guard or reward the devotees who honor their Lord; they have black, blue, red, and white faces, and usually hold a sword, guitar, umbrella, and snake in their hands. Opposite the door is a shrine containing an image of Maitreya Buddha, or the Merciful One, a very fat, jolly personage, who is to have an avatar three thousand years hence; images of Kwantí, the God of War, and of Wei-to, a general under the Four Kings, clad in armor, are often seen near the shrine. Going behind a screen, the next great hall contains a high gilded image of Sakya-muni sitting on a lotus flower, with smaller statues of Ananda and Kashiapa on his sides; their shrine often has standing images of attendants. In this hall are other images or pictures of the Eighteen Arhans, deified missionaries who propagated their faith early in China. In the rear of these is represented some form of Kwanyin, the Goddess of Mercy, the popular idol of the sects. In large temples the five hundred Arhans, placed on as many seats, each having some distinguishing attribute, fill a large hall. Besides these occur the disciples of Buddha listening to his teachings, the horrible punishments of hell, and various honored deities, sages, or local gods, so that few temples are alike in all respects. In all of them are guest-chambers of various sizes, refectories, study rooms, and cloisters, according to the wants and resources of the fraternity.

The hold of the Buddhist priesthood upon the mass of Chinese consists far more in the position they occupy in relation to the rites performed in honor of the dead than in their tenets. This brings us to the consideration of the real religion of the Chinese, that in which more than anything else they trust, and to which they look for consolation and reward—the worship of deceased ancestors. The doctrines of Confucius and the cerèmonial of the State religion, exhibit the speculative, intellectual dogmas of the educated literati and thinkers, who have early been taught the high ideal of the Princely Man set forth by their sages. The tenets of Lau-tsz' and the sorcery and incantations of his followers show the mystic and marvellous part of the popular belief. Buddhism takes hold of the common life of man, offers relief in times of distress, escape from a future hell at a cheap rate, and employment in a round of prayers, study, or work, ending in the nirvana. But the heart of the nation reposes more upon the rites offered at the family shrine to the two "living divinities" who preside in the hall of ancestors than to all the rest. This sort of family worship has been popular in other countries, but in no part of the world has it reached the consequence it has received in Eastern Asia; every natural feeling serves, indeed, to strengthen its simple cultus.

In the *Shí King*, whose existence, as we have already pointed out, is coeval with Samuel or earlier, are many references to this worship, and to certain rites connected with its royal observance. At some festivals the dead were personated by a younger relative, who was supposed to be taken possession of by their spirits, and thereby became their visible image. He was placed on high, and the sacrificer, on appearing in the temple, asked him to be seated at his ease, and urged him to eat, thereby to prepare himself to receive the homage given to the dead. When he had done so he gave the response in their name; the defied spirits returned to heaven, and their personator came down from his seat. In one ode the response of the ancestors through their personator is thus given:

What said the message from your sires?
"Vessels and gifts are clean;
And all your friends, assisting you,
Behave with reverent mien.

"Most reverently you did your part,
And reverent by your side
Your son appeared. On you henceforth
Shall ceaseless blessings bide.

"What shall the ceaseless blessings be ?
That in your palace high,
For myriad years you dwell in peace,
Rich in posterity." [1]

The teachings of this ancient book intimate that the protecting favor of the departed could be lost by the vile, cruel, or unjust conduct of their descendants—thus connecting ancestral worship and reward with personal character. Another ode sums up this idea in the expression, "The mysterious empyrean is able to strengthen anything; do not disgrace your imperial ancestors, and it will save your posterity." Many stories occur in the native literature exemplifying this idea by actual experiences of blessing and cursing, all flowing from the observance or neglect of the required duties.

The great sages Confucius and Mencius, with the earlier rulers, King Wăn and Duke Chau, and their millions of followers, have all upheld these sentiments, and those teachings and examples are still as powerful as ever. In every household, a shrine, a tablet, an oratory, or a domestic temple, according to the position of the family, contains the simple legend of the two ancestral names written on a slip of paper or carved on a board. Incense is burned before it, daily or on the new and full moons; and in April the people everywhere gather at the family graves to sweep them, and worship the departed around a festive sacrifice. To the children it has all the pleasant associations of our Christmas or Thanksgiving; and all the elder members of the family who can do so come together around the tomb or in the ancestral hall at the annual rite. Parents and children meet and bow before the tablet, and in their simple cheer contract no associations with temples or idols, monasteries or priests, processions, or flags and music. It is the family, and a stranger intermeddleth not with it; he has his own tablet to look to, and can get no good by worshipping before that bearing the names of another family.

As the children grow up the worship of the ancestors, whom they never saw, is exchanged for that of nearer ones who bore and nurtured, clothed, taught, and cheered them in helpless

[1] Legge's *She King*, p. 309, London, 1876.

childhood and hopeful youth, and the whole is thus rendered more personal, vivid, and endearing. There is nothing revolting or cruel connected with it, but everything is orderly, kind, and simple, calculated to strengthen the family relationship, cement the affection between brothers and sisters, and uphold habits of filial reverence and obedience. Though the strongest motive for this worship arises out of the belief that success in worldly affairs depends on the support given to parental spirits in hades, who will resent continued neglect by withholding their blessing, yet, in the course of ages, it has influenced Chinese character, in promoting industry and cultivating habits of domestic care and thrift, beyond all estimation.

It has, moreover, done much to preserve that feature of the government which grows out of the oversight of heaven as manifested to the people through their Emperor, the Son of Heaven, whom they regard as its vicegerent. The parental authority is also itself honored by that peculiar position of the monarch, and the child grows up with the habit of yielding to its injunctions, for to him the family tablet is a reality, the abode of a personal Being who exerts an influence over him that cannot be evaded, and is far more to him as an individual than any of the popular gods. Those gods are to be feared and their wrath deprecated, but the "illustrious ones who have completed their probation" represent love, care, and interest to the worshippers if they do not fail in their duties.

Another indirect result has been to define and elevate the position of the wife and mother. All the laws which could be framed for the protection of women would lack their force if she were not honored in the household. As there can be only one "illustrious consort" (*hien pí*) named on the tablet, there is of course only one wife (*tsí*) acknowledged in the family. There are concubines (*tsieh*), whose legal rights are defined and secured, and who form an integral part of the family; but they are not admitted into the ancestral hall, and their children are reckoned with the others as Dan and Asher were in Jacob's household. Polygamous families in China form a small proportion of the whole; and this acknowledged parity of the mother with the father, in the most sacred position she can be placed, has done much to maintain the purity and right influence of woman amid all the degradations, pollutions, and moral weakness of heathenism. It is one of the most powerful supports of good order. It may even be confidently stated that woman's legal, social, and domestic position is as high in China as it has ever been outside of Christian culture, and as safe as it can be without the restraints of Christianity. Another benefit to the people, that of early marriages, derives much of its prevalence and obligation from the fear that, if neglected, there may be no heirs left to carry on the worship at the family tomb.

The three leading results here noticed, viz., the prevention of a priestly caste, the confirmation of parental authority in its own sphere, and the elevation of the woman and wife to a parity with the man and husband, do much to explain the perpetuity of Chinese institutions. The fact that filial piety in this system has overpassed the limit set by God in his Word, and that deceased parents are worshipped as gods by their children, is both true and sad. That the worship rendered to their ancestors by the Chinese is idolatrous cannot be doubted; and it forms one of the subtlest phases of idolatry—essentially evil with the guise of goodness—ever established among men.

The prevalence of infanticide and the indifference with which the crime is regarded may seem to militate against this view of Chinese social character, and throw discredit on the degree of respect and reverence paid to parents; for how, some will ask, can a man thus worship and venerate parents who once imbrued their hands in his sister's blood? Such anomalies may be found in the distorted minds and depraved hearts educated under the superstitions of heathenism in every country, and the Chinese are no exception. It is exceedingly difficult, however, to ascertain the extent of infanticide in China, and all the reasons which prompt to the horrid act. Investigations have been made about Canton, and evidence obtained to show that it is comparatively rare, and strongly discountenanced by public opinion; though by no means unknown, nor punished by law when done. Similar investigations at Amoy have disclosed a fearful extent of murders of this nature; yet while the latter are believed, the assertions of the former are regarded as evasions of the truth from the fear of being reproached for it or a sense of shame. The whole nation has been branded as systematic murderers of their children from the practice of the inhabitants of a portion of two provinces, who are generally regarded by their countrymen as among the most violent and poorest fraction of the whole. Sir John Barrow heard that the carts went about the streets of Peking daily to pick up dead and dying infants thrown out by their unnatural parents, but he does not mention ever having seen a single corpse in all his walks or rides about the capital. It has now been ascertained that this cart contains so many dead bodies of both sexes, that the inference by Dr. Dudgeon that not one in a hundred was killed seems to be sustained. The bodies of children are not as often seen in the lanes and creeks of Canton as those of adults, and the former are as likely to have died natural deaths as the latter.

In Fuhkien province, especially in the departments of Tsiuen-chau and Changchau, infanticide prevails to a greater extent than in any other part of the Empire yet examined. Mr. Abeel extended his inquiries to forty different towns and villages lying in the first, and found that the percentage was between seventy and eighty down to ten, giving an average of about forty per cent. of all girls born in those places as being murdered. In Changchau, out of seventeen towns, the proportion lies between one-fourth and three-tenths in some places, occasionally rising to one-third, and in others sinking to one-fifth, making an average of one-fourth put to death. In other departments of the province the practice is confessed, but the proportion thought by intelligent natives to be less, since there is less poverty and fewer people than formerly. The examination was conducted in as fair a manner as possible, and persons of all classes were questioned as to the number of children they had killed themselves, or knew had been killed by their relatives or neighbors. One of eight brothers told him that only three girls were left among all their children, sixteen having been killed. On one occasion he visited a small village on Amoy Island, called Bo-au, where the whole population turned out to see him and Dr. Cumming, the latter of whom had recently cut out a large tumor from a fellow villager. He says:

From the number of women in the crowd which turned out to greet us, we were pretty well persuaded that they were under as little restraint as the men from indulging their curiosity; and upon inquiry, found it to be so. We were conducted to a small temple, when I had the opportunity of conversing with many who came around us. On a second visit, while addressing them, one man held up a child, and publicly acknowledged that he had killed five of the helpless beings, having preserved but two. I thought he was jesting, but as no surprise or dissent was expressed by his neighbors, and as there was an air of simplicity and regret in the individual, there was no reason to doubt its truth. After repeating his confession he added with affecting simplicity, "It was before I heard you speak on this subject; I did not know it was wrong; I would not do so now." Wishing to obtain the testimony of the assembled villagers, I put the question publicly, "What number of female infants in this village are destroyed at birth?" The reply was, "More than one-half." As there was no discussion among them, which is not the case when they differ in opinion, and as we were fully convinced from our own observation of the numerical inequality of the sexes, the proportion of deaths they gave did not strike us as extravagant.

The reasons assigned for committing the unnatural deed are various. Poverty is the leading cause; the alternative being, as the parents think, a life of infamy or slavery, since if they cannot rear their offspring themselves they must sell them. The fact of the great numbers of men who emigrate to the Archipelago from the coast districts has no doubt also had its effect in inducing parents to destroy daughters for whom they had little expectation of finding husbands if they did rear them. Many who are able to support their daughters prefer to destroy them rather than incur the expenses of their marriage, but the investigation showed that the crime was rather less among the educated than the ignorant, and that they had done something to dissuade their poor neighbors from putting their girls to death. In the adjoining departments of Chauchau and Kiaying in Kwangtung, the people admit the practice, and, as their circumstances are similar, it is probable that it is not much less than around Amoy Dr. Dudgeon, of Peking, has had very favorable opportunities for prosecuting inquiries in that region, and has shown that the stories formerly credited are wrong, and that most of the children thus disposed of are born of nuns. Inquiries instituted at Hankow by Dr. F. P. Smith, of the hospital, showed a wide prevalence of the crime among the poor and rural population, for which he ascribes several reasons; the proportion of the sexes is ten men to seven women.

While one of the worst features of the crime is the little degree of detestation everywhere expressed at it, yet the actual proportion is an important inquiry, and this, taking the whole nation, has been much exaggerated, chiefly from applying such facts and estimates as the preceding to the whole country. The governor of Canton once issued a dissuasive exhortation on this subject to the people, telling them that if they destroyed all their daughters they would soon have no mothers. Until investigations have been made elsewhere, it is not fair to charge all the Chinese with the atrocities of a small portion, nor to disbelieve the affirmations of the inhabitants of Canton, Ningpo, and Shanghai, and elsewhere, that they do not usually put their daughters to death, until we have overwhelming testimony that they deny and conceal what they are ashamed to confess.[1]

Comparing their lamentable practice with those of other and European nations, we find, according to Hume, that "the exposure of new-born infants was an allowed practice in almost all the States of Greece and Rome; even among the polite and civilized Athenians, the abandoning of one's child to hunger or wild beasts was regarded without blame or censure. This practice was very common; and it is not spoken of by any author of those times with the horror it deserves, or scarcely even with disapprobation. Plutarch, the humane, good-natured Plutarch, mentions it as a merit in Attalus, king of Pergamus, that he murdered, or, if you will, exposed all his own children, in order to leave his crown to the son of his brother Eumenes. It was Solon, the most celebrated of the sages of Greece, that gave parents permission by law to kill their children." Aristotle

[1] *Chinese Repository*, Vol. XVII., p. 11, for a native essay against it; Vol. XVI., p. 513; Vol. XII., pp. 540–548; Vol. XI., p. 508; Vol. VII., p. 54. Bishop Smith's *China*, p. 443. *Report of Peking Hospital*, 1865. Dr. F. P. Smith's *Five Annual Reports of Hankow Hospital*, 1870, pp. 45–52. Doolittle, *Social Life*, II., pp. 203–209. *Notes and Queries on C. and J.*, Vol. III., pp. 156, 172. *L'infanticide et l'Oeuvre de la Ste.-Enfance en Chine*, par Père G. Palatre, Changhai. *Autographie de la Mission Catholique à l'orphelinat de Tou-sè-wè*, 1878. M. E. Martin, *Étude Médico-Légale sur l'Infanticide et l'Avortement dans l'Empire Chinois*, Paris, 1872.

thought it should be encouraged by the magistrates, and Plato maintained the same inhuman doctrine. It was complained of as a great singularity that the laws of Thebes forbade the practice. In all the provinces, and especially in Italy, the crime was daily perpetrated.[1]

The ceremonies attendant upon the decease of a person vary in different parts of the country, though they are not necessarily elaborate or expensive anywhere, and all the important ones can be performed by the poorest mourner. The inhabitants of Fuhkien put a piece of silver in the mouth of the dying person, and carefully cover his nose and ears. Scarcely is he dead when they make a hole in the roof to facilitate the exit of the spirits proceeding from his body, of which they imagine each person possesses seven animal senses which die with him, and three souls, one of which enters elysium and receives judgment, another abides with the tablet, and a third dwells in the tomb. In some places, as a man approaches his last hour, the relatives come into the room to array him in his best garments and carry him into the main hall to breathe his life away while dressed in the costume with which he is to appear in Hades. The popular ideas regarding their fate vary so much that it is difficult to describe the national faith in this respect; transmigration is more or less believed in, but the detail of the changes the good or evil spirit undergoes before it is absorbed in Buddha varies almost according to the fancy of the worshipper. Those who are sent to hell pass through every form of suffering inflicted upon them by hideous monsters, and are at last released to wander about as houseless demons to torment mankind, or vex themselves in the bodies of animals and reptiles.

When the priests come the corpse is laid out upon the floor in the principal room, and a tablet set up by its side; a table is near, on which are placed meats, lamps, and incense. While the priests are reciting prayers to deliver the soul from purgatory and hell, they occasionally call on all present to weep and lament, and on these occasions the females of the household are particularly clamorous in their grief, alternately uttering the

[1] McIlvaine, *Evidences of Christianity*, p. 291.

most doleful accents, and then tittering with some of the new-comers. Papers having figures on them and Peter's pence in the form of paper money are burned; white lanterns, instead of the common red ones, and a slip of paper containing the name, titles, age, etc., of the dead are hung at the door; a mat porch is put up for the musicians and the priests.[1] The soul, having crossed the bridge leading out of hell with the aid of the priests, gets a letter of recommendation from them to be admitted into the western heavens.

Previous to burial a lucky place for interment, if the family have moved away from its paternal sepulchre, must be found. The body is coffined soon after death, arrayed in the most splendid habiliments the family can afford; a fan is put in one hand and a prayer on a piece of paper in the other. The form of a Chinese coffin resembles the trunk of a tree; the boards are three or four inches thick and rounded on top (from whence a coffin is called "longevity boards"), making a very substantial case. When the corpse is put in it is laid in a bed of lime or cotton, or covered with quicklime, and the edges of the lid are closed with mortar in the groove so that no smell escapes; the coffin is varnished if it is to remain in the house before burial. The Chinese often expend large sums in the purchase and preparation of a coffin during their lifetime; the cheapest are from five to ten dollars, and upward to five hundred and even two thousand dollars, according to the materials and ornamenting.

Bodies are sometimes kept in or about the house for many years and incense burned morning and evening. They are placed either on trestles near the doorway and protected by a covering in the principal hall, or in the ancestral chamber, where they remain until the fortunes of the family improve so as to enable them to bury the remains, or a lucky place is found, or until opportunity and means allow the survivors to lay them in their patrimonial sepulchre.

The lineal relatives of the deceased are informed of his death,

---

[1] Ball says that money is put into the mouth of the dead by rich people to buy favor and passage into heaven; others affirm that the money is to make the spirit ready of speech. The phrase "no silver to hit the mouth" has reference to this custom.

and as many as can do so repair to the house to condole with and assist the family. The eldest son or the nearest descendant repairs to an adjoining river or well with a bowl in his hand, and accompanied by two relatives, to "buy water" with money which he carries and throws into it. Upon the way to the well it is customary to carry lanterns—even at noon—and to make a great wailing: with the water thus obtained he washes the corpse before it is dressed. After the body is laid in the coffin and before interment the sons of the deceased among the poor are frequently sent around to the relatives and friends of the family to solicit subscriptions to buy a grave, hire mourners, or provide a suitable sacrifice, and it is considered a good act to assist in such cases; perhaps fear of the ill-will of the displeased spirit prompts to the charity. The coffin is sometimes seized or attached by creditors to compel the relatives to collect a sum to release it, and instances of filial sons are mentioned who have sold themselves into temporary or perpetual slavery in order to raise money to bury their parents. In other cases a defaulting tenant will retain a coffin in the house to forestall an ejectment for the back rent. On the day of burial an offering of cooked provisions is laid out near the coffin. The chief mourners, clothed in coarse white sackcloth, then approach and kneel before it, knocking their heads upon the ground and going through with the full kotow; two persons dressed in mourning hand them incense-sticks, which are placed in jars. After the male mourners have made their parting prostrations the females perform the same ceremonies, and then such friends and relations as are present; during these observances a band of music plays. The funeral procession is formed of all these persons—the band, the tablets, priests, etc. In Peking, where religious processions are prohibited, great display is made in funerals according to the means and rank of the deceased. The coffin is borne on an unwieldy bier carried by sixty-four men or more and covered by a richly embroidered catafalque, attended by musicians, mourners, priests, etc. Sometimes the carts are covered with white cloth and the mules wear white harness.

Burial-places are selected by geomancers, and their location has important results on the prosperity of the living. The supposed connection between these two things has influenced the science, religion, and customs of the Chinese from very early days, and under the name of *fung-shui*, or 'wind and water' rules, still contains most of their science and explains most of their superstitions. As true science extends this travestie of natural philosophy will fade away and form a subject of fascination among the people as it now does a source of terror. Every strange event is interpreted by *fung-shui*, and its professors employ the doctrines of Buddhists and Taoists to enforce their dicta, as they do their little knowledge of astronomy, medicine, and natural science to explain them. The whole has gradually grown into a system of geomancy, involving, however, their cosmogony, natural philosophy, spiritualism, and biology so far as they have these sciences. It was in the twelfth century that it became systematized, and its influence has spread ever since. Were it only a picturesque kaleidoscope of facts and fancies it would be a harmless pastime; but it now enters into every act of life, since the human soul and body, whether in this world or the next, are regarded as constantly influenced by their actions, their relatives, and their locations. Thus the choice of a burial-place is supposed to affect the past, present, and future, and the *fung-shui siensăng*, or 'wind and water doctors,' know therein how to benefit their customers and themselves.

Regarding all nature as a living organism and each person surrounded by invisible beings, the Chinese try to propitiate these essences through their departed relatives. They consider them as restrained by their animal nature to the tomb where their bodies lie, while the spiritual nature seeks to hover about its old scenes and children. If a tomb is placed so that the spirit dwelling therein is comfortable, the inference is that the deceased will grant those who supply its wants all that the spirit world can grant. A tomb located where no star on high or dragon below, no breath of nature or malign configuration of hills, can disturb the repose of the dead, must therefore be lucky, and worth great effort to secure.

The principles of geomancy depend much on two supposed currents running through the earth, known as the dragon and the tiger; a propitious site has these on its left and right. A skilful observer can detect and describe them, with the help of the compass, direction of the watercourses, shapes of the male and female ground, and their proportions, color of the soil, and the permutations of the elements. The common people know nothing of the basis on which this conclusion is founded, but give their money as their faith in the priest or charlatan increases.[1]

At the south, uncultivated hills are selected because they are dry and the white ants will not attack the coffin; and a hill-side in view of water, a copse, or a ravine near a hill-top, are all lucky spots. At the north, where ants are unknown, the dead are buried in fields; but nowhere collected in graveyards in cities or temples. The form of the grave is sometimes a simple tumulus with a tombstone at the head; in the southern provinces oftener in the shape of the Greek letter Ω, or that of a huge arm-chair. The back of the supposed chair is the place for the tombstone, while the body is interred in the seat, the sides of which are built around with masonry and approach each other in front. A tomb is occasionally built of stone in a substantial manner, and carved pillars are placed at the corners, the whole often costing thousands of dollars. The case of one necromancer is recorded, who, after having selected a grave for a family, was attacked with ophthalmia, and in revenge for their giving him poisonous food which he supposed had caused the malady, hired men to remove a large mass of rock near the grave, whereby its efficacy was completely spoiled. The position is thought to be the better if it command a good view. Some of the graves occupy many hundred square feet, the corners being defined by low stones bearing two characters, importing whose *chih*, or 'house,' it is. The shapes of graves vary more at the north; some are conical mounds planted with shrubs or flowers, others made of mason-work shaped like little houses, others mere square tombs or earthly tumuli; not a few coffins are simply left upon the ground. It is seldom the Chinese hew graves out of

[1] Compare Dr. Edkins in the *Chinese Recorder*, Vol. IV., 1871–72. *Feng-shui; or the Rudiments of Natural Science in China*, by Ernest J. Eitel, London, 1873. The *Cornhill Magazine* for March, 1874. *Notes and Queries on C. and J.*, Vol. II., p. 69.

the rock or dig large vaults; their care is to make a showy grave, and at the same time a convenient one for performing the prescribed rites. The mausolea of emperors and grandees occupy vast enclosures laid out as parks and adorned with ornamental buildings to which lead avenues of stone guardians.[1] The tomb of Yungloh (A.D. 1403–1425) is reached through a *dromos* of gigantic statues nearly a mile long—two pairs each of lions, unicorns, elephants, camels, and horses, one erect, the other couchant, and six pairs of civil and military officers; each figure is a monolith. The origin of this custom can be traced back nearly to the tenth century, but was probably known in the Tang dynasty. Officials are allowed to erect a few statues to become their guardians.[2]

When the day of interment arrives, which is usually the nearest lucky day to the third seventh after death, the friends assemble at the house. A band of musicians accompanies the procession, in which is also carried the ancestral tablet of the deceased in a separate sedan, accompanied sometimes by a sacrifice and the red tablets of the offices held by the family. The mourners are dressed entirely in white, or wear a white fillet around the head; the sons of the deceased must put on the expression and habiliments of woe, and the eldest one is at times supported along the street to the grave in all the eloquence and attitude of grief, although it may have been years since his father went to "wander among the genii." The women and children of the family follow, and at intervals cry and wail. A man goes ahead and scatters paper money to purchase the goodwill of such stray spirits as are prowling about. Different figures and banners are carried according to the means and rank of the family, which, with the friends and crowd attracted by the show, sometimes swell the train to a great length. The grave is deep, and lime is freely mixed with the earth thrown

---

[1] In the Yih chin the custodian reported in the *Peking Gazette* of January 3, 1871, that there were 92,690 trees, mostly fir, pine, elm, etc. The people in charge of such grounds are used to girdling the timber, in order afterward to get the dead trees as firewood for themselves.

[2] Mayers in *North China Br. Royal Asiatic Society Journal*, No. XII., 1878. Doolittle, *Social Life*, II., p. 337.

in; a body is never put into an old grave while anything remains of the former occupant; crackers are fired, libations poured out, prayers recited, and finally paper models of houses, clothes, horses, money, and everything he can possibly want in the land of shadows (which Davis calls a *wise economy*) are burned. The tablet and sacrifice are then carried back; the family feast on the latter or distribute it among the poor around the door, while the former is placed in the ancestral hall. The married daughters of the dead are not considered part of the family, and wear no mourning; nor are they invited to their father's funeral.

The period of mourning for a father is nominally three years, but actually reduced to twenty-seven months; the persons required to observe this are enumerated in the Code, and Sections CLXXIX.–CLXXXI. contain the penalties for concealing the death of a parent, or misrepresenting it, and of omitting the proper formalities. Burning the corpse, or casting it into the water, unfeelingly exposing it in the house longer than a year, and making the funeral ceremony and feast an occasion of merrymaking and indecorous meeting of males and females, are also prohibited. For thirty days after the demise the nearest kindred must not shave their heads nor change their dress, but rather exhibit a slovenly, slipshod appearance, as if grief had taken away both appetite and decorum. In the southern districts half-mourning is blue, usually exhibited in a pair of blue shoes and a blue silken cord woven in the queue, instead of a red one; grass shoes neatly made are now and then worn. In the northern provinces white is the only mourning color seen. The visiting cards also indicate that the time of mourning has not passed. The expenses incurred by the rich are great, and the priests receive large sums for masses, ten thousand dollars being often spent. In the north still greater expenses are incurred in buying a piece of land for a burial plot and its glebe. Here they erect a lodge, where the keeper of the grave lives, cultivating the land and keeping the tomb in order.[1]

When the Empress dies officers put on mourning, take the

[1] *Chinese Repository*, Vol. IV., p. 352; Vol. II., p. 499.

buttons and fringes from their caps, stamp their seals with blue ink, and go through a prescribed set of ceremonies; they must not shave their heads for a hundred days, nor the people for a month. Full details of the ceremonies ordered on the occasion of the decease of the Empress, or "interior assistant, who for thirteen years had held the situation of earth to heaven," were published in 1833, in both Manchu and Chinese. When the Emperor dies all his subjects let their hair grow for a hundred days, marriages are postponed, theatres and sports disallowed, and a ceremonial gloom and dishabille pervades the Empire. On the morning after the death of the Emperor Tungchí, January 12, 1875, the streets of Peking presented a surprising contrast to their usual gaiety in the removal of everything red. In early times human beings were immolated at the obsequies of rulers, and voluntary deaths of their attendants and women are occasionally mentioned. De Guignes says that the Emperor Shunchí ordered thirty persons to be immolated at the funeral of his consort; but Kanghí, his son, forbade four women from sacrificing themselves on the death of his Empress.[1]

The hall of ancestors is found in the house of almost every member of the family, but always in that of the eldest son. In rich families it is a separate building; in others a room set apart for the purpose, and in many a mere shelf or shrine. The tablet, or *shin chu*, is a board about twelve inches long and three wide, placed upright in a block. The inscriptions on two are like the following: "The tablet of Hwang Yung-fuh (late Ching-teh), the head of the family, who finished his probation with honor during the Imperial Tsing dynasty, reaching a sub-magistracy." His wife's reads: "The tablet of Madame, originally of the noble family Chin, who would have received the title of lady, and in the Imperial Tsing dynasty became his illustrious consort." A receptacle is often cut in the back, containing pieces of paper bearing the names of the higher ancestors, or other members of the family. Incense and papers are daily burned before them, accompanied by a bow or act of homage, forming

[1] *N. C. Br. R. As. Soc. Journal*, No. II., 1865, pp. 173 ff. De Guignes' *Voyages*, Tome II., p. 304. *Mémoires conc. les Chinois*, Tome VI., pp. 346 ff. *Chinese and Japanese Repository* for May, 1864.

in fact a sort of family prayer. The tablets are ranged in chronological order, those of the same generation being placed in a line. When the hall is large, and the family rich, no pains are spared to adorn it with banners and insignia of wealth and rank, and on festival days it serves as a convenient place for friends to meet, or for any extraordinary family occasion. A person residing near Macao spent about one thousand five hun-

Ancestral Hall and Mode of Worshipping the Tablets.

dred dollars in the erection of a hall, and on the dedication day the female members of his family assembled with his sons and descendants to assist in the ceremonies. The portraits of the deceased are also suspended in the hall, but effigies or images are not now made.

In the wood-cut adjoining, the tablets are arranged on the

same level, and the sacrifice laid on the altar before them; the character *shao*, 'longevity,' is drawn on the wall behind. During the ceremonies fire-crackers are let off and papers burned; after it the feast is spread.

In the first part of April, one hundred and six days after the winter solstice, during the term called *tsing-ming*, a general worship of ancestors is observed. In Kwangtung this is commonly called *pai shan*, or 'worshipping on the hills,' but the general term is *siu făn tí*, or 'sweeping the tombs.' The whole population, men, women, and children, repair to their family tombs, carrying a tray containing the sacrifice, libations for offering, and candles, paper, and incense for burning, and there go through a variety of ceremonies and prayers. The grave is at this season repaired and swept, and at the close of the service three pieces of turf are placed at the back and front of the grave to retain long strips of red and white paper; this indicates that the accustomed rites have been performed, and these fugitive testimonials remain fluttering in the wind long enough to announce it to all the friends as well as enemies of the family; for when a grave has been neglected three years it is sometimes dug over and the land resold. The enormous amount of litigation connected with sepulchral boundaries, transfer of grave glebes or sale of the ancient plats, injury, robbery, and repairs of tombs, all indicate the high importance of this kind of property.

"Such are the harmless, if not meritorious, forms of respect for the dead," says Davis, "which the Jesuits wisely tolerated in their converts, knowing the consequences of outraging their most cherished prejudices; but the crowds of ignorant monks who flocked to the breach which those scientific and able men had opened, jealous, perhaps, of their success, brought this as a charge against them until the point became one of serious controversy and reference to the Pope. His Holiness espoused the bigoted and unwiser part, which led to the expulsion of the monks of all varieties." And elsewhere he says the worship paid to ancestors is "not exactly idolatrous, for they sacrifice to the invisible spirit and not to any representation of it in the figure of an idol." This distinction is much the same as that alleged by the Greek church, which disallows images but permits gold and silver pictures having the face and hands only painted, for Sir John Davis, himself being a Protestant, probably admits that worship paid to any other object besides the true God is idolatry; and that the Chinese do truly worship their ancestors is evident from a prayer, such as the following, offered at the tombs:

Taukwang, 12th year, 3d moon, 1st day. I, Lin Kwang, the second son of the third generation, presume to come before the grave of my ancestor, Lin Kung. Revolving years have brought again the season of spring. Cherishing sentiments of veneration, I look up and sweep your tomb. Prostrate I pray that you will come and be present, and that you will grant to your posterity that they may be prosperous and illustrious. At this season of genial showers and gentle breezes I desire to recompense the root of my existence and exert myself sincerely. Always grant your safe protection. My trust is in your divine spirit. Reverently I present the five-fold sacrifice of a pig, a fowl, a duck, a goose, and a fish; also an offering of five plates of fruit, with libations of spirituous liquors, earnestly entreating that you will come and view them. With the most attentive respect this annunciation is presented on high.

It is not easy to perceive, perhaps, why the Pope and the Dominicans were so much opposed to the worship of ancestral penates among the Chinese when they performed much the same services themselves before the images of Mary, Joseph, Cecilia, Ignatius, and hundreds of other deified mortals; but it is somewhat surprising that a Protestant should describe this worship as consisting of "harmless, if not meritorious, forms of respect for the dead." Mr. Fortune, too, thinks "a considerable portion of this worship springs from a higher and purer source than a mere matter of form, and that when the Chinese periodically visit the tombs of their fathers to worship and pay respect to their memory, they indulge in the pleasing reflection that when they themselves are no more their graves will not be neglected or forgotten." This feeling does actuate them, but there can be no dispute, one would think, about its idolatrous character. The Chinese who have embraced the doctrines of the New Testament, and who may be supposed qualified to judge of their own acts and feelings, regard the rites as superstitious and sinful. It is a form of worship, indeed, which presents fewer revolting features than most systems of false religion—consisting merely of pouring out libations and burning paper and candles at the grave, and then a family meeting at a social feast, with a few simple prostrations and petitions. No bacchanalian companies of men and women run riot over the hills, as in the Eleusinian mysteries, nor are obscene rites practised in the house; all is pleasant, decorous, and harmonious. The junior members of the family come from a distance, sometimes two or three hundred miles, to observe it, and the family meeting on this occasion is looked forward to by all with much the same feelings that Christmas is in Old England or Thanksgiving in New England. Brothers and sisters, cousins and other relatives join in the worship and feast, and it is this pleasant reunion of dear ones, perhaps the most favorable to the cementing of family affection to be found in heathen society, which constitutes much of its power and will present such an obstacle to the reception of the Gospel and removal of the "two divinities" from the house.

The funeral ceremonies here described are performed by sons for their parents, especially for the father; but there are few or no ceremonies and little expense for infants, unmarried children, concubines, or slaves. These are coffined and buried without parade in the family sepulchre; the poor sometimes tie them up in mats and boards and lay them in the fields to shock the eyes and noses of all who pass. The municipal authorities of Canton issued orders to the people in 1832 to bring such bodies as had no place of burial to the potter's field, where they would be interred at public expense; societies, moreover, exist in all the large cities whose object is to bury poor people. In some parts the body is wrapped in cloth or coffined and laid in graveyards on the surface of the ground. When one dies far away from home the coffin is often lodged in *larariums*, or public depositories maintained by societies, where they remain many years. Few acts during the war of 1841 irritated the people about Canton against the English more than forcing open the coffins found in these mausolea and mutilating the corpses. One building contained hundreds of coffins from which, when opened, a pungent aromatic smell was perceptible, while the features of the corpses presented a dried appearance. One traveller tells a story of his guide, when he was conducting him over the hills in Hupeh, ordering him to conceal his blue eyes by putting on green spectacles as they were approaching some houses, and describes his surprise at finding them all filled with coffins arranged in an orderly manner. Graves are not enclosed; cattle pasture among them and paths lead over and through them.

Tombstones are usually made of granite and their inscriptions soon become defaced. Epitaphs are short, giving the name of the dynasty, his place of birth, number of his generation in the family, and his temple name. Laudatory expressions are rare, and quotations from the classics or stanzas of poetry to convey a sentiment entirely unknown. The corpses of officers who die at their stations are carried to their paternal tombs, sometimes at public expense. The Emperor, in some instances, orders the funeral rites of distinguished statesmen to be defrayed. This was done during the war with England in the cases of Commissioner Yukien and General Hailing, who burned himself at Chinkiang fu.[1]

Besides these funeral rites and religious ceremonies to their departed ancestors the Chinese have an almost infinite variety of superstitious practices, most of which are of a deprecatory character, growing out of their belief in demons and genii who trouble or help people. It may be said that most of their religious acts performed in temples are intended to avert misfortune rather than supplicate blessings. In order to ward off malignant influences amulets are worn and charms hung up, such as money-swords made of coins of different monarchs strung together in the form of a dagger; leaves of the sweet-flag (*Acorus*) and Artemisia tied in a bundle, or a sprig of peach-blossoms; the first is placed near beds, the latter over the lintel, to drive away demons. A man also collects a cash or two from each of his friends and gets a lock made which he hangs to his son's neck in order to lock him to life and make the subscribers surety for

[1] *Chinese Repository*, Vol. XVIII., pp. 363–384. Doolittle, *Social Life*, II., pp. 45–48. M. T. Yates, *Ancestral Worship*, *Missionary Conference* (of 1867), p. 367. Johnson, *Oriental Religions: China*, pp. 693–708. Gray's *China*, I., pp. 320–328. *China Review*, Vol. IV., p. 296. P. D. de Thiersant, *La Piété Filiale en Chine*, Paris, 1877. E. Faber in the *Chinese Recorder*, Vol. IX., pp. 329, 401.

his safety; adult females also wear a neck lock for the same purpose. Charms are common. One bears the inscription, "May you get the three *manys* and the nine *likes;*" another, "To obtain long eyebrowed longevity." The three *manys* are many years of happiness and life and many sons. Old brass mirrors to cure mad people are hung up by the rich in their halls, and figures or representations of the unicorn, of gourds,

Buddhist Priests.

tigers' claws, or the eight diagrams, are worn to insure good fortune or ward off sickness, fire, or fright. Stones or pieces of metal with short sentences cut upon them are almost always found suspended or tied about the persons of children and women, which are supposed to have great efficacy in preventing evil. The rich pay large sums for rare objects to promote this end.

In addition to their employment in the worship and burial of the dead and cultivation of glebe lands (some of which are very extensive[1]), priests resort to many expedients to increase their incomes, few of which have the improvement of their countrymen as a ruling motive. Some go around the streets collecting printed or written paper in baskets, to burn them lest the venerable names of Confucius or Buddha be defiled; others obtain a few pennies by writing inscriptions and charms on doors; and many in rural places get a good living off the lands owned by their temples. The priests of both sects are under the control of officials recognized by and amenable to the authorities, so that the vicious and unprincipled among them are soon restrained.

The Buddhists issue small books, called *Girdle Classics*, containing prayers addressed to the deity under whose protection the person has placed himself. Spells are made in great variety, some of them to be worn or pasted up in the house, while others are written on leaves, paper, or cloth, and burned, and their ashes thrown into a liquid for the patient or child to drink. These spells are sold by Rationalists, and consist of characters, like *fuh* ('happiness') or *shao* ('longevity'), fancifully combined. The god of doors, of the North Pole, Pwanku, the heavenly astronomer, the god of thunder and lightning, or typhoons, the god of medicine, demigods and genii of almost every name and power, are all invoked, and some of them by all persons. In shops the word *shin* is put up in a shrine and incense placed before it, all objects of fear and worship being included under this general term. The threshold is peculiarly sacred, and incense-sticks are lighted morning and evening at its side.[2]

The Chinese dread wandering and hungry ghosts of wicked men, and the priests are hired to celebrate a mass called *ta tsiao*, to appease these disturbers of human happiness, which, in its general purport, corresponds to All Souls' Day, and from its splendor and the general interest taken in its success is very popular. The streets at Canton are covered with awnings, and

[1] *Lettres Edifiantes*, Tome III., p. 33.

[2] *Lettres Edifiantes*, Tome IV., p. 310—where other ceremonies of the Taoists, to ward off pestilence, are described.

festoons of cheap silk, of brilliant colors, are hung across and along the streets. Chandeliers of glass are suspended at short intervals, alternating with small trays, on which paper figures in various attitudes, intended to illustrate some well-known scene in history, amuse the spectators. At night the glare of a thousand lamps shining through myriads of lustres lights up the whole scene in a gorgeous manner. The priests erect a staging somewhere in the vicinity, for the rehearsal of prayers to *Yen wang* (Yama or Pluto), and display tables covered with eatables for the hungry ghosts to feed on. Their acolytes mark the time when the half-starved ghosts, who have no children or friends to care for them, rush in and shoulder the viands, which they carry off for their year's supply. Bands of music chime in from time to time, to refresh these hungry spirits with the dulcet tones they once heard; for the Chinese, judging their gods by themselves, provide what is pleasing to those who pay for the entertainment, as well as to those who are supposed to be benefited by it. After the services are performed the crowd carry off what is left, but when this is permitted the priests sometimes cheat them with merely a cover of food on the tops of the baskets, the bottoms being filled with shavings.

Another festival in August is connected with this, called *shau i*, or 'burning clothes,' at which pieces of paper folded in the form of garments are burned for the use of the suffering ghosts, with a large quantity of what may be properly called *fiat money*, paper ingots which become valuable chiefly when they are burned. Paper houses with proper furniture, and puppets to represent household servants, are likewise made. Medhurst adds that "writings are drawn up and signed in the presence of witnesses to certify the conveyance of the property, stipulating that on its arrival in hades it shall be duly made over to the individuals specified in the bond; the houses, servants, clothes, money and all are then burned with the bond, the worshippers feeling confident that their friends obtain the benefit of what they have sent them." Thus "they make a covenant with the grave, and with hell they are at agreement." This festival, like all others, is attended with feasting and music. In order still further to provide for childless ghosts, their ancestral tablets are collected in temples and placed together in a room set apart for the purpose, called *wu sz' tan*, or 'orbate temple,' and a man hired to attend and burn incense before them. The sensations which arise on going into a room of this sort, and seeing one or two hundred small wooden tablets standing in regular array, and knowing that each one, or each pair, is like the silent tombstone of an extinct family, are such as no hall full of staring idols can ever inspire. The tablets look old, discolored, and broken, covered with dust and black with smoke, so that the gilded characters are obscured, and one cannot behold them long in their silence and forgetfulness without almost feeling as if spirits still hovered around them. All these ghosts are supposed to be propitiated by the sacrifices on All Souls' Day.

The patronage given to idolatry and superstition is constant and general among all classes, and thousands of persons get their livelihood by shrewdly availing themselves of the fears of their countrymen. The peepul, *pu-tí* (*Ficus religiosa*) at the south and the Sophora at the north, with perhaps other aged trees, are worshipped for long life.[1] Special efforts are made from time to time to build or repair a temple or pagoda, in order to insure or recall prosperity to a place, and large sums are subscribed by the devout. A case occurred in 1843, which illustrates this spirit. One of the English officers brought an image of *Wa-kwang*, the god of fire, from Chinkiang fu, which he presented as a curiosity to a lady in Macao. It remained in her house several months, and on the breaking up of the establishment, previous to a return to India, it was exposed for sale at auction with the furniture. A large crowd collected, and the attention of the Chinese was attracted to this image, which they examined carefully to see if it had the genuine marks of its ordination upon it; for no image is supposed to be properly an object of worship until the spirit has been inaugurated into it by the prescribed ceremonies. Having satisfied themselves, the idol was purchased for thirty dollars by two or three zealous

[1] Compare C. F. Koeppen, *Die Religion des Buddha*, Berlin, 1857, who describes the peepul (Bôdhi) tree—the "symbol of the spread and growth of the Buddhist church"—in India. E. Bernouf, *Introduction à l'histoire du Buddhisme Indien*, Paris, 1844. *Notes and Queries on C. and J.*, Vol. III., p. 100.

persons, and carried off in triumph to a shop and respectfully installed in a room cleared for the purpose. A public meeting was shortly after called, and resolutions passed to improve the propitious opportunity to obtain and preserve the protecting power of so potent a deity, by erecting a pavilion where he would have a respectable lodgment and receive due worship. A subscription was thereupon started, some of its advocates putting down fifty and others thirty dollars, until about one thousand two hundred dollars were raised, with which a small lot was purchased on the island west of Macao, and a pavilion or temple erected where *Wa-kwáng* was enshrined with pompous parade amid theatrical exhibitions, and a man hired to keep him and his domicile in good order.

No people are more enslaved by fear of the unknown than the Chinese, and none resort more frequently to sortilege to ascertain whether an enterprise will be successful or a proposed remedy avail to cure. This desire actuates all classes, and thousands and myriads of persons take advantage of it to their own profit. The tables of fortune-tellers and the shops of geomancers are met at street corners, and a strong inducement to repair to the temples is to cast lots as to the success of the prayers offered. One way of divining is to hold a bamboo root cut in halves, resembling in size and color a common potato, and let it drop as the petition is put up. Sometimes the worshipper drops it many times, in order to see if a majority of trials will not be favorable, and when disappointed the first time not unfrequently tries again, if mayhap he can force the gods to be more propitious. The devotee may determine himself what position of the blocks shall be deemed auspicious, but usually one face up and one down is regarded as promising. The countenances of worshippers as they leave the shrines, some beaming with hope and resolution to succeed, and others, notwithstanding their repeated knockings and divinings, going away with vexation and gloom written on their faces at the obduracy of the gods and sadness of their prospects, offer a study not less melancholy than instructive. "Such is the weakness of mortals: they dread, even after mature reflection, to undertake a project, and then enter blindly upon it at a chance after consulting chance itself as blind."

The fortune-tellers also consult fate by means of bamboo slips bearing certain characters, as the sixty-four diagrams, titles of poetical responses, or lists of names, etc. The applicant comes up to the table and states his desire; he wishes to know whether it will be fair weather, which of a dozen doctors shall be selected to cure his child, what sex an unborn infant will be, where his stolen property is, or any other matter. Selecting a slip, the diviner dissects the character into its component parts, or in some other way, and writes the parts upon a board lying before him, joining to them the time, the names of the person, five planets, colors, viscera, and other heterogeneous things, and from them all, putting on a most cabalistic, sapient look, educes a sentence which contains the required answer.

Consulting a Fortune-teller.

The man receives it as confidently as if he had entered the sybil's cave and heard her voice, pays his fee, and goes away. Others, less shrewd, refer to books in which the required answer is contained in a sort of equivocal delphian distich. The Chinese method of sortilege is not far different from that practised by the ancient Romans. "The lots preserved at Preneste were slips of oak with ancient characters engraved on them. They were shaken up together by a boy, and one of them was drawn for the person who consulted the oracle. They remind us of the Runic staves. Similar divining lots were found in other places."[1]

[1] Niebuhr, *History of Rome*, Vol. I., p. 246. See, further, Doolittle's *Social Life*, Vol. II., Chap. IV. Gray's *China*, Chap. XII. Prof. Douglas, *China*, Chap. XV.

The purchase of a building lot, and especially the selection of a grave, involve much expense, sortilege, and inquiry. When a succession of misfortunes comes upon a family, they will sometimes disinter all their relatives and bury them in a new place to remove the ill luck. Before a house is built a written prayer is tied to a pole stuck in the ground, petitioning for good luck, that no evil spirits may arise from beneath; when the ridge-pole is laid another prayer is pasted on and charms hung to it to insure the building against fire; and lastly, when the house is done it is dedicated to some patron, and petitions offered for its safety. Prayers are sometimes offered according to forms, at others the suppliant himself speaks. Two middle-aged women, attended by a maid-servant, were once found opposite Canton in the fields among the graves. They had placed a small paper shrine upon a tomb near the pathway, and one of them was kneeling before it, her lips moving in prayer; there was nothing in the shrine, but over it was written the most common petition known in China, "Ask and ye shall receive."

Answers are looked for in various ways. A man was once met at dusk repairing a lonely grave before which candles were burning and plates of rice and cups of spirits arranged. He knelt, and knocking his head began to repeat some words in a half audible manner, when he was asked if the spirits of his ancestors heard his supplications. At the instant a slight puff of air blew the candles, when he replied, "Yes; see, they have come; don't interrupt me." Contingent vows are often made, and useful acts performed in case the answer be favorable. A sick man in Macao once made a vow that if he recovered he would repave a bad piece of road—which he actually performed, aided a little by his neighbors; but it was deemed eminently unlucky that a toper who was somewhat flustered, passing soon after, should fall into the public well. Persons sometimes insult the gods, spit at them or whip them, or even break the ancestral tablets, in their vexation at having been deluded into foolish deeds or misled by divination. Legends are told of the vengeance which has followed such impiety, as well as the rewards attending a different course; and the *Kanying*

Pien, or 'Book of Rewards and Punishments,' has strengthened these sentiments by its stories of the results of human acts.

The worship of street divinities is not altogether municipal; some of the shrines in Canton are resorted to so much by women as to obstruct the path. The unsocial character of heathenism is observable at such places and in temples; however great the crowd may be, each one worships by himself as much as if no one else were present. Altars are erected in fields, on which a smooth stone is placed, where offerings are presented and libations poured out to secure a good crop. Few farmers omit all worship in the spring to the gods of the land and grain; and some go further and present a thanksgiving after harvest. Temples are open night and day, and in towns are the resort of crowds of idle fellows. Worshippers go on with their devotions amid all the hubbub, strike the drum and bell to arouse the god, burn paper prayers, and knock their heads upon the ground to implore his blessing, and then retire.

The Chinese collectively spend enormous sums in their idolatry, though they are more economical of time and money than the Hindus. Rich families give much for the services of priests, papers, candles, etc., at the interment of their friends, but when a large sacrifice is provided none goes to the priests, who are prohibited meat. The aggregate outlay to the whole people is very large, made up of repairs of temples, purchasing idols, petty costs, such as incense-sticks, candles, paper, etc., charms and larger sacrifices prepared from time to time. The sum cannot of course be ascertained, but if the daily expenditure of each person be estimated at one-third of a cent, or four cash, the total will exceed four hundred millions of dollars per annum, and this estimate is more likely to be under than over the mark, owing to the universality and constancy of the daily service.

This brief sketch of Chinese religious character will be incomplete without some notice of the benevolent institutions found among them. Good acts are required as proofs of sincerity; the classics teach benevolence, and the religious books of the Buddhists inculcate compassion to the poor and relief of the sick. Private alms of rice or clothes are frequently given, and the modes of collecting the poor-tax are very direct and economical, bringing the householders into some intercourse with the beggars in their neighborhoods, but offering no rewards to tramps and idlers. A retreat for poor aged and infirm or blind people is situated near the east side of Canton, the expenses of which are stated at about seven thousand dollars, but the number of persons relieved is not mentioned. The peculation and bad faith of the managers vitiate many of these institutions, and indispose the charitable to patronize them. Lazarettos are established in all large towns in Southern China, where a large entrance fee will secure a comfortable living for these outcasts to the end of their days; the prevalence of the disease leads everybody to aid the measures taken to restrict its ravages. A full account of the report issued by the directors of a long-established foundling hospital in Shanghai is given in the *Chinese Repository* (Vol. XIV.), and shows the methodical character of the people, and that no priests are joined in its management. In the report full credit is given to the benefactors, and an appeal made for funds to carry it on, as it is nearly out of supplies. Various modes of raising money are proposed, and arguments are brought forward to induce people to give, all in the same manner as is common with charitable institutions in western lands, as its closing paragraph shows:

> If, for the extension of kindness to our fellow creatures, and to those poor and destitute who have no father and mother, all the good and benevolent would daily give one cash ($\frac{1}{1100}$ of a dollar), it would be sufficient for the maintenance of the foundlings one day. Let no one consider a small good unmeritorious, nor a small subscription as of no avail. Either you may induce others to subscribe by the vernal breeze from your mouth, or you may nourish the blade of benevolence in the field of happiness, or cherish the already sprouting bud. Thus by taking advantage of opportunities as they present themselves, and using your endeavors to accomplish your object, you may immeasurably benefit and extend the institution.

The deaths are reported as being nearly one-half of the admissions, and the number of inmates about one hundred and thirty in all. The details of the receipts and expenditures are given at the end of the report in a business-like manner. The annual disbursement was about one thousand five hundred and fifty dollars, and the receipts from all sources more than that, so that a balance of five thousand dollars is reported on hand, four-fifths of which was derived from interest on subscriptions invested and on wares from pawnbrokers.

Similar establishments are found in all large towns, some of them partly supported by the government. That in Canton was founded in 1698, and contains accommodations for three hundred children, whose annual support was reckoned at three thousand five hundred dollars in 1833, at which date the money was filched from foreigners by a tax on their ships. These hospitals seem to be of modern origin, less than two centuries old, and may have been imitated from or suggested by the Roman Catholics. Candida, a distinguished convert about 1710, did much to establish them and show the excellence of the religion she professed. Mr. Milne, who visited one at Ningpo, says, after entering the court: "A number of coarse-looking women were peeping through the lattice at us, with squallababies at their breasts and squalid boys and girls at their heels; these women are the nurses, and these children are the foundlings, each woman having two or three to look after. But I have rarely beheld such a collection of filthy, unwashen, ragged brats. There are at present between sixty and seventy children, the boys on one side, the girls on the other. Boys remain here till the age of fourteen, when they are hired out or adopted; girls stay till sixteen, when they are betrothed as wives or taken as concubines or servants. It is supported by the rental of lands and houses, and by an annual tax of thirty-six stone or *shih* (about five hundred pounds) of rice from each district in the department."

In large towns other voluntary societies are found, having for their object the relief of suffering, which ought to be mentioned, as the Chinese have not been fairly credited with what they do in this line. Humane societies for restoring life to persons rescued from the water, and providing coffins if they are dead, exist along the riverine towns. Associations to give decent interment to the poor in a public potter's field are found in large cities, where gratuitous vaccination is often given to all who apply. Soup-kitchens are constantly opened as cold weather comes on, and houses prepared for vagrants and outcasts who have been suddenly reduced. Societies for the relief of indigent and virtuous widows are of long standing, and a kind of savings bank for the purpose of aiding a man to get married or to bury his parent exists among the people.[1]

Charity is a virtue which thrives poorly in the selfish soil of heathenism, but even badly managed establishments like these are praiseworthy, and promise something better when higher teachings shall have been engrafted into the public mind. The government is obliged to expend large sums almost every year for relieving the necessities of the starving and the distressed, and strong calls are made on the rich to give to these objects. During the great famine in 1877–78 in the north-eastern provinces, the common habits of industry, thrift, and order were united with these practices of voluntary benevolence among the people, and aided greatly in enabling those who distributed food and money to reach the greatest number possible with the means. The sufferers had already learned that violence and robbery would only increase their miseries and hasten their end.

The general condition of religion among the Chinese is effete; and the stately formalities of imperial worship, the doctrines of Confucius, the ceremonies of the Buddhists, the sorceries of the Rationalists, alike fail to comfort and instruct. But the fear of evil spirits and the worship of ancestors, the two beliefs which hold all ranks and abilities in their thrall, are still strong; and the principal sway the two sects exert is owing to the connection of their priests with the ceremonies of burial. Each has exerted its greatest possible power over the people, but all have failed to impart present happiness or assure future joy to their votaries. Confucianism is cold and unsatisfactory to the affectionate, the anguished, or the inquiring mind, and the transcendentalism of Rationalism or the vagaries of Bud-

[1] *Chinese Repository*, Vol. XIV., pp. 177–195. Lockhart, *Medical Missionary in China*, Chapter II., London, 1861.

dhism are a little worse. All classes are the prey of unfounded fears and superstitions, and dwell in a mist of ignorance and error which the light of true religion and knowledge alone can dissipate.

Besides the two leading idolatrous sects, there are also many combinations existing among the people, partly religious and partly political, one of which, the *Pih-lien kiao*, or the Triad Society, has already been mentioned in Chapter VIII. The *Wăn kiang*, or 'Incense-burning sect,' is also denounced in the *Sacred Commands*, but has not been mentioned in late times. The Triad Society is comparatively peaceful throughout China Proper in overt acts, the members of the auxiliary societies contenting themselves with keeping alive the spirit of resistance to the Manchus, getting new members, and countenancing one another in their opposition; but in Siam, Singapore, Malacca, and the Archipelago, it has become a powerful body, and great cruelties are committed on those who refuse to join. The members are admitted with formalities bearing strong resemblance to those of the Freemasons, and the professed objects of the society are the same. The novice swears before an idol to maintain inviolate secrecy, and stands under naked swords while taking the oath, which is then read to him; he afterward cuts off a cock's head, the usual form of swearing among all Chinese, intimating that a like fate awaits him if treacherous. There are countersigns known among the members, consisting of grips and motions of the fingers. Such is the secrecy of their operations in China, however, that very little is known of their numbers, internal organization, or character; the dislike of their machinations is the best security against their ultimate success. Local delusions, caused by some sharp-witted fellow, now and then arise in one part and another of the country, but they are speedily put down or dissipate of themselves. There has transpired not an item of news concerning any of these seditious organizations since the suppression of the Tai-ping rebellion in 1868. None of them are allowed to erect temples or make a public exhibition or procession, and exhortations are from time to time issued by the magistrates against them; while the penalties annexed to the statute against all illegal associations give the rulers great power to crush whatever they may deem suspicious or treasonable.[1]

The introduction of Islamism into China was so gradual that it is not easy to state the date or manner. The trade between China and ports lying on the Arabian Sea early attracted its adherents (called *Hwui-hwui kiao*) to the Middle Kingdom, and as long ago as the Tang dynasty its missionaries came to the seaports, especially of Canton and Hangchau. They likewise formed a large portion of the caravans which went to and fro through Central Asia, and seem to have been received without resistance, if not with favor, until they grew by natural increase to be a large and an integral part of the population. Mosques were built, schools taught, pilgrimages made, books printed, and converts allowed to exercise their rites without serious hindrance almost from the first. The two great features of the faith—the existence of one only true God and the wickedness of idolatry—have not been kept hidden; but, though promulgated, they have not been accepted outside of the sect and have not made the least impression upon the State religion.

The reasons for this are not far to seek. The rigid rule that the Koran must not be translated has kept this book out of reach of the literati, and the faithful could not even appeal to it in support of their belief, for not one in thousands knew how to read it. The Chinese naturally neither could nor would learn Arabic, and there was no sword hanging over them, as was the case in Persia, to force them into Moslem ranks. The simplicity of the State religion and ancestral worship gave very little handle to iconoclasts to declaim against polytheism and idolatry. The prohibition of pork to all true believers seemed a senseless injunction among a frugal people which depended largely on swine for meat and had never felt any the worse, bodily or mentally, from its use. The inhibition of wine, moreover, was needless among so temperate a race as the Chinese. Those who liked to keep Fridays or other days as fasts, practise circumcision as a symbol of faith, and worship in a temple with-

[1] Compare the *Chinese Repository*, Vol. XVIII., p. 281.

out images, could do so if they chose; but they must obey the laws of the land and honor the Emperor as good subjects. They have done so, and, generally speaking, have never been molested on account of their beliefs. Their chief strength lies in the northern part. The recent struggle in the north-western provinces, which cost so many lives, began almost wholly at the instigation of Turk or Tartar sectaries, and was a simple trial of strength as to who should rule. While cities and towns in Kansuh occupied by them were destroyed (in 1860–73), the two hundred thousand Moslems in Peking remained perfectly quiet and were unmolested by the authorities.

Some hold office, and pass through the examinations to obtain it, most of them being military men. In their mosques they exhibit a tablet with the customary ascription of reverence to the Emperor, but place the Prophet's name behind. They have no images or other tablets in the mosques, but suspend scrolls referring to the tenets of the faith. The Plain Pagoda in Canton was built during the Tang dynasty and called 'Remember-the-Holy Temple;' it is one hundred and sixty-five cubits high; it was built by foreigners, who used to go to the top during the fifth and sixth moons at dawn and pray to a golden weathercock there, crying out in a loud voice. These notices are taken from the native *Topography*, where also is reference to the tomb of a maternal uncle of Mohammed buried north of the city. The mosques throughout China are similar in their arrangement and resemble temples in many respects, the large arches and inscriptions in Arabic on the walls forming the chief peculiarities. Arabic is studied under great difficulties by the mollahs, and few of the faithful can read or speak it, contenting themselves with observing its ritual relating to circumcision, abstinence from pork, and idolatry. So far as can be seen, their worship of the true God under the name of *Chu*, or Lord, has not had the least influence on the polytheism of the nation or in elevating the tone of morals. A well-digested summary of their tenets has been published at Canton by an unknown author under the title of *True Comments on the Correct Doctrine*, in two volumes, pp. 240, 1801. No restrictions have been laid on this sect by the government during the present dynasty; the struggle which continued during the last twenty years between them was simply a question of dominion, not of religion.

Mr. Milne visited the mosque in Ningpo and made the acquaintance of the mollah. "He is a man about forty-five years of age, of a remarkably benign and intelligent countenance and gentlemanly bearing. His native place is Shantung, but his ancestors came from Medina. He readily reads the Arabic scriptures and talks that language fluently, but can neither read nor write Chinese, which is somewhat surprising considering he can talk it well, was born in China, and is a minister of religion among the Chinese. His supporters number between twenty and thirty families, and one or two of his adherents are officers. He took me into the place of worship which adjoins his apartments. A flight of steps leads into a room, covered with a plain roof, on either side of which lay a mass of dusty furniture and agricultural implements; the pillars are ornamented with sentences out of the Koran. Facing you is an ornamented pair of small doors hung upon the wall, within which the sacred seat is supposed to lie, and on one side is a convenient bookcase containing their scriptures. He showed me his usual officiating dress—a white robe with a painted turban—but he never wears this costume except at service, appearing in the Chinese habit at other times. They have a weekly day of rest, which falls on our Thursday. On asking if I might be permitted to attend any of their services, he replied that if their adherents had business on that day they did not trouble themselves to attend. The stronghold of his religion is in Hangchau fu, where are several mosques, but the low state of Mohammedanism seemed to dampen his spirits. Happening to see near the entrance a tablet similar to that found in every other temple, with the inscription, 'The Emperor, ever-living, may he live forever!' I asked him how he could allow such a blasphemous monument to stand in a spot which he regarded as consecrated to the worship of Aloha, as he styles the true God. He protested he did not and never could worship it, and pointed to the low place given it as evidence of this, and added that it was only for the sake of expediency it was allowed lodgment in the building, for if they were ever charged with disloyalty by the enemies of their faith they could appeal to it! His reigning desire was to make a pilgrimage to Mecca, and he inquired particularly respecting the price of a passage."[1]

Since the introduction of steamers great numbers of pilgrims visit Mecca, who cannot fail to extend the knowledge of western lands as they return among their people. The Mohammedan inhabitants of Turkestan and Ílí are distinguished into three classes by the color and shape of their turbans; one has red and another white sugar-loaf, the third the common Arab turban. The number throughout the region north of the Yangtsz' River cannot be stated, but it probably exceeds ten millions. In some places they form a third of the population; a missionary in Sz'chuen reckons eighty thousand living in one of its cities.[2]

The existence of Jews in China has long been known, but the information possessed relative to their past number, condition, and residences is very imperfect. They were once numbered by thousands, and are supposed by Mr. Finn to have belonged to the restoration from Chaldea, as they had portions of Malachi and Zechariah, adopted the era of Seleucus, and had many rabbinical customs. They probably entered China through the north-western route, and there is no good reason for rejecting their own date, during the Han dynasty. Within the last three centuries all have lived in Kaifung, the capital of Honan, wherever they may have lived in earlier days. Marco Polo just mentions their existence at Cambaluc, as do John of Montecorvino and Marignolli about the same time, and Ibn Batuta at an earlier date. In the Chinese annals of the Mongol dynasty the Jews are first referred to in 1329, and again in 1354, when they were invited to Peking in the decline of its power to join the army of the Imperialists. They are styled *Shu-hwuh*, or Jehudi, and must have been numerous enough

---

[1] Compare Milne's *Life in China*, p. 96, London, 1857.

[2] *Chinese Repository*, Vols. XIII., p. 32; XX., pp. 77–84; II., p. 256. De Guignes, *Voyages à Peking*, Tome II., p. 68. Gray, *China*, I., pp. 137–142. Edkins, *Religions in China*, Chap. XV. *Annales de la Foi*, II., p. 245. Reinaud, *Relation des Voyages à la Chine*.

to make them worth noticing with Mohammedans, and their help in men and means implored; but no hint is given of their places of abode. Further research into Chinese histories may disclose other notices of their existence.

The Jews were early known by the term of *Tiao-kin kiao*, or the 'sect which pulls out the sinew.' De Guignes says they are also called *Lan-mao Hwui-tsz'*, or 'Mohammedans with Blue Caps,' because they wore a blue cap in the synagogue; but this latter must be a local name. The first description of this colony was written by the Jesuit Gozani, about the year 1700, and shows that the *Tsing-chin sz'*, or 'Pure and True Temple,' was then a large establishment consisting of four separate courts, various buildings enclosed for residence, worship, and work. The *Lí-pai sz'*, or Synagogue, measured about sixty by forty feet, having a portico with a double row of four columns before it. In the centre of the room, between the rows of pillars, is the throne of Moses, a magnificent and elevated chair with an embroidered cushion, upon which they place the book of the law while it is read.

This account of Gozani remained as the latest information until Bishop Smith sent two native Christians from Shanghai to Kaifung to learn the present condition of the Jews. They were ignorant of Hebrew, but had been instructed how to copy the letters, and did their work very creditably, bringing away with them some portions of the Old Testament written on vellum-like paper of an old date. The synagogue had suffered during the great inundation of 1849, and the colony of two hundred individuals was found in abject poverty, ignorance, and dejection. Not one of them knew a word of Hebrew, and many of their buildings had been sold for the materials to support their lives.

In February, 1866, Rev. W. A. P. Martin, President of the Tung-wăn Kwan at Peking, visited Kaifung, and learned that during the interval of fifteen years they had become still more impoverished. Having learned from the mollah of a mosque where they lived, he "passed through streets crowded with curious spectators to an open square, in the centre of which there stood a solitary stone. On one side was an inscription commemorating the erection of the synagogue in A.D. 1183, and on the other of its rebuilding in 1488. . . . 'Are there among you any of the family of Israel?' I inquired. 'I am one,' responded a young man, whose face corroborated his assertion; and then another and another stepped forth, until I saw before me representatives of six of the seven families into which the colony is divided. There, on that melancholy spot where the very foundations of the synagogue had been torn from the ground, and there no longer remained one stone upon another, they confessed, with shame and grief, that their holy and beautiful house had been demolished by their own hands. It had long been, they said, in a ruinous condition; they had no money to make repairs. They had lost all knowledge of the sacred tongue; the traditions of the fathers were no longer handed down, and their ritual worship had ceased to be observed. They had at last yielded to the pressure of necessity, and disposed of the timbers and stones of the venerable edifice to obtain relief for their bodily wants."

They estimated their number at between three hundred and four hundred persons, all of them poor, and, now that the centre of attraction had disappeared, likely to become dispersed and lost. The entrance tablet in gilt characters, stating that the building was "Israel's Possession," had been placed in a mosque, and some of the colony had entered its worship.

Since that date one of their own race, now Bishop Schereschewsky, of Shanghai, has also visited them, but the literati of the city refused to allow him to remain among them. A company of the colony came up to Peking about twelve years ago, but, finding that no money was to be obtained for their support, ere long went back. It is probable that in a few years their unity will be so destroyed in the removal of their synagogue that they will be quite mingled with their countrymen. One or two are now Buddhist priests, others are literary graduates, and all of them are ignorant of their peculiar rites and festivals. Like the Mohammedans, they have never translated their sacred books into Chinese; but during their long existence in China they have remained indeed, as Dr. Martin says, like "a rock rent from the sides of Mount Zion by some great national catastrophe, and projected into the central Plain of China, which has stood there while the centuries rolled by, sublime in its antiquity and solitude."[1]

[1] *Chinese Repository*, Vol. XX., pp. 436–466. Yule's *Marco Polo*, 1871, Vol. I., p. 309. *Cathay*, pp. 225, 341, 497. James Finn, *Jews in China*, 1843. Bp. Smith, *Mission of Inquiry to Jews at Kai-fung*, 1851. Dr. Martin, *The Chinese*, N. Y., 1881. *Journal of Royal Geog. Soc.*, London, Vol. XXVII., p. 297. *Versuch einer Geschichte der Juden in Sina, nebst P. J. Kögler's Beschreibung ihrer heiligen Bücher*, herausg. von C. G. von Murr, Halle, 1806. Milne, *Life in China*, p. 403.

CHAPTER XIX.

CHRISTIAN MISSIONS AMONG THE CHINESE.

THE earliest recorded attempt to impart the knowledge of the true God to the Chinese ascribes it to the Nestorian church in the seventh century; though the voice of tradition, and detached notices in ecclesiastical writers of the Eastern Empire collated by Fabricius, lead to the belief that not many years elapsed after the times of the apostles before the sound of the gospel was heard in China and Chin-India. If the tradition contained in the breviary used among the Malabar Christians, that by Saint Thomas himself the Chinese were converted to the truth, be not received, Mosheim well remarks that "we may believe that at an early period the Christian religion extended to the Chinese, Seres, and Tartars. There are various arguments collected from learned men to show that the Christian faith was carried to China, if not by the apostle Thomas, by the first teachers of Christianity." Arnobius, A.D. 300, speaks of the Christian deeds done in India, and among the Seres, Persians, and Medes. The Nestorian monks who brought the eggs of the silk-worm to Constantinople (A.D. 551) had resided long in China, where it is reasonable to suppose they were not the first nor the only ones who went thither to preach the gospel. The extent of their success must be left to conjecture, but "if such beams have travelled down to us through the darkness of so many ages, it is reasonable to believe they emanated from a brighter source."

The time of the arrival of the Nestorians in China cannot be specified certainly, but there are grounds for placing it as early as A.D. 505. Ebedjesus Sobiensis remarks that "the Catholicos Salibazacha created the metropolitan sees of Sina and Samarcand, though some say they were constituted by Achæus and Silas." Silas was patriarch of the Nestorians from A.D. 505 to 520; and Achæus was archbishop at Seleucia in 415. The metropolitan bishop of Sina is also mentioned in a list of those subject to this patriarch, published by Amro, and it is placed in the list after that of India, according to the priority of foundation.

The only record yet found in China itself of the labors of the Nestorians is the celebrated monument which was discovered at Sí-ngan fu in Shensí, in 1625; and though the discussion re-

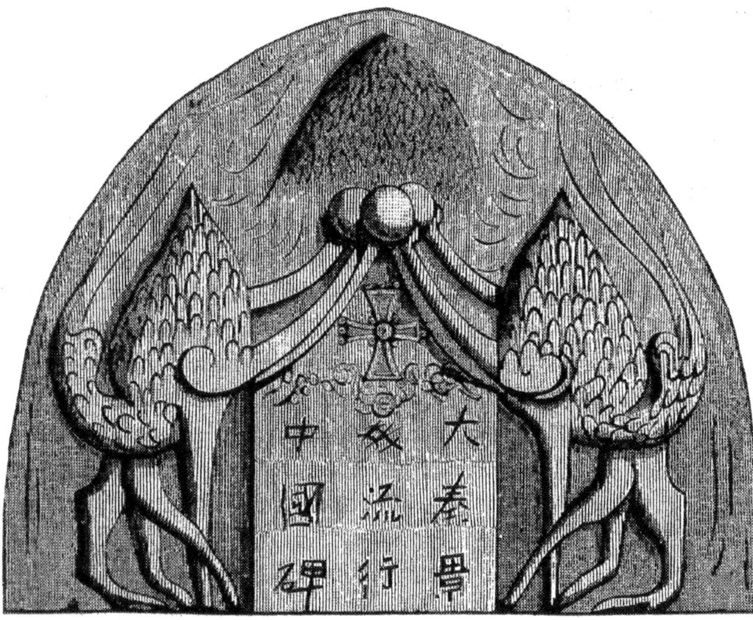

Head of Nestorian Tablet at Sí-ngan.

garding its authenticity has been rather warm between the Jesuits and their opponents, the weight of evidence, both internal and external, leaves no doubt regarding its verity. It has been found quite recently to be in good preservation, and rubbings taken from it are nearly perfect. The Syriac characters composing the signatures of Olopun and his associates have made it an object of much interest to the natives; these, as well as the singular cross on its top (seen in the illustration), have doubtless contributed to its preservation. It was set up in 1859 by a

Chinese who had so much regard for it as to rebuild it in the brick wall where it had once stood outside of the city. The stone seems to be a coarse marble.

It has been often translated since the first attempt by Boime, published with the original by Kircher in Holland. In 1845 Dr. E. C. Bridgman published Kircher's Latin translation with the French version of Dalquié, and another of his own, which brought it more into notice. The style is very terse, and the exact meaning not easily perceived even by learned natives. As Dr. Bridgman says, "Were a hundred Chinese students employed on the document they would probably each give a different view of the meaning in some parts of the inscription." This is apparent when four or five of them are compared. The last one, by A. Wylie, of the London Mission at Shanghai, goes over the whole subject with a fullness and care which leaves little to be desired.[1]

TABLET EULOGIZING THE PROPAGATION OF THE ILLUSTRIOUS RELIGION IN CHINA, WITH A PREFACE; COMPOSED BY KING-TSING, A PRIEST OF THE SYRIAN CHURCH.

Behold the unchangeably true and invisible, who existed through all eternity without origin; the far-seeing perfect intelligence, whose mysterious existence is everlasting; operating on primordial substance he created the universe, being more excellent than all holy intelligences, inasmuch as he is the source of all that is honorable. This is our eternal true lord God, triune and mysterious in substance. He appointed the cross as the means for determining the four cardinal points, he moved the original spirit, and produced the two principles of nature; the sombre void was changed, and heaven and earth were opened out; the sun and moon revolved, and day and night commenced; having perfected all inferior objects, he then made the first man; upon him he bestowed an excellent disposition, giving him in charge the government of all created beings; man, acting out the original principles of his nature, was pure and unostentatious; his unsullied and expansive mind was free from the least inordinate desire; until Satan introduced the seeds of falsehood, to deteriorate his purity of principle; the opening thus commenced in his virtue

[1] Visdelou in *Bibliotheque Oriental*, Vol. IV. Kircher's *China Illustrata*, Part I., Antwerp, 1667. *Chinese Repository*, XIV., pp. 201–229. Huc, *Christianity in China*, I., pp. 49–58. Wylie, *North China Herald*, 1855, reprinted in *Journal of Am. Oriental Soc.*, Vol. V., p. 277. Archimandrite Palladius published a Russian version. Williamson, *Journeys in North China*, I., p. 382. *Le Catholicisme en Chine au VIIIe Siècle de notre ère avec une nouvelle traduction de l'inscription de Sy-nganfou*, par P. D. de Thiersant, Paris, 1877.

gradually enlarged, and by this crevice in his nature was obscured and rendered vicious; hence three hundred and sixty-five sects followed each other in continuous track, inventing every species of doctrinal complexity; while some pointed to material objects as the source of their faith, others reduced all to vacancy, even to the annihilation of the two primeval principles; some sought to call down blessings by prayers and supplications, while others by an assumption of excellence held themselves up as superior to their fellows; their intellects and thoughts continually wavering, their minds and affections incessantly on the move, they never obtained their vast desires, but being exhausted and distressed they revolved in their own heated atmosphere; till by an accumulation of obscurity they lost their path, and after long groping in darkness they were unable to return. Thereupon, our Trinity being divided in nature, the illustrious and honorable Messiah, veiling his true dignity, appeared in the world as a man; angelic powers promulgated the glad tidings, a virgin gave birth to the Holy One in Syria; a bright star announced the felicitous event, and Persians[1] observing the splendor came to present tribute; the ancient dispensation, as declared by the twenty-four holy men,[2] was then fulfilled, and he laid down great principles for the government of families and kingdoms; he established the new religion of the silent operation of the pure spirit of the Triune; he rendered virtue subservient to direct faith; he fixed the extent of the eight boundaries,[3] thus completing the truth and freeing it from dross; he opened the gate of the three constant principles,[4] introducing life and destroying death; he suspended the bright sun to invade the chambers of darkness, and the falsehoods of the devil were thereupon defeated; he set in motion the vessel of mercy by which to ascend to the bright mansions, whereupon rational beings were then released; having thus completed the manifestation of his power, in clear day he ascended to his true station. Twenty-seven sacred books[5] have been left, which disseminate intelligence by unfolding the original transforming principles. By the rule for admission, it is the custom to apply the water of baptism, to wash away all superficial show and to cleanse and purify the neophytes. As a seal, they hold the cross, whose influence is reflected in every direction, uniting all without distinction. As they strike the wood, the fame of their benevolence is diffused abroad; worshipping toward the east, they hasten on the way to life and glory; they pre-

---

[1] *Po-sz'*, 'Persians.' This name was well known to the Chinese at that time, being the designation of an extensive sect then located in the Empire, and the name of a nation with which they had held commercial and political intercourse for several centuries. The statement here is in admirable harmony with the general tradition of the early church, that the Magi or wise men mentioned in Matthew's gospel were no other than philosophers of the Parsee sect.

[2] The "holy men" denote the writers of the books of the Old Testament.

[3] The "eight boundaries" are inexplicable; some refer them to the beatitudes.

[4] The "three constant principles" may perhaps mean faith, hope, and charity.

[5] Exactly the number we have in the New Testament.

serve the beard to symbolize their outward actions, they shave the crown to indicate the absence of inward affections; they do not keep slaves, but put noble and mean all on an equality; they do not amass wealth, but cast all their property into the common stock; they fast, in order to perfect themselves by self-inspection; they submit to restraints, in order to strengthen themselves by silent watchfulness; seven times a day they have worship and praise, for the benefit of the living and the dead; once in seven days they sacrifice, to cleanse the heart and return to purity.

It is difficult to find a name to express the excellence of the true and unchangeable doctrine; but as its meritorious operations are manifestly displayed, by accommodation it is named the Illustrious Religion. Now without holy men, principles cannot become expanded; without principles, holy men cannot become magnified; but with holy men and right principles, united as the two parts of a signet, the world becomes civilized and enlightened.

In the time of the accomplished Emperor Taitsung, the illustrious and magnificent founder of the dynasty, among the enlightened and holy men who arrived was the Most-virtuous Olopun, from the country of Syria. Observing the azure clouds, he bore the true sacred books; beholding the direction of the winds, he braved difficulties and dangers. In the year A.D. 635 he arrived at Chang-an; the Emperor sent his Prime Minister, Duke Fang Hiuenling; who, carrying the official staff to the west border, conducted his guest into the interior; the sacred books were translated in the imperial library, the sovereign investigated the subject in his private apartments; when becoming deeply impressed with the rectitude and truth of the religion, he gave special orders for its dissemination. In the seventh month of the year A.D. 638 the following imperial proclamation was issued:

"Right principles have no invariable name, holy men have no invariable station; instruction is established in accordance with the locality, with the object of benefiting the people at large. The Greatly-virtuous Olopun, of the kingdom of Syria, has brought his sacred books and images from that distant part, and has presented them at our chief capital. Having examined the principles of this religion, we find them to be purely excellent and natural; investigating its originating source, we find it has taken its rise from the establishment of important truths; its ritual is free from perplexing expressions, its principles will survive when the framework is forgot; it is beneficial to all creatures; it is advantageous to mankind. Let it be published throughout the Empire, and let the proper authority build a Syrian church in the capital in the Í-ning Way, which shall be governed by twenty-one priests. When the virtue of the Chau dynasty declined, the rider on the azure ox ascended to the west; the principles of the great Tang becoming resplendent, the Illustrious breezes have come to fan the East."

Orders were then issued to the authorities to have a true portrait of the Emperor taken; when it was transferred to the wall of the church, the dazzling splendor of the celestial visage irradiated the Illustrious portals. The sacred traces emitted a felicitous influence, and shed a perpetual splendor over the holy precincts. According to the Illustrated Memoir of the Western Regions, and the historical books of the Han and Wei dynasties, the kingdom of Syria reaches south to the Coral Sea; on the north it joins the Gem Mountains; on the west it extends toward the borders of the immortals and the flowery forests; on the east it lies open to the violent winds and tideless waters. The country produces fire-proof cloth, life-restoring incense, bright moon-pearls, and night-lustre gems. Brigands and robbers are unknown, but the people enjoy happiness and peace. None but Illustrious laws prevail; none but the virtuous are raised to sovereign power. The land is broad and ample, and its literary productions are perspicuous and clear.

The Emperor Kautsung respectfully succeeded his ancestor, and was still more beneficent toward the institution of truth. In every province he caused Illustrious churches to be erected, and ratified the honor conferred upon Olopun, making him the great conservator of doctrine for the preservation of the State. While this doctrine pervaded every channel, the State became enriched and tranquillity abounded. Every city was full of churches, and the royal family enjoyed lustre and happiness. In the year A.D. 699 the Buddhists, gaining power, raised their voices in the eastern metropolis; [1] in the year A.D. 713, some low fellows excited ridicule and spread slanders in the western capital. At that time there was the chief priest Lo-han, the Greatly-virtuous Kie-leih, and others of noble estate from the golden regions, lofty-minded priests, having abandoned all worldly interests; who unitedly maintained the grand principles and preserved them entire to the end.

The high-principled Emperor Hiuentsung caused the Prince of Ning and others, five princes in all, personally to visit the felicitous edifice; he established the place of worship; he restored the consecrated timbers which had been temporarily thrown down; and re-erected the sacred stones which for a time had been desecrated.

In 742 orders were given to the great general Kau Lih-sz', to send the five sacred portraits and have them placed in the church, and a gift of a hundred pieces of silk accompanied these pictures of intelligence. Although the dragon's beard was then remote, their bows and swords were still within reach; while the solar horns sent forth their rays, and celestial visages seemed close at hand.[2]

In 744 the priest Kih-ho, in the kingdom of Syria, looking toward the star (of China), was attracted by its transforming influen e, and observing the sun (*i.e.*, Emperor), came to pay court to the most honorable. The Emperor commanded the priest Lo-han, the priest Pu-lun, and others, seven in all, together with the Greatly-virtuous Kih-ho, to perform a service of merit in the Hing-king palace. Thereupon the Emperor composed mottoes for the sides of the church, and the tablets were graced with the royal inscriptions; the accumulated gems emitted their effulgence, while their sparkling brightness vied with the ruby clouds; the transcripts of intelligence suspended in the

---

[1] "Eastern metropolis" is *Tung Chau*, literally 'Eastern Chau.' The Empire was at this time under the government of the Empress Wu Tsih-tien, who had removed her residence from Chang-an to Lohyang in Honan.

[2] These personages are the first five Emperors of the Tang dynasty, Hiuentsung's predecessors. Their portraits were so admirably painted that they seemed to be present, their arms could almost be handled, and their foreheads, or "horns of the sun," radiated their intelligence.

void shot forth their rays as reflected by the sun; the bountiful gifts exceeded the height of the southern hills; the bedewing favors were deep as the eastern sea. Nothing is beyond the range of right principle, and what is permissible may be identified; nothing is beyond the power of the holy man, and that which is practicable may be related.

The accomplished and enlightened Emperor Suhtsung rebuilt the Illustrious churches in Ling-wu and four other places; great benefits were conferred, and felicity began to increase; great munificence was displayed, and the imperial State became established.

The accomplished and military Emperor Taitsung magnified the sacred succession, and honored the latent principle of nature; always, on the incarnation-day, he bestowed celestial incense, and ordered the performance of a service of merit; he distributed of the imperial viands, in order to shed a glory on the Illustrious Congregation. Heaven is munificent in the dissemination of blessings, whereby the benefits of life are extended; the holy man embodies the original principle of virtue, whence he is able to counteract noxious influences.

Our sacred and sage-like, accomplished and military Emperor Kienchung appointed the eight branches of government, according to which he advanced or degraded the intelligent and dull; he opened up the nine categories, by means of which he renovated the illustrious decrees; his transforming influence pervaded the most abstruse principles, while openness of heart distinguished his devotions. Thus, by correct and enlarged purity of principle, and undeviating consistency in sympathy with others; by extended commiseration rescuing multitudes from misery, while disseminating blessings on all around, the cultivation of our doctrine gained a grand basis, and by gradual advances its influence was diffused. If the winds and rains are seasonable, the world will be at rest; men will be guided by principle, inferior objects will be pure; the living will be at ease, and the dead will rejoice; the thoughts will produce their appropriate response, the affections will be free, and the eyes will be sincere; such is the laudable condition which we of the Illustrious Religion are laboring to attain.

Our great benefactor, the Imperially-conferred-purple-gown priest,[1] Î-sz', titular Great Statesman of the Banqueting-house, Associated Secondary Military Commissioner for the Northern Region, and Examination-palace Overseer, was naturally mild and graciously disposed; his mind susceptible of sound doctrine, he was diligent in the performance; from the distant city of Râjagriha,[2] he came to visit China; his principles more lofty than those of the

[1] It was no rare occurrence for priests to occupy civil and military offices in the State during the Tang and preceding dynasties. Of the three titles here given, the first is merely an indication of rank, by which the bearer is entitled to a certain emolument from the State; the second is his title as an officer actively engaged in the imperial service; and the third is an honorary title, which gives to the possessor a certain status in the capital, without any duties or emolument connected therewith.

[2] *Wang-shih*, literally 'Royal residence,' which is also the translation of the Sanskrit word Râjagriha, is the name of a city on the banks of the Ganges,

three dynasties, his practice was perfect in every department; at first he applied himself to duties pertaining to the palace, eventually his name was inscribed on the military roll. When the Duke Koh Tsz'-í, Secondary Minister of State and Prince of Făn-yang, at first conducted the military in the northern region, the Emperor Suhtsung made him (Í-sz') his attendant on his travels; although he was a private chamberlain, he assumed no distinction on the march; he was as claws and teeth to the duke, and in rousing the military he was as ears and eyes; he distributed the wealth conferred upon him, not accumulating treasure for his private use; he made offerings of the jewelry which had been given by imperial favor, he spread out a golden carpet for devotion; now he repaired the old churches, anon he increased the number of religious establishments; he honored and decorated the various edifices, till they resembled the plumage of the pheasant in its flight; moreover, practising the discipline of the Illustrious Religion, he distributed his riches in deeds of benevolence; every year he assembled those in the sacred office from four churches, and respectfully engaged them for fifty days in purification and preparation; the naked came and were clothed; the sick were attended to and restored; the dead were buried in reposo; even among the most pure and self-denying of the Buddhists, such excellence was never heard of; the white-clad members of the Illustrious Congregation, now considering these men, have desired to engrave a broad tablet, in order to set forth a eulogy of their magnanimous deeds.

ODE.

The true Lord is without origin,
Profound, invisible, and unchangeable;
With power and capacity to perfect and transform,
He raised up the earth and established the heavens.

Divided in nature, he entered the world,
To save and to help without bounds;
The sun arose, and darkness was dispelled,
All bearing witness to his true original.

The glorious and resplendent, accomplished Emperor,
Whose principles embraced those of preceding monarchs,
Taking advantage of the occasion, suppressed turbulence;
Heaven was spread out and the earth was enlarged.

When the pure, bright Illustrious Religion
Was introduced to our Tang dynasty,
The Scriptures were translated, and churches built,
And the vessel set in motion for the living and the dead;
Every kind of blessing was then obtained,
And all the kingdoms enjoyed a state of peace.

---

which occurs in several Buddhist works. As this was one of the most important of the Buddhist cities in India, it is natural to suppose that Í-sz' was a Buddhist priest.

When Kautsung succeeded to his ancestral estate,
He rebuilt the edifices of purity;
Palaces of concord, large and light,
Covered the length and breadth of the land.

The true doctrine was clearly announced,
Overseers of the church were appointed in due form;
The people enjoyed happiness and peace,
While all creatures were exempt from calamity and distress.

When Hiuentsung commenced his sacred career,
He applied himself to the cultivation of truth and rectitude;
His imperial tablets shot forth their effulgence,
And the celestial writings mutually reflected their splendors.

The imperial domain was rich and luxuriant,
While the whole land rendered exalted homage;
Every business was flourishing throughout,
And the people all enjoyed prosperity.

Then came Suhtsung, who commenced anew,
And celestial dignity marked the imperial movements;
Sacred as the moon's unsullied expanse,
While felicity was wafted like nocturnal gales.

Happiness reverted to the imperial household,
The autumnal influences were long removed;
Ebullitions were allayed, and risings suppressed,
And thus our dynasty was firmly built up.

Taitsung the filial and just
Combined in virtue with heaven and earth;
By his liberal bequests the living were satisfied,
And property formed the channel of imparting succor.

By fragrant mementoes he rewarded the meritorious,
With benevolence he dispensed his donations;
The solar concave appeared in dignity,
And the lunar retreat was decorated to extreme.

When Kienchung succeeded to the throne,
He began by the cultivation of intelligent virtue;
His military vigilance extended to the four seas,
And his accomplished purity influenced all lands.

His light penetrated the secresies of men,
And to him the diversities of objects were seen as in a mirror;
He shed a vivifying influence through the whole realm of nature,
And all outer nations took him for example.

The true doctrine how expansive!
Its responses are minute;
How difficult to name it!
To elucidate the three in one.

The sovereign has the power to act!
While the ministers record;
We raise this noble monument!
To the praise of great felicity.

This was erected in the 2d year of Kienchung, of the Tang dynasty (A.D. 781), on the 7th day of 1st month, being Sunday.

Written by Lu Siu-yen, Secretary to Council, formerly Military Superintendent for Taichau; while the Bishop Ning-shu had the charge of the congregations of the Illustrious in the East.

The two lines of Syriac, of which the following is a transcript, are in the Estrangelo character, and run down the right and left sides of the Chinese respectively:

Adam Kasiso Vicur-apiskupo va Papasi de Zinstan.
Beyumi aba dabahotha Mar Hana Jesua katholika patriarchis.

Kircher translates this as follows:

"Adam, Deacon, Vicar-episcopal and Pope of China.
In the time of the Father of Fathers, the Lord John Joshua, the Universal Patriarch."

The transcript of the Syriac at the foot of the stone is given here on the authority of Kircher:

Besanath alf utisaain vtarten diavanoiê. Mor Jibuzad Kasiso Vcurapiskupo de Cumdan medinah malcutho bar nihh napso Milis Kasiso dmen Balehh medintho Tahhurstan Akim Lucho hono Papa dictabon beh medabarnutho dpharukan Vcaruzuthon dabhain daluat malche dizinio.

"In the year of the Greeks one thousand and ninety-two, the Lord Jazedbuzid, Priest and Vicar-episcopal of Cumdan the royal city, son of the enlightened Mailas, Priest of Balach a city of Turkestan, set up this tablet, whereon is inscribed the Dispensation of our Redeemer, and the preaching of the apostolic missionaries to the King of China."

After this, in Chinese characters, is "The Priest Lingpau." Then follows:

Adam meschamschóno Bar Jidbuzad Curapiskupo.
Mar Sargis Kasiso, Vcurapiskupo.
Sabar Jesua Kasiso.
Gabriel Kasiso Varcodiakun, Vrisch medintho de Cumdan vdasrag.

"Adam the Deacon, son of Jazedbuzid, Vicar-episcopal.
The Lord Sergius, Priest and Vicar-episcopal.
Sabar Jesus, Priest.
Gabriel, Priest, Archdeacon, and Ecclesiarch of Cumdan and Sarag."

The following subscription is appended in Chinese:

"Assistant Examiner: the High Statesman of the Sacred rites, the Imperially-conferred-purple-gown Chief Presbyter and Priest Yí-lí."

On the left hand edge are the Syriac names of sixty-seven priests, and sixty-one are given in Chinese.

This truly oriental writing is the most ancient Christian inscription yet found in Asia, and shows plainly that Christianity had made great progress among the Chinese. Kircher and Le Comte claimed it as a record of the success of the Romish church in China, but no one now doubts that it commemorates the exertions of the Nestorians.

Timothy, a patriarch, sent Subchal-Jesus in 780, who labored in Tartary and China for many years, and lost his life on his return, when his place was supplied by Davidis, who was consecrated metropolitan. In the year 845 an edict of Wu-tsung commanded the priests that belonged to the sect that came from Ta Tsin, amounting to no less than three thousand persons, to retire to private life. The two Arabian travellers in the ninth century report that many Christians perished in the siege of Canfu. Marco Polo's frequent allusions lead us to conclude that the Nestorians were both numerous and respected.

He mentions the existence of a church at Hangchau, and two at Chinkiang, built by the prefect Marsarchis, who was himself a member of that church, and alludes to their residence in most of the towns and countries of Central Asia.

The existence of a Christian prince called Prester John, in Central Asia, is spoken of by Marco Polo and Montecorvino. The exact position of his dominions, and the extent of his influence in favor of that faith, have been examined by Col. Yule and

M. Pauthier in their editions of the Venetian, and the glamour which once surrounded him has been found to have arisen mostly from hearsay reports, and from confounding different persons under one name. When the conquests of Genghis khan and his descendants threw all Asia into commotion, this Prester John, ruler of the Kara Kitai Tartars in northern China, fell before him, A.D. 1203. The Nestorians suffered much, but maintained a precarious footing in China during the time of the Yuen dynasty, having been cut off from all help and intercourse with the mother church since the rise of the Moslems. They had ceased long before this period to maintain the purity of the faith, however, and had apparently done nothing to teach and diffuse the Bible, which the tablet intimates was in part or in whole translated by Olopun, under the Emperor's auspices.

At the present time no works composed by their priests, or remains of any churches belonging to them or buildings erected by them, are known to exist in the Empire, though perhaps some books may yet be found. The buildings erected by the Nestorians for churches and dwellings were, of course, no better built than other Chinese edifices, and would not long remain when deserted; while, to account still further for the absence of books, the Buddhists and other opposers may have sought out and destroyed such as existed, which even if carefully kept would not last many generations. The notices of the tablet in Chinese authors, which Mr. Wylie has brought together, prove that those writers had confounded the *King kiao* with Zoroastrianism and Manicheism, and such a confusion is not surprising. The records of futurity alone will disclose to us the names and labors of the devoted disciples and teachers of true Christianity in the Nestorian church, who lived and died for the gospel among the Chinese.[1]

The efforts of the Roman Catholics in China have been great, but not greater than the importance of the field demanded.

---

[1] Yule's *Marco Polo*, Vol. I., p. 275, passim. *N. C. As. Soc. Journal*, Arch. Palladius' notes on it, Vol. X., pp. 20–23. Huc, *Christianity in China*, Chap. II. Pauthier's *Marco Polo*, Chaps. XLVIII.–L. Yule, *Cathay and the Way Thither*, Vol. I., pp. 174–183.

They have met with varied success, and their prudence in the choice of measures and zeal in the work of evangelizing have reflected the highest credit upon them, and would probably, if their object had simply been that of preaching the gospel, have gradually made the entire mass of the population acquainted with the leading doctrines of Christianity. The history of their missions is voluminous, and the principles on which they have been conducted can be learned from their own writings, especially the *Lettres Édifiantes*, the *Annales de la Foi*, and in the elaborate works of Huc and Marshall in later times. The present sketch need embrace only the principal points, for which we shall depend chiefly upon those writers who have already examined these sources.

The first epoch of their missions in China is the thirteenth century. Subsequent to the mission of John of Plano Carpini to Kuyuk khan in 1246–47, there were several envoys sent by one party to the other whose intercourse resulted in nothing permanent. The first attempt which can be called a settled mission was that of John of Montecorvino, from Nicholas IV., in 1288. Corvino arrived in India in 1291, and after preaching there a twelvemonth, during which time he baptized a hundred persons, he joined a caravan going to Cathay and was kindly received by Kublai khan. The Nestorians opposed his progress, and for eleven years he carried on the work alone, but not till the latter part of this period with much success. He built a church at Cambaluc, "which had a steeple and belfry with three bells that were rung every hour to summon the new converts to prayer." He baptized nearly six thousand persons during that time, "and bought one hundred and fifty children, whom he instructed in Greek and Latin and composed for them several devotional books." [1]

Clement V., hearing of Corvino's success, appointed him archbishop in 1307 and sent him seven suffragan bishops as assistants. Two letters of his are extant in which he gives a pleasing account of his efforts to preach the gospel, but of the

[1] *Chinese Repository*, Vol. III., p. 112; Vol. XIII., passim. Lowrie, *Land of Sinim.*

subsequent success of the endeavors made by him and his coadjutors to propagate the faith there are only imperfect records. Corvino was ordered to have the mysteries of the Bible represented by pictures in all his churches, for the purpose of captivating the eyes of the barbarians. He died in 1328, when about eighty years of age, "after having converted more than thirty thousand infidels." One of the accounts relates that at his funeral "all the inhabitants of Cambaluc, without distinction, mourned for the man of God, and both Christians and pagans were present at the funeral ceremony, the latter rending their garments in token of grief, . . . and the place of his burial became a pilgrimage to which the inhabitants of Cambaluc resorted with pious eagerness." It is not easy to estimate the real value of the labors of this priest and his successors, nor to decide how much better they were than those of the Nestorians in making known the Cross of Christ among the Mongols. The short record preserved of Corvino speaks well of his character and favorably of the toleration granted by the Mongols to his efforts to instruct them. It is affecting to hear him say, "It is now twelve years since I have heard any news from the West. I am become old and grayheaded, but it is rather through labors and tribulations than through age, for I am only fifty-eight years old. I have learned the Tartar language and literature, into which I have translated the whole New Testament and the Psalms of David, and have caused them to be transcribed with the utmost care. I write and read and preach openly and freely the testimony of the law of Christ."

The Pope sent Nicholas to succeed Montecorvino at Peking, and a company of twenty-six Franciscans with him, but no authentic record of their arrival there has been preserved. In 1336 the last Mongol Emperor, Shuntí, whose reign was then called Chíyuen, sent André, a Frank, as his ambassador to the Pope, to whom was also addressed a letter from the Alain Christians asking for a bishop to take Corvino's place, Nicholas not having then reached his see. Benedict XII. sent four nuncios, one of whom, John of Florence, returned to Europe in 1353, after residing and travelling in China twelve years, bringing friendly letters from the Emperor Shuntí. At this period there was another bishopric among the Mongols at Ílí, or Kuldja, and a letter from Pascal, a Spanish friar, dated from that city in 1338, has been preserved. It would seem that during the sway of the Mongol princes these missionaries carried on their work chiefly among their tribes. It is, if such was the case, less surprising, therefore, that we hear nothing of them and their converts after the Chinese troops had expelled Kublai's weak descendants from the country in 1368, since they would naturally follow them into Central Asia. After the final establishment of the Ming dynasty almost nothing is known concerning either them or the Nestorians, and it is probable that during the wanderings of the defeated Mongols the adherents of both sects gradually lapsed into ignorance and thence easily into Mohammedanism and Buddhism. There is no reasonable doubt, however, that during the three centuries ending with the accession of Hungwu, the greater part of Central Asia and Northern China was the scene of many flourishing Christian communities.

The second period in the history of Romish missions in China includes a space of one hundred and fifty years, extending from the time when Matteo Ricci first established himself at Shauking in 1582 to the death of the Emperor Yungching in 1736. Before Ricci entered the country there had been some efforts made to revive the long-deferred work among the Chinese, but the Portuguese and Spanish merchants were opposed to the extension of a faith which their flagitious conduct so outrageously belied. The Chinese government was still more strongly opposed to the residence of the foreign missionaries. Francis Xavier started from Goa in 1552 in company with an ambassador to China, but the embassy was hindered by the Governor of Malacca, who detained Pereyra and his ship, and Xavier was obliged to go alone. He died, however, at Shangchuen, Sançian, or St. John's, an island about thirty miles south-west of Macao, disappointed in his expectations and thwarted in his plans by the untoward opposition of his countrymen. Other attempts were made to accomplish this design, but it was reserved for the Jesuits to carry it into effect. Valignani, the Superior of their missions in the East, selected Michael Ruggiero, or Roger, for this enterprise. He arrived at Macao in 1580 and commenced the study of the language. Soon after he was joined by Matthew Ricci, and after a series of efforts and disappointments they succeeded, in 1582, in obtaining lodgment at Shauking, then the residence of the Governor of Kwangtung. He granted them permission to build a house there, as they had told him that "they had at last ascertained with their own eyes that the Celestial Empire was even superior to its brilliant renown. They therefore desired to end their days in it, and wished to obtain a little land to construct a house and a church where they might pass their time in prayer and study, in solitude and meditation, which they could not do at Macao on account of the tumult and bustle which the perpetual activity of commerce occasioned." A beginning like this indicated the policy which has marked the progress of their work during the three centuries now passed. Nothing is said of making known Christ and him crucified as the great theme of their preaching. Huc tells us, too, that they took down the picture of the Virgin, because "the report had been spread that the strangers worshipped a woman," and replaced it by an image of the Saviour; and in this also they set the example, which successive ages have strengthened, of upholding the native idolatry. In their intercourse with the people of all classes they won good opinions by their courtesy, presents, and scientific attainments, and Huc sums up their principles in his approving remark, "they thought justly that the philosopher would make more impression than the priest upon minds so sceptic and so imbued with literary conceit." The appointed means given by the Founder of Christianity for its propagation are never mentioned as their guide and authority, and the building corresponds to the foundations laid.

In 1594 Valignani advised Ricci and his associates to exchange their garb of Buddhist priests for the more respected dress of the literati; and soon after he set out from Shauchau, in the north of Kwangtung, for Nanchang, the capital of Kiangsí, and thence made his way to Nanking, still a place of great importance, although not the capital of the Empire. He was directed to depart, and returned to Nanchang, where he was permitted to lay the foundation of a religious institution and establish his associates. He then left again for Nanking, but finding many obstacles proceeded to Suchau, the capital of Kiangnan, and there, too, established a school. The times becoming favorable, he appeared a third time at Nanking, in 1598, where he was received with amity, frankness, and good breeding, and his lectures on the exact sciences listened to with rapture. The progress of the mission had been so considerable that Valignani had appointed Ricci its Superior-General, which gave him power to regulate its internal concerns, for which he was well fitted.

An officer whom he had known in Shauchau, and who had been appointed President of the Board of Civil Office, was induced to take him to Peking on his return there from a mission to Hainan; but opposition arising this friend, Kwang, advised him to return with him to Nanking, as the officials at the capital were much disappointed to find that he knew nothing about making silver and gold, which was wanted to pay for the expedition to Japan. After Kwang's departure he and his colleague, Cataneo, found themselves nearly penniless, and he decided to return south, although it was winter. He reached Suchau in a very weak condition, but, having recovered, went to Nanking in 1599, where the high provincial authorities visited and aided him, heard his discourses on astronomy, and enabled him to get a house.

Everything progressed favorably, and Cataneo had returned from Macao with funds and presents. Ricci availed himself of a timely proposal from a eunuch to go with him to Peking, and started in a junk with his presents. The eunuch, however, wished to keep the latter, and by misrepresentations contrived to detain Ricci and his companion, Pantoja, at Tientsin for six months, at the end of which the villany was exposed, and the foreigners invited to court by imperial orders. They reached Peking January 4, 1601, twenty-one years after Ricci landed in Macao. The pleasing manners and extensive acquirements of Ricci, joined to a distribution of presents, gained him the favor of men in authority. He soon numbered some of them among his adherents, among whom Sü, baptized Paul, was one of his earliest and most efficient co-operators, and assisted him in translating Euclid.

The Emperor Wanleih received him with kindness, and allowed him and Pantoja to be accommodated at the place where foreign envoys usually remained; he subsequently permitted them to hire a house, and assigned them a stipend. In the meantime other Jesuits joined him at Peking, and were also settled in all the intermediate stations, where they carried on the work of their missions under his direction with success and favor. Paul Sü and his widowed daughter, who took the baptismal name of Candida, proved efficient supporters of the new faith. The new religion encountered many obstacles, and the officers who saw its progress felt the necessity of checking its growth before it got strength to set at naught the commands of government. Much excitement arose in 1605 between the Portuguese and the officials at Canton in consequence of a rumor of the former going to attack the city; and it was carried to such a height that the latter seized a convert named Martinez and punished him so severely that he died. A decree in 1617 ordered the missionaries to depart from court to Canton, there to embark for Europe, but, like many others of the same import subsequently issued, it received just as much obedience as they thought expedient to give it—and properly too; for if they were not disturbers of the peace or seditious, they ought not to be sent out of the country. This edict hindered their work only partially, and such was their diligence that by the year 1636 they had published no fewer than three hundred and forty treatises, some of them religious, but mostly on natural philosophy and mathematics. Ricci formulated a set of rules for their guidance, in which he allowed the converts to practise the rites of ancestral worship, because he considered them purely civil in their nature. The matter subsequently became a bone of contention between the Jesuits and Franciscans.

The talented founder of these missions died in 1610, at the age of fifty-eight, and for skill, perseverance, learning, and tact, his name deservedly stands highest among their missionaries. His withholding the Bible from the Chinese, and substitution of image worship, ritualism, and priestly ordinances for the pure truths of the gospel, have been maintained by his successors, for they are essential features of the church which sent them forth. He has been extolled by the Jesuits as a man possessed of every virtue. Another writer of the same church gives him the following character: "Ricci was active, skilful, full of schemes, and endowed with all the talents necessary to render him agreeable to the great or to gain the favor of princes; but at the same time so little versed in matters of faith that, as the Bishop of Conon said, it was sufficient to read his work on the true religion to be satisfied that he was ignorant of the first principles of theology. Being more a politician than a theologian, he discovered the secret of remaining peacefully in China. The kings found in him a man full of complaisance; the pagans a minister who accommodated himself to their superstitions; the mandarins a polite courtier skilled in all the trickery of courts; and the devil a faithful servant, who, far from destroying, established his reign among the heathen, and even extended it to the Christians. He preached in China the religion of Christ according to his own fancy; that is to say, he disfigured it by a faithful mixture of pagan superstitions, adopting the sacrifices offered to Confucius and ancestors, and teaching the Christians to assist and co-operate at the worship of idols, provided they only addressed their devotions to a cross covered with flowers, or secretly attached to one of the candles which were lighted in the temples of the false gods."[1] His work was described by Trigault in 1616, when full materials were accessible, so that his actions and motives are known more fully than many who have come after him.

After his death his place was filled by Longobardi, whose experience, learning, and judgment well fitted him for the post. The efforts of many enemies caused a reaction in 1616, and an edict was issued ordering all missionaries to leave the country; but they were sheltered by their converts, especially through the exertions of Sü, who in 1622 obtained the reversal of the edict of expulsion, and thereby caused the persecution

[1] *Anecdotes de la Chine*, Tome I., Pref. vi, vii. Huc, *Christianity in China*, Vol. II., Chaps. II. to V. Rémusat, *Nouveaux Mélanges*, Tome II., p. 207.

to cease.[1] The talents and learning of Schaal, a German Jesuit, who was recommended by Sü to the Emperor's regard in 1628, soon placed him at the head of all his brethren and ranked him among the most distinguished men in the Empire. The Dominicans and Franciscans also flocked to the land which had thus been opened by the Jesuits, but they were not welcomed by those who wished to build up their own power. After the death of Wanleih, in 1620, and those converts within the palace who had favored the cause, new influences against it arose, and during the short reign of his young grandson, Tienhí, troubles increased. Amid the breaking up of the Ming dynasty and the establishment of the present family on the throne (1630–1660), the missions suffered much, their spiritual guides retired to places of safety from the molestations of soldiers and banditti, and converts were necessarily left without instruction. The missionaries in the north sided with the Manchus, and Schaal became a favorite with the new monarch and his advisers, by whom he was appointed to reform the calendar. He succeeded in showing the incompetency of the persons who had the supervision of it, and after its revision was appointed president of the *Kin Tien Kien*, an astronomical board established for this object, and invested with the insignia and emoluments of a grandee of the first class. He employed his influence and means in securing the admission of other missionaries, and to build two churches in the capital and repair many of those which had fallen to decay in the provinces.

The exertions of the native converts did much to advance the cause of religion, and the baptismal names of Leon, Michel, etc., have been preserved among these early confessors; but none are more famous than Sü and his daughter, Candida. He gave his influence in its favor and his property to assist in building churches, while his revision of their writings made them acceptable to fastidious scholars. His daughter also spent her life in good works. According to Du Halde, she exhibited the sincerity of her profession by building thirty-nine churches

---

[1] Sü's *Apology* is given in full in the *Chinese Repository*, Vol. XIX., p. 118.

in different provinces, and printing one hundred and thirty Christian books for the instruction of her countrymen. Having heard that the pagans in several of the provinces were accustomed to abandon their children as soon as born, she established a foundling hospital; and seeing many blind people telling idle stories in the streets for the sake of gain, she got them instructed and sent forth to relate the different events of the gospel history. A few years before her death the Emperor conferred on her the title of *sho jin*, or 'virtuous woman,' and sent her a magnificent habit and head-dress adorned with pearls, which it is said she gradually sold, expending the proceeds in benevolent works. She received the last sacrament with a lively faith of being united to that God whom she had so zealously loved and served. She and her father have since been deified by the people, and are worshipped now at Shanghai for their good deeds. The large mission establishment at Sikawé (properly *Sü Kia-wei*, or the 'Sü Family Hamlet'), situated near that city, under the care of the Roman Catholics, now covers the same ground once owned by this eminent man. Candida's example was emulated by another lady of high connections, named Agatha, who was zealous in carrying on the same works. We can but hope that although the worship of these converts was mixed with much error, and Mary, Ignatius, and others received their homage as well as Christ, their faith was genuine and their works done by an actuating spirit of humble love.[1]

The Romish missionaries had friends among the high families in the land during the first hundred years of their labors, besides converts of both sexes. Few missions in pagan countries have been more favored with zealous converts, or their missionaries more aided and countenanced by rich and noble supporters, than the early papal missions to China. Le Comte speaks of the high favor enjoyed by all the laborers in this work through the reputation and influence of Schaal at court. One of those who obtained celebrity was Faber, whose efforts in Shensí were attended with great success, and who wrought many

[1] Medhurst's *China*, p. 188. Du Halde's *China*, Vol. II., p. 8.

miracles during his ministry in that province. Among others he mentions that "the town of Hang ching was at a certain time overrun with a prodigious multitude of locusts, which ate up all the leaves of the trees and gnawed the grass to the very roots. The inhabitants, after exhausting all the resources of their own superstitions and charms, applied to Faber, who promised to deliver them from the plague provided they would become Christians. When they consented he marched in ceremony into the highways in his stole and surplice, and sprinkled up and down the holy water, accompanying this action with the prayers of the church, but especially with a lively faith. God heard the voice of his servant, and the next day all the insects disappeared. But the people refused to perform their promise, and the plague grew worse than before. With much contrition they came to the father, confessing their fault and entreating his renewed interposition; again he sprinkled the holy water, and the insects a second time disappeared. Then the whole borough was converted, and many years afterward was reckoned one of the devoutest missions in China. His biographer mentions that Faber was carried over rivers through the air; he foretold his own death, and did several other such wonders; but the greatest miracle of all was his life, which he spent in the continual exercise of all the apostolical virtues and a tender devotion to the mother of God."

The increase of churches and converts in the northern provinces was rapid during the reign of Shunchí, but the southern parts of the Empire not being completely subdued, the claimant to the throne of Ming was favored by the missionaries there, and his troops led on by two Christian Chinese officers, called Thomas Kiu and Luke Chin. His mother, wife, and son were baptized with the names of Helena, Maria, and Constantine, and the former wrote a letter to Pope Alexander VII., expressing her attachment to the cause of Christianity, and wishing to put the country through him under the protection of God. He kindly answered her, but the expectations of the Romanists were disappointed by the death of Tunglieh, the Emperor.

During the reign of Shunchí Schaal and his coadjutors stood high at Peking, and missions prospered in the provinces; but on the Emperor's death the administration fell into the hands of four regents, and as they were known to be opposed to the new sect, a memorial was sent to court setting forth the evils likely to arise if it was not repressed. It should be mentioned that several monks of the Dominican and Franciscan orders, especially of Fuhkien province, where Capellas, a Spaniard, had been martyred in 1648, had resumed the labors of Archbishop John of Montecorvino at Peking, more than thirty years before this date. "Their presence had been resisted by the Jesuits [so ran the memorial], and the strifes between these orders about the meaning and worship of *tien* and *shangtí* (words used for the Supreme Being) revealed the important secret that the principles of the new doctrine were made to subserve the purposes of those who were aspiring to influence. It was remembered also that while the Catholics continued in Japan, nothing but intrigue, schism, and civil war was heard of, calamities that might sooner or later befal China if the criminal eagerness of the missionaries in enlisting people of all classes was not checked. The members of the different orders wore distinctive badges of medals, rosaries, crosses, etc., and were always ready to obey the calls of their chiefs, who could have no scruple to lead them on to action the moment a probability of success in subverting the existing political order and the ancient worship of China should offer." The regents took the memorial into consideration, and in 1665 the tribunals under their direction decreed that "Schaal and his associates merited the punishment of seducers, who announce to the people a false and pernicious doctrine."

Notwithstanding the honorable position Schaal held as tutor of the young Emperor Kanghí, he was proscribed and degraded with several high officers who had been baptized. Some of them perished, Schaal himself dying of grief and suffering August 16th of the same year, at the age of seventy-eight, having been thirty-seven years in imperial employ, under five monarchs. Verbiest and others were imprisoned, one of whom died; and twenty-one Jesuits, with some of other sects, were sent out of the country. Magaillans says he himself was "loaden for four whole months together with nine chains, three about his neck, his arms, and his legs; he was also condemned to have forty lashes, and to be banished out of Tartary as long as he lived. But a great earthquake that happened at that time at Peking delivered both him and the rest of his companions."[1] Their relief, however, was probably owing more to the favor of Kanghí on taking the reins of government in 1671 than to the earthquake; he soon released Verbiest to appoint him astronomer, and allowed the missionaries to return to their stations, though he forbade his subjects embracing Christianity. This favorable change is partly ascribed, too, to the errors Verbiest pointed out in the calendar, which showed an utter ignorance of the commonest principles of astronomy on the part of those who prepared it. An intercalary month had been erroneously introduced, and the unfortunate astronomers were made to exchange places with the imprisoned missionaries, while their intercalary month was discarded and the year shortened, to the astonishment of the common people. It may reasonably be doubted whether the priest acted with sagacity and prudence in thus exasperating those in high places by this public ridicule of their incompetency. Verbiest also prepared an astronomical work entitled "The Perpetual Astronomy of the Emperor Kanghí," which he graciously received and conferred the title of *tajin*, or 'magnate,' on him, and ennobled all his kindred. "He had no relatives in China, but as the Jesuits called each other brother, they did not hesitate to use the same title. The greatest part of the religious caused it to be inscribed on the doors of their houses."

The favor of the Emperor continued, and the missionaries requited his kindness with many signal services, besides those of a literary and astronomical nature, among which was casting cannon for his army. In 1636 Schaal had made a number for Tsungching, and Verbiest, his successor, cast several hundreds in all for the Emperor Kanghí. On one occasion, in 1680, the pieces, three hundred and twenty of all sizes, were to be tested in the presence of the court; but before doing so Verbiest "had an altar prepared on which he placed a cross. Then, clothed in his surplice and stole, he worshipped the true God, prostrating himself nine times, and striking the earth nine times with his forehead, in

[1] Magaillans' *China*, p. 147. *Chinese Repository*, Vol. I., p. 434.

the Chinese manner of expressing adoration; and after that he read the prayers of the church and sprinkled the cannon with holy water, having bestowed on each of them the name of a female saint, which he had himself drawn on the breech."[1] Some of the high officers were still opposed to the toleration of foreign priests, and the Governor of Chehkiang undertook to carry into effect the laws against their admission into the country and their proselyting labors; but Verbiest, on informing the Emperor of their character as excellent mathematicians and scholars, obtained their liberation. No foreigner has ever enjoyed so great favor and confidence from the rulers of China as this able priest. He seems indeed to have deserved this for his diligence, knowledge, and purity of conduct in devoting all his energies and opportunities to their good. His residence of thirty years at Peking (1658–1688) was passed under the eyes of suspicious observers; but his modesty in the end won their confidence as his writings and devotions called forth their approval.

During all this time—or at least since the other sects came to assist in the work—there had been constant disputes, as has already been intimated, between the disciples of Loyola, Dominic, and Francis, excited probably by rivalry, but ostensibly relating to the rites paid to deceased ancestors and to Confucius. Ricci had drawn up rules for the regulation of the Jesuits, in which he considered these customs to be merely civil and secular, and such as might be tolerated in their converts. Morales, a Spanish Dominican, however, opposed this view, declaring them to be idolatrous and sinful, and they were condemned as such by the Propaganda, which sentence was confirmed by Innocent X. in 1645. This decree of the see at Rome gave the Jesuits some annoyance, and they set themselves at work to procure its revision. Martinez was sent to Rome as their principal agent in this, and by many explanations and testimonials proved to the satisfaction of the tribunal of inquisitors their civil nature, and Alexander VII., in 1656, approved this opinion. There were thus two infallible decrees nearly opposed to each other, for Alexander took care not to directly contradict the bull of Inno-

[1] Huc, *Christianity in China*, Vol. III., p. 81.

cent, and worded his decision so that both claimed it. When all the missionaries were imprisoned or sent to Canton, a good opportunity offered for mutual consultation and decision upon these and other points. Twenty-three priests met in the Jesuit seminary at Canton in 1665, and drew up forty-two articles to serve hereafter for rules of conduct, all of which were unanimously adopted. The one relating to the ceremonies was as follows:

In respect to the customs by which the Chinese worship Confucius and the deceased, the answer of the congregation of the universal Inquisition, sanctioned in 1656 by his Holiness Alexander VII., shall be invariably followed; for it is founded upon the most probable opinion, without any evident proof to the contrary; and this probability being admitted, the door of salvation must not be shut against innumerable Chinese, who would abandon our Christian religion were they forbidden to attend to those things that they may lawfully and without injury to their faith attend to, and forced to give up what cannot be abandoned without serious consequences.

One member of this meeting, the Dominican Navarette, soon expressed his dissent, and the dispute was renewed as virulently as ever. The opponents of the Jesuits complained that they taught their converts that there was but little difference generally between Christianity and their own belief, and allowed them to retain their old superstitions; they were charged, moreover, with luxury and ambition, and neglecting the duties of their ministry that they might meddle in the affairs of State. These allegations were rebutted by the Jesuits, though it appears from Mosheim that some of them partially acknowledged their truth. In 1693 Maigrot, a bishop and apostolic vicar living in China, issued a mandate on his own authority diametrically opposed to the decision of the Inquisition and the Pope, in which he declared that *tien* signified nothing more than the material heavens, and that the Chinese customs and rites were idolatrous. In 1699 the Jesuits brought the matter before the Emperor in the following memorial:

We, your faithful subjects, although originally from distant countries, respectfully supplicate your Majesty to give us clear instructions on the following points. The scholars of Europe have understood that the Chinese practise certain ceremonies in honor of Confucius, that they offer sacrifices to heaven, and that they observe peculiar rites toward their ancestors; but persuaded that these ceremonies, sacrifices, and rites are founded in reason, though ignorant of their true intention, earnestly desire us to inform them. We have always supposed that Confucius was honored in China as a legislator, and that it was in this character alone, and with this view solely, that the ceremonies established in his honor were practised. We believe that the ancestral rites are only observed in order to exhibit the love felt for them, and to hallow the remembrance of the good received from them during their life. We believe that the sacrifices offered to heaven are not tendered to the visible heavens which are seen above us, but to the Supreme Master, Author, and Preserver of heaven and earth, and of all they contain. Such are the interpretation and the sense which we have always given to these Chinese ceremonies; but as strangers cannot be considered competent to pronounce on these important points with the same certainty as the Chinese themselves, we presume to request your Majesty not to refuse to give us the explanations which we desire concerning them. We wait for them with respect and submission.[1]

The Emperor's reply in 1700 to this petition, and another one presented to him, was sent to the Pope; in it he declared that "*tien* means the true God, and that the customs of China are political." The enemies of the Jesuits say that they "confirmed the sentiments expressed in the imperial rescript by the oaths which they exacted from a multitude of Chinese, among whom were many from the lowest classes, not only entirely ignorant of the meaning of many characters in their own language, but even of Christian doctrine." The strongest efforts were made by both parties to influence the decision of the Pope, but the Jesuits failed. In 1704 a decree of Clement XI. confirmed the decision of Bishop Maigrot. It had been reached after careful and candid examination, and was substantially as follows: "As the true God cannot conveniently be named in the Chinese language with European words, we must employ the words *Tien Chu*, *i.e.*, 'Lord of Heaven,' in use for a long time in China, and approved by both missionaries and their converts. We must, on the contrary, absolutely reject the appellation of *Tien* (Heaven) and *Shangtí* (August Emperor); and for this reason it must on no account be permitted that tablets shall be suspended in churches with the inscription *King Tien* (Adore Heaven)." The court of the Vatican had already dispatched a legate *à latere* and apostolic visitor to China in the person of

[1] *Life of Saint-Martin*, p. 292.

Tournon, who was consecrated Patriarch of Antioch in order to give him a title of sufficient dignity in the distant regions to which he was bound.

The legate landed at Macao in April, 1705, and was received with a show of honor by the governor and bishop. He arrived at Peking in December, but the Jesuits had already prejudiced the Emperor against him, and at an audience accorded to him in June, 1706, the former brought forward the subject to learn the legate's views. After some delay, however, the patriarch issued the Pope's mandate, which was contrary to the monarch's decision. Kanghí was not the man who would transfer to a pope the right of legislating over his own subjects, and in December, 1706, he decreed that he would countenance those missionaries who preached the doctrines of Ricci, but persecute those who followed the opinion of Maigrot. Examiners were appointed for ascertaining their sentiments, but Tournon, who had been banished to Macao, forbade the missionaries, under pain of excommunication, holding any discussion on these points with the examiners. The Bishop of Macao confined the legate in a private house, and when he used his ecclesiastical authority and powers against his enemies, stuck up a monitory on the very door of his residence, exhorting him to revoke his censures within three days under pain of excommunication, and exhibit proofs of his legation to his diocesan. This was re-echoed from Tournon by a still severer sentence against the bishop. Three new missionaries reached Macao at this juncture in January, 1710, and one of them, Père Ripa, gives an account of a nocturnal visit they paid the legate in his prison after eluding the vigilance of his guards. Ripa remarks that about forty missionaries of different religious orders were confined with Tournon, who had lately been made a cardinal, but he himself and his companions were left at liberty. His eminence sent a remonstrance to the Governor of Canton against his imprisonment, and also a memorial to the Emperor stating that six missionaries had arrived from Europe, three of whom were acquainted with mathematics, music, and painting. Ripa, who was to be the painter, says that he knew only the rudiments of the art, and records his dissatisfaction at this change in his vocation, but soon resigned himself to obedience. Tournon died in his confinement in July of the same year.

The proceedings of Tournon were mainly confirmed by the Pope, and in 1715 he dispatched Mezzabarba, another legate, by way of Lisbon, who was favorably received at Peking. He "was instructed to express the Pope's sincere gratitude to Kanghí for his magnanimous kindness toward the missionaries, to beg leave to remain in China as their head or as superior of the whole mission, and to obtain from Kanghí his consent that the Christians in China might submit to the decision of his Holiness concerning the rites." The Emperor evaded all reference to the rites, and the legate, soon perceiving that his Majesty would not surrender any part of his inherent authority, solicited and obtained permission at his last audience to return to Europe, which he did March 3, 1721. The first fifteen years of the eighteenth century was the period of the greatest prosperity to the Romish missions in China. It is stated that in the governor-generalship of Kiangnan and Kiangsí alone there were one hundred churches and a hundred thousand converts. The survey of the Empire was carried on by the Emperor's command from 1708 to 1718, under the direction of ten Jesuits, of whom Regis, Bouvet, and Jartoux were the most prominent.[1] It was a great work for that day, and considering the instruments they had, the vast area they traversed, and the imperfect education of their assistants, its accuracy and completeness form the best index of the ability of the surveyors.

The disputes between the various orders of missionaries and the resistance of some converts to the Emperor's commands respecting the ancestral rites, together with the representations of his own officers upon the tendency of the new religion to undermine his own authority, gradually opened his eyes to the true character of the propagandists. In 1718 he forbade any missionary remaining in the country without permission from himself, given only after their promise to follow the rules of Ricci. Yet no European missionary could repair to China

---

[1] An additional re-survey was made and presented to the Emperor Kienlung in 1761 by Benoit and Allerstein.

without subscribing a formula in which he promised fully and entirely to obey the orders of Clement XI. upon these ceremonies, and observe those injunctions without any tergiversation. Kanghí was made acquainted with all these matters and took his measures, gradually restraining the missionaries in their work and keeping them about him at court, while he allowed persecuting measures to be carried on in the provinces. The work of Ripa affords evidence of this plan, and it was characteristic of Chinese policy.

After the death of Kanghí in 1723 the designs of the government under his son Yungching were still more evident. In 1724 an order was promulgated in which every effort to propagate the *Tien Chu kiao*, or 'Religion of the Lord of Heaven,' as it was then and has ever since been called, was strictly prohibited. All missionaries not required at Peking for scientific purposes were ordered to leave the country, by which more than three hundred thousand converts were deprived of teachers. Many of the missionaries secreted themselves, and the converts exhibited the greatest fidelity in adhering to them even at the risk of death. When the missionaries reached Canton, where they were allowed to remain, they devised measures to return to their flocks, and frequently succeeded. The influence of those remaining at Peking was exerted to regain their former toleration, but with partial success. Their enemies in the provinces harassed the converts in order to extort money, and found plenty of assistants who knew the names and condition of all the leading adherents of the proscribed faith, and aided in compelling them to violate their consciences or lose their property.

The edict of Yungching forms an epoch in the Romish missions in China. Since that time they have experienced various degrees of quiet and storm, but on the whole decreasing in number and influence until the new era inaugurated by the treaties of 1858. The troubles in France and Europe toward the latter part of the eighteenth century withdrew the attention of the supporters of missions from those in China, while in the country itself the maintenance of the laws against the propagation of Christianity, and an occasional seizure of priests and converts by a zealous officer, caused a still further diminution. The edicts of Kienlung, soon after his accession in 1736, showed that no countenance was to be expected from court; the rulers were thoroughly dissatisfied with the foreigners, and ready to take almost any measures to relieve the country of them. Perhaps their personal conduct had something to do with this course of procedure, for Ripa, who cannot be accused of partiality, says, when speaking of the number of converts, that "if our European missionaries in China would conduct themselves with less ostentation, and accommodate their manners to persons of all ranks and conditions, the number of converts would be immensely increased. Their garments are made of the richest materials; they go nowhere on foot, but always in sedans, on horseback, or in boats, and with numerous attendants following them. With a few honorable exceptions, all the missionaries live in this manner; and thus, as they never mix with the people, they make but few converts. The diffusion of our holy religion in these parts has been almost entirely owing to the catechists who are in their service, to other Christians, or to the distribution of Christian books in the Chinese language. Thus there is scarcely a single missionary who can boast of having made a convert by his own preaching, for they merely baptize those who have been already converted by others."[1] But this missionary himself afterward assigns a much better reason for their not preaching, when he adds that, up to his time in 1714, "none of the missionaries had been able to surmount the language so as to make himself understood by the people at large." This remark must, however, be taken with some explanations. There had been about five hundred missionaries sent from Europe between 1580 and 1724, which was less than an annual average of four individuals during a century and a half.

When the intentions of the new Emperor were known, there would not long be wanting occasions to harass the Christians. In 1747 a persecution extended over all the provinces, and Bishop Sanz and five Dominican priests in Fuhkien lost their lives. All the foreign priests who could be found elsewhere were

---

[1] *Residence at Peking*, p. 43.

sent away—a mark of leniency the more striking when it was supposed by the Chinese that some of them had already once returned from banishment. The missions in Sz'chuen and Shansí suffered most, but through the zeal of their pastors maintained themselves better than elsewhere; their bishops, Mullener, and after him Pottier, contrived to remain in the country most of the time between 1712 and 1792. The missions in Yunnan and Kweichau were not so flourishing as that in Sz'chuen. In this province M. Gleyo was apprehended in 1767, and endured much suffering for the faith he came to preach; he remained in prison ten years, when he was liberated through the efforts of a Jesuit in the employ of government. For several years after this the order enjoyed comparative quiet, but in 1784 greater efforts than ever were made to discover and apprehend all foreign priests and their abettors, owing to the detection of four Europeans in Hukwang while they were going to their mission. M. de la Tour, the procureur of the mission at Canton, through whose instrumentality they were sent through the country, was apprehended and carried to Peking; and the hong merchant who had been his security was glad to purchase his own safety by the sacrifice of one hundred and twenty thousand taels of silver.

Didier Saint-Martin, who was then in Sz'chuen, gives a long account of his own capture, trial, and imprisonment, and many particulars of the sufferings of his fellow missionaries. Eighteen Europeans were taken away from the missions by it, but none of them were actually executed; twelve were sentenced to perpetual imprisonment, six having died, but for some reason the Emperor revoked the decree soon after it was made, and gave them all the choice to enter his service or leave the country; nine of the twelve preferred to depart, the other three joining the priests at the capital. This search was so close that few of the foreigners escaped. Pottier was not taken, though he was obliged at one time to conceal himself for a month in a small house, and in so confined a place that he hardly dared either to cough or to spit for fear of being discovered. Saint-Martin and Dufresse retired to Manila, where they were received with great honors, and were enabled to return after a time to Sz'chuen. The former died in 1801 in peace, but Dufresse was beheaded in 1814;[1] in 1816 M. Triora was strangled in Hupeh, and M. Clet three years after; in the interval, Schoeffler, Bounard, and Diaz perished, and Chapdelaine in 1856. But no data are available to show the number of native priests and converts who suffered death, torture, imprisonment, and banishment in these storms. The records of constancy and cheerful fortitude exhibited under tortures and cruel mockings, given in the writings of the time, show their faith in Christ. The details are summarized in Marshall's work, and probably the number may reasonably be estimated by hundreds.

The period which elapsed after the promulgation of the edicts of 1767 up to 1820 contains less to interest the reader than since the last date. At that time restored quiet in Europe urged a resumption of the work; and the *Annales de la Foi* henceforth continue the narratives of the missions, formerly recorded in the *Lettres Édifiantes*, with the approval of the directors and bishops. It is not easy at any period to learn their condition and number, for only vague estimates of hundreds of churches, hundreds of thousands of converts, scores of missionaries, schools, catechists, priests, and stations, comprise the data given in the flourishing days of Verbiest and Parennin. Perhaps many of the early statistics have perished, yet it has never been easy to obtain accurate data, and often they have been withheld from public knowledge. There is no responsibility or reckoning required from the managers of the missions by the body of the church as to what is done with the funds, as among Protestant missions. In 1820 an estimate gives 6 bishops, 2 coadjutors, 23 foreign missionaries, 80 native priests, and 215,000 converts. In 1839 a table in the *Annales* gives for that year, 8 bishops, 57 foreigners, 114 native priests, and 303,000 converts. In 1846 the record shows 12 bishops, 7 or 8 coadjutors, 80 foreign missionaries, 90 natives, and 400,000 converts; 54 boys' and 114 girls' schools are put down for Sz'chuen. In 1866 they report 20 bishops,

---

[1] *Annales de la Foi*, Tome I., pp. 25, 53, 68. Dufresse was afterward canonized.

233 foreign missionaries, 237 native priests, 12 colleges, 331 students in seven of them, and 363,000 converts; these figures include only those in the Eighteen Provinces. In 1870 the tables show 254 foreigners, bishops and missionaries, 138 native priests in nine provinces, and 404,530 converts.

Lastly, from the Hong Kong *Catholic Register* we learn that the statistics in 1881 were: Bishops, 41; European priests, 664; native priests, 559; converts *in toto*, 1,092,818; colleges, 34; convents, 34. The paper which publishes this summary, "from a most reliable source," gives no information as to where the missions or colleges are located, or what numbers are found in the different provinces. It is, moreover, somewhat difficult to learn what constitutes a college, or whether the grade in these institutions is uniform throughout the land. In addition to the education imparted at home, a number of Chinese are yearly sent to Rome to be educated at the College of the Propaganda. The total number of converts includes all the members of the various families who give an outward adherence to the rites of the church. In the persecutions which these adherents have endured at various times, some have left the faith, but a large number of the descendants of these early converts have remained faithful, generation after generation, to the religion which their ancestors had embraced under more favorable auspices. Hence this estimate represents the number now adhering to them, many of them being the descendants of early converts; and this number of followers has become so numerous largely by natural increase. We have no information as to the number of converts year by year. In one village of South China, where there are some Roman Catholics resident, it has been noted that the increase is almost entirely by natural generation. The girls of Catholic families are only permitted co-religionists. The men marry heathen wives on the promise that they will become Romanists. One man and his wife of this village first became converts. The number of adherents now here is over one hundred, all descendants of this first pair; and this increase is entirely by natural descent and by marriage.

With the increased openings since the treaties of 1858 the regulation of the missions has devolved on different societies, which have apportioned their laborers in the provinces. The Lazarists have Chihlí, Kiangsí, and Chehkiang; the Franciscans, Shantung, Shansí, Shensí, and Hukwang; the Jesuits, Kíangnan and eastern Chihlí; the Dominicans, Fuhkien; the Gallic church, all the western and south-western regions, with Manchuria; one society in Milan has charge of Honan, and another in Belgium labors in Mongolia. The successful efforts of M. Lagrené, the French envoy to China in 1844, to obtain formal recognition of the Christian religion and protection to its professors from their own rulers, entitle him to the thanks of every well-wisher of missions. The intention of the Chinese authorities in tolerating such efforts was to limit them to the newly opened ports, where alone churches could be erected, for the missionaries are disallowed free entrance into the country. This partial permission of 1844 prepared the way for the toleration articles in the treaties of 1858, when the four Powers present at Tientsin obtained a more explicit acknowledgment from the Emperor of the rights of Christian laborers and professors among the Chinese. Those articles have been in force during the past twenty years, and have proved a safeguard and a warrant for the faith of Christ and its adherents even beyond the hopes of those who first proposed them.

The exclusive labors of the Roman Catholics among the Chinese comprise a period of about two hundred and fifty years from the date of Ricci's reception at Peking. The various works written by them during this period contained not only the details of their labors, but nearly everything that was then known relating to the Chinese. The essays, translations, histories, travels, etc., of Visdelou, Mailla, Trigault, Semido, Amiot, Le Comte, and scores of others, still remain to inform those who seek to learn their acts.[1] Every reader must honor the men who thus suffered and labored, prospered and died, in the prosecution of their work. It is worthy of consideration, as to the self-supporting character of this work, that their constant experience has shown that, however numerous and zealous the converts, the presence of European pastors and overseers is

---

[1] Rémusat, *Nouveaux Mélanges*, pp. 207 ff.

indispensable to their spiritual prosperity.[1] Whether this is owing to the character of the Chinese mind, or to the little Christian instruction and principle these converts really have, cannot in most cases be easily decided. It can hardly be expected that pagans should perceive much difference immediately between their old worship and the ceremonies of the new faith in the presence of pictures, images, and crosses, before which they were taught to prostrate themselves. The native priests and catechists were not instructed to maintain the authority of the law and word of God above all human teachings in this respect, for the second commandment had been early expunged from the Decalogue, and thus the command of God made void, which prohibits man to make, to serve, or to bow down to such things. It may be this defect in their religious training which keeps these native priests in tutelage under the foreigners, and prevents the maintenance of self-supporting, indigenous churches under their oversight.

In former days the entrance of missionaries into the interior of China was attended with considerable hazard, delay, and uncertainty, arising from the weakness or ignorance of those guides to whose care they were entrusted, and the risks they ran if detected. This has now all passed away, and access to all parts of the Empire is even more free than it was in the days of the Emperor Kanghí. In those early times the development of missionary work was not as well understood as it is now after long experience, and less attention was paid to education and self-support. Those points were not appreciated even in Europe, and we should not look for stronger growth in the branches of the tree than in its trunk. Within the last twenty years, not only have the theological schools of the Romish missions increased so that eighteen were open in 1859, but with the introduction of the Sisters of Charity many thousands of young children are taught needlework, reading, and various handicrafts to prepare them for useful lives. These schools and orphanages exert a widespread and lasting influence.

The baptism of children and adults has ever been a very

---

[1] *Lettres Édifiantes*, Tome IV., p. 77.

important work with the Roman Catholic missionaries, and especially (if its frequent mention is an evidence) the baptism of *moribunds*, or dying children of heathens. The agents in this work are usually elderly women, says Verolles, "who have experience in the treatment of infantile diseases. Furnished with innocent pills and a bottle of holy water whose virtues they extol, they introduce themselves into the houses where there are sick infants, and discover whether they are in danger of death; in this case they inform the parents, and tell them that before administering other remedies they must wash their hands with the purifying waters of their bottle. The parents, not suspecting this *pieuse ruse*, readily consent, and by these innocent frauds we procure in our mission the baptism of seven or eight thousand infants every year." Another missionary, Dufresse, one of the most distinguished of late years, says: "The women who baptize the infants of heathen parents announce themselves as consecrated to the healing of infants, and to give remedies gratis, that they may satisfy the vow of their father who has commanded this as an act of charity." The number of baptized children thus saved from perdition is carefully detailed in the annual reports, and calculations are made by the missionaries for the consideration of their patrons in France and elsewhere as to the expense incurred for this branch of labor, and the cost of each soul thus saved; and appeals for aid in sending out these female baptists are based upon the tabular reports. It may, however, be a question, even with a candid Romanist who believes that unbaptized infants perish eternally, whether baptism performed by women and unconsecrated laymen is valid; and still more so, whether it is ritual when done by stealth and under false pretences. The number thus annually baptized in all the missions cannot be placed much under fifty thousand, and some years it exceeds a hundred thousand. No attention seems to be given to the child in ordinary cases if it happen to live after this surreptitious baptism.

The degree of instruction given to the converts is trifling, partly owing to the great extent of a single diocese and partly to imperfect knowledge of the language on the part of missionaries. The vexations constantly experienced urge them to be cautious; and truly if a missionary believes that baptism, confirmation, confession, and absolution, are all the evidences of faith that are required in a convert to entitle him to salvation, it cannot be supposed he will deem it necessary to give them long-continued instruction. The causes which usually bring the converts into trouble with their countrymen or the officials were thus described many years ago by the Bishop of Caradre in Sz'chuen; they are still partly applicable.

First. Christians are frequently confounded with the members of the Triad Society, or of the White Lily sect, both by their enemies and by persons belonging to those associations.

Second. The Christians refuse to contribute to the erection or repair of temples, or subscribe to idolatrous feasts and superstitious rites; though, according to the *Annales*, they sometimes defray the charges of the theatrical exhibitions which follow, in order to avoid the malice of their adversaries.

Third. "Espousals are almost indissoluble in China, and whenever the Christians refuse to ratify them by proceeding to a marriage already commenced, they are regarded as law-breakers and treated as such."[1] This is the most common source of trouble, especially when the parents of the girl have become converts since the betrothment, and the other party is anxious to fulfil the contract. These engagements are sometimes broken in a sufficiently unscrupulous manner, and nothing draws so much odium upon Christians as their refusal to adhere to these contracts. On one occasion this bishop assisted in breaking up such an engagment, when the parents, on the death of a sister of the girl, asserted that the deceased was the one who had been betrothed. He adds: "I think the faith of the parents and the purity of their motives will readily excuse them before God for the sin of lying." On other occasions the missionaries endeavor to dissolve these engagements by exhorting the believing party to take vows of celibacy.

Fourth. All communication with Europeans being interdicted, the magistrates seek diligently for every evidence of their exist-

[1] *Lettres Édifiantes*, Tome III., p. 37, where there appear two or three cases of this and Saint-Martin's reasoning on the point.

ence in the country, by searching for the objects used in worship, as crosses, breviaries, etc.

Fifth. The little respect the converts have for their ancestors is always an offence in the eyes of the pagans, and leads to recrimination and vexatious annoyances.

Sixth. As the converts are obliged to take down the ancestral tablets in order to put up those of their own religion, they are seldom forgiven in this change, and occasion is taken therefrom to persecute.

Seventh. The indiscreet zeal of the neophytes leading them to break the idols or insult the objects of public worship is one of the most common causes of persecution.

Eighth. The disputes between the missionaries themselves, regarding the ceremonies, have frequently excited troubles.

In addition to these causes, some of which are now removed, there are others which have grown up since the toleration granted to Christianity by the treaties, and which may develop still more. They are discussed in the minute drawn up by the Chinese government in 1871, after the Tientsin riot, in which eight rules for their regulation are proposed. The grievances refer to the seclusion of children in orphanages; to the presence of women in religious assemblies; to missionaries interfering in legal cases so as to screen criminals, and their interchanging passports; to the neophytes rescuing criminals from justice; to the missionaries affecting the style of native officials; and, lastly, to their demand for land alleged to have once belonged to them, whatever may have been its ownership meanwhile. This has since ceased, and the others have been somewhat restrained.

Christians sometimes refuse to have their deceased friends buried with the idolatrous ceremonies required by their relatives, upon which the latter occasionally carry the matter before the officers, or resort to petty annoyances. In order to keep up the spirit of devotion among the neophytes, crucifixes, reliquaries, and other articles were given them, and "God wrought several miracles among them to authorize the practice." These articles, in the estimation of both priest and people, probably have no little influence over the demons which vex and harass the pagans, but which never trouble Christians. Saint-Martin, writing to his father from the capital of Sz'chuen in 1774, says: "The most sensible proof for the pagans, and one always in force, is the power the Christians have over demons.[1] It is astonishing how these poor infidels are tormented, and they can find remedy only in the prayers of Christians, by whose help they are delivered and then converted. Seven or eight leagues from this spot is a house which has been infested with demons for a month; they maltreat all who come near them, and have set the dwelling on fire at different times. They have had recourse to all kinds of superstitious ceremonies, calling in the native priests, but all to no effect; and the master of the family where I am staying has now gone to assist them. He is a man of lively faith, and has already performed many miraculous cures."[2]

It is interesting to compare with this the account of Friar Odoric, "How the friars deal with devils in Tartary." In his *Travels* we read that "God Almighty hath bestowed such grace upon the Minor friars that in Great Tartary they think it a mere nothing to expel devils from the possessed, no more, indeed, than to drive a dog out of the house. For there be many in those parts possessed of the devil, both men and women, and these they bind and bring to our friars from as far as ten days' journey off. The friars bid the demons depart forth instantly from the bodies of the possessed, in the name of Jesus Christ, and they do depart immediately in obedience to this command. Then those who have been delivered from the demon straightway cause themselves to be baptized; and the friars take their idols, which are made of felt, and carry them to the fire, while all the people of the country round assemble to see their neighbor's gods burnt. The friars accordingly cast the idols into the fire, but they leap out again. And so the friars take holy water and sprinkle it upon the fire, and that straightway drives away the demon from the fire; so the friars again casting the idols into the fire, they are consumed.

---

[1] *Lettres Édifiantes*, Tomes I., pp. 39 and 151, passim, and IV., p. 27.

[2] *Life of Didier Saint-Martin*, p. 35.

And then the devil in the air raises a shout, saying: 'See then! see then! how I am expelled from my dwelling place!' And in this way our friars baptize great numbers in that country."[1]

When persons educated in a country like France allow their converts to entertain such ideas, even if they do not favor them

Roman Catholic Altar near Shanghai.

themselves, and countenance their endeavors to exorcise the possessed, we cannot look for a very high degree of knowledge or piety. If they are brought out of pagan darkness, it is but little if any better than into light hardly bright enough to enable them even to distinguish trees from men.

The points of similarity between Buddhism and Romanism have already been noticed, and the converts from one to the

[1] Yule, *Cathay and the Way Thither*, Vol. I., p. 155.

other see but little more change than they do when going from Buddhism to the metaphysical speculations of the learned *ju kiao*. If Romish priests have allowed their converts to worship before pagan images, provided a cross is put into the candles, it would not be difficult for the latter to put the names of their departed parents behind the "tablets of religion," and worship them together. Similar to such a permission is the combination of the cross and dragon carved on a Romish altar near Shanghai, given on the preceding page, and at which both pagans and Christians could alike worship.

Agnuses, crosses, etc., are easily substituted for coins and charms, and it does not surely require much faith to believe the former as effectual as the latter. The neophyte takes away the tablet in his house or shop having *shin*, 'æon' or 'spirit,' written on it,[1] and puts up another, on which is written *shin, chin chu, tsao tien ti jin-wuh*, or 'God, true Lord, Creator of heaven, earth, man, and all things,' and burns the same incense before this as before that. Chinese demigods are changed for foreign saints, with this difference, that now they worship they know not what, while before they knew something of the name and character of the ancient hero from popular accounts and historical legends. They cease, indeed, to venerate the queen of Heaven, holy mother Ma tsupu, but what advance in true religion has been made by falling down before the Queen of Heaven, holy mother Mary? The people call the Buddhist idols and the Romish images by the same name, and apply much the same terms to their ceremonies. Such converts can easily be numbered by thousands; and it is a wonder, indeed, when one considers the nature of the case, that the whole population of China have not long since become "devout confessors" of this faith. Conversions depend, in such cases, on almost every other kind of influence than that of the Holy Spirit blessing his own word in an intelligent mind and a quickened conscience. The missionaries write that "being forced in three or four months after their arrival to preach

[1] Converts in Sz'chuen sometimes steal the idols from the roadside. *Lettres Édifiantes*, Tome I., p. 219.

when they do not know the language sufficiently either to be understood or to understand themselves, they have seen their auditors immediately embrace Christianity."

We pass no decision upon these converts, except what is given or drawn from the writings of their teachers. Human nature is everywhere the same in its great lineaments, and the effect of living godly lives in Christ Jesus will everywhere excite opposition, calumny, persecution, and death, according to the liberty granted the enemies of the truth. There may have been true converts among the adherents to Romanism; but what salutary effects has this large body of Christians wrought in the vast population of China during the three hundred years since Ricci established himself at Nanking? None, absolutely none, that attract attention. The letters of some of the missionaries written to their friends breathe a spirit of pious ardor and true Christian principle worthy of all imitation. Among the best letters contained in the *Annales* is one from Dufresse to his pupils then at Penang. It is a long epistle, and contains nothing (with one exception) which the most scrupulous Protestant would not approve. The same may be said of most of the letters contained in the same collection written in prison by Gagelin, a missionary who was strangled in Annam in 1833. It is hardly possible to doubt, when reading the letters of these two men, both of whom were martyred for the faith they preached, that they sincerely loved and trusted in the Saviour they proclaimed. Many of their converts also exhibit the greatest constancy in their profession, preferring to suffer persecution, torture, imprisonment, banishment, and death rather than to deny their faith, though every inducement of prevarication and mental reservation was held out to them by the magistrates in order to avoid the necessity of proceeding to extreme measures. If undergoing the loss of all things is an evidence of piety, many of them have abundantly proved their title to this virtue. But until there shall be a complete separation from idolatry and superstition; until the confessional shall be abolished, and the worship of the Virgin, wearing crosses and rosaries, and reliance on ceremonies and penances be stopped; until the entire Scriptures and Decalogue be taught to the converts; until, in short, the essential doctrine of justification by faith alone be substituted for the many forms of justification by works, the mass of converts to Romanism in China can hardly be considered as much better than baptized pagans.[1]

Turn we now to a brief survey of the efforts of Protestants among the Chinese, and the results which have attended their labors. Hardly forty years have passed since the treaty of Nanking opened the five ports to their direct work in the Empire, and the results thus far necessarily partake of the incompleteness of new enterprises. The radical distinction between their modes of operation and those of their predecessors is indicated in the names 'Religion of Heaven's Lord' and 'Religion of Jesus;' the Romanists depend much on their teachings and ceremonies to convert men, the Protestants on the preaching of the word of God and a blessing on its vital truths.

The first Protestant missionary to China was Rev. Robert Morrison, of Morpeth, England, who was sent out by the London Missionary Society. He arrived at Canton, by way of New York, in September, 1807, and lived there for a year, in a quiet manner, in the factory of Messrs. Milner and Bull, of New York. He early made the acquaintance of Sir George T. Staunton, one of his firmest friends, and already well versed in Chinese studies; Mr. Robarts, the chief of the British factory, advised him to avow his intention to the Chinese of translating the Scriptures into their language, on the ground that it was a divine book which Christians highly esteemed and which the Chinese should have the opportunity of examining. In consequence of difficulties connected with the trade, he was obliged to leave Canton in 1808 with all British subjects and repair to Macao, where he deemed it prudent to maintain a careful retirement in

---

[1] An exhaustive collection of the titles of every work of importance upon Catholic missions in China, as well as a *résumé* of their periodical publications, may be found in M. Cordier's *Dictionnaire bibliographique des ouvrages Chinois*, Tome I., pp. 330–578, and following these pages are the works concerning Protestant missions, pp. 578–633. Compare also Thos. Marshall, *Christian Missions: their Agents and their Results*, London, 1863, and Chr. H. Kalkar, *Geschichte der christlichen Mission unter den Heiden*, Gütersloh, 1879–80.

order not to attract undue notice from the Portuguese priests. His associate, Dr. Milne, observed, with reference to these traits in his character, that "the patience that refuses to be conquered, the diligence that never tires, the caution that always trembles, and the studious habit that spontaneously seeks retirement were best adapted for the first Protestant missionary to China."

He married Miss Mary Morton in 1809, and accepted the appointment of translator under the East India Company, in whose service he continued until 1834. His position was now a well-understood one, and his official connexion obtained for him all necessary security so that he could prosecute his work with diligence and confidence. He no doubt did wisely in the circumstances in which he was placed, for his dictionary could hardly have been printed, or his translation of the Scriptures and other works been so successfully carried on, without the countenance and assistance of that powerful body. The entire New Testament was published in 1814, about half of it having been translated by Morrison and the remainder revised from a manuscript which had been deposited in 1739 in the British Museum.

Rev. W. Milne arrived in July, 1813, as his associate, and resided in Canton, leaving his wife at Macao. In 1814 he sailed for the Indian Archipelago, provided with about seventeen thousand copies of Testaments and tracts for distribution among the Chinese there. He stopped at Banca on his route, and then proceeded to Java, where he was received by Sir Stamford Raffles, a man far in advance of the times in his support and patronage of missions. Milne was enabled to travel over the island and distribute such books as he had. From Java he went to Malacca, then a Dutch settlement, afterward returning to Canton, where he remained undisturbed, though a severe persecution, in which Dufresse lost his life, was waging against the Christians throughout the Empire. Milne, finding it difficult to prosecute his labors in China (for the East India Company would not countenance him), embarked for Malacca in 1815, accompanied by a teacher and workmen for printing Chinese books; here he resided till his death in 1822.

The leading objects in sending Morrison to Canton, namely, the translation of the Bible and preparation of a dictionary, occupied the greater portion of his time. He soon commenced a Sabbath service with his domestics and acquaintances in his own apartments, which he never relinquished, though it did not expand into a regular public congregation during his lifetime. He considered this as one of the most important parts of his work, and was much encouraged when in 1814 one of his audience, Tsai A-ko, made a profession of his faith and was baptized. He was the first convert, and it is reasonably to be hoped, judging from his after-life, that he sincerely believed to salvation.

The compilation of the dictionary progressed so well that in 1814 a few members of the Company's establishment, among whom Mr. Elphinstone and Sir George Staunton were prominent, interested themselves in getting it printed. The Court of Directors responded to the application on the most liberal scale, sending out as printer P. P. Thoms, together with a printing office. The first volume was issued in 1817, and the whole was completed in six quarto volumes, containing four thousand five hundred and ninety-five pages, in 1823, at an expense of about twelve thousand pounds sterling. It consisted of three parts, viz., characters arranged according to their radicals, according to their pronunciation, and an English and Chinese part. This work contributed much to the advancement of a knowledge of Chinese literature, and its aid in missions has been manifold greater. The plan was rather too comprehensive for one man to fill up, and also involved much repetition; a reprint of the second part was issued in a smaller volume, in 1854, without material addition.

While the dictionary was going through the press, the translation of the Old Testament was progressing by the joint labors of Morrison and Milne, and in November, 1818, the entire Bible was published. Another version, by Dr. Marshman at Serampore, was completed and printed with movable types in 1822. A second edition of the Baptist version was never struck off, and comparatively few copies have ever been circulated among the Chinese. Both these versions are such that a sincere inquirer after the truth cannot fail to comprehend the meaning, though both are open to criticisms and contain mistakes incident to first translations. They are now numbered among superseded versions like those of Wiclif and Tyndal, the Italic and Ulfilas in other languages, but will ever be regarded with gratitude.[1]

During the years he was thus engaged Morrison published a tract on Redemption, a translation of the Assembly's Catechism, church of England liturgy, a synopsis of Old Testament history, a hymn book, and a Tour of the World; altogether, nearly thirty thousand copies were printed and distributed. He prepared a Chinese grammar on the model of a common English grammar, which was printed at Serampore in 1815; also a volume of miscellaneous information on the chronology, festivals, geography, and other subjects relating to China, under the title of *View of China for Philological Purposes.* The list of his writings comprises thirty-one titles, of which nineteen are in English; each work bears witness to his learning and piety.

In 1821 Mrs. Morrison died, and about eight months after he visited Malacca and Singapore, where he was much delighted by what he saw. The Anglo-Chinese College was then under the care of Collie, and this visit from its founder encouraged both principal and students. In 1824 he returned to England and was honorably received by his Majesty George IV., and obtained the approbation of all who took an interest in the promotion of religion and learning. He published a volume of sermons and a miscellany called *Horæ Sinicæ* while in England; and having formed a second matrimonial connection, left his native land again in May, 1826, under different circumstances from the first time. During his absence the mission at Canton was left in charge of the first native preacher, Liang Kung-fah, or Liang A-fah, whom Morrison had ordained as an evangelist. This worthy man carried on his useful labors in preaching and writing until his death in 1855 at that city, from whence, in 1834, he had been forced to flee for his life. He takes a deservedly high position at the head of the native Protestant Christian min-

---

[1] Medhurst's *China*, p. 217. *Chinese Repository*, Vol. IV., p. 249. *Life of Morrison*, by his widow, passim, 2 Vols., London, 1839. Wylie in *Chinese Recorder*, Vol. I., pp. 121, 145. *Lives of the Leaders of our Church Universal*, p. 819, Phila., 1879.

istry among the Chinese in respect to time, and his writings have been highly successful and beneficial.

During the years which elapsed between the return and death of Morrison, he was principally occupied by his duties as translator to the Company and in literary labors. His *Memoirs* furnish all the particulars of their contents, as well as the details of his useful and uneventful life. His last years were cheered by the arrival of five fellow-laborers from the United States, the first who had come to his assistance since Milne left him in 1814. On the dissolution of the East India Company's establishment, in April, 1834, he was appointed interpreter to the King's Commission, but his death took place August 1, 1834, at the age of fifty-two, even then much worn out with his unaided labors of twenty-seven years.

Perhaps no two persons were ever less alike than the founders of the Romish and Protestant missions to China, but no plans of operations could be more dissimilar than those adopted by Ricci and Morrison. We have already sketched the life-work of the former, obtained from friendly sources. When Morrison was sent out the directors of the London Missionary Society thus expressed their views of his labors: "We trust that no objection will be made to your continuing in Canton till you have accomplished your great object of acquiring the language; when this is done, you may probably soon afterward begin to turn this attainment into a direction which may be of extensive use to the world; perhaps you may have the honor of forming a Chinese dictionary, more comprehensive and correct than any preceding one, or the still greater honor of translating the sacred Scriptures into a language spoken by a third part of the human race." The enterprise thus committed to the hands of a single individual was only part of a system which neither the projectors nor their collaborator supposed would end there. They knew that the great work of evangelizing and elevating a mass of mind like that using the Chinese language required large preparatory labors, of which those here mentioned were among the most important. China was a sealed country when Morrison landed on its shores, and he could not have forced his way into it if he had tried, with any prospect of ultimate success, even by adopting the same plans which Ricci did. It is doubtful if he could have lived there at all had it not been for the protection of the East India Company. After all his toil, and faith, and prayer, he only saw three or four converts, no churches, schools, or congregations publicly assembled; but his last letter breathes the same desires as when he first went out: "I wait patiently the events to be developed in the course of Divine Providence. The Lord reigneth. If the kingdom of God our Saviour prosper in China, all will be well; other matters are comparatively of small importance." He died just as the day of change and progress was dawning in Eastern Asia, but his life was very far from being a failure in its results or influence. The principles of these two missionaries have been followed out by their successors, and we are quite willing to let their results be the test of their foundation upon the Chief Corner Stone.

Protestant missions among the Chinese emigrants in Malacca, Penang, Singapore, Rhio, Borneo, and Batavia have never taken much hold upon them, and they are at present all suspended or abandoned. The first named was established in 1815 by Milne, and was conducted longest and with the most efficiency, though the labors at the other points have been carried on with zeal and a degree of success. The comparatively small results which have attended all these missions may be ascribed to two or three reasons, besides the fewness of the laborers. The Chinese residing in these settlements consist chiefly of emigrants who have fled or left their native countries, in all cases without their families, some to avoid the injustice or oppression of their rulers, but more to gain a livelihood they cannot find so well at home. Consequently they lead a roving life; few of them marry or settle down to become valuable citizens, and fewer still are sufficiently educated to relish or care for instruction or books. These communities are much troubled by branches of the Triad Society, and the restless habits of the Malays are congenial to most of the emigrants who enter among them. The Chinese, coming as they do from different parts of their own land, speak different dialects, and soon learn the Malay language as a lingua franca; their children also learn it still more thoroughly from their mothers, notwithstanding the education their fathers give them in Chinese. The want of fixedness in the Chinese population therefore partly accounts for the little permanent impression made on it in these settlements by missionary efforts.

It was at Malacca that the Anglo-Chinese College was established in 1818 by Dr. Morrison, assisted by other friends of religion. Its objects were to afford Europeans the means of acquiring the Chinese language and enable Chinese to become acquainted with the religion and science of the West. It was productive of good up to the time of its removal to Hongkong in 1844. About seventy persons were baptized while the mission remained at Malacca, and about fifty students finished their education, part of whom were sincere Christians and all of them respectable members of society. Three or four of the converts have become preachers. There is little hesitation, however, in saying that the name and array of a college were too far in advance of the people among whom it was situated. The efforts made in it would probably have been more profitably expended in establishing common schools among the people, in which Christianity and knowledge went hand in hand. It is far better among an ignorant pagan people that a hundred persons should know one thing than that one man should know a hundred; the widest diffusion of the first elements of religion and science is most desirable. The mission was not, however, large enough at any one time for its members to superintend many common schools. Among the books issued besides Bibles and tracts were a periodical called the *Indo-Chinese Gleaner*, edited by Dr. Milne; a translation of the Four Books, by Mr. Collie; an edition of Prémare's *Notitia Linguæ Sinicæ;* a life of Milne, and a volume of sermons by Morrison. The number of volumes printed in Chinese was about half a million.

The mission at Georgetown, in the island of Penang, like that at Malacca, was established in 1819 by the London Missionary Society, and continued till 1843, at which time it was suspended. The mission at Singapore was commenced in 1819 by Mr. Milton; the colonial government granted a lot, and a chapel and other buildings were erected in the course of a few years. Messrs. Smith and Tomlin came to the settlement in 1827, but did not remain long. Gutzlaff came over from the Dutch settlement at Rhio, but did not remain long enough to effect anything; nor did Abeel, who came from China in 1831 and left soon after for Siam. The German missionary at this station, Thomsen, when about to leave in 1834, sold his printing apparatus to the mission newly established there under the American Board by Tracy. The prospects in China appearing unpromising at this time, it was designed by the directors of the American society to establish a well-regulated school for both Chinese and Malays, which was by degrees to become a seminary, and as many primary schools as there were means to support; besides the usual labors in preaching and visiting, a type foundry and printing office for manufacturing books in Chinese, Malay, Bugís, and Siamese were also contemplated. In December, 1834, Tracy was joined by the Rev. P. Parker, M.D., who opened a hospital in the Chinese part of the town for the gratuitous relief of the sick; in 1835 Wolfe arrived from England, and two years afterward Rev. Messrs. Dickinson, Hope, and Travelli, and North from the United States, to take charge of the schools and printing office. The school established by the American mission was carried on until 1844, when the mission was removed to China and the Malay portion of it given up.

The English mission, after the death of Wolfe in 1837, was under the care of Messrs. Dyer and Stronach, the former of whom had removed there from Penang and Malacca. Dyer had been for many years engaged in preparing steel punches for a font of movable Chinese type, and his patient labors had already overcome the principal difficulties in the way when the work was arrested by his death in 1843. He had, however, finished matrices for so many characters of two fonts that the enterprise needed only to be carried on by a practised mechanic to assure its success. This was afterward done by Messrs. Cole and Gamble of the American Presbyterian Board. In their superior styles and the different sizes now in use we must not forget Dyer's initiatory steps. This gentleman labored nearly seventeen years with a consecration of energy and singleness of purpose seldom exceeded, and won the affectionate respect of the natives wherever he lived. The mission was continued until 1845, when the printing office was removed to Hongkong, and nearly all proselyting efforts in the colony by British Christians suspended. This point of influence has peculiar claims on them as a radiating centre for the various nations and tribes which trade in Singapore.

The mission to the Chinese in Java was commenced by Slater in 1819 and reinforced in 1822 by Medhurst, who continued in charge of it, with some interruptions, until 1843, when he removed to Shanghai. The Dutch churches have carried on evangelizing work in all their colonies, aided and guided somewhat by the government officials, but have done almost nothing for the Chinese, except as they have been addressed in Malay. Such labors in the Dutch colonies have been left to them, and foreign societies have now withdrawn from the Archipelago in a great measure. The efforts of the American missionaries were confined to Borneo and Singapore up to 1844, when they all removed to China. The suspicious and restrictive bearing of the Dutch authorities toward such efforts had its influence in making this change.

A summary of labors at the stations was given by Medhurst in 1837, who refers in it almost exclusively to the English missionaries, as the Americans had at that time only recently commenced operations. "Protestant missionaries, considering themselves excluded from the interior of the Empire of China, and finding a host of emigrants in the various countries in the Malayan Archipelago, aimed first to enlighten these, with the hope that if properly instructed and influenced they would, on their return to their native land, carry with them the gospel they had learned and spread it among their countrymen. With this view they established themselves in the various colonies around China, studied the language, set up schools and seminaries, wrote and printed books, conversed extensively with the people, and tried to collect congregations to whom they might preach the word of life. Since the commencement of their missions they have translated the Holy Scriptures and printed two thousand complete Bibles in two sizes, ten thousand Testaments and thirty thousand separate books, and upward of half a million of tracts in Chinese; besides four thousand Testaments and one hundred and fifty thousand tracts in the languages of the archipelago, making about twenty millions of printed pages. About ten thousand children have passed through the mission schools, nearly one hundred persons have been baptized, and several native preachers raised up, one of whom has proclaimed the gospel to his countrymen and endured persecution for Jesus' sake."

Since this was written the number of pages printed and circulated has more than doubled, the number of scholars taught has increased many thousands, and preaching proportionably extended; while a few more have professed the gospel by baptism and a generally consistent life. All these missions, so far as the Chinese are concerned, are now suspended, and, unless the Dutch resume them, are not likely to be soon revived. The greater openings in China itself, and the small number of qualified men ready to enter them, invited all the laborers away from the outskirts and colonies to the borders, and into the mother country itself. The idea entertained, that the colonists would react upon their countrymen at home, proved illusive; for the converts, when they returned to dwell among their heathen countrymen, were lost in the crowd, and though they may not have adopted or sanctioned their old heathen customs, were too few to work in concert and too ignorant and unskilled to carry on such labors.[1]

When Robert Morrison died at Canton in 1834, the prospect of the extension of evangelistic work among the people was nearly as dark as when he landed; in China itself during that time only three assistants had come to his help, for there were few encouragements for them to stay. Bridgman, the first missionary from the American churches to China, in company with D. Abeel, seaman's chaplain at Whampoa, arrived in February, 1830. Abeel remained nearly a year, when he went to Singapore, and subsequently to Siam. They were received in Canton

[1] Besides the regular publications of the societies engaged in this branch of missions which give authentic details, see the memoirs of Abeel, Dyer, Milne, and Morrison, Tomlin's *Missionary Letters*, and Abeel's *Residence in China* and the neighboring countries.

by the house of Olyphant & Co., in whose establishment one or both were maintained during the first three years, and whose partners remained the friends and supporters of all efforts for the evangelization of the Chinese till its close, fifty years afterward. Bridgman took four or five boys as scholars, but his limited accommodations prevented the enlargement of the school, and in 1834 it was disbanded by the departure of its pupils, whose friends feared to be involved in trouble.

During the summer of 1833 Liang A-fah distributed a large number of books in and about Canton, a work which well suited his inclinations. Many copies of the Scriptures and his own tracts had reached the students assembled at the literary examinations, when the officers interfered to prevent him. In 1834 the authorities ordered a search for those natives who had "traitorously" assisted Lord Napier in publishing an appeal to the Chinese, and Liang A-fah and his assistants were immediately suspected. Two of the latter were seized, one of whom was beaten with forty blows upon his face for refusing to divulge; the other made a full disclosure, and the police next day repaired to his shop and seized three printers, with four hundred volumes and blocks; the men were subsequently released by paying about eight hundred dollars. Liang A-fah fled, and a body of police arrived at his native village to arrest him, but not finding him or his family they seized three of his kindred and sealed up his house. He finally made his way to Macao and sailed to Singapore.

Few books were distributed after this at Canton until ten years later, but numerous copies were circulated along the coast as far north as Tientsin, accompanied with such explanations as could be given. The first and most interesting of these voyages was made by Gutzlaff, on board a junk proceeding from Bangkok to Tientsin, June 9, 1831, in which the sociable character of the Chinese and their readiness to receive and entertain foreigners when they could do so without fear of their rulers was plainly seen.[1] After his arrival at Macao, December 13th,

[1] For an account of a trip much like it, see *Annales de la Foi*, Tome VII., p. 356.

he was engaged by the enlightened chief of the English factory, Charles Marjoribanks, as interpreter to accompany Lindsay in the ship Lord Amherst, on an experimental commercial voyage which occupied about seven months (February 26 to September 5, 1832), and presented further opportunities for learning the feelings of the Chinese officers regarding foreign intercourse. Many religious and scientific books were distributed, among which was one giving a general account of the English nation that was eagerly received by all classes. Within a few weeks after his return Gutzlaff started a third time, October 20th, in the Sylph, an opium vessel in the employ of a leading English firm at Canton, and went as far as Manchuria while the winds were favorable. She returned to Macao April 29, 1833, visiting many places on the downward trip. The interest aroused in England and America among political, commercial, and religious people, fifty years ago, by the reports of these three voyages can now hardly be appreciated. They opened the prospect of new relations with one-half of mankind, and the other half who had long felt debarred from entering upon their rightful fields in all these diversified interests prepared for great efforts.

Great Britain took the lead in breaking down the barriers, and the religious world urged on the work of missions. Contributions were sent to Gutzlaff from England and America, encouraging him to proceed, and grants were made to aid in printing Bibles and tracts. In 1835 he gave up his connection with the opium trade and took the office of interpreter to the English consular authorities on a salary of eight hundred pounds sterling, which he retained till his death, August 9, 1851, aged forty-eight. He was a man of great industry and knowledge of Chinese, and carried on a missionary organization at Hongkong by means of native Christians for several years. His publications in the Chinese, Japanese, Dutch, German, English, Siamese, Cochinchinese, and Latin languages number eighty-five in all; they are now seldom seen.

In 1835 Medhurst visited China, and, assisted by the house of Olyphant & Co., embarked in the brig Huron, accompanied by the American missionary Stevens and furnished with a supply of books. During the three months of the voyage, they "went through various parts of four provinces and many villages, giving away about eighteen thousand volumes, of which six thousand were portions of the Scriptures, among a cheerful and willing people, without meeting with the least aggression or injury; having been always received by the people with a cheerful smile, and most generally by the officers with politeness and respect." Medhurst's ability to speak the Amoy dialect introduced him to the people in the junks at all the ports on the coast. Years after this voyage the Methodist missionaries at Fuhchau found that some of the books given away on Haitan Island had been read and remembered, and thus prepared the people there for listening to further preaching.

The most expensive enterprise for this object was set on foot in 1836, and few efforts to advance the cause of religion among the Chinese have been planned on a scale of greater liberality. The brig Himmaleh was purchased in New York by the firm of Talbot, Olyphant & Co., principally for the purpose of aiding missionaries in circulating religious books on the coasts of China and the neighboring countries, and arrived in August, 1836. Gutzlaff, who was then engaged as interpreter to the English authorities, declined going in her, because in that case he must resign his commission, and there was no other missionary in China acquainted with the dialects spoken on the coast. The brig remained unemployed, therefore, until December, when she was dispatched on a cruise among the islands of the archipelago under the direction of Mr. Stevens, accompanied by G. T. Lay, agent of the British and Foreign Bible Society, recently arrived. This decision of Gutzlaff, who had again and again urged such a measure, and had himself ceased his voyages on the coast because of his implied connection thereby with the opium trade, was quite unexpected. The death of Mr. Stevens at Singapore, in January, threw the chief responsibility and direction of the undertaking upon Capt. Frazer, who seems to have been poorly qualified for any other than the maritime part. Rev. Messrs. Dickinson and Wolfe went in Stevens' place, but as none of these gentlemen understood the Malayan language, less direct intercourse was had with the people at the places where they stopped than was anticipated. The Himmaleh reached China in July, 1837, and as there was no one qualified to go in her, she returned to the United States. An account of the voyage was written by Lay and published in New York, in connection with that of the ship Morrison to Japan in August, 1837, by C. W. King, of the firm of Olyphant & Co., under whose direction the trip of the latter was taken for the purpose of restoring seven shipwrecked Japanese to their native land. Gutzlaff accompanied this vessel as interpreter, for three of the men were under the orders of the English superintendent; the expedition failed in its object, and all the men were brought back. Probably fifty thousand books in all were scattered on the coast in these and other voyages, and more than double that number about Canton, Macao, and their vicinity.

This promiscuous distribution of books has been criticised by some as injudicious and little calculated to advance the objects of a Christian mission. The funds expended in printing and circulating books, it was said by these critics, who have never undertaken aught themselves, could have been much better employed in establishing schools. To scatter bcoks broadcast among a people whose ability to read them was not ascertained, and under circumstances which prevented any explanation of the design in giving them or inquiries as to the effects produced, was not, at first view, a very wise or promising course. But it must be remembered that prior to the treaty of Nanking this was the only means of approaching the people of the country. The Emperor forbade foreigners residing in his borders except at Canton, and Protestant missionaries did not believe that it was the best means of recommending their teachings to come before his subjects as persistent violators of his laws; God's providence would open the way when the laborers were ready. No one supposed that the desire to receive books was an index of the ability of the people to understand them or love of the doctrines contained in them. If the plan offered a reasonable probability of effecting some good, it certainly could do almost no harm, for the respect for printed books assured us that they would not be wantonly destroyed, but rather, in most cases, carefully preserved. The business of tract distribution and colportage may, however, be carried too far in advance of other parts of missionary work. It is much easier to write, print, and give away religious treatises, than it is to sit down with the people and explain the leading truths of the Bible; but the two go well together among those who can read, and in no nation is it more desirable that they should be combined. If the books be given away without explanation, the people do not understand the object and feel too little interest in them to take the trouble to find out; if the preacher deliver an intelligible discourse, his audience will probably remember its general purport, but they will be likely to read the book with more attention and understand the sermon better when the two are combined; the voice explains the book and the book recalls the ideas and teachings of the preacher.

It is not surprising that the fate of these books cannot be traced, for that is true of such labors in other lands. On the one hand, they have been seen on the counters of shops cut in two for wrapping up medicines and fruit—which the shopman would not do with the worst of his own books; on the other, a copy of a gospel containing remarks was found on board the admiral's junk at Tinghai, when that town was taken by the English in 1840. They certainly have not all been lost or contemptuously destroyed, though perhaps most have been like seed sown by the wayside. In missions, as in other things, it is impossible to predict the result of several courses of action before trying them; and if it was believed that many of those who receive books can read them, there was a strong inducement to press this branch of labor, when, too, it was the only one which could be brought to bear upon large portions of the people.

In 1832 the *Chinese Repository* was commenced by Bridgman and encouraged by Morrison, who, with his son, continued to furnish valuable papers and translations as long as they lived. Its object was to diffuse correct information concerning China, while it formed a convenient repertory of the essays, travels, translations, and papers of contributors. It was issued monthly for twenty years under the editorship of Messrs. Bridgman and Williams, and contains a history of foreign intercourse and missions during its existence. The *Chinese Recorder* has since chronicled the latter cause and the *China Review* taken the literary branch.

In 1834 Dr. Parker joined the mission at Canton, and opened a hospital, in October, 1835, for the gratuitous relief of such diseases among the Chinese as his time and means would allow, devoting his attention chiefly to ophthalmic cases and surgical operations. This branch of Christian benevolence was already not unknown in China. Morrison in 1820 had, in connection with Dr. Livingstone, commenced dispensing medicines at Macao, while T. R. Colledge, also of the East India Company, opened a dispensary at his own expense, in 1827, and finding the number of patients rapidly increasing, he rented two small houses at Macao, where in four years more than four thousand patients were cured or relieved. The benevolent design was encouraged by the foreign community, and about six thousand five hundred dollars were contributed, so that it was, after the first year, no other expense to the founder than giving his time and strength. It was unavoidably closed in 1832, and a philanthropic Swede, Sir Andrew Ljungstedt, prepared a short account of its operations, and inserted several letters written to Dr. Colledge, one of which is here quoted:

To knock head and thank the great English doctor. Venerable gentleman: May your groves of almond trees be abundant, and the orange trees make the water of your well fragrant. As heretofore, may you be made known to the world as illustrious and brilliant, and as a most profound and skilful doctor. I last year arrived in Macao blind in both eyes; I have to thank you, venerable sir, for having by your excellent methods cured me perfectly. Your goodness is as lofty as a hill, your virtue deep as the sea; therefore all my family will express their gratitude for your new-creating goodness. Now I am desirous of returning home. Your profound kindness it is impossible for me to requite; I feel extremely ashamed of myself for it. I am grateful for your favors, and shall think of them without ceasing. Moreover, I am certain that since you have been a benefactor to the world and your good government is spread abroad, heaven must surely grant you a long life, and you will enjoy every happiness. I return to my mean province. Your illustrious name, venerable sir, will extend to all time; during a thousand ages it will not decay. I return thanks for your great kindness. Impotent are my words to sound your fame and to express my thanks. I wish you everlasting tranquillity.

Presented to the great English doctor and noble gentleman in the 11th year of Taukwang, by Ho Shuh, of the district of Chau-ngan, in the department of Changchau in Fuhkien, who knocks head and presents thanks.

Another patient, in true Chinese style, returned thanks for the aid he had received in a poetical effusion:

This I address to the English physician: condescend, sir, to look upon it. Diseased in my eyes, I had almost lost my sight, when happily, sir, I met with you. You gave me medicine; you applied the knife; and, as when the clouds are swept away, now again I behold the azure heavens. My joys know no bounds. As a faint token of my feelings, I have composed a stanza in heptameter, which, with a few trifling presents, I beg you will be pleased to accept. Then happy, happy shall I be!

He lavishes his blessings, but seeks for no return;
Such medicine, such physician, since Tsin were never known:
The medicine—how many kinds most excellent has he!
The surgeon's knife—it pierced the eye, and spring once more I see.
If Tung has not been born again to bless the present age,
Then sure 'tis Sü reanimate again upon the stage.
Whenever called away from far, to see your native land,
A living monument I'll wait upon the ocean's strand.

When Dr. Parker's scheme was made known to Howqua, the hong merchant, he readily fell in with it and let his building for the purpose, and after the first year gave it rent free till its destruction in 1856. It was opened for the admission of patients November 4, 1835. The peculiar circumstances under which this enterprise was started imposed some caution on its superintendent, and the hong merchants themselves seem to have had a lurking suspicion that so purely a benevolent object, involving so much expense of time, labor, and money, must have some latent object which it behooved them to watch. A linguist's clerk was often in attendance, partly for this purpose, for three or four years, and made himself very useful. The patients, who numbered about a hundred daily, were often restless, and hindered their own relief by not patiently awaiting their turn; but the habits of order in which they are trained made even such a company amenable to rules. The surgical operations attracted much notice, and successful cures were spoken of abroad and served to advertise and recommend the institution to the higher ranks of native society. It is difficult at this date to fully appreciate the extraordinary ignorance and prejudice respecting foreigners which the Chinese then entertained, and which could be best removed by some such form of benevolence. On the other hand, the repeated instances of kind feeling between friends and relatives exhibited among the patients, tender solicitude of parents for the relief of children, and the fortitude shown in bearing the severest operations, or faith in taking unknown medicines from the foreigners' hands, all tended to elevate the character of the Chinese in the opinion of every beholder, as their unfeigned gratitude for restored health increased his esteem.

The reports of this hospital in Sin-tau-lan Street gave the requisite information as to its operations, and means were taken to place the whole system upon a surer footing by forming a society in China. Suggestions for this object were circulated in October, 1836, signed by Messrs. Colledge, Parker, and Bridgman, in which the motives for such a step and the good effects likely to result from it were thus explained:

We cannot close these suggestions without adverting to one idea, though this is not the place to enlarge upon it. It is affecting to contemplate this Empire, embracing three hundred and sixty millions of souls, where almost all the light of true science is unknown, where Christianity has *scarcely* shed one genial ray, and where the theories concerning matter and mind, creation and providence, are wofully destitute of truth; it is deeply affecting to see the multitudes who are here suffering under maladies from which the hand of charity is able to relieve them. Now we know, indeed, that it is the glorious gospel of the blessed God only that can set free the human mind, and that it is only when enlightened in the true knowledge of God that man is rendered capable of rising to his true intellectual elevation; but while we take care to give this truth the high place which it ought ever to hold, we should beware of depreciating other truth. In the vast conflict which is to revolutionize the intellectual and moral world, we may not underrate the value of any weapon. As a means, then, to waken the dormant mind of China, may we not place a high value upon medical truth, and seek its introduction with good hope of its becoming the handmaid of religious truth? If an inquiry after truth upon any subject is elicited, is there not a great point gained? And that inquiry after medical truth may be provoked, there is good reason to expect; for, exclusive as China is in all her systems, she cannot exclude disease nor shut her people up from the desire of relief. Does not, then, the finger of Providence point clearly to one way that we should take with the people of China, directing us to seek the introduction of the remedies for sin itself by the same door through which we convey those which are designed to mitigate or remove its evils? Although medical truths cannot restore the sick and afflicted to the favor of God, yet perchance the spirit of inquiry about it once awakened will not sleep till it inquires about the source of truth; and he who comes with the blessings of health may prove an angel of mercy to point to the Lamb of God. At any rate, this seems the only open door; let us enter it. A faith that worketh not may wait for other doors. None can deny that *this* is a way of charity that worketh no ill, and our duty to walk in it seems plain and imperative.[1]

This paper was favorably received, and in February, 1838, a public meeting was convened at Canton for the purpose of forming a society, "the object of which shall be to encourage gentlemen of the medical profession to come and practise gratuitously among the Chinese by affording the usual aid of hospitals, medicines, and attendants; but that the support or remuneration of such medical gentlemen be not at present within its contemplation." Some other rules were laid down, but the principle here stated has been since adhered to in all the similar establishments opened in other places. It has served, moreover, to retain them under the oversight and their resident physicians in the employ of missionary societies. No directions were given by the framers of the first society concerning the mode of imparting religious instruction, distributing tracts, or doing missionary work as they had opportunity. The signers of the original paper of suggestions also issued an address, further setting forth their views and expectations:

To restore health, to ease pain, or in any way to diminish the sum of human misery, forms an object worthy of the philanthropist. But in the prosecution of our views we look forward to far higher results than the mere relief of human suffering. We hope that our endeavors will tend to break down the walls of prejudice and long-cherished nationality of feeling, and to teach the Chinese that those whom they affect to despise are both able and willing to become their benefactors. They shut the door against the teachers of the gospel; they find our books often written in idioms which they cannot readily understand; and they have laid such restrictions upon commerce that it does not awaken among them that love of science, that spirit of invention, and that love of thought which it uniformly excites and fosters whenever it is allowed to take its own course without limit or interference. In the way of doing them good our opportunities are few; but among these that of practis-

---

[1] *Chinese Repository*, Vol. V., p. 372; Vol. VII., pp. 33–40. Lockhart's *Medical Missionary in China*, 1861, p. 134.

ing medicine and surgery stands pre-eminent. Favorable results have hitherto followed it, and will still continue to do so. It is a department of benevolence peculiarly adapted to China. . . .

In the department of benevolence to which our attention is now turned, purity and disinterestedness of motive are more clearly evinced than in any other. They appear unmasked; they attract the gaze and excite the admiration and gratitude of thousands. *Heal the sick* is our motto, constituting alike the injunction under which we act and the object at which we aim; and which, with the blessing of God, we hope to accomplish by means of scientific practice in the exercise of an unbought and untiring kindness. We have called ours a missionary society because we trust it will advance the cause of missions, and because we want men to fill our institutions who to requisite skill and experience add the self-denial and high moral qualities which are looked for in a missionary.

The undertaking so auspiciously begun at Canton, in 1835, has been carried on ever since, and was the pattern of many similar hospitals at the stations afterward occupied. The greatest part of the funds needed for carrying them on has been contributed in China itself by foreigners, who certainly would not have done so had they not felt that it was a wise and useful charity, and known something of the way their funds were employed. The hospital at Canton has exceeded even the hopes of its founders, and its many buildings and wards attest the liberality of the community which presented them to the society. The native rulers, gentry, and merchants are now well acquainted with the institution, and contribute to carry it on. During the forty-five years of its existence it has been conducted by Drs. Parker and Kerr nearly all the time, who have relieved about seven hundred and fifty thousand patients entered on the books; the outlay has been over one hundred and twenty-five thousand dollars. Several dispensaries in the country have also been carried on with the society's grants in aid. A separate hospital was conducted in Canton from 1846 to 1856 by B. Hobson, F.R.C.S., who has left an enduring record of his labors in eighteen medical works in Chinese, many of them illustrated. J. G. Kerr, M.D., has also issued several small treatises, and the publications of this kind in Chinese suitable for the people, issued by them and other missionary physicians, already number nearly fifty.

In these details of the inception of the plan of combining

medical labors with the work of Christian missions in China, it will be seen how the confined position of foreigners at Canton proved to be an incentive and an aid to its prosecution for some years—long enough to show its place and fitness. On the cessation of hostilities between China and Great Britain in 1842, other fields were opened, where its benefits were even more strongly shown. The war had left the people amazed and irritated at what they deemed to be a causeless and unjust attack by superior power. This was the case at Amoy, where no foreigners had lived until the British army took possession in August, 1841. In February, 1842, Revs. D. Abeel and W. J. Boone went there and made the acquaintance of the people on Kulang su, who were much pleased to meet with those who could converse with them and answer their inquiries. Dr. Cumming was able, by their assistance, as soon as he opened his dispensary, to inform the people of his designs; and the missionaries, on their part, preached the gospel to the patients, distributing in addition suitable books. The people were so ready to accept the proffered relief that it was soon impossible for one man to do more than wait upon the blind, lame, diseased, and injured who thronged his doors. A few months more equally proved that while the physician was attending to the patients in one room, the preacher could not ask for a better audience than those who were waiting in the adjoining one. An invitation to attend more formal services on the Sabbath was soon accepted by a few, whose curiosity led them to come and hear more of foreigners and their teachings. The reputation of the hospital was seen when taking short excursions in the vicinity, for persons who had been relieved constantly came forward to express their heartfelt thanks. Thus suspicion gave way to gratitude, enemies were converted to friends, and those who had enjoyed no opportunity of learning the character of foreigners, and had been taught to regard them as barbarians and demons, were disabused of their error. The favorable impression thus made at Amoy, forty years ago, has never been suspended, and numerous native churches have been gathered in all that region. Just the same union of preaching and practice was begun at Shanghai by Dr. W.

Lockhart after the capture of that city in 1844, and has been continued to this time. Ningpo and Fuhchau received similar benefits soon after; these and many others have received aid from foreigners residing in the Empire. Several thousand dollars were sent from Great Britain and the United States to further the object, and one society was formed in Edinburgh in 1856 to develop this branch of missionary work.

The proposition in the original scheme of educating Chinese youth as physicians and surgeons has not been carried out to a great extent. The practising missionary has hardly the time to do his students justice, and unless they show great aptitude for operations, the assistants get weary of the routine of attending to the patients and go away. Dr. Lockhart speaks of his own disappointments in this respect. Dr. Parker had only one pupil, Kwan A-to, who took up the profession among his countrymen. Dr. Wong A-fun received a complete medical education in Edinburgh, and rendered efficient help for many years in the hospital at Canton till his death. The college at Peking has now a chair of anatomy and physiology, which will aid in introducing better practice. Dr. Kerr gives some other reasons for the small number of skilled physicians educated in the missionary hospitals, yet some of his pupils had obtained lucrative practice. Others had imposed themselves in remote places on the people as such, who had only been employed as students a few months—a gratifying index of progress. It is not likely, however, that the Chinese generally will immediately discard their own mode of practice and adopt another from their countrymen so far as to support them in their new system. They have not enough knowledge of medicine to appreciate the difference between science and charlatanism; and a native physician himself might reasonably have fears of the legal or personal results of an unsuccessful or doubtful surgical case among his ignorant patients, so far as often to prevent him trying it.

The successive annual reports issued from the various missionary hospitals in China furnish the amplest information concerning their management, and numerous particulars respecting the people who resort to them. At the Missionary Conference in Shanghai (1877) Drs. Kerr and Gould presented papers relating to this branch of labor in all its various aspects. The latter discussed the advantages of hospital versus itinerary practice; the modes of bringing the patients under religious instruction; how to limit their number so as to not wear out the physician; oversight of assistants and education of pupils; how far this gratuitous relief should be extended; what was the best mode of getting a fee from those natives who were able to pay something; and, finally, the reasons for not uniting the ministerial functions with the medical. These various points show clearly how the experience of past years had manifested the wisdom and foresight of those who originated the work, and the manner it has developed in connection with other branches. If kept as an auxiliary agency, there seems to be no reason for reducing the efforts now made by foreign societies until native physicians and surgeons are able to take up this work, just as native preachers are to oversee their own churches.

Another benevolent society, whose name and object was the Diffusion of Useful Knowledge in China, was established in December, 1834. The designs of the association were "by all means in its power to prepare and publish, in a cheap form, plain and easy treatises in the Chinese language, on such branches of useful knowledge as are suited to the existing state and condition of the Chinese Empire." It published six or eight works and a magazine during the few years of its existence, and their number would have been larger if there had been more persons capable of writing treatises. Since then this kind of mission work has been taken up by various agencies better fitted to develop its several departments, and, excepting newspapers, the preparation of suitable histories, geographies, and scientific books has been done by Protestant missionaries. The Chinese government has directed its employés in the arsenal schools to translate such works as will furnish the scholars with good elementary books.

Their usefulness as aids and precursors of the introduction of the gospel is very great. Among a less intelligent population they are not so important until the people get a taste for knowledge in schools; but where the conceit of false learning and pride of literary attainments cause such a contempt for all other than their own books, as is the case in Chinese society, entertaining narratives and notices of other people and lands, got up in an attractive form, tend to disabuse them of these ideas (the offspring of arrogant ignorance rather than deliberate rejection) and incite them to learn and read more. The influence of newspapers and other periodical literature will be very great among the Chinese when they begin to think for themselves on the great truths and principles which are now being introduced among them. They have already begun to discuss political topics, and the great advantage of movable types over the old blocks tends to hasten the adoption of foreign modes of printing. It may, by some, be considered as not the business of a missionary to edit a newspaper; but those who are acquainted with the debased inertness of heathen minds know that any means which will convey truth and arouse the people tends to advance religion. The influence of the *Dnyanodya* in Bombay, and other kindred publications in various places in India, is great and good; hundreds of the people read them and then talk about the subjects treated in them, who would neither attend religious meetings, look at the Scriptures, nor have a tract in their possession. The same will be the case in China, and it is not irrelevant to the work of a missionary to adopt such a mode of imparting truths, if it be the most likely way of reaching the prejudiced, proud, and ignorant people around him. When the native religious community has begun to take form, this mode of instruction and disputation will be left to its most intelligent members.

In January, 1835, the foreign community in China established a third association, which originated entirely with a few of its leading members. Soon after the death of Dr. Morrison, a paper was circulated containing suggestions for the formation of an association to be called the Morrison Education Society, intended both as a testimonial of the worth and labors of that excellent man, more enduring than marble or brass, and a means of continuing his efforts for the good of China. A provisional committee was formed from among the subscribers to this paper, consisting of Sir G. B. Robinson, Bart., Messrs. W. Jardine, D.

W. C. Olyphant, Lancelot Dent, J. R. Morrison, and Rev. E. C. Bridgman; five thousand nine hundred and seventy-seven dollars were immediately subscribed, and about one thousand five hundred volumes of books presented to its library. This liberal spirit for the welfare of the people among whom they sojourned reflected the highest credit on the gentlemen interested in it, as well as upon the whole foreign community, inasmuch as, with only four or five exceptions, none of them were united to the country by other than temporary business relations.

The main objects of the Morrison Education Society were "the establishment and improvement of schools in which Chinese youth shall be taught to read and write the English language in connection with their own, by which means shall be brought within their reach all the instruction requisite for their becoming wise, industrious, sober, and virtuous members of society, fitted in their respective stations of life to discharge well the duties which they owe to themselves, their kindred, their country, and their God." The means of accomplishing this end by gathering a library, employing competent teachers, and encouraging native schools were all pointed out in this programme of labors, whose comprehensiveness was equalled only by its philanthropy. Applications were made for teachers both in England and America; from the former, an answer was received that there was no likelihood of obtaining one; a person was selected in the latter, the Rev. S. R. Brown, who with his wife arrived at Macao in February, 1839. In the interval between the formation of the Society and the time when its operations assumed a definite shape in its own schools, something was done in collecting information concerning native education and in supporting a few boys, or assisting Mrs. Gutzlaff's school at Macao. The Society's school was opened at Macao in November, 1839, with six scholars; four years afterward it removed to Morrison Hill in Hongkong, into the commodious quarters erected by its president, Lancelot Dent, on a site granted by the colonial government for the purpose. In 1845 Brown had thirty pupils, who filled all the room there was in the house. He stated in his report of that year, as a gratifying evidence of confidence on their part, that no parent had asked to have his child leave during the year. "When the school was commenced," observes Mr. Brown, "few offered their sons as pupils, and even they, as some of them have since told me, did it with a good deal of apprehension as to the consequences. 'We could not understand,' says one who first brought a boy to the school, 'why a foreigner should wish to feed and instruct our children for nothing. We thought there must be some sinister motive at the bottom of it. Perhaps it was to entice them away from their parents and country, and transport them by and by to some foreign land.' At all events, it was a mystery. 'But now,' said the same father to me a few weeks ago, 'I understand it. I have had my three sons in your school steadily since they entered it, and no harm has happened to them. The eldest has been qualified for service as an interpreter. The other two have learned nothing bad. The religion you have taught them, and of which I was so much afraid, has made them better. I myself believe its truth, though the customs of my country forbid my embracing it. I have no longer any fear; you labor for others' good, not your own. I understand it now.' "

This suspicion was not surprising, considering the common estimate of foreigners among the people, and indicates that it was high time to attempt something worthy of the Christianity which they professed. The school was conducted as it would have been if removed to a town in New England; and when its pupils left they were fitted for taking a high rank in their own country. Their attachment to their teacher was great. One instance is taken from the fourth report: "Last spring the father of one in the older class came to the house and told his son that he could not let him remain here any longer but that he must put him out to service and make him earn something. His father is a poor miserable man, besotted by the use of opium, and has sold his two daughter into slavery to raise money. The boy ran away to his instructor and told him what his father had said, adding, 'I cannot go.' Willing to ascertain the sincerity of the boy and the strength of his attachment to his friends, his teacher coolly replied, 'Perhaps it will be well for you to go, for probably you could be a table-boy in some gentleman's house and so get two dollars a month, which is two more than you get here, where only your food is given you.' The little fellow looked at him steadily while he made these remarks, as if amazed at the strange language he used, and when he had done, turned hastily about and burst into tears, exclaiming, 'I cannot go; if I go away from this school I shall be lost.' He did not leave, for his father did not wish to force him away."

Another case shows the confidence of a parent on the occasion of the death of one of the pupils, his only child: "He heard of his son's illness too late to arrive before he died, and when he came it was to bury his remains. He was naturally overwhelmed with grief at the affliction that had come upon him, and his apprehensions of the effect of the tidings upon the boy's mother were gloomy enough. After the funeral was over, I conversed with him. To my surprise he made not the least complaint as to what had been done for the sick lad, either in the way of medical treatment or otherwise, but expressed many thanks for the kind and assiduous attentions that had been bestowed upon him. He said he had entertained great hope of his son's future usefulness, and in order to promote it had placed him here at school. But now his family would end in himself. I showed him some specimens of his son's drawing, an amusement of which he was particularly fond. The tears gushed faster as his eyes rested on these evidences of his son's skill. 'Do not show them to me,' said he; 'it is too much. I cannot speak now. I know you have done well to my son. I pity *you*, for all your labor is lost.' I assured him I did not think so. He had been a very diligent and obedient learner, and had won the esteem of his teachers and companions. He had been taught concerning the true God and the way of salvation, and it might have done him everlasting good. As the old man was leaving me, he turned and asked if, in case he should adopt another boy, I would receive him as a pupil, to which I replied in the affirmative."

An assistant teacher, Wm. A. Macy, joined Mr. Brown in 1846; the latter returned to America in 1847, and the school was closed in 1849, owing chiefly to the departure of its early patrons from China and the opening of new ports of trade, scattering the foreign community so that funds could not be obtained. Mission societies began to enlarge their work at these ports and occupy the same department of education as the Morrison School. It, however, did a good work in its education of half a score of men who now fill high places in their country's service, or occupy posts of usefulness most honorably to themselves. The boy mentioned in a previous paragraph afterward went through a medical course at Edinburgh, became a practising surgeon and physician at Canton, and died there in 1878, honored by foreigners and natives during a life of usefulness and benevolence. In that year Mr. Brown visited China for his health, and was received by this Dr. Wong and others of his old pupils with marks of regard honorable and gratifying to both; they fitted up a house there for him, presented him with a beautiful piece of silver plate, and paid his passage up to Peking and back to Shanghai.

The efforts of Protestants for the evangelization of China were largely of a preparatory nature until the year 1842. Most of the laborers were stationed out of China, and those in the Empire itself were unable to pursue their designs without many embarrassments. Mrs. Gutzlaff experienced many obstacles in her endeavors to collect a school at Macao, partly from the fears of the parents and the harassing inquiries of the police, the latter of which naturally increased the former; partly again from the short period the parents were willing to allow their children to remain. The Portuguese clergy and government of Macao have done nothing themselves to impede Protestant missionaries in their labors in the colony since 1833, when the governor ordered the Albion press, belonging to Dr. Morrison's son, to be stopped, on account of his publishing a religious newspaper called the *Miscellanea Sinicæ;* and this he was encouraged to do from knowing that the East India Company was opposed to its continuance. The governor intimated to one of the American missionaries in 1839 that no tracts must be distributed or public congregations gathered in the colony, but no objection would be made to audiences collected in his own house for instruction. No obstacle was put in the way of printing, and the press that was interdicted in 1833 was carried back to Macao in 1835, after the dissolution of the East

India Company, under the direction of the American mission. Several aids in the study of the Chinese language were issued from it during the nine years it was there under the author's charge.

The city of Canton was long in China one of the most unpromising fields for missionary labors, not alone when it was the only one in the Empire, but until recently. This was owing to several causes. The pursuits of foreigners were limited to trade. Their residence was confined to an area of a few acres held by the guild of hong merchants allowed to trade with them, and all intercourse was carried on in the jargon known as *Pigeon-English.* They were systematically degraded by the native rulers in the eyes of the people, who knew no other appellation for the strangers than *fan-kwei*, or 'foreign devil.' The opium war of 1839–42 had aroused the worst passions of the Cantonese, and their conceit had been increased by the unsuccessful attempts to take the city in 1841 and 1847 by the English forces. Since 1858 the citizens have been accessible to other influences, and learned that their isolation and ignorance brought calamity on themselves.

When Morrison died, Dr. Bridgman and the writer of these pages were the only fellow-laborers belonging to any missionary society then in China; the Christian church formed in 1835 contained only three members. It was indeed a day of small things, but from henceforth grew more and more bright. The contrast even in twelve years is thus described in Dr. Hobson's report of his hospital; the extract shows the little freedom then enjoyed in comparison with what it now is, nearly forty years after:

The average attendance of Chinese has been over a hundred, and none have been more respectful and cordial in their attention than those in whom aneurism has been cured or sight restored, from whom the tumor has been extirpated or the stone extracted. These services must be witnessed to understand fully their interest. Deep emotions have been awakened when contrasting the restrictions of the first years of Protestant missions in China with the present freedom. Then, not permitted to avow our missionary character and object lest it might eject us from the country; nor could a Chinese receive a Christian book but at the peril of his safety, or embrace that religion without hazarding his life. Now he may receive and practise the doctrines of Christ, and transgress no law of the Empire. Our interest may be more easily conceived than expressed as we have declared the truths of the gospel, or when looking upon the evangelist Liang A-fah, and thought of him fleeing for his life and long banished from his native land, and now returned to declare boldly the truths of the gospel in the city from which he had fled. Well did he call upon his audience to worship and give thanks to the God of heaven and earth for what he had done for them. With happy effect he dwelt upon the Saviour's life and example, and pointing to the paintings suspended on the walls of the room, informed his auditors that these were performed by his blessing and in conformity to his precepts and example. Portions of the Scriptures and religious tracts are given to all the hearers on the Sabbath, and likewise to all the patients during the week, so that thousands of volumes have been sent forth from the hospital to scores of villages and to distant provinces.

Before the capture of the city the people had become quite friendly to all missionary labors, through the ameliorating influences of the hospitals. While the city was beleaguered by the insurgents in 1855, the wounded soldiers were attended to by Dr. Hobson, who sometimes had his house full. After Canton was occupied by the allies in 1858 there was an enlargement of mission work in the city and environs, which has been growing in depth and extent till the changes draw the attention of the most casual observer. Foreigners are now seldom addressed as *fan-kwei*, and their excursions into the country and along the streams are made in safety. The Germans have established stations in many places between Canton and Hongkong, and easterly along the river up to Kia-ying, where the people are more turbulent than around the city or toward the west.

The occupation of Hongkong in 1841 induced the American Baptists to make it a station immediately, and Messrs. Roberts and Shuck began the mission work, followed by the London Mission two years after, when Dr. Legge removed there from Malacca. The Roman Catholic missionaries also moved over from Macao at the earliest date. The colonial authorities in time began a system of common schools for all their subjects, so that mission schools have been less necessary since that date, but are still opened to some extent. The benevolent labors by German, British, and American missionaries in Hongkong and its vicinity have been zealously carried on in harmony, and there are fully fifty separate stations on the mainland northerly from the island which are worked from this colony. The number in the whole province of Kwangtung amounts to more than seventy-five, all of them efficiently established since 1858.

The mission at Amoy was commenced in 1842 by Messrs. Abeel and Boone under the most favorable auspices. The English expedition took that city in August, 1841, and on leaving it stationed a small naval and military force on the island of Kulang su. The people of Amoy and its environs cared perhaps little for the merits of the war then raging, but they knew that they had suffered much from it, and no interpreters were available to carry on communication between the two parties. Both these gentlemen could converse in the local dialect, and were soon applied to by many desirous of learning something of the foreigners or who had business with them. The Chinese authorities were also pleased to obtain the aid of competent interpreters, and the good opinion of these dignitaries exercised considerable influence in inducing the people to attend upon the ministrations of the missionaries. Both officers and private gentlemen invited them to their residences, where they had opportunity to answer their reasonable inquiries concerning foreign lands and customs, and convey an outline of the Christian faith. One of these officers was Seu Ki-yu, afterward governor of the province and author of the *Ying Hwan Chí Lioh*, in which he mentions Abeel's name and speaks of his indebtedness to him in preparing that work. The number of books given away was not great, but part of every day was spent in talking with the people; when the hospital was opened by Dr. Cumming, greater facilities were afforded for intercourse. The irritation caused by what the people naturally looked upon as an unprovoked outrage was gradually allayed. There had been no long education of intercommunication between natives and foreigners in Amoy as at Canton. The work so pleasantly begun in 1842 in Kulang su has extended over most parts of the province of Fuhkien, and westward into the prefecture of Chauchau in Kwangtung. There are more converts, native pastors, and schools in this province than any other in China.

Its capital was never visited by a foreign enemy, nor did it suffer from the Tai-ping rebels, so that the gentry of Fuhchau have never been scattered nor their influence broken, like those of many other provincial centres. The mission work was commenced there in 1847 by Rev. Stephen Johnson, from Bangkok, who was soon joined by other American and English colleagues. He speaks of the great prejudices against all foreigners among the citizens in consequence of the evil effects of opium-smoking, which destroyed the people who would not cease to buy it. An experience of thirty years has not altogether removed this dislike, which even lately found an opportunity to exhibit itself in removing the Church Missionary Society's mission from the Wu-shih Hill, where it had rented buildings for that period and "injured the good luck of the city." These prejudices will gradually give way with a new generation of scholars and merchants, and we can afford to be patient with them when we reflect on their slow progress in other things.

The American Board, American Methodist, and Church Missionary Societies have each extended their stations beyond the city into the country almost to the borders of Chehkiang and Kiangsí, occupying in all nearly two hundred localities with their assistants. Besides these agencies, the China Inland mission has occupied three cities on the eastern coast and about sixteen other stations. The whole number of places in the province of Fuhkien where Protestants have opened their work in one form and another is now over two hundred and fifty, under seven separate societies. In most of these towns the good will of the people has remained with them when their objects have been fully understood; and the contrasts of destroying their chapels or book-shops, as at Kien-ning, have been found to be mixed up with other causes. Since the year 1863 the island of Formosa has been occupied by two or three British societies, and the work of their missionaries in the chief towns has been greatly prospered. Dr. Maxwell has carried on his hospital at Taiwan with eminent success as a means of winning the good opinion of suspicious natives and aborigines and inclining them to listen to the gospel. Native churches have been gathered in various parts remote from the coast, and thirty-five stations are now worked by the two British societies which have taken up this field. This progress has not been without opposition, for two of the converts were martyred a few years ago by their countrymen.

The first missionary efforts north of Canton of a permanent nature were made in 1840 by Dr. Lockhart, in the establishment of a hospital at Tinghai in Chusan. They were resumed by Milne in 1842, and while the island was under the control of British troops. Gutzlaff occupied the office of Chinese magistrate of Tinghai in 1842, and endeavored to hold meetings. Milne left Ningpo in June, 1843, and came to Hongkong overland dressed in a native costume. After his departure, some time elapsed before his place was supplied. The journal of his residence in that city indicated a great willingness on the part of people of all ranks to cultivate intercourse with such foreigners as could converse with them. Drs. Macgowan and McCarty went there in 1843 and 1844 to open a hospital, and were followed by Messrs. Lowrie, Culbertson, Loomis, and Cole, the latter in charge of a printing office of English and Chinese type and a type foundry. Religious services are held at the hospitals in that city, and Dr. Macgowan says: "Each patient is exhorted to renounce all idolatry and wickedness and to embrace the religion of the Saviour. They are admitted by tens into the prescribing room, and before being dismissed are addressed by the physician and the native Christian assistant on the subject of religion. Tracts are given to all who are able to read." The more such labors are carried on the better will the prospect of peace and a profitable intercourse between China and western nations become; the more the people learn of the science and resources, the character and designs, and partake of the religion and benevolence of western nations, the less chance will there be of collisions, and the more each party will respect the other. The fear is, however, that the disruptive and disorganizing influences will preponderate over the peaceful, and precipitate new outbreaks before these influences obtain much hold upon the Chinese.

The occupation of Ningpo in 1841 by the British troops, and their excursions into the country, had the effect of preparing the people of Chehkiang province to listen to foreigners. The mission work begun at Ningpo by three or four societies in 1842–48 has been carried on with marked success and completeness in its agencies. The various missions have taken different parts of the province for their particular fields, and by means of chapels, hospitals, schools, printing offices, itinerating and preaching excursions, and the sale of religious books, have made known the truth. A large part of the province was ravaged by the Tai-ping rebels, and after their dispersion in 1867 Hangchau and Shauking were occupied. These two cities were well nigh destroyed, but their inhabitants are learning that no force or governmental influence accompanies the preaching of the doctrines of Jesus. This idea has considerable strength among all the Chinese, and no disclaimer or explanations have much effect at first. The people of Chehkiang province have less energy and individuality than their countrymen in the southern provinces, but they have received the faith in simplicity, maintaining its ordinances and bearing its expenses in many cases without foreign aid. In the seventy stations now occupied by six societies from England and America, the advance is seen to be great since the capture of Ningpo and Tinghai forty years ago, even by the confession of those who still hold aloof. The good reputation of the missionaries was shown in the amicable settlement of an irritating question in Hangchau city in 1874. It arose from the occupation of the hillside by the Americans, who had bought the spot when it was bare of houses and erected their own dwellings. These were deemed to be detrimental to its prosperity, and a riot arose which was quelled by the authorities. A proposal was then made by the gentry to remove them by getting another site in the lower city, and this harmonized all parties while establishing a good precedent for future observance.

The great city of Shanghai was almost unknown to foreign nations until the treaty of Nanking opened it to their trade in 1842. Its inhabitants suffered greatly at its capture, but the growing commerce ere long brought prosperity. As soon as arrangements could be made the London Mission moved its hospital from Chusan Island to Shanghai (in 1844), and Dr. Lockhart immediately commenced his work. His rooms were thronged, and it is stated that ten thousand nine hundred and seventy-eight patients were attended to between May, 1844, and June, 1845. The knowledge of this charity spread over the province of Kiangsu, and removed much of the ill-will and ignorance of the people toward foreigners. One effect in the city was to incite the inhabitants to open a dispensary during four summer months, for the gratuitous relief of the sick. It was called *Shí Í Kung-kiuh*, or 'Public Establishment for Dispensing Healing.' "It was attended by eight or nine native practitioners, who saw the patients once in five days; this attendance was gratuitous on the part of some of them, and was paid for in the case of others. The medicines are supplied from the different apothecary shops, one furnishing all that is wanted during one day, which is paid for by subscriptions to the dispensary. The patients vary from three hundred to five hundred. The reason given for the recent establishment of this dispensary for relieving the sick is that it has been done by a foreigner who came to reside at the place, and therefore some of the wealthy natives wished to show their benevolence in the same way." Such a spirit speaks well for the inhabitants of Shanghai, for nothing like competition in doing good has ever been started elsewhere, nor even a public acknowledgment made of the benefits conferred by the hospitals.

During the voyage along the coast of China made by Messrs. Medhurst and Stevens, in 1835, they visited Shanghai; and an abstract of Medhurst's interview with the officers on that occasion is taken from his journal. He had already been invited by them to enter a temple hard by the landing-place, to the end that they might learn the object of the visit, and was conversing with them.

The party was now joined by another officer named Chin, a hearty, rough-looking man, with a keen eye and a voluble tongue. He immediately took the lead in the conversation, and asked whether we had not been in Shantung and had communication with some great officers there? He inquired after Messrs. Lindsay and Gutzlaff, and wished to know whither we intended to proceed. I told him these gentlemen were well; but we could hardly tell where we should go, quoting a Chinese proverb, "We know not to day what will take place to-morrow." But, I continued, as your native conjurors are reckoned very clever, they may perhaps be able to tell you. "I am conjuror enough for that," said Chin; "but what is your profession?" I told him that I was a teacher of religion. . . . After a little time a great noise was heard outside, and the arrival of the chief magistrate of the city was announced, when several officers came in and requested me to go and see his worship. He appeared to be a middle-aged man, but assumed a stern aspect as I entered, though I paid him the usual compliments and took my seat in a chair placed opposite. This disconcerted him much, and as soon as he could recover himself from the surprise at seeing a barbarian seated in his presence, he ordered me to come near and stand before him, while all the officers called out, "Rise! Rise!" I arose accordingly, and asked whether I could not be allowed to sit at the conference, and as he refused, I bowed and left the room. I was soon followed by Chin and Wang, who tried every effort to persuade me to return; this, however, I steadfastly refused to do unless I could be allowed to sit, as others of my countrymen had done in like circumstances. . . .

Having been joined by Mr. Stevens (who had been distributing books among the crowd without), we proceeded to converse more familiarly and to deliver out books to the officers and their attendants, as well as to some strangers that were present, till they were all gone. A list of such provisions as were wanted had been given to Wang, whom we requested to purchase them for us, and we would pay for them. By this time the articles were brought in, which they offered to give us as a present, and seeing that there was no other way of settling the question, we resolved to accept of the articles and send them something in return. The rain having moderated, we arose to take a walk and proceeded toward the boat, where the sailors were busy eating their dinner. Wishing to enter the city we turned off in that direction, but were stopped by the officers and their attendants, and reluctantly returned to the temple. After another hour's conversation, and partaking of refreshments with the officers, they departed. On the steps near the boat we observed a basket nearly full of straw, and on the top about half a dozen books torn in pieces and about to be burnt. On inquiry, they told us that these were a few that had been torn in the scuffle, and in order to prevent their being trodden under foot they were about to burn them. Recollecting, however, that Chin had told his servant to do something with the books he had received, it now occurred to us that he had directed them to be burned in our presence. On the torch being applied, therefore, we took the presents which were lying by and threw them on the fire, which put it out. The policeman, taking off the articles, applied the torch again, while we repeated the former operation; to show them that if they despised our presents, we also disregarded theirs. Finally the basket was thrown into the river and we left, much displeased at this insulting conduct.[1]

This extract might be thought to refer to an event which took place in the days of Ricci instead of one within the memory of the living. The progress and changes since it occurred in that city typify what has been going on throughout the

[1] *China: Its State and Prospects*, pp. 371–377. *Chinese Repository*, Vol. IV., pp. 330, 331.

whole land. Medhurst came back to Shanghai to live, within nine years after this incident, and when his failing health compelled his retirement in 1856, he closed an honorable service of thirty-nine years in the mission field. His dictionaries, translations, and writings in Chinese and English (ninety-three in all) indicate his industry; and through them he, being dead, yet speaketh to the Chinese upon his favorite themes of redemption. The work which he began was reinforced by colleagues from Great Britain and America until the whole population was reached, and towns lying south of the Yangtsz' River were all visited. After the rebellion was quelled in 1867 other cities were occupied, until about forty-five localities in all parts of Kiangsu are now held as preaching stations. People are returning to their deserted homes, and lands that lay fallow for years are retilled; thither foreign and native preachers and colportors bring the living word without hindrance.[1]

The consequences of the introduction of the gospel into China are likely to be the same that they have been elsewhere, in stirring up private and public antagonism to what is so opposed to the depravity of the human heart. There are some grounds for hoping that there will not be much systematic opposition from the imperial government when once the chiefs of the nation learn the popular sentiments and will. The principal reasons for this are found in the character of the people, who are not cruel or disposed to take life for opinions when those opinions are held by numbers of respectable and intelligent men. The fact that the officers of government all spring from the body of the people, and that these dignitaries are neither governed nor influenced by any State hierarchy—by any body of priestly men, who, feeling that the progress of the new faith will cause the loss of their influence and position, are determined to use the power of the State to put it down—leads us to hope that such officers as may adopt the new faith will not, on account of their profession, be banished or disgraced. Such was the case with Sü, who assisted and countenanced Ricci.

[1] In this connection the work of Dr. Lockhart (*Medical Missionary in China*, London, 1861) may profitably be read for the details and results of mission labors in Shanghai.

The general character of the Chinese is irreligious, and they care much more for money and power than they do for religious ceremonies of any kind; they would never lose a battle as the Egyptians did because the Persians placed cats between the armies. There are no ceremonies which they consider so binding as to be willing to fight for them, and persecute others for omitting, except those pertaining to ancestral worship;—these are of so domestic a nature that thousands of converts might discard them before much would be known or done by the people in relation to the matter. The conscientious Christian magistrate would be somewhat obnoxious to his master, and liable to be removed for refusing to perform his functions at the *ching-hwang miao* before the tutelar gods of the Empire. These and other reasons, growing out of the character of the people and the nature of their political and religious institutions, lead to the hope that the leaven of truth will permeate the mass of society and renovate, purify, and strengthen it without weakening, disorganizing, or destroying the government. There are, also, some causes to fear that such will not be the case, arising from the ignorance of the people of the proper results of Christian doctrines; from a dread of the government respecting its own stability from foreign aggression; from the evil consequences of the use of opium, and the drainage of the precious metals; and from the disturbing effects of the intercourse with unscrupulous foreigners and irritated natives often leading to riots and the interference of government authorities.

The toleration of the Christian religion had been allowed throughout the Empire by imperial edicts issued in the reign of Shunchí and his son; and often and often discountenanced and persecuted after those dates. The governmental policy had been long settled to disallow its profession by its subjects or the residence of the Roman Catholic missionaries in its borders. In 1844 the French envoy, M. de Lagrené, brought their disabilities to the notice of Kíying, who memorialized the throne and received the following rescript, which reversed the bloody decrees of 1722 and later years. For his efforts in this matter he deserves the thanks and remembrance of every friend of Christianity and the Chinese.

Kíying, imperial commissioner, minister of State, and governor-general of Kwangtung and Kwangsí, respectfully addresses the throne by memorial.

On examination it appears that the religion of the Lord of Heaven is that professed by all the nations of the West; that its main object is to encourage the good and suppress the wicked; that since its introduction to China during the Ming dynasty it has never been interdicted; that subsequently, when Chinese, practising this religion, often made it a covert for wickedness, even to the seducing of wives and daughters, and to the deceitful extraction of the pupils from the eyes of the sick,[1] government made investigation and inflicted punishment, as is on record; and that in the reign of Kiaking special clauses were first laid down for the punishment of the guilty. The prohibition, therefore, was directed against evil-doing under the covert of religion, and not against the religion professed by the western foreign nations.

Now the request of the French ambassador, Lagrené, that those Chinese who, doing well, practise this religion, be exempt from criminality, seems feasible. It is right therefore to make the request, and earnestly to crave celestial favor to grant that, henceforth, all natives and foreigners without distinction, who learn and practise the religion of the Lord of Heaven, and do not excite trouble by improper conduct, be exempted from criminality. If there be any who seduce wives and daughters, or deceitfully take the pupils from the eyes of the sick, walking in their former paths, or are otherwise guilty of criminal acts, let them be dealt with according to the old laws. As to those of the French and other foreign nations who practise the religion, let them only be permitted to build churches at the five ports opened for commercial intercourse. They must not presume to enter the country to propagate religion. Should any act in opposition, turn their backs upon the treaties, and rashly overstep the boundaries, the local officers will at once seize and deliver them to their respective consuls for restraint and correction. Capital punishment is not to be rashly inflicted, in order that the exercise of gentleness may be displayed. Thus, peradventure, the good and the profligate will not be blended, while the equity of mild laws will be exhibited.

This request, that well-doers practising the religion may be exempt from criminality, I (the commissioner), in accordance with reason and bounden duty, respectfully lay before the throne, earnestly praying the august Emperor graciously to grant that it may be carried into effect. A respectful memorial.

Taukwang, 24th year, 11th month, 19th day (December 28, 1844), was received the vermilion reply: "Let it be according to the counsel [of Kíying]." This is from the Emperor.[2]

---

[1] This is thus explained by a Chinese: "It is a custom with the priests who teach this religion, when a man is about to die, to take a handful of cotton, having concealed within it a sharp needle, and then, while rubbing the individual's eyes with the cotton, to introduce the needle into the eye and puncture the pupil with it; the humors of the pupil saturate the cotton and are afterward used as a medicine." This foolish idea has its origin in the extreme unction administered by Catholic priests to the dying. See, moreover, the *Lettres Édifiantes*, Tome IV., p. 44.

[2] *Chinese Repository*, Vol. XIV., p. 195.

This rescript granted toleration to the Christians already in the country, known only by the term *Tien Chu kiao*, or 'Religion of the Lord of Heaven,' and referring only to those persons who profess Catholicism. Subsequently the French minister was asked to state whether, in making this request of the Chinese officers, he intended to include Christians of all sects, as there had been some doubts on that point. He therefore brought the subject again before Kíying, who issued an explanatory notice, without making a second appeal to his sovereign. It is not necessary to quote the entire reply, which granted as complete toleration to all Christian sects as its writer was able to do from his knowledge of their differences. The term *Yésu kiao*, since adopted for Protestants, was not then current. After quoting the purport of M. de Lagrené's communication, Kíying thus sums up his conclusions:

> Now I find that, in the first place, when the regulations for free trade were agreed upon, there was an article allowing the erection of churches at the five ports. This same privilege was to extend to all nations; there were to be no distinctions. Subsequently the commissioner Lagrené requested that the Chinese who, acting well, practised this religion, should equally be held blameless. Accordingly, I made a representation of the case to the throne, by memorial, and received the imperial consent thereto. After this, however, local magistrates having made improper seizures, taking and destroying crosses, pictures, and images, further deliberations were held, and it was agreed that these [crosses, etc.] might be reverenced. Originally I did not know that there were, among the nations, these differences in their religious practices. Now with regard to the religion of the Lord of Heaven—no matter whether the crosses, pictures, and images be reverenced or be not reverenced—all who, acting well, practise it, ought to be held blameless. All the great western nations being placed on an equal footing, only let them by acting well practise their religion, and China will in no way prohibit or impede their so doing. Whether their customs be alike or unlike, certainly it is right that there should be no distinction and no obstruction.—December 22, 1845.

The sentence in this document which speaks of local magistrates making improper seizures probably refers to something which had occurred in the country. At Shanghai the intendant of circuit issued a proclamation in November, 1845, based upon the Emperor's rescript, in which he defines the *Tien Chu kiao* "to consist in periodically assembling for unitedly worshipping the Lord of Heaven, in respecting and venerating the cross, with pictures and images, as well as in reading aloud the works of the said religion; these are customs of the said religion in question, and practices not in accordance with these cannot be considered as the religion of the Lord of Heaven." The various associations and sects found throughout China are all included under the vague name of *kiao*, or 'doctrine;' they are an annoyance to the government and well disposed people, and are referred to and excepted against in this proclamation. In a decree received by Kíying at Canton, February 20, 1846, relating to the restoration of the houses belonging to Romanists, the views of the Chinese government respecting the foreign missionaries were further made known.

On a former occasion Kíying and others laid before Us a memorial, requesting immunity from punishment for those who doing well profess the religion of Heaven's Lord; and that those who erect churches, assemble together for worship, venerate the cross and pictures and images, read and explain sacred books, be not prohibited from so doing. This was granted. The religion of the Lord of Heaven, instructing and guiding men in well-doing, differs widely from the heterodox and illicit sects; and the toleration thereof has already been allowed. That which has been requested on a subsequent occasion, it is right in like manner to grant.

Let all the ancient houses throughout the provinces, which were built in the reign of Kanghí, and have been preserved to the present time, and which, on personal examination by proper authorities, are clearly found to be their *bona fide* possessions, be restored to the professors of this religion in their respective places, excepting only those churches which have been converted into temples and dwelling-houses for the people.

If, after the promulgation of this decree throughout the provinces, the local officers irregularly prosecute and seize any of the professors of the religion of the Lord of Heaven, who are not bandits, upon all such the just penalties of the law shall be meted out.

If any, under a profession of this religion, do evil, or congregate people from distant towns, seducing and binding them together; or if any other sect or bandits, borrowing the name of the religion of the Lord of Heaven, create disturbances, transgress the laws, or excite rebellion, they shall be punished according to their respective crimes, each being dealt with as the existing statutes of the Empire direct.

Also, in order to make apparent the proper distinctions, foreigners of every nation are, in accordance with existing regulations, prohibited from going into the country to propagate religion.

For these purposes this decree is given. Cause it to be made known. From the Emperor.[1]

[1] *Chinese Repository*, Vol. XV., p. 155, where the original is given.

The directors of Protestant missions did not think it right to violate the last paragraph in this rescript, and confined their efforts to the open ports, where their agents had much preliminary work to do. This went on quietly, and on the whole peaceably, as the inhabitants found that the missionaries were their friends. Chapels, schools, hospitals, printing offices, and dwellings were erected at all the ports, so that by the year 1858 about one hundred Protestants were carrying them on. The number of converts was few, and there was not much result to show in tabular lists. It was a time of seed-sowing.

In 1849 the adherents of Hung Siu-tsuen began to make trouble in the west of Kwangtung, and to be called the *Shangtí hwui;* and the Peking authorities were unable to distinguish them from Protestants, who had thus rendered the name for God in the version of the Bible used by these misguided men. Their rapid successes against the imperial troops soon roused the utmost energies of the government to suppress them and retake Nanking. In 1856 a more dangerous struggle was precipitated by the impolitic action of Yeh Ming-chin, the governor-general at Canton, in respect to the Arrow, a smuggling lorcha carrying the British flag, which ended in a declaration of war against China. When hostilities ceased in 1858 by signing treaties of peace at Tientsin with envoys of the four nations there assembled, it was deemed to be a favorable time to introduce some definite stipulations respecting the toleration of Christianity in China. The rescripts of the Emperor Taukwang in 1844 had never carried any real weight among rulers or people, nor had the Romanists ever been able to re-possess their old churches and other real estate taken from them. The largest part had long been occupied or destroyed.

Any opposition to such a proposal was not likely to be very persistent on the part of the Chinese plenipotentiaries in face of the force at the call of those who had just captured the forts at Taku and held the city of Tientsin under their guns. The four nations, Great Britain, France, the United States, and Russia, were, as representatives of Christendom, in the providence of God brought face to face with China, the representative of paganism. They came to demand an arrangement of commercial, diplomatic, civil, and ex-territorial rights, and the introduction of religious privileges did not enter into their plans. The war on the part of the two first-named powers had no reference to religion, and their two colleagues would doubtless have omitted the articles on toleration if the Chinese had held out on those alone. At this singular and most unexpected correlation of moral and physical forces among the nations of the world, involving the greater part of its inhabitants, the freedom of the rising church of Christ in China was quietly secured by the four following articles of toleration inserted in the treaties signed in June, 1858. They are here given in the order of their dates:

Russian. Art. VIII.—The Chinese government having recognized the fact that the Christian doctrine promotes the establishment of order and peace among men, promises not to persecute its Christian subjects for the exercise of the duties of their religion; they shall enjoy the protection of all those who profess other creeds tolerated in the Empire. The Chinese government, considering the Christian missionaries as worthy men who do not seek worldly advantages, will permit them to propagate Christianity among its subjects, and will not hinder them from moving about in the interior of the Empire. A certain number of missionaries setting out from the open ports, or cities, shall be provided with passports signed by Russian authorities.

American. Art. XXIX.—The principles of the Christian religion, as professed by the Protestant and Roman Catholic churches, are recognized as teaching men to do good, and to do to others as they would have others do to them. Hereafter, those who quietly profess and teach these doctrines shall not be harassed or persecuted on account of their faith. Any person, whether citizen of the United States or Chinese convert, who according to these tenets peaceably teaches and practises the principles of Christianity, shall in no case be interfered with or molested.

British. Art. VIII.—The Christian religion, as professed by Protestants or Roman Catholics, inculcates the practice of virtue, and teaches man to do as he would be done by. Persons teaching it or professing it, therefore, shall alike be entitled to the protection of the Chinese authorities; nor shall any such, peaceably pursuing their calling, and not offending against the laws, be persecuted or interfered with.

French. ART. XIII.—La religion Chrétienne, ayant pour objet essentiel, de porter les hommes à la vertu, les membres de toutes communions Chrétiennes jouiront d'une entière sécurité pour leurs personnes, leurs propriétés, et le libre exercice de leurs pratiques religieuses; et une protection efficace sera donnée aux missionnaires qui se rendront pacifiquement dans l'intérieur du pays, munis des passeports réguliers dont il est parlé dans l'Article VIII. Aucune entrave ne sera apportée par les autorités de l'Empire Chinois au droit qui est reconnu à tout individu en Chine d'embrasser, s'il le veut, le Christianisme et d'en suivre les pratiques, sans être passible d'aucune peine infligée pour ce fait. Tout ce qui a été précédemment écrit, proclamé, ou publié en Chine par ordre du gouvernement contre le culte Chrétien, est complètement abrogé, et reste sans valeur dans toutes les provinces de l'Empire.

An article similar to these in its general import has been inserted in nearly all the treaties subsequently signed with the Chinese. They contain as much freedom of faith and practice by converts as could be desired by any reasonable man; but many missionaries were disappointed that their provisions were violated or disregarded by native officials. These sanguine persons often forgot that forbearance and time were both needed to bring the people and their rulers up to an appreciation of the new liberties and obligations contained in the treaties, and that their ignorance would be best and thoroughly removed by the living evidences of the purity and power of Christianity among its converts. These have already begun to show their faith by their works.

The only additional action of the Chinese government in this direction that needs to be noticed is Article VI., agreed upon with the French envoy and contained in the convention signed at Peking in October, 1860, in relation to the restoration of property once owned by the Romanists. The translation is as follows:

ART. VI.—It shall be promulgated throughout the length

and breadth of the land, in the terms of the imperial edict of February 20, 1846, that it is permitted to all people in all parts of China to propagate and practise the teachings of the Lord of Heaven, to meet together for preaching the doctrines, to build churches and to worship; further, all such as indiscriminately arrest [Christians] shall be duly punished, and such churches, schools, cemeteries, lands, and buildings as were owned on former occasions by persecuted Christians shall be paid for, and the money handed to the French representative at Peking for transmission to the Christians in the locality concerned. *It is in addition permitted to French missionaries to rent and purchase land in all the provinces, and to erect buildings thereon at pleasure.*[1]

In carrying out the details of this article, so much injustice and violence were exhibited by native Romanists, supported by the missionaries in claiming lands alleged to have belonged to them as far back as the days of Ricci and in the Ming dynasty, and forcing their owners and occupants to yield them without any or sufficient compensation, that riots and hatreds arose in many parts of China. Temples, houses, and shops which had been in the legal possession of natives for one or two centuries were claimed under this stipulation, and they forcibly resisted the surrender. The discontent became so great that the French minister at last issued a notice, about 1872, that no more claims of this kind would be received from the missionaries, and further complaints ceased. The imbroglio was heightened by the murder of two or three missionaries in Kweichau and Sz'chuen during the previous years, and the escape of the guilty parties into other provinces.

The feelings of all the Romish missionaries at the removal of the many disabilities under which they had long lived and bravely suffered were expressed by the Bishop of Shantung in

---

[1] This sentence in italics is not contained in the French text of the convention; but as that language is made, in Art. III of the Treaty of Tientsin, the *only* authoritative text, the surreptitious insertion of this important stipulation in the Chinese text makes it void. The procedure was unworthy of a great nation like France, whose army environed Peking when the convention was signed.

an encyclical letter to his people, in which he exhorts them to "maintain and diligently learn the holy religion. . . . Let them also pray that the holy religion may be greatly promoted, remembering that the kind consideration of the Emperor toward our holy religion springs entirely from the favor of the Lord of Heaven. After the reception of this order, let thanks be offered up to God for his mercies in the churches, for three Lord's days in succession. While the faithful rejoice in this extraordinary favor, let Ave Marias be recited to display grateful feelings."

The subject of the thorough revision of the Chinese Bible had long occupied the thoughts of those best acquainted with the need of such a work; and when the English missionaries met at Hongkong in 1843, a general conference of all Protestant missionaries was called to take measures for the preparation of so desirable a work. The version of Morrison and Milne was acknowledged by themselves to be imperfect, and the former had begun some corrections in it before his death. Messrs. Medhurst, Gutzlaff, Bridgman, and J. R. Morrison had united their labors in revising the New Testament, and published it in 1836.

The greatest harmony existed at this meeting, and the books of the New Testament were distributed among the missionaries at the several stations without regard to denomination. Some discussion arose as to the best word for *baptism*, for all agreed that it could not well be transliterated. The question was referred to a committee, which, finding itself unable to agree upon a term, recommended that in the proposed version this word should be left for each party to adopt which it liked. The term *sí lí*, which had been in use to denote this rite since the days of Ricci, by Romanists of all opinions, had been taken by Morrison and Medhurst, and by those associated with them. Marshman preferred another word, *tsan*, which was so unusual that it would almost always require explanation; and in fact could only be fully explained by the ceremony itself. Some of the American Baptist missionaries have taken Marshman's term, and others have proposed a third one, *yuh*. Their joint action with their brethren in regard to a common version was afterward repudiated by the societies in the United States, which directed them to prepare separate translations.

The question of the proper word for God in Chinese was also referred to a committee at this meeting in Hongkong, which reported its inability to agree; and this point, like the word for baptism, was therefore left to the decisions of the respective missions, after the version itself was finished. The delegates on the projected translation were chosen by the body of missionaries at each station, and met at Shanghai in June, 1847. They consisted of Rev. Messrs. Medhurst, J. Stronach, and Milne from the London Missionary Society, and Rev. Messrs. Bridgman, Boone, Shuck, Lowrie, and Culbertson from American societies; of the last five, Culbertson took Lowrie's place after his death, and Bp. Boone was never able to take an active share in the work. The New Testament was finished July 25, 1850, and was published soon after with different terms for God and Spirit.

The Old Testament was translated by the three first named in 1853; while another, more adapted to common readers, was completed in 1862 by Messrs. Bridgman and Culbertson. Gutzlaff also issued two or three revisions by himself. In 1865 a committee was formed in Peking for the purpose of making a version of the SS. in the Mandarin dialect, especially that prevalent in the northern provinces. It was done by Rev. Messrs. Blodget, Edkins, Burdon, and Schereschewsky; the New Testament was completed by them jointly in 1872, and the Old Testament in 1874 by the last named alone. It made the sixth complete translation of the Bible into Chinese during this century. Other translations have been made into the five southern patois of several books of the Bible—and at Ningpo and Amoy they are issued in the Romanized letters, and not in the Chinese character. These last, of course, are unintelligible to all natives not taught in mission schools.

The influence and labors of female missionaries in China is, from the constitution of society in that country, likely to be the only, or principal means of reaching their sex for a long time to come, and it is desirable, therefore, that they should engage in the work by learning the language and making the acquaintance of the families around them. No nation can be elevated, or Christian institutions placed upon a permanent basis, until females are taught their rightful place as the companions of men, and can teach their children the duties they owe to their God, themselves, and their country. Female schools are the necessary complement of boys', and a heathen wife soon carries a man back to idolatry if he is only intellectually convinced of the truths of Christianity. The comparatively high estimation the Chinese place upon female education is an encouragement to multiply girls' schools. The formation of mission boards in western lands, conducted entirely by women, has made these schools and medical work among women in China both practical and necessary. No large mission is now regarded as complete without one or more women to carry on such parts of the work as belong to them; and this is true of the Romish missions as well as Protestants.

The advance in the work of evangelization since the opening of the Empire in 1842 by the Treaty of Nanking has been in the highest degree encouraging. It was soon ascertained that the hatred and contempt of foreigners which were supposed to dwell in the minds of all Chinese, needed only to be met with kindness and patient teachings to give place to respect and confidence. The sufferings from the war with England, and the evils resulting from the smuggling and use of opium among the people, had embittered the minds of dwellers along the coast; but as most of this was local, the enlargement of mission work did much to remove the ignorance which nursed the dislike. The free relief of disease and pain in the hospitals aided greatly to improve intercourse, so that at this day the natives in and around the open ports have become entirely changed in their feelings.

This outline of Protestant mission work in China may be closed by a notice of the conference held at Shanghai in May, 1877, at which one hundred and twenty-six men and women, connected with twenty different bodies, assembled to discuss their common work in its various departments. The report of their proceedings gives fuller statistics of the work then going on than is to be found elsewhere, and the twenty-seven papers read and discussed in the three-days' sessions contain the ripened views of competent thinkers upon the most serious questions connected with the welfare of China. The following table has been taken from this report, and exhibits a remarkable development in education and preaching, considering that most of the stations have been opened since 1860.

STATISTICS OF PROTESTANT MISSIONS TO CHINA FOR THE YEAR 1877.

Branches of Mission Work.	American Missions.	British Missions.	Continental Missions.	Total.
Stations where missionaries reside	41	43	8	92
Out-stations	215	290	27	532
Organized churches	150	156	12	318
(*a*) Wholly self-supporting	11	7	....	18
(*b*) Partially self-supporting	115	149	....	264
Communicants, males	3,117	4,504	687	8,308
Communicants, females	2,183	2,440	584	5,207
Pupils in 31 boys' boarding-schools	347	154	146	647
" 177 boys' day-schools	1,255	1,470	265	2,991
" 39 girls' boarding-schools	464	206	124	794
" 82 girls' day-schools	957	335	15	1,307
" 21 theological schools	94	120	22	236
" 115 Sunday-schools	2,110	495	....	2,605
Pastors and preachers ordained	42	28	3	73
Assistant preachers	212	273	34	519
Colportors	28	46	3	77
Bible women	62	28	2	92
Church buildings for worship	113	118	15	246
Chapels and preaching places	183	249	25	457
In-patients, in 18 hospitals, 1876	1,390	3,905	....	5,295
Out-patients, in 18 hospitals, 1876	47,635	41,170	....	88,805
Patients treated in 24 dispensaries, 1876	25,107	16,174	....	41,281
Medical students	19	13	1	33
Contributions of native Christians, 1876	$4,482	$5,089	....	$9,571

The total number of men who have joined the Protestant missions to the Chinese up to 1876, as nearly as can be ascertained, has been 484. Of these 41 were laymen, chiefly physicians, and no women or natives are included. Twelve American societies had sent out 212 ordained missionaries, and the same number of British societies had sent 196; all the agents of the 8 or 10 continental societies amounted to 35. The number in 1847 was 112 of all nations; in 1858, this figure had increased to 214; and a table made out in 1877 by the Shanghai Conference gives 473 as the total number of persons then engaged in active missionary work in China, including 15 not employed by any of the 25 societies enumerated. Of these 210 belonged to 10 American, 242 to 13 British, and 26 to 2 German societies; 172 of the whole number being wives of missionaries, and 63 unmarried females.

No one acquainted with the practical evangelical work in China needs to be told that these statistics give no idea of the character and attainments of the fourteen thousand converts which have joined native churches, or the extent and thoroughness of the education given the five thousand seven hundred children counted in. Those who look for more than the merest beginnings of faith and culture in the minds of natives just brought out of the ignorance, sottishness, and impurity of heathenism into the brightness of Christianity, or those who harshly criticise these results of mission work, will do well to examine for themselves more fully the limitations and nature of all its branches.

No mention is made in these items of the amount of printing done at mission presses, for those particulars are scattered over hundreds of reports issued during the last score or two years. The presses formerly conducted by Williams, Wylie, and Cole at Canton, Shanghai, and Hongkong during an aggregate of nearly forty years, have been superseded by more and larger establishments; moreover, the facilities for transporting books render their issues more available at the remotest parts of the country. The manufacture of Chinese and Japanese types by the Presbyterian Mission press and foundry furnishes native workmen with the means of printing newspapers and books, which otherwise could never have been done (so as to become self-supporting) by means of blocks. At this establishment over thirty millions of pages are annually sent forth, and this amount is more than doubled by all the other mission presses. The effects of this literature upon the native mind, which these agencies are scattering wider every year, will be apparent in the near future.

The worth and labors of many men comprised in this number of missionaries have long been known to the Christian public. Milne and Collie ardently longed and labored diligently for the coming and extension of the kingdom of Christ in China, though not allowed to live in its borders. Few men in the missionary corps have exceeded Edwin Stevens in sound judgment and steady pursuit of a well-formed purpose, which in his case was to aid in perfecting the version of the Bible. He was employed nearly three years as seamen's chaplain at Whampoa before entering the service among the Chinese, and his labors in that department were highly acceptable to those who frequented the port.

The warm-hearted, humble piety and singleness of purpose of Samuel Dyer were also well known to every one engaged with him. His long and assiduous labors to complete a fount of Chinese metallic type, amid many obstacles and hindrances, were prompted by the hope that, when once finished, books could be printed with more elegance, cheapness, and rapidity than in any other way. He lived to see it brought into partial use, and to satisfy himself concerning the feasibility of this plan. If the impulses of private friendship and the esteem generally entertained for David Abeel should prompt a notice of his character and labors, it would soon extend to many pages; they have been well worthy the fuller notice which is given in his memoir. Among other biographies may be mentioned those of Walter M. Lowrie, William C. Burns, D. Sandeman, J. Henderson, Samuel Dyer, E. C. Bridgman, and W. Aitcheson, which will furnish information upon the details of their labors. Female missionaries have also done much, and will do more, in this work, which requires minds and labors in large variety. Mrs. Mary Morrison, Mrs. Sarah Boone, Mrs. Theodosia Dean, Mrs. Lucy Ball, Mrs. Henrietta Shuck, Mrs. Doty, and Mrs. Pohlman, all died in China before 1846—the first of scores of honorable women who have since thus ended their lives.

Before closing this brief sketch of Christian missions among the Chinese, it may be well to mention some of the peculiar facilities and difficulties which attend the work. The business of transforming heathen society and reconstructing it on Christian principles is a great and protracted undertaking, and is to be commenced in all communities by working on individuals. The opposition of the unregenerate heart can be overcome only by the transforming influences of the Spirit, but the intellect must be enlightened, and the moral sense instructed by a system of means, before the truths of the Bible can be intelligently received or rejected. This opposition is not peculiar to China, but it will probably assume a more polemic and argumentative cast there than in some other countries. The proud literati are not disposed to abase Confucius below the Saviour, but rather inclined to despise the reiteration of his name and atonement as a seesaw about "one Jesus who was dead, whom we affirm to be alive." Medhurst notices a tract written against him by a Chinese, in which it is argued that "it was monstrous in barbarians to attempt to improve the inhabitants of the Celestial Empire when they were so miserably deficient themselves. Thus, introducing among the Chinese a poisonous drug, for their own benefit to the injury of others, they were deficient in benevolence; sending their fleets and armies to rob other nations of their possessions, they could make no pretentions to rectitude; allowing men and women to mix in society and walk arm in arm through the streets, they showed that they had not the least sense of propriety; and in rejecting the doctrines of the ancient kings they were far from displaying wisdom; indeed, truth was the only good quality to which they could lay the least claim. Deficient, therefore, in four out of the five cardinal virtues, how could they expect to renovate others? Then, while foreigners lavished money in circulating books for the renovation of the age, they made no scruple of trampling printed paper under foot, by which they showed their disrespect for the inventors of letters. Further, these would-be exhorters of the world were themselves deficient in filial piety, forgetting their parents as soon as dead, putting them off with deal coffins only an inch thick, and never so much as once sacrificing to their manes, or burning the smallest trifle of gilt paper for their support in the future world. Lastly, they allowed the rich and noble to enter office without passing through any literary examinations, and did not throw open the road to advancement to the poorest and meanest in the land. From all these, it appeared that foreigners were inferior to Chinese, and therefore most unfit to instruct them."

To these arguments, which commend themselves to a Chinese with a force that can hardly be understood by a foreigner, they often add the intemperate, immoral lives and reckless cupidity of professed Christians who visit their shores, and ask what good it will do them to change their long-tried precepts for the new-fangled teachings of the Bible? The pride of learning is a great obstacle to the reception of the humiliating truths of the Gospel everywhere, but perhaps especially in China, where letters are so highly honored and patronized. The language is another difficulty in the way of the diffusion of the Gospel, both on the part of the native and the missionary. The mode of education among the Chinese is admirably fitted for the ends they propose, viz., of forming the mind to implicit belief and reverence for the precepts of Confucius, and obedience to the government which makes those precepts the outlines of its actions, but it rather weakens the intellect for independent thought on other subjects. The language itself, as we have had opportunity to observe, is an unwieldy vehicle for imparting new truths, either by writing or speaking, chiefly because of the additional burden every new character or term imposes upon the memory. The immense number, who read and speak this language, reconciles one, however, to extra labor and patience to become familiar with its forms of speech, and ascertain the best modes of conveying truth.

When the five ports were opened in 1845 to practical missionary work among the two or three millions of people living in and around them, it was soon found that they were tolerably well-disposed to foreigners when they understood what was said to them. Fifteen years of constant labor changed the ignorance and suspicion with which they regarded the first missionaries, into respectful regard if not acceptance of their message. At the end of this period, the capture of Peking and the ratification of the treaties of Tientsin completed the opening of China to such labors as far as diplomatic agency could go. Congregations are now collected, and truth explained to them with a good degree of acceptance every Sabbath, and all that is wanted to get more congregations is more preachers; long before missionary labors are accomplished in all the ports, the whole land will afford every choice of climate and position. Facilities for learning the language are constantly increasing. Dictionaries, vocabularies, phrase books, grammars, and chrestomathies in all the dialects will soon be prepared; and the list now is not small. They have all, with few exceptions, been made and printed by Protestant missionaries.

Churches have increased since the first one was formed in Canton in 1835, and some of them are served by native evangelists, two of whom, Liang A-fah and Tsin Shen, of the London Mission, deserve mention as among the first of their countrymen who became educated, earnest preachers of the gospel. The future is full of promise, and the efforts of the church with regard to China will not cease until every son and daughter of the race of Han has been taught the truths of the Bible, and has had them fairly propounded for reception or rejection. They will progress until all the cities, towns, villages, and hamlets of that vast Empire have the teacher and professor of religion living in them; until their children are educated, their civil liberties understood, and political rights guaranteed; their poor cared for, their literature purified, their condition bettered in this world by the full revelation of another made known to them. The work of missions will go on until the government is modified, and religious and civil liberty granted to all, and China takes her rank among the Christian nations of the earth, reciprocating all the courtesies due from people professing the same faith.

CHAPTER XX.

COMMERCE OF THE CHINESE.

It is probable that the applications made in remote times to the rulers of China for liberty to trade with their subjects, partook in their opinion very much of the nature of an acknowledgment of their power; the presents accompanying the request were termed *kung*, and regarded as tribute, while the traders themselves also looked upon the intercourse in somewhat the same light. The chapter of the *Book of Records*, called the "Tribute of Yu," is one of the most ancient documents in existence relating to the products of a country, and indicates a trade in them of no small extent. Silk, lacquer, furs, grass-cloth, salt, gems, gold, silver, and other metals, ivory and manufactured goods are enumerated; they are mostly identified with articles still produced, as Legge has shown in his translation. The records of the origin and early course of this trade are lost to a great extent, but the Chinese annals furnish proof of similar traffic for two thousand years after the days of Yu. It had the effect of extending the influence of Chinese institutions among less civilized neighbors, and of making foreign commerce a means of benefit to all parties. The restrictions and charges upon all trade were of small amount at this early period; as it extended, the cupidity of local officers led them to burden it with numerous illegal fees, which gradually reduced its value, and finally, in some instances, drove it away altogether.

The materials in Chinese literature for investigating this subject after the period of the Han dynasty are abundant, and they will reward the careful analysis of foreign scholars. Marco Polo, the two Arab travellers in A.D. 850 and 878, and Ibn Batuta, in 1330, have each contributed their narratives, hinting therein more than they could carefully investigate of the wide range and value of the Chinese foreign commerce. During the Ming dynasty this trade fell off, owing to the impoverishment of the land by the Mongols; but when (about 1600) the stimulus of European ships along the coast began to develop and reward native manufactures, foreign nations and merchants appreciated the fact that it was more profitable to trade with China than attack her.

The principal items of export and import have not materially changed during the last century; the splendid fabrics of Chinese looms, their tea, lacquered ware, and products of their kilns, being still bartered for the cottons, metals, furs, and woollens of the west. Such articles as possess peculiar interest, and have not been already described, together with a few notices respecting the present extent and mode of conducting the trade, will suffice to explain its general features.[1] The history of the culture and trade in tea by Samuel Ball of Canton in 1835, may yet be considered as an authority upon the subject. The growth in the use of tea is instructive, too, rising from an importation of about eighty pounds into England in 1670, till it had so well vindicated its virtues and enlarged its use among that people, that in 1880 one hundred and eighty million pounds were required to supply them; and more than that was exported elsewhere from China.

The first item which attracts attention in the table of trade with China is opium, whose growth and momentous consequences require a detailed account. The use of opium as a medicine has not long been known to Chinese doctors, though, from the way the poppy is mentioned in the *Herbal*, there is reason to suppose it to be indigenous. The drug is called *apien*, in imitation of the word *opium*, while the plant is called *afuyung*, a transliteration of the Arabic name *Afyun*, from which country it was brought about the ninth century. It has many

[1] Ample materials are now provided in the full reports of the Custom's service and the Exhibition Catalogues of Vienna, Paris, Philadelphia, etc.; the reports of Rondot, Hedde, and other members of the French Legation in 1844 are still valuable.

names, as *great smoke*, *black commodity*, *black earth*, *foreign medicine;* the last is the term used in the tariff. The compiler of the *Herbal*, who wrote two centuries ago, speaks of the plant and its inspissated juice, saying that both were formerly but little known; he then concisely describes the mode of collecting it, which leads to the inference that it was then used in medicine. None was imported coastwise for scores of years after that date, but the poppy is now grown in every province and in Manchuria, and no real restraint is anywhere put on its cultivation. The juice is collected and prepared by the people for their own consumption in much the same manner as in India; as long ago as 1830 we find one official observing in respect to the cultivation, which was extending, that it was "not only bringing injury on the good, but greatly retarding the work of the husbandmen."

The mode of raising the poppy in the Patna district in India is thus described: The ryot or cultivator having selected a piece of ground, always preferring (*cæteris paribus*) that which is nearest his house, fences it in. He then, by repeated ploughings and manuring, makes it rich and fine, and removes all the weeds and grass. Next, he divides the field into two or more beds by small dikes of mould, running lengthwise and crosswise according to the slope and nature of the ground, and again into smaller squares by other dikes leading from the principal ones. A tank is dug about ten feet deep at one end of the field, from which by a leathern bucket, water is raised into one of the principal dikes and carried to every part as required; this irrigation is necessary because the cultivation is carried on in the dry weather. The seed is sown in November, and the juice collected in February and March, during a period, usually, of about six weeks; weeding and watering commence as soon as the plants spring up, and are continued till the poppies come to maturity. Cuts are then made in the capsule with a *nusktur* or notched iron instrument made of three or four sharp lancet-like plates; this is done at sunrise, and the exudation is scraped off next morning by a scoop or *sittuha*, and deposited in the dish hanging at the ryot's side. He takes it home and after draining it dry in a large shallow dish, turns it over and over in the air for a month till the mass is equally dried, and it is fit to carry to the godown. Here it is thrown into a great tank, and kneaded to a uniform consistence; when ready it is rolled into balls according to the size of a brass bowl; these balls are covered with a coating of poppy petals, and stored in a drying-house till ready for packing. The quality of the article depends very much upon the care taken in the drying and covering with *liwa* or opium paste when the ball is prepared.

The cultivator must deliver a certain quantity at the stipulated price to the collector, the amount being fixed by a survey of the field when in bloom; he receives about one dollar and sixty-five cents for a seer (one pound thirteen ounces) of the poppy juice, which must be of a certain consistence. The ryot has, in most cases, already received the advance money, and if he sell this crude opium to any other than the collector, or if he fail to deliver the estimated quantity, and there is reason for supposing he has embezzled it, he is liable to punishment. In all parts of India, the cultivation of the poppy, the preparation of the drug, and the traffic in it until it is sold at auction for exportation, are under a strict monopoly. Should an individual undertake the cultivation without having entered into engagements with the government to deliver the produce at the fixed rate, his property would be immediately attached, and he compelled either to destroy the poppies, or give security for the faithful delivery of the product. The cultivation of the plant is compulsory, for if the ryot refuse the advance for the year's crop, the simple plan of throwing the rupees into his house is adopted; should he attempt to abscond, the agents seize him, tie the advance up in his clothes, and push him into his house. There being then no remedy, he applies himself as he may to the fulfilment of his contract. The chief opium district is on the Ganges valley, occupying the best land in Benares and Behar, to the extent of about a thousand square miles. The northern and central parts of India are now covered with poppies, while other plants used for food or clothing have nearly been driven out. In Turkey, Persia, India, and China many myriads of acres and millions of people are employed in the cultivation of poppies.[1] The growth has extended so much in Persia that opium has lately come from thence to China.

The preparation of the opium is superintended by official examiners, and is a business of some difficulty, from the many substances put into the juice to adulterate or increase its weight. Wetting it so that the mass shall be more fluid than it naturally is, mixing sand, soft clayey mud, sugar, coarse molasses, cow-dung, pounded poppy-seeds, and the juice of stramony, quinces, and other plants, are all resorted to, though with the almost certain result of detection and loss. When the juice has been dried properly, to about seventy per cent. spissitude, it appears coppery brown in the mass, and when spread thin on a white plate, shows considerable translucency, with a gallstone yellow color and a slightly granular texture. When cut with a knife it exhibits sharp edges without drawing out into threads; and is tremulous like strawberry-jam, to which it has been aptly compared. It has considerable adhesiveness, a handful of it not dropping from the inverted hand for some seconds.

All the opium grown is brought to Calcutta and stored in government warehouses, until it is exposed for sale at auction, at an upset price, graduated according to the market price in China. It is supposed not to cost much more than seven hundred rupees a chest, and is sold at as high an advance as it will bear. Great care is taken to suit the taste of the Chinese; on one occasion, the East India Company refunded part of the price on a lot which had been differently prepared, to try whether that people would prefer it. There are several sorts of opium: Turkey and Persian, which sell cheapest, and reach China from Aden; Patna and Benares which are sold at Calcutta; and Malwa, which is cultivated out of British jurisdiction. In order to equalize its competition, an export duty was until 1842 put on each chest of one hundred and twenty-five rupees, which has been increased to six hundred rupees. The drug is rolled in balls, and then packed in strong boxes, weighing from one hundred and sixteen pounds for

[1] *Chinese Repository*, Vol V., p. 472.

Patna, to one hundred and thirty-four pounds or one hundred and forty pounds for Malwa. Malwa opium is grown and prepared by natives, and is often extensively adulterated; between four hundred and five hundred cakes are in a chest, and the cultivator there receives double the wages of the ryot in Bengal.

Opium chests are made of mango wood in Patna and Benares and consist of two parts, in each of which there are twenty partitions; the balls are carefully rolled in dry poppy leaves. The chest is covered with hides or gunny bags, and the seams closed so as to render it as impervious to the air as possible. After the drug is sold at auction, there is no further tax on it. The revenue from this monopoly has become so great and important, that its continuance is described by a leading editor in India as a matter of life and death to the Government. In 1840, the income was somewhat over two millions sterling; it has since steadily increased, till in 1872 it amounted to £7,657,000; the average annual sum between the years 1869 to 1876 was £6,524,000, and it has been over five millions ever since the peace of Tientsin. The purity and flavor of the drug has been carefully maintained by competent scientists, and by this date the prejudice in its favor has become so strong among the Chinese, as to induce them to pay an enormous premium for the Indian article over any native product.

The use of opium among the Chinese two centuries ago must have been very little, or the writings of Romish missionaries, from 1580 down to the beginning of the nineteenth century, would certainly have contained some account of it. It was not till the year 1767 that the importation reached a thousand chests, and continued at that rate for some years, most of the trade being in the hands of the Portuguese. The East India Company made a small adventure in 1773; and seven years after, a dépôt of two small vessels was established by the English in Lark's Bay, south of Macao; the price was then about $550 a chest. In 1781 the company freighted a vessel to Canton, but were obliged to sell the lot of 1,600 chests at $200 a chest, to Sinqua, one of the hong-merchants, who, not being able to dispose of it to advantage, reshipped it to the Archipelago. The price in

1791 was about $370 a chest, and was imported under the head of medicine at a duty of about seven dollars a hundredweight, including charges. The authorities at Canton began to complain of the two ships in Lark's Bay in 1793, and their owners being much annoyed by the pirates and revenue boats, and inconvenienced by the distance from Canton, loaded the opium on board a single vessel, and brought her to Whampoa, where she lay unmolested for more than a year. She was then loaded and sent out of the river, and the drug introduced in another ship; this practice continued until 1820, when the governor-general and collector of customs issued an edict, forbidding any vessel to enter the port in which opium was stored, and making the pilots and hong-merchants responsible for its being on board. The Portuguese were also forbidden to introduce it into Macao, and every officer in the Chinese custom-house there was likewise made responsible for preventing it, under the heaviest penalties. "Be careful," says his excellency in conclusion, "and do not view this document as mere matter of form, and so tread within the net of the law, for you will find your escape as impracticable as it is for a man to bite his own navel."

The importation had been prohibited by the Emperor Kiaking in 1800, under heavy penalties, on account of its use wasting the time and destroying the property of the people of the Inner Land, and exchanging their silver and commodities for the "vile dirt" of foreign countries. The supercargoes of the Company therefore recommended the Directors to prohibit its shipment to China from England and India, but this could not be done; and they contented themselves by forbidding their own ships bringing it to China. The hong-merchants were required to give bonds, in 1809, that no ship which discharged her cargo at Whampoa had opium on board; but they contrived to evade the restriction. The traffic was carried on at Whampoa and Macao by the connivance of local officers, some of whom watched the delivery of every chest and received a fee; while their superiors, remote from the scene of smuggling, pocketed an annual bribe for overlooking the violation of the imperial orders.

The system of bribery and condoning malpractices, so common

in China, is well illustrated by a case which occurred in connection with this business. In September, 1821, a Chinese inhabitant of Macao, who had been the medium of receiving from the Portuguese, and paying to the Chinese officers the several bribes annually given for the introduction of opium, was arrested by government for hiring banditti to assault one of his personal opponents. Having got the man in their power, quicksilver was poured into his ears, to injure his head without killing him; they also forced him to drink a horrible potion of scalding tea mixed with the short hairs shaved from his head. The vile wretch who originated this cruel idea and paid the perpetrators of it, was a pettifogging notary, who brought gain to the officials by intimidating the people, until he was the pest and terror of the neighborhood. An official enemy at last laid his character and doings before the governor, who had him seized and thrown into prison, when he turned his wrath on his former employers, and confessed that he held the place of bribe-collector, and that all the authorities received so much per chest, even up to the admiral of the station. The governor, though doubtless aware of these practices, was now obliged to notice them; but instead of punishing those who were directly guilty, he accused the senior hong-merchant, a rich man, nicknamed the "timid young lady," and charged him with neglecting his suretyship in not pointing out every foreign ship which contained opium. It was in vain for him to plead that he had never dealt in opium, nor had any connection with those who did deal in it; nor could he search the ships to ascertain what was in them, or control the authorities who encouraged and protected the smuggling of opium: notwithstanding all his pleas, the governor was determined to hold him responsible. He was accordingly disgraced, and a paper, combining admonition, with exhortation and entreaty, was addressed by his excellency to the foreigners, Portuguese, English, and Americans. The gods, he said, would conduct the fair dealers in safety over the ocean, but over the contraband smugglers of a pernicious poison, the terrors of the royal law on earth, and the wrath of the infernal gods in hades were suspended. The Americans brought opium, he observed, "because they had no king to rule them." The opium ships thus being driven from Whampoa, and the Portuguese unwilling or afraid to admit it into Macao unless at a high duty, the merchants established a floating dépôt of receiving-ships at Lintin, an island between Macao and the Bogue. In summer, the ships moved to Kumsing moon, Kapshui moon, Hongkong, and other anchorages off the river, to be more secure against the tyfoons; remaining near Lintin during the north-east monsoon, until 1839.[1]

The mode of introducing opium into the country, when the prohibitions against its use were upheld by the moral approval of the best portion of the native society, has hardly any interest now, except as a matter of history. It is a sad exhibition of power, habit, skill, and money all combining to weaken and overpower the feeble, desultory resistance of a pagan and ignorant people against the progress of what they knew was destroying them. The finality of such a struggle could hardly be doubted, and when the tariff of 1858 allowed opium to enter by the payment of a duty, the already enfeebled moral resistance seemed to die out with the extinction of the smuggling trade in opium, now raised to a licensed commerce. The rise and course of the trade up to that year can be learned from the volumes of the *Chinese Repository* and newspapers issued in China.

The utensils used in preparing the opium for smoking, consist chiefly of three hemispherical brass pans, two bamboo filters, two portable furnaces, earthen pots, ladles, straining-cloths, and sprinklers. The ball being cut in two, the interior is taken out, and the opium adhering to or contained in the leafy covering is previously simmered three several times, each time using a pint of spring water, and straining it into an earthen pot; some cold water is poured over the dregs after the third boiling, and from half a cake (weighing at first about twenty-eight pounds, and with which this process is supposed to be conducted), there will be about five pints of liquid. The interior of the cake is then boiled with this liquid for about an hour, until the whole is reduced to a paste, which is spread out with a spatula in two pans, and exposed to the fire for two or three minutes at

[1] *Chinese Repository*, Vol. V., pp. 546–553.

a time, till the water is driven off; during this operation it is often broken up and re-spread, and at the last drying cut across with a knife. It is all then spread out in one cake, and covered with six pints of water, being allowed to remain several hours or over night for digestion. When sufficiently soaked, a rag filter is placed on the edge of the pan, and the whole of the valuable part drips slowly through the rag into a basket lined with coarse bamboo paper, from which it falls into the other brass pan, about as much liquid going through as there was water poured over the cake. The dregs are again soaked and immediately filtered till found to be nearly tasteless; this weaker part usually makes about six pints of liquid.

The first six pints are then briskly boiled, being sprinkled with cold water to allay the heat so as not to boil over, and removing the scum by a feather into a separate vessel. After boiling twenty minutes, five pints of the weak liquid are poured in and boiled with it, until the whole is evaporated to about three pints, when it is strained through paper into another pan, and the remaining pint thrown into the pan just emptied, to wash away any portion that may remain in it, and also boiled a little while, when it is also strained into the three pints. The whole is then placed over a slow fire in the small furnace, and boiled down to a proper consistency for smoking; while it is evaporating a ring forms around the edge, and the pan is taken off the fire at intervals to prolong the process, the mass being the while rapidly stirred with sticks, and fanned until it becomes like thick treacle, when it is taken out and put into small pots for smoking. The boxes in which it is retailed are made of buffalo's horn, of such a size as easily to be carried about the person. The dregs containing the vegetable residuum, together with the scum and washings of the pans, are lastly strained and boiled with water, producing about six pints of thin, brownish liquid, which is evaporated to a proper consistence for selling to the poor. The process of seething the crude opium is exceedingly unpleasant to those unaccustomed to it, from the overpowering narcotic fumes which arise, and this odor marks every shop where it is prepared and every person who smokes it. The loss in weight by this mode of preparation is about one-half. The Malays prepare it in much the same manner. The custom in Penang is to reduce the dry cake made on the first evaporation to a powder, and when it is digested and again strained and evaporated, reducing it to a consistence resembling shoemaker's wax.

The opium pipe consists of a tube of heavy wood furnished at the head with a cup which serves to collect the residuum or ashes left after combustion; this cup is usually a small cavity in the end of the pipe, and serves to elevate the bowl to a level with the lamp. The bowl of the pipe is made of earthenware, of an ellipsoid shape, and sets down upon the hole, itself having a small rimmed orifice on the flat side. The opium-smoker always lies down, and the impossible picture given by Davis of a "Mandarin smoking an opium-pipe," dressed in his official robes and sitting up at a table, becomes still more singular if the author ever saw a smoker at his pipe. Lying along the couch, he holds the pipe, aptly called *yen tsiang*, *i.e.*, 'smoking-pistol,' so near the lamp that the bowl can be brought close up to the flame. A pellet of the size of a pea being taken on the end of a spoon-headed needle, is put upon the hole of the bowl and set on fire at the lamp, and inhaled at one whiff so that none of the smoke shall be lost. Old smokers will retain the breath a long time, filling the lungs and exhaling the fumes through the nose. The taste of the half-fluid extract is sweetish and oily, somewhat like rich cream, but the smell of the burning drug is rather sickening. When the pipe has burned out, the smoker lies listless for a moment while the fumes are dissipating, and then repeats the process until he has spent all his purchase, or taken his prescribed dose. When the smoking commences, the man becomes loquacious, and breaks out into boisterous, silly merriment, which gradually changes to a vacant paleness and shrinking of the features, as the quantity increases and the narcotic acts. A deep sleep supervenes from half an hour to three or four hours' duration, during which the pulse becomes slower, softer, and smaller than before the debauch. No refreshment is felt from this sleep, when the person has become a victim to the habit, but a universal sinking of the powers of the body and mind is experienced, and complete recklessness of all consequences, if only the craving for more can be appeased.

A novice is content with one or two whiffs, which produce vertigo, nausea, and headache, though practice enables him to gradually increase the quantity; "temperate smokers," warned by the sad example of the numerous victims around them, endeavor to keep within bounds, and walk as near the precipice as they can without falling over into hopeless ruin. In order to do this, they limit themselves to a certain quantity daily, and take it at, or soon after meals, so that the stomach may not be so much weakened. A "temperate smoker" (though this term is like that of a *temperate* robber, who only takes shillings from his employer's till, or a *temperate* blood-letter, who only takes a spoonful daily from his veins) can seldom exceed a mace weight, or about as much of prepared opium as will balance a pistareen or a franc piece; this quantity will fill twelve pipes. Two mace weight taken daily is considered an immoderate dose, which few can bear for any length of time; and those who are afraid of the effects of the drug upon themselves endeavor not to exceed a mace. Some persons, who have strong constitutions and stronger resolution, continue the use of the drug within these limits for many years without disastrous effects upon their health and spirits though most of even these moderate smokers are so much the slaves to the habit that they feel too wretched, nerveless, and imbecile to go on with their business without the stimulus.

The testimony regarding the evil effects of the use of this pernicious drug, which deserves better to be called an "article of destruction" than an "article of luxury," are so unanimous that few can be found to stand up strongly in its favor. Dr. Smith, a physician in charge of the hospital at Penang, says: "The baneful effects of this habit on the human constitution are particularly displayed by stupor, forgetfulness, general deterioration of all the mental faculties, emaciation, debility, sallow complexion, lividness of lips and eyelids, languor and lack-lustre of eye, and appetite either destroyed or depraved, sweetmeats or sugar being the articles that are most relished." These symptoms appear when the habit has weakened the physical powers, but the unhappy man soon begins to feel the power of the drug in a general languor and sinking, which disables him, mentally more than bodily, from carrying on his ordinary pursuits. A dose of opium does not produce the intoxication of ardent spirits, and so far as the peace of the community and his family are concerned, the smoker is less troublesome than the drunkard; the former never throws the chairs and tables about the room, or drives his wife out of doors in his furious rage; he never goes reeling through the streets or takes lodgings in the gutter; but contrariwise, he is quiet or pleasant, and fretful only when the effects of the pipe are gone. It is in the insupportable languor throughout the whole frame, the gnawing at the stomach, pulling at the shoulders, and failing of the spirits that the tremendous power of this vice lies, compelling the "victimized" slave "to seek it yet again." There has not yet been opportunity to make those minute investigations respecting the extent opium is used among the Chinese, what classes of people use it, their daily dose, the proportion of reprobate smokers, and many other points which have been narrowly examined into in regard to the use of alcohol; so that it is impossible to decide the question as to which of the two is the more dreadful habit. These statistics have, heretofore, been impossible to obtain in China, and it will be very difficult to obtain them, even when a person who may have the leisure and abilities shall undertake the task.

Various means have been tried by benevolent natives to dissuade their countrymen from using it, such as distributing tracts showing its ruinous effects, compounding medicines for the smoker to take to aid him in breaking off the habit, and denouncing the smoking-shops to government. A painter at Canton made a series of admonitory pictures, showing the several steps in the downward course of the opium-smoker, until beggary and death ended the scene; one of them, showing the young debauchee at his revels, is here introduced.

A Chinese scholar thus sums up the bad effects of opium, which, he says, is taken at first to raise the animal spirits and prevent lassitude: "It exhausts the animal spirits, impedes the regular performance of business, wastes the flesh and blood, dissipates every kind of property, renders the person ill-favored, promotes obscenity, discloses secrets, violates the laws, attacks the vitals, and destroys life." Under each of these heads he lucidly shows the mode of the process, or gives examples to uphold his assertions: "In comparison with arsenic, I pronounce it tenfold the greater poison; one swallows arsenic because he has lost his reputation, and is so involved that he cannot extricate himself. Thus driven to desperation, he takes

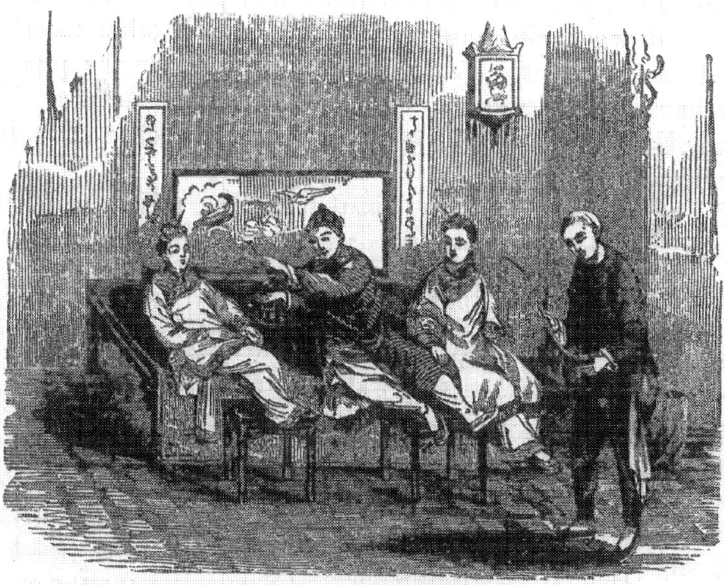

Manner of Smoking Opium.

the dose and is destroyed at once; but those who smoke the drug are injured in many ways. It may be compared to raising the wick of a lamp, which, while it increases the blaze, hastens the exhaustion of the oil and the extinction of the light. Hence, the youth who smoke will shorten their own days and cut off all hopes of posterity, leaving their parents and wives without any one on whom to depend. From the robust who smoke the flesh is gradually consumed and worn away, and the skin hangs like a bag. Their faces become cadaverous and black, and their bones naked as billets of wood. The habitual smokers doze for days over their pipes, without appetite; when the desire for opium comes on, they cannot resist its impulse. Mucus flows from their nostrils and tears from their eyes; their very bodies are rotten and putrid. From careless observers the sight of such objects is enough to excite loud peals of laughter. The poor smoker, who has pawned every article in his possession, still remains idle; and when the periodical thirst comes on, will even pawn his wives and sell his daughters. In the province of Nganhwui I once saw a man named Chin, who, being childless, purchased a concubine and got her with child; afterward, when his money was expended and other means all failed him, being unable to resist the desire for the pipe, he sold her in her pregnancy for several tens of dollars. This money being expended, he went and hung himself. Alas, how painful was his end!"[1]

The thirst and burning sensation in the throat which the wretched sufferer feels, only to be removed by a repetition of the dose, proves one of the strongest links in the chain which drags him to his ruin. At this stage of the habit his case is almost hopeless; if the pipe be delayed too long, vertigo, complete prostration, and discharge of water from the eyes ensue; if entirely withheld, coldness and aching pains are felt over the body, an obstinate diarrhœa supervenes, and death closes the scene. The disastrous effects of the drug are somewhat delayed or modified by the quantity of nourishing food the person can procure, and consequently it is among the poor who can least afford the pipe, and still less the injury done to their energies, that the destruction of life is the greatest. The evils suffered and crimes committed by the desperate victims of the opium pipe are dreadful and multiplied. Theft, arson, murder, and suicide are perpetrated in order to obtain it or escape its effects. Some try to break off the fatal habit by taking a tincture of the opium dirt in spirits, gradually diminishing its strength until it is left off entirely; others mix opium with tobacco and smoke the compound in a less and less proportion, until tobacco alone remains. The general belief is that the vice can be overcome without

---

[1] *Chinese Repository*, Vol. VII., p. 108.

fatal results, if the person firmly resolve to forsake it and keep away from sight and smell of the pipe, laboring as much as his strength will allow in the open air until he recovers his spirits and no longer feels a longing for it. Few, very few, however, emancipate themselves from the tyrannous habit which enslaves them; they are able to resist its insidious effects until the habit has become strong, and the resolution to break it off is generally delayed until their chains are forged and deliverance felt to be hopeless.

Swallowing opium is commonly resorted to as a means of suicide; the papers published in China constantly report cases where physicians have tried to save the patient by injections of atrophine before life is gone, and the number of these applications painfully show how lightly the Chinese esteem life. A comparison is sometimes drawn between the opium-smoker and drunkard, and the former averred to be less injured by the habit; but the balance is struck between two terrible evils, both of which end in the loss of health, property, mind, influence, and life. Opium imparts no benefit to the smoker, impairs his bodily vigor, beclouds his mind, and unfits him for his station in society; he is miserable without it, and at last dies by what he lives upon.

The import having been legalized in 1858, under the pressure of war, it was useless for the imperial government longer to prevent the cultivation of the poppy, and the growth has rapidly extended throughout the provinces. Since all the opium brought to China reaches it through Hongkong, and the consumption upon that island must be comparatively insignificant, the table on the following page, taken from the Chinese Customs Reports, will convey a very fair idea of the amount and value of the import during the past six years.

Although it is difficult to make a general statement regarding an import of such varying quantity and value, the average total may be safely enough put at between twelve and thirteen million pounds, the approximate value of which is something over sixty million dollars, per annum. The prices range from $540 to $580 per pecul for Benares, $740 for Malwa, $560 for Patna, $540 for Persian, and nearly $1,500 for the prepared drug. The imports of Persian and Turkish, though steadily increasing, amount as yet to hardly one-fiftieth of the total. But the merest guesses can be made at the production of native opium.

TOTAL IMPORT OF OPIUM AT HONGKONG.

Year.	Quantity.	Value.
	Peculs.	*Hk. Tls.*[1]
1876............	96,985	36,491,288
1877............	94,200	32,303,963
1878............	94,899	37,470,465
1879............	107,970	41,479,892
1880............	96,839	42,823,721
1881............	89,688	38,115,154

The British consul at Canton reported in 1877 "on good authority" that the out-turn came to 32,000 peculs, while in the Customs Special Report on Opium of 1881 the estimates of the several commissioners vary from 12,000 (Mr. McKean, of Canton) to 265,000 peculs (Mr. Drew, of Ningpo). In this report only seven out of the nineteen trade ports present any figures upon this head.[2]

This *résumé* of facts connected with the growth and condition of this trade are enough, probably, for the present purpose. "Opium is the only article of all her imports that China cannot

[1] The *Haikwan tael* is equivalent to $1.36½ in American gold. The *pecul* weighs 133⅓ pounds avoirdupois.

[2] Compare *Returns of Trade at the Treaty Ports* for 1881, and *Opium* (Special, Series II., No. 4), published by the Im. Mar. Customs at Shanghai. *Portfolio Chinensis*, by J. Lewis Shuck, Macao, 1840. Rev. A. S. Thelwall, *The Iniquities of the Opium Trade with China*, London, 1839. *L'Opium en Chine, Étude statistique et morale*, par le Dr. E. Martin, Paris, 1871. Alonzo Calkins, *Opium and the Opium Appetite*, Philadelphia, 1871. F. S. Turner, *British Opium Policy and its Results to India and China*, London, 1876. Dr. D. J. Macgowan in *Transactions of the N. C. Br. R. A. S.*, Part IV., Art. II. Fernand Papillon, *Revue des Deux Mondes*, 1er Mai, 1873. Dr. H. H. Kane, *Opium Smoking*, New York, 1882. *The Friend of China*, published at London bi-monthly; and publications of the Anglo-Oriental Society for the Suppression of the Opium Trade.

do without now," said a British minister once in a sorrowing mood, as he acknowledged its evils; but there are many other commodities, and a survey of the native and foreign commerce will exhibit the extent and variety of the resources of the Empire. The Chinese trade with foreign ports in native vessels is at present nearly extinct, in consequence of the increase of foreign shipping and advantages of insurance enabling the native trader to send and receive commodities with less risk and more speed than by junks. The facilities and security of commerce in a country are among the best indices of its government being administered, on the whole, in a tolerably just manner, and on those principles which give the mechanic, farmer, and merchant a good prospect of reaping the fruits of their industry. This security is afforded in China to a considerable degree—far more than in Western Asia—and is one of the most satisfactory proofs, amid all the extortions and depravity seen in their courts and in society at large, that the people, generally speaking, enjoy the rewards of industry. Tranquillity may often be owing to the strong arm of power, but trade, manufactures, voyages, and large commercial enterprises must remunerate those who undertake them, or they cease. The Chinese are eminently a trading people; their merchants are acute, methodical, sagacious, and enterprising, not over-scrupulous as to their mercantile honesty in small transactions, but in large dealings exhibiting that regard for character in the fulfilment of their obligations which extensive commercial engagements usually produce. The roguery and injustice which an officer of government may commit without disgrace would blast a merchant's reputation, and he undertakes the largest transactions with confidence, being guaranteed in his engagements by a combination of mercantile security and responsibility, which is more effectual than legal sanctions. These are like the rings and guilds, the corporations, patents, co-operative societies, etc., which are found in Europe and America, and enter into all branches of industry.

The coasting trade is disproportionately small compared with the inland commerce; large junks cross the seas, but smaller ones proceed cautiously along the coast from one headland to another, and sail chiefly by day. Their cargoes consist of rice, stockfish, vegetables, timber, poles, coal, stones, and other bulky articles. Between the unopened ports the native trade still employs thousands of small craft, whose crews know no other homes; but the progress of steam and sailing ships has gradually turned the coasting trade into foreign bottoms.

The foreign ports now visited by Chinese junks are Singapore, Labuan, Borneo, Bangkok and elsewhere in Siam, Manila, Corea, and Japan. The cargoes carried to these places comprise coarse crockery, fruits, cottons, cheap silks, and metallic articles of great variety. European goods are not brought to any great amount by junks, but the variety of articles of food or domestic use and raw materials for manufactures, known under the general denomination of *Straits produce*, is large. Rice is the chief import from Bangkok and Manila; rattans, pepper, and betelnut from Singapore and Borneo; biche-de-mer from the Sulu Sea. Of the amount of capital embarked in this commerce, the number of vessels, the mode in which it is carried on, and the degree of risk attending it, little is known. It is gradually decreasing, and all the valuable portions are already transferred to foreign bottoms.

The natural facilities for inland navigation in China are, as the first chapters of this work have pointed out, unusually great, and have been, moreover, improved by art for travel and transportation. It will be a hazardous experiment for the peace of the country to hastily supplant the swarms of boats on its rivers and canals by shallow-draught steamers and launches, and throw most of their poor and ignorant crews out of employment. The sugar, oil, and rice of the southern provinces, the tea, silk, cotton, and crockery of the eastern, the furs, grain, and medicines of the northern, and the metals and minerals of the western, are constantly going to and fro and demand myriads of boats; add thereto the immense number of governmental boats required for the transportation of salt and the taxes paid in kind, the passage-boats plying in great numbers between contiguous towns, the pleasure and official barges and revenue cutters, and lastly, the far greater number used for family residences, and the total of the inland shipping, it will be seen, must be enormous. It is, however, impossible to state the amount in any satisfactory manner, or give an idea of the proportion between the different kinds of boats. The transit duties levied on the produce carried in these vessels partake of the nature of an excise duty, and afford a very considerable revenue to the government, the greatest so, probably, next to the land tax. It was estimated that the additional charges for transit duty and transportation on only those teas brought to Canton overland for exportation amounted to about a million of dollars. Whenever a boat loaded with produce passes the custom-house, the supercargo presents his manifest, stating his name and residence, the name of the boat and its crew, and the description of the cargo, and when the charges are paid proceeds on his voyage. The tariff on goods at these places is light, but their number in a journey of any length, and the liability to unforeseen detention and exaction by the tidewaiters, greatly increase the expense and delay.

Since the treaties of 1842 and 1858, the Chinese and British authorities have been in constant dispute about the right and mode of levying transit dues on foreign and native produce going through the country—a dispute which involves and disturbs the whole revenue system of the country.

The mode of conducting the foreign trade with China now presents few of those peculiarities which formerly distinguished it, for the monopoly of the hong merchants and of the East India Company both being abolished, native and foreign traders are free to choose with whom they will deal. The introduction of regular printed permits, clearances, and other customs blanks to facilitate trade, followed the treaty of 1842, and their acceptance has now extended to every port. The employment of foreigners to conduct the details of the trade in connection with native officers and clerks has worked easily, and its extension to all commerce is gradually perfecting.

The articles of trade are likely to increase in variety and amount, and a brief account of the principal ones, taken from the *Chinese Commercial Guide*, may be interesting to those unacquainted with the character of this commerce. The foreign export and import trade divides itself into two branches, that between India and the Archipelago and China, and that beyond the Isthmus of Suez; the former comprises the greatest variety, but its total value is much less. *Alum* of an inferior quality is sent to India to use in dyeing, making glass, and purifying water. *Aniseed stars*, seeds of many sorts of *amomum*, *cubebs*, and *turmeric* are all sought after for their aromatic properties. The first is the small five-rayed pod of the *Illicium anisatum;* the pods and seeds are both prized for their aromatic qualities, and a volatile oil, used in perfumery and medicine in Europe, is obtained from them; the Asiatics employ them in cooking. *Cubebs*, the produce of a vine (*Cubeba officinalis*), are externally distinguished from black pepper chiefly by their lighter color, and a short process where the seed is attached to the stalk. The taste is warm or pungent and slightly bitter, with a pleasant aromatic smell; the Chinese article goes to India, the consumption of Europe being supplied from Java. Turmeric is the root of the *Curcuma longa*, and is used over the Archipelago and India for its coloring and aromatic properties, and for food. The roots are uneven and knotty, of a yellowish-saffron color; the smell resembles ginger, with a bitterish taste; and the two are usually combined in the composition of curry-powders. Its color is too fugacious for a dye, no mordant having yet been found to set it.

Cassia and *cassia oil* are sent abroad in amounts far exceeding the whole of the preceding; *cassia buds* also form an article of commerce. Cassia oil is used for confectionery and perfumery, and the demand is usually much greater than the supply. *Arsenic* is exported to India for medicinal purposes, and the native sulphuret or orpiment is sometimes shipped under the Hindustani name of *hartall*, as a yellow coloring drug. Wrist and ankle rings, known by the Hindu name of *bangles*, are exported largely, with false pearls, coral, and beads; the Chinese imitate jade and chalcedony in their manufacture, in which the Hindus do not succeed so well. The universal use and brittle nature of these ornaments render their consumption enormous in Eastern Asia. *Brass foil*, or *tinsel*, is made into the *kin hwa*, or 'golden flowers,' which are placed before shrines and adorn the rooms of houses, imitating bouquets and tableaux with cunning art; it is also used for coatings of toys. *Bones* and *horns* are manufactured into buttons, opium-boxes, hair-pins, etc., some of which go abroad. Many kinds of useful and fancy articles are made from bamboo and rattan, and their export forms an item of some importance. Chairs, baskets, canes and umbrella handles, fishing-rods, furniture, and similar articles are still made in vast variety. The same may be said of the great assortment of articles comprised under the head of *curiosities*, as vases, pots, jars, cups, images, boxes, plates, screens, statuettes, etc., made of copper, iron, bronze, porcelain, stone, wood, clay, or lacquered-ware. During the last twenty years the native shops have been nearly cleared of the choicer specimens of Chinese art and skill in these various departments.

Capoor cutchery, corrupted from the Hindu name *kafúr-kuchri*, or camphor root, is the aromatic root of the *Hedychium*, and also of the *Kœmpferia*; it goes to Bombay for perfumery, plasters, and other medicinal ends, as well as preserving clothes from insects. It is about half an inch in diameter, and cut up when brought to market; it has a pungent, bitterish taste. *Galangal* is another aromatic root exported for perfumery and medicine. The name is probably a corruption of *Kao-liang*, or *Ko-long*, meaning 'mild ginger,' from Kauchau, in the southwest of Kwangtung, where the best is found. It is the dried root of the *Alpinia officinarum* (Hance) and other species, and thousands of peculs reach Europe and America, where it is used as a cordial and tonic. There are two or three sorts; the smaller is a reddish-colored root, light and firm in texture, with an acrid, peppery taste.

The larger is from a different plant (*Kœmpferia galanga*), and inferior in every respect. Both are used as spicery, and the powder is mixed in tea among the Tartars, and to flavor a liquor called *nastoika* drank in Russia. All the plants whose roots have the aromatic sharp taste of ginger are prized by the Chinese. *China-root* is a commercial name applied to two different products, for which the native name *fuh-ling* rather misleads. One is the root of *Smilax China*, a vine-like dodder in appearance; it is a knotty and jointed brown tuber, white and starchy when cut, and sweetish. The other is a curious fungus (*Pachyma*) produced by fir roots apparently as it is found under that tree. The article is whitish and reddish when cut, bitterish and sharp to the taste, and eaten hot as a stomachic in rice-cakes where it is cheap. It is similar to the Indian bread, or *tuck-ahoo*, of the Carolinas.

The exportation of *porcelain* and *chinaware*, which was so great last century, diminished as European skill produced finer sorts at cheaper rates, and ceased altogether about twenty-five years ago, when the Tai-ping rebellion dispersed the workmen in Kingteh chin. Since the peace, those kilns have resumed work, and the demand for their finest pieces has arisen once more from western lands, so that China bids fair to regain her original reputation. She still supplies most parts of Asia with coarse stoneware and crockery for domestic use. *Glue* of a tolerably good quality, made from ox-hides, supplies the Chinese and furnishes an article for export to India. *Isinglass*, or fish-glue, is made from the sounds and noses of sturgeons and other sorts of fish, as the bynni carp, or *Polynemus;* it is used in sizing silk and in cookery, as well as in manufacturing of india-ink, water-colors, and false pearls.

A kind of parasol, made of oiled paper, or silk called *kittysol* (*i.e.*, *quitté sol*), is exported to India; the article is durable, considering its material, and its cheapness induces a large consumption. *Tobacco*, one of the most widely cultivated plants in China (for men, women, and children smoke), is also sent to the Indian Islands in considerable quantity, for use among the natives. Ware made from ivory, tortoise-shell, mother-o'-pearl, and gold and silver constitutes altogether a considerable item in the trade, for the beautiful carving of the Chinese always commands a market. The workmen easily imitate new patterns for boxes, combs, and buttons of mother-o'-pearl or tortoise-shell, while the cheapness and beauty with which silver table furniture is made cause a large demand. *Lacquered-ware* is not so much sent abroad now as formerly, the foreign imitations of the trays and tables having nearly superseded the demand for the Chinese ware. *Marble slabs* of a clouded blue limestone are wrought out in Kwangtung province for floors, and some go abroad; square tiles are used everywhere for pavements, roofing, brick stoves, and drains. In the southern provinces they are well burned and make serviceable floors.

Mats of rattan for table furniture, and of grass for floors, are all made by hand. The latter is manufactured of two or three sorts of grass in different widths and patterns, and though the amount annually sent to the United States and elsewhere exceeds five million yards, it forms a very small proportion to the home consumption. Floor matting is put up in rolls containing twenty mats, or forty yards. *Musk*, though still in demand, is often and much adulterated, or its quality impaired by disease. It comes in bags about as large as a walnut; when good, it is of a dark purplish color, dry and light, and generally in concrete, smooth, and unctuous grains; its taste is bitter and smell strong; when rubbed on paper the trace is of a bright yellow color, and the feel free from grittiness. A brown unctuous earth is sometimes mixed with it, and the bags are frequently artificial; the price is about forty-five dollars a pound for the best quality.

Nankeen is a foreign name given to a kind of reddish cotton cloth manufactured near Nanking and Tsungming Island; it was once largely exported, but the product has now nearly ceased. It is the most durable kind of cotton cloth known, and its excellence always repays the cultivator. The opening of the country to foreigners, and the disorders ensuent on the Tai-ping rebellion, altered the character of the *silk* trade. The loss of capital and dispersion of workmen in the vicinity of Canton nearly destroyed the export of raw silk and piece-goods formerly made at Fatshan, and the pongees once woven there are seldom seen. The elegant crape shawls and scarfs, gauzes and checked lustrings, satins and lining silks, which were sent abroad from Canton, have all dwindled away. Raw silk makes the bulk of the export, amounting to over a hundred thousand bales, of which nearly two-thirds goes to Great Britain. The annual average for the six years ending 1860 was seventy-eight thousand five hundred bales; in 1836 it was twenty-one thousand; the price of the best sorts was about five hundred and fifty dollars a pecul. Silk goods are exported to the annual value of about two million taels; they consist chiefly of gauzes, pongees, handkerchiefs, scarfs, sarsnet, senshaws, levantines, and satins; ribbons, sewing-thread, and organzine, or thrown silk, are not much shipped. The silk trade is more likely to increase than any other branch of the commerce, after tea, and the Chinese can furnish almost any amount of raw and manufactured silks, according to the demand for them. *Soy* is a name derived from the Japanese *sho-ya ;* it is made by boiling the beans of the *Dolichos soja*, adding an equal quantity of wheat or barley, and leaving the mass to ferment ; a layer of salt and three times as much water as beans are afterward put in, and the whole compound stirred daily for two months, when the liquid is pressed and strained. Another method of making the condiment has already been mentioned in Volume I., p. 365.

Besides the articles above-mentioned, there are many others which singly form very trifling items in the trade, but their total exportation annually amounts to many lacs of dollars. Among them fire-crackers, and straw braid woven in Shantung from a variety of wheat, are both sent to the United States. Among other sundries, vermilion, gold leaf, amber, sea-shells, preserved insects, fans, ginger, sweetmeats and jellies, rhubarb, gamboge, camphor, grass-cloth, artificial flowers, insect wax, fishing-lines, joss-sticks, spangles, window-blinds, vegetable tallow, and pictures are the most deserving of mention. Some of them may perhaps become important articles of commerce, and all of them, except vermilion, gamboge, and rattans, are the produce of the country.

The imports make a much longer list than the exports, for almost everything that should or might sell there is from time to time offered in the market ; and if the Chinese at Canton had had any inclination or curiosity to obtain the productions or manufactures of other lands, they have had no want of specimens. It will only be necessary to mention articles of import whose names are not of themselves a sufficient description. Opium, rice, raw cotton, longcloths, domestics and sheetings among manufactured cottons, ginseng, tin, lead, bar, rod, and hoop iron, and woollen goods, constitute the great bulk of the import trade. Rice is brought from southern islands, and a bounty used to be paid on its importation into Canton by taking off the tonnage dues on ships laden with this alone—a bonus of about three thousand dollars on a large vessel.

The importations from the Indian Archipelago comprise a

large variety of articles, though their total amount and value are not very great. *Agar-agar*, or *agal-agal*, is the Malay name for the *Plocaria tenax*, *Gracillaria*, and other sorts of seaweed; it is boiled and clarified to make a vegetable glue which is largely employed in lantern and silk manufacture instead of isinglass; it is also made into a jelly, but the *seaweed* (*Laiminaria*) from Japan has supplanted it. *Betel-nut* is the fruit of the areca palm, and is called *betel-nut* because it is chewed with the leaf of the betel pepper (*Chavica*) as a masticatory. The nut is the only part brought to China, the leaf being raised along the southern coast; it resembles a nutmeg in shape and color, is a little larger, and the whole of the nut is chewed. They are boiled or eaten raw, the former being cut into slices and boiled with a small quantity of cutch and then dried. Those brought to China are simply deprived of the husk and dried. When chewed, a slice of the nut is wrapped in the fresh leaf smeared with a mixture of gambier or shell-lime colored red, and the whole masticated to a pulp before spitting it out. The teeth become dark red from using it, but the Chinese are careful to remove this stain. The taste of the fresh pepper leaf is herbaceous and aromatic with a little pungency, and those who chew have it seldom out of their mouths; the habit is not general where the fresh leaf cannot be obtained.

Biche-de-mer, *i.e.*, slug of the sea, or tripang, is a marine gasteropod (*Holothuria*) resembling, when alive, a crawling sausage more than anything else; it is sometimes over a foot long and two or three inches through; it inhabits the shallow waters around the islands of the Pacific and Indian Archipelago, and is obtained by diving or spearing, and prepared by cleansing and smoking it. In the market it appears hard and rigid, of a dirty brown color; when soaked in water it resembles pork-rind, and when stewed is not unlike it in taste. The Chinese distinguish nearly thirty sorts of *hai săng*—'sea ginseng;' in commerce, however, all are known as white or black, the prices ranging from two dollars up to eighty dollars a pecul.

Birds' nests, *sharks' fins*, and *fish-maws* are three other articles of food prized by Chinese epicures for their supposed stimulating quality, and they readily fetch high prices. The first is the nest of a species of swallow (*Collocalia*), which makes the gelatinous fibres from its own crop out of the seaweed (*Gelidium*) it feeds on. These nests resemble those of the chimney swallow in shape, and are collected in most dangerous places along the cliffs and caves in the Indian Islands. The article varies from thirty dollars to three dollars a pound, and its total import is hardly five hundred peculs a year. The taste of the Chinese for the gelatinous fins and stomachs of the shark aids in clearing the seas of that ferocious fish even as far as the Persian Gulf. The soup made from the fins resembles that from isinglass, and is worthy of acceptance on other tables.

Amber is found on various eastern shores, along the Mozambique coast, in the Indian Islands, and localities in Annam and Yunnan. The consumption for court beads and other ornaments is great, and shows that the supply is permanent, for none is brought from Prussia. The Chinese use the powder of amber in their high-priced medicines. Their artists have also learned to imitate it admirably in a variety of articles made of copal, shell-lac, and colophony.

The *bezoars*, or biliary calculi from ruminating and other animals, always find a ready market in China for drugs; that from the cow is most prized, and is often imitated with pipe-clay and ox-gall mixed with hair, or adulterated by the camel bezoar. The Mongols prize these substances very highly; the pure goat and cow bezoars are ground for paints by the Cantonese.

Cutch, or terra japonica, is a gummy resin, obtained from a species of areca palm and the *Acacia catechu*, and was for a long time supposed to be a sort of earth found in Japan; it is called *cutch* from the Runn of Cutch, near which the tree grows. The best is friable between the fingers, is of a reddish-brown color, and used in China as a dye. There are two kinds, *black* and *pale*; the former is made by boiling the heart-wood of the acacia and putting the resin into small cakes; it is now brought in small quantities, as gambier has supplanted it.

Rose-maloes, corrupted from *rasamala*, the Javanese name of the *Altingia excelsa*, is a liquid storax obtained from the *Styrax*; it is a scented gummous oil of the consistency of tar, and is brought from Bombay to China for medicine. *Gum benzoin*, or *benjamin*, is one of the gum-resins brought from abroad, and highly prized by Chinese doctors; its Chinese name indicates that it came from Parthia; but it is collected from the *Styrax benzoin* in Sumatra and Borneo by making incisions in the bark in much the same manner as opium, until the plant withers and dies. It comes to market in cakes, which in some parts of those islands formerly served as standards of value. Good benzoin is full of clear light-colored spots, marbled on the broken surface, and giving off an agreeable odor when heated or rubbed; it is the frankincense of the far East, and has been employed by many nations in their religious ceremonies; for what was so acceptable to the worshippers was soon inferred to be equally grateful to the gods, and sought after by all devotees as a delightful perfume. The quantity of benzoin imported is, however, small, and the Arabian frankincense, or *olibanum*, is more commonly seen in the market, and is employed for the same purposes. This gum-resin exudes from the *Boswellia thurifera* cultivated in Coromandel; the drops have a pale reddish color, a strong and somewhat unpleasant smell, a pungent and bitterish taste, and when chewed give the saliva a milky color; it burns with a pleasant fragrance and slight residuum. *Dragon's blood* is probably an equivalent of the Chinese name *lung-yen hiang*, given to this resin from its coming to market in lumps formed from the agglutinated tears. It is the gummy covering of the seeds of a rattan palm (*Dæmonorops draco*) common in Sumatra, which is separated by shaking them in a basket or bag; an inferior sort is made by boiling the nuts. It is used in varnishing, painting, and medical preparations.

Cloves are consumed but little by the Chinese, and mostly in expressing an oil which forms an ingredient in condiments and medicines, like the oil of peppermint made by themselves. *Pepper* is much more used than cloves, the tea being considered beneficial in fevers; the good effects as a febrifuge seem to be doubted lately, for the importation is only twenty thousand peculs, not one-half what it was fifty years ago. *Baroos camphor* is still imported from Borneo, the people supposing that the drops and lumps found in the fissures of the tree (*Dryobalanops*) in that island are more powerful than their own gum; the proportion between the two, both in price and quantity, is about eighteen to one.

Gambier is obtained from the gambier vine (*Uncaria*) by boiling the leaves and inspissating the decoction; a soapy substance of a brownish-yellow color remains, which is both chewed with betel-nut and forms a good and cheap material for tanning and dyeing. *Putchuck* is the root of a kind of thistle (*Aucklandia*) cultivated in Cashmere; it comes in dry, brown, broken pieces, resembling rhubarb in color and smell, and affording an agreeable perfume when burned; the powder is employed in making incense-sticks and the thin shavings mixed in medicines.

Cornelians, agates, and other stones of greater or less value are purchased by the Chinese for manufacturing into official insignia, rings, beads, and other articles of ornament; they are brought chiefly from India or Central Asia. *Seed pearls*, to the amount of three hundred thousand dollars, are annually brought from Bombay to Canton, where they are run on strings to be worn in ladies' head-dresses; *coral* is also a part of cargoes from the Archipelago. *Mother-o'-pearl* shells and *tortoise-shell* are brought from the same region and the Pacific islands, Muscat, and Bombay, a large part of which is re-exported in the shape of buttons, combs, and other productions of Chinese skill.

Ivory still comes from Africa *via* Bombay, and Malaysia, mostly from Bangkok; the fossil ivory of Siberia has furnished the material for the inlaid tables of Ningpo; but the cost of fine ivory has prevented the manufacture of many articles once common at Canton. *Rhinoceros' horns* are all brought to China to be carved into ornaments, or served in remedies and tonics.[1] But the principal use of these horns is in medicine and for amulets, for only one good cup can be carved from the end of each horn; the parings and fragments are carefully preserved to serve for the other purposes. The teeth of the sperm whale, walrus, lamantine, and other phocine animals, form an article of import in limited quantities under the designation

[1] The elegant plumage of the turquois kingfisher and some other birds is also worked into ornaments and head-dresses.

of "sea-horse teeth;" these tusks weigh from sixteen to forty ounces, their ivory being nearly as compact though not so white as that of the elephant.

Several kinds of *wood* are brought for cabinet and inlaid work, medical preparations, and dyeing. Among these are *ebony* and *camagon* (*mao tsz'*), both obtained from species of *Diospyros* growing in India and Luzon; they are often very cleverly imitated by covering teak and other hard woods with a black stain. *Gahru wood*—also called eagle or agila wood (*Aquilaria*)—furnishes the calambak timber, highly prized for its perfume; the diseased heart-wood of this tree is the precious aloes wood, the lign aloes of the Bible.[1] Among dye-stuffs the *laka* wood (*Tanarius*) from Sumatra, mangrove bark, sapan wood (*Cæsalpinia*), and red wood are important articles; the imports of sandal wood for incense, rosewood, satin wood, amboyna or knot wood, camphor and *kranjee* are employed in various ways for junks, buildings, and furniture.

The greater facilities of trade with foreign countries since 1860 have vastly enlarged the list of imports and exports, and brought many new and useful articles within reach of the natives living far from the ports. In their fear and ignorance the Chinese associated everything dreadful with the name and coming of those whom they called devils and barbarians, and knew chiefly in connection with war and opium. By degrees, however, they are learning the benefits of a wider commercial as well as intellectual intercourse. One of the most notable among the imports, which carries with it something of this broadening influence, is kerosene; the traveller in China, as well as in Algeria, Greece, and Egypt, can hardly fail to note with interest the multitude of benefits arising from the introduction of a cheap and brilliant lamp into a house whose only light before has been a water-lamp or tallow candle. Electric lighting is now employed in certain of the foreign settlements, and will doubtless become as popular in the far East as among Western nations. It is needless, however, to enumerate the novelties in which the Chinese are constantly urged and tempted to invest.

The mode of conducting the trade is described in the author's

[1] *Chinese Commercial Guide*, Fifth Edition, p. 106.

Chinese Commercial Guide (fifth edition, Hongkong, 1863), which contains the treaties, tariffs, regulations, etc., of other nations as well as of China. A peculiar feature of this trade is the fact that the natives have always conducted it in English,—that is, they do business in the jargon called *pigeon-English*, whose curious formation has already received some attention in a previous chapter. The Chinaman using it deems no sentence complete until it contains the same number of words and in the same idiom as its equivalent phrase in his own language. A sample of this hybrid lingo, with its *mélange* of Chinese, Portuguese, and Malay words and grammatical constructions, may not be out of place here. We will suppose a shopkeeper is soliciting custom from a foreigner: "My chin-chin you," he says, "one good fleen [friend], take care for my [patronize me]; 'spose you wanchee any first chop ting, my can catchee for you [obtain]. I secure sell 'em plum cash [prime cost], alla same cumsha [present]; can do?" The foreigner, with great gravity, replies: "Just now my no wanchee anyting; any teem [time] 'spose you got vely number one good ting, p'rhaps I come you shop look see." After hearing for a few days such sentences, the foreigner begins to imitate them, soon learning to adapt his speech to his interlocutor's, and thus perpetuating the jargon. Other nationalities are also obliged to learn it, and the whole trade is conducted in this meagre gibberish, which the natives suppose, however, to be correct English, but which hardly enables the two parties to exchange ideas upon even household subjects. Much of the misunderstanding and trouble experienced in daily intercourse with the Chinese is doubtless owing to this imperfect medium.[1]

The trade at the five ports opened by the treaty of Nanking in 1842 was conducted by native custom-house officers, as it had been previously at Canton, but under regulations which insured more honesty and efficiency. In 1853, however, the capture of Shanghai by insurgents threw the whole trade into such confusion that the collector, who had been formerly

[1] Mr. Schuyler mentions hearing some Chinese residents at Vierny speaking a mongrel with the Russian officers of the post, which might be called "pigeon-Russian." *Turkistan*, Vol. II., p. 147.

a hong merchant at Canton, called in the aid of foreigners to carry on his duties. A trio of inspectors was nominated for this purpose by the British, American, and French ministers from their nationalities; and so well did it work in honestly collecting the revenue for the imperial coffers, that when the city was recaptured the system was made permanent for that port. In the negotiations growing out of the treaties of Tientsin in 1858, the Chinese government felt so much confidence in the feasibility of the plan, that it was extended to all the ports and placed under the entire control of an inspector-general. By thus utilizing the experience and integrity of foreign employés in carrying on this important branch of its administration, the rulers broke through their long seclusion and isolation, and opened the way for removing the impediments to their own progress in every branch of polity.

The following tables, compiled or abridged from the so-called "Yellow Books," or Trade Reports, issued by the Imperial Maritime Customs, will furnish a general idea of the foreign trade with China and some statistics concerning its domestic commerce. It is hardly necessary to add, however, that concerning the latter when unconnected with foreigners, there are almost no figures of value attainable. The *Haikwan tael*, it may be well to repeat, is valued at $1.36½, or 5*s.* 6½*d.* The *pecul* weighs 133⅓ pounds.

ANNUAL VALUE OF THE FOREIGN TRADE OF CHINA, 1871 TO 1881.

YEAR.	Net Imports.[1]	Exports.	Total.
	Hk. Tls.	*Hk. Tls.*	*Hk Tls.*
1871	70,103,077	66,853,161	136,956,238
1872	67,317,049	75,288,125	142,605,174
1873	66,637,209	69,451,277	136,088,486
1874	64,360,864	66,712,868	137,073,732
1875	67,803,247	68,912,929	136,716,176
1876	70,269,574	80,850,512	151,120,086
1877	73,233,896	67,445,022	140,678,918
1878	70,804,027	67,172,179	137,976,206
1879	82,227,424	72,281,262	154,508,686
1880	79,293,452	77,883,587	157,177,039
1881	91,910,877	71,452,974	163,363,851

[1] Meaning the value of foreign goods imported direct from foreign countries, less the value of the foreign goods re-exported to foreign countries during the year.

CUSTOMS REVENUE, 1871 TO 1881.

YEAR.	DUTIES ON NATIVE PRODUCE EXPORTED TO—		TOTAL REVENUE FROM—		
	Foreign Countries.	Chinese Ports.	Foreign Trade.	Home Trade.	Total.
	Hk. Tls.	*Hk. Tls.*	*Hk. Tls.*	*Hk. Tls.*	*Hk. Tls.*
1871........	5,246,467	1,138,116	9,508,972	1,707,174	11,216,146
1872........	5,840,261	1,099,724	10,029,050	1,649,586	11,678,636
1873........	4,978,179	1,158,938	9,238,675	1,738,407	10,977,082
1874........	5,535,041	1,147,686	9,775,743	1,721,529	11,497,272
1875........	5,640,062	1,291,922	10,030,226	1,937,883	11,968,109
1876........	5,772,709	1,222,860	10,318,631	1,834,290	12,152,921
1877........	5,703,321	1,140,442	10,356,415	1,710,663	12,067,078
1878........	5,803,485	1,306,118	10,524,811	1,956,177	12,483,988
1879........	5,958,176	1,426,894	11,391,329	2,140,341	13,531,670
1880........	6,696,290	1,572,392	11,899,995	2,358,588	14,258,583
1881........	6,869,486	1,460,182	12,494,889	2,190,273	14,685,162

EXPORT OF TEA FROM CHINA DURING TEN YEARS.

YEAR.	Black.	Green.	Leaf.	Dust.	Brick.	Total.
	Peculs.	*Peculs.*	*Peculs.*	*Peculs.*	*Peculs.*	*Peculs.*
1872........	1,420,170	256,464	85	950	96,994	1,774,663
1873........	1,274,232	235,413	372	416	107,330	1,617,763
1874........	1,444,249	212,834	....	3,504	74,792	1,735,379
1875........	1,438,611	210,282	....	2,594	166,900	1,818,387
1876........	1,415,349	189,714	74	3,799	153,951	1,762,887
1877........	1,552,174	197,522	36	12,158	147,810	1,909,700
1878........	1,517,617	172,826	....	14,236	194,277	1,898,956
1879........	1,523,419	183,234	....	5,270	275,540	1,987,463
1880........	1,661,325	188,623	....	14,201	232,969	2,097,118
1881........	1,636,724	238,064	....	15,186	247,498	2,137,472

EXPORT OF NATIVE CHINESE GOODS TO FOREIGN COUNTRIES, 1880 AND 1881.

Description of Goods.	Classifier of Quantity.	1880.		1881.	
		Quantity.	Value.	Quantity.	Value.
			Hk. Tls.		*Hk. Tls.*
Silk, all kinds	Peculs.	114,821	29,831,444	106,632	26,868,200
Tea, all kinds	"	2,097,119	35,728,169	2,137,473	32,890,268
Bags, all kinds	Pieces.	749,383	20,555	860,558	31,002
Bamboo, all kinds	Value.	....	74,597	....	86.167
Beans and beancake	Peculs.	154,645	159,996	112,628	139,066
Cassia lignea	"	38,785	225,692	57,456	300,303
Camphor	"	12,327	100,679	9,317	79,625
Chinaware and pottery	"	75,142	379,574	78,503	387,006
Coal	"	161	34	1,478	308
Clothing, boots, and shoes	Value.	....	327,548	....	358,301
Cotton, raw and waste	Peculs.	20,315	182.918	23,139	228,391
Curios	Value.	....	44,948	....	43,364
Dyes, colors, and paints	Peculs.	676	3,196	20	183
Fans, all kinds	Pieces.	6,287,989	38,881	2,017,157	27,710
Fish, provisions, and vegetables	Peculs.	68,940	165,922	66,008	146,262
Fire-crackers	"	27,051	260,010	34,380	322,522
Flour, grain, and pulse	"	149,394	139,653	39,911	49,361
Fruits, all kinds	"	73,720	92,913	87,140	106,756
Grasscloth	"	1,185	104,719	1,589	148,985
Hemp	"	19,548	160,602	20,771	158,143
Hides and hoops	"	20,786	253,548	38,526	473,555
Indigo	"	2,847	13,768	1,764	7,168
Lung-ngans	"	8,080	34,669	7,592	30,753
Mats and matting	Pieces.	384,680	533,027	360,827	358,537
Medicines	Peculs.	28,676	194,451	31,916	194,090
Metals, manufactured	"	14,284	147,405	14,804	135,778
Metals, unmanufactured	"	217	875	2	4
Nankeens and wool	"	6,511	122,815	8,750	172,205
Nutgalls and preserves	"	47,690	432,774	44,260	402,017
Oil, all kinds	"	3,692	70,295	9,442	159,516
Paper, books, tin, and brass foil	"	43.581	512,720	53,438	597,496
Rattans and rattanware	"	2,085	8,975	2,757	11,901
Rhubarb	"	6,153	212,527	6,814	245,957
Skins, all kinds	Pieces.	244,193	152,486	330,922	262,780
Straw braid	Peculs.	48,970	1,227,670	50,502	1,363,984
Sugar, white, brown, candy	"	1,138,196	3,263,889	957,564	2,584,000
Tobacco	"	19,077	167,931	7,250	73,386
Vermicelli and macaroni	"	26,991	125,422	40,122	154,159
Sundries, unenumerated	Value.	....	2,366,290	....	1,853,865
Total value	....	....	77,883,587	....	71,452,974

CHAPTER XXI.

FOREIGN INTERCOURSE WITH CHINA.

THE most important notices which the research of authors had collected respecting the intercourse between China and the West, and the principal facts of interest of a political and commercial nature down to the year 1834, are carefully arranged in the first three chapters of Sir John Davis' work.[1] In truth, the terms *intercourse* and *ambassies*, so often used with reference to the nations of Eastern Asia, indicate a peculiar state of relations with them; for while other courts send and receive resident ministers, those of China, Japan, Corea, and Cochinchina have until very recently kept themselves aloof from this national interchange of civilities, neither understanding its principles nor appreciating its advantages. Embassies have been sent by most European nations to the two first, which have tended rather to strengthen their assumptions of supremacy than to enlighten them as to the real objects and wishes of the courts proposing such courtesies. The commercial intercourse has, like the political, either been forced upon or begged of these governments, constantly subject to those vexatious restrictions and interruptions which might be expected from such ill-defined arrangements; and though mutually advantageous, has never been conducted on those principles of reciprocity and equality which characterize commerce at the West. As yet, the rulers and merchants of oriental nations are hardly well enough acquainted with their own and others' rights to be able or willing

[1] *The Chinese*, 2 Vols., Harper's Family Library, 1837. See also Murray's *China*, Vol. I., 1843. Montgomery Martin's *China*, passim, 1847. *Mémoires conc. les Chinois*, Tome V., pp. 1–23. T. W. Kingsmill in *N. C. Br. R. A. Soc. Journal*, N. S., No. XIV., 1879.

to enter into close relations with European powers. Both magistrates and people are ignorant and afraid of the resources, power, and designs of Christian nations, and consequently disinclined to admit them or their subjects to unrestrained intercourse. When western adventurers, as Pinto, Andrade, Weddell, and others came to the shores of China and Japan in the sixteenth and seventeenth centuries, they found the governments disposed to traffic, but the conquests subsequently made by Europeans in the neighboring regions of Luçonia, Java, and India, and their cruel treatment of the natives, led these two powers to apprehend like results for themselves if they did not soon take precautionary measures of exclusion and restriction. Nor can there be much doubt that this policy was the safest measure, in order to preserve their independence and maintain their authority over even their own subjects. Might made right more generally among nations then than it does now, and the belief entertained by most Europeans at that period, that all pagan lands belonged justly to the Pope, only wanted men and means to be everywhere carried into effect. Had the Chinese and Japanese governments allowed Portuguese, Spanish, French, and English colonists to settle and increase within their borders, they would, probably, long since have crumbled to pieces and their territories have been possessed by others.

The data brought together by Davis in 1838 on this subject has since been enlarged and illustrated by Col. Yule in his admirable "Preliminary Essay" of 1866, prefixed to *Cathay and the Way Thither*, and by Richthofen, the latter half of whose first volume on China is devoted to an exhaustive treatise upon the "Development of the Knowledge of China."[1] A digest of these elaborate works would be too long for our purpose here,

---

[1] *China, Ergebnisse eigener Reisen und darauf gegründeter Studien*, Berlin, 1877. This author's arrangement of the subject into "Periods" is as follows: I.—Legendary notices of intercourse before the year 1122 B.C. II.—From the accession of the Chaus to the building of the Great Wall (1122–212 B.C.). III.—From the building of the Great Wall to the accession of the Tangs (212 B.C.–619 A.D.). IV.—From the Tangs to the Mongols (619–1205). V.—From the rise of the Mongol power to the arrival of the Portuguese in China (1205–1517). VI.—From the arrival of the Portuguese to the present time.

where only the most interesting points can be noticed. The first recorded knowledge of China among the nations of the West does not date further back than the geographer Ptolemy, A.D. 150, who seems himself to have been indebted to the Tyrian author Marinus. The Periplus of the Erythræan Sea, however, refers to the same land under the name Θὶν, or *Thin*, at perhaps an earlier date. Previous to this time, moreover, accounts of the existence of the land of Confucius, and an appreciation and demand for the splendid silks made there, had reached Persia, judging from the legends found in its writers alluding to ancient wars and embassies with China, in which the country, the government, people, and fabrics are invested with a halo of power and wealth which has not yet entirely vanished. These legends strengthen the conclusion that the Prophet Isaiah has the first mention now extant of the Flowery Land under the name *Sinim*. The interchange of the initial in *China*, *Thina* or *Tina*, and *Sina* ought to give no trouble in identifying the land, for such changes in pronunciation are still common in it; *e.g.*, *Chau-chau fu* into *Tiè-chiu hu*.

The Periplus of Arrian places the city of Thina perhaps as far east as Sí-ngan, but too vaguely to be relied on; that great city must certainly have then been known, however, among the traders of Central Asia, who probably were better acquainted with its geography than the authors who have survived them. Under the term *Seres* the Chinese are more clearly referred to at even an earlier date than *Sina*, and among the Latin writers it was about the only term used, its association with the silks brought thence keeping it before them. The two names were used for different regions,[1] the Seres being understood as lying to the north. Mela places them between the Indians and Scythians; Ptolemy calls the country *Serice* and the capital *Sera*, but regarded them as distinct from the *Sinæ*, precisely as a Chinese geographer might confuse Britain and England. He says there

[1] The different appellations seem to have been employed according as it was regarded as the terminus of a southern sea route or a journey across the continent. In the former aspect the name has nearly always been some form of *Sin*, *Chin*, Sinæ, China; in the latter, to the ancients as the land of the *Seres*, to the middle ages as the Empire of *Cathay*.—Yule.

was a long and dangerous land route leading to Sera through Persia to Bactria, over mountain defiles and perilous paths, which occupied the largest part of a year. Besides Ptolemy, there are notices by Pliny of the Seres, and these two authors furnished their successors with most of their knowledge down to the reign of Justinian. Col. Yule concisely summarizes the knowledge of China down to that date among the Romans: "The region of the Seres is a vast and populous country, touching on the east the ocean and the limits of the habitable world; and extending west nearly to Imaus and the confines of Bactria. The people are civilized men, of mild, just, and frugal temper; eschewing collisions with their neighbors, and even shy of close intercourse, but not averse to dispose of their own products, of which raw silk is the staple, but which include also silk stuffs, furs, and iron of remarkable quality." He further explains how authors writing at Rome and Constantinople were quite unable to traverse and rectify what was said of the marts and nations spoken of in the farthest East, and place them with any precision. They were, in truth, in the same difficulty in coming to an accurate conclusion that the Chinese geographer Seu Kí-yu was when writing at Fuhchau in 1847; he could not explain the discrepancies he found between Rhodes and its colossus and Rhode Island in the United States.

Among the marts mentioned in the various authors, Greek, Roman, and Persian, only a few can be identified with even fair probability. The "Stone Tower" of Ptolemy seems to have denoted *Tashkend*, a name of the same meaning, and a town still resorted to for trade. His port of Cattigara may have been a mart at the mouth of the Meinam, the Meikon, the Chu Kiang, or some other large stream in that region, where seafaring people could exchange their wares with the natives, then quite independent of the Chinese in Shensí, who were known to him as Seres. Cattigara is more probably to be looked for near Canton, for its annals state that in the reign of Hwan tí (A.D. 147–168) "Tienchuh (India), Ta-tsin (Rome, Egypt or Arabia), and other nations came by the southern sea with tribute, and from this time trade was carried on at Canton with foreigners." During the same dynasty (the Eastern Han), foreigners came from Cantoo, Lu-hwang-chí, and other nations in the south. The nearest was about ten days' journey, and the farthest about five months'.[1]

On the land frontier, the Chinese annals of the Han dynasty record the efforts of Wu tí (B.C. 140–86) to open a communication with the Yuehchí, or Getæ, who had driven out the Greek rulers in Bactria and settled themselves north of the River Oxus, in order to get their help against his enemies the Huns. He sent an envoy, Chang Kiang, in 135, who was captured by the Huns and kept prisoner for ten years, when he escaped with some of his attendants and got to *Ta-wan*, or Ferghana, and thence reached the Yuehchí further south. He was unsuccessful in his mission, and attempted to return home through Tibet, but was re-taken by the Huns, and did not succeed in reporting himself at Chang-an till thirteen years had elapsed. The introduction of the vine into China is rather doubtfully ascribed to this brave envoy.

De Guignes concludes that this notice about trade at Canton refers to the embassy sent in A.D. 166 by the Emperor Marcus Aurelius (whom the Chinese call *An-tun*), which entered China by the south at Tongking, or Canton. The Latin author Florus, who lived in Trajan's reign, about fifty years before, has a passage showing, as proof of the universal awe and veneration in which the power of Rome was held under Augustus, that ambassadors from the remotest nations, the Seres and the Indians, came with presents of elephants, gems, and pearls—a rhetorical exaggeration quite on a par with the Chinese account of the tribute sent from An-tun, and not so well authenticated. Whether, indeed, the *Ta-tsin kwoh* mentioned by Chinese writers meant Judea, Rome, or Persia, cannot now be exactly ascertained, though Yule concludes that this name almost certainly means the Roman Empire, otherwise called the Kingdom of the Western Sea. The title was given to these regions because of the analogy of its people to those of the Middle King-

[1] *Chinese Repository*, I., p. 365. Heeren, *Asiatic Researches*, II., pp. 285–295. Murray's *China*, I., p. 141. Yule's *Cathay*, Vol. I., pp. xli–xlv. Smith, *Classical Dictionary*, Art. SERES.

dom.[1] The envoys sent to that country reported that "beyond the territory of the Tau-shí (perhaps the Persians) there was a great sea, by which, sailing due west, one might arrive at the country where the sun sets." Like most attempts of the kind in subsequent days, the mission of Antoninus appears to have been a failure, and to have returned without accomplishing any practical benefit to intercourse or trade between the two greatest empires in the world. It was received, no doubt, at Lohyang, then the capital, with ostentatious show and patronizing kindness, and its occurrence inscribed in the national records as another evidence of the glory and fame of the Son of Heaven. That a direct trade between Rome and China did not result at this period may have been largely due to the jealousy of the Parthian merchants, who reaped great profits as middle-men in the traffic, and disposed of their own woven and colored stuffs to the Romans, all of which gain they knew would have passed over their heads had the extreme East and West come into more intimate relations.

It is worthy of observation how, even from the earliest times, the traffic in the rich natural and artificial productions of India and China has been the great stimulus to urge adventurers to come from Europe, who on their part offered little in exchange besides precious metals. The *Serica vestis*, whether it was a silken or cotton fabric, and other rarities found in those regions, bore such a high price at Rome as to tempt the merchants to undertake the longest journeys and undergo the greatest hardships to procure them; and such was the case likewise during the long period before the discovery of the Cape of Good Hope. The existence of this trade early enabled the Nestorian missionaries to penetrate into those remote regions, and keep up a communication with their patrons at home; the more extended

[1] *Cathay and the Way Thither*, p. lvi. Klaproth, *Tableaux Historiques de l'Asie* (Paris, 1826), p. 68. So Richthofen (*China*, Bd. I., p. 470), who adds: "It is accepted now, by almost all those who have written on the subject, that the Chinese by *Ta-tsin* meant to denote 'Great-China,' and through this, on the other hand, we have a proof that the Chinese called their own country *Tsin*. It will hardly do, however, to suppose that so prejudiced a people as they would recognize another folk as greater. The appellation *Ta* (great) is given to every nation whose power the Chinese feel to be considerable."

voyages of modern commerce likewise assist benevolent persons in reaching the remotest tribes and carrying on their labors, through their patrons on the other side of the world, probably with less danger and delay than a mission at Cadiz could have been directed from Jerusalem in the days of the apostles.

The notices in Cosmas (a Greek monk who had been a merchant, and wrote his "Universal Christian Topography" between 530 and 550 A.D.) of China and its products refer to the maritime trade under the Byzantine emperors. This country he locates very correctly as occupying the extreme east of Asia, and calls *Tzinista*, a name probably picked up from the Persians or old Hindus, and nearly similar to the *Tzinisthan* of the tablet at Sí-ngan. Another Greek, Theophylact, in the next century describes the internal intercourse in Central Asia, and a great Turkish people, the *Taugas*, whom he was unaware were the Chinese. It may be that he miswrote *Tang* in a grecized form for the dynasty just about that time settling its power. The indirect commerce between China and the Greek Empire increased by sea and land until the rise of the Moslem power. The same indifference on the part of the Chinese respecting the power, resources, and position of other lands is seen through all their notices of those western kingdoms. The products carried west were silk in various forms, but the demand for this article diminished after the worms had been successfully taken to Greece about A.D. 550. Cotton fabrics, medicines, and spices went westward as well as silk, but it is impossible to distinguish the trade with China from that with India. The leaf called *malabathrum* in the Periplus was not a Chinese plant, but the *tamalapatra*, a kind of cassia (*Cinnamomum nitidum*, whose leaves were purchased in Rome for three hundred denarii per pound), and now called Malabar leaf; it was probably mixed or confounded with the Indian *nard* and with camphor. The people called *Sesatæ* in the Periplus are probably to be looked for in Assam or Sikkim, where wild cassia grows, and where the real tea plant is native; but neither tea nor betel-leaf can be regarded as the ancient malabathrum.[1]

---

[1] Heeren's *Asiatic Researches*, II., p. 294; Yule's *Cathay*, pp. xlvi, cxliv.

Within the last few years the translations of the travels of Buddhist pilgrims between China and India have furnished more satisfactory details of the peoples inhabiting the central and western parts of Asia than all the Greek and Latin authors. Those of Fahian (399–414), of Hiuen-tsang (628–645), and of Hwui-sing (518), are the most extensive. Further researches into conventual libraries in China and Tibet are encouraged by what has been found on their shelves, and from them enough has already been gained to reward the labor. Of greater worth than these, perhaps, are the official histories of the Han, Tsin, and Tang dynasties, reaching from B.C. 200 to A.D. 900, only portions of which have yet been made accessible in full. Their trivialties are so numerous that their entire translation into English would hardly repay the printing, as the experiment by Mailla, in 1785, of the *Tang Kien Kang-muh*, in thirteen volumes quarto, shows. These histories, on the whole, supply more accurate information about Syria, Persia, Greece, and Parthia, than the writers of those countries give about China;—for example, the notices of *Fulin*, or Constantinople, are more minute than any account of Chang-an in western writers. But as Yule well remarks, there is much analogy between the fragmentary views each party had, the same uncertainty as to exact position, and the same application of facts belonging to the nearer skirts of a half-seen empire to the whole land. It can well be paralleled by reading some of our own travellers who applied all that they saw and heard at Canton to the Eighteen Provinces. Only a few embassies from *Ta-tsin* and *Fulin* are enumerated by Pauthier in his *Chine* as coming down to the year 1091; but the tractate by Dr. E. Bretschneider, of the Russian Legation at Peking,[1] shows how constant were the visits of the Arabs down to the Sung (A.D. 1086), and especially during the Tang dynasty. During the Tsin and Wei dynasties the visits of envoys from Ceylon were frequent, all of them an outgrowth of Buddhism, but repaid in more ways than one by the trade and its results—as shown by Sir E. Tennent in his *History of Ceylon*. In 1266 the King of Ceylon had Chinese soldiers in

[1] *On the Knowledge of the Arabs and Arabian Colonies possessed by the Ancient Chinese*, London, 1871.

his service, and envoys came to him to buy Buddha's sacred alms-dish. In 1405 the Emperor Yungloh of the Ming dynasty, taking umbrage at the indignities offered to his representative by Wijayabahu IV., despatched Ching Ho with a fleet of sixty-two ships and a land force to cruise along the coasts of Cambodia, Siam, and other places, demanding tribute and conferring gifts as the successor of the throne held by the great Kublai. Going again the next year as far as Ceylon, Ching Ho evaded a snare set by the king, and captured him and his whole family and officials, carrying them all to Peking. In 1411 the latter were set free, but a new king was appointed to the vacant throne, who reigned fifty years and sent tribute till 1459; this was only thirty-eight years before Gama arrived at Calicut. It was the last attempt of the Chinese to assert their sway beyond the limits of the Middle Kingdom seaward.[1]

One intimation of a continuance of the intercourse with China from the time of Justinian to that of the Arab travellers Wahab and Abu Zaid, is the Nestorian inscription (page 277). The narratives of the Arabs (A.D. 850 and 877) are trustworthy in their general statements as to the course pursued in the voyage, the port to which they sailed in China, the customs of the people there, and the nature and mode of conducting the trade; they form, in fact, the first authentic accounts we have of the Chinese from western writers, and make us doubt a little whether others like them have not been lost, rather than suppose that such were never written. These interesting relics were translated by Reinaud in 1845, with the text and notes.[2] The second traveller speaks of the sack of the city of Canfu, then the port of all the Arabian merchants, in which one hundred and twenty thousand Mohammedans, Jews, Christians, and Magians, or Parsees, engaged in traffic, were destroyed. This shows the extent and value of the trade. Canfu was Kanpu, a fine port near the modern town of the same name, twenty-five miles from Hangchau, and near Chapu on the Bay of Hangchau; the

[1] Tennent's *Ceylon*, I., pp. 607–626. Yule's *Cathay*, pp. lxvi–lxxvi.

[2] *Relation des Voyages faits par les Arabes et les Persans dans l'Inde et à la Chine dans le IXme Siècle de l'ère Chrètienne*, 2 Vols., Paris, 1845.

Gates of China were probably in the Chusan Archipelago and its numerous channels. Much of the statement made by Abu Zaid respecting the wealth, extent, and splendor of Canfu really refers to the city of Hangchau. The bore in the Tsientang River makes it impossible for ships to lie off that place, and this had its effect in developing Kanpu. The destruction of the capital in 877 contributed to direct part of the trade to Canton, which even then and long after was comparatively a small place, and the people of that part of the country but little removed from gross barbarism. In Marco Polo's time Ganpu was frequented by all the ships that bring merchandise from India.[1]

Prior to the date when he reached the confines of the Pacific, the ravages of the Mongols, under Genghis and his successors, in the regions between the Mediterranean and Caspian, and their great victory near Lignitz, April 12, 1241, had aroused the fears of the Pope and other potentates for their own safety. After the sudden recall of the hosts of Okkodai, in the same year, at his death, and their retreat from Bohemia and Poland to the Dneiper, the Pope determined to send two missions to the Tartars to urge them to greater humanity. One was a Franciscan monk, John of Plano Carpini, who carried the following letter to Batu khan on the Wolga:

INNOCENT, BISHOP, SERVANT OF THE SERVANTS OF GOD, TO THE KING AND PEOPLE OF THE TARTARS.

Since not only men, but also irrational animals, and even the mechanical mundane elements, are united by some kind of alliance, after the example of superior spirits, whose hosts the Author of the universe has established in a perpetual and peaceful order, we are compelled to wonder, not without reason, how you, as we have heard, having entered many lands of Christians and others, have wasted them with horrible desolation, and still, with continued fury, not ceasing to extend further your destroying hands, dissolving every natural tie, neither sparing sex nor age, direct indifferently against all the fury of the sword. We therefore, after the example of the Prince of Peace, desiring to unite all mankind in unity and the fear of God, warn, beseech, and exhort you henceforth to desist wholly from such outrages, and especially from

[1] *Chinese Repository*, Vol. I., pp. 6, 42, 252; Vol. III., p. 115. Yule's *Marco Polo*, Vol. II., pp. 149, 156. *Cathay*, p. cxciii.

the persecution of Christians; and since, by so many and so great offences, you have doubtless grievously provoked the wrath of the Divine majesty, that you make satisfaction to him by suitable penitence; and that you be not so daring as to carry your rage further, because the omnipotent God has hitherto permitted the nations to be laid prostrate before your face. He sometimes thus passes by the proud men of the age; but if they do not humble themselves, he will not fail to inflict the severest temporal punishment on their guilt. And now, behold, we send our beloved brother John, and his companions, bearers of these presents, men conspicuous for religion and honesty, and endued with a knowledge of sacred Scripture, whom we hope you will kindly receive and honorably treat as if they were ourselves, placing confidence in what they may say from us, and specially treat with them on what relates to peace, and fully intimate what has moved you to this extermination of other nations, and what you further intend, providing them in going and returning with a safe conductor, and other things needful for returning to our presence. We have chosen to send to you the said friars, on account of their exemplary conduct and knowledge of the sacred Scriptures, and because they would be more useful to you as imitating the humility of our Saviour, and if we had thought they would be more grateful and useful to you, we would have sent other prelates or powerful men.[1]

M. D'Avezac's essay contains a full account of the travels and proceedings of Carpini and his companion, Benedict, in their hazardous journey of a hundred days from Kiev, across the plains of Russia and Bokhara, to the court of Kuyuk, who had succeeded Okkodai. They were first sent forward by the commanding officers of the several posts to Batu's camp, where the Pope's letter was translated; from hence they were again despatched at the most rapid rate, on horseback, to Kara-korum, where they arrived July 22, 1246, almost exhausted. After they had been there a few days the election was decided, and all ambassadors were introduced to an audience to the khan. when the Pope's envoys alone were without a present. The letter was read, and an answer returned in a few weeks in the same style. These two potentates, so singularly introduced to each other in their mutual ignorance by the letters carried by John, had much more in common in their pretensions to universal dominion by the command of God than they suspected. The khan's letter was as follows:

---

[1] Murray's *Marco Polo*, p. 49. Yule's *Cathay*, p. cxxiii ff. D'Avezac's essay in the *Recueil de Voyages*, IV., p. 399.

LETTER OF THE KING OF THE TARTARS TO THE LORD POPE.

The strength of God, Kuyuk khan, the ruler of all men, to the great Pope. You and all the Christian people who dwell in the West have sent by your messengers sure and certain letters for the purpose of making peace with us. This we have heard from them, and it is contained in your letter. Therefore, if you desire to have peace with us, you Pope, emperors, all kings, all men powerful in cities, by no means delay to come to us for the purpose of concluding peace, and you will hear our answer and our will. The series of your letters contained that we ought to be baptized and to become Christians; we briefly reply, that we do not understand why we ought to do so. As to what is mentioned in your letters, that you wonder at the slaughter of men, and chiefly of Christians, especially Hungarians, Poles, and Moravians, we shortly answer, that this too we do not understand. Nevertheless, lest we should seem to pass it over in silence, we think proper to reply as follows: It is because they have not obeyed the precept of God and of Genghis khan, and, holding bad counsel, have slain our messengers;[1] wherefore God has ordered them to be destroyed, and delivered them into our hands. But if God had not done it, what could man have done to man? But you, inhabitants of the West, believe that you only are Christians, and despise others; but how do you know on whom he may choose to bestow his favor? We adore God, and, in his strength, will overwhelm the whole earth from the east to the west. But if we men were not strengthened by God, what could we do?[2]

The khan took the precaution, which the Pope did not, of putting his reply into an intelligible language, and when it was written in Tartar he had it carefully explained to the friars, who translated it into Latin, and were soon after dismissed. They left the court on November 13, 1246, and "travelled all winter through a wide open country, being commonly obliged to sleep on the ground after clearing away the snow, with which in the morning they often found themselves covered." They reached Kiev the next June, and Carpini was rewarded for his hardships by being appointed Archbishop of Antivari in Dalmatia. As Yule remarks, "they were the first to bring to western Europe the revived knowledge of a great and civilized nation lying in the extreme East upon the shores of the ocean."

Louis XI. of France having heard that Sartach, the son of Batu, then commanding on the western frontier, was a Chris-

---

[1] Allusion is here made to Tartar ambassadors, whom the Russians murdered before the battle of Kalka.

[2] Murray's *Marco Polo*, p. 59.

tian, sent a mission to him, consisting of the friar William Rubruquis[1] and three companions. They left Constantinople May 7, 1253, and proceeded to the Crimea, from whence they set out with a present of wines, fruits, and biscuits intended for the khan. In three days they met the Tartars, who conducted them first to Scacatai, a chieftain by whom, after considerable delay and vexation, they were furnished with everything necessary for a journey across the plains of southern Russia to the Wolga and the camp of Sartach. The monks attempted to convert the rude nomads, but ignorance of the language and suspicions of their intentions interposed great obstacles on both sides. On arriving at the end of their journey, they were disappointed at finding the ruler of these warriors a besotted infidel, who expected all persons admitted into his presence to bring him costly presents. A Nestorian named Cojat, whom Rubruquis regarded as no better than a heretic, was high in authority, and the only medium of communication with the khan. He told the friar to bring his books and vestments and make himself ready to appear before the khan on the morrow; their elegance was such that at the close of the audience Cojat seized most of them under an idle pretext that it was improper to appear in them a second time before Batu khan, to whom Rubruquis and his companions were to be sent.

Their journey was soon after prosecuted by following up the Wolga some distance, and when they arrived at the encampment of Batu khan, he made many inquiries about the resources and power of the French king and the war he was waging with the Saracens. On his introduction, "the friar bent one knee, but finding this unsatisfactory did not choose to contend, and dropped on both. Misled by his position, instead of answering questions he began a prayer for the conversion of the khan, with warning of the dreadful consequences of unbelief. The prince merely smiled; but the derision which was loudly expressed by the surrounding chiefs threw him into a good deal of confusion." The interview was followed by an order to proceed to the court

[1] Or, more correctly, Rubruk, as D'Avezac has pointed out (*Bull. de la Soc. de Géogr.*, 1868), and in whose conclusions Yule joins (*Marco Polo*, second edition, p. 536).

of Mangu, who had succeeded Kuyuk as Grand khan. This long journey occupied four months, through the high land of Central Asia (farther eastward than where Carpini found Kuyuk's court), and subjected them to severe hardships. Mangu received the mission hardly with civility, but having been examined by some Nestorian priests, they were admitted to an audience. The same ceremonies were required as at Batu's court, and inquiries made as to the possessions of the French king, especially the number of rams, horses, and oxen he owned, which, the friar was amazed to learn, were soon to be attacked by the Tartars. No permission to remain could be obtained, but he was furnished with a house and allowed to tarry till the cold mitigated. In this remote region he found a European architect, William Bourchier, and his wife, from Mentz, besides many Armenians, Saracens, and Nestorians, all of whom the khan received. He accompanied the court to Kara-korum, where he nearly became involved in dangerous religious disputes, and on the approach of milder weather was compelled to return to Batu khan, by whom he was sent on, in a south-westerly direction, until he entered Armenia, and thence found his way to Iconium, having been absent nearly two years.

These ambassadors had not the aid of printing to diffuse their narratives, and it was perhaps chiefly owing to the high standing of those who sent them that their relations have been preserved. In the case of many travellers of humbler origin or pretensions, there was no inducement to write what they had seen; these therefore only told their stories, which were lost with the narrators. Even the travels of Marco Polo would perhaps never have been given to the world if the leisure of captivity had not induced him to adopt this method of relieving its tedium. Every examination of his record has added to its reputation for accuracy, both in the position of the cities he mentions or visited and in the events he details; and when it is considered that he dictated it several years after his return to a fellow-prisoner, Rusticiano of Pisa, who wrote it in French, his accuracy is wonderful. The edition by Marsden in 1818 remained for fifty years the chief authority, but the recent editions by Pauthier and Yule, with their full notes, have made the traveller's record vastly better understood, while adding much to our knowledge of mediæval Asia.

Ser Marco Polo, the Venetian, was the son of Nicolo Polo, who with his brother Matteo, nobles and merchants of Venice, first left that city about 1254, and Constantinople in 1260, on a mercantile voyage to the Crimea, from which point a series of events led them eastward as far as China, then lately conquered by Kublai, the Grand Khan and successor of Mangu khan, whom Rubruquis visited. They were favorably received, and when they left Kublai it was under a promise to return, which they did about December, 1274, bearing letters from Gregory X., and accompanied by young Marco, then about sixteen years old. He soon became a favorite with the Emperor, and was able to travel to many parts of the country, spending in all about twenty-one years in the East; the three Polos reached Venice again in 1295. Marco was prefect at Yangchau on the Grand Canal for three years, and this involves a knowledge of Mongolian and Chinese speech and writing, without which he could hardly have administered its official duties. His possession of these accomplishments was nearly indispensable to the post, though Col. Yule infers, from an easily explained mistake in Chapter LXXV., that he did not have them. On reaching Venice, by way of India and Persia, the long-lost travellers appeared so completely altered that their friends and countrymen did not recognize them. Their wealth and entertaining recitals, however, soon restored them to the highest ranks of society. The industry of recent editors has probably brought together all that can be learned of their subsequent history, which is now so well known as to require no further words here.

In the year 1254, Hethum, or Hayton, king of Little Armenia, undertook a journey to Mangu khan, to petition for an abatement of the tribute which he had been obliged to pay the Mongols. Having first sent forth his brother, Sempad, or Sinibald (in 1246), to Kuyuk khan, Hayton himself set out upon the accession to the throne of his successor. Passing through Kars and Armenia Proper to the Wolga, he was there received by Batu and forwarded by a route to the north of that traversed by Carpini to Kara-korum and the Grand khan. At the end of a six weeks' sojourn with the court, during which time he appears to have been kindly received, Hayton commenced his homeward journey via Bishbalig and Songaria to Samarkand, Bokhara, Khorasan, and thence to Tabriz. The accounts of these two embassies, wherein are described many wonderful things concerning the heathens of the East and barbarians upon the route, made up, doubtless, a large part of the "History" (written in 1307) by the king's relative, Hayton of Gorigos.[1] The different positions held by these men and the Polos naturally led each of them to look upon the same people and events with vastly different feelings. The efforts of John of Montecorvino to propagate Christianity in China were undertaken just as the Polos returned, but no detailed accounts of his labors (beyond what Col. Yule has gathered in his *Cathay*) have been preserved.

Among the most important mediæval travellers in Asia was the Moor, Ibn Batuta, who at the age of twenty-one set out (in 1325) upon his journeys, from which he did not return until thirty years later.[2] Abu-Abdullah Mahomed (nicknamed Ibn Batuta, "The Traveller") commenced his wanderings, which were contemporaneous with those of the more doubtful Englishman, Sir John Mandeville, by a series of pilgrimages to the sacred places of his religion; among other excursions, he found time at one period to continue three years in Mecca. Going from one city to another, along the shores of the Mediterranean, and in the countries between it and the Caspian, he at length reached Delhi, where he resided eight years, enjoying—until the latter end of his stay—high favor from the Sultan Mahomed. The versatile Moor occupied the position of judge, though there is good reason to doubt his serious attention to any business while at this magnificent court, other than that of spending his master's money. In the spring of 1342, having recovered

[1] The chapter concerning Cathay appears in Yule's *Cathay*, p. cxcv. A translation of the elder Hayton's narrative is given by Klaproth in the *Journal Asiatique*, IIe Séries, Tome XII., pp. 273 ff.

[2] His work has been very ably edited and translated into French by M. Defrémery and Dr. Sanguinetti (four volumes, Paris, 1858–59), under the patronage of the Asiatic Society of Paris. Several partial translations of the journal have appeared from time to time within the present century.

from a temporary disgrace, he was despatched on an ambassy to China by the Sultan. It seems that a Chinese envoy had arrived at Delhi to request permission for the natives to rebuild a temple in Butan, as they were poor and dependent upon the inhabitants of the plain, and had besought the Chinese government to intercede for them. Ibn Batuta was sent with lavish presents to the Emperor, but a refusal to assist in the building project unless that sovereign would go through the form of paying a poll-tax to the Sultan. This embassy was attacked by a body of Hindus when scarcely out of Delhi, and obliged to return. Again it was sent out, going to Calicut on the Malabar coast, where were found fifteen Chinese vessels or galleys at anchor, whose crews and guard amounted to a thousand men each. The envoy embarked his attendants on one of these ships, but while he remained on shore to pray for a prosperous voyage, a storm sunk the vessel and all on board. After this second mishap the luckless Moor was afraid to return to his master, and went to Sumatra, from whence he found his way to China, landing at Zayton, the present Chinchew, in Fuhkien.

Though it is doubtful if Ibn Batuta, notwithstanding his description of the place, ever reached Peking, his spirited accounts of Zayton, Sinkalan (Canton), Khansa (Hangchau), Kanjanfu, and other centres of trade in the south, are both entertaining and important. Spite of exaggerations, confusion of names and dates, and certain cases of positive fiction, one can hardly fail to put faith in the generality of his statements and conclude in favor of his veracity and genuine character. He mentions that the circulation of paper money, which Marco Polo thought so excellent a device for a king to raise funds, had entirely driven out the use of metallic currency. In every large town he found Mohammedans, ruled by officers of their own persuasion.

The journal of Friar Odoric (1286–1331) contains much of interest in connection with China of the middle ages. This worthy priest landed at "Censcalan" (Canton), after a long and tedious trip from Bagdad round by Sumatra and thence northeast by land to Zayton. Here, says he, "we friars minor have two houses, and there I deposited the bones of our friars who suffered martyrdom for the faith of Jesus Christ." He had brought these relics from Tana, near Bombay. Thence he journeyed to Fuhchau, Hangchau, and Nanking, going on northward to Peking, where the aged archbishop, Corvino, was still living, and remained there three years. His return journey as far as H'lassa was not very different from that of Huc and Gabet in 1843; from the Tibetan capital he probably continued on a westerly course to Cabul and Tabriz, reaching Venice in 1330, after an absence of thirteen years. His itinerary was taken down the following year by William of Solagna, a brother of the order, at Padua.

In this narrative there is mention of a number of characteristics of the Chinese, well known to all the world of to-day, but left wholly unnoticed by other travellers of his age. "His notices of the custom of fishing with cormorants, of the habits of letting the finger-nails grow long, and of compressing the women's feet, as well as of the divisions of the khan's Empire into twelve provinces, with four chief vizirs, are peculiar to him, I believe, among all the European travellers of the age. Polo mentions none of them. The names which he assigns to the Chinese post-stations, and to the provincial Boards of Administration, the technical Turki term which he uses for a sack of rice, etc., are all tokens of the reality of his experience."[1] On the other hand, the influence of superstition upon their own minds rendered most of the religious travellers into Central Asia—Odoric as well as the others—less trustworthy and observant than they would perhaps have been either centuries before or after that period. Everything of a religious sort they regarded as done under the direct agency of the powers of darkness, into whose dominions they were venturing. Too fearful, moreover, to examine candidly or record accurately what they beheld, these pious adventurers were constantly misled by endeavors to explain any uncommon experience by referring the same to their own imperfect or erroneous conceptions. This is true as well of the Romish priests connected with the Peking mission, a few of whose letters have been preserved and re-

[1] Yule, *Cathay and the Way Thither*, p. 21.

cently made known to the public by Col. Yule; among these are Friar Jordanus, Bishop Andrew of Zayton, Pascal of Vittoria, together with the Archbishop of Soltania, author of the "Book of the Estate and Governance of the Great Caan of Cathay."[1]

But much fairer than these missionaries, in his reputation for veracity, was the Jesuit Benedict Goës, who in the century preceding what may be termed the modern period of our knowledge of China, undertook a journey across the desert, to die on the threshold of the Empire. Born in one of the islands of the Azore group, Goës spent his youth in the profession of a soldier on board of the Portuguese fleet. Becoming suddenly converted, he entered the service of the Jesuits as a lay brother—which humble rank he resolutely held during the rest of his career—and was sent to the court of Akbar. His residence in India gained him a high reputation for courage, judgment, and skill in the Persian tongue, the *lingua franca* of Asia at that date. He was selected, therefore, to undertake a journey to the Cathay of Marco Polo, in the capital of which Jerome Xavier thought he had hopes of finding the Christian ruler and descendant of Prester John. Goës set out from Agra in 1602, joined a company of merchants, and with them took a route passing through Cabul, the Hindu kush, along the River Oxus to its head-waters on the Pamir table-land, and so to Yangi Hissar, Yarkand, Aksu, and Suh-chau, where he was detained seventeen months, and finally died, shortly after assistance had been sent him from the mission at Peking.

His journey was full of terrible hardships, and it was to these as well as to the careless treatment he suffered in Suh-chau that he owed his untimely end. Could we have Goës' own narrative of his experience, the information concerning the unknown regions of Central Asia over which he toiled would be of priceless worth. His journals, however, were either lost or destroyed during his miserable detention at the frontier town, and nothing remained save a few meagre notes

[1] About 1330. See ibid., pp. 238–250.

and his faithful Armenian servant Isaac, whose language no one at Peking could understand. Such as it was, an account was compiled from these sources by Ricci himself, and published soon after that missionary's death in the work of Trigautius, *De Christiana Expeditione apud Sinas.*[1] To Benedict Goës we may give the credit of the discovery that *Cathay* and *China* (*Sina*) were in reality one and the same land. It is a curious illustration of the condition of intercommunication between distant parts of the world in those days, that this fact must have been known to the earliest Jesuit missionaries in Peking, though the friars of the same order stationed in India held to a belief in Cambaluc and its Christian prince until far into the seventeenth century.

In many particulars the practical descriptions of Abu Zaid, Masudi,[2] Ibn Wahab, and Marco Polo stand in decided contrast to the details noted down by such as Rubruquis and Odoric. The accounts of all these writers convey the impression that China was in their time free to all travellers. Ibn Wahab, speaking of the regulations practised under the Tang dynasty, observes:

If a man would travel from one province to another, he must take two passes with him, one from the governor, the other from the eunuch [or lieutenant]. The governor's pass permits him to set out on his journey and contains the names of the traveller and those also of his company, also the ages of the one and the other and the clan to which he belongs. For every traveller in China, whether a native or an Arab, or other foreigner, cannot avoid carrying a paper with him containing everything by which he can be verified. The eunuch's pass specifies the quantities of money or goods which the traveller and those with him take along; this is done for the information of officers at the frontier places where these two passes are examined. Whenever a traveller arrives at any of them, it is registered that "Such a one, son of such a one, of such a calling, passed here on such a day, month, and year, having

[1] A translation of this notice appears in Col. Yule's oft-quoted *Cathay and the Way Thither*, pp. 529–591. Trigautius' work appeared in 1615, and was subsequently translated into all the continental languages. Compare Purchas, *His Pilgrimes*, Vol. III., pp. 380, ff.—*A Discourse of the Kingdome of China, taken out of Riccius and Trigavtivs, contayning the Countrey, People, Gouernment*, etc., etc.

[2] Reinaud, *Relation des Voyages*, etc. MM. Barbier de Meynard and Pavet de Courteille, *Les Praries d'Or*, Paris, 1861–66.

such things with him." The government resorts to this means to prevent danger to travellers in their money or goods; for should one suffer loss or die, everything about him is immediately known and he himself or his heirs after his death receive whatever is his.[1]

The same writer speaks of the Mabed, a nation dwelling in Yunnan, on the south-west, who sent ambassadors every year with presents to the Emperor; and in return he sent presents annually to them. These embassies, indeed, were simply trading companies in disguise, who came from the Persians, Arabs, and other nations, with every protestation of respect and humility, bearing presents to the Son of Heaven. The dignity of the Emperor demanded that these should be returned with gifts three or four times the value of this "tribute," and that the ambassadors should be royally entertained during their sojourn at the capital. It is needless to add that such missions were repeated by the merchants as often as circumstances would permit. Entrance into the country overland otherwise than by some such ruse seems to have been withheld after the fall of the Mongol dynasty.

It was, however, not until the subjugation of the Empire by the Manchus that foreign trade was limited to Canton, the jealous conduct of the present rulers being to a certain extent actuated by a fear of similar reprisals from some quarter, which the Mongols experienced. The outrageous behavior of foreign traders themselves must, moreover, be regarded as a chief cause of the watchful seclusion with which they were treated. "Their early conduct," says Sir John Davis, referring to the Portuguese, "was not calculated to impress the Chinese with any favorable idea of Europeans; and when in course of time they came to be competitors with the Dutch and the English, the contests of mercantile avarice tended to place them all in a still worse point of view. To this day the character of the Europeans is represented as that of a race of men intent alone on the gains of commercial traffic, and regardless altogether of the means of attainment. Struck by the perpetual hostilities which existed among these foreign adventurers, as-

---

[1] Reinaud, *Relation*, Tome I., p. 41.

similated in other respects by a close resemblance in their costumes and manners, the government of the country became disposed to treat them with a degree of jealousy and exclusion which it had not deemed necessary to be exercised toward the more peaceable and well ordered Arabs, their predecessors."[1]

These characteristics of avarice, lawlessness, and power have been the leading traits in the Chinese estimate of foreigners from their first acquaintance with them, and the latter have done little to effectually disabuse orientals upon these points. The following record of their first arrival, taken from a Chinese work, is still good authority in the general opinion of the natives:

> During the reign of Chingtih [1506], foreigners from the West, called Fah-lan-kí [Franks], who said that they had tribute, abruptly entered the Bogue, and by their tremendously loud guns, shook the place far and near. This was reported at court, and an order returned to drive them away immediately and stop their trade. At about this time also the Hollanders, who in ancient times inhabited a wild territory and had no intercourse with China, came to Macao in two or three large ships. Their clothes and their hair were red; their bodies tall; they had blue eyes, sunk deep in their heads. Their feet were one cubit and two-tenths long; and they frightened the people by their strange appearance.[2]

The Portuguese Rafael Perestrello sailed in a junk for China in 1516, five years after the conquest of Malacca, and was the first person who ever conducted a vessel to China under a European flag. Ferdinand Andrade came in the next year, in four Portuguese and four Malay ships, and gave great satisfaction to the authorities at Canton by his fair dealings; his galleons were allowed to anchor at Shangchuen, or St. John's Island. His brother Simon came the following year, and by his atrocious conduct entirely reversed the good opinion formed of his countrymen; the Chinese besieged him in port and drove him away in 1521. Others of his countrymen followed him, and one of the earliest ships accompanied some Chinese junks along the coast, and succeeded in establishing a factory

---

[1] *The Chinese*, Vol. I., p. 20.

[2] The term *Hung-mao*, or 'red-haired,' then applied to the Dutch, has since been transferred to the English.

at Ningpo; trade was also conducted at Amoy. In 1537 there were three Portuguese settlements near Canton, one at St. John's, one at a smaller island called Lampaçao (Lang-peh-kau), lying north-west of the Grand Ladrones, and the third just begun on Macao.[1] In 1542 traders had left St. John's for Lampaçao, and ten years afterward, at the time of Xavier's death, trade was concentrated at the latter, where five or six hundred Portuguese constantly resided in 1560. Macao was commenced under the pretext of erecting sheds for drying goods introduced under the appellation of tribute, and alleged to have been damaged in a storm. In 1573 the Chinese government erected a barrier wall across the isthmus joining Macao to the island of Hiangshan, and in 1587 established a civil magistracy to rule the Chinese. By their ill conduct at Ningpo the Portuguese drew upon them the vengeance of the people, who rose upon them and "destroyed twelve thousand Christians, including eight hundred Portuguese, and burned thirty-five ships and two junks." One of their provocative acts is stated to have been going out in large parties into the neighboring villages and seizing the women and virgins, by which they justly lost their privileges in one of the provinces and ports best adapted to European trade. Four years later, in 1549, they were also driven from their newly formed settlement at Chinchew.

The Portuguese have sent four embassies to the Emperor of China. The first envoy, Thomé Pires, was appointed by the Governor at Goa, and accompanied Ferdinand Andrade to Canton, in 1517, where he was received and treated in the usual style of foreign ambassadors. When his mission was reported at Peking the Emperor Chingtih was influenced against it by a subject of the Sultan of Malacca, and detained Pires at Canton three years; the flagitious conduct of Andrade's brother

[1] There stood originally on the site of this town an idol known as *Ama*. *Amau-gau*, or *Ama-kau*, then, meant the 'Harbor of Ama,' which in Portuguese was written *Amacao*, and afterward shortened to *Macao*. Comp. Trigautius, *De Christiana Expeditione apud Sinas*, 1615. Nieuwhof, *Nauwkeurige Beschryvinge van't Gesandschap*, etc., Amsterdam, 1664. Sir A. Ljungstedt, *Historical Sketch of the Portuguese Settlements in China*, Boston, 1836. *Chinese Commercial Guide*, fifth edition, p. 229.

and the character of the Portuguese induced the Emperor to appoint a court to examine whether the embassy was legitimate or spurious, and Pires and his companions were adjudged to be spies and sent back to Canton to be detained till Malacca was restored. This not being done, he and others suffered death in September, 1523; other accounts lead to the inference that he died in prison. Thus the innocent were made to suffer for the guilty. The next embassy was undertaken in 1552, at the suggestion of Xavier, by the Viceroy of Goa, but the mission proceeded no farther than Malacca, the governor of that town refusing to allow it to leave the place—a significant intimation of the degree of subordination and order maintained by the Portuguese in the administration of their new colonies. The third was also sent from Goa in 1667, in the name of Alfonso VI., on occasion of the suspension of the trade of Macao by Kanghí; the expense was defrayed by that colony (about forty thousand dollars), and "the result of it so little answered their expectations that the Senate solicited his Majesty not to intercede in behalf of his vassals at Macao with the government of China, were it not in an imperious and cogent case."

A good opportunity and necessity for this, it was thought, presented itself in 1723, when Magaillans returned to China carrying the answer of the Pope to Kanghí, to send an envoy, Alexander Metello, along with him to Peking. He arrived at court in May, 1727, and had his audience of leave in July, receiving in exchange for the thirty chests of presents which he offered, and which Yungching received with pleasure "as evidences of the affection of the King of Portugal," as many for his master, besides a cup of wine and some porcelain dishes, sent from the Emperor's table, and other presents for himself and his retinue, which were "valuable solely because they were the gifts of a monarch." No more advantage resulted from this than the embassy sent a century previous, though it cost the inhabitants of Macao a like heavy sum. Another and last Portuguese embassy reached Peking in 1753, conducted and ending in much the same manner as its predecessors; all of them exhibiting, in a greater or less degree, the spectacle of humiliating submission of independent nations through their envoys to a court which took pleasure in arrogantly exalting itself on the homage it received, and studiously avoided all reference to the real business of the embassy, that it might neither give nor deny anything. But in estimating its conduct in these respects, it must not be overlooked that the imperial court never associated commercial equality and regulations with embassies and tribute.

The influence and wealth of the Portuguese in China for the last century and a half have gradual decreased. A Swedish knight, Sir Andrew Ljungstedt, published a historical sketch of their doings down to 1833, including an account of the colony, which is still the fullest book on the subject. In 1820 the opium trade was removed to Lintin, and that being the principal source of income, the commerce of the place for many years was at a low ebb. The imperial commissioner Kíying granted some additional privileges to the settlement in 1844, among others, permitting the inhabitants to build and repair new houses, churches, and ships without a license, and to trade at the five ports open to foreign commerce on the same terms as other nations; it was just three centuries before this that the Portuguese were driven away from Ningpo. The anchorage of the Typa was included in the jurisdiction of Macao, but the application of the Portuguese commissioner to surcease payment of the annual ground-rent of five hundred taels to the Chinese met with a decided refusal. Its advantages as a summer resort and its accessibility to a densely peopled region west invite visitors and traders to some extent, but the proximity and wealth of Hongkong make it secondary to that. Its short-lived prosperity in 1839–50, during the opium war and early days of Hongkong, was followed by the enlargement of the coolie trade, which for twenty-five years was the only real business. The Chinese have never ceded the peninsula to the Portuguese crown, although they were powerless to prevent the export of coolies; the relations now between the two countries are not distinctly defined. In 1862 a treaty was negotiated at Peking by Governor Guimaraēs, in which the supremacy of the Portuguese authority over the territory within the Barrier was implied rather than declared in Article IX., wherein the equal appointment of consular officers was mutually agreed to. The Chinese found out, however, that this virtually acknowledged the independence of the colony, and refused to ratify the treaty without an express stipulation asserting their right of domain to the peninsula. It has never been ratified, therefore, but trade is unfettered, and the Chinese inhabitants continue to increase; no rental has been paid for the ground-tax since 1849. The cessation of the coolie trade in 1873 has reduced Macao lower than ever, and it now hardly pays its own officials; all the thrifty or wealthy foreign citizens have removed elsewhere.

The trade between the Spaniards and Chinese has been smaller, and their relations less important than most other European nations. The Spanish admiral Legaspi conquered the Philippines in 1543, and Chinese merchants soon began to trade with Manila; but the first attempt of the Spaniards to enter China was not made until 1575, when two Augustine friars accompanied a Chinese naval officer on his return home from the pursuit of a famous pirate named Li-ma-hon, whom the Spaniards had driven away from their new colony. The missionaries landed at Tansuso, a place on the coast of Kwangtung, and went up to Canton, where they were courteously received. The prefect sent them to the governor at Shauking, by whom they were examined; they stated that their chief object was to form a close alliance between the two nations for their mutual benefit, adding at the same time what their countrymen had done against Li-ma-hon; a second object was their wish to learn the language of China and teach its inhabitants their religion. The governor kept them in a sort of honorable bondage several weeks, and at last sent them back to Manila, doubtless by orders from court, though he alleged as a reason that the pirate Li-ma-hon was still at large. After the return of this mission the governor of the Philippines deemed it advisable to let the trade take its own course, and therefore refused the proposal of a body of Franciscans to enter the country. They, however, made the attempt in a small native vessel, and passed up the river to Tsiuenchau, where they were seized and examined as to their designs. Not being acquainted with the language, they were both themselves deluded and misrepresented to the prefect by a professed native friend who understood Portuguese; after many months' delay they were mortified to learn that no permission to remain would be given, and in 1580 they returned to Manila, not at all disposed to renew the enterprise.

Philip II., however, having received the suggestion made by the Chinese admiral that he should send an embassy to Peking, had already ordered the governor to undertake such an enterprise. He fitted out a mission, therefore, in 1580, at the head of which was Martin Ignatius. It gives one a low idea of the skill of navigators at that day to learn that in this short trip, the vessel being carried up the coast northward of Canton, the party thought it better to land than to try to beat back to their destination. The envoy and all with him were brought before the Chinese officers, who, probably entirely misunderstanding their object, imprisoned them; after considerable delay they were brought before a higher officer and sent on to Canton, where they were again imprisoned; the Portuguese governor of Macao subsequently obtained their liberation. This unlucky attempt, if Mendoza is right in calling it an embassy, was the only one ever made by the Spanish government to communicate with the court of Peking until the mission of Don Sinibaldo de Mas in 1847 and his treaty of 1864. The pecular feature of that treaty was the privilege, first granted to Spanish merchants, of engaging coolies as contract laborers for Cuba. The harsh treatment they received there led the Chinese to send a commission of inquiry in 1873, and to suspend the validity of this article until the truth could be ascertained. This procedure has resulted in a cessation of imported Chinese laborers at Havana.

The Chinese have carried on a valuable trade at Manila, but the Spaniards have treated them with peculiar severity. They are burdened with special taxes, and their immigration is rather restrained. than encouraged. The harsh treatment of Chinese settlers there excited the attention and indignation of one of their countrymen many years ago, and on his return to Canton he exercised all his influence with officers of his own government, making what he had seen the model and the motive to induce them to treat all foreigners at Canton in the same way. It ended in perfecting the principal features of the system of espionage and restriction of the co-hong which existed for nearly a century, until the treaty of 1842;—another instance of the treatment requited upon foreigners for their own acts.

The Dutch commerce with the East commenced after their successful struggle against the Spanish yoke, and soon after completing their independence they turned their arms against the oriental possessions of their enemies, capturing Malacca, the Spice Islands, and other places. They appeared before Macao in 1622 with a squadron of seventeen vessels, but being repulsed with the loss of their admiral and about three hundred men, they retired and established themselves on the Pescadores in 1624. Their occupation of this position was a source of great annoyance both to the Spaniards and to the Chinese authorities in Fuhkien. According to the custom of those days, they began to build a fort, and forced the native Chinese to do their work, treating them with great severity. Many of the laborers were prisoners, whom the Dutch had taken in their attacks. Alternate hostilities and parleys succeeded, the Chinese declaring that the Dutch must send an envoy to the authorities on the mainland; they accordingly despatched Von Mildert to Amoy, and the sub-prefect forwarded him to Fuhchau to the governor. He decided to send a messenger to the Dutch to state to them that trade would be allowed if they would remove to Formosa, but this proposition was refused. However, after a series of attacks and negotiations, the Chinese constantly increasing their forces and the Dutch diminishing in their supplies, the latter acceded to the proposition, and removed to Formosa, where they erected Fort Zealandia in 1624. It is recorded that the Chinese landed five thousand troops on one of the Pescadore Islands; and their determined efforts in repelling the aggressions or occupation of their soil by the Dutch probably raised their reputation for courage, and prevented the repetition of similar acts by others. It was doubtless a good stroke of policy on their part to propose the occupation of Formosa to the Dutch in exchange for the Pescadores, for they had not the least title to it themselves, and hardly knew its exact size or the character of the inhabitants. The Dutch endeavored to extend their power over it, but with only partial success; in the villages around Fort Zealandia they introduced new laws among the inhabitants, and instead of their councils of elders, constituted one of their chief men supervisor in every village, to administer justice and report his acts to the governor of the island.

The moral interests of the natives were not neglected, and in 1626 George Candidius, a Protestant minister, was appointed to labor among them, and took great pains to introduce Christianity. The natives were ignorant of letters, their superstitions resting only on traditions or customs which were of recent origin; the prospects, therefore, of teaching them a better religion were favorable. In sixteen months he had instructed over a hundred in the leading truths of Christianity. The work was progressing favorably, churches and schools were multiplying, the intermarriages of the colonists and natives were bringing them into closer relationship with each other, and many thousands of the islanders had been baptized, when the Dutch governors in India, fearful of offending the Japanese, who were then persecuting the Christians in Japan—in which the Dutch helped them, to their lasting disgrace—restricted these benevolent labors, and discouraged the further conversion of the islanders. Thus, as often elsewhere in Asia, the interests of true religion were sacrificed upon the altar of mammon, and the trade thus bought died from inanition.

During the struggles ensuent upon the overthrow of the Ming dynasty, many thousands of families emigrated to Formosa, some of whom settled under the Dutch, while others planted separate colonies; their industry soon changed the desolate island into a cultivated country, and increased the produce of rice and sugar for exportation. The immigration went on so rapidly as to alarm the Dutch, who, instead of taking wise measures to conciliate and instruct the colonists, tried to prevent their landing, and thereby did much to irritate them and lead them to join in any likely attempt to expel the foreigners.

Meanwhile, their trade with China itself was trifling compared with that of their rivals, the Portuguese, and when the undoubted ascendancy of the Manchus was evident, the government of Batavia resolved to despatch a deputation to Canton to petition for trade. In January, 1653, Schedel was sent in a richly freighted ship, but the Portuguese succeeded in preventing any further traffic, even after the envoy had spent considerable sums in presents to the authorities, and obtained the governor's promise to allow his countrymen to build a factory. Schedel was informed, however, that his masters would do well to send an embassy to Peking, a suggestion favorably entertained by the Company, which, in 1655, appointed Goyer and Keyzer as its envoys. The narrative of this embassy by Nieuwhof, the steward of the mission, made Europeans better acquainted with the country than they had before been—almost the only practical benefit it produced, for as a mercantile speculation it proved nearly a total loss. Their presents were received and others given in return; they prostrated themselves not only before the Emperor in person, but made the *kotow* to his name, his letters, and his throne, doing everything in the way of humiliation and homage likely to please the new rulers. The only privilege their subserviency obtained was permission to send an embassy once in eight years, at which time they might come in four ships to trade.

This mission left China in 1657, and very soon after, the Chinese chieftain, Ching Ching-kung (Koshinga, or Koxinga as his name is written by the Portuguese), began to prepare an attack upon Formosa. The Dutch had foreseen the probability of this onset, and had been strengthening the garrison of Zealandia since 1650 while they were negotiating for trade; Koxinga, too, had confined himself to sending emissaries among his countrymen in Formosa, to inform them of his designs. He set about preparing an armament at Amoy, ostensibly to strengthen himself against the Manchus, meanwhile carrying on his ordinary traffic with the colony to lull all apprehensions until the council had sent away the admiral and force despatched from Java to protect them, when in June, 1661, he landed a force of twenty-five thousand troops, and took up a strong position. The communication between the forts being cut off, the governor sent two hundred and forty men to dislodge the enemy, only half of whom returned alive; one of the four ships in the harbor was burned by the Chinese, and another hastened to Batavia for reinforcements. Koxinga followed up these successes by cutting off all communication between the garrison and the surrounding country, and compelling the surrender of the garrison and cannon in the small fort. Fort Zealandia was now closely invested, but finding himself severely galled, he turned the siege into a blockade, and vented his rage against the Dutch living in the surrounding country, and such Chinese as abetted them. Some of the ministers and schoolmasters were seized and crucified, under the pretext that they encouraged their parishioners to resist; others were used as agents to treat concerning the surrender of the fort. Valentyn has given a clear history of the occupation of Formosa by his countrymen in his great work, and especially of their defeat at Zealandia. He narrates an incident of Rev. A. Hambroek, as does also Nieuwhof, from whose travels it is quoted.

Among the Dutch prisoners taken in the country, was one Mr. Hambroek, a minister. This man was sent by Koxinga to the governor, to propose terms for surrendering the fort; and that in case of refusal, vengeance would be taken on the Dutch prisoners. Mr. Hambroek came into the castle, being forced to leave his wife and children behind him as hostages, which sufficiently proved that if he failed in his negotiation, they had nothing but death to expect from the chieftain. Yet was he so far from persuading the garrison to surrender, that he encouraged them to a brave defence by hopes of relief, assuring them that Koxinga had lost many of his best ships and soldiers, and began to be weary of the siege. When he had ended, the council of war left it to his choice to stay with them or return to the camp, where he could expect nothing but present death; every one entreated him to stay. He had two daughters within the castle, who hung upon his neck, overwhelmed with grief and tears to see their father ready to go where they knew he must be sacrificed by the merciless enemy. But he represented to them that having left his wife and two other children as hostages, nothing but death could attend them if he returned not: so unlocking himself from his daughters' arms, and exhorting everybody to a resolute defence, he returned to the camp, telling them at parting that he hoped he might prove serviceable to his poor fellow-prisoners. Koxinga received his answer sternly; then causing it to be rumored that the prisoners excited the Formosans to rebel, he ordered all the Dutch male prisoners to be slain; some being beheaded, others killed in a more barbarous manner, to the number of five hundred, their bodies stripped quite naked and buried; nor were the women and children spared, many of them likewise being slain, though some of the best were preserved for the use of the commanders, and the rest sold to the common soldiers. Among the slain were Messrs. Hambroek, Mus, Winsam, Ampzingius, and Campius, clergymen, and many schoolmasters.

A force of ten ships and seven hundred men arriving from Batavia, the besieged began to act on the offensive, but were unable to drive Koxinga from the town, though they checked his operations and brought down the garrisons from Kílung and Tamsui to their aid. A letter from the governor of Fuhkien to Coyet, the Dutch governor, came soon after, suggesting a junction of their forces to drive Koxinga away from the coast, after which both could easily conquer him in Formosa. This proposal was followed, but no sooner had the five vessels gone than Koxinga made his advances so vigorously that the garrison was forced to surrender, after a siege of nine months and the loss of one thousand six hundred men. Thus ended the Dutch rule in Formosa, after twenty-eight years' duration.[1]

This loss induced the council at Batavia to prosecute their former enterprise against Amoy, where Koxinga still had a garrison. Twelve vessels were fitted out under Bort, who arrived, in 1662, at the mouth of the River Min, where he was visited by deputies from the governor, and induced to send two of his officers to arrange with him concerning operations. The governor was in the country, and the two officers, on reaching his camp, soon saw that there could be no cordiality between their leaders; this proposal of a foreign power to assist them against the Chinese was too much like that of Wu San-kwei to their chieftains in 1644 for the Manchus to entertain it. Bort, desirous of doing something, commenced a series of attacks on the fleet and garrisons of Koxinga, burning and destroying them

[1] *Chinese Repository*, Vols. I., p. 414, and XX., p. 543. *Journal N. C. Br. R. As. Soc.*, Vol. XI. (1876), Art. I. Moreau de St.-Mêry, *Voyage de l'Ambassade de la Compagnie des Indes orientales Hollandaises vers l'Empereur de la Chine, tiré du journal d'André Everard van Braam Houckgeest*, translated and published in London, 2 Vols., 1798. J. Nieuwhof, *Nauwkeurige Beschryvinge van't Gesandschap der Nederlandtsche Oost-Indische Compagnie van Batavia nar Peking in Sina, door de Heeren Pieter de Goyer en Jacob de Keyser*, Amsterdam, 1664.

in a piratical manner, that was not less ineffectual toward regaining Formosa and obtaining privilege of trade at Canton than harassing to the Chinese on the coast. He returned to Batavia in 1663, and was despatched to Fuhkien in a few months with a stronger force, and ordered to make reprisals on both Manchus and Chinese, if necessary, in order to get satisfaction for the loss of Formosa. The governor received him favorably, and after a number of skirmishes against the rebellious Chinese, Amoy was taken and its troops destroyed, which completed the subjugation of the province to the Manchus. As a reward for this assistance, the real value of which cannot, however, be easily ascertained, the governor lent *two junks* to the Dutch to retake Formosa, but Koxinga laughed at the pitiful force sent against him, and Bort sailed for Batavia.

These results so chagrined the council that they fitted out no more expeditions, preferring to despatch an embassy, under Van Hoorn, to Peking, to petition for trade and permission to erect factories. He landed at Fuhchau in 1664, where he was received in a polite manner. The imperial sanction had been already received, but he unwisely delayed his journey to the capital until his cargo was sold. While discussing this matter the Dutch seized a Chinese vessel bringing bullion from Java contrary to their colonial regulations, and the governor very properly intimated that until restitution was made no amicable arrangement could be completed; consequently Van Hoorn, in order to save his dignity and not contravene the orders of his own government, was obliged to allow the bullion to be carried off, as if by force, by a police officer.

These preliminary disputes were not settled till nearly a year had elapsed, when Van Hoorn and his suite left Fuhchau, and after a tedious journey up the River Min and across the mountains to Hangchau, they reached the canal and Peking, having been six months on the way, "during which they saw thirty-seven cities and three hundred and thirty-five villages." The same succession of prostrations before an empty throne, followed by state banquets, and accompanied by the presentation and conferring of presents, characterized the reception of this embassy as it had all its predecessors. It ended with a similar farce, alike pleasing to the haughty court which received it, and unworthy the Christian nation which gave it; and the "only result of this grand expedition was a sealed letter, of the contents of which they were wholly ignorant, but which did not, in fact, grant any of the privileges they so anxiously solicited." They had, by their performance of the act of prostration, caused their nation to be enrolled among the tributaries of the Grand khan, and then were dismissed as loyal subjects should be, at the will of their liege lord, with what he chose to give them. It was a fitting end to a career begun in rapine and aggression toward the Chinese, who had never provoked them.

The Dutch sent no more embassies to Peking for one hundred and thirty years, but carried on trade at Canton on the same footing as other nations. The ill success of Macartney's embassy in 1793 induced Van Braam, the consular agent at Canton, to propose a mission of salutation and respect from the government of Batavia, on the occasion of Kienlung reaching the sixtieth year of his reign. He hoped, by conforming to Chinese ceremonies, to obtain some privileges which would place Dutch trade on a better footing, but one would have supposed that the miscarriage of former attempts might have convinced him that nothing was to be gained by new humiliations before a court which had just dismissed a well-appointed embassy. The Company appointed Isaac Titsingh, late from Japan, as chief commissioner, giving Van Braam the second place, and making up their cortege with a number of clerks and interpreters, one of whom, De Guignes, wrote the results of his researches during a long residence in Canton, and his travels with the embassy to Peking, under the title of *Voyages à Peking.* It is needless to detail the annoyances, humiliations, and contemptuous treatment experienced by the embassy on its overland journey in midwinter, and the degrading manner in which the Emperor received the envoys: his hauteur was a befitting foil to their servility, at once exhibiting both his pride and their ignorance of their true position and rights. They were brought to the capital like malefactors, treated when there like beggars, and then sent back to Canton like mountebanks to perform the three-times-three prostration at all times and before everything their conductors saw fit; who on their part stood by and laughed at their embarrassment in making these evolutions in their tight clothes. They were not allowed a single opportunity to speak about business, which the Chinese never associate with an embassy, but were entertained with banquets and theatrical shows, and performed many skilful evolutions themselves upon their skates, greatly to the Emperor's gratification, and received, moreover, a present of broken victuals from him, which had not only been honored by coming from his Majesty's own table, but bore marks of his teeth and good appetite; "they were upon a dirty plate, and appeared rather destined to feed a dog than form the repast of a human creature." Van Braam's account of this embassy is one of the most humiliating records of ill-requited obsequiousness before insolent government lackeys which any European was ever called upon to pen. The mission returned to Canton in April, 1796, having attained no more noble end than that of saluting the Emperor, and this, indeed, was all the Chinese meant should be done when themselves suggesting the entire performance; for in order to understand much of their conduct toward their guests, the feelings they entertained toward them must not be lost sight of.

In 1843 the governor-general at Batavia sent T. Modderman to Canton to make inquiries respecting trade at the newly opened ports and establish consulates. The council there had, in 1839, forbidden Chinese to settle in any of their Indian colonies, owing to their skill in engrossing the native trade; but when this prohibition was removed about 1875, the Chinese showed no disposition to emigrate to Java. In 1863 a treaty was negotiated by M. Van der Hoeven at Tientsin, which placed the trade on the same footing as other nations.

The French Government has never sent a formal mission to the capital to petition for trade and make obeisance, though through their missionaries that nation has made Europeans better acquainted with China and given the Chinese more knowledge of western countries than all other Christian nations together. In the year 1289 Philip the Fair received a letter from Argun khan in Persia, and in 1305 another from Oljaitu, both of them proposing joint action against their enemies the Saracens. The originals are still to be seen in Paris. In 1688 Louis XIV. addressed a letter to Kanghí, whom he called "Most high, most excellent, most puissant, and most magnanimous prince, dearly beloved good friend;" and signed himself "Your most dear and good friend, Louis." In 1844 diplomatic relations were resumed by the appointment of a large mission, at the head of which was M. Lagrené, by whom a treaty was formed between France and China.[1]

The Russians have sent several embassies to Peking, and compelled the Chinese to treat them as equals. The first recorded visit of Russian agents at Peking is that of two Cossacks, Petroff and Yallysheff, in 1567, who, however, did not see the Emperor Lungking, who succeeded to the throne that year, because they had brought no presents. In 1619 Evashko Pettlin reached that city, having come across the desert from Tomsk; but he and his companion, having no presents, could not see the "dragon's face," and were dismissed with a letter, which all the learning at Tobolsk and Moscow could not decipher. Thirty-four years after, the Czar Alexis (1653) sent his envoy Baikoff, who refused to prostrate himself before the Emperor Shunchí, and was promptly dismissed. This repulse did not interfere with trade, for in the years 1658, 1672, and 1677 three several trading embassies reached Peking. During all this time Russian and Chinese subjects and soldiers frequently quarrelled, especially along the banks of the Amur, and the necessity of settling these disturbances and pretexts for trouble by fixing the boundary line being evident to both nations, commissioners were appointed and met at Nipchu, where, on August 27, 1689, they signed the first treaty ever agreed upon by the court of Peking. The principal points in it were the retirement of the Russians from Albazin and Manchuria, where they had held their own for thirty-eight years, the freedom of trade, and defining the frontier along the Daourian Mountains. The missionary Gerbillon was mainly instrumental

---

[1] *Chinese Repository*, Vol. XIX., pp. 526–535. Yule's *Cathay*, p. cxxx. Rémusat in *Mém. de l'Acad. Ins.*, Vol. VII., pp. 367, 391 ff.

in settling these disputes, and neither party would probably have lowered its arrogant claims if it had not been through his influence; the Chinese were far the most difficult to please.[1]

Peter sent Ysbrandt Ides in 1692 as his envoy to Peking to exchange the ratifications. His journey across the wilds and wastes of Central Asia took up more time than a voyage by sea, for it was not till a year and eight months that "he could return thanks to the great God, who had conducted them all safe and well to their desired place." Ides' own account of his mission contains very slight notices regarding its object or how he was received; but it is now credibly believed that he performed the *kotow* before the Emperor. About twenty years after his departure, Kanghí sent a Manchu envoy, Tulishen, through Russia to confer with the khan of the Tourgouth Tartars about their return to China, which a portion of them accomplished some years after. Tulishen executed his mission so well that he was sent again as envoy to the Czar about 1730, and reached Petersburg in the reign of Peter II. In 1719 Peter the Great despatched another embassy, under Ismailoff, to arrange the trade then conducted on a precarious footing—an account of which was drawn up by John Bell in 1763. Ismailoff refused to prostrate himself until it was agreed that a Chinese minister, whenever sent to Petersburg, should conform to the usages of the Russians; a safe stipulation, certainly, to a court which never demeans itself to send missions. The evident desirableness of keeping on good terms with the Russians led the Chinese to treat their envoys with unusual respect and attend to the business they came to settle. One of the most instructive books on the kind of intercourse carried on during this period is the *Journal* of Lange, who went first in 1716, and thrice afterward, and has left an account of his residence at Kanghí's capital.[2]

---

[1] *Chinese Repository*, Vol. VIII., pp. 417, 506. Du Halde, *Description géographique, historique, chronologique, politique et physique de l'Empire de la Chine et de la Tartarie chinoise*, 4 vols., Paris, 1735. G. Timkowski, *Travels of the Russian Mission through Mongolia to China*, etc., 2 vols., London, 1827. Klaproth, *Mémoires sur l'Asie*, Tome I., pp. 1–81.

[2] Published in one volume with Bell: *Journey from St. Petersburgh in Russia to Ispahan in Persia*, etc., London, 1715.

In 1727 a fifth mission was sent by the Empress Catherine under Count Vladislavitch, which succeeded in establishing the intercourse on a still better basis, viz., that a mission, consisting of six ecclesiastical and four lay members, should remain at Peking to study the Chinese and Manchu languages, so that interpreters could be prepared and communications carried on satisfactorily; the members were to be changed decennially. The caravans, which had been the vehicles of trade, were regulated about 1730 by the establishment, at Kiakhta and Maimaichin, of two marts on the frontier, where it could be brought under regulations; the last reached Peking in 1755. This embassy was the most successful of all, and partly owing to the Emperor Yungching's desire to counterbalance Jesuit intrigues by raising up other interpreters. This treaty, signed August 27, 1727, remained in force till June, 1858—the longest lived treaty on record. The narrative of George Timkowski, who conducted the relief sent in 1821, gives an account of his trip from Kiakhta across the desert, together with considerable information relating to the Kalkas and other Mongol tribes subject to China. The archimandrite, Hyacinth Batchourin, has given a description of Peking, but such works as the members of the Russian college have written are for the most part still in that language. Up to the present date there have been sixteen archimandrites (1736 to 1880) and many monks attached to the ecclesiastical mission in Peking.[1]

The intercourse of the English with China, though it commenced later than other maritime nations of Europe, has been far more important in its consequences, and their trade greater in amount than all other foreign nations combined. This intercourse has not been such as was calculated to impress the Chinese with a just idea of the character of the British nation as a leading Christian people; for the East India Company, which had the monopoly of the trade between the two countries for nearly two centuries, systematically opposed every effort to diffuse Christian doctrine and general knowledge among them down to the end of their control in 1834.

---

[1] Dudgeon's monograph on *Russian Intercourse with China* contains notices of all events of any importance between the two nations, digested with great care, pp. 80, Peking, 1872. Also, Martin's *China*, Vol. I., p. 386.

The first English vessels anchored off Macao in July, 1635, under the command of Weddell, who was sent to China in accordance with a "truce and free trade" which had been entered into between the English merchants and the viceroy of Goa, who gave letters to the governor of Macao. The fleet was coldly received and Weddell deluded with vain promises until the Portuguese fleet had sailed for Japan, when he was denied permission to trade. Two or three of his officers having visited Canton, he was very desirous to participate in the traffic, and proceeded with his whole fleet up to the Bogue forts, where this desire was made known to the commanders of the forts, who promised to return an answer in a week. Meanwhile the Portuguese so misrepresented them to the Chinese that the commander of the forts concluded to end the matter by driving them away. Having made every preparation during the period the fleet was waiting, an attack was first made upon a watering-boat by firing shot at it when passing near the forts.

"Herewith the whole fleet, being instantly incensed, did, on the sudden, display their bloody ensigns; and, weighing their anchors, fell up with the flood, and berthed themselves before the castle, from whence came many shot, yet not any that touched so much as hull or rope; whereupon, not being able to endure their bravadoes any longer, each ship began to play furiously upon them with their broadsides; and after two or three hours, perceiving their cowardly fainting, the boats were landed with about one hundred men: which sight occasioned them, with great distractions, instantly to abandon the castle and fly; the boats' crews, in the meantime, without let, entering the same and displaying his Majesty's colors of Great Britain upon the walls, having the same night put aboard all their ordnance, fired the council-house and demolished what they could. The boats of the fleet also seized a junk laden with boards and timber, and another with salt. Another vessel of small moment was surprised, by whose boat a letter was sent to the chief mandarins at Canton, expostulating their breach of truce, excusing the assailing of the castle, and withal in fair terms requiring the liberty of trade."[1] This letter was shortly answered,

[1] Staunton's *Embassy*, Vol. I., pp. 5–12.

and after a little explanatory negotiation, hastened to a favorable conclusion on the part of the Chinese by what they had seen, trade was allowed after the captured guns and vessels were restored and the ships supplied with cargoes.

No other attempt to open a trade was made till 1664, and during the change of dynasty which took place in the interim, the trade of all nations with China suffered. The East India Company had a factory at Bantam in Java, and one at Madras, but their trade with the East was seriously incommoded by the war with the Dutch; when it was renewed in 1664, only one ship was sent to Macao, but such were the exactions imposed upon the trade by the Chinese, and the effect of the misrepresentations of the Portuguese, that the ship returned without effecting sale. This did not discourage the Company, however, who ordered their agents at Bantam to make inquiries respecting the most favorable port and what commodities were most in demand. They mentioned "Fuhchau as a place of great resort, affording all China commodities, as raw and wrought silk, tutenague, gold, china-root, tea, etc." A trade had been opened with Koxinga's son in Formosa and at Amoy, but this rude chieftain had little other idea of traffic than a means of helping himself to every curious commodity the ships brought, and levying heavy imposts upon their cargoes. A treaty was indeed entered into with him, in which the supercargoes, as was the case subsequently in 1842, stipulated for far greater privileges and lighter duties than Chinese goods and vessels would have had in English ports. Besides freedom to go where they pleased without any one attending them, access at all times to the king, liberty to choose their own clerks and trade with whom they pleased, it was also agreed "that what goods the king buys shall pay no custom; that rice imported pay no custom; that all goods imported pay three per cent. *after sale*, and all goods exported be custom free." The trade at Amoy was more successful than at Zealandia, and a small vessel was sent there in 1677, which brought back a favorable report. In 1678 the investments for these two places were $30,000 in bullion and $20,000 in goods; the returns were chiefly in silk goods, tutenague, rhubarb, etc.;

the trade was continued for several years, apparently with considerable profit, though the Manchus continually increased the restrictions under which it labored. In 1681 the Company ordered their factories at Amoy and Formosa to be withdrawn, and one established at Canton or Fuhchau, but in 1685 the trade was renewed at Amoy.

The Portuguese managed to prevent the English obtaining a footing at Canton until about 1684; and, as Davis remarks, the stupid pertinacity with which they endeavored to exclude them from this port and trade is one of the most striking circumstances connected with these trials and rivalries. It is the more inexplicable in the case of the Portuguese, for they could carry nothing to England, nor could they force the English to trade with them at second hand; theirs was truly the "dog in the manger" policy, and they have subsequently starved upon it. In 1689 a duty of five shillings per pound was laid upon tea imported into England; and the principal articles of export are stated to have been wrought silks of every kind, porcelain, lacquered-ware, a good quantity of fine tea, some fans and screens. Ten years after, the court of directors sent out a consul's commission to the chief supercargo, Mr. Catchpoole, which constituted him king's minister or consul for the whole Empire of China and the adjacent islands. In 1701 an attempt was made by him to open a trade, and he obtained permission to send ships to Chusan or Ningpo; an investment in three vessels, worth £101,300, was accordingly made, but he found the exactions of the government so grievous, and the monopoly of the merchants so oppressive, that the adventure proved a great loss, and the traders were compelled to withdraw. The Company's hopes of trade at that port must, however, have been great, for their investment to Amoy that year was only £34,400, and to Canton £40,800. In 1702 Catchpoole also established a factory at Pulo Condore, an island near the coast of Cochinchina which had been taken by the English. The whole concern, however, experienced a tragical end in 1705, when the Malays rose upon the English, murdered them all, and burned the factory. The Cochinchinese are said to have instigated this treacherous attack to regain the island, which was claimed by them.

The extortions and grievances suffered by the traders at Canton were increased in 1702 by the appointment of an individual who alone had the right of trading with them and of farming it out to those who had the means of doing so. The trade seems hardly, even at this time, to have taken a regular form, but by 1720 the number and value of the annual commodities had so much increased that the Chinese established a uniform duty of four per cent. on all goods, and appointed a body of native merchants, who, for the privilege of trading with foreigners, became security for their payment of duties and good behavior. The duty on imports was also increased to about sixteen per cent. and an enormous fee demanded of purveyors before they could supply ships with provisions, besides a heavy measurement duty and cumshaw to the collector of customs. These exactions seemed likely to increase unless a stand was taken against them. This was done by a united appeal to the governor in person in 1728 ; yet the relief was only temporary, for the plan was so effectual and convenient for the government that the co-hong was ere long re-established as the only medium through which the foreign trade could be conducted. An additional duty of ten per cent. was laid upon all exports, which no efforts were effectual in removing until the accession of Kienlung in 1736. This apparently suicidal practice of levying export duties is, in China, really a continuation of the internal excise or transit duties paid upon goods exported in native vessels as well as foreign.

The Emperor, in taking off the newly imposed duty of ten per cent., required that the merchants should hear the act of grace read upon their knees; but the foreigners all met in a body, and each one agreed on his honor not to submit to this slavish posture, nor make any concession or proposal of accommodation without acquainting the rest. The Emperor also required the delivery of all the arms on board ship, a demand afterward waived on the payment of about ten thousand dollars. The hong merchants shortly became the only medium of communication with the government, themselves being the exactors of the duties and contrivers of the grievances, and when complaints were made, the judges of the equity of their own acts.

In 1734 only one English ship came to Canton, and one was sent to Amoy, but the extortions there were greater than at the other port, whereupon the latter vessel withdrew. In 1736 the number of ships at Canton was four English, two French, two Dutch, one Danish, and one Swedish vessel; the Portuguese ships had been restricted to Macao before this date.

Commodore Anson arrived at Macao in 1742, and as the Centurion was the first British man-of-war which had visited China, his decided conduct in refusing to leave the river until provisions were furnished, and his determination in seeking an interview with the governor, no doubt had a good effect. A mixture of decision and kindness, such as that exhibited by Anson when demanding only what was in itself right, and backed by an array of force not lightly to be trifled with or incensed, has always proved the most successful way of dealing with the Chinese, who on their part need instruction as well as intimidation. The constant presence of a ship of war on the coast of China would perhaps have saved foreigners much of the personal vexations, and prevented many of the imposts upon trade which the history of foreign intercourse exhibits, making it in fact little better than a recital of annoyances on the part of a government too ignorant and proud to understand its own true interests, and recriminations on the part of traders unable to do more than protest against them.

In consequence of the exactions of the government and the success of the co-hong in preventing all direct intercourse with the local authorities, the attempt was again made to trade at Amoy and Ningpo. The Hardwicke was sent to Amoy in 1744, and obliged to return without a cargo. Messrs. Flint and Harrison were despatched to Ningpo in 1755, and were well received; but when the Holderness subsequently came to trade, it was with difficulty that she procured a cargo, and an imperial edict was promulgated soon after restricting all foreign ships to Canton. In 1759 the factory at Ningpo was demolished, so that Mr. Flint, who repaired there that year, was unable to do anything toward restoring the trade. This gentleman was a person of uncommon perseverance and talents, and had mastered the difficulties of the Chinese language so as to act as interpreter at Canton twelve years before he was sent on his mission. "The ungrateful return which his energy and exertions in their service met with from his employers," justly observes Sir John Davis, "was such as tended in all probability, more than any other cause, to discourage his successors from undertaking so laborious, unprofitable, and even hazardous a work of supererogation."

On his arrival at Ningpo, Mr. Flint, finding it useless to attempt anything there, proceeded in a native vessel to Tientsin, from whence he succeeded in making his case known to the Emperor Kienlung. A commissioner was deputed to accompany him overland to Canton; Mr. Flint proceeded to the English factory soon after his arrival, and the foreigners of all nations assembled before the commissioner, who informed them that the hoppo had been superseded, and all duties remitted over six per cent. on goods and the cumshaw and tonnage dues on ships. The sequel of Mr. Flint's enterprise was unfortunate, and the mode the Chinese took to bring it about thoroughly characteristic.

It proved, however, that these fair appearances were destined only to be the prelude to a storm. Some days afterward the governor desired to see Mr. Flint for the purpose of communicating the Emperor's orders, and was accompanied by the council of his countrymen. When the party had reached the palace, the hong merchants proposed their going in one at a time, but they insisted on proceeding together; and on Mr. Flint being called for, they were received at the first gate and ushered through two courts with seeming complaisance by the officers in waiting; but on arriving at the gate of the inner court they were hurried, and even forced into the governor's presence, where a struggle ensued with their brutal conductors to force them to do homage after the Chinese fashion until they were overpowered and thrown down. Seeing their determination not to submit to these base humiliations, the governor ordered the people to desist; and then telling Mr. Flint to advance, he pointed to an order, which he called the Emperor's edict, for his banishment to Macao, and subsequent departure for England, on account of his endeavoring to open a trade at Ningpo contrary to orders from Peking. He added that the native who had written the petition in Chinese was to be beheaded that day for traitorously encouraging foreigners, which was performed on a man quite innocent of what these officers were pleased to call a crime. Mr. Flint was soon after conveyed to Tsienshan, a place near Macao, called Casa Branca by the Portuguese, where he was imprisoned two years and a half and then sent to England.[1]

[1] Davis, *Chinese*, Vol. I., p. 58.

Mr. Flint stated to the Company that a fee of one thousand two hundred and fifty dollars to the governor would set him at liberty, but they contented themselves with a petition. The punishment he received from the Chinese for this attempt to break their laws would not have been considered as unmerited or unjust in any other country, but the neglect of the Company to procure the liberation of one who had suffered so much to serve them reflects the greatest reproach upon that body.

The whole history of the foreign trade, as related by Auber in his chronological narrative, during the one hundred and fifty years up to 1842 is a melancholy and curious chapter in national intercourse. The grievances complained of were delay in loading ships and plunder of goods on their transit to Canton; the injurious proclamations annually put up by the government accusing foreigners of horrible crimes; the extortions of the underlings of office; and the difficulty of access to the high authorities. The hong merchants, from their position as traders and interpreters between the two parties, were able to delude both to a considerable extent, though their responsibility for the acts and payments of foreigners, over whom they could exercise no real restraint, rendered their situation by no means pleasant. The rule on which the Chinese government proceeded in its dealings with foreigners was this: "The barbarians are like beasts, and not to be ruled on the same principles as citizens. Were any one to attempt controlling them by the great maxims of reason, it would tend to nothing but confusion. The ancient kings well understood this, and accordingly ruled barbarians by misrule; therefore, to rule barbarians by misrule is the true and best way of ruling them." The same rule in regard to foreign traders was virtually acted on in England during the reign of Henry VII., and the ideas among the Chinese of their power over those who visit their shores are not unlike those which prevailed in Europe before the Reformation.

The entire ignorance of foreign traders of the spoken and written language of China brought them into contempt with all classes, and where all intercourse was carried on in a jargon which each party despised, the results were often misunderstanding, dislike, and hatred. Another fruitful source of difficulty was the turbulent conduct of sailors. The French and English seamen at Whampoa, in 1754, carried their national hatred to such a degree that they could not pursue their trade without quarrelling; and a Frenchman having killed an English sailor, the Chinese stopped the trade of the former nation until the guilty person was given up, though he was subsequently liberated. The Chinese allotted two different islands in the river at Whampoa for the recreation of the seamen of each nation, in order that such troubles might be avoided in future. A similar case occurred at Canton in 1780, when a Frenchman killed a Portuguese sailor at night in one of the merchants' houses and fled to the consul's for refuge. The Chinese demanded the criminal, and after some days he was given up to them and publicly strangled; this punishment he no doubt merited, although it was the first case in which they had interfered where the matter was altogether among foreigners. In 1784 a native was killed by a ball left in a gun when firing a salute, and the Chinese, on the principle of requiring life for life, demanded the man who had fired the gun. Knowing that the English were not likely to give him up, the police seized Mr. Smith, the supercargo of the vessel, and carried him a prisoner into the city. On the seizure of this gentleman the ships' boats were ordered up from Whampoa with armed crews to defend the factories. A messenger from the Chinese, however, declared that their purpose in seizing Smith was simply to examine him on the affair, to which statement the captive himself added a request that the gunner should be sent up to the authorities and submit to their questions. Trusting too much to their promises, the man was allowed to go alone before the officials within the city walls, when Mr. Smith was immediately liberated and the unhappy gunner strangled, after some six weeks' confinement, by direct orders of the Emperor. The man, probably, underwent no form of trial intelligible to himself, and his condemnation was the more unjust, as by Section CCXCII. of the Chinese code he was allowed to ransom himself by a fine of about twenty dollars. As a counterpart of this tragedy, the Chinese stated (and there was reason for believing them) that a native who had accidentally killed a British seaman about the same time was executed for the casualty.

The Chinese mode of operations, when it was impracticable to get possession of the guilty or accused party, was well exhibited in the case of a homicide occurring in 1807. A party of sailors had been drinking at Canton, when a scuffle ensued, and the sailors put the populace to flight, killing one of the natives in the onset. The trade was promptly stopped, and the hong merchant who had *secured* the ship held responsible for the delivery of the offender. Eleven men were arrested and a court instituted in the Company's hall before Chinese judges, Captain Rolles, of H. B. M. ship Lion, being present with the committee. The actual homicide could not be found, but one Edward Sheen was detained in custody, which satisfied the Chinese while he remained in Canton; but when the committee wished to take him to Macao with them they resisted, until Captain Rolles declared that otherwise he should take the prisoner on board his own ship, which he did. Being now beyond their reach, the authorities were fain to account for the affair to the supreme tribunal at the capital by inventing a tale, stating that the prisoner had caused the death of a native by raising an upper window and accidentally dropping a stick upon his head as he was passing in the street below. This statement was reported to his Majesty as having been concurred in by the English after a full examination of witnesses who attested to the circumstances; the imperial rescript affirmed the sentence of the Board of Punishments, which ordered that the prisoner should be set at liberty after paying the usual fine of twenty dollars provided by law to defray the funeral expenses. The trade was thereupon resumed.[1]

Another case of homicide occurred at Whampoa in 1820, when the authorities reported that the butcher of another ship, who had committed suicide the day of the inquest, was the guilty person. The court of directors very properly blamed their agents at Canton for their complicity in this subterfuge, and spoke of "the paramount advantages which must invari-

[1] Sir G. T. Staunton, *Penal Code of China*, p. 516.

ably be derived from a strict and inflexible adherence to truth as the foundation of all moral obligations."[1]

Other cases of murder and homicide have since occurred between foreigners and natives. In the instance of the British frigate Topaze at Lintin Island in 1822, whose crew had been attacked on shore, her captain successfully resisted the surrender of a British subject for the death of two natives in the affray. The dignified and united action of the British authorities on this occasion was a striking contrast to the weakness of the Americans the year before in the case of Terranova. It proved the beneficial results of a stand for the right, for no foreigner has since been executed by the Chinese. It also proved the necessity and advantages of competent interpreters and translators, inasmuch as the case owed much of its success to Dr. Morrison's aid, which had been rejected by the hong merchants the previous year.[2]

These cases are brought together to illustrate the anomalous position which foreigners once held in China. They constituted a community by themselves, subject chiefly to their own sense of honor in their mutual dealings, but their relations with the Chinese were like what lawyers call a "state of nature." The change of a governor-general, of a collector of customs, or senior hong merchant, involved a new course of policy according to the personal character of these functionaries. The committee of the East India Company had considerable power over British subjects, especially those living in Canton, and could deport them if they pleased; but the consuls of other nations had little or no authority over their countrymen. Trade was left at the same loose ends that politics were, and the want of an acknowledged tariff encouraged smuggling and kept up a constant spirit of resistance and dissatisfaction between the native and foreign merchants, each party endeavoring to get along as advantageously to itself as practicable. Nor was there any acknowledged medium of communication between them, for the

---

[1] Auber, *China: An Outline of its Government, Laws, Policy*, etc., p. 286, London, 1834.

[2] *Chinese Repository*, Vol. II., pp. 513–515. Morrison's *Memoirs*, Vol. II. App., p. 10. Auber, *China, its Government*, etc., pp. 288–309.

consuls, not being credited by the Chinese Government, came and went, hoisted or lowered their flags, without the slightest notice from the authorities. Trade could proceed, perhaps, without involving the nations in war, since if it was unprofitable it would cease; but while it continued on such a precarious footing national character suffered, and the misrepresentations produced thereby rendered explanations difficult, inasmuch as neither party understood or believed the other.

The death of the unfortunate gunner in 1784, and the large debts owed to the English by the hong merchants, which there seemed no probability of recovering, induced the British Government to turn its attention to the situation of the king's subjects in China with the purpose of placing their relations on a better footing. The flagitious conduct of a Captain M'Clary, who seized a Dutch vessel at Whampoa in 1781, which Davis narrates,[1] and the inability of the Company to restrain such proceedings, also had its weight in deciding the crown to send an embassy to Peking. Colonel Cathcart was appointed envoy in 1788, but his death in the Straits of Sunda temporarily deferred the mission, which was resumed on a larger scale in 1792, when the Earl of Macartney was sent as ambassador, with a large suite of able men, to place the relations between the two nations, if possible, on a well-understood and secure footing. Two ships were appointed as tenders to accompany his Majesty's ship Lion (64), and nothing was omitted, either in the composition of the mission or the presents to the Emperor, to insure its success. Little is known regarding its real impression upon the Chinese; they treated it with great consideration while it remained in the country, although at an estimated cost of $850,000, and probably dismissed it with the feeling that it was one of the most splendid testimonials of respect that a tributary nation had ever paid their court. The English were henceforth registered among the nations who had sent tribute-bearers, and were consequently only the more bound to obey the injunctions of their master.[2]

---

[1] *The Chinese*, Vol. I., p. 63.

[2] Sir G. L. Staunton, *Authentic Account of an Embassy from the King of Great Britain to the Emperor of China*, 3 vols., London, 1798.

To the European world, as well as to the British nation, however, this expedition may be said to have opened China, so great was the interest taken in it and so well calculated were the narratives of Staunton and Barrow to convey better ideas of that remote country. "Much of the lasting impression which the relations of Lord Macartney's embassy leave on the mind of his reader," to quote from a review of it, "must be ascribed, exclusive of the natural effect of clear, elegant, and able composition, to the number of persons engaged in that business, the variety of their characters, the reputation they already enjoyed or afterward acquired; the bustle and stir of a sea voyage; the placidity and success which finally characterized the intercourse of the English with the Chinese; the splendor of the reception the latter gave to their European guests; the walks in the magnificent gardens of the 'Son of Heaven;' the picturesque and almost romantic navigation upon the imperial canal; and perhaps, not less for the interest we feel for every grand enterprise, skilfully prepared, and which proves successful, partly in consequence of the happy choice of the persons and the means by which it was to be carried into effect." This impression of the grandeur and extent of the Chinese Empire has ever since more or less remained upon the minds of all readers of Staunton's narrative; but truer views were imparted than had before been entertained concerning its real civilization and its low rank among the nations.

That the embassy produced some good effect is undeniable, though it failed in most of the principal points. It also afforded the Chinese an opportunity of making arrangements concerning that future intercourse which they could not avoid, even if they would not negotiate, and of acquiring information concerning foreign nations which would have proved of great advantage to them. Their contemptuous rejection, ignorant though they decided to remain of the real character of these courtesies, of peaceful missions like those of Macartney, Titsingh, and others, takes away much of our sympathy for the calamities which subsequently came upon them. With characteristic shortsightedness they looked upon the very means taken to arrange existing ill-understood relations as a reason for considering those relations as settled to their liking, and a motive to still further exactions.

For many years subsequent to this embassy the trade went on without interruption, though the demands and duties were rather increased than diminished, and the personal liberty of foreigners more and more restricted. The government generally, down to the lowest underling, systematically endeavored to degrade and insult foreigners in the eyes of the populace and citizens of Canton, in order, in case of any disturbance, to have their co-operation and sympathy against the "barbarian devils." The dissolute and violent conduct of many foreigners toward the Chinese gave them, alas, too many arguments for their aspersions and exactions, and both parties too frequently considered the other fair subjects for imposition.

In 1802 the English troops occupied Macao by order of the governor-general of India, lest it should be attacked by the French, but the news of the treaty of peace arriving soon after, they re-embarked almost as soon as the Chinese remonstrated. The discussion was revived, however, in 1808, when the French again threatened the settlement; and the English, under Admiral Drury, landed a detachment to assist the Portuguese in defending it. The Chinese, who had previously asserted their complete jurisdiction over this territory, and which a little examination would have plainly shown, now protested against the armed occupation of their soil, and immediately stopped the trade and denied provisions to the ships. The English traders were ordered by the Committee to go aboard ship, and the governor refused to have the least communication with the admiral until the troops were withdrawn. He attempted to proceed to Canton in armed boats, but was repulsed, and finally, in order not to implicate the trade any further (a step not at all apprehended in protecting the Portuguese), he wisely withdrew his troops and sailed for India. The success of the native authorities greatly rejoiced them; a temple was built on the river's bank to commemorate their victory, and a fort, called "Howqua's Folly" by foreigners (since washed away), erected to guard the river at that point.

The Chinese, ignorant of the principles on which international intercourse is regulated among western powers, regarded every hostile demonstration between them in their waters as directed toward themselves, and demanding their interference. Though often powerless to defend themselves against their own piratical subjects, as has been manifested again and again—for example, in 1810, and also in 1660, when Koxinga ravaged the coast—they still assume that they are able to protect all foreigners who "range themselves under their sway." This was exhibited in 1814, when the British frigate Doris, against all the acknowledged rights of a nation over its own waters, and simply because it could be done with impunity, cruised off the port of Canton to seize American vessels. The provincial authorities ordered the Committee to send her away, saying that if the English and Americans had any petty squabbles they must settle them between themselves and not bring them to China. The Committee stated their inability to control the proceedings of men-of-war, whereupon the Chinese began a series of annoyances against the merchants and shipping, prohibiting the employment of native servants, entering their houses to seize natives, molesting and stopping ships' boats proceeding up and down the river on business, hindering the loading of the ships, and other like harassing acts so characteristic of Asiatic governments when they feel themselves powerless to cope with the real object of their fear or anger. These measures proceeded at last to such a length that the Committee determined to stop the British trade until the governor would allow it to go on, as before, without molestation, and they had actually left Canton for Whampoa, and proceeded down the river some distance, before he showed a sincere wish to arrange matters amicably. A deputation from each party accordingly met in Canton, and the principal points in dispute were at last gained. In this affair the Chinese would be adjudged to have been altogether in the right according to international law. At this time the governor-general conceded three important points to the Committee, viz., the right of corresponding with the government, under seal, in the Chinese language, the unmolested employment of native servants, and the assurance that the houses of foreigners should not be entered without permission; nor were these stipulations ever retracted or violated.

The proceedings in this affair were conducted with no little apprehension on both sides, for the value of the traffic was of such importance that neither party could really think of stopping it. Besides the revenue accruing to government from duties and presents, the preparation and shipment of the articles in demand for foreign countries give employment to millions of natives in different parts of the Empire, and had caused Canton to become one of the greatest marts in the world. The governor and his colleagues were responsible for the revenue and peaceful continuance of the trade; but through their ignorance of the true principles of a prosperous commerce, their fear of the consequences resulting from any innovation or change, or the least extension of privileges to the few half-imprisoned foreigners, they thought their security lay rather in restriction than in freedom, in a haughty bearing to intimidate, and not in conciliation to please their customers. On the other hand, the existence of the East India Company's charter depended in a good degree upon keeping a regular supply of tea in England, and therefore the success of the Committee's bold measure of stopping the trade depended not a little upon the ignorance of the Chinese of the great power a passive course of action would give them.

The government at home, on learning these proceedings, resolved to despatch another ambassy to Peking in order to state the facts of the case at court, and if possible agree upon some understood mode of conducting trade and communicating with the heads of government. Lord Amherst, who like Lord Macartney had been governor-general of India, was appointed ambassador to Peking, and Henry Ellis and Sir George T. Staunton associated with him as second and third commissioners. A large suite of able men, with Dr. Morrison as principal interpreter, accompanied the ambassy, and the usual quantity and variety of presents.[1] The mission reached the capital August 28, 1816, but was summarily dismissed without an audience, because the ambassador would not perform the kotow

[1] Ellis, *Embassy to China*, London, 1840. Sir J. F. Davis, *Sketches of China*, 2 Vols., London, 1841. Clarke Abel, *Narrative of a Journey in the Interior of China and a Voyage to and from that Country in* 1816 *and* 1817, London, 1818. R. Morrison, *A View of China*, etc., Macao, 1817.

or appear before his Majesty as soon as he arrived; the intrigues of the authorities at Canton with the high officers about the Emperor to defeat the ambassy by deceiving their master have also been adduced as reasons for its failure. Its real failure, as we can now see, was owing to the utter misconception of their true position by the Emperor and his officials, arising from their ignorance, pride, isolation, and mendacity, all combining to keep them so until resistless force should open them to meliorating influences. It was the last attempt of the kind, and three alternatives only remained: the resort to force to compel them to enter into some equitable arrangement, entire submission to whatever they ordered, or the withdrawal of all trade until they proposed its resumption. The course of events continued the second until the first was resorted to, and eventuated in laying open the whole coast to the enterprise of western nations.

At the close of the East India Company's exclusive rights in China, the prospect for the continuance of a peaceful trade was rather dubious. The enterprising Mr. Marjoribanks despatched a vessel to ascertain how far trade could be carried on along the coast, which resulted in satisfactorily proving that the authorities were able and determined to stop all traffic, however desirous the people might be for it. The contraband trade in opium was conducted in a manner that threatened ere long to involve the two nations, but the Company nominally kept itself aloof from it by bringing none in its ships: the same Company, however, did everything in India to encourage the growth and sale of the drug, and received from it at the time of its dissolution an annual revenue of nearly two millions sterling. During its whole existence in China the East India Company stood forward as the defenders of the rights of foreigners and humanity, in a manner which no community of isolated merchants could have done, and to some extent compelled the Chinese to treat all more civilly. As a body it did little for the encouragement of Chinese literature or the diffusion of Christian truth or of science among the Chinese, except the printing of Morrison's Dictionary and an annual grant to the Anglo-Chinese College; and although Dr. Morrison was their official translator for twenty-five years, the directors never gave him the empty compliment of enrolling him in the list of their servants, nor contributed one penny for carrying on his great work of translating and printing the Bible in Chinese. They set themselves against all such efforts, and during a long existence the natives of that country had no means put into their hands, by their agency, of learning that there was any great difference in the religion, science, or civilization of European nations and their own.

The trade of the Americans to China commenced in 1784, the first vessel having left New York February 22d of that year, and returned May 11, 1785; it was commanded by Captain Green, and the supercargo, Samuel Shaw, on his return, gave a lucid narrative of his voyage to Chief Justice Jay. His journal, published in 1847, contains the only record of this voyage, and furnishes many curious facts about the political and social relations existing between foreigners then in China. Our trade with China steadily increased after this date, and has been the second in amount for many years. The only political event in the American intercourse up to 1842 was the suspension of trade in October, 1821, in consequence of the homicide of a Chinese by a sailor at Whampoa. The American merchants were really helpless to carry the trial of Terranova to a just conclusion against the Chinese law, which peremptorily required life for life wherever foreigners were concerned, and gave him up on the assurance that his life was in no danger. They are stated, in a narrative published in the *North American Review*, to have told Howqua at the trial on board the Emily at Whampoa, "We are bound to submit to your laws while we are in your waters; be they ever so unjust, we will not resist them." The poor man was taken out of the ship by force, while all the Americans present protested against the unfair trial he had had; he was then promptly carried to Canton and strangled at the public execution ground (October 25); his body was given up next day, and the trade reopened.[1]

[1] Shaw's *Journal*, Boston, 1847. *North American Review*, January, 1835. *Chinese Repository*, September, 1836. Sir Geo. T. Staunton's *Notices of China*, second edition, pp. 409–432, 1850.

The American Government neither took notice of this affair nor made remonstrance against its injustice, but still left the commerce, lives, and property of its citizens wholly unprotected, and at the mercy of Chinese laws and rulers. The consuls at Canton were merely merchants, having no salary from their government, no funds to employ interpreters when necessary, or any power over their countrymen, and came and went without the least notice or acknowledgment from the Chinese.

The trade and intercourse of the Swedes, Danes, Prussians, Italians, Austrians, Peruvians, Mexicans, or Chilians, at Canton, have been attended with no peculiarities or events of any moment. None of these nations ever sent "tribute" to the court of the Son of Heaven, and their ships traded at Canton on the same footing with the English. The voyage of Peter Osbeck, chaplain to a Swedish East Indiaman, in 1753, contains considerable information relating to the mode of conducting the trade and the position of foreigners, who then enjoyed more liberty and suffered fewer extortions than in later years.[1]

The term *fan-kwei*, by which they were all alike called by the Cantonese, indicated the popular estimation, and this epithet of '*foreign devil*' did much, in the course of years, to increase the contempt and ill will which it expressed, not only there but throughout the Empire, for they were thereby maligned before they were known. Another term, *i*, has been raised into notice by its condemnation in the British Treaty as an epithet for British subjects or countries. This word, there rendered '*barbarian*,' conveys to a native but little more than the idea that the people thus called do not understand the Chinese language and usages, and are consequently less civilized. This epithet *barbarian* meant to the Greeks those who could not speak Greek, as it did to Shakspeare those who were not English; likewise among the Chinese, under *i* were included great masses of their own subjects. By translating *wai i* as '*outside barbarians*,' foreigners have been misrepresented in the status they

[1] *A Voyage to China and the East Indies, translated from the German by* John R. Forster, 2 vols., London, 1771.

held among educated natives, which was not that of savages but of the illiteracy growing out of their ignorance of the language and writings of Confucius.

The ancient Chinese books speak of four wild nations on the four sides of the country, viz., the *fan*, *í*, *tih*, *man*; the first two seem to have been applied to traders from the south and west, and grew into more distinct expressions because these traders often acted so outrageously. Other terms, as "western ocean men," "far-travelled strangers," and "men from afar," have occasionally been substituted when *í* was objected to. When used as a general term, without an opprobrious addition, *í* is as well adapted as any to denote all foreigners; but the most recent usage gives prominence to the terms *wai kwoh* and *yang jăn* ('outside country' and 'ocean man'). Among educated natives the national names are becoming more and more common, as *Ying kwoh*, *Fah kwoh*, *Mei kwoh*, *Teh kwoh*, for England, France, America, Germany, etc.

CHAPTER XXII.

ORIGIN OF THE FIRST WAR WITH ENGLAND.

THE East India Company's commercial privileges ceased in 1834, and it is worthy of note that an association should have been continued in the providence of God as the principal representative of Christendom among the Chinese, which by its character, its pecuniary interests, and general inclination was bound in a manner to maintain peaceful relations with them, while every other important Asiatic kingdom and island, from Arabia to Japan, was at one time or another during that period the scene of collision, war, or conquest between the nations and their visitors. Its monopoly ceased when western nations no longer looked upon these regions as objects of desire, nor went to Rome to get a privilege to seize or claim such pagan lands as they might discover, and when, too, Christians began to learn and act upon their duty to evangelize these ignorant races. China and Japan were once open to such agencies as well as trade, but no effective measures were taken to translate or distribute the pure word of God in them.

Believing that the affairs of the kingdoms of this world are ordered by their Almighty Governor with regard to the fulfilment of his promises and the promulgation of his truth, the first war between England and China is not only one of great historical interest, but one whose future consequences cannot fail to exercise increasing influence upon many millions of mankind. This war was extraordinary in its origin as growing chiefly out of a commercial misunderstanding; remarkable in its course as being waged between strength and weakness, conscious superiority and ignorant pride; melancholy in its end as forcing the weaker to pay for the opium within its borders against all its laws, thus paralyzing the little moral power its feeble government could exert to protect its subjects; and momentous in its results as introducing, on a basis of acknowledged obligations, one-half of the world to the other, without any arrogant demands from the victors or humiliating concessions from the vanquished. It was a turning-point in the national life of the Chinese race, but the compulsory payment of six million dollars for the opium destroyed has left a stigma upon the English name.

In 1834 the select Committee of the East India Company repeated its notice given in 1831 to the authorities at Canton, that its ships would no longer come to China, and that a king's officer would be sent out as chief to manage the affairs of the British trade. The only "chief" whom the Chinese expected to receive was a commercial headman, qualified to communicate with their officers by petition, through the usual and legal medium of the hong merchants. The English Government justly deemed the change one of considerable importance, and concluded that the oversight of their subjects and the great trade they conducted required a commission of experienced men. The Rt. Hon. Lord Napier was consequently appointed as chief superintendent of British trade, and arrived at Macao July 15, 1834, where were associated with him in the commission John F. Davis and Sir G. B. Robinson, formerly servants of the Company, and a number of secretaries, surgeons, chaplains, interpreters, etc., whose united salaries amounted to $91,000. On arriving at Canton the tide-waiters officially reported that three "foreign devils" had landed. As soon as Governor Lu had learned that Lord Napier had reached Macao, he ordered the hong merchants to go down and intimate to him that he must remain there until he obtained legal permission to come to Canton; for, having received no orders from court as to the manner in which he should treat the English superintendent, he thought it the safest plan to adhere to the old regulations.

Lord Napier had been ordered to report himself to the governor at Canton *by letter*. A short extract from his instructions will show the intentions of the English Government in constituting the commission, and the entirely wrong views it had of the notions of the Chinese respecting foreign intercourse, and the character they gave to the English authorities. Lord Palmerston says:

In addition to the duty of protecting and fostering the trade of his Majesty's subjects with the port of Canton, it will be one of your principal objects to ascertain whether it may not be practicable to extend that trade to other parts of the Chinese dominions. . . . It is obvious that, with a view to the attainment of this object, the establishment of direct communications with the port of Peking would be desirable; and you will accordingly direct your attention to discover the best means of preparing the way for such communications, bearing constantly in mind, however, that peculiar caution and circumspection will be indispensable on this point, lest you should awaken the fears or offend the prejudices of the Chinese Government, and thus put to hazard even the existing opportunities of intercourse by a precipitate attempt to extend them. In conformity with this caution you will abstain from entering into any new relations or negotiations with the Chinese authorities, except under very urgent and unforeseen circumstances. But if any opportunity for such negotiations should appear to you to present itself, you will lose no time in reporting the circumstance to his Majesty's government, and in asking for instructions; but previously to the receipt of such instructions you will adopt no proceedings but such as may have a general tendency to convince the Chinese authorities of the sincere desire of the king to cultivate the most friendly relations with the Emperor of China, and to join with him in any measures likely to promote the happiness and prosperity of their respective subjects.

Governor Lu's messengers arrived too late to detain the British superintendent at Macao, and a military officer despatched to intercept him passed him on the way; so that the first intimation the latter received of the governor's disposition was in an edict addressed to the hong merchants, from which two paragraphs are extracted:

On this occasion the barbarian *eye*, Lord Napier, has come to Canton without having at all resided at Macao to wait for orders; nor has he requested or received a permit from the superintendent of customs, but has hastily come up to Canton—a great infringement of the established laws! The custom-house waiters and others who presumed to admit him to enter are sent with a communication requiring their trial. But in tender consideration for the said barbarian *eye* being a new-comer, and unacquainted with the statutes and laws of the Celestial Empire, I will not strictly investigate. . . . As to his object in coming to Canton, it is for commercial business. The Celestial Empire appoints officers, civil ones to rule the people, military ones to intimidate the wicked. The petty affairs of commerce are to be directed by the merchants themselves; the officers have nothing to hear on the subject. . . . If any affair is to be newly commenced, it is necessary to wait till a respectful memorial be made, clearly reporting it to the great Emperor, and his mandate be received; the great ministers of the Celestial Empire are not permitted to have intercourse by letters with outside barbarians. If the said barbarian eye *throws in* private letters, I, the governor, will not at all receive or look at them. With regard to the foreign factory of the Company without the walls of the city, it is a place of temporary residence for foreigners coming to Canton to trade; they are permitted only to eat, sleep, buy and sell in the factories; they are not allowed to go out to ramble about.[1]

How unlike were these two documents and the expectations of their writers! The governor felt that it was safest to wait for an imperial mandate before commencing a new affair, and refused to receive *a letter* from a foreign officer. Had he done so he would have laid himself open to reprimand and perhaps punishment from his superiors; and in saying that the superintendent should report himself and apply for a permit before coming to Canton, he only required what the members of the Company had always done when they returned from their summer vacation at Macao. Lord Napier thought he had the same liberty to come to Canton without announcing himself that other and private foreigners exercised; but an officer of his rank would have pleased the Chinese authorities better by observing their regulations. He had thought of this contingency before leaving England, and had requested "that in case of necessity he might have authority to treat with the government at Peking;" this request being denied, he desired that his appointment to Canton might be announced at the capital; this not being granted, he wished that a communication from the home authorities might be addressed to the governor of Canton; but this was deemed inexpedient, and he was directed to "go to Canton and report himself by letter." These reasonable requests involved no loss of dignity, but the court of St. James chose to send out a superintendent of trade, an officer partaking of both ministerial and consular powers, and ordered him to act in a certain manner, involving a violation of the regulations of the country where he was going, without providing for the alternative of his rejection.

---

[1] *Correspondence relating to China* (Blue Book), p. 4. *Chinese Repository*. Vol. III., p. 188; Vol. XI., p. 188.

To Canton, therefore, he came, and the next day reported himself by letter to the governor, sending it to the city gates. His lordship was directed to have nothing to do with the hong merchants; and therefore when they waited upon him the morning of his arrival, with the edict they had been sent down to Macao to "enjoin upon him," he courteously dismissed them, with an intimation that "he would communicate immediately with the viceroy in the manner befitting his Majesty's commission and the honor of the British nation." The account of the reception of his communication is taken from his correspondence:

On the arrival of the party at the city gates, the soldier on guard was despatched to report the circumstance to his superior. In less than a quarter of an hour an officer of inferior rank appeared, whereupon Mr. Astell offered my letter for transmission to the viceroy, which duty this officer declined, adding that his superior was on his way to the spot. In the course of an hour several officers of nearly equal rank arrived in succession, each refusing to deliver the letter on the plea that higher officers would shortly attend. After an hour's delay, during which time the party were treated with much indignity, not unusual on such occasions, the linguists and hong merchants arrived, who entreated to become the bearers of the letter to the viceroy. About this time an officer of rank higher than any of those who had preceded him joined the party, to whom the letter was in due form offered, and as formally refused. The officer having seen the superscription on the letter, argued, that "as it came from the superintendent of trade, the hong merchants were the proper channels of communication:" but this obstacle appeared of minor importance in their eyes, upon ascertaining that the document was styled a *letter*, and not a *petition*. The linguists requested to be allowed a copy of the address, which was of course refused.

About this time the *kwang-hieh*, a military officer of the rank of colonel, accompanied by an officer a little inferior to himself, arrived on the spot, to whom the letter was offered three several times and as often refused. The senior hong merchant, Howqua, after a private conversation with the colonel, requested to be allowed to carry the letter in company with him and ascertain whether it would be received. This being considered as an insidious attempt to circumvent the directions of the superintendents, a negative was made to this and other overtures of a similar tendency. Suddenly all the officers took their departure for the purpose, as it was afterward ascertained, of consulting with the viceroy. Nearly three hours having been thus lost within the city, Mr. Astell determined to wait a reasonable time for the return of the officers, who shortly afterward reassembled; whereupon Mr. Astell respectfully offered the letter in question three separate times to the colonel and afterward to the other officers, all of whom distinctly refused even to touch it; upon which the party returned to the factory.[1]

---

[1] *Chinese Repository*, Vol. XI., p. 27.

The governor reported this occurrence at court in a memorial, in which, after stating that his predecessor had instructed the Company's supercargoes to make arrangements that "a *taipan* [or supercargo, the word being applied to all foreign consuls] acquainted with affairs should still be appointed to come to Canton to control and direct the trade," he states what had occurred, and adds:

> The said barbarian eye would not receive the hong merchants, but afterward repaired to the outside of the city to present a letter to me, your Majesty's minister, Lu. On the face of the envelope the forms and style of equality were used, and there were absurdly written the characters *Ta Ying kwoh* ['Great English nation']. Now it is plain on the least reflection, that in keeping the central and outside [people] apart, it is of the highest importance to maintain dignity and sovereignty. Whether the said barbarian eye has or has not official rank there are no means of thoroughly ascertaining. But though he be really an officer of the said nation, he yet cannot write letters on equality with the frontier officers of the Celestial Empire. As the thing concerned the national dignity, it was inexpedient in the least to allow a tendency to any approach or advance by which lightness of esteem might be occasioned. Accordingly orders were given to Han Shau-king, the colonel in command of the military forces of this department, to tell him authoritatively that, by the statutes and enactments of the Celestial Empire, there has never been intercourse by letters with outside barbarians; that, respecting commercial matters, petitions must be made through the medium of the hong merchants, and that it is not permitted to offer or present letters. . . . On humble examination it appears that the commerce of the English barbarians has hitherto been managed by the hong merchants and *taipans;* there has never been a barbarian eye to form a precedent. Now it is suddenly desired to appoint an officer, a superintendent, which is not in accordance with old regulations. Besides, if the said nation has formed this decision, it still should have stated in a petition the affairs which, and the way how, such superintendent is to manage, so that a memorial might be presented requesting your Majesty's mandate and pleasure as to what should be refused, in order that obedience might be paid to it and the same be acted on accordingly. But the said barbarian eye, Lord Napier, without having made any plain report, suddenly came to the barbarian factories outside the city to reside, and presumed to desire intercourse to and fro by official documents and letters with the officers of the Central Flowery Land; this was, indeed, far out of the bounds of reason.[1]

The governor here intimates that the intention of his government in requesting a *taipan* to come to Canton was only to have a responsible officer with whom to communicate. In refusing

[1] *Chinese Repository*, Vol. III., p. 327.

to receive an 'eye,' or superintendent, therefore, he did not, in his own view of the case, suppose that he was refusing, nor did he or the court of Peking intend to refuse, the residence of a supercargo, for they were desirous to have responsible heads appointed over the commerce and subjects of every nation trading at Canton. These occurrences were discussed by the Hon. John Quincy Adams in his lecture upon the war with China, delivered in 1841, in which he alleged that the rejection of Lord Napier's letter and mission was a sufficient reason for the subsequent contest. He showed the impolicy of allowing the Chinese ideas of supremacy over other nations, and exhibited their natural results in the degraded position of foreigners. He had, however, only an imperfect conception of the strength of this assumption, but it was not debated in this contest between Governor Lu and Lord Napier. The former was not blameworthy for endeavoring to carry the laws of his own country into execution, while the latter was doing his best to obey the instructions of his own sovereign. The question of the propriety of those laws, involving as they did the supremacy of the Emperor over the English, or the feasibility of those instructions, could only be discussed and settled by their principals. Whether this assumption was a proper ground of hostilities is altogether another question. When Lord Napier's letter was rejected he would probably have referred home to his government for further instructions if it had intended to settle the question of supremacy, but he did not do so, nor did the ministry refer to it or remonstrate against the unhandsome treatment their representative received.

The refusal of Lord Napier to confer with the hong merchants, and of the governor to receive any communication except a petition, placed the two parties in an awkward position. In his letter the former stated the object of his coming to Canton, and requested that his excellency would accord him an interview in order that their future intercourse might be arranged; and considering the desirableness of giving him accurate views, the party at the gate would have acted wisely in permitting the hong merchants to take it to him. The governor was irritated and alarmed, and vented his anger upon the unfortunate hong merchants. These had two or three interviews with Lord Napier after the rejection of the letter, but as they now said it would not be received unless superscribed *pin*, or 'petition,' they were dismissed. Having heard that there was a party among the British residents in Canton who disapproved of the proceedings of the superintendent, they vainly endeavored to call a meeting of the disaffected on the 10th of August, while his lordship assembled all of his countrymen next day, and found that they generally approved of his conduct. On the 14th he reviews his position in consequence of the rejection of his letter and the subsequent conduct of the governor. After recommending the renewal of the effort to open better understood relations with the court of Peking by a demand upon the Emperor to allow the same privileges to all foreigners residing in China which Chinese received in foreign countries, he goes on to say:

My present position is, in one point of view, a delicate one, because the trade is put in jeopardy on account of the difference existing between the viceroy and myself. I am ordered by his Majesty to "go to Canton and there report myself by letter to the viceroy." I use my best endeavors to do so; but the viceroy is a presumptuous savage, and will not grant the same privileges to me that have been exercised constantly by the chiefs of the committee. He rakes up obsolete orders, or perhaps makes them for the occasion; but the fact is, the chiefs used formerly to wait on the viceroy on their return from Macao, and continued to do it until the viceroy gave them an order to wait upon him, whereupon they gave the practice up. Had I even degraded the king's commission so far as to petition through the hong merchants for an interview, it is quite clear by the tenor of the edicts that it would have been refused. Were he to send an armed force and order me to the boat, I could then retreat with honor, and he would implicate himself; but they are afraid to attempt such a measure. What then remains but the stoppage of the trade or my retirement? If the trade is stopped for any length of time the consequences to the merchants are most serious, as they are also to the unoffending Chinese. But the viceroy cares no more for commerce, or for the comfort and happiness of the people as long as he receives his pay and plunder, than if he did not live among them. My situation is different; I cannot hazard millions of property for any length of time on the mere score of etiquette. If the trade shall be stopped, which is probable enough in the absence of the frigate, it is possible I may be obliged to retire to Macao to let it loose again. Then has the viceroy gained his point and the commission is degraded. Now, my lord, I argue that whether the commission retires by force of arms or by the injustice practised on the merchants, the viceroy has committed an outrage on the British crown which should be equally chastised. The whole system of government here is that of subterfuge and shifting the blame from the shoulders of the one to the other. . . . I shall not go, however, without publishing in Chinese and disseminating far and wide the base conduct of the viceroy in oppressing the merchants, native as well as foreign, and of my having taken the step out of pure compassion to them. I can only once more implore your lordship to force them to acknowledge my authority and the king's commission, and if you can do that you will have no difficulty in opening the ports at the same time.[1]

Such were the sentiments and desires which filled the mind of the English superintendent. He is in error in saying that the governor would not grant him the same privileges as had been accorded to the chiefs of the Company. The present question was not about having an interview, but regarding the superscription of his letter; for the chiefs of the Company sent their sealed communications through the hong merchants as petitions. The governor stopped the English trade on the 16th, and two days after issued an explanatory paper in reply to the report that his orders on that subject had been carried into effect. This document sets forth his determination to uphold the old regulations, and a few sentences from it are here introduced as a contrast with the preceding despatch. The conviction of the governor in the supremacy of his Emperor over all foreign nations which had sent embassies to his court, and his own official position making him responsible for successfully maintaining the laws over foreigners, must be borne in mind:

To refer to England: should an official personage from a foreign country proceed to the said nation for the arrangement of any business, how could he neglect to have the object of his coming announced in a memorial to the said nation's king, or how could he act contrary to the requirements of the said nation's dignity, doing his own will and pleasure? Since the said barbarian eye states that he is an official personage, he ought to be more thoroughly acquainted with these principles. Before, when he offered a letter, I, the governor, saw it inexpedient to receive it, because the established laws of the Celestial Empire do not permit ministers and those under authority to have private intercourse by letter with outside barbarians, but have, hitherto, in commercial affairs, held the merchants responsible; and if perchance any barbarian merchant should have any petition to make requesting the investigation of any affair, [the laws require] that by the said *taipan* a duly prepared petition should be in form presented, and an answer by proclamation awaited. There has never been such a thing as outside barbarians sending in a letter.

---

[1] *Chinese Repository*, Vol. XV., p. 68.

He then says that there had never been any official correspondence to and fro between the native officers and the barbarian merchants; by this he means a correspondence of equality, which the Chinese Government had indeed never yielded. The idea of supremacy never leaves him—witness, for example, the following strain, peculiarly Chinese:

The hong merchants, because the said barbarian eye will not adhere to the old regulations, have requested that a stop should be put to the said nation's commerce. This manifests a profound knowledge of the great principles of dignity. It is most highly praiseworthy. Lord Napier's perverse opposition necessarily demands such a mode of procedure, and it would be most right immediately to put a stop to buying and selling. But considering that the said nation's king has hitherto been in the highest degree reverently obedient, he cannot in sending Lord Napier at this time have desired him thus obstinately to resist. The some hundreds of thousands of commercial duties yearly coming from the said country concern not the Celestial Empire the extent of a hair or a feather's down. The possession or absence of them is utterly unworthy of one careful thought. Their broadcloths and camlets are still more unimportant, and of no regard. But the tea, the rhubarb, the raw silk of the Inner Land, are the sources by which the said nation's people live and maintain life. For the fault of one man, Lord Napier, must the livelihood of the whole nation be precipitately cut off? I, the governor, looking up and embodying the great Emperor's most sacred, most divine wish, to nurse and tenderly cherish as one all that are without, feel that I cannot bring my mind to bear it! Besides, all the merchants of the said nation dare dangers, crossing the seas myriads of miles to come from far. Their hopes rest wholly in the attainment of gain by buying and selling. That they did not attend when summoned by the hong merchants to a meeting for consultation, was because they were under the direction of Lord Napier; it assuredly did not proceed from the several merchants' own free will. Should the trade be wholly cut off in one morning, it would cause great distress to many persons, who, having travelled hither by land and sea, would by one man, Lord Napier, be ruined. They cannot in such case but be utterly depressed with grief. . . . I hear the said eye is a man of very solid and expansive mind and placid speech. If he consider, he can himself doubtless distinguish right and wrong: let him on no account permit himself to be deluded by men around him. . . . Hereafter, when the said nation's king hears respecting these repeated orders and official replies, [he will know] that the whole wrong lies on the barbarian eye; it is in nowise owing to any want on the part of the Celestial Empire of extreme consideration for the virtue of reverential obedience exercised by the said nation's king.[1]

He consequently sent a deputation of officials to Lord Napier to inquire why he had come to Canton, what business he

[1] *Chinese Repository*, Vol. III., p. 235.

was appointed to perform, and when he would retire to Macao. The letter was again handed them, but the superscription still remained, and they refused to touch it. They, however, learned enough to be able to inform their master what he wished to know: the real point of dispute between the two could only be settled between their sovereigns. The governor by this depu tation showed a desire to make some arrangement, and the trade would probably have been shortly reopened had not Lord Napier carried out his idea, two days after, of appealing to the people in order to explain the reasons why the governor had stopped the trade and brought distress on them. The paper simply detailed the principal events which had occurred since his arrival, laying the blame upon the "ignorance and obstinacy" of the governor in refusing to receive his letter, and closing with—"The merchants of Great Britain wish to trade with all China on principles of mutual benefit; they will never relax in their exertions till they gain a point of equal importance to both countries; and the viceroy will find it as easy to stop the current of the Canton River as to carry into effect the insane determination of the hong."

In many of the former proceedings between the Chinese and foreigners, based as they were upon incorrect ideas, the rules of diplomacy elsewhere observed formed no guide; but the publication of this statement was unwise and dangerous. Not only did it jeopardize the lives and property of British subjects, but of all other foreigners residing at Canton, to whose safety and interests, as involved with his own dispute, Lord Napier makes no reference in his despatches. Happily, Governor Lu did not appease his irritation by letting loose the populace of Canton, which was highly excited, but by imprisoning members of the co-hong for allowing the superintendent to come to the city.

The governor and his colleagues stopped the English trade on September 2d, in a proclamation containing many inaccurate statements and absurd reasonings, in which he forbade either natives or foreigners to give aid or comfort to Lord Napier. Communication with the shipping at Whampoa was also interdicted, so that, in reality, the entire foreign trade was interrupted. A guard of Chinese troops was placed near the Company's factory, but no personal distress was felt on account of the interdict. H. B. M. frigates Andromache and Imogene were ordered up to protect the shipping and persons of British subjects, and the two vessels anchored at Whampoa on the 11th. In their passage through the Bogue they returned the fire from the forts, with little damage to either; and on anchoring, a lieutenant and boat's crew were despatched to Canton to protect the English factory. These decisive proceedings troubled the native authorities not a little, who, on their part, prepared for stronger measures by blocking up the river and stationing troops about Whampoa, but were relieved when they found that the ships remained at their anchorage.

Lord Napier sent a protest against the proceedings of the governor in stopping the trade, through the Chamber of Commerce and hong merchants; but at this juncture his health gave way so rapidly that three days after the frigates had anchored he decided to return to Macao and wait for instructions. The Chinese detained him on his passage down until the ships were out of the river; but he sank and died October 11th, a fortnight after reaching that city. As soon as he left Canton the trade was reopened. On hearing that the ships had reached Whampoa, the Emperor degraded or suspended all the officials who had been in any way responsible; but when he learned that "Lord Napier had been driven out, and the two ships of war dragged over the shallows and expelled," he restored most of those whom he had thus punished. The governor also vented his indignation upon ten of his subordinates, by subjecting them to torture in order to "ascertain if they were guilty of illicit connection with foreigners." The drama was closed on the part of the Chinese by an imperial mandate: "The English barbarians have an open market in the Inner Land, but there has hitherto been no interchange of official communications. Yet it is absolutely requisite that there should be a person possessing general control, to have the special direction of affairs; wherefore let the governor immediately order the hong merchants to command the said separate merchants, that they send a letter back to their country calling for the appointment of another person as *taipan*, to come for the control and direction of commercial affairs, in accordance with the old regulations."

The principles on which the Chinese acted in this affair are plainly seen. To have granted official intercourse by letter would have been to give up the whole question, to consider the king of England as no longer a tributary, and so release him and his subjects from their allegiance. To do so would not only permit them to come into their borders as equals, subject to no laws or customs, but would further open the door for resistance to their authority, armed opposition to their control, and ultimate in possession of their territory. The governor hints at this when speaking of the necessity of restraining the barbarian eye: "With regard to territory, it would also have its consequences." These would be the probable results of allowing such a mode of address from the Kalkas, or Tibetans, and the Emperor felt the importance of its concession in a way that Lord Napier himself could not appreciate. Nevertheless, with the inconsistency of children, the Son of Heaven and his courtiers, in the mandate just quoted, yield their obligations to justly govern the far-travelled strangers, by requiring them to get a countryman "to exercise general control" and live among them —thus establishing the principle of ex-territoriality within their borders which they now find so irksome.

It is pitiable, and natural too, that the Chinese should have had notions so incorrect and dangerous, for it led them to misinterpret every act of foreigners. Their entire intercourse with Europeans, since the Portuguese first came to their shores, had conspired to strengthen the opinion that all traders were crafty, domineering, avaricious, and contumacious, and must be kept down in every possible way to insure safety to the Chinese natives. The indignation of the Emperor on hearing of the entrance of the ships of war was mixed with great apprehension, "lest there were yet other ships staying at a distance ready to bring in aid to him" [Lord Napier]. Ignorant as he was of the true character of the embassies which had been received at Peking, he was still more likely to take alarm at any attempt to open an equal intercourse, and disposed to resist it as he would a forcible occupation of his territory, of which it was, in his view, only the precursor.

That these were the feelings of the rulers at Peking cannot be doubted; and we must know what views and fears actuated them in order to understand their proceedings. If the position of England in the eyes of the Chinese had been fully known in London, the unequal contest imposed upon Lord Napier would either have been avoided or directed against the imperial government. The offer of an amicable intercourse was given to the Chinese, but through the inapplicable instructions which his lordship received this offer was not made to the weaker and ignorant party in such a way as not to excite its fears, while it fully explained the real position and intentions of England, and through her all Christendom, in seeking intercourse with China. Yet so long as the court of Peking, in virtue of the Emperor's vicegerency over mankind, claimed supremacy over other nations, the struggle to maintain that assumption was sure to come. This false notion did, however, really continue among them for about forty years, till five foreign ministers had their first audience with the Emperor Tungchí, June, 1873, and stood before his throne as they presented their credentials.

The British residents at Canton saw the point of difficulty clearly, and in a petition to the king in council, dated December 4, 1834, recommended that a commissioner be sent to one of the northern ports with a small fleet to arrange the matter of future intercourse. In this petition they "trace the disabilities and restrictions under which British commerce now labors to a long acquiescence in the arrogant assumption of supremacy over the monarchs and people of other countries claimed by the Emperor of China for himself and his subjects," and conclude that "no essentially beneficial result can be expected to arise out of negotiations in which such pretensions are not decidedly repelled." The recommendations of the petitioners were disregarded in England. The cabinet disapproved of the spirit of Lord Napier's despatches, and intimated to him that it was "not by force and violence that his Majesty intended to establish a commercial intercourse between his subjects and China, but by conciliatory measures." After the events of 1834 if a commissioner, backed by a small fleet, had been immediately appointed to Peking to arrange the terms of future intercourse, the subsequent war might have been averted, though it is more likely that the imperial court would have rejected all overtures until compelled to treat by force.

As things were situated at Canton, it was really impossible for the Chinese Government to carry on a line of policy with respect to foreign intercourse which would at once maintain its assumptions, avoid the risk of a rupture, squeeze all the money possible out of the trade, and repress the complaints of the British merchants. The cessation of the Company's monopoly, as well as its control over all British subjects, had weakened the leverage of the local authorities to manage them, to a greater degree than they were aware.

The trade was conducted during the next season to the satisfaction of all parties. That of other nations had been practically stopped with that of the English, but the suspension was at a dull season of the year. Their consuls took no official part in the dispute, though they had some ground for complaint in the suspension of their trade and the imprisonment of their countrymen. The Chinese shopkeepers known as "outside merchants" having been interdicted trading at all with foreigners, went to the governor's palace in a large body and soon obtained a removal of the restriction. The hong merchants themselves instigated this decree, for these shopkeepers, while deriving large profits from their business, were almost free from the extortions which the monopolists suffered. All the extraordinary expenses incurred by the provincial exchequer in the late affair were required of these unfortunate men; and they *must* get it out of the trade in the best way they could. Amelioration could not be expected from such a system; for as soon as the foreigners began to complain, the hong merchants were impelled by every motive to misrepresent their complaints to the governor and quash every effort to obtain redress. The situation of foreigners there was aptly likened by a writer on the subject to the inmates of the Zoölogical Garden in Regent's Park: "They [the animals] have been free to play what pranks they pleased, so that they made no uproar nor escaped from confinement. The keepers looked sharply after them and tried to keep them quiet, because annoyed by the noise they made and responsible for the mischief they might commit if they got at liberty. They might do what was right in their own eyes with each other. The authorities of China do not expect from wild and restless barbarians the decorum and conduct exemplified in their own great family."

The peculiar position of the relations with the Chinese and the value of the trade, present and prospective, was so great that these events called out many pamphleteers both in England and the East. The servants of the Company naturally recommended a continuance of the peaceable system, urging that foreigners should obey the laws of the Empire where they lived and not interfere with the restrictions put upon them. Others counselled the occupation of an island on the coast, to which Chinese traders would immediately resort, and which was to be held only so long as the Emperor refused to open his ports and allow a fair traffic with his people. Others deprecated resort to force until a commissioner to Peking had explained the designs and wishes of his government, demanded the same privileges for foreigners in China that the Chinese enjoyed abroad, and then, in the event of a refusal, compel acquiescence. Some advised letting things take their own course and conducting trade as it could be at Canton until circumstances compelled the Chinese to act. "That which we now require is not to lose the enjoyment of what we have got," said the Duke of Wellington, and his advice was followed in most respects. A few thought it would be the wiser way to disseminate juster ideas of the position, power, and wishes of England and all foreign nations among the Chinese in their own language. They argued very properly that ignorance on these points would neutralize every attempt to bring about a better state of things; that although the Chinese were to blame for their uncompromising arrogance, it was also their great misfortune that they really had had little opportunity to learn the truth respecting their visitors. All these suggestions looked forward to no long continuance of the present undefined, anomalous relations, and all of them contained much pertinent advice and many valuable items of information; but it was a question not more difficult than important what course of procedure was the best. While the point of supremacy seemed to be settled in favor of the Son of Heaven, the virus of the contraband opium trade was working out its evil effects among his subjects and hastening on a new era.

The British superintendents now lived in Macao pending the action of their government, merely keeping a clerk at Canton to sign manifests. The foreign residents established the Society for the Diffusion of Useful Knowledge, and other benevolent projects mentioned in a previous chapter; they also sent two or three vessels along the coast to see what openings existed for entering the country, preaching the gospel, or living on shore. The results of the voyages fully proved the impossibility of entering the country in an open manner without the permission of the rulers, and the limited intercourse with the people also showed that the character of foreigners was generally associated with the opium trade. The dwellers immediately on the coast were eager for an extension of the traffic, because it brought them large gains, and the officers at the principal ports were desirous of participating in the emoluments of their fellows at Canton; but those who had the good of the country at heart (and there are many such in China) thought that the extension of foreign trade would bring with it unmitigated evil from the increased use of opium.

Sir G. B. Robinson, the superintendent, remained at Lintin on board a cutter among opium ships anchored there during the season of 1835-36, and was so well satisfied with his position that he recommended his government to purchase a small ship for the permanent accommodation of the commission there beyond the reach of the Chinese officers, and to vest its powers in a single individual. He also expressed his conviction that there was little hope of establishing a proper understanding with the Chinese Government, except by a resort to force and the occupation of an island off the mouth of the river:

I see no grounds to apprehend the occurrence of any fearful events on the north-east coast, nor can I learn what new danger exists. I am assured from the best authority that the scuffles between different parties of smugglers and mandarins, alike engaged and competing in the traffic, are not more serious or frequent than in this province. In no case have Europeans been engaged in any kind of conflict or affray: and while this increasing and lucrative trade is in the hands of the parties whose vital interests are so totally dependent on its safety and continuance, and by whose prudence and integrity it has been brought into its present increasing and flourishing condition, I think little apprehension may be entertained of dangers emanating from imprudence on their part. Should any unfortunate catastrophe take place, what would our position at Canton entail upon us but responsibility and jeopardy, from which we are now free? On the question of smuggling opium I will not enter in this place, though, indeed, smuggling carried on actively in the government boats can hardly be termed such. Whenever his Majesty's government directs us to prevent British vessels engaging in the traffic, we can enforce any order to that effect, but a more certain method would be to prohibit the growth of the poppy and the manufacture of opium in British India; and if British ships are in the habit of committing irregularities and crimes, it seems doubly necessary to exercise a salutary control over them by the presence of an authority at Lintin.

Taking all things into consideration, this is a remarkable despatch to be sent by the representative of a Christian government writing from the midst of a fleet of smugglers on the shores of a pagan country. "The scuffles caused by the introduction of opium are," he remarks, "*not more* serious or frequent on the coast than about Canton;" though even there, probably, not one-half which did occur were known; but Europeans never personally engaged in any of them. They only brought the cause and object of these collisions where the people could get it, and then quietly looked on to see them fight about it. The "prudence and integrity" of the merchants were engaged in cherishing it to a high degree of prosperity, and they were not likely to act imprudently. The orders of the supreme government for its officers on the coast to stop the traffic were utterly powerless, through the cupidity and venality of those officers and their underlings; yet their almost complete failure to execute them does not impugn the sincerity of the court in issuing them. There is not the least evidence to show that the court of Peking was not sincere in its desire to suppress the trade, from the first edict in 1800 till the war broke out in 1840. The excuse that the government smuggled because its revenue cruisers engaged in it and the helpless provincial authorities winked at it, is no more satisfactory than to make the successful bribery of custom-house officers in England or elsewhere a proof of the corruption of the treasury department. The temptation of an "increasing and lucrative" trade was as strong to the unenlightened pagan Chinese smuggler as it was to the Christian merchants and monopolists who placed the poisonous drug constantly within his reach. It would have been far more frank on the part of the British superintendent to have openly defended a traffic affording a revenue of more than two millions sterling to his own government, and suggested that such an "increasing and lucrative" business should not be impeded, than to say that he could stop British ships engaging in it as soon as he received orders to that effect.

The existence of the commission at the outer anchorages was fully known to the authorities at Canton, but no movement toward reopening the intercourse was made by either party. Lord Palmerston instructed the superintendent not to communicate with the governor-general through the hong merchants, nor to give his written communications the name of petitions. Captain Elliot succeeded Sir George in 1836, and immediately set about reopening the communication with the Chinese officers in the same way that the supercargoes of the Company had conducted it. He defended this course upon the grounds that he had no right to direct official communication with the governor, and that the remarkable movements of the Chinese and the state of uncertainty in respect to the whole foreign trade rendered it desirable to be at Canton. The successor of Lu, Tăng Ting-ching, willingly responded to this proposition by sending a deputation of three officers to Macao with the hong merchants to make some inquiries before memorializing the Emperor. In his report the governor avoided all reference to Lord Napier, and requested his Majesty's sanction to the present request as being in accordance with the orders that the English merchants should send home to have a supercargo come out to manage them. It was of course granted; and the British commission, having received a "red permit" from the collector of customs, returned to Canton April 12, 1837, after an absence of about thirty months. In his note to the governor upon receiving the imperial sanction, Captain Elliot says: "The undersigned respectfully assures his excellency that it is at once his duty and his anxious desire to conform in all things to the imperial pleasure; and he will therefore heedfully attend to the points adverted to in the papers now before him." This language was decided, and his excellency afterward called upon the superintendent to do as he had promised.

The remarkable movements of the supreme government here referred to grew out of a memorial from Hü Nai-tsí, formerly salt commissioner and judge at Canton, proposing the legalization of the opium trade. In this paper he acknowledges that it is impossible to stop the traffic or use of the drug; if the foreign vessels be driven from the coast, they will go to some island near by, where the native craft will go off to them; and if the laws be made too severe upon those who smoke the drug they will be disregarded. By legalizing it, he says, the drain of specie will be stopped, the regular trade rendered more profitable and manageable, and the consumption of the drug regulated. He proposes instant dismissal from office as the penalty for all functionaries convicted of smoking, while their present ineffectual attempts to suppress the trade, which resulted in general contempt for all law, would cease, and consequently the dignity of government be better maintained. The trade on the coast would be concentrated at Canton, and the fleet at Lintin broken up, thereby bringing all foreigners more completely under control.

This unexpected movement at the capital caused no little stir at Canton, and the hong merchants presently advertised the foreigners that soon there would no longer be any use for the receiving-ships at Lintin. Captain Elliot wrote that he thought legalization had come too late to stop the trade on the coast, and, with a prescient eye, adds that the "feeling of independence created among British subjects from the peculiar mode of conducting this branch of the trade," would ere long lead to graver difficulties and acts of violence requiring the armed interference of his government. The impression was general at Canton that the trade would be legalized, and increased preparations were accordingly made in India to extend the cultivation. The governor and his colleagues recommended its legalization on the grounds that "the tens of millions of precious money which now annually ooze out of the Empire will be saved," the duties be increased, the evil practices of transporting contraband goods by deceit and violence suppressed, numberless quarrels and litigations arising therefrom and the crimes of worthless vagrants diminished. They also deluded themselves with the idea that if the officers were dismissed as soon as convicted, the intelligent part of society would not indulge their depraved appetites, but let the "victims of their own self-sacrificing folly," the poor opium-smokers, be found only among the lower classes. In connection with this report, the hong merchants replied to various inquiries respecting the best mode of carrying on the opium trade in case it should be legalized, and their mode of conducting commerce generally; adding that it was beyond their power to control the smuggling traffic or restrain the exportation of sycee, and showed that the balance of trade would naturally leave the country in bullion. These papers are fairly drawn up, and their perusal cannot fail to elevate the character of the Chinese for consideration, carefulness, and business-like procedure.[1]

There were other statesmen, however, who regarded Hü Naitsí's memorial as a dangerous step in the downward path, and sounded the alarm. Among these the foremost was Chu Tsun, a cabinet minister, who sent in a counter-memorial couched in the strongest terms. He advised that the laws be more strictly maintained, and cited instances to show that when the provincial authorities earnestly set about it they could put the trade down; that the people would soon learn to despise all laws if those against opium-smoking were suspended; and that recreant officers should be superseded and punished. His indignation warms as he goes on: "It has been represented that advantage is taken of the laws against opium by extortionate underlings and worthless vagrants, to benefit themselves. Is it not known, then, that when government enacts a law, there is necessarily an infraction of that law? And though the law should sometimes be relaxed and become ineffectual, yet surely it should not on that account be abolished; any more than we

[1] *Chinese Repository*, Vol. V., pp. 139, 259, 385 ff.

should altogether cease to eat because of stoppage of the throat. The laws which forbid the people to do wrong may be likened to the dikes which prevent the overflowing of water. If any one urging, then, that the dikes are very old and therefore useless, we should have them thrown down, what words could express the consequences of the impetuous rush and all-destroying overflow! Yet the provincials, when discussing the subject of opium, being perplexed and bewildered by it, think that a prohibition which does not *utterly* prohibit is better than one which does not effectually prevent the importation of the drug. . . . If we can but prevent the importation of opium, the exportation of dollars will then cease of itself, and the two offences will both at once be stopped. Moreover, is it not better, by continuing the old enactments, to find even a partial remedy for the evil, than by a change of the laws to increase the importation still further?"

He then proceeds to show that the native article could not compete with the foreign, for it would not be as well manufactured, and moreover "all men prize what is strange and undervalue whatever is in ordinary use." Its cultivation would occupy rich and fertile land now used for nutritive grains: "To draw off in this way the waters of the great fountain requisite for the production of food and raiment, and to lavish them upon the root whence calamity and disaster spring forth, is an error like that of the physician who, when treating a mere external disease, drives it inward to the heart and centre of the body. Shall the fine fields of Kwangtung, which produce their three crops every year, be given up for the cultivation of this noxious weed?" He says the question does not concern property and duties, but the welfare and vigor of the people; and quotes from the *History of Formosa* a passage showing the way in which the natives there were enervated by using it, and adds that the purpose of the English in introducing opium into the country has been to weaken and enfeeble it. Kanghí long ago (1717) remarked, he observes, "There is cause for apprehension, lest in the centuries or millenniums to come China may be endangered by collisions with the various nations of the West who come hither from beyond the seas." And now, in less than two centuries, "we see the commencement of that danger which he apprehended."

The suggestion of Hü Nai-tsí, to allow it to the people and interdict the officers, is called bad casuistry, "like shutting a woman's ears before you steal her earrings." He shows that this distinction will be vain, for it will be impossible to say who is of the people and who are officers, for all the latter are taken from the body of the former. The permission will induce people to use it who now refrain from fear of the laws; for even the proposal has caused "thieves and villains on all hands to raise their heads and open their eyes, gazing about and pointing the finger under the notion that when once these prohibitions are repealed, thenceforth and forever they may regard themselves far from every restraint and cause of fear." He asserts that nothing but strong laws rigidly carried into effect will restrain them from their evil ways, and concludes by recommending increased stringency in their execution as the only hope of reformation.

This spirited paper was supported by another from a sub-censor, Hü Kiu, on the necessity of checking the exportation of silver, and recommending that a determined officer be sent to punish severely the native traitors, which would add dignity to the laws; and then the barbarians would be awed and consequently reform and be entirely defeated in their designs of conquering the country. He cites several instances of their outrageous violation of the laws, such as levelling graves in Macao for the purpose of making a road over them, landing goods there for entering them at Canton in order to evade the duties and port charges, and even riding in sedans with four bearers, like Chinese officers. Force needed only to be put forth a little and they would again be humbled to subjection; but if they still brought the pernicious drug, then inflict capital punishment upon them as well as upon natives. The sub-censor agrees with Chu Tsun regarding the designs of foreigners in doing so, that they wished first to debilitate and impoverish the land as a preparatory measure, for they never smoked the drug in their own country, but brought it all to China. This prevailing impression was derived mainly from the abstinence of foreign merchants and seamen.

Both these papers were transmitted to Canton for deliberation, although the local officers had already sent a memorial to the cabinet approving the suggestions of Hü Nai-tsí. At this time, however, it was properly remarked that "there had been a diversity of opinion in regard to it, some requesting a change in the policy hitherto adopted, and others recommending the continuance of the severe prohibitions. It is highly important to consider the subject carefully in all its bearings, surveying at once the whole field of action so that such measures may be adopted as shall continue forever in force, free from all failure." This subject, the most important, it cannot be doubted, which had ever been deliberated upon by the Emperor of China and his council, was now fairly brought before the whole nation; and if all the circumstances be taken into consideration, it was one of the most remarkable consultations of any age or country. A long experience of the baneful effects of opium-smoking upon the health, minds, and property of those who used it, had produced a deep conviction in the minds of well-wishers of their country of the necessity of some legal restraint over the people; while the annual drainage of specie at the rate of three or four million sterling for what brought misery and poverty in its train, alarmed those who cared only for the stability and prosperity of the country. The settlement or management of the question was one of equal difficulty and importance, and the result proved that it was quite beyond the reach of both their power and wisdom. Fully conscious of the weak moral principle in themselves and in their countrymen, they considered it right to restrain and deter the people by legislative enactments and severe penalties. Ignorant of the nature of commercial dealings, they thought it both practicable and necessary to limit the exportation of specie; for not having any substitute for coin or any system of national credit, there was serious hazard, otherwise, that the government would ultimately be bankrupted. It is unjust to the Chinese to say, as was argued by those who had never felt these sufferings, that all parties were insincere in their efforts to put down this trade, that it was a mere affectation of morality, and that no one would be more chagrined to see it stop than those apparently so strenuous against it. This assertion was made by Lord Palmerston in Parliament and re-echoed by the Indian officials; but those who have candidly examined the proceedings of the Chinese, or have lived among the people in a way to learn their real feelings, need not be told how incorrect is the remark. The highest statesman and the debilitated, victimized smoker alike agreed in their opinion of its bad effects, and both were pretty much in the position of a miserable lamb in the coil of a hungry anaconda.

The debate among the Chinese excited a discussion among foreigners, most of whom were engaged in the traffic. Here the gist of the question turned upon the points whether opium was really a noxious stimulant *per se*, and whether the Chinese government was sincere in its prohibitions in the face of the notorious connivance of the officers along the coast from Hainan to Tientsin. One writer conclusively proved its baneful effects upon the system when taken constantly, and that its habitual use in the smallest degree almost certainly led to intemperate or uncontrollable use; he then charges the crime of murder upon those who traffic in it, and asserts that "the perpetuating and encouraging and engaging in a trade which promotes disease, misery, crime, madness, despair, and death, is to be an accomplice with the guilty principals in that tremendous pursuit." He exposes the fallacy, hypocrisy, and guilt of the question whether it be less criminal for a man to engage in a pursuit which he knows to be injurious to his fellow-men, because if he does not do so some one else will. The Court of Directors, even, whom all the world knows to be chief managers of the cultivation, manufacture, and sale of the drug, says in one of its despatches that "so repugnant are their feelings to the opium trade, they would gladly, in compassion to mankind, put a total end to the consumption of opium if they could. But they cannot do this, and as opium will be grown somewhere or other, and will be largely consumed in spite of all their benevolent wishes, they can only do as they do"!

Another Englishman engaged in the traffic defended it on the ground that what is bad now was always bad; and the Emperor and his ministers had doubtless other grounds for their sudden opposition. He asserts that opium is "a useful soother, a harmless luxury, and a precious medicine, except to those who abuse it," and that while a few destroy themselves, the prudent many enjoy a pleasing solace, to get which tends to produce the persevering economy and the never-ceasing industry of the Chinese. He estimates that at a daily allowance of one and one-third ounce not more than one person in three hundred and twenty-six touches the pipe, and that there were not *more* than nine hundred and twelve thousand victimized smokers in the Empire. He also remarked that the present mode of conducting the trade by large capitalists kept it respectable, and that if their characters were held up to odium and infamy it would get into the hands of desperadoes, pirates, and marauders. He looked upon the efforts to put it down as utterly futile as the proclamations of Elizabeth were to put down hops, or the Counterblaste of James to stop tobacco.

This rejoinder was responded to by two writers, who clearly exhibited its unsoundness and ridiculed the plea that the trade should be kept in the hands of gentlemen and under the direction of a monopoly. The smuggler brought his vessel on the coast, and there waited till the people came off for his merchandise, disposing of it without the least risk to himself, "coolly commenting on the injustice of the Chinese government in refusing the practice of international law and reciprocity to countries whose subjects it only knows as engaged in constant and gross infraction of laws, the breaking of which affects the basis of all good government, the morals of the country." The true character of the smuggling trade is well set forth:

Reverse the picture. Suppose, by any chance, that Chinese junks were to import into England, as a foreign and fashionable luxury, so harmless a thing as arsenic or corrosive sublimate; that after a few years it became a rage; that thousands, yea, hundreds of thousands used it, and that its use was, in consequence of its bad effects, prohibited. Suppose that, in opposition to the prohibition, junks were stationed in St. George's Channel with a constant supply, taking occasional trips to the Isle of Wight and the mouth of the Thames when the officers were sufficiently attentive to their duty at the former station to prevent its introduction there. Suppose the consumption to increase annually, and to arouse the attention of the government and of those sound-thinking men who foresaw misery and destruction from the rapid spread of an insidious, unprofitable, and dangerous habit. Suppose, in fact, that, *mutato nomine*, all which has been achieved here had been practised there. Suppose some conservators of the public morals to be aroused at last, and to remonstrate against its use and increase; and that among the nation sending forth this destroyer to prey on private happiness and public virtue, one or two pious and well-meaning *bonzes* were to remonstrato with their countrymen on the enormity of their conduct:—how wonderfully consolatory to one party, and unanswerable to the other, must be the remark of the well-dressed and well-educated Chinese merchant: "Hai ya! my friend, do not you see my silk dress and the crystal knob on my cap; don't you know that I have read and can quote Confucius, Mencius, and all the Five Books; do you not see that the barbarians are passionately fond of arsenic, that they will have it, and even go so far as to pay for it; and can you, for one moment, doubt that it would not be much worse for them if, instead of my bringing it, it were left to the chance, needy, and uncertain supply which low men of no capital could afford to bring?"[1]

The writer shows that instead of only one person in every three hundred and twenty-six using the pipe, it was far more probable that at least one out of every one hundred and fifty (or about two million five hundred thousand in all) of the population was a victimized smoker. The assertion of its being a harmless luxury to the many, like wine or beer, is disputed, and the sophisticated argument of its use as a means of hospitality exploded. "What would a benevolent and sober-minded Chinese think," he asks, "were the sophistry of the defenders of this trade translated for him? Where would he find the high-principled and high-minded inhabitants of the far-off country? How could he be made to comprehend that the believers in and practisers of Christian morality advocated a trade so ruinous to his country? That the government of India compelled the growth of it by unwilling ryots; and that, instead of its being brought to China by 'desperadoes, pirates, and marauders,' it was purveyed by a body of capitalists, not participating certainly in what they carry, but supplying the Indian revenue safely and peaceably; that the British government and others encouraged it; and that the agents in the traffic were constantly residing at Canton, protected by the government whose laws they outraged, but monstrously indignant, and appealing to their governments, if No. 2 longcloths are classed as No. 1 through the desperate villany of some paltry custom-house servant?"

The other writer exposes the sinful fallacy of the argument

[1] *Chinese Repository*, Vol V., p. 409.

of expediency, and then proceeds to show how great an obstacle it is in the way of diffusing the gospel among the Chinese. We must refer to their own remarks[1] for the fuller development of the arguments, but this one showed the earnestness of his convictions by offering a premium of £100 for the best essay "showing the effects of the opium trade on the commercial, political, and moral interests of the nations and individuals connected therewith, and pointing out the course they ought to pursue in regard to it." There was, however, so little interest in the subject that this premium was never awarded, though the proposal was extensively advertised both in China and England.

The governor of Canton and his colleagues soon learned that the feeling at court was rather against legalizing the drug, though they were directed to report concerning the amount of duty proper to be levied on it; and to show their zeal, arrested several brokers and dealers. A-ming, one of the linguists, was severely tortured and exposed in the cangue for exporting sycee; others escaped similar treatment by absconding. The chief superintendent naïvely expressed his opinion that "the legalization of the trade in opium would afford his Majesty's government great satisfaction," but suggested that the gradual diversion of British capital into other channels would be attended with advantageous consequences. To one situated between his own government, which promoted the preparation and importation of opium, and the Chinese government, which was now making extraordinary efforts to regulate it, and deeply sensible of the injury resulting from its use to the people around him, and to the reputation of his own and all foreign nations from the constant infraction of the laws, the proposed step of legalization offered a timely relief. No one was more desirous of putting a stop to this destructive traffic than Captain Elliot, but knowing the impossibility of checking it by laws, he naturally wished to see the multitude of political and commercial evils growing out of smuggling done away with. There were, indeed, many things to urge in favor of this

---

[1] *Chinese Repository*, Vol. V., pp. 407, 413, and passim.

course; but the fact ought never to be lost sight of, and be mentioned to the lasting credit of the Emperor Taukwang and his advisers, in the midst of their perplexity and weakness, that he would not admit opium because it was detrimental to his people.

The conflict was now fairly begun; its issue between the parties, so unequally matched—one having almost nothing but the right on its side, the other assisted by every material and physical advantage—could easily be foreseen. Captain Elliot, as the recognized head of the British trade, received an order through the hong merchants from the provincial authorities to drive away the receiving-ships from Lintin, and send the Emperor's commands to his king, that henceforth they be prohibited coming. He replied that he could not transmit any orders to his own sovereign which did not come to him direct from the government, and quoted the recent instance of the governor-general of Fuhkien communicating directly with the captain of a British ship of war. The governor was therefore forced to send his orders to the prefect and colonel of the department to be enjoined on Captain Elliot. He replied by promising to send it to his country, and adds, in true diplomatic style, unworthy of himself and his nation: "He has already signified to your excellency, with truth and plainness, that his commission extends only to the regular trade with this Empire; and further, that the existence of any other than this trade has never yet been submitted to the knowledge of his own gracious sovereign." Captain Elliot transmitted with these "orders" a minute account of the condition of the opium trade, and a memorandum respecting the desirableness of opening communication with the court. Lord Palmerston, in reply, intimates that "her Majesty's government do not see their way in such a measure with sufficient clearness to justify them in adopting it at the present moment." He adds that no protection can be afforded to "enable British subjects to violate the laws of the country to which they trade. Any loss, therefore, which such persons may suffer in consequence of the more effectual execution of the Chinese laws on this subject, must be borne by the parties who have brought that loss on themselves by their own acts." A most paradoxical but convenient position for this "honorable" officer of the English government to assume, and worthy to be recorded in contrast to the utterances from Peking.

Near the close of 1837 the British flag was again hauled down at Canton, and the superintendent returned to Macao because he refused to superscribe the word *pin*, or 'petition,' upon his communications, according to his instructions, and the governor declined to receive them without it. In July, 1838, Sir Frederick Maitland arrived in the Wellesley (74), and was brought into correspondence with the Chinese Admiral Kwan, in consequence of the forts firing upon an English schooner passing the Bogue and stopping her to inquire whether he or any of his crew or women were on board. The Wellesley and her two consorts were anchored near the forts, and the Chinese admiral made a full apology for the mistake; his conduct in the affair was very creditable both to his judgment and temper. As soon as Sir Frederick arrived, Captain Elliot vainly endeavored to reopen correspondence with the governor by sending an open letter to the city gates, which was received and taken to him, but returned in the evening because it had not the required superscription.

Having now fully taken the sense of the Empire in the replies received from all its highest officials, the Emperor Taukwang increased his efforts to suppress the trade. In April, 1838, a native named Kwoh Sí-ping was publicly strangled at Macao by express command of the Emperor, as a warning to others not to engage in exporting sycee or introducing opium. The execution was conducted by the district magistrate and subprefect with dignity and order in the presence of a crowd of natives and foreigners. More than fifty small craft under the English or American flag were constantly plying off the port of Canton, most of them engaged in smuggling. Sometimes the government exerted its power; boats were destroyed, smugglers seized and tortured, and the sales checked; then it went on again as briskly as ever. These boats were easily caught, for the government could exercise entire control over its own subjects; but when the foreign schooners, heavily armed and manned, sailed up and down the river delivering the drug, the revenue cruisers were afraid to attack them. The hong merchants addressed a note to all foreign residents concerning them, the close of which vividly exhibits their unlucky position as the "responsible advisers" of the barbarians: "Lately we have repeatedly received edicts from the governor and hoppo severely reprimanding us; and we have also written to you, gentlemen of the different nations, several times, giving you full information of the orders and regulations, that you might perfectly obey them and manage accordingly; but you, gentlemen, continue wholly regardless."

Collisions became more and more frequent between the Chinese and their rulers, in consequence of the increased stringency of the orders from court. In September, in an affray near Whampoa between the military and villagers, several persons were killed and scores arrested. The retailers at Canton were imprisoned, and those found in other places brought there in chains. In Hupeh it was reported that the officers had punished arrested smokers by cutting out a portion of the upper lip to incapacitate them from using the pipe. Still, such was the venality of the officers that even at this time the son of Governor Tăng himself was engaged in the traffic, and many of the underlings only seized the drug from the smuggling-boats to retail it themselves. The memorial of Hwang Tsioh-tsz', advising the penalty of death, was promulgated in Canton; and the Emperor's rescript urged to stronger measures. In a rapid survey of the ill effects from the use of the drug, Hwang acknowledges that it had extended to Manchuria, and pervaded all ranks of official and humble life. The efflux of silver "into the insatiate depths of transmarine regions" had caused the rate of exchange for cash to rise until it was difficult to carry on the business of government. He then reviews the different plans proposed for checking the cause of all this evil, such as guarding the ports, stopping the entire foreign trade, arresting the smugglers, shutting up the shops, and, lastly, encouraging the home growth. He confesses that the bribes paid the coast-guard service and the maritime officers are so great as entirely to prevent their vigilance; and that the home-prepared drug does not yield the same stimulus as the foreign article. As a last resort, he proposes to increase the penalties upon the consumers, laying all the blame upon them, and advises death to be awarded all who smoke opium after a year's warning has been given them. The well-known subdivision of responsibility was to be made doubly strong by requiring bonds of every tithing and hundred that there were no smokers within their limits. Officers found guilty were not only to be executed, but their children deprived of the privilege of competing at the public examination. One cannot withhold a degree of sympathy for the helpless condition of the officers and statesmen of a great Empire sincerely desirous of doing their country service, and yet so sadly ignorant of their false position by their assumption of supremacy over the very nation whom they could not restrain, and whose officials they rejected for a formality. They might as well have tried to concert a measure to stop the Yangtsz' River in its impetuous flow, as to check the opium trade by laws and penalties.

On December 3, 1838, about two peculs of opium were seized while landing at the factories, and the coolies carried into the city. They declared that they had been sent to Whampoa by Mr. Innes, a British merchant, to obtain the opium from an American ship consigned to Mr. Talbot. The governor ordered the hong merchants to expel these two gentlemen and the ship within three days, on the garbled testimony of the two coolies. Mr. Talbot sent in a communication, stating that neither the ship nor himself had anything to do with the opium, and obtained a reversal of the order to leave. The hong merchants were justly irritated, and informed the Chamber of Commerce that they would not rent their houses to any who would not give a bond to abstain from such proceedings, and refusing to open the trade until such bonds were given; they furthermore declared their intention to pull Mr. Innes' house down if he refused to depart. The Chamber protested that "the inviolability of their personal dwellings was a point imperatively necessary" for their security; the hong merchants then resorted to entreaty, stating their difficult position between their own rulers on one side, who held them responsible for executing their orders, and the foreigners on the other, over whom they had little or no power. The Chamber could only express its regret at the unjust punishment inflicted on a hong merchant, Punhoyqua, for this, and reassert its inability to control the acts of any foreigner.

The governor had put himself in this helpless condition by refusing Captain Elliot's letters; and it is remarkable that he hesitated to arrest Mr. Innes, when one word would have set the populace on the factories and their tenants, and destroyed them all. As an alternative, he now resolved to show foreigners what consequences befel natives who dealt in opium; and while Mr. Innes still remained in Canton, he sent an officer with fifteen soldiers to execute Ho Lau-kin, a convicted dealer, in front of the factories. The officer was proceeding to carry his orders into effect near the American flag-staff, when the foreigners sallied out, pushed down the tent he was raising, and told him in loud tones not to execute the man there. Quite unprepared for this opposition, he hastily gathered up his implements and went into a neighboring street, where the man was strangled. Meanwhile a crowd collected to see these extraordinary proceedings, whom the foreigners endeavored to drive away, supposing that a little determination would soon scatter them. Blows, however, were returned, the foreigners driven into their factories, and the gates shut; the crowd had now become a mob, and under the impression that two natives had been seized, they began to batter the fronts and break the windows with stones and brickbats. They had had possession of the square about three hours, and the danger was becoming imminent, when the Pwanyu hien, or 'district magistrate,' came up, with three or four other officers, attended by a small body of police. Stepping out of his sedan he waved his hand over the crowd, the lictors pouncing upon three or four of the most active, whom they began to chastise upon the spot, and the storm was quelled. About twenty soldiers, armed with swords and spears, took their stand in a conspicuous quarter; the magistrate and his retinue seated themselves, leaving the hong merchants and the police to disperse the crowd. The foreigners were also assured that all should be kept quiet during the night, but not a word was said to them regarding their conduct in interfering with the execution or their folly in bringing this danger upon themselves. This occurrence tended to impress both the government and people with contempt and hatred for foreigners and their characters, fear of their designs, and the necessity of restraining them. The majority of them were engaged in the opium trade, and all stood before the Empire as violators of the laws, while the people themselves suffered the dreadful penalty.

There is no room for the details and correspondence connected with this remarkable incident.[1] Captain Elliot now reappeared in Canton, and at a general meeting expressed his conviction of the cause of these untoward events in the smuggling traffic on the river, declaring his intention of ordering all the British-owned vessels to leave it within three days; he moreover expressed the hope that the further step of opening communication with the provincial authorities to obtain their co-operation to drive them out would be prevented by their speedy departure. Injunctions and entreaties to his countrymen were, however, alike unavailing, and he accordingly addressed the governor, stating his wish to co-operate in driving them out. In a public notice he remarked that "this course of traffic was rapidly staining the British character with deep disgrace" and exposing the regular commerce to imminent jeopardy, and that he meant to shrink from no responsibility in drawing it to a conclusion. The governor, as was expected, praised the superintendent for his offer, but left him to do the whole work; remarking, in that peculiar strain of Chinese conceit which so effectually forestalls our sympathy for their difficulties, that "it may well be conceived that these boats trouble me not one iota:"—as if all he had to do was to arise in his majesty, and they were gone. The boats, however, gradually left the river. Mr. Innes retired, and the regular trade was resumed in January.

No British consular officer has been placed in a more difficult and humiliating dilemma, and Captain Elliot did himself honor in his efforts. The English newspapers ridiculed him as a tide-waiter of the Chinese custom-house, a man who aided the

---

[1] *Chinese Repository*, Vol. VII., pp. 437–456.

cowardly authorities to carry their orders into effect, thereby staining the honor of her Majesty's commission. Although he did not intend to draw a line between the heinousness of the opium trade inside of the Bogue and its harmlessness beyond that limit, still there were good reasons, under his peculiar position, for some action to show the Chinese government that British power would not protect British subjects in violating the laws of China.

At this period the Peking government had taken its course of action. Reports had been received from the provincial authorities almost unanimously recommending increased stringency to abolish the traffic. History, so far as we know, does not record a similar example of an arbitrary, despotic, pagan government taking the public sentiment of its own people before adopting a doubtful line of conduct. It was a far more momentous and difficult question than even the cabinet deemed it to be, while their conceit and ignorance incapacitated them from dealing with it prudently or successfully. There can be no reasonable doubt that the best part of his people and the moral power of the nation were with their sovereign in this attempt. Hü Nai-tsí was dismissed for proposing legalization, and three princes of the blood degraded for smoking opium; arrests, fines, tortures, imprisonments, and executions were frequent in the provinces on the same grounds, all showing the determination to eradicate it. The governor of Hukwang, Lin Tseh-sü, was ordered to proceed to Canton, with unlimited powers to stop the traffic. The trade there was at this time almost suspended, the deliveries being small and at losing prices. Many underlings were convicted and summarily punished, and on February 26th Fung A-ngan was strangled in front of the factories for his connection with opium and participation in the affray at Whampoa. The foreign flags, English, American, Dutch, and French, were all hauled down in consequence. The entire stoppage of all trade was threatened, and the governor urged foreigners to send all opium ships from Chinese waters.

Commissioner Lin arrived in Canton March 10th. The Emperor sent him to inquire and act so as thoroughly to remove the source of the evil, for, says he, "if the source of the evil be not clearly ascertained, how can we hope that the stream of pernicious consequences shall be stayed? It is our full hope that the long-indulged habit will be forever laid aside, and every root and germ of it entirely eradicated; we would fain think that our ministers will be enabled to substantiate our wishes, and so remove from China the dire calamity." It was reported in Canton that the monarch, when recounting the evils which had long afflicted his people by means of opium, paused and wept, and turning to Lin, said: "How, alas! can I die and go to the shades of my imperial father and ancestors, until these direful evils are removed!" Such was the chief purpose of this movement on the part of the Chinese government, and Lin was invested with the fullest powers ever conferred on a subject. Although long experience of the ineffectiveness of Chinese edicts generally lead those residing in the country to regard them as mere verbiage, still, to say that they are all insincere and formal because they are ineffectual, is to misjudge and pervert the emotions of common humanity. Lin appears to have been well fitted for the mission; and if he had been half as enlightened as he was sincere, he would perhaps have averted the war which followed, and been convinced that legalization was the most judicious step he could recommend.

The commissioner spent a week making inquiries, during which time nothing was publicly heard from him; while natives and foreigners alike anxiously speculated as to his plans. It was not until March 18th that his first proclamations were issued to the hong merchants and foreigners; that to the latter required them to deliver up all the opium in the storeships, and to give bonds that they would bring no more, on penalty of death. The poor hong merchants were, as usual, instructed regarding their responsibility to admonish the foreigners, and strictly charged to procure these bonds, or they would be made examples of. Three days were allowed for compliance with these demands. The hoppo had already issued orders detaining all foreigners in Canton—in fact, making them prisoners in their own houses; communication with the shipping was suspended, troops were assembled about the factories, and armed cruisers stationed on the river. The Chamber of Commerce wrote to the hong merchants on the 20th, through their chairman, W. S. Wetmore, an American, stating that they would send a definite reply in four days, and adding that "there is an almost unanimous feeling in the community of the absolute necessity of the foreign residents of Canton having no connection with the opium traffic."

This paper was taken to the commissioner, and about ten o'clock P.M. the hong merchants again met the Chamber, and told them that if *some* opium was not given up two of their number would be beheaded in the morning. The merchants present, including British, Parsees, Americans, and others, acting as individuals, then subscribed one thousand and thirty-seven chests, to be tendered to the commissioner; but the hong merchants reported next morning that this amount was insufficient. In the afternoon Lin sent an invitation to Mr. Dent, a leading English merchant, to meet him at the city gates, who expressed his willingness to go if the commissioner would give him a safe-warrant guaranteeing his return within a day. The hong merchants returned without him; and the next morning two of them, Howqua and Mowqua, came again to his house with chains upon their necks, having been sent with an express order for him to appear. They repaired to the Chamber of Commerce then assembled, but all soon returned to Mr. Dent's house, where an animated debate took place, which resulted in the unanimous decision on the part of the foreign residents that he should not go into the city without the safe-warrant. This unexpected demand caused much discussion among foreigners, as it was doubtless a contrivance to secure a hostage; and the refusal of the former to give a written safe-warrant would probably have ended in seizing Mr. Dent and imprisoning him, if Howqua, the senior hong merchant, had not allowed everything to wait over one day till Monday. Mr. Dent's partner had that day seen the *an-chah sz'*, or 'provincial judge,' in the city to explain why he hesitated to go to Lin.

On the 22d Captain Elliot sent a note to the governor expressing his readiness to meet the Chinese officers, and use "his sincere efforts to fulfil the pleasure of the great Emperor as soon as it was made known to him." The Chinese could hardly draw any other conclusion from this admission than that he had the power, as well as the inclination to put down the opium trade, which he certainly could not do; it tended therefore to deceive them. This note was followed by a letter to Captain Blake, of the Larne, requesting his assistance in defending British property and life, and by a circular ordering all British ships, opium and others, to proceed to Hongkong and prepare themselves to resist every act of aggression. A second circular to British subjects detailed the reasons which compelled him to withdraw all confidence in the "justice and moderation of the provincial government," and demand passports for all his countrymen who wished to leave Canton, while counselling every one to make preparations to remove on board ship. Elliot now proceeded to Canton, which he safely reached about sunset Sunday evening, dressed in naval uniform and closely attended by cruisers watching his movements. The British flag was then hoisted, and Captain Elliot, conducting Mr. Dent to the consulate in the most conspicuous manner, summoned a public meeting, read his notice of the previous day, and told the hong merchants to inform the commissioner that he was willing to let Mr. Dent go into the city if he could accompany him.

His coming up the river had excited the apprehensions of the Chinese that he meant to force his way out again, and orders were issued to close every pass around the factories. By nine o'clock that evening the foreigners, about two hundred and seventy-five in number, were the only inmates of their houses. Patrols, sentinels, and officers, hastening hither and thither, with the blowing of trumpets and beating of gongs, added confusion to the darkness of the night.

On the 25th most of the foreign merchants of all nations signed a paper pledging themselves "not to deal in opium, nor to attempt to introduce it into the Chinese Empire:" how many of the individuals subsequently broke this pledge on the ground that it was forced from them cannot be stated, but part of the firms which signed it afterward actively engaged in the trade. Captain Elliot applied for passports for himself and countrymen, and requested the return of the servants, avoiding all reference to his promise of three days before, or mention of the cause of these stringent proceedings. His requests were refused; no native was allowed to bring food or water to the factories; letters could not be sent to Whampoa or Macao, except at imminent risk; the confinement was complete, and had been effected without the least personal harm. The heavy punishment which had fallen on Kwoh Sí-ping, Ho Lau-kin, and Fung A-ngan had now come near to the foreign agents of the traffic; but not an individual had been touched.

The commissioner next issued an exhortation to all foreigners, urging them to deliver the drug on four grounds, viz., because they were men and had reason; because the laws forbade its use, under severe penalties; because they should have feelings for those who suffered from using it; and because of their present duress, from which they would then be released. This paper, as were all those issued by Lin, was characterized by an unusual vigor of expression and cogency of reasoning, but betrayed the same arrogance and ignorance which had misled his predecessors. One extract will suffice. Under the first reason why the opium should be delivered up, he says that otherwise the retribution of heaven will follow them, and cites some cases to prove this:

> Now, our great Emperor, being actuated by the exalted virtue of heaven itself, wishes to cut off this deluge of opium, which is the plainest proof that such is the intention of high heaven! It is then a traffic on which heaven looks with disgust, and who is he that may oppose its will? Thus in the instance of the English chief Robarts, who violated our laws; he endeavored to get possession of Macao by force, and at Macao he died! Again, in 1834, Lord Napier bolted through the Bocca Tigris, but being overwhelmed with grief and fear he almost immediately died; and Morrison, who had been darkly deceiving him, died that very year also! Besides these, every one of those who have not observed our laws have either been overtaken with the judgments of heaven on returning to their country, or silently cut off ere they could return thither. Thus then it is manifest that the heavenly dynasty may not be opposed!

Two communications to Captain Elliot, from Lin through the prefect and district magistrates, accompanied this exhortation, stating his view of the superintendent's conduct in contumaciously resisting his commands and requiring him to give up the opium. For once in the history of foreign intercourse with China, these commands were obeyed, and after intimating his readiness to comply, Captain Elliot issued a circular on March 27th, which from its important results is quoted entire:

I, Charles Elliot, chief superintendent of the trade of British subjects in China, presently forcibly detained by the provincial government, together with all the merchants of my own and the other foreign nations settled here, without supplies of food, deprived of our servants, and cut off from all intercourse with our respective countries (notwithstanding my own official demand to be set at liberty that I might act without restraint), have now received the commands of the high commissioner, issued directly to me under the seals of the honorable officers, to deliver into his hand all the opium held by the people of my own country. Now I, the said chief superintendent, thus constrained by paramount motives affecting the safety of the lives and liberty of all the foreigners here present in Canton, and by other very weighty causes, do hereby, in the name and on the behalf of her Britannic Majesty's government, enjoin and require all her Majesty's subjects now present in Canton, forthwith to make a surrender to me for the service of her said Majesty's government, to be delivered over to the government of China, of all the opium under their respective control: and to hold the British ships and vessels engaged in the opium trade subject to my immediate direction: and to forward me without delay a sealed list of all the British-owned opium in their respective possession. And I, the said chief superintendent, do now, in the most full and unreserved manner, hold myself responsible for, and on the behalf of her Britannic Majesty's government, to all and each of her Majesty's subjects surrendering the said British-owned opium into my hands, to be delivered over to the Chinese government. And I, the said chief superintendent, do further especially caution all her Majesty's subjects here present in Canton, owners of or charged with the management of opium the property of British subjects, that failing the surrender of the said opium into my hands at or before six o'clock this day, I, the said superintendent, hereby declare her Majesty's government wholly free of all manner of responsibility in respect of the said British-owned opium. And it is specially to be understood that proof of British property and value of all British-owned opium surrendered to me agreeable to this notice, shall be determined upon principles, and in a manner hereafter to be defined by her Majesty's government.[1]

The guarantee offered in this notice was deemed sufficient by the merchants, though Captain Elliot had no authority to take such a responsibility, and exceeded his powers in giving it; being the authorized agent of the crown, however, his government was responsible for his acts, though the notice did not, nor could it, set any price upon the surrendered property.

At the time it was given it could not be honestly said that

[1] *Chinese Repository*, Vol. VII., p. 633.

the lives of foreigners were in jeopardy, and Lin had promised to reopen the trade as soon as the opium was delivered and the bonds given. What the other "very weighty causes" were must be guessed; but the requisition was promptly answered, and before night twenty thousand two hundred and eighty-three chests of opium had been surrendered, which Captain Elliot the next day tendered to the commissioner. Their market value at the time was not far from nine millions of dollars, and the cost price nearly eleven millions. Directions were sent to twenty-two vessels to anchor near the Bogue, to await orders for its delivery, the commissioner and the governor themselves going down forty miles to superintend the transfer. On April 2d the arrangements for delivering the opium were completed, and on May 21st it was all housed near the Bogue.

When the guard was placed about the factories, no native came near them for three days, but on the 29th a supply of sheep, pigs, poultry, and other provisions was "graciously bestowed" upon their inmates, most of whom refused them as gifts, which impressed Lin with the belief that they were not actually suffering for food. On May 5th the guards and boats were removed, and communication resumed with the shipping. Sixteen persons, English, Americans, and Parsees, named as principal agents in the opium trade, were ordered to leave the country and never return. On the 24th Captain Elliot left Canton, accompanied by the ten British subjects mentioned among the sixteen outlawed persons. In order still further to involve her Majesty's ministers in his acts, he forbade British ships entering the port, or any British subject living in Canton, on the ground that both life and property were insecure; there were, however, no serious apprehensions felt by other foreigners remaining there; and the propriety of the order was questioned by those who were serious sufferers from its action.

This success in getting the opium encouraged Lin to demand the bond, but although the captains of most of the ships signed it when the port was first opened, it was not required long after. The British merchants at Canton prepared a memorial to the foreign secretary of their government, recapitulating the aggressive acts of the Chinese government in stopping the legal trade, detaining all foreigners in Canton until the opium was surrendered, and requiring them to sign a bond not to bring it again, which involved their responsibility over those whom they could not control; but nothing was said in it of their own unlawful acts, no reference to their promises of a few months before, no allusion to the causes of these acts of aggression. Its burden was, however, to urge the government to issue a notice of its intentions respecting the pledge given them by the superintendent in his demand for the opium.

Lin referred to Peking for orders concerning the disposal of the opium, and his Majesty commanded the whole to be destroyed by him and his colleagues in the presence of the civil and military officers, the inhabitants of the coast, and the foreigners, "that they may know and tremble thereat." Captain Elliot, on the other hand, before it had all been delivered, wrote to his government, April 22d, his belief that the Chinese intended to sell it at a high price, remunerating the owners and pocketing the difference, preparatory to legalizing the traffic, and making some arrangements to limit the annual importation to a certain number of chests; consequently he recommended an "immediate and strong declaration to exact complete indemnity for all manner of loss" from the Chinese. He calls Lin "false and perfidious," though it is difficult to see why he applies these epithets to one who seems to have sincerely endeavored to carry out instructions, while his own communications certainly tended to mislead him. The sense of the responsibility he had assumed, and the irritating confinement under which it was written, account, in a measure, for this despatch, so different in its tenor from his previous declarations.

The opium was destroyed in the most thorough manner, by mixing it in parcels of two hundred chests, in trenches, with lime and salt water, and then drawing off the contents into the adjacent creek at low tide. Overseers were stationed to prevent the workmen or villagers from purloining the opium, and one man was summarily executed for attempting to carry away a small quantity. No doubt remained in the minds of persons who visited the place and examined the operation, that the entire quantity of twenty thousand two hundred and ninety-one chests received from the English (eight more having been sent from Macao) was completely destroyed:—a solitary instance in the history of the world of a pagan monarch preferring to destroy what would injure his subjects, rather than to fill his own pockets with its sale. The whole transaction will ever remain one of the most remarkable incidents in human history for its contrasts, and the great changes it introduced into China.[1]

The course of events during the remainder of the year 1839 presents a strange mixture of traffic and hostility. The British merchants were obliged to send their goods to Canton in ships sailing under other flags, which led the commissioner to issue placards exhorting British captains to bring their ships into port. This procedure brought out a rejoinder from Captain Elliot, giving the reasons why he had forbidden them to do so, and complaining of his own unjust imprisonment as unbecoming treatment to the "officer of a friendly nation, recognized by the Emperor, who had always performed his duty peacefully and irreproachably." Captain Elliot's own correspondence shows, however, that this is an unfair statement of the political relations between them.

While this matter of trade was pending, a drunken affray occurred at Hongkong with some English sailors, in which an inoffensive native named Lin Wei-hí lost his life. The commissioner ordered an inquest to be held, and demanded the murderer, according to Chinese law. The superintendent empanelled a regular court of criminal and admiralty jurisdiction at Hongkong, to try the seamen who had been arrested. He also offered

[1] Sir Robert Peel declared that this property was obtained by her Majesty's agent without any authority; but when the six millions of dollars were received from the Chinese as indemnity, the British government made its subjects receive their money in London, charged them with all expenses instead of paying it in China, and priced the opium at scarcely half what the East India Company had received from it, by taking the market rates when the trade at Canton was nominal. The merchants lost, with accruing interest, about two millions sterling, and "Sir R. Peel transferred a million sterling from their pockets to the public treasury."—*Chinese Repository*, Vol. XIII., p. 54 (from London paper).

a reward of $200 for such evidence as would lead to the conviction of the offenders; and advanced in all $2,000 to the friends of the deceased as some compensation for their heavy loss, and to the villagers for injuries done to them in the riot. Having formed the court, he politely invited the provincial officers to attend the trial; and when it was over, informed them that he had been unable to ascertain the perpetrator of the deed. Five sailors were convicted and punished for riotous conduct by fine and imprisonment, and sent to England under arrest, but to everybody's surprise were all liberated on their arrival. The proceedings in this matter were perfectly fair, and the commissioner should have been satisfied; but his subsequent violent conduct really placed the dispute on an entirely new ground, though he regarded his action as simply exercising the same prerogative of control over foreigners in both cases. Finding his demand for the murderer disregarded, he took measures against the English then in Macao which were calculated to bring serious loss upon the Portuguese population. His course was prompted by anger at losing the trade, and only injured his own cause. In order to relieve the unoffending and helpless people in Macao, Captain Elliot and all British subjects who could do so left the settlement August 26th, and went on board ship for a time. During this interval Lin and Governor Tăng visited Macao under an escort of Portuguese troops, but retired the same day. This move placed the English beyond his reach, but did not advance his efforts to drive the opium ships from the coast, or induce the regular traders to enter the port. The sales of opium had begun again even before the destruction of the drug, and rapidly increased when it was known that that immense quantity had really been destroyed. Lin now began to see that his plan of proceedings might not ultimately prove so successful as he had anticipated, for he was bound to remain at Canton until he could report the complete suppression of the contraband and safe continuance of the legal trade.

Finding that the British fleet at Hongkong was too strong to drive away, he forbade the inhabitants supplying the ships with provisions. This led to a collision between the British and three junks near Kowlung, which resulted, however, in no serious damage. On September 11th, Captain Elliot, having ordered all British vessels engaged in the opium trade to leave the harbor and coast, they mostly proceeded to Namoh. The Chinese burned the next day a Spanish vessel, the Bilbaino, in Macao waters, under the impression that she was English.

In unison with all the strange features of this struggle, while hostilities were going on, negotiations for continuing trade were entered into in October, when the commissioner signed the agreement, and Captain Elliot furnished security for its being conducted fairly. But the unauthorized entrance of the English ship Thomas Coutts, whose captain signed the bond, led to a rupture and the renewed demand for the murderer of Lin Wei-hí. Captain Elliot ordered all British ships to reassemble at Tungku under the protection of the ships of war Volage and Hyacinth. He also proceeded to the Bogue to request a withdrawal of the threats against the British until the two governments could arrange the difficulties, when an engagement ensued between Admiral Kwan, with a fleet of sixteen junks, and the two ships of war; three junks were sunk, one blown up, and the rest scattered. The commissioner had been foiled in all his efforts to destroy the opium trade and continue the legal commerce. As a last effort against the British, he declared their trade at an end after December 6, 1839, and issued an edict like that of Napoleon at Berlin, November 19, 1806, forbidding their goods to be imported in any vessels. An enormous amount of property now lay at Canton and on board ship waiting to be exchanged in the course of regular trade, but only the opium traffic flourished.

The close of the year 1839 saw the two nations involved in serious difficulties, and as the events here briefly recounted were the cause of the war, it will be proper to compare the opinions of the two parties, in order to arrive at a better judgment upon the character of that contest. The degree of authority to be exercised over persons who visit their shores is acknowledged by Christian nations among themselves to be nearly the same as that over their own subjects; but none of these nations have conceded this authority to unchristian powers, as Turkey, Persia, or China, mainly because of the little security and justice to be expected. The Chinese have looked upon foreigners resorting to their ports as doing so by sufferance; they entered into no treaty to settle the conditions of authority on either side, for the latter considered themselves as sojourners and aliens, and the natives were unaware of their rights in the matter. Their right to prohibit the introduction of any particular articles was acknowledged, and the propriety of making regulations as to duties allowed. But traders from western nations often set light by the fiscal regulations of such countries as China, Siam, etc., if they can do so without personal detriment or loss of character; and where there is a want of power in the government, joined to a lack of moral sense in the people, all laws are imperfectly executed. No one acquainted with these countries is surprised at frequent and flagrant violations of law, order, justice or courtesy, both among rulers and ruled; yet the obligation of foreigners to obey just laws made known to them surely is not to be measured solely by the degree of obedience paid by a portion of the people themselves.

The Chinese government discussed the measure of legalizing a trade it could not suppress, but before constructing a law to that effect, it determined to make a final and more vigorous effort to stamp it out. Might makes right, or at least enforces it; had the Chinese possessed the power to destroy every ship found violating their laws, although the loss of life would have been dreadful, no voice would have been raised against the proceeding. "Her Majesty's government," said Lord Palmerston, "cannot interfere for the purpose of enabling British subjects to violate the laws of the country to which they trade." But in that case this power would not have been dared; the known weakness of the government emboldened both sellers and buyers, until Captain Elliot told the Foreign Secretary that "it was a confusion of terms to call the opium trade a smuggling trade."

Lin probably wished to get Mr. Dent as a hostage for the delivery of the opium in the hands of his countrymen, not to punish him for disobedience to previous orders; expecting no opposition to this demand, he seems to have been unwilling to seize him immediately, preferring to try persuasion and command longer, and detain him and other foreigners until he was obeyed; Captain Elliot he viewed as a mere head merchant. When, therefore, the attempt was made, as he supposed, to take Mr. Dent out of his hands, he was apprehensive of a struggle, and instantly took the strongest precautionary measures to prevent the prey escaping. Considerate allowance should be granted for the serious mistake he made of imprisoning the innocent with the guilty; but when Captain Elliot took Mr. Dent thus under his protection, the commissioner felt that his purpose would be defeated, and no opium obtained, if he began to draw a distinction. Besides, conscious that he possessed unlimited power over a few defenceless foreigners, nearly all of whom were in his eyes guilty, he cared very little where his acts fell. There is no good evidence to show that *he* seriously meditated anything which would hazard their lives. When he had received this vast amount of property, success evidently made him careless as to his conduct, and judging the probity and good faith of foreigners by his own standard, he deemed it safest to detain them until the opium was actually in his possession. Concluding that Captain Elliot did attempt to abscond with Mr. Dent, it is less surprising, therefore, that he should have looked upon his offers to "carry out the will of the great Emperor," when set at liberty, as a lure rather than a sincere proposition. In imprisoning him he had no more idea he was imprisoning, insulting, threatening, and coercing the representative of a power like Great Britain, or violating rules western powers call *jus gentium*, than if he had been the envoy from Siam or Lewchew. Whether he should not have known this is another question, and had he candidly set himself, on his arrival at Canton, to ascertain the power, position, and commerce of western countries, he would have found Captain Elliot sincerely desirous of meeting him in his endeavors to fulfil his high commission. Let us deal fairly by the Chinese rulers in their desire to restrain a traffic of which they knew and felt vastly more of its evil than we have ever done, and give Lin his due, though his endeavors failed so signally.

The opium was now obtained; no lives had been lost, nor any

one endangered; but the British government felt bound to pay its own subjects for their chests. The only source Captain Elliot suggested was to make the Chinese refund. The Emperor ordered it to be destroyed, and the commissioner, after executing that order, next endeavored to separate the legal from the contraband trade by demanding bonds; they had been taken in vain from the hong merchants, but there was more hope if taken directly from foreigners. The bonds were not made a pretext for war by the English ministry; that, on the part of England, according to Lord John Russell, was "set afoot to obtain reparation for insults and injuries offered her Majesty's superintendent and subjects; to obtain indemnification for the losses the merchants had sustained under threats of violence; and, lastly, to get security that persons and property trading with China should in future be protected from insult and injury, and trade maintained upon a proper footing." Looking at the war, therefore, as growing out of this trade, and waged to recover the losses sustained by the surrendry to the British superintendent, it was an *unjust* one. It was, moreover, an *immoral* contest, when the standing of the two nations was examined, and the fact could not be concealed that Great Britain, the first Christian power, really waged this war against the pagan monarch who had vainly endeavored to put down a vice hurtful to his people. The war was looked upon in this light by the Chinese; it will always be so looked upon by the candid historian, and known as the Opium War.

On the other hand, the war was felt by every well-wisher to China to involve far higher principles than the mere recovery of the opium; and had it been really held to be so by the English ministry, they would have done well to have alluded to them. Lin's reiterated demands for the murderer of Lin Wei-hí, though told that he could not be found, was only one form of the supremacy the Chinese arrogantly assumed over other nations. In all their intercourse with their fellow-men they maintained a patronizing, unfair, and contemptuous position, which left no alternative but withdrawal from their shores or a humiliating submission that no one feeling the least independence could endure. Not unjustly proud of their country in comparison with those near it, her Emperor, her rulers, and her people all believed her to be impregnably strong, portentously awful, and immensely rich in learning, power, wealth, and territory. None of them imagined that aught could be learned or gained from other nations; for the "outside barbarians" were dependent for their health and food upon the rhubarb, tea, and silks of the Inner Land. They had seen, indeed, bad specimens of western power and people, but there were equal opportunities for them to have learned the truth on these points. The reception of the religion of the Bible, the varied useful branches of science, and the many mechanical arts known in western lands, with the free passage of their own people abroad, were all forbidden to the millions of China by their supercilious rulers; they thereby preferred to remain the slaves of debasing superstitions, ignorant of common science, and deprived of everything which Christian benevolence, philanthropy, and knowledge could and wished to impart to them. This assumption of supremacy, and a real impression of its propriety, was a higher wall around them than the long pile of stones north of Peking. Force seemed to be the only effectual destroyer of such a barrier, and in this view the war may be said to have been necessary to compel the Chinese government to receive western powers as its equals, or at least make it treat their subjects as well as it did its own people. There was little hope of an adjustment of difficulties until the Chinese were compelled to abandon this erroneous assumption; the conviction that it was unjust, unfounded, and foolish in itself could safely be left to the gradual influences of true religion, profitable commerce, and sound knowledge.

The report of the debate in the British Parliament on this momentous question hardly contains a single reference to this feature of the Chinese government. It turned almost wholly upon the opium trade, and whether the hostilities had not proceeded from the want of foresight and precaution on the part of her Majesty's ministers. The speeches all showed ignorance of both principles and facts: Sir James Graham asserted that the governors of Canton had sanctioned the trade; Sir George Staunton that it would not be safe for British power in India if these insults were not checked, and that the Chinese had far exceeded in their recent efforts the previous acknowledged laws of the land! Dr. Lushington maintained that the connivance of the local rulers acquitted the smugglers; Sir John Hobhouse truly stated that the reason why the government had done nothing to stop the opium trade was that it was profitable; and Lord Melbourne, with still more fairness, said: "We possess immense territories peculiarly fitted for raising opium, and though I would wish that the government were not so directly concerned in the traffic, I am not prepared to pledge myself to relinquish it." The Duke of Wellington thought the Chinese government was insincere in its efforts, and therefore deserved little sympathy; while Lord Ellenborough spoke of the million and a half sterling revenue "derived from foreigners," which, if the opium monopoly was given up and its cultivation abandoned, they must seek elsewhere. No one advocated war on the ground that the opium had been seized, but the majority were in favor of letting it go on because it was begun. This debate was, in fact, a remarkable instance of the way in which a moral question is blinked even by conscientious persons whenever politics or interest come athwart its course. No declaration of war was ever published by Queen Victoria, further than an order in council to the admiralty, in which it was recited that "satisfaction and reparation for the late injurious proceedings of certain officers of the Emperor of China against certain of our officers and subjects shall be demanded from the Chinese government;" the object of this order was, chiefly, to direct concerning the disposal of such ships, vessels, and cargoes belonging to the Chinese as might be seized. Perhaps the formality of a declaration of war against a nation which knew nothing of the law of nations was not necessary, but if a minister plenipotentiary from Peking had been present at the debate in Parliament in April, 1840, he would have declared the motives and proceedings of his government strangely misrepresented. It was time that better ideas of one another should find place in their councils, and that means snould be afforded the rulers of each nation to learn the truth.

The Chinese apparently foresaw the coming struggle, and

began to collect troops and repair their forts; Lin, now governor-general of Kwangtung, purchased the Chesapeake, a large ship, and appointed an intendant of circuit near Macao, to guard the coasts. The English carried on their trade under neutral flags, and Lin made no further efforts to annoy them. He, however, wrote two official letters to Queen Victoria, desiring her assistance in putting down the opium trade, in which the peculiar ideas of his countrymen respecting their own importance and their position among the nations of the earth were singularly exhibited.[1] Notwithstanding the causes of complaint he had against the English, he behaved kindly to the surviving crew of the Sunda, an English vessel wrecked on Hainan, and sent them, on their arrival at Canton, to their countrymen.

---

[1] *Chinese Repository*, Vol. VIII., pp. 9–12, 497–503; Vol. IX., pp. 241–257.

CHAPTER XXIII.

PROGRESS AND RESULTS OF THE FIRST WAR BETWEEN ENGLAND AND CHINA.

On June 22, 1840, before the advance part of the British force reached China, Sir Gordon Bremer published a notice of the blockade of the port of Canton. The Americans living there had requested Lin to let all their ships arriving before it was laid on come directly up the river. He granted the application, but declared it "to be an egregious mistake, analogous to an audacious falsehood, that the English contemplated putting on a blockade." Captain Elliot also issued a manifesto to the people, which was widely dispersed, setting forth the grievances which had been suffered by the English at the hands of Lin, and assuring them that no harm would come while they pursued their peaceful occupations—for the quarrel was entirely between the two governments, and the Queen had deputed high officers to make known the truth to the Emperor.

Sir Gordon Bremer's force of five ships of war, three steamers, and twenty-one transports reached Tinghai harbor July 4th. In reply to a summons to surrender, the Chinese officers declared their determination to resist as far as their means allowed; but complained of the hardship of being made answerable for wrongs done at Canton, upon which place the blow should properly fall. The attack was made on Sunday, July 5th, when the Wellesley (74) opened her guns on the town, which were answered by the junks and batteries. A few minutes sufficed to silence the latter, and three thousand men landed and menaced Tinghai, whose walls were lined with soldiers. The town was evacuated during the night, most of the respectable inhabitants going to Ningpo; many of the Chinese high officials were killed, which, with the experience of the terrible foreign force brought against them, disheartened their troops beyond measure.

Two days after this attack the joint plenipotentiaries, Admiral G. Elliot and Captain Elliot, arrived in the Melville (74) at Chusan. To the authorities at Amoy and Ningpo they sent copies of Lord Palmerston's letter to the Emperor, with a request to forward them to Peking; the officials declined, however, undertaking any such responsibility.

The prefect of Ningpo took measures to prevent the people of Chusan from "aiding and comforting" their conquerors by sending police-runners to mark those who supplied them; a purveyor from Canton was seized and brought back. An idea that the Chinese people wished to throw off the Manchu yoke, and a desire to conciliate the islanders, led the British to take less decided measures for supplying themselves with provisions than they otherwise would. A small party was sent to recapture the purveyor, but its unsuccessful trip over the island showed the unwillingness of the people to have anything to do with their invaders, while their dread was increased by the arrest of several village elders. Mr. Gutzlaff was stationed at Chusan, doing his best to reassure the people; and as he went around exhorting them to act peaceably, some of them asked him, "If you are so desirous of peace, why did you come here at all?"

After arranging the government of the island, the stations of the troops, and blockading of Amoy, Ningpo, and the mouths of the Min and Yangtsz' Rivers, the two plenipotentiaries left Tinghai and anchored off the Pei ho August 11th. Captain Elliot went ashore, and finding that Kíshen, the governor-general of Chihlí, was at Taku, delivered the letter to his messenger, who returned with a request for ten days' delay in which to lay it before the Emperor. During this interval the ships visited the coast of Liautung to procure provisions, which they obtained with some difficulty. No message coming off, a strong boat-force was sent ashore on the 28th, with a menacing letter to Kíshen, when it was ascertained that the reply had in reality been awaiting the return of the ships during several days. Arrangements were now made for a personal interview at Taku between Kíshen and Captain Elliot, on Sunday, August 30th, in a large tent. Kíshen argued his side of the question with great tact and ability, sincerely urging the argument that his master had the most unquestionable right to treat the English as he had done, for they were and had enrolled themselves his tributary subjects. He could not treat definitely on all the points in dispute, and obtained a further delay of six days in order to refer again to Peking. The conclusion was the reasonable arrangement that Kíshen should meet the English plenipotentiaries at Canton, where the truth could be better ascertained; and on September 15th the squadron returned to Chusan.

While these things were taking place at Taku, there had occurred a few skirmishes elsewhere. A shipwrecked crew had fallen into Chinese hands and been carried to Ningpo, and some foraging parties were roughly handled. Lin tried to inspirit his troops by offering large rewards for British ships and subjects, and a force of about one thousand two hundred men was stationed in and around the Barrier at Macao. Captain Smith, however, moved two sloops and a steamer near their position, and soon drove the soldiers away, destroying their guns and barracks.

Lin was busy enlisting volunteers and preparing the defences of Canton, but in the summer he was ordered to return "with the speed of flames" to Peking. His Majesty was unnecessarily severe upon his servant: "You have not only proved yourself unable to cut off their trade," he says, "but you have also proved yourself unable to seize perverse natives. You have but dissembled with empty words, and so far from having been any help in the affair, you have caused the waves of confusion to arise, and a thousand interminable disorders are sprouting; in fact, you have been as if your arms were tied, without knowing what to do: it appears, then, you are no better than a wooden image. When I meditate on all these things, I am filled with anger and melancholy." Trade was carried on notwithstanding the blockade, by sending tea and goods through Macao; and many ships loaded for England and the United States.

Admiral Elliot entered into a truce with Îlípu, governor-general of Chehkiang, by which each party agreed to observe certain boundaries. Sickness and death had made sad inroads into the health and numbers of the troops at Tinghai, owing to their bad location, malaria, and improper food; more than four hundred out of the four thousand landed in July having died, and three times that number being in the hospitals. The people dared not reopen their shops until after the truce; the visits paid to various parts of the island better informed the inhabitants of the personal character of their temporary rulers, and a profitable trade in provisions encouraged them to farther acquaintance.

The two plenipotentiaries returned November 20th, and immediately sent a steamer bearing a despatch from Îlípu to Kíshen; the vessel was fired upon by an officer unacquainted with the meaning of a white flag—the intent and privileges of which were after this understood; Kíshen made an ample apology for this mishap. Negotiations were resumed during the month of December, but the determination of the Chinese to resist rather than grant full indemnity for the opium was more and more apparent. Kíshen probably found more zeal among the people for a fight than he had supposed, but his own desires were to settle the matter "more soon, more better." What demands were made as a last alternative are not known, but one of them, the cession of the island of Hongkong, he refused to grant, and broke off the discussion. Commodore Bremer thereupon attacked and took the forts at Chuenpí and Taikok-tau on January 7th, when the further progress of his forces was stayed by Kíshen, who was present and saw enough to convince him of the folly of resistance.

On January 20th the suspended negotiations had proceeded so far that Captain Elliot announced the conclusion of preliminary arrangements upon four points, viz., the cession of the island and harbor of Hongkong to the British crown, an indemnity of six millions of dollars in annual instalments, direct official intercourse upon an equal footing, and the immediate resumption of English trade at Canton. By these arrangements Chusan and Chuenpí were to be immediately restored to the Chinese, the prisoners at Ningpo released, and the English allowed to occupy Hongkong. One evidence of Kíshen's "scrupulous good faith," mentioned in Captain Elliot's notice, is the edict he put up on Hongkong, telling the inhabitants they were now under English authority. Two interviews took place after this, at the last of which it was plain that two of the four stipulations, viz., the first instalment of a million of dollars, and opening of trade by February 1st, would not be fulfilled. The intimations of the designs of the court were so evident that the treaty was probably never even presented to the Emperor for ratification.

Kíshen carried his negotiations thus far, with the hope perhaps that an adjustment of the difficulties on such terms would be accepted by his imperial master. On the other hand, Lin and his colleagues memorialized him as soon as Kíshen came to Canton against peaceful measures, and their recommendations as to the necessity of resistance were strongly backed by the mortifying loss of Chusan. The approach of a large force to the Pei ho alarmed his Majesty, and conciliatory measures were taken, and a reference to Canton proposed before settling the dispute; when the men-of-war left, he was inclined for peace, and issued orders not to attack the ships while the discussions were going on. But the memorials had already changed his mind, and war was determined on at the date of signing the treaty. It is probable if, instead of seizing Chusan, which had given no cause of provocation, the English had gone up the Yangtsz' kiang and Pei ho, and stationed themselves there until their demands were granted, peace would have been soon made. But, in that case, would the vain notion of their supremacy have left the Chinese?

Looking back forty years, one can recognize the benefit to both parties which resulted from the failure of this treaty. The great desire of Christian people, who believed that China was finally to receive the gospel, was that it might be opened to their benevolent efforts, but this treaty left the country as closed as ever to all good influences, commercial, political, social, and religious, while the evils of smuggling, law-breaking, and opium-smoking remained unmolested. The crisis which had brought out this expedition was not likely soon to recur, and if this failed to break down its seclusiveness, no other nation would attempt the task. Every well-wisher of China cherished the hope that, since this unfortunate conflict must needs be, its outcome would leave the entire land fully accessible to the regenerating, as well as shielded from the evil influences of Christian nations.

Captain Elliot appreciated the dilemma into which the Emperor had been brought by the acts of Lin, and knew that ignorance was much more the misfortune than the fault of both; he acted humanely, therefore, in pursuing a mild course at first, until the points at issue had been fairly brought before the people as well as the cabinet. However justly some parts of his conduct may have merited criticism, this praiseworthy feature of his policy by no means earned the torrent of abuse he received for consistently pursuing such a course. His countrymen would have had him burn, kill, and destroy, as soon as the expedition reached the coast, before even stating his demands at court; and during his negotiations with Kíshen, and when Chusan was restored, a smile of contempt at his supposed gullibility was everywhere seen. The treaty of the Bogue, though formed in good faith by both commissioners, was rejected by both sovereigns, though for opposite reasons; by Victoria, because it did not grant enough, by Taukwang, because it granted too much.

The Emperor issued orders to resume the war, collect troops from the provinces upon Canton and Tinghai, in order to "destroy and wipe clean away, to exterminate and root out the rebellious barbarians," and urged the people to regard them with the same bitterness they did their personal enemies. His mandate is couched in strong terms, saying that his enemies have been rebellious against heaven, opposing reason, one in spirit with the brute beasts, "beings that the overshadowing vault and all-containing earth can hardly suffer to live," obnoxious to angels and men, and that he must discharge his heaven-conferred trust by sweeping them from the face of the earth. This decree exhibited the true principles of action of this proud government, which deliberately rejected the offer of peace, and determined to uphold its fancied supremacy to the utmost. China must now win or break.

Hostile intentions had become so evident that Captain Elliot announced that Commodore Bremer would return to the Bogue with the force ; the boats of the Nemesis were fired upon while sounding, and the battery near Anunghoy was attacked the same day that Chusan was evacuated. Rewards of $50,000 were offered for Elliot, Bremer, Morrison, and other ringleaders, and all the defences put in the best condition. On February 26th the Bogue forts were all taken, Admiral Kwan falling at his post. The British had nine ships, assisted by less than five hundred troops, and two steamers. The Chinese force was probably over three thousand, but it made no resistance after the batteries were taken; the total loss was supposed to be not far from a thousand. The forts were built so solidly that few were killed by the broadsides of the ships, and their magazines so well protected that no explosions took place; the powder found in them was used to demolish the walls. There were in all eight large forts on the sides of the river and Wangtong Island, forming altogether a line of batteries which would have been impregnable in the hands of European troops, and was not without reason deemed to be so by the Chinese themselves.

The next day the small ships moved up to the First Bar, where a long fortification on the river bank, and an intrenched camp of two thousand troops, defended by upward of a hundred cannon, with a strong raft thrown across the river, showed a resolution to make a stand. The ships and steamers opened a hot fire upon the batteries and camp, which returned it as well as they could, but the loss of life was greatest when the English landed. Many instances of personal bravery showed that the Chinese were not all destitute of courage, but without discipline and better weapons it was of no avail. Nearly one-fourth were killed, their camp burned, the Chesapeake and all her stores blown up, and most of the crew killed. The raft was easily removed by the steamers, to the mortification of the Chinese, who had trusted that this might prove a permanent barrier to the approach of ships to the city. From this point the way was open to within five miles of Canton, and when the forts at that place were taken, the prefect met Captain Elliot on March 3d with a flag of truce proposing a suspension of hostilities for three days.

Kíshen had already been ordered to return to Peking to await his trial; his memorial[1] on hearing of his degradation does him credit. Íliang was left in command of the province until four general officers, leading large bodies of troops, should arrive. The highest of these was Yihshan, a nephew of the Emperor, assisted by Yang Fang, Lungwăn, and Tsíshin. On the part of the English, Major-General Sir Hugh Gough arrived from India to take command of the land forces, and Sir Gordon Bremer sailed for Calcutta to procure recruits. Bodies of troops were gathering in and around Canton to the amount of five or six thousand, most of whom had come from the North-West Provinces, and were not less strange and formidable to the citizens than were their foreign enemies.

After the truce had expired the English moved toward Canton by both the channels leading to the city, the iron steamer Nemesis proceeding up the Inner Passage, subduing all obstacles in her way until every fort, raft, battery, camp, and stockade between the ocean and Canton had been taken or destroyed, and the city lay at their mercy. The factories had been kept safely, and were occupied by British troops just two years after Lin had imprisoned the foreigners there. A second truce was agreed upon March 20th, by which trade was allowed to proceed on the old mode; merchant ships accordingly advanced up the river, and for about six weeks trade went on uninterruptedly—one party getting their tea and the other their duties. The new governor, Kí Kung, together with the "rebel-quelling general" Yihshan, then arrived, and the people, thinking that a slight cause would disturb the truce, took advantage of it to remove their effects, well aware how much they would suffer from their own army in case of trouble.

Toward the middle of May the hostile intentions of the Chinese were manifest, though cloaked under professions of amity; and on the 21st Captain Elliot notified all foreigners to go

[1] *Chinese Repository,* Vol. X., p. 235.

aboard ship. The secret preparations for attack were very extensive. Large fire-boats and rafts were prepared, masked batteries erected along the river, troops quartered in the temples, and large cannon placed in the streets. The day before the notice of Captain Elliot was issued, the prefect had the impudence to publish a proclamation assuring all classes of the peaceful intentions of the commissioners. Finding their prey gone, a night attack was made by land and water on the ships, but none were seriously injured. As daylight advanced the Nemesis went in pursuit of the fire-boats and junks, and burned upward of sixty, while three men-of-war silenced the batteries along shore. Meantime the Chinese troops searched the factory buildings for arms and pillaged three of the hongs, to the consternation of the prefect, who told the commissioner that he would be forced to pay for losses thus sustained. On the 24th the land and naval forces under Sir Hugh Gough and Sir Fleming Senhouse arrived from Hongkong and prepared to invest the city. Most of the troops debarked above it, at Neishing, under the personal directions of Sir Fleming, who had provided many boats in which the force of two thousand six hundred men, besides followers, guns, and stores, were towed about twelve miles. A detachment landed and took possession of the factories. Sir Hugh Gough remained near the place of debarkation till the next morning, when the whole body moved onward to attack the forts and camps behind the city. As the English advanced the Chinese found that their shot did not reach them, so that after an hour's firing they began to collect outside of the forts, preparatory to retiring. The advance pushed on, and sent them scampering down the hills toward the city; the intrenched camp was carried with considerable loss to its defenders, who everywhere ran as soon as the fight came to close quarters; but in the forts there were many furious struggles.

On the 26th a driving rain stopped all operations; and a parley was also requested from the now deserted city walls by two officers, who agreed to send a deputation to make arrangements for surrender. Night came on before any heralds appeared, so that it was not till morning that the troops were in

WALL OF CANTON CITY. (FROM FISHER.)

position, the guns loaded and primed, port-fires lighted, and everything in readiness to open fire, when a messenger arrived from Captain Elliot, desiring further operations to be delayed until he had concluded his negotiations. The terms were: that the forces should remain in position until a ransom of $6,000,000 was paid; that the three imperial commissioners and all their troops should march sixty miles from the city; that compensation for the loss of property in the factories and burning the Spanish brig Bilbaino should be at once handed over or secured; and that the Chinese troops, nearly fifty thousand in number, should evacuate the city. Captain Elliot ought indeed to have demanded a personal apology from Yihshan and his colleagues for their infamous treachery before letting them go. His acceptance of this ransom and sparing the city from capture were sharply criticised at the time, and the contemptuous bearing of the citizens during the sixteen ensuing years of their possession proved that it was an ill-timed mercy. How much influence the orders from home to be careful of the tea-trade had in this course cannot be learned.

While the English forces were occupying the heights the lawless soldiers from Kweichau and Kwangsí began to plunder the citizens, who retaliated till blood was shed and more than a thousand persons were killed in the streets; a patriot mob of villagers, numbering about fifteen thousand, attacked the few British troops left on the hills north of the city, but a prompt advance on the part of Sir Hugh drove this rabble a rout of some three miles. Upon their reappearance next day, the prefect was told that if they were not instantly dispersed the city would be bombarded; the threats and persuasions of the commissioners, aided by a British officer, finally induced the mob to retire. The superiority of discipline over mere numbers was probably never more remarkably exhibited; though the Chinese outnumbered the English more than forty to one, not a single foreigner was killed.

On the 31st the prefect furnished five hundred coolies to assist in transporting the guns and stores to the river side, and ten days after Captain Elliot's first notice everything was restored to the Chinese. The casualties among the British forces were fourteen killed and one hundred and twelve wounded, but about three hundred died from sickness. The losses of the Chinese from first to last could hardly have been much under five thousand men, besides thousands of cannon, ginjals, and matchlocks. In posting their forces, placing their masked batteries, and equipping their troops and forts, the Chinese showed considerable strategy and skill, but lack of discipline and confidence rendered every defence unavailing. Yihshan and his associates memorialized the Emperor, detailing their reasons for ransoming the city and requesting an inquiry into their conduct.[1]

The sickness of the troops compelled the British force to remain at Hongkong to recruit and wait for reinforcements. Commodore Bremer returned as joint plenipotentiary, bringing additional forces from Calcutta, and the expedition was on the point of sailing northward when both he and Captain Elliot were wrecked in a tyfoon, and this detained the ships a few days longer. Before they sailed Sir Henry Pottinger and Admiral Sir William Parker arrived direct from England to supersede them both. Sir Henry announced his appointment and duties, and also sent a communication to the governor of Canton, assuring him that the existing truce would be observed as long as the Chinese did not arm their forts, impede the regular trade, which had been lately reopened to British ships by imperial command, or trouble the merchants residing in the factories. The trade went on at Canton, after this, without any serious interruption during the war, the usual duties and charges being paid as if no hostilities existed.

The expedition moved northward, August 21st, under the joint command of Sir Hugh Gough and Admiral Parker, consisting of two seventy-fours and seven other ships of war, four steamers, twenty-three transports, and a surveying vessel, carrying in all about three thousand five hundred troops. Six ships and four or five hundred Indian troops remained off Canton and at Hongkong, to compel the observance of the truce. The force reached Amoy, and after a hasty reconnoissance attacked

[1] *Chinese Repository*, Vol. X. (p. 402), in which, and in Vols. VIII., IX., and XI., most of the official papers issued from the Chinese and English authorities during the war are contained.

all its defences, which were carried without much loss of life on either side. The city was taken on the 27th, and all the arms and public stores, wall-pieces, ginjals, matchlocks, shields, uniforms, bows, arrows, spears, and quantities of powder were destroyed; five hundred cannon were found in the forts. When H. M. S. Blonde came into this harbor, fourteen months previous, to deliver the letter for Peking, the fortifications consisted only of two or three forts near the city, but every island and protecting headland overlooking the harbor had since been occupied and armed, while a line of stone wall more than a mile long, with embrasures roofed by large slabs covered with earth to protect the guns, had been built, and batteries and bastions erected at well-chosen points. The broadsides of the ships had little effect here, and it was not until the troops landed and drove out the garrisons, who "stood right manfully to their guns," that the fire slackened, and the Chinese retreated. The city was completely pillaged by native robbers, who ran riot during several weeks until the craven authorities came back and resumed their functions. The island of Kulang su was garrisoned by a detachment of five hundred and fifty troops, and three ships left to protect them. The British found one two-decker among the war junks, built on a foreign model, launched and ready for sea, carrying twenty guns; all were burned.

The English fleet again entered the harbor of Tinghai, September 29th, and found the beach much altered since February. Stone walls and fortifications extended two miles in front of the suburbs, besides sand-bags and redoubts thrown up on well-selected positions. They were taken after a defence marked with unusual courage; the general commanding the battery and all his suite were killed at their posts, and many hand-to-hand conflicts took place. But bravery and numbers were alike unavailing, and in two hours their defences were cleared, the walls of the town escaladed, the whole force scattered, and the island subdued, with the estimated loss to the Chinese of a thousand men. Great quantities of ordnance, among which were forty brass guns made in imitation of foreign howitzers, with military stores and provisions in abundance, were seized. A detachment was sent throughout the island to drive off the enemy's troops, and announce to the inhabitants that they were now under English authority. They evinced none of the alarm they had done the year before; provisions came in, shops were opened, and confidence in these proclamations generally exhibited. A military government was appointed, and a garrison of four hundred men left to protect the island.

The military operations in Chehkiang were conducted by Yukien and Yu Pu-yun; both these men had urged war, and had done all they could to fortify Tinghai and Chinhai, whose batteries and magazines showed the vigor of their operations. The English fleet proceeded to Chinhai October 9th, and a force of about two thousand two hundred men, with twelve field pieces and mortars, landed next morning to attack the citadel and intrenched camp. There were nearly five thousand men in this position, who formed in good order as the English advanced, opening a well-directed fire upon the front column, but quite neglecting two detachments on their flanks; as the three opened upon them nearly simultaneously, their force was completely bewildered, and all soon broke and fled. Knowing nothing of the mode of asking for quarter, while some fled into the country, the greater part retreated toward the water, pursued by the three columns, hundreds being shot and hundreds drowned. Sir Hugh Gough sent out a flag with Chinese written upon it, to inform them that their lives would be spared if they yielded, but not more than five hundred either could or would throw down their arms. The water was soon covered with bodies, and fully fifteen hundred soldiers lost their lives. The town and its defences were bombarded, and the troops driven out. Yukien endeavored to drown himself on seeing the day was lost, but being prevented he retreated to Yüyau, where he committed suicide, as was said, by swallowing gold leaf. He was a Manchu, and could not brook his master's displeasure; but his atrocious cruelty to two Englishmen who fell into his hands, one of whom was flayed and then burnt to death, had aroused general detestation against him. About one hundred and fifty pieces of brass ordnance, with great quantities of gunpowder and other military stores, were destroyed. The guns and carriages in the fort and batteries were so well made and placed that in some cases the victors on entering turned them against the flying Chinese. The frame of a wheel vessel, intended to be moved by human power, was found near Chinhai, showing, as did the brass guns, traversing carriages, and frigate at Amoy, that the Chinese were already imitating the machinery of war from their foes.

Ningpo was taken without resistance on the 13th. Many of the people left the city, and those who remained shut themselves in their houses, writing *shun min*, 'submissive people,' on the doors. Captain Anstruther took possession of his old prison—where he found the identical cage he had been carried in—and released all the inmates to make way for his detachment of artillery. About $100,000 in sycee were found in this building, upward of $70,000 in the treasury, many tons of copper cash in the mint, and rice, silk, and porcelain in the public stores, forming altogether the most valuable prizes yet secured. Sir Henry Pottinger intended at first to burn the city, but, happily for his reputation, he decided to occupy it as winter quarters. Leaving a garrison at Chinhai, he returned to Hongkong in February, 1842, Sir Hugh and the admiral remaining at the north.

The fall of Amoy, Tinghai, Chinhai, and Ningpo, instead of disheartening the Emperor, served rather to inspirit him. His commissioners, generals, and high officers generally did the best their knowledge and means enabled them to do, and when defeated, endeavored to palliate the discomfiture they could not entirely conceal by misrepresenting the force brought against them, and laying the blame upon the common people, the elements, the native traitors who aided the British, or the inefficiency of the naval armaments. The troops sent home with tokens of victory from Canton stimulated the war spirit in the western provinces. After they had gone Yihshan concocted measures of defence, one of which was to enlist two or three thousand volunteers, or "village braves," near the city, and place them under their own officers. The people having been taught to despise foreigners were easily incensed against them, and several cases of insult and wantonness were repeated and magnified in order to stir up a spirit of revenge. These patriots supposed, moreover, that if the great Emperor had called on *them*, instead of entrusting the conduct of the quarrel to truckling traitorous poltroons like Kíshen and the prefect, they could have avenged him of his enemies.

Consequently the truce was soon broken in an underhand manner by sinking hundreds of tons of stones in the river. H. M. S. Royalist levelled the fortifications at the Bogue, and Captain Nias destroyed a number of boats at Whampoa. After the destruction of these forts and his retirement from the river, Yihshan directed his attention to erecting forts near the city, casting guns, and drilling the volunteers, who numbered nearly thirty thousand at the new year. He also gave a public dinner to the rich men of the city, in order to learn their willingness to contribute to the expenses of these measures. However, since no serious obstacles were placed in the way of shipping teas by the provincial officers, from the duties on which they chiefly derived the funds for these undertakings, the British officers deemed it advisable to let them alone.

The case was different at other points. The imperial government had supposed that Amoy would be attacked, because the visit of the Blonde showed that the barbarians, "sneaking in and out like rats," knew of its existence; but the people of that province, except near Amoy, took no particular interest in the dispute, and probably knew far less of it than was known in most parts of England and the United States; no newspapers, with "own correspondents" to write the "latest accounts from the seat of war," narrated the progress of this struggle, which to them was like the silent reflection of distant lightning in their own quiet firmament. The sack of Amoy was a heavy blow to its citizens, but the plunderers were mostly their countrymen; and when Captain Smith of the Druid had been there a short time in command, and his character became known, they returned to their houses and shops, supplied the garrison with provisions, and even brought back a deserter, and assisted in chasing some pirates. Rumors of attack were always brought to him, and his declarations allayed their fears, so that after the sub-prefect resumed his authority no disturbance occurred. The explanations of the missionaries on Kulang su, in diffusing a better understanding of the object in occupying that island, also contributed to this result.

The loss of Chinhai and Ningpo threw the eastern parts of Chehkiang open to the invaders, and alarmed the court far more than the destruction of Canton would have done. The Emperor appointed his nephew, Yihking, to be "majesty-bearing generalissimo," and with him Tih-í-shun and Wănwei, all Manchus, to command the grand army and arouse the dwellers on the sea-coast to arm and defend themselves. "Ministers and people! Inhabitants of our dominions! Ye are all the children of our dynasty! For two centuries ye have trod our earth and eaten our food. Whoever among you has heavenly goodness must needs detest these rebellious and disorderly barbarians even as ye do your personal foes. On no account allow yourselves to be deceived by their wiles, and act or live abroad with them." Such was the closing exhortation of an imperial proclamation issued to encourage them. In order to raise funds for its operations, the government resorted to the sale of office and titles of nobility, and levied benevolences from rich individuals and contributions from the people; which, when large in amount, were noticed and rewarded. Kíshen, who had been tried at Peking and sentenced to lose his life, was for some reason reprieved to be associated with Yihking as an adviser, but never proceeded beyond Chihlí. Lin was also recalled from Îlí, if indeed he ever went beyond the Great Wall, and Îlípu, whose treatment and release of the prisoners at Ningpo had gained him the good-will of the English, was also sentenced to banishment, but neither did he go beyond the Desert.

Defences were thrown up at Tientsin and Taku to guard the passage to the capital, but the bar at the mouth of the Pei ho was its sufficient protection. Fearing that the English would advance upon the city of Hangchau, the troops of the province and all its available means were put into requisition. Sir Hugh Gough could only approach it by a land march from Ningpo, and deemed it advisable to wait for reinforcements, his available force being reduced to six hundred men on entering that city. The rewards given to the families of those who had fallen in battle, and the posthumous honors conferred by the Emperor, stimulated others to deeds of valor and a determination to accomplish their master's vengeance. Yukien, "who gave his life for his country, casting himself into the water," received high titular honors in the hall of worthies, and his brother was permitted to bring his corpse within the city of Peking. The names of humbler servants were not forgotten in the imperial rescripts, and a place was granted them among those whom the "king delighteth to honor." Thus did the Chinese endeavor to reassert their supremacy, though their counsels and efforts to chastise the rebellious barbarians were not unlike the deliberations of the rats upon "how to bell the cat."

The occupation of Ningpo was an eyesore to the Chinese generals, but the citizens had learned their best interests and generally kept quiet. They showed their genius in various contrivances to carry off plunder, such as putting valuable articles in coffins and ash-baskets, wrapping them around corpses, packing them under vegetables or rubbish. One party overtook two persons near Ningpo running off with a basket between them; on overtaking and recovering it, a well-dressed lady was found coiled up, who, however, did not scream when detected. Another was found in a locker on board a junk, and as the captain was desirous of examining the mode of bandaging her feet, he told his men to lift the body out of the closet, when a scream explained the trick; she was dismissed, and the money she had endeavored to hide put into her hands. Opium was found in most of the official residences; its sale received no serious check from the war, and no reference was made to it by either party.

Toward the end of the year 1841, information was received of the collection of a large force at Yüyau. Two iron steamers soon landed seven hundred men, who took up a position for the night, intending to escalade the walls in the morning; but their defenders evacuated the place. The marines and seamen took the circuit of the walls, and found the troops, about a thousand strong, drawn up in array; and the two, after exchanging their fire, started on the run. The public stores were destroyed, and the town left to the care of its citizens, without much loss of life on either side. On his return the general visited Tsz'kí, but the troops and the authorities had decamped. The rice found in the granaries was distributed to the townsmen, and the detachment returned to Ningpo December 31st. On a similar visit to Funghwa it was found that the authorities and troops had fled, so that to destroy the government stores and distribute the rice to the people was all that remained to be done. These two expeditions so terrified the "majesty-bearing generalissimo," Yihking, and his colleagues, that they fled to Suchau, in Kiangsu. With such leaders it is not strange that the villagers near Ningpo wished to enrol themselves under British rule; and the effect of the moderation of the English troops was seen in the people giving them little or no molestation after the first alarm was over, and supplying their wants as far as possible.

The force had fairly settled in its quarters at Ningpo, when the Chinese opened the campaign, March 10th, by a well-concerted night attack on the city. During the preceding day, many troops entered the city in citizen's clothes, and stationed themselves near the gates; and about three o'clock in the morning the western and southern gates were attacked and driven in. Colonel Morris ordered a party to retake the south gate, which was done, with considerable loss to the enemy; as usually happened, the moment the Chinese were opposed their main object was forgotten, and every man sought his own safety, thereby exposing himself more fully to destruction. On the approach of daylight the garrison assembled at the western gate, and dragging two or three howitzers through it, came upon the main force of the enemy drawn up in compact form, headed by an officer on horseback. The volleys poured into this dense mass mowed them down so that the street was choked with dead bodies, and the horse of the leader actually covered with corpses, from which he was seen vainly endeavoring to release himself. Those who escaped the fire in front were attacked in rear; at last about six hundred were killed, and the whole force of five thousand scattered by less than two hundred Europeans, with the loss of one man killed and six wounded.

The British then prepared to attack an intrenched camp of eight thousand troops near Tsz'ki, and about twelve hundred were embarked in the steamers. The Chinese had chosen their ground well, on the acclivity of two hills behind the town, and in order to confound and disperse their enemy completely, the attacking force was divided so as to fall upon them on three sides simultaneously, which was done with great slaughter. The Chinese did not run until they began to close in with their opponents, when they soon found that their intimidating gesticulations and cheers, their tiger-faced shields and two-edged swords, were of no avail in terrifying the barbarians or resisting their pistols, bayonets, and furious onset. In these cases, emulation among the different parties of English troops to distinguish themselves occasionally degenerated into unmanly slaughter of their flying enemy, who were looked upon rather as good game than fellow-men, and pursued in some instances several miles. Most of the Chinese troops in this engagement and in the attack on Ningpo were from the western provinces, and superior in size and bodily strength to those hitherto met. They had been encouraged to attack Ningpo by a bounty to each man of four or five dollars, and pieces of sycee were found on their bodies. The Chinese lost a thousand slain on the field, many by their own act; the English casualties were six killed and thirty-seven wounded.

The conquerors set fire to the Chinese camp in the morning, consuming all the houses used as arsenals, with arms and ammunition of every kind. The force then proceeded to the Changkí pass, a defile in the mountains, but the imperialists had abandoned their camp, leaving only "a considerable quantity of good bread." In his despatch Sir Hugh speaks of the forbearance shown by his men toward the inhabitants; and efforts were taken by the English, throughout the war, to spare the people and respect their property. The English thus dispersed that part of the Grand Army which had been called out by the Emperor and his "majesty-bearing generalissimo" to annihilate the rebels. The fugitives spread such dismay among their comrades near Hangchau that the troops began to desert and exhibit symptoms of disbanding altogether; the spirit of dissatisfaction was, moreover, increased by the people, who very naturally grumbled at being obliged to support their unsuccessful defenders, as well as submit to their tyrannous exactions.

The Chinese near Ningpo and Chinhai had so much confidence in the English, and were so greatly profited by their presence, that no disturbances took place. The rewards offered by the Chinese generals for prisoners induced the people to lay in wait for stragglers. One, Sergeant Campbell, was seized near Tinghai, put into a bag to be carried to the coast, where he was shipped in a junk and landed at Chapu, before being relieved of his hood. One of his ears was cut off with a pair of scissors, but after reaching Hangchau he was well treated. During his captivity there he was often questioned by the Chinese officers as to the movements, forces, and arms of his countrymen, and received a high idea of their intelligence from the character of their inquiries.

The entire strength with Sir Hugh Gough, in May, consisted of parts of four English regiments, a naval brigade of two hundred and fifty, and a few Indian troops, in all about two thousand five hundred men; the fleet comprised seven ships of war and four steamers. On the 17th the whole anchored in the harbor of Chapu, about forty miles above Chinhai. About six thousand three hundred Chinese troops and one thousand seven hundred Manchus were posted here in forts and intrenched camps. The English landed in three columns, as usual without opposition, and promptly turned the orderly arranged army and garrisons of their opponents into a mass of fugitives, each man throwing away his arms and uniform and flying *à pas de géant*. A body of three hundred Manchus, seeing their retreat cut off, retired into an enclosed temple, whose entrance was both narrow and dark. Every one who attempted to enter it was either killed or wounded, one of whom was Lieutenant-Colonel Tomlinson. At length a part of the wall was blown in, which exposed the inmates to the rifles of their foes, and a rocket or two set the building on fire, by which the inmates were driven from their position to the rooms below; when resistance ceased only fifty were taken prisoners, the others having been burned to death or suffocated. The total loss of the invaders was thirteen killed and fifty-two wounded.

The defences of Chapu being carried, with a loss to the enemy of about one thousand five hundred, the English moved on the city. This was the first time the Manchus had really come in contact with the English; and either fearing that indiscriminate slaughter would ensue on defeat, as it would have done had *they* been the victors, or else unable to brook their disgrace, they destroyed themselves in great numbers, first immolating their wives and children, and then cutting their own throats. Scores of bodies were found in their quarters, some not entirely dead; others were prevented from self-destruction, and in many instances, young children were found attending upon their aged or infirm parents, awaiting in dread suspense the visit of the conquerors, from whom they expected little less than instant destruction. The English surgeons endeavored to bind up the wounds of such Chinese as fell in their way, and these attentions had a good effect upon the high Chinese officers, Ílípu himself sending a letter in which he thanked the general and admiral for their kindness in giving the hungry rice to eat and caring for the wounded. The old man endeavored to requite it by making the condition of his prisoners as easy as he could, and paid them money on their release. When the English generals, having destroyed all the government stores, re-embarked, the prisoners were released with a small present, and on their return to Hangchau loudly proclaimed their praises of the foreigners.

The expedition proceeded northward to the mouth of the Yangtsz' kiang, and reached the embouchure of the Wusung, where the ships took their allotted positions, June 16th, before the well-built stone batteries, extending full three miles along the western banks of the river. One of these works enclosed the town of Paushan and mounted one hundred and thirty-four guns; the others counted altogether one hundred and seventy-five guns, forty-two of which were brass. These defences were manned by a well-selected force, under the command of Chin Hwa-ching. The ships had scarcely taken their stations when the batteries opened, and both sides kept up a cannonading for about two hours, the Chinese working their guns with much skill and effect. When the marines landed and entered, they bravely measured weapons with them, and died at their posts. Among the war junks were several new wheel-boats, having two wooden paddle-wheels turned by a capstan, which interlocked its cogs into those upon the shaft, and was worked by men on the gun-deck. These were paddling out of danger, when the steamers overtook and silenced them. The number of Chinese killed was about one hundred, out of not less than five thousand men composing the garrison and army. The governor-general, Niu Kien, who was present, in reporting the loss of the forts and dispersion of the troops, says he braved the hottest of the fight, "where cannon-balls innumerable, flying in awful confusion through the expanse of heaven, fell before, behind, and on either side of him; while in the distance he saw the ships of the rebels standing erect, lofty as the mountains. The fierce daring of the rebels was inconceivable; officers and men fell at their posts. Every effort to resist and check the onset was in vain, and a retreat became inevitable."

Among the killed was General Chin, who had taken unwearied pains to drill his troops, appoint them to their places, and inspirit them with his own courageous self-devotion. In a memoir of him, it is said that on the morning of the attack "he arrayed himself in his robes of state, and having prayed to heaven and earth, ordered all his officers and soldiers to get their arms and ammunition ready." Niu Kien's conduct was not such as to cheer them on, and most of the officers "came forward and begged to retire" when they saw the dilapidated state of the batteries. Chin's second suggested a retreat when the marines entered the battery, but he drew his sword upon him, saying, "My confidence in you has been misplaced." He again inspirited his men, himself loading and firing the ginjals, and fell pierced with wounds on the walls of the fort, bowing his head as he died in the direction of the Emperor's palace. His Majesty paid him high honors, by erecting shrines to him in his native village and at the place where he fell; in the *Ching-hwang miao* at Shanghai there is a sitting image of him in his robes of state, before which incense is burned. A reward of a thousand taels was given his family, and his son was made a *kü-jin* by special patent. In this notice it is stated as a current rumor in Shanghai, that about a fortnight after his death Chin sent down the news through the divining altar at Sungkiang, that he had been promoted by the Supreme Ruler of

Heaven to the rank of second general-in-chief of the Board of Thunder, so that although he could not, while alive, repay the imperial favor by exterminating the rebels, he could still afford some aid to his country.

The stores of every kind were destroyed, except the brass pieces, among which were one Spanish gun of old date, and a Chinese piece more than three centuries old, both of them of singular shape, the latter being like a small-mouthed jar. The British landed on the 19th, two thousand in all, and proceeded to Shanghai by land. After the capture of Wusung, Mr. Gutzlaff, who accompanied the admiral as interpreter, succeeded in reassuring the people and inducing them to stay in their dwellings; he was also employed in procuring provisions. The ships silenced two small batteries near the city with a single broadside, and the troops entered it without resistance. The good effects of previous kindness shown the people in respecting their property were here seen. Captain Loch says that on the march along the banks he passed through two villages where the shops were open, with their owners in them, and that groups of people were assembled on the right and left to see them pass. The troops occupied the arsenals, the pawnbrokers' shops, and the temples, destroying all the government stores and distributing the rice in the granaries among the people. The total number of cannon taken was three hundred and eighty-eight, of which seventy-six were of brass; some of the latter were named "tamer and subduer of the barbarians;" others, "the robbers' judgment," and one piece twelve feet long was called the "Barbarian." The citizens voluntarily came forward to supply provisions, and stated that there had been a serious affray in the city a few days before between them and their officers, who wished to levy a subsidy for the defence of the city, which even then they were on the point of abandoning. The boats before the walls were crowded with inhabitants flying with their property, many of whom returned in a few days.

The troops retired from Shanghai June 23d, leaving it less injured than any city yet taken, owing chiefly to the efforts made by the people themselves to protect their property. The eight hundred junks and upward lying off the town were unharmed, but their owners no doubt were made to contribute toward the $300,000 exacted as a ransom. Sir Henry Pottinger now rejoined the expedition, accompanied by Lord Saltoun, with large reinforcements for both arms, and immediate preparations were made for proceeding up the Yangtsz', to interrupt the communication by the Grand Canal across that river. The Chinese officers, unable to read any European language, learned the designs of their enemy chiefly by rumors, which natives in the employ of the English brought them, and consequently not unfrequently misled his Majesty—unwittingly, in mentioning the wrong places likely to be attacked, but wilfully as to their numbers and conduct in the hour of victory. The fall of Shanghai and the probable march upon Sungkiang and Suchau greatly alarmed him, and he now began to think that the rebels really intended to proceed up to Nanking and the Grand Canal, which he had been assured was not their purpose.

He accordingly concentrated his troops at Chinkiang, Nanking, Suchau, and Tientsin, four places which he feared were in danger, and associated Kíying and Ilípu as commissioners with the governor-general, Niu Kien, to superintend civil affairs; military matters were still left under the management of the imbecile Yihking. Only a few places on the Yangtsz' kiang offered eligible positions for forts, and Niu Kien wisely declined to stake the Great River at Chinkiang, lest it should alarm the inhabitants. Fire-rafts and boats were, however, ordered for the defence of that city, and reinforcements of troops collected there and at Nanking, some of whom were encamped without the city, and part incorporated with the garrison. The tone of the documents which fell into the hands of the English showed the anxiety felt at court regarding the result of this movement up the river.

The British plenipotentiary published and circulated a manifesto at this date for "the information of the people of the country." In this paper he enumerated, in much the same manner as Captain Elliot had done, the grievances the English had suffered at Canton from the spoliations, insults, and imprisonment inflicted upon them by Lin in order to extort opium, which was given up by the English superintendent to rescue himself and his countrymen from death. The duplicity of the Chinese government in sending down Kíshen as a commissioner to Canton to arrange matters, and then, while he was negotiating, to break off the treaty and treacherously resort to war, was another "grand instance of offence against England." The bad treatment of kidnapped prisoners, the mendacious reports of victories gained over the English, which misled the Emperor and retarded the settlement of the war, was another cause of offence. The restriction of the trade to Canton, establishment of the monopoly of the hong merchants, the oppressive and unjust exactions imposed upon it through their scheming, and many other minor grievances which need not be enumerated, formed the last count in this indictment. Three things must be granted before peace could be made, viz., the cession of an island for commerce and the residence of merchants; compensation for losses and expenses; and allowing a friendly and becoming intercourse between the officers of the two countries on terms of equality. This proclamation, however, made no mention of the real cause of the war, the opium trade, and in that respect was far from being an ingenuous, fair statement of the question. It was much more like one of Napoleon's bulletins in the *Moniteur*, and considering the moral and intellectual condition of Great Britain and China, failed to uphold the high standing of the former.

While Sir Henry Pottinger knew that the use of this drug was one of the greatest evils which afflicted the people, he should have, in a document of this nature, left no room for the supposition, on the part of either ruler or subject, that the war was undertaken to uphold and countenance the opium trade. He could not have been ignorant that the Emperor and his ministers supposed the unequal contest they were waging was caused by their unsuccessful efforts to suppress the traffic; and that if they were defeated the opium trade must go on unchecked. The question of supremacy was set at rest in this proclamation; it must be given up; but no encouragement was held out to reassure the Chinese government in their lawful desire to restrain the tremendous scourge. Why should he? If he encouraged any action against the trade, he could expect little promotion or reward from his superiors in India or England, who looked to it for all the revenue it could be made to bring; or consideration from the merchants, who would not thank him for telling the Chinese they might attack the opium clippers wherever they found them, and seize all the opium they could, and English power would not interfere.

The Emperor issued a proclamation about the same time, recapitulating his conduct and efforts to put a stop to the war, stating what he had done to ward off calamity and repress the rebels. The opium trade, and his efforts for a long time to repress it, and especially the measures of Lin, are in this paper regarded as the causes of the war, which concludes by expressing his regrets for the sufferings and losses occasioned his subjects by the attacks of the English at Amoy, Chusan, Ningpo, and elsewhere, and exhorting them to renewed efforts. It is a matter of lasting regret that the impression has been left upon the minds of the Chinese people that the war was an opium war, and waged chiefly to uphold it. But nations, like individuals, must usually trust to might more than right to maintain their standing; and when conscious weakness leads them to adopt underhand measures to regain their rights, the temptation which led to these acts is rarely thought of in the day of retribution. The money demands of England were not deemed at the time to be exacting, but she should, and could at this time in an effectual manner, through her plenipotentiary, have cleared herself from all sanction of this traffic. If Lord Melbourne could wish it were a less objectionable traffic, Sir Henry Pottinger might surely have intimated, in as public a manner, his regret at its existence. He probably did not deem the use of opium very deleterious.

The number of ships, steamers, transports, and all in the expedition, when it left Wusung, July 6th, was seventy-two, most of them large vessels. They were arranged in five divisions, with an advance squadron of five small steamers and tenders to survey the river, each division having a frigate or seventy-four at its head. The world has seldom seen a more conspicuous instance of the superiority of a small body possessing science, skill, and discipline, over immense multitudes of undisciplined, ignorant, and distrustful soldiers, than was exhibited in this bold manœuvre. Not to speak alone of the great disparity in numbers, the distant quarters of the globe whence the ships were collected, the many languages and tribes found in the invading force, the magnitude of their ships, abundance of their supplies, and superiority of their weapons of war, the moral energy and confidence of power in this small troop over its ineffective adversary was not less conspicuous. The sight of such a fleet sailing up their Great River struck the inhabitants with mingled astonishment and dread.

Chinkiang lies half a mile from the southern bank of the Yangtsz', surrounded by a high wall four miles in circuit, and having hills of considerable elevation in its rear. The canal comes in from the south, close to the walls on its western side, and along the shores of both river and canal are extensive suburbs—at this time completely under the command of the guns of the ships, which could also bombard the city itself from some positions. A bluff hill on the north partly concealed the town from the ships, and it was not till this hill-top had been gained that the three Chinese encampments behind the city could be seen. The general divided his small force of seven thousand men into three brigades, under the command of Major-Generals Lord Saltoun, Schoedde, and Bartley, besides an artillery brigade of five hundred and seventy rank and file, under Lieutenant-Colonel Montgomerie. The Chinese encampments contained more than three thousand men, most of them soldiers from Hupeh and Chehkiang provinces. The Manchu garrison within the city consisted of one thousand two hundred regular troops and eight hundred Mongols from Koko-nor, together with eight hundred and thirty-five Chinese troops, making altogether from two thousand six hundred to two thousand eight hundred fighting men; the entire force was under the command of Hailing, who had made such a disposition of his troops and strengthened his means of defence as well as the time allowed. He closes his last communication to the Emperor with the assurance that "he cannot do otherwise than exert his whole heart and strength in endeavors to repay a small fraction of the favors he has enjoyed from his government."

The right brigade, under Lord Saltoun, soon drove the imperialists out of their camp, who did not wait for his near approach, but broke and dispersed after firing three or four distant volleys. Captain Loch says that while the party of volunteers were approaching the camp, they passed through a small hamlet on the hills; "the village had not been deserted; some of the houses were closed, while the inhabitants of others were standing in the streets staring at us in stupid wonder; and although they were viewing a contest between foreigners and their fellow-countrymen, and in danger themselves of being shot, were coolly eating their meals."

The centre brigade, under Major-General Schoedde, landed on the northern corner of the city, to escalade the walls on that side and prevent the troops from the camp entering the gates. He was received by a well-sustained fire, his men placing their ladders and mounting in the face of a determined resistance; as soon as they gained the parapet they drove the Tartars before them, though their passage was bravely disputed. While they were mounting the walls a fire was kept up on the city on the northern and eastern sides, under cover of which, after clearing the ramparts, they proceeded to the western gate, conquering all opposition in the northern part of the city, and driving the Tartars to the southern quarter.

The left brigade, under Major-General Bartley, did not reach the western side as soon as was expected, being delayed by the canal, here between seventy and eighty feet broad, which formed a deep ditch on this side. The western gate was blown in, the blast carrying before it a high pile of sand-bags heaped against the inside to strengthen the bars. While this work was going on, seven boats carrying artillerymen entered the canal to proceed up to the gate; but when nearly opposite they were repulsed by a severe fire from the walls, and the men compelled to abandon the three leading boats and take refuge in the houses along the banks; the others halted under cover of some houses until their comrades rejoined them, when all returned to the ships. Two hundred marines now landed, and with three hundred sepoys soon recovered the boats and carried back the wounded men. The party then planted their ladders in the face of a spirited fire from the walls, and succeeded in carrying them against all opposition.

All resistance at the three gateways having been overcome, it was supposed that the city was nearly subdued. Sir Hugh consequently ordered a halt for his men on account of the heat, and despatched a small force to proceed along the western ramparts to occupy the southern gate. This squad had proceeded about half a mile when it met a body of eight hundred or one thousand Tartars regularly drawn up in an open space. They fired with steadiness and regularity, but their bravery was of no avail, for the party, giving them one volley, charged down the bank and scattered them immediately, though not without some resistance. The dispersed Tartars, however, kept up a scattering fire along the streets and from the houses, which served chiefly to irritate their enemies and increase their own loss.

The heat of the day having passed, the commander-in-chief, guided by Mr. Gutzlaff and some Chinese, marched with two regiments into the southern quarter of the city. The scenes of desolation and woe which he met seem to have sickened the gray-haired warrior, for he says in his despatches, "finding dead bodies of Tartars in every house we entered, principally women and children, thrown into wells or otherwise murdered by their own people, I was glad to withdraw the troops from this frightful scene of destruction, and place them in the northern quarter." It was indeed a terrific scene. Captain Loch, who accompanied Sir Hugh, says they went to a large building thought to be the prefect's house, which was forced open and found entirely deserted, though completely furnished and of great extent; "we set fire to it and marched on." What the object or advantage of this barbarous act was he does not say. Leaving the general, he turned down a street and burst open the door of a large mansion; the objects which met his view were shocking.

After we had forced our way over piles of furniture placed to barricade the door, we entered an open court strewed with rich stuffs and covered with clotted blood; and upon the steps leading to the hall of ancestors there were two bodies of youthful Tartars, cold and stiff, who seemed to be brothers. Having gained the threshold of their abode, they had died where they had fallen from loss of blood. Stepping over these bodies we entered the hall, and met face to face three women seated, a mother and two daughters, and at their feet lay two bodies of elderly men, with their throats cut from ear to ear, their senseless heads resting upon the feet of their relations. To the right were two young girls, beautiful and delicate, crouching over and endeavoring to conceal a living soldier. In the heat of action, when the blood is up and the struggle is for life between man and man, the anguish of the wounded and the sight of misery and pain is unheeded; humanity is partially obscured by danger; but when excitement subsides with victory, a heart would be hardly human that could feel unaffected by the retrospection. And the hardest heart of the oldest man who ever lived a life of rapine and slaughter could not have gazed on this scene of woe unmoved. I stopped, horror-stricken at what I saw. The expression of cold, unutterable despair depicted on the mother's face changed to the violent workings of scorn and hate, which at last burst forth in a paroxysm of invective, afterward in floods of tears, which apparently, if anything could, relieved her. She came close to me and seized me by the arm, and with clenched teeth and deadly frown pointed to the bodies, to her daughters, to her yet splendid house, and to herself; then stepped back a pace, and with firmly closed hands and in a husky voice, I could see by her gestures, spoke of her misery, her hate, and, I doubt not, her revenge. I attempted by signs to explain, offered her my services, but was spurned. I endeavored to make her comprehend that, however great her present misery, it might be in her unprotected state a hundredfold increased; that if she would place herself under my guidance, I would pass her through the city gates in safety into the open country; but the poor woman would not listen to me, and the whole family was by this time in loud lamentation. All that remained for me to do was to prevent the soldiers bayoneting the man, who, since our entrance, had attempted to escape.[1]

The destruction of life was appalling. Some of the Manchus shut the doors of their houses, while through the crevices persons could be seen deliberately cutting the throats of their women, and destroying their children by throwing them into wells. In one house a man was shot while sawing his wife's throat as he held her over a well into which he had already thrown his children; her wound was sewed up and the lives of the children saved. In another house no less than fourteen dead bodies, principally women, were discovered; while such was their terror and hatred of the invaders, that every Manchu preferred resistance, death, suicide, or flight, to surrender. Out of a Manchu population of four thousand, it was estimated that not more than five hundred survived, the greater part having perished by their own hands.

[1] Capt. G. G. Loch, *Narrative of Events in China*, p. 109.

The public offices were ransacked and all arms and stores destroyed; only $60,000 in sycee were found in the treasury. The populace began to pillage, and in one instance, fearing a stop might be put to their rapacity, they set fire to the buildings at each end of a street in order to plunder a pawnbroker's shop without interference. The streets and lanes were strewed with silken, fur, and other rich dresses which the robbers had thrown away when they saw something more valuable, and the sepoys and camp-followers took what they could find. Parties were accordingly stationed at the gates to take everything from the natives as they went out, or which they threw over the walls, and in this way the thieves were in their turn stripped. Within twenty-four hours after the troops landed, the city and suburbs of Chinkiang were a mass of ruin and destruction; part of the eastern wall was subsequently blown in and all the gates dismantled to prevent any treachery. The total loss of the English was thirty-seven killed and one hundred and thirty-one wounded.

A curious contrast to the terrible scenes going on at Chinkiang was seen at Iching hien, on the northern side of the river. Four days before, the approach of the steamer Nemesis had caused no little consternation, and in the evening a Chinese gentleman came off to her with a few presents to learn if there was any intention of attacking the town. He was told that if he would send supplies of meat and provisions no harm would be done, and all he brought should be paid for. In the morning provisions were furnished, and he remained on board to see the steamer chase and bring junks to; being much amazed at these novel operations, which gave him a new idea of the energy of the invaders. In the evening commands were given him to bring provisions in larger quantities, and three boats went up to the town to procure them. The people showed no hostility, and through his assistance the English opened a market in the courtyard of a temple, at which supplies were purchased, put aboard small junks, and conveyed to the fleet. On the 21st the same person came, according to agreement, to accompany a large party of English from the ships to his house, where he had prepared an entertainment for them. Through the medium of a Chinese boy communication was easily carried on, and the alarms of the townspeople quieted; a proclamation was also issued stating that every peaceable person would be unharmed. This gentleman had invited a large company of his relatives and friends, and served up a collation for his guests; all this time the firing was heard from Chinkiang, where the countrymen of those so agreeably occupied were engaged in hostile encounter. On returning to their boats an additional mark of respect was shown by placing a well-dressed man each side of every officer to fan him as he walked. At the market-temple another entertainment was also served up. No injury was done by either side, and the forbearance of the English was not without good effect. Such queer contrasts as this have frequently characterized the contests between the Chinese and British.

Some of the large ships were towed up to Nanking, and the whole fleet reached it August 9th, at which time preparation had been made for the assault; but desirous of avoiding a repetition of the sad scenes of Chinkiang, the British leaders had also sent a communication to Niu Kien, offering to ransom the city for $3,000,000.

This celebrated city lies about three miles south of the river, but the north-east corner of an outer wall reaches within seven hundred paces of the water; the western face runs along the base of wooded hills for part of its distance, and is then continued through flat grounds around the southern side, both being defended by a deep ditch. The suburbs are on this low ground, where Sir Hugh Gough intended to bombard the place and make an entrance on the eastern side, while diversions at other points perplexed the garrison. His force consisted of only four thousand five hundred effective men; there were, as nearly as could be learned, six thousand Manchu and nine thousand Chinese troops within the city. On the 11th Lord Saltoun's brigade landed at a village from whence a paved road led to one of the eastern gates, and other detachments were stationed in the neighborhood. Everything was in readiness for the assault by daylight of August 15th, and the governor-general was told that it would assuredly be made unless the commissioners produced their authority for treating.

In the interval between the downfall of Chinkiang and investment of Nanking, several communications were received from the Chinese officers, and one from Kíying, couched in conciliatory language, and evincing a desire for peace. Sir Henry Pottinger replied in the same strain, deploring the war and calamities caused by its continuance, but stating that he could have no interview with any individual, however exalted, who was not properly commissioned to treat for peace. It is probable that the Emperor did not receive any suggestion from his ministers in regard to making peace until after the fall of Chinkiang, and it was a matter of some importance, therefore, for Ílípu and his colleague to delay the attack on Nanking until an answer could be received from the capital. The usual doubts in the minds of the English as to their sincerity led them to look upon the whole as a scheme to perfect the defences, and gain time for the people to retire; consequently the preparations for taking the city went on, in order to deepen the conviction that if one party was practising any deception, the other certainly was in earnest.

On the night of the 14th, scarcely three hours before the artillery was to open, Ílípu, Kíying, and Niu Kien addressed a joint letter to Sir Henry Pottinger requesting an interview in the morning, when they would produce their credentials and arrange for further proceedings. This request was granted with some reluctance, for the day before the *puching sz'* and Tartar commandant had behaved very unsatisfactorily, refusing to exhibit the credentials or discuss the terms of peace or ransom. The distress ensuent upon the blockade was becoming greater and greater; more than seven hundred vessels coming from the south had been stopped at Chinkiang, and a large fleet lay in the northern branch of the canal, so that some possibility existed of the whole province falling into anarchy if the pressure were not removed. The authorities of the city of Yangchau, on the canal, had already sent half a million dollars as the ransom of that place, while Niu Kien would only offer a third of a million to ransom the capital.

The Emperor's authority to treat with the English was, however, exhibited at this meeting, and in return Sir Henry's was fully explained to them. The delegates on the part of the commissioners were Hwang Ngăn-tung, secretary to Kíying, and Chin, the Manchu commandant, while Major Malcom, secretary of legation, and Mr. J. R. Morrison acted on the part of the plenipotentiary. Captain Loch, who was present, humorously describes the solemn manner in which the Emperor's commission was brought out from the box in which it was deposited, and the dismay of the lower attendants at seeing the foreigners irreverently handle it and examine its authenticity with so little awe. The skeleton of the treaty was immediately drafted for Hwang to take to his superiors. General Chin laughingly remarked that though the conditions were hard, they were no more so than the Chinese would have demanded if they had been the victors. The bearing of these officers was courteous, and Hwang especially found favor with all who were thrown into his company.

The utmost care being requisite in drawing up the articles, most of the work falling upon Mr. Morrison, it was not till late at night on the 17th that the final draft was sent to the Chinese. The plenipotentiary, on the 18th, desired the general and admiral to suspend hostilities, at which time arrangements were also made for an interview the next day between the representatives on both sides. The English officers meantime explored the vicinity of the city, and the demand for provisions to supply the force caused a brisk trade highly beneficial to the Chinese, and well calculated to please them.

On the 19th Kíying, Îlípu, and Niu Kien, accompanied by a large suite, paid their first visit to the English. The steamer Medusa brought them alongside the Cornwallis, and Sir Henry Pottinger, supported by the admiral and general, received them on the quarter-deck. The ship was decked with flags, and the crowd of gayly dressed officers in blue and scarlet contrasted well with the bright crapes and robes of the Chinese. This visit was one of ceremony, and after partaking of refreshments and examining the ship the commissioners retired, expressing their gratification at what they saw. They conducted themselves with decorum in their novel position, and Kíying and Îlípu, though both brought up in the full persuasion of the supremacy of their sovereign over the rulers of all other nations, and particularly over the English, manifested no ill-concealed chagrin. They had previously sent up a report of the progress of the expedition after the capture of Chinkiang, requesting in it that the demands of the invaders might be conceded; the inefficiency of their troops is acknowledged, and a candid statement of the impossibility of effectual resistance laid before his Majesty, with cogent reasons for acceding to the demands of the English as the wisest course of procedure. The further disasters which will ensue if the war is not brought to a close are hinted at, and the concession of the points at issue considered in a manner least humbling to imperial vanity. The sum of $21,000,000 to be paid is regarded by them as a present to the soldiers and sailors before sending them home; partly as the liquidation of just debts due from the hong merchants, whose insolvency made them chargeable to the government, and partly as indemnification for the opium. Trade at the five ports was to be allowed, because four of them had already been seized, and this was the only way to induce the invaders to withdraw, while Hongkong could be ceded inasmuch as they had already built houses there. The memorial is a curious effort to render the bitter pill somewhat palatable to themselves and their master.

The English plenipotentiary, accompanied by a large concourse of officers, returned the visit on shore in a few days, and were met at the entrance of a temple by the commissioners, who led them through a guard of newly uniformed and unarmed soldiers into the building, the bands of both nations striking up their music at the same time. This visit continued the good understanding which prevailed; the room had been carpeted and ornamented with lanterns and scrolls for the occasion, while the adjacent grounds accommodated a crowd of natives. On the 26th Sir Henry Pottinger and his suite, consisting of his secretary, Major Malcom, Messrs. Morrison, Thom, and Gutzlaff, the three interpreters, and three other gentlemen, proceeded about four miles to the landing-place on the canal, where they were met by a brigadier and two colonels; the banks of the canal were lined with troops. The party then took their horses, and, preceded by a mounted escort, were received at the city gate by the secretaries of Ílípu; the procession advanced to the place of meeting, guarded by a detachment of Manchu cavalry, whose shaggy ponies and flowing dresses presented a singular contrast to the envoy's escort and their beautiful Arabs. He himself was conducted through the outer gate, up the court and through the second gateway, ascending the steps into the third entrance, where he dismounted and entered the building with the commissioners and governor-general. The room had been elegantly fitted up, and a crowd of official attendants dressed in their ceremonial robes stood around. Sir Henry occupied the chief seat between Kíying and Ílípu, their respective attendants being seated in proper order, with small tables between every two persons, while dinner was served up in usual Chinese style.

These formalities being over, the thirteen articles of this most important treaty were discussed:

I.—Lasting peace between the two nations.

II.—The ports of Canton, Amoy, Fuhchau, Ningpo, and Shanghai to be opened to British trade and residence, and trade conducted according to a well-understood tariff.

III.—"It being obviously necessary and desirable that British subjects should have some port whereat they may careen and refit their ships when required," the island of Hongkong to be ceded to her Majesty.

IV.—Six millions of dollars to be paid as the value of the opium which was delivered up "as a ransom for the lives of H. B. M. Superintendent and subjects," in March, 1839.

V.—Three millions of dollars to be paid for the debts due to British merchants.

VI.—Twelve millions to be paid for the expenses incurred in the expedition sent out "to obtain redress for the violent and unjust proceedings of the Chinese high authorities."

VII.—The entire amount of $21,000,000 to be paid before December 31, 1845.

VIII.—All prisoners of war to be immediately released by the Chinese.

IX.—The Emperor to grant full and entire amnesty to those of his subjects who had aided the British.

X.—A regular and fair tariff of export and import customs and other dues to be established at the open ports, and a transit duty to be levied in addition which will give goods a free conveyance to all places in China.

XI.—Official correspondence to be hereafter conducted on terms of equality according to the standing of the parties.

XII.—Conditions for restoring the places held by British troops to be according to the payments of money.

XIII.—Time of exchanging ratifications and carrying the treaty into effect.

The official English and Chinese texts of this compact and a literal translation of the Chinese text are given in the *Chinese Repository*, Vols. XIII. and XIV.; in that serial is also to be found a full account of the struggle which was thus brought to a close. Looked at in any point of view, political, commercial, moral, or intellectual, it will always be considered as one of the turning points in the history of mankind, involving the welfare of all nations in its wide-reaching consequences.

When matters connected with the treaty had been arranged, Sir Henry proposed to say a few words upon "the great cause that produced the disturbances which led to the war, viz., the trade in opium." But upon hearing this (Captain Loch says) they unanimously declined entering upon the subject, until they were assured that he had introduced it merely as a topic for private conversation.

They then evinced much interest, and eagerly requested to know why we would not act fairly toward them by prohibiting the growth of the poppy in our dominions, and thus effectually stop a traffic so pernicious to the human race. This, he said, in consistency with our constitutional laws could not be done; and he added that even if England chose to exercise so arbitrary a power over her tillers of the soil, it would not check the evil, so far as the Chinese were concerned, while the cancer remained uneradicated among themselves, but that it would merely throw the market into other hands. It, in fact, he said, rests entirely with yourselves. If your people are virtuous, they will desist from the evil practice; and if your officers are incorruptible and obey your orders, no opium can enter your country. The discouragement of the growth of the poppy in our territories rests principally with you, for nearly the entire produce cultivated in India travels east to China; if, however, the habit has become a confirmed vice, and you feel that your power is at present inadequate to stay its indulgence, you may rest assured your people will procure the drug in spite of every enactment. Would it not, therefore, be better at once to legalize its importation, and by thus securing the co-operation of the rich and of your authorities, from whom it would thus be no longer debarred, thereby greatly limit the facilities which now exist for smuggling? They owned the plausibility of the argument, but expressed themselves persuaded that their imperial master would never listen to a word upon the subject.

To convince them that what he said was not introduced from any sinister wish to gain an end more advantageous for ourselves, he drew a rapid sketch of England's rise and progress from a barbarous state to a degree of wealth and civilization unparalleled in the history of the world; which rapid rise was principally attributable to benign and liberal laws, aided by commerce, which conferred power and consequence. He then casually mentioned instances of governments having failed to attain their ends by endeavoring to exclude any particular objects of popular desire; tobacco was one of those he alluded to, and now that it was legalized, not only did it produce a large revenue to the crown, but it was more moderately indulged in in Britain than elsewhere.[1]

To the well-wisher of his fellow-men this narrative suggests many melancholy reflections. On the one hand were four or five high Chinese officers, who, although pagans and unacquainted with the principles of true virtue, had evidently sympathized with and upheld their sovereign in his fruitless, misdirected endeavors to save his people from a vicious habit. "Why will you not act fairly toward us by prohibiting the growth of the poppy?" is their anxious inquiry; for they knew that there was no moral principle among themselves strong enough to resist the opium pipe. "Your people must become virtuous and your officers incorruptible, and then you can stop the opium coming into your borders," is the reply; precisely the words that the callous rumseller gives the broken-hearted wife of the besotted drunkard when she beseeches him not to sell liquor to her enslaved husband. "Other people will bring it to you if we should stop the cultivation of the poppy; if England chose to exercise so arbitrary a power over her tillers of the soil, it would not check the evil," adds the envoy; "you cannot do better than legalize it." Although nations are somewhat different from individuals in respect to their power of resisting and suppressing a vice,

---

[1] Loch's *Events in China*, p. 173, London, 1843. This same point is slightly referred to by Lieutenant Ouchterlony, on page 448 of his *Chinese War*, where he states that Sir Henry had prepared a paper for the information of the Chinese officials, proposing to them to permit the traffic in opium to be by barter

and Sir Henry did right to speak of the legal difficulty in the way of restraining labor, yet how heartless was the excuse, "if we do not bring it to you others will." No suggestion was made to them as to the most judicious mode of restraining what they were told they could not prohibit; no hint of the farming system, which would have held out to them a medium path between absolute freedom and prohibition, and probably been seriously considered by the court; no frank explanation as to the real position the English government itself held in respect to the forced growth of this pernicious article in its Indian territories. How much nobler would that government have stood in the eyes of mankind if its head and ministers had instructed their plenipotentiary, that when their other demands were all paid and conceded no indemnity should have been asked for smuggled opium entirely destroyed by those who had seized it within their borders under threats of worse consequences. That government and ministry which had paid a hundred millions for the emancipation of slaves could surely afford to release a pagan nation from such an imposed obligation, instead of sending their armies to exact a few millions which the revenue of one year, derived from this very article alone, would amply discharge to their own subjects. For this pitiful sum must the great moral lesson to the Emperor of China and his subjects, which could have been taught them at this time, be lost.

Sir Henry inquired if an envoy would be received at Peking, should one be sent from England, which Kíying assured him would no doubt be a gratification to his master, though what ideas the latter connected with such a suggestion can only be inferred. The conference lasted three or four hours, and when the procession returned to the barges, through an immense crowd of people, nothing was heard from them to indicate dislike or dread; all other thoughts were merged in overpowering curiosity. It was remarkable that this was the anniversary of the day when English subjects, among whom were the three interpreters here present, left Macao in 1839, by order of Lin; on August 26, 1840, the plenipotentiaries entered the Pei ho to seek an interview with Kíshen; that day, the next year, Amoy and its extensive batteries fell; and now the three years' game is won and China is obliged to bend, her magnates come down from their eminences, and her wall of supremacy, isolation, and conceit is shattered beyond the possibility of restoration. Her rulers apparently submitted with good grace to the hard lesson, which seemed to be the only effectual means of compelling them to abandon their ridiculous pretensions; though it cannot be too often repeated that the effect of kindness, honorable dealing, and peaceful missions had not been fairly tried.

Arrangements were made on the 29th to sign the treaty on board the Cornwallis. After it was signed all sat down to table, and the admiral, as the host in his flagship, gave the healths of their Majesties, the Queen of England and the Emperor of China, which was announced to the fleet and army by a salute of twenty-one guns and hoisting the Union Jack and a yellow flag at the main and mizzen. The treaty was forwarded to Peking that evening. The embargo on the rivers and ports was at once taken off, the troops re-embarked, and preparations made to return to Wusung. The six millions were paid without much delay, and on September 15th the Emperor's ratification was received. The secretary of legation, Major Malcom, immediately left to obtain the Queen's ratification, going by steam the entire distance (except eighty miles in Egypt) from Nanking to London—an extraordinary feat in those days.

The imperial assent was also published in a rescript addressed to Kíying, in reply to his account of the settlement of affairs, in which he gives directions for disbanding the troops, rebuilding such forts as had been destroyed, and cultivating peace as well as providing for the fulfilment of the articles. It is, on the whole, a dignified approval of the treaty, and breathes nothing of a spirit of revenge or intention to prepare for future resistance.

The fleet of ships and transports returned down the river and reassembled at Tinghai, at the end of October, not a vessel having been lost. Even before leaving Nanking, and in the passage down the river, the troops and sailors, especially the Indian regiments, were reduced by cholera, fever, and other diseases, some of the transports being nearly disabled; the deaths amounted to more than a thousand before reaching Hongkong.

On arriving at Amoy the plenipotentiary was highly incensed on hearing of the melancholy fate of the captive crews of the Nerbudda and Ann, wrecked on Formosa. The first, a transport, contained two hundred and seventy-four souls, and when she went ashore all the Europeans abandoned two hundred and forty Hindus to their fate, most of whom fell into the hands of the Chinese. The Ann was an opium vessel, and her crew of fifty-seven souls were taken prisoners and carried to Taiwan fu. The prisoners were divided into small parties and had little communication with each other during their captivity, which was aggravated by want of food and clothing, filthy lodgings, and other hardships of a Chinese jail, so that many of the Indians died. The survivors, on August 13th, with the exception of ten persons, were carried out to a plain near the city, one of whom, Mr. Newman, a seacunnie on board the Ann and the last in the procession, gave the following account:

On being taken out of his sedan, to have his hands shackled behind his back, he saw two of the prisoners with their irons off and refusing to have them put on. They had both been drinking and were making a great noise, crying out to him that they were all to have their heads cut off. He advised them to submit quietly, but they still refusing, he first wrenched off his own and then put them into theirs, to the great pleasure of the soldiers, but when the soldiers wished to replace his he declined. As they were on the point of securing him he accidentally saw the chief officer seated close to him. Going before him he threw himself on his head and commenced singing a few Chinese words which he had frequently heard repeated in a temple. The officer was so pleased with this procedure that he turned round to the soldiers and ordered them to carry him back to the city. All the rest, one hundred and ninety-seven in number, were placed at small distances from each other on their knees, their feet in irons and hands manacled behind their backs, thus waiting for the executioners, who went round and with a kind of two-handed sword cut off their heads without being laid on a block. Afterward their bodies were thrown into one grave and their heads stuck up in cages on the seashore.[1]

A journal was kept by Mr. Gully to within three days of his death, and another by Captain Denham of the Ann, one of the prisoners saved to send to Peking.[2] Both contain full accounts

[1] *Chinese Repository*, Vol. XII., p. 248.

[2] *Journals of Mr. Gully and Captain Denham during a Captivity in China in* 1842. London: Chapman & Hall, 1844.

of the treatment of the unhappy captives, and diminish the sympathy felt for the defeat of the government which allowed such slaughter. It was said to have been done by orders from court, grounded on a lying report sent up by the Manchu commandant, Tahungah. When their sad fate was learned Sir Henry Pottinger published two proclamations in Chinese, in which the principal facts were detailed, so that all might know the truth of the matter; a demand made for the degradation and punishment of the lying officers who had superintended it, and the confiscation of their property for the use of the families of the sufferers. Iliang, the governor-general, expressed his sincere regret to the English envoy at what had taken place, and examined into the facts himself, which led to the degradation and banishment of the commandant and intendant. While the prisoners were still at Taiwan fu, H. M. S. Serpent was sent over from Amoy to reclaim them, by which expedition the truth of the barbarous execution was first learned; this vessel afterward went there to receive the shipwrecked crew of the Herculaneum transport.

The citizens of Amoy, Ningpo, and Shanghai hailed the cessation of the war and the opening of their ports to foreign trade; but not so at Canton. The discharged volunteers still remained about the city, notwithstanding orders to return home and resume their usual employments, most of whom probably had neither. Scheming demagogues took advantage of a rumor that the English army intended to form a settlement opposite the city, and issued a paper in the name of the gentry, calling upon all to combine and resist the aggression. The enthusiasm it caused was worked up to a higher pitch by an inflammatory manifesto, in which desperate measures were plainly intimated; but the district magistrates took no steps against them. An invitation was circulated for the citizens and gentlemen from other provinces to meet at the public assembly hall to consult upon public affairs. A counter but less spirited manifesto was pasted up in the hall, which had the effect of inducing about half the people to disperse. The writers of this paper dissuaded their countrymen from hasty measures, by telling them that no land could be taken or dwellings occupied without permission from the provincial authorities, and urged upon them to live at peace with the English, in accordance with the injunctions of their wise sovereign.

A brawl occurred in Hog Lane on December 6th, between some hucksters and lascars, who were pursued into the Square, where the mob rapidly increased, and about two o'clock began pulling down a brick wall around the Company's garden and forcing open one of the factories, which was speedily pillaged, the inmates escaping through the back doors. The British flag-staff was fired by a party which kept guard around it, and the flames communicating to the verandah, other parts soon caught, and by midnight the three hongs east of Hog Lane were burning furiously. The ringleaders, satisfied with firing the British consulate, endeavored to prevent thieves carrying away the plunder; but they were forced to escape about midnight. These wretches soon began to quarrel among themselves for the dollars found in the ruins, and it was not till noon that the police and soldiers ventured to attack the knotted groups of struggling desperadoes and arrest the most conspicuous, and with the aid of boats' crews from the shipping recapture some of the specie. Full compensation was subsequently made to the foreigners for the losses sustained, amounting to $67,397, and some of the ringleaders were executed.

A large part of the officers in the army and navy engaged in the war received promotion or honorary titles. Sir Hugh was made a baronet, and, after more service in India, elevated to the peerage, with the title of Lord Gough, Baron of Chinkiang fu; the plenipotentiary and the admiral obtained Grand Crosses of the Bath. The three interpreters, Messrs. Morrison, Thom, and Gutzlaff, whose services had been arduous and important, received no distinctive reward from their government. The amount of prize money distributed among the soldiers and sailors was small. The losses of the English from shipwreck, sickness, and casualties during the war amounted to more than three thousand; the mortality was greatest among the Indian regiments and the European recruits, especially after the operations behind Canton and the capture of Chinkiang.

While the English government rewarded its officers, the Emperor expressed his displeasure at the conduct of the major part of his surviving generals, but distributed posthumous honors to those who had died at their posts. Hailing, with his wife and grandson, were honored with a fane, and his sons promoted. Kíying was appointed governor-general at Nanking. Though many civil and military officers were condemned to death, none actually lost their lives, except Yu Pu-yun, the governor of Chehkiang, who fled from Ningpo in October, 1841.

The settlement of the duties and regulations for carrying on foreign commerce immediately engaged the attention of the plenipotentiary. He called on the British merchants for information, but so utterly desultory was the manner in which the duties had been formerly levied, that they could give him little or no reliable information as to what was really done with the money. The whole matter was placed by both parties in the hands of Mr. Thom, who had been engaged in business at Canton, and Hwang Ngăn-tung, secretary to Kíying. To settle these multifarious affairs and restore quiet, Ílípu was sent to Canton as commissioner. On his arrival, he set about allaying the popular discontent at the treaty, and his edict[1] is a good instance of the mixture of flattery and instruction, coaxing and commanding, which Chinese officers frequently adopt when they are not sure of gaining their end by power alone, and do not wish to irritate. In this instance it did much to remove misapprehension and allay excitement, but its author had not long been engaged in these arduous duties before he "made a vacancy," aged seventy-two, having been more than half his life engaged in high employments in his country's service; his conduct and foresight in the last two years did credit to himself and elevated his nation. His associate, Kíying, took his place and exchanged the ratifications of the treaty of Nanking at Hongkong with Sir Henry Pottinger, ten months after it had been signed by the same persons. The island was then taken possession of on behalf of the Queen by proclamation, and the warrant read ap-

[1] *Chinese Repository*, Vol. XII., p. 106.

pointing Sir Henry governor of the colony. Its influence on the well-being of China since that period has been less than was anticipated by those who looked to the higher welfare and progress of a British colony so near to it as likely to be an example for good. A free port has encouraged smuggling to a degree that constantly irritates and baffles the native authorities on the mainland, and leads to armed resistance to their efforts toward collecting lawful revenue, especially on opium; while the influx of Chinese traders, attracted by its greater security, is gradually converting the island into a Chinese settlement protected by British rule. The peninsula of Kowlung, on the north side of the harbor, was added in 1860, to furnish ground for the commissary departments of the forces. The influence of a well-ordered Christian government exercising a beneficent rule over a less civilized race under its sway, is soon neutralized by licensing the opium farms and gambling saloons and lending its moral sanction to smuggling.

The tariff and commercial regulations were published July 22d. In this tariff, all emoluments and illegal exactions superimposed upon the imperial duties were prohibited, and a fixed duty put on each article, which seldom exceeded five per cent. on the cost; all kinds of breadstuffs were free. Commercial dealings were placed on a well-understood basis, instead of the former loose way of conducting business; the monopoly of the hong merchants was ended, the fees exacted on ships were abolished, and a tonnage duty of five mace per ton substituted; the charge for pilotage was reduced so much that the pilots were nearly stripped of all they received after paying the usual fees to the tidewaiters along the river. Disputes between English and Chinese were to be settled by the consuls, and in serious cases by a mixed court, when, upon conviction, each party was to punish its own criminals.

The proclamation giving effect to these regulations was one of the most important documents ever issued by the Chinese government; as an initiation of the new order of things, it was creditable to the people whose rulers were of themselves and could utter such words to them. After referring to the war and treaty of peace, Kíying goes on to say, respecting the tariff, that as soon as replies shall be received from the Board of Revenue, "it will then take effect with reference to the commerce with China of all countries, as well as of England. Henceforth, then, the weapons of war shall forever be laid aside, and joy and profit shall be the perpetual lot of all; neither slight nor few will be the advantages reaped by the merchants alike of China and of foreign countries. From this time forward, all must free themselves from prejudice and suspicions, pursuing each his proper avocation, and careful always to retain no inimical feelings from the recollection of the hostilities that have before taken place. For such feelings and recollections can have no other effect than to hinder the growth of a good understanding between the two peoples." It should be moreover added, as due praise to the imperial government, that none of the many hundreds who served the English on ship and shore against their country were afterward molested in any way for so doing. Many were apprehended, but the commissioner says he "has obtained from the good favor of his august sovereign, vast and boundless as that of heaven itself, the remission of their punishment for all past deeds; . . . they need entertain no apprehension of being hereafter dragged forward, nor yield in consequence to any fears or suspicions."[1]

These new arrangements pleased the leading Chinese merchants better than they did the hoppo and others who had lined their pockets and fed their friends with illegal exactions. The never-failing sponge of the co-hong could no longer be sucked, but for a last squeeze the authorities called upon the merchants for five millions of dollars, which they refused to pay, and withdrew from business with so much determination and union that the hoppo and his friends were foiled; they finally contributed among themselves about one million seven hundred thousand dollars, which was nearly or quite their last benevolence to their rulers. Howqua, the leading member of the body during thirty years, died about this time, aged seventy-five; he was, altogether, the most remarkable native known to foreigners, and while he filled the difficult station of senior merchant, exhibited

[1] *Chinese Repository*, Vol. XII., p. 443.

great shrewdness and ability in managing the delicate and difficult affairs constantly thrown upon him. He came from Amoy when a young man, and his property, probably over-estimated at four millions sterling, passed quietly into the hands of his children.[1]

The foreign community also suffered a great loss at this time in the death of John Robert Morrison, at the age of twenty-nine. He was born in China, and had identified himself with the best interests of her people and their advancement in knowledge and Christianity. At the age of twenty, on his father's decease, he was appointed Chinese secretary to the British superintendents, and filled that responsible situation with credit and efficiency during all the disputes with the provincial authorities and commissioner Lin, and of the war, until peace was declared. His intimate acquaintance with the policy of the Chinese government and the habits of thought of its officers eminently fitted him for successfully treating with them, and enlightening them upon the intentions and wishes of foreign powers; while his unaffected kindness to all natives assured them of the sincerity of his professions. The successful conduct of the negotiations at Nanking depended very much upon him, and the manner in which he performed the many translations to and from Chinese, connected with that event, was such as to secure the confidence of the imperial commissioners, in their ignorance of all foreign languages, that they were fairly dealt with.

He was eminently a Christian man, and whenever opportunity allowed, failed not to speak of the doctrines of the Bible to his native friends. The projected revision of the Chinese version of the Scriptures by the Protestant missionaries engaged his attention, and it was expected would receive his assistance. With his influence, his pen, his property, and his prayers, he contributed to the welfare of the people, and the confidence felt in him by natives who knew him was often strikingly exhibited

[1] Compare *The Fan Kwae at Canton before Treaty Days, by an Old Resident* (Mr. W. C. Hunter), London, 1882; a little volume which, besides many personal reminiscences of the characters mentioned in this narrative, furnishes an interesting picture of life in Canton a half century ago.

at Canton during the commotions of 1841 and the negotiations of 1843. He died at Macao August 29th, a year after the treaty of Nanking was signed, and was buried by the side of his parents in the Protestant burying-ground. Sir Henry Pottinger announced his death as a "positive national calamity," and it was so received by the government at home. He also justly added that "Mr. Morrison was so well known to every one, and so beloved, respected, and esteemed by all who had the pleasure and happiness of his acquaintance or friendship, that to attempt to pass any panegyric upon his private character would be a mere waste of words;" while his own sorrow was but a type of the universal feeling in which his memory and merit are embalmed. As a testimony of their sense of his worth, the foreign community, learning that he had died poor, leaving a maiden sister who had been dependent upon him, and that his official accounts were in some confusion, immediately came forward and contributed nearly fourteen thousand dollars to relieve his estate and relatives from all embarrassment.

The negotiations were concluded by the English and Chinese plenipotentiaries signing a supplementary treaty on October 8th (the day was a lucky one in the Chinese calendar), at the Bogue. This treaty provided, among other things, for the admission of all foreigners to the five open ports on the same terms as English subjects; it was inserted at the request of Kíying, that all might appreciate the intentions of his government; for neither he nor his master knew anything of that favorite phrase, "the most favored nation," and expected and wished to avoid all controversy by putting every ship and flag on the same footing.

It might have been expected that the Chinese government would have now taken some action upon the opium trade, which was still going on unchecked and unlicensed. Opium schooners were passing in and out of Hongkong harbor, though the drug sold by the Indian government at Calcutta was not allowed by the colonial British government at Hongkong to be stored on shore. Yet no edicts were issued, few or no seizures made, no notice taken of it; no proposition to repress, legalize, or manage it came from the imperial commissioner. The old laws denouncing its use, purchase, or sale under the penalty of death still remained on the statute book, but no one feared or cared for them. This conduct is fully explained by the supposition that, having undergone so much, the Emperor and his ministers thought safety from future trouble with the British lay in enduring what was past curing; they had already suffered greatly in attempting to suppress it, and another war might be caused by meddling with the dangerous subject, since too it was now guarded by well-armed British vessels. Public opinion was still too strong against it, or else consistency obliged the monarch to forbid legalization.[1]

Sir Henry Pottinger, hearing that persons were about sending opium to Canton under the pretense that unenumerated articles were admissible by the new tariff at a duty of five per cent., issued a proclamation in English and Chinese, to the intent that such proceedings were illegal. He also forbade British vessels going beyond lat. 32° N., and intimated to the Chinese that they might seize all persons and confiscate all vessels found above that line, or anywhere else on the coast besides the five ports; and, moreover, published an order in council which restricted, under penalty of $500 for each offence, all British vessels violating the stipulations of the treaty in this respect. All this was done chiefly to throw dust in their eyes, and put the onus of the contraband traffic on the Chinese government and the violation of law on those who came off to the smuggling vessels, and these proclamations and orders, like their edicts, were to be put "on record." This was shown when Captain Hope, of H.M.S. Thalia, for stopping two or three of the opium vessels proceeding above Shanghai, was recalled from his station and ordered to India, where he could not "interfere in such a manner with the undertakings of British subjects"—to quote Lord Palmerston's despatch to Captain Elliot. This effectually deterred other British officers from meddling with it.

Yet the commercial bearings of this trade were clearly seen in England, and a memorial to Sir Robert Peel, signed by two hundred and thirty-five merchants and manufacturers, was drawn

[1] Montgomery Martin, *China; Political, Commercial, and Social*, Vol. II., Chap. IV. (London, 1847)—a chapter containing some most suggestive reflections on this subject by a member of her Majesty's government at Hongkong.

up, in which they proved that the "commerce with China cannot be conducted on a permanently safe and satisfactory basis so long as the contraband trade in opium is permitted. Even if legalized, the trade would inevitably undermine the commerce of Great Britain with China, and prevent its being, as it otherwise might be, an advantageous market for our manufactures. It would operate for evil in a double way: first, by enervating and impoverishing the consumers of the drug, it would disable them from becoming purchasers of our productions; and second, as the Chinese would then be paid for their produce chiefly as now in opium, the quantity of that article imported by them having of late years exceeded in value the tea and silk we receive from them, our own manufactures would consequently be to a great extent precluded." The memorial shows that between 1803–08 the annual demand for woollens alone was nearly $750,000 more than it was for *all* products of British industry between 1834–39; while in that interval the opium trade had risen from three thousand to thirty thousand chests annually. Nothing in the annals of commerce ever showed more conclusively how heartless a thing trade is when it comes in contact with morality or humanity, than the discussions respecting the opium traffic. These memorialists plead for their manufactures, but the East India Company would have been sorry to have had their market spoiled: what could Sir Robert Peel, or even Wilberforce, if he had been premier, do against them in this matter? The question was which party of manufacturers should be patronized. But none of these "merchants and manufacturers of the highest standing and respectability" refer to the destruction of life, distress of families, waste of mind, body, and property, and the many other evils connected with the growth and use of opium, except as connected with the sale of their goods. One paper, in order to compound the matter, recommended the manufacture of morphine to tempt the Chinese, in order that, if they would smoke it, they might have a delicate preparation for fashionable smokers.

The conduct of the ministry in remunerating the merchants who had surrendered their property to Captain Elliot was appropriate to the character of the trade. The $6,000,000, instead of being divided in China among those who were to receive it —as could have been done without expense—was carried to England to be coined, which, with the freight, reduced it considerably. Then by the manner of ascertaining the market value at the time it was given up, and the holders of the opium script got their pay, they received scarcely one-half of what was originally paid to the East India Company, either directly or indirectly, thereby reducing it nearly a million sterling. Furthermore, by the form of payment they lost nearly one-fifth even of the promised sum, or about one million two hundred thousand dollars. Then they lost four years' interest on their whole capital, or about four million dollars more. What the merchants lost, the government profited. The Company gained during these four years at least a million sterling by the increased price of the drug, while Sir Robert Peel also transferred that amount from the pockets of the merchants to the public treasury. It was an undignified and pitiful haggling with the merchants and owners of the opium, whom that ministry had encouraged for many years in their trade along the Chinese coast, and then forced to take what was doled out.

Public opinion will ever characterize the contest thus brought to an end as an *opium war*, entered into and carried on to obtain indemnity for opium seized, and—setting aside the niceties of western international law, which the Chinese government knew nothing of—most justly seized. The British and American merchants who voluntarily subscribed one thousand and thirty-seven chests to Commissioner Lin, acknowledged themselves to be transgressors by this very act. Yet war seemed to be the only way to break down the intolerable assumptions of the court of Peking; that a war would do it was quite plain to every one acquainted with the character of that court and the genius of the people, and the result has shown the expectation to have been well based. Members of Parliament expressed their gratification at being at last out of a bad business; their desire, frequently uttered, that the light of the gospel and the blessings of Christian civilization might now be introduced among the millions of China, was a cheap peace-offering of good wishes, somewhat in the manner of the old Hebrews sacrificing a kid when they had committed a trespass. The short but pithy digest of the whole war by Justin McCarthy, in Chapter X. of the *History of Our Own Times*, brings out its leading features in a fairly candid manner.

The announcement of the treaty of Nanking caused considerable sensation in Europe and America, chiefly in commercial circles. M. Auguste Moxhet, the Belgian consul at Singapore, was sent on to China to make such inquiries for transmission to his government as would direct it in its efforts to open a trade. The Netherlands government sent orders to the authorities at Batavia, who despatched M. Tonco Modderman for the same purpose. The king of Prussia appointed M. Grube to proceed to China to prosecute researches as to the prospect of finding a market for German manufactures. The Spanish ministry, through the authorities at Manila, designated Don Sinibaldo de Mas in this new sphere. The governor of Macao, M. Pinto, before returning home, was appointed commissioner on behalf of H. M. F. Majesty, to treat respecting the rights and privileges of Macao under the new order of things, and succeeded in obtaining some stipulations favorable to the trade of the place, but could not get the Chinese to cede it to Portugal. These gentlemen arrived in China during the latter part of 1843, and most of them had interviews or communication with Kíying before he returned to court in December.

The governments of the United States and France early appointed ministers extraordinary to the court of Peking. Caleb Cushing, commissioner on behalf of the United States, brought a letter from the President to the Emperor, which is inserted in full as an instance of the singular mixture of patronizing and deprecatory address then deemed suitable for the Grand Khan by western nations:

LETTER TO THE EMPEROR OF CHINA FROM THE PRESIDENT OF THE UNITED STATES OF AMERICA.

I, John Tyler, President of the United States of America—which States are: Maine, New Hampshire, Massachusetts, Rhode Island, Connecticut, Vermont, New York, New Jersey, Pennsylvania, Delaware, Maryland, Virginia, North Carolina, South Carolina, Georgia, Kentucky, Tennessee, Ohio, Louisiana, Indiana, Mississippi, Illinois, Alabama, Missouri, Arkansas, and

Michigan—send you this letter of peace and friendship, signed by my own hand.

I hope your health is good. China is a great Empire, extending over a great part of the world. The Chinese are numerous. You have millions and millions of subjects. The twenty-six United States are as large as China, though our people are not so numerous. The rising sun looks upon the great mountains and great rivers of China. When he sets, he looks upon rivers and mountains equally large in the United States. Our territories extend from one great ocean to the other; and on the west we are divided from your dominions only by the sea. Leaving the mouth of one of our great rivers, and going constantly toward the setting sun, we sail to Japan and to the Yellow Sea.

Now, my words are that the governments of two such great countries should be at peace. It is proper, and according to the will of heaven, that they should respect each other, and act wisely. I therefore send to your court Caleb Cushing, one of the wise and learned men of this country. On his first arrival in China, he will inquire for your health. He has strict orders to go to your great city of Peking, and there to deliver this letter. He will have with him secretaries and interpreters.

The Chinese love to trade with our people, and to sell them tea and silk, for which our people pay silver, and sometimes other articles. But if the Chinese and the Americans will trade, there shall be rules, so that they shall not break your laws or our laws. Our minister, Caleb Cushing, is authorized to make a treaty to regulate trade. Let it be just. Let there be no unfair advantage on either side. Let the people trade not only at Canton, but also at Amoy, Ningpo, Shanghai, Fuhchau, and all such other places as may offer profitable exchanges both to China and the United States, provided they do not break your laws nor our laws. We shall not take the part of evil-doers. We shall not uphold them that break your laws. Therefore, we doubt not that you will be pleased that our messenger of peace, with this letter in his hand, shall come to Peking, and there deliver it; and that your great officers will, by your order, make a treaty with him to regulate affairs of trade—so that nothing may happen to disturb the peace between China and America. Let the treaty be signed by your own imperial hand. It shall be signed by mine, by the authority of our great council, the Senate.

And so may your health be good, and may peace reign.

Written at Washington, this twelfth day of July, in the year of our Lord one thousand eight hundred and forty-three. Your good friend.

Mr. Cushing arrived in China in the frigate Brandywine, Commodore Parker, February 24, 1844. The announcement of the general objects of his mission, and the directions he had to proceed to Peking, was made to Governor Ching, who instantly informed the court of his arrival; and with a promptitude indicative of the desire of the Emperor to give no cause of offence, Kíying was reappointed commissioner, with higher powers than before. The frigate had brought out a flagstaff and vane for the consulate at Canton; the vane was in the form of an arrow, and as it turned its barb to the four points of the compass, the superstitious people thought it conveyed destructive influences around, transfixing all the benign operations of heaven and earth, and thereby causing disease and calamity among them. An unusual degree of sickness prevailed at this time in the city and its environs, which the geomancers and doctors declared would not cease until the deadly arrow was removed. The people accordingly waited on the consul, Mr. Forbes, to request the removal of the arrow, which he acceded to, and substituted a vane of another shape. The gentry issued a placard the next day, commending its removal, and requesting the people to harbor no ill-will toward the Americans as the cause of the sickness.

Kíying having announced his appointment and powers to the people, proceeded to the Bogue to meet Sir Henry Pottinger, and be introduced to Governor Davis, from whence he went to Macao and took up his residence in the village of Wanghia, in the suburbs of that city. He had associated three assistants with himself, viz., Hwang Ngăn-tung, Pwan Sz'-shing, one of the late hong merchants, and Chau Chang-ling, a prefect. H. E. Hon. Caleb Cushing was sole commissioner and envoy extraordinary; Fletcher Webster, Esq., was secretary; Rev. E. C. Bridgman, D.D., and Rev. Peter Parker, M.D., were joint Chinese secretaries, and Dr. Bridgman, chaplain; Messrs. J. H. O'Donnell, R. McIntosh, S. Hernisz, T. R. West, and John R. Peters, Jr., were attached to the legation.

Mr. Cushing had already prepared the general outline of the treaty, which greatly abridged the negotiations, and the few disputed or doubtful points in the draft having been modified and settled, it was signed at Wanghia on July 3, 1844, by the two plenipotentiaries, Commodore Parker, and a few other Americans, a large company of Chinese being present. Its fulness of details and clear exhibition of the rights conceded by the Chinese government to foreigners dwelling within its borders, made it the leading authority in settling disputes among them until 1860.

Soon after Kíying left Canton the populace began to show signs of disturbance. A party of gentlemen were walking in the Company's garden, when the gate was burst open by a mob and they were obliged to escape by boats. On the next evening the mob again collected, with the intention of getting possession of the large garden, but were driven out of the passage without much opposition. Two or three Americans, in escorting one of their countrymen to his house, were attacked by missiles on their return; whereupon one of them fired low to drive the people back, but unhappily killed a native, named Sü A-mun. The case was investigated by the district magistrate, and a report made by the governor to Kíying; but Ching took no pains to send a sufficient force to repress the populace. In a communication to the American consul he says, after ordering him to deliver up the murderer: "It has been ascertained that the man who was killed was from the district of Tsingyuen, having no relatives in Canton. But if he had been a citizen, it would have become at the moment an occasion for attack, for it would have been told to the populace, and they would have revenged it by again setting fire to the factories and plundering their contents, or something of that sort. The people are highly irritated against the offender, and it is impossible but that they have constant debates among themselves until they are revenged."

A party of marines from the corvette St. Louis came up to Canton the next day, and quiet was restored. Kíying brought the case before Mr. Cushing, stating it to be his conviction that "the murderer ought to forfeit his life," and begging him to give orders for a speedy examination of the case. In his reply Mr. Cushing expressed his regret at what had occurred, his willingness to institute an inquiry, and added a few remarks upon the necessity of better protecting foreigners at Canton, in order to prevent the recurrence of such scenes, and embroiling the two countries. Kíying replied in a considerate manner, still upholding the authority of his government and laws: "It seems from this that, regarding our nations and their subjects, the people of our land may be peaceful, and the citizens of the United States may be peaceful, and yet, after their governments have become amicable, that then their people may become inimical; and albeit the authorities of the two governments may day after day deliberate upon friendship, it is all nothing but empty words. Thus, while we are deliberating and settling a treaty of peace, all at once the people of our two countries are at odds and taking lives." He also speaks of the overbearing and violent character of the people of Canton:

Since the period when the English brought in soldiers, these ladrones have been banding together and forming societies; and while some, taking advantage of their strength, have plundered and robbed, others have called upon the able-bodied and valiant to get their living. Therefore, employing troops, which is the endangering of the authorities and [peaceable] people, is the profit of these miscreants; peace and good order which traders, both native and foreign, desire, is what these bad men do not at all wish. . . . I have heard that usually the citizens of Canton have respected and liked the officers and people of the United States, as they were peaceable and reasonable; that they would, even when there was a cause of difference, endeavor to settle it, which is very unlike the English. But unexpectedly, on the 16th instant, a cause for animosity was given in the shooting of Sü A-mun. I have heard different accounts of this affair; I judge reasonably in thinking that the merchants of your country causelessly and rashly took life. But the populace are determined to seek a quarrel, and I very much fear lest they will avail of this to raise commotion, perhaps under the pretence of avenging his death, but doubtless with other ideas too.

The American minister referred in a subsequent communication to the death of the boy Sherry, in May, 1841, when the boat's crew from the ship Morrison was captured. This affair had been already brought to the notice of the Chinese government by Commodore Kearny, and a sum of $7,800 paid for losses and damages sustained; but the present was a fitting opportunity for reviving it, since it and the case of Sü A-mun furnished a mutual commentary upon the necessity of securing better protection for foreigners. Kíying made an investigation of the case, and reported the successive actions of his predecessor, Kí Kung; so thoroughly indeed was his reply divested of all the rhodomontade usually seen in Chinese state papers, that one could hardly believe it was written by a governor-general of Canton. The exciting circumstances of the first casualty did indeed go far to extenuate it; though now both Kíying and his superiors could not but see that the time for demanding life for life had passed away. The commissioner was, however, in a dilemma. He could only appease the populace by stating in his proclamations that he was making every effort to ascertain who was the murderer and bring him to justice, and they must leave the management of the case in the hands of the regular authorities. On the other hand, the arguments of Mr. Cushing and the stipulations in the English treaty, both convinced him that foreign nations would not give up their treaty right of judging their own countrymen. He finally escaped the trouble by deferring the petitioners and relatives of the deceased awhile, and then appeasing them by a small donation.

In conducting these negotiations, and settling this treaty "between the youngest and oldest empires in the world," Mr. Cushing exhibited both ability and knowledge of his subject. In his instructions he was directed to deliver the President's letter to the Emperor in person, or to an officer of rank in his presence; and, therefore, on his arrival he informed the governor that he had been sent to the imperial court, and being under the necessity of remaining a few weeks at Macao, he improved the first opportunity to inquire after the health of his Majesty. Whether he regarded the mere going to court as important cannot be inferred from his correspondence, but if so, he should have gone directly to the mouth of the Pei ho and waited there for a commissioner to be sent to meet him. Yet the real advantages of such a proceeding at this time would have been trifling, and its risks and contingencies very serious; as the Emperor was not disposed to forego that homage required of all who appeared before him, however willing he might be to grant commercial privileges, it was undesirable to excite discussions on this point. Moreover, the appointment of Kíying with such unusual powers indicated a favorable disposition toward the Americans. It was fortunate that the two plenipotentiaries were at hand when the riot and homicide occurred, while the discussion which grew out of those events was no small benefit to the local government. The secret of much of the power of the Emperor of China consists in the acknowledgment by his subjects of his sacred character as the Son of Heaven; and although that lofty assumption must come down before the advance of western civilization, and will ere long crumble of itself, to have asked for an audience when this formality was known to be inadmissible would have irritated him, and put the foreign minister in an indefensible position. The subsequent discussions proved how deeply rooted in the Chinese mind was this attribute; the peaceful settlement of the question in 1873 could not have been anticipated in 1844.

The French ambassador, H. E. Th. de Lagrené, arrived in China August 14th. In addition to the two secretaries, MM. le Marquis de Ferrière le Voyer and le Comte d'Harcourt, five other gentlemen were sent out to make investigations into the commerce, arts, and industrial resources of the Chinese. M. de Lagrené took possession of the lodgings prepared for him at Macao, in the same building which Mr. Cushing had occupied. Kíying immediately made arrangements for opening the negotiations by sending his three associates to congratulate the French minister on his arrival; he himself reached Macao September 29th. The gratification of the Chinese statesmen at finding that the missions from the American and French governments were not sent, like the English expedition, to demand indemnity and the cession of an island, was great. Their arrival had been foreshadowed among the people of Canton, the number of ships of war had been exaggerated, and the design of the ambassadors strangely misrepresented as including the seizure of an island. These reports could hardly fail to reach and have some effect upon the highest officers in the land. The time, therefore, was favorable, not merely to obtain the same political and commercial advantages which had been granted to England, but further to explain to the Chinese officers something of the relations their nation should enter into with the other powers of the earth. The first interviews between Kíying and M. de Lagrené were held in October, and the treaty of Wanghia taken as the basis of agreement. The negotiations were amicably settled by the signing of the treaty at Whampoa on October 23d. This act may be said to have concluded the opening of China, so far as its government was prepared for the extension of this intercourse.

The instalments due according to the treaty of Nanking were

not yet all paid, but the Chinese had shown their desire to fulfil their engagements, and the $21,000,000 were received by the English within a short period of the specified time. This was a minor consideration, however, in comparison with the great advantages gained by England for herself and all Christendom over the seclusive and exclusive system of former days, which had now received such a shock that it could not only never recover from it, but was not likely even to maintain itself where the treaties had defined it. The intercourse begun by these treaties went on as fast as the two parties found it for their benefit. The war, though eminently unjust in its cause as an opium war—and even English officers and authors do not try to disguise that the seizure of the opium was the real reason for an appeal to arms, though the imprisonment of Captain Elliot and other acts was the pretext—was still, so far as human sagacity can perceive, a wholesome infliction upon a government which haughtily refused all equal intercourse with other nations, or explanations regarding its conduct, and forbade its subjects having free dealings with their fellow-men.

If in entering upon the conflict England had published to the world her declaration of the reasons for engaging in it, the merits of the case would have been better understood. If she had said at the outset that she commenced the struggle with the Emperor because he would not treat her subjects resorting to his shores by his permission with common humanity, allowing them no intercourse with his subjects, nor access to his officers; because he contemptuously discarded her ambassadors and consular agents, sent with friendly design; because he made foolish regulations (which his own subjects did not observe) an occasion of offence against others when it suited him, and had despoiled them of their property by strange and arbitrary proceedings, weakening all confidence in his equity; lastly, because he kept himself aloof from other sovereigns, and shut out his people from that intercourse with their fellow-men which was their privilege and right; her character in this war would have appeared far better. But it is the prerogative of the Governor of nations to educe good out of evil, and make the wrath, the avarice, and the ambition of men to serve his purposes and advance his own designs, although their intentions may be far otherwise.

The external and internal relations of the Chinese Empire at the close of the year 1844 were in a far better state than one would have supposed they could have become in so short a time after such a convulsion. The cities and provinces where the storm of war had beat most violently were reviving, the authority of the officers was becoming re-established, the bands of lawless desperadoes were gradually dispersing, and the people resuming their peaceful pursuits. No ill-will was manifested in Amoy on account of the losses its citizens had sustained, nor at Ningpo or Shanghai for their occupation by English troops. The English consuls at the five ports had all been received, and trade was commencing under favorable auspices. The opium trade—for this dark feature everywhere forces itself into the prospect—was also extending, and opium schooners plying up and down the coast, and anchoring on the outside limits of every port to deliver the drug.

The citizens of Canton, however, maintained their hereditary ill-will toward foreigners, and proceeded to such lengths that the local government became powerless to carry the stipulation of the British treaty, to enter its city gates, into effect. Governor Davis proceeded to Canton in May, 1847, with several vessels of war, capturing all the guns at the Bogue in his progress up the river, and compelled the authorities to grant a larger space for residences and warehouses on the south side of the Pearl River, to be occupied as soon as arrangements could be made. It was also agreed that the gates should be unconditionally opened within two years, so that foreigners might have the same access to this city as to the other four ports. When the time came for this to be carried out, the Emperor ordered Governor-General Sü to mind the voice of the people and disregard this engagement, which had probably never received his sanction. A careful examination of the Chinese text of all the treaties showed that an explicit permission to enter the citadel (*ching*), or walled portion of the marts opened to foreign commerce, was not given. In consequence of this vagueness the Hongkong authorities, acting under instructions from London, did not press the point, and the gates of Canton remained inviolate till January, 1858.[1]

[1] *Chinese Repository*, Vols. XVIII., pp. 216, 275; XV., p. 46 ff. Davis, *China during the War and since the Peace*, 1852, Vol. II., Chaps. V. and VI., *passim*. Among other authorities on the war may be mentioned Lord Jocelyin, *Six Months with the Chinese Expedition*, London, 1841; K. Stewart Mackenzie, *Narrative of the Second Campaign in China*, London, 1842; Col. Arthur Cunynghame, *Recollections of Service in China*, 1853; Lieut. John Ouchterlony, *The Chinese War*, 1844; *The Last Year in China to the Peace of Nanking*, by a Field Officer, London and Philadelphia, 1843; Auguste Haussmann, *La Chine, résumé historique*, etc., Paris, 1858; Ad. Barrot in the *Revue des Deux Mondes* for February 15, March 1, June 1, and July 1, 1842.

CHAPTER XXIV.

THE TAI-PING REBELLION.

THE war, which was brought to an end by the treaty of Nanking, left the imperial government astonished and crippled, but not paralyzed or dejected. It had, moreover, the effect of arousing it from the old notions of absolutism and security; and though the actual heads of bureaus at Peking were unable, from their secluded position and imperfect education, to ascertain and appreciate the real nature of the contest, the maritime officials could see that its results were likely to be lasting and serious. A few thoughtful men among them, as Ílípu, Seu Kí-yu, Kíying and his colleagues, understood better than their superiors at the capital that the advent of the 'Western Ocean people' at the five open ports introduced a permanent influence upon the Black-haired race. They could not, of course, estimate what this influence would become, but a sense of its power and vitality had the effect of preventing them from petty opposition in carrying out the treaty stipulations. With the major part of the officials, on the other hand, life-long prejudice, joined to utter ignorance as to the numbers, position, and resources of foreign nations, led them to withdraw from even such a measure of intercourse with consular and diplomatic officials as they could easily have held. The tone of official society was opposed to having any personal relations with their foreign colleagues, and after the old Emperor Taukwang had passed off the stage in 1850, his son showed—even eight years after the peace—that promotion was incompatible with cultivating a closer acquaintance with them.

It is not surprising that this reaction took on the form of doing as little as possible, and that its stringency was increased in reality by the device of making the governor-general at Canton the only channel of correspondence with foreign ministers. This magnate was surrounded in that city by subordinates whose training had been inimical to extending intercourse with foreigners, because they had reaped the advantages of the old system in their monopoly of the trade. The intendants at the other open ports were directed to refer difficult questions relating to foreigners to this high functionary, but as they were more disposed to let such disputes settle themselves, if possible, few cases were ever sent to him. The animus of the whole governing class gradually assumed a settled determination to keep aloof from those who had humbled them in the eyes of their subjects, and yet give no handle to these potent outsiders to repeat their descent on the coast. It was a poor policy in every point of view, only serving to hasten the evils they dreaded.

Sir John Davis was appointed governor of Hongkong in 1844, and during four years' service so soon after the war saw much of this proud and foolish spirit. His two volumes, published in 1852 (*China during the War and since the Peace*), contain a digest of the official records and acts of the Chinese government which is highly instructive. It is remarkable that he should show so much surprise at the mendacity, ill-will, and weakness of the officers in these reports to their master, or at the Emperor's persistency in wreaking his wrath on those whose poltroonery had done him so much harm. A residence of nearly thirty years in the country should have developed, in his case, an intimate acquaintance with native ideas of honor and mercy, and shown him how little of either are practised in time of war. If he blames the Chinese leaders for their ignorance and silly mistakes in its conduct, one can readily see that they never had an opportunity to learn the truth about their enemies. Their struggle against the impossible was not altogether in vain, therefore, if it prepared them for accepting the inevitable. Had Sir John manifested a little sympathy for their plight in such an unequal contest, and shown more humanity for their sufferings under the evils which afflicted them, his opinion of the best remedies would have carried much weight. As an instance of the result of his own training in the East India Company's school, he remarks respecting the imperial edicts against opium, that they fell into disuse, and that the subject had never been revived since the war; adding, "But at no time was the traffic deserving the full load of infamy with which many were disposed to heap it, for at most it only supplied the poison, which the Chinese were not obliged to take. The worst effect, perhaps, was the piracy it engendered, for this has told against the honest trade."[1] In his first interview with Kíying, in May, 1844, he proposed that the Chinese government should legalize the opium trade, for "such a wise and salutary measure would remove all chances of unpleasant occurrences between the two governments; it might provide an ample revenue for the Emperor, and check to the same extent the consumption of a commodity which was at present absolutely untaxed."[2] He, however, brought it more directly to his notice the next year in consequence of the revival of smuggling at Whampoa to as great a degree as in 1839, and the opium vessels all left the Reach.

Kíying was entirely indisposed to move, or even aid, in this matter, which he knew would be distasteful to the Emperor, other than by a truly Chinese device—that the officials of both nations should let it go on by mutual connivance. Sir John naïvely remarks on this: "The only thing wanting was that the Emperor should publicly sanction what he had once publicly condemned. . . . The trade, however, was practically tolerated, and to us this made a great difference. The Chinese government was not sufficiently honest to make a public avowal of this change in its system, but the position in which Great Britain stood became materially altered. China had distinctly declined a conventional arrangement for the remedy of the evil, and expressed a desire that we should not bring the existing abuse to its notice."[3] With two such men in command, of course nothing was ever done by either side to restrain the evils growing out of this contraband and demoralizing trade, until another war and new treaties changed the national relations.

---

[1] *China during the War*, etc., Vol. I., p. 19.
[2] *Ibid.*, Vol. II., p. 44.
[3] *Ibid.*, Vol. II., p. 203.

At Canton the long-cherished dislike to foreigners was fomented by demagogues and idlers. These worked upon the fears of the people by telling them that their lands were to be taken to build warehouses upon; and this rumor was so far believed that it soon became unsafe for foreigners to venture far into the suburbs. In December, 1847, not long after the arrangement with Sir John Davis respecting an entrance into Canton city was made, six Englishmen were attacked by a mob at Hwang-chuh-kí while on a ramble, and all killed, some of them with refined cruelty. Kíying took immediate measures—extremely creditable to his sense of what he owed to justice and maintenance of peace—to punish these villagers. A number of men whom their fellows indicated as leaders in the outrage were arrested; the prisoners were tried at Canton by the regular courts. Four were presently decapitated in the sight of a military deputation sent from Hongkong, and two others by orders from Peking. This well-timed justice secured the safety of foreigners peaceably going about the city and environs; but it was credibly stated afterward that there were numerous placards already posted in that region informing the people that foreigners would perhaps be coming thither to select sites for themselves. These unfortunate Englishmen, indeed, would perhaps have been allowed to return home, if they had been able to speak to the villagers and explain their object.

This incident makes it proper to notice a common misapprehension abroad in respect to the influence of the treaties which had been signed with China upon the people themselves. It was inferred that as soon as the three treaties with England, France, and America had been ratified, the great body of educated Chinese at least would inquire and learn what were their provisions, and a natural curiosity would be manifested to know something about the peoples of those lands. Nothing could be more likely—nothing was farther from the reality. No efforts were ever made by the imperial officers at the capital or in the provinces to promulgate these national compacts, whose original and ratified copies were never even transmitted to Peking. Consequently, the existence and nature of these *hwo yoh*, or 'peace contracts,' had to be continually taught to the natives, who on their part did not usually feel themselves under much obligation to obey them. In China, as elsewhere, just laws never execute themselves, and it is hardly surprising that not an officer of the Emperor should go out of his way to enforce their distasteful stipulations.

It was therefore uphill work to see that the treaties did not become a dead letter, and all the hardest part of this labor fell to the lot of the British consuls. They alone stood forth among foreign officials as invested with some power of their own; and being generally able to use the Chinese language, they came into personal relations with the local officers, and thus began the only effectual mode through which the treaties could become agencies for breaking down the hoary wall of prejudice, ignorance, and contempt which had so long kept China out of the pale of progress. In doing this, no fixed course could be laid down; though the constant tendency of the consuls was to encroach on the power of the mandarins, these latter were generally able to recur to the treaties, and thus learn the necessity and benefits of adherence to them. Their education was a colossal undertaking, and considering the enormous difficulties, its progress has been as rapid as was consistent with the welfare of themselves or their subjects. In this progress they bear the greatest share of the burden; its responsibilities and costs, its risks and results, almost wholly come upon them, while foreign nations, with the immense undefined rights of exterritoriality on their side, are interested on-lookers, ready to take advantage of every *faux pas* to compel them to conform to their interpretation of the treaties. Very little consideration is given to their ignorance of international law, to their full belief in the power of China, or to their consequent disinclination to accept the new order of things so suddenly forced on them. On the other hand, no one who knows all the features of this period will withhold the praise due to the British authorities in China for their conduct in relations with its functionaries; it might fairly be added that the improved state of international intercourse is mostly due to them.

The condition of the Empire at the close of the war was most discouraging to its rulers, who had not dreamed of receiving so crushing a defeat. It is creditable to them that they honorably paid up the $21,000,000 exacted of them by the British, who of course restored Chusan at the stipulated time. The name of R. Montgomery Martin, then treasurer of Hongkong colony, must be awarded due mention as being the only Queen's official who endeavored to resist its surrender, on the plea of its great benefit to her eastern empire and influence. Sir John Davis speaks of the "political and military considerations" which gave importance to it; but the proposal of Mr. Martin was promptly rejected by his superiors, and the whole archipelago has since been neglected. At the four northern ports opened by treaty, with the exception of Fuhchau, trade began without difficulty. This city having entirely escaped the ravages of the war, its proud gentry influenced the citizens against foreigners and their trade; the first European residents there met with some ill-usage, but this bitter feeling gradually wore off as the parties became better known.

At Canton the case was aggravated by the prejudices of race and the turbulence of the unemployed braves who had flocked into it on the invitation and inducements of Commissioner Lin to enlist against the English. They had been disbanded by Kíying, but had not returned to their homes; their lawlessness increased till it threatened the supremacy of the provincial government, and required the strongest measures of repression. The disorders spread rather than diminished under an impoverished treasury and ill-paid soldiery, and prepared the way for the rebellion which during the next twenty years tasked the utmost resources of the nation. The ignorance of one part of its people of what was taking place in another province—which during the foreign war so greatly crippled the Emperor's efforts to interest his subjects in this struggle—here did much to preserve them from uniting against him to his overthrow. It was plain to every candid observer that however weak, unprincipled, and tyrannical the Manchu rulers might be, they were as efficient sovereigns as the people could produce, and no substituted sway could possibly elevate and purify them until higher principles of social and political life had been adopted by the nation at large.

The protracted convulsion, known abroad as the Tai-ping

Rebellion, owed much of its duration as well to the exposure of the government's internal rottenness as to its weakness against foreign nations; but many other causes were at work. The body of the Chinese people are well aware that their rulers are no better than themselves in morals, honesty, or patriotism; but they are all ready to ascribe the evils they suffer from robbers, taxation, exactions, and unjust sentences to those in authority. The rulers are conscious that their countrymen consider it honorable to evade taxes, defy the police when they can safely do so, and oppose rather than aid in the maintenance of law and order. There is no basis of what in Christian lands is regarded as the foundation of social order and just government—the power of conscience and amenableness to law; nevertheless, from the habits of obedience taught in the family and in the schoolroom, the people have attained a good degree of security for themselves and show much regard to just rulers. The most serious evils and sufferings in Chinese society are caused by its disorderly members, not its rapacious rulers; and both can only be removed and reformed by the reception of a higher code which raises the standard of action from expediency to obligation.

In giving an account of the rise and overthrow of the Tai-ping Rebellion, it will be necessary to limit the narrative to the most important religious, political, and military events connected with it up to its suppression in 1867. The phrase "Tai-ping Rebellion" is wholly of foreign manufacture; at Peking and everywhere among those loyal to the government the insurgents were styled *Chang-mao tseh*, or 'Long-haired rebels,' while on their side, by a whimsical resemblance to English slang, the imperialists were dubbed *imps*. When the chiefs assumed to be aiming at independence in 1850, in order to identify their followers with their cause they took the term *Ping Chao*, or 'Peace Dynasty,' as the style of their sway, to distinguish it from the *Tsing Chao*, or 'Pure Dynasty,' of the Manchus. Each of them prefixed the adjective *Ta* (or *Tai*, in Cantonese), 'Great,' as is the Chinese custom with regard to dynasties and nations; thus the name *Tai-ping* became known to foreigners. The leader took the style *Tien-teh*, or 'Heavenly Virtue,' for his reign, thereby indicating his aim in seeking the throne. His own personal name, Hung Siu-tsuen, was regarded as too sacred to be used by his followers. The banners and edicts used at Nanking and in his army bore the inscription, *Tien-fu*, *Tien-hiung*, *Tien-wang Tai-ping Tien-kwoh*, or 'Heavenly Father, Heavenly Elder Brother, Heavenly King of the Great Peace [Dynasty] of the Heavenly Kingdom' (*i.e.*, China).

The incidents of this man's early life and education were ascertained in 1854, from his relative Hung Jin, by the Rev. Theodore Hamberg, whose narrative[1] bears the marks of a trustworthy recital. Hung Siu-tsuen was the youngest son of Hung Jang, a well-to-do farmer living in Hwa hien, a district situated on the North River, about thirty miles from Canton city, in a small village of which he was the headman. The family was from Kiaying prefecture, on the borders of Kiangsí, and the whole village was regarded as belonging to the Hakkas, or Squatters, and had little intercourse with the Pun-tis, or Indigenes, on that account. Siu-tsuen was born in 1813, and at the usual age of seven entered school, where he showed remarkable aptitude for study. His family being too poor to spare his services long, he had to struggle and deny himself, as many a poor aspirant for fame in all lands has done, in order to fit himself to enter the regular examinations. In 1826 his name appeared on the list of candidates in Hwa hien, but Hung Jin says: "Though his name was always among the first upon the board at the district examinations, yet he never succeeded in attaining the degree of Siu-tsai." In 1833 he was at Canton at the triennial examination, when he met with the native evangelist Liang A-fah, who was distributing and selling a number of his own writings near the Kung yuen to the candidates as they went in and out of the hall. Attracted by the venerable aspect of this man, he accepted a set of his tracts called *Kiuen Shí Liang Yen*, or 'Good Words to Exhort the Age.' He took them home with him, but threw them aside when he found that they advocated Christianity, then a proscribed doctrine.

In 1837 he was again in the provincial tripos, where his re-

[1] *Visions of Hung Siu-tshuen and Origin of the Kwang-si Insurrection*, Hongkong, 1854. Mr. W. Sargent in the *North American Review* for July, 1854, Vol. LXXIX., p. 158.

peated disappointment and discontent aggravated an illness that seized him. On reaching his home he took to his bed and prepared for death, having had several visions foretokening his decease. He called his parents to his bedside and thus addressed them: "My days are counted and my life will soon be closed. O my parents! how badly have I returned the favor of your love to me; I shall never attain a name that shall reflect lustre on you." After uttering these words he shut his eyes and lost all strength and command over his body, and became unconscious of what was going on around him. His outward senses were inactive, his body appeared as dead, but his soul was acted upon by a peculiar energy, seeing and remembering things of a very extraordinary nature.

At first, when his eyes were closed he saw a dragon, a tiger, and a cock enter the room; a great number of men playing upon instruments then approached, bearing a beautiful sedan-chair in which they invited him to be seated. Not knowing what to make of this honor, he was carried away to a luminous and beautiful place wherein a multitude of fine men and women saluted him on arrival with expressions of joy. On leaving the sedan an old woman took him down to a river, saying: "Thou dirty man, why hast thou kept company with yonder people and defiled thyself? I must now wash thee clean." After the washing was over he entered a large building in company with a crowd of old and virtuous men, some of whom were the ancient sages. Here they opened his body, took out the heart and other organs, and replaced them by new ones of a red color; this done, the wound closed without leaving a scar. The whole assembly then went on to another larger hall, whose splendor was beyond description, in which an aged man, with a golden beard and dressed in black robes, sat on the highest place. Seeing Siu-tsuen, he began to shed tears and said: "All human beings in the world are produced and sustained by me; they eat my food and wear my clothing, but not one among them has a heart to remember and venerate me; what is worse, they take my gifts and therewith worship demons; they purposely rebel against me and arouse my anger. Do thou not imitate them." Hereupon he gave him a sword to destroy the demons, a seal to overcome the evil spirits, and a sweet yellow fruit to eat. Siu-tsuen received them, and straightway began to exhort his venerable companions to perform their duties to their master. After doing so even to tears, the high personage led him to a spot whence he could behold the world below, and discern the horrible depravity and vice of its inhabitants. The sight was too awful to be endured, and words were inadequate to describe it. So he awoke from his trance, and had vigor enough to rise and dress himself and go to his father. Making a bow, Siu-tsuen said: "The venerable old man above has commanded that all men shall turn to me, and that all treasures shall flow to me." This sickness continued about forty days, and the visions were multiplied. He often met with a man in them whom he called his elder brother, who instructed him how to act and assisted him in going after and killing evil spirits. He became more and more possessed with the idea, as his health returned, that he had been commissioned to be Emperor of China; and one day his father found a slip on which was written "The Heavenly King of Great Reason, the Sovereign King Tsuen." As time wore on, this lofty idea seems to have more and more developed his mind to a soberness and purity which overawed and attracted him. Nothing is said about his utterances while the war with England was progressing, but he must have known its progress and results. His cataleptic fits and visions seem not to have returned, and he pursued his avocation as a school-teacher until about 1843, having meanwhile failed in another trial to obtain his degree at Canton. In that year his wife's brother asked to take away the nine tracts of Liang A-fah to see what they contained; when he returned them to Siu-tsuen he urged him to read them too.

They consisted of sixty-eight short chapters upon common topics, selected from the Bible, and not exactly fitted to give him, in his excited state and total ignorance of western books and religion, a fair notion of Christianity. As he read them he saw, as he thought, the true meaning of his visions. The venerable old man was no other than God the Father, and his guide was Jesus Christ, who had assisted him in slaying the demons. "These books are certainly sent purposely by heaven to me to confirm the truth of my former experience. If I had received them without having gone through the sickness, I should not have dared to believe in them, and by myself to oppose the customs of the whole world. If I had merely been sick, but not also received the books, I should have had no further evidence as to the truth of my visions, which might also have been considered as mere products of a diseased imagination."

This sounds reasonable, and commends itself as wholly unlike the ravings of a madman. Nevertheless, while it would be unwise for us to closely criticise this narrative in its details, and assert that Siu-tsuen's pretensions were all hypocritical, we must bear in mind the fact that he had certainly, neither at this time nor ever afterward, a clear conception of the true nature of Christianity, judging from his writings and edicts. The nature of sin, and the dominion of God's law upon the sinner; the need of atonement from the stain and effects of sin; Christ's mediatorial sacrifice; were subjects on which he could not possibly have received full instruction from these fragmentary essays. In after days his conviction of his own divine calling to rule over China, seems to have blinded his understanding to the spiritual nature of the Christian church. His individual penchant was insufficient to resist or mould the subordinates who accepted his mission for their own ends. But he was not a tool in their hands at any time, and his personal influence permeated the ignorant mass of reckless men around him to an extraordinary degree, while his skill in turning some of the doctrines and requirements of the Bible as the ground and proofs of his own authority indicated original genius, since the results were far beyond the reach of a cunning impostor. From first to last, beginning with poverty, obscurity, and weakness in Hwa, continuing with distinction, power, and royalty at Nanking and throughout its five adjacent provinces, and ending with defeat, desertion, and death in his own palace, Hung never wavered or abated one jot of his claim to supreme rule on earth. When his end was reported at Peking in August, 1864, thirty-one years after his receiving Liang A-fah's tracts, the imperial rescript sadly said: "Words cannot convey any idea of the misery and desolation he caused; the measure of his iniquity was full, and the wrath of both gods and men was roused against him."

A career so full of exceptional interest and notable incidents cannot, of course, be minutely described in this sketch. After Hung's examination of the tracts which had lain unnoticed in his hands for ten years, followed by his conviction of the real meaning of his visions in 1837, he began to proclaim his mission and exhort those around him to accept Christianity. Hung Jin (who furnished Mr. Hamberg with his statements) and a fellow-student, Fung Yun-shan, were his first converts; they agreed to put away all idols and the Confucian tablet out of their schools, and then baptized or washed themselves in a brook near by, as a sign of their purification and faith in Jesus. As they had no portion of the Sacred Scriptures to guide them, they were at a loss to understand many things spoken of by Liang A-fah, but his expositions of the events and doctrines occurring in them were deeply pondered and accepted. The Mosaic account of creation and the flood, destruction of Sodom, sermon on the Mount, and nature of the final judgment, were given in them, as well as a full relation of Christ's life and death; and these prepared the neophytes to receive the Bible when they got it. But the same desire to find proof of his own calling led Siu-tsuen to fix on fanciful renderings of certain texts, and, after the manner of commentators in other lands, to extract meanings never intended. A favorite conceit, among others, was to assume that wherever the character *tsuen*, 全, meaning 'whole,' 'altogether,' occurred in a verse, it meant himself, and as it forms a part of the Chinese phrase for *almighty*, he thus had strong reasons (as he thought) for his course. The phrase *Tien kwoh*, denoting the 'Kingdom of Heaven' in Christ's preaching, they applied to China. With such preconceived views it is not wonderful that the brethren were all able to fortify themselves in their opinions by the strongest arguments. All those discourses in the series relating to repentance, faith, and man's depravity were apparently entirely overlooked by them.

The strange notions, unaffected earnestness, moral conduct, and new ideas about God and happiness of these men soon began to attract people to them, some to dispute and cavil, others to accept and worship with them. Their scholars, one and all, deserted them as soon as the Confucian tablet was removed from the schoolroom, and they were left penniless and unemployed, sometimes subjected to beatings and obloquy for embracing an outlandish religion, and other times ridiculed for forsaking their ancestral halls. The number of their adherents was too few to detain them at home, and in May, 1844, Siu-tsuen, Yun-shan, and two associates resolved to visit a distant relative who lived near the Miaotsz' in Kwangsí, and get their living along the road by peddling ink-stones and pencils. They reached the adjoining district, Tsingyuen, where they preached two months and baptized several persons; some time after Hung Jin took a school there, and remained several years, baptizing over fifty converts. Siu-tsuen and Yun-shan came to the confines of the Miaotsz' in Sinchau fu in three months, preaching the existence of the true God and of redemption by his Son, and after many vicissitudes reached their relative's house in Kwei hien among the mountains. Here they tarried all summer, and their earnest zeal in spreading the doctrines which they evidently had found so cheering to their own hearts, arrested the attention of these rude mountaineers, and many of them professed their faith in Christ. Siu-tsuen returned home in the winter, and was disappointed in not finding his colleague Yun-shan there as well as the other two, nor could he give any account of his course. It appeared afterward that Yun-shan had met some acquaintances on his road, and became so much interested in preaching to them at Thistle-mount that he remained there two years, teaching school and gathering churches.

Siu-tsuen continued to teach and preach the truth as he had learned it from the books in his hands. In 1846 he heard of I. J. Roberts, the American missionary, living at Canton, and the next spring received an invitation to come there and study. He and Hung Jin did so; the former remained with Mr. Roberts about two months, giving him a narrative of his own visions, conversion, and preaching, at the same time learning the nature and extent of foreign mission work in that city. He made a visit home with two native Christians, who had been sent to Hwa to learn more about him. They seem to have obtained good reports of his character; but others in Mr. Roberts' employ were afraid of his influence if he should enter their church, and therefore intrigued to have him refused admission just then. Mr. Roberts appears to have acted discreetly according to the light he had respecting the applicant's integrity, and would no doubt have baptized him had not the latter soon after left Canton, where he had no means of support. At this time the political disturbances in Kwangtung seem to have greatly influenced Siu-tsuen's course, and when he reached home he made a second visit to his relative, and thence went to Thistle-mount to rejoin Fung Yun-shan. Hung Jin states that before this date he had expressed disloyal sentiments against the Manchus, but these are so common among the Cantonese that they attracted no notice. On seeing Yun-shan and meeting the two thousand converts he had gathered, it is pretty certain that hopes of a successful resistance must have revived in his breast. A woman among them also began to relate some visions she had seen ten years before, foretelling the advent of a man who should teach them how to worship God. The number of converts rapidly increased in three prefectures adjacent to the River Yuh in the eastern part of Kwangsí, and no serious hindrance was met with from the officials, though there were not wanting enemies, by one of whom Yun-shan was accused and then thrown into prison. However, the prefect and district magistrate to whom the case was referred, finding no sufficient cause for punishment, liberated him; though the new sectaries had made themselves somewhat obnoxious to the idolaters by their iconoclasm—so hard is it to learn patience and toleration in any country. In very many villages in that region the *Shangtí hwui*, or 'Associations for worshipping God,' began to be recognized, but they do not seem to have quoted the toleration edict obtained in 1844 in favor of Christianity, as that only spoke of the *Tien-chu kiao*, or Catholics. The worship of Shangtí is a peculiar function of the Emperor, as has been already explained; and it is not surprising to be told by Hung Jin that the new sect was regarded as treasonable.

In 1848 Siu-tsuen's father died trusting in the new faith and directing that no Buddhist services be held at his funeral; the whole family had by this time become its followers, and when the son and Yun-shan met them soon after, they began to discuss their future. The believers in Kwangsí were left to take care of themselves during the whole winter, and appear to have gone on with their usual meetings without hindrance. In June, 1849, the two leaders left Hwa for Kwangsí, assisted by the faithful, and found much to encourage them in their secret plans in the general unity which pervaded the association. Some members had been favored with visions, others had become exhorters, denouncing those who behaved contrary to the doctrines; others essayed to cure diseases. Siu-tsuen was immediately acknowledged by all as their leader; he set himself to introduce and maintain a rigid discipline, forbade the use of opium and spirits, introduced the observance of the Sabbath, and regulated the worship of God. No hint of calling in the aid of a foreign teacher to direct them in their new services appears to have been suggested by any member, nor even of sending to Canton to engage the services of a native convert, though Liang A-fah was still living then. The whole year was thus passed at Thistle-mount, and the nucleus of the future force thoroughly imbued with the ideas of their leader, who had, by June, 1850, gathered around him his own relatives and chosen his lieutenants.[1]

The existence of such a large body of people, acting together under the orders of one man, whose aspirations and teachings had gradually filled their minds with new ideas, could not remain unnoticed by the authorities. The governor-general lived at Canton, and received his information through local magistrates and prefects, whose policy was rather to understate the truth. But Sü Kwang-tsin felt that he was not fitted for the coming struggle. His place was therefore filled by the appoint-

[1] The insurgents cut off the tail, allowed their hair to grow, and decided that all who joined the insurrectional movement should leave off the *chang* and the Tartar tunic, and should wear the robe open in the front, which their ancestors had worn in the time of the Mings.—Callery and Yvan, *History of the Insurrection in China*, translated by John Oxenford, p. 61. London, 1853.

ment of Lin, then living in Fuhchau, who started to fulfil his new charge, but died in October, as he entered the province. Governor Sü was obliged to leave Canton on duty, but he never met the enemy nor returned to his post. The populace of the city made themselves merry over his violent conduct toward a poor paper-image maker near the landing, who had just set out to dry some effigies dressed in high official costume, each one lacking a head. Sü chose to regard this proceeding as an intentional insult, as the artisan must have known that he was to pass by that way, and ordered him to be bambooed and his effigies destroyed to neutralize the bad omen. The Peking government had just sent three Manchus to superintend operations in Kwangsí; their predecessors, Lí and Chau, with the provincial governor, Ching, were all degraded, but these new imperial officials did no better, nor did those on the spot expect that they would succeed. Tahungah was the ruffian who had executed one hundred and eighty British prisoners in Formosa nine years before; and Saishangah was the prime minister of the young Emperor Hienfung, as worthless as he was depraved. Uruntai, who had long been in command of the Manchu garrison at Canton, was also sent, in May, 1851, to check the growing power of the insurgents. They were well posted in Wusiuen hien, near the junction of two rivers, and this chieftain naïvely expresses his surprise in his report to the Emperor that the rebels should occupy an important post which he had just decided to fortify. However, his official report[1] explains the reasons for the imperial reverses better than anything which had hitherto appeared. Corruption, venality, idleness, opium-smoking, and peculation had made the whole army a mass of rottenness; no one can wonder that the Tai-pings marched without danger through the land to their goal at Nanking.

A year previous to this date, however, the conflict had been begun by the followers of Siu-tsuen. In their zeal against idolatry they had destroyed temples and irritated the people, which ere long aroused a spirit of distrust and enmity; this was further increased by the long-standing feud and mutual hatred

---

[1] *Chinese Repository*, Vol. XX., p. 493.

between the *pun-tis* and *hakkas* (natives and squatters) which ran through society. Siu-tsuen and his chiefs were mostly of the latter class, and whenever villages were attacked and the hakkas worsted, they moved over to Thistle-mount and professed to worship Shangtí with Siu-tsuen. In this way the whole population had become more or less split up into parties. When a body of imperial soldiers sent to arrest him and Yunshan were driven off, they availed themselves of the enthusiasm of their followers to gather them and occupy Lienchu, a large market-town in Kwei hien. This proceeding attracted to their banner all the needy and discontented spirits in that region, but their own partisans were now able to regulate and employ all who came, requiring a close adherence to their religious tenets and worship. This town of Lienchu was soon fortified, and the order of a camp began to appear among its possessors, who, however, spared the townspeople. The drilling of the force, now increased to many thousands, commenced; its vitality was soon tested when it was deemed best to cross the river and advance on Taitsun in order to obtain more room. The imperialists were hoodwinked by a simple device, and when they found their enemy had marched off, their attack on the rear was repulsed with much loss. Like all their class, they turned their wrath on the peaceful inhabitants of Lienchu, killing and burning till almost nothing was left. This needless cruelty recoiled on themselves, and all the members of the *Shangtí hwui*, loyal and disaffected alike, felt that their very name carried sedition in it, and they must join Siu-tsuen's standard or give up their faith. He had induced some recent comers belonging to the Triad Society to put their money into the military chest and to submit to his rules. One of his religious teachers had been detected embezzling the funds while on their way to the commissariat, but the public trial and execution of the man had served both as a warning and an encouragement to the different classes who witnessed the affair. Most of the Triad chiefs, however, were afraid of such discipline, and drew off to the imperialists with the greater number of their followers. The defection furnished Siu-tsuen an opportunity to make known his settled opposition to this fraternity, and that every man joining his party must leave it. At this time the discipline and good order exhibited in the encampment at Taitsun must have struck the people around it with surprise and admiration, if the meagre accounts we have received are at all trustworthy.

About one year elapsed between the conflict near Lienchu and the capture of Yung-ngan chau, a city on the River Mei in Pingloh prefecture. During this period Siu-tsuen had become more and more possessed with the idea of his divine mission from the *Tien-fu*, or 'Heavenly Father,' as God was now commonly called, and the *Tien-hiung*, or 'Heavenly Elder Brother,' as he termed Jesus Christ. He began to seclude himself from the gaze of his followers, and deliver to them such revelations as he received for the management of the force committed to him to clear the land of all idolatry and oppression, and cheer the hearts of those pledged to the glorious cause. This course was destructive of all those peculiar tenets which Christianity teaches, and, so far as can be learned, neither he nor Yun-shan any longer prominently set forth the doctrines of salvation by repentance and faith in Christ, as they had done in their first journey among the Miaotsz', but held their followers together by fanaticism and the hope of final triumph. In its main features, his course was copied from that of Moses and Aaron when they withdrew into the tabernacle, and it was easy to impress upon his uninstructed followers the repetition in his person of the same mode of making known the will of Heaven. An adequate reason can also be found in this scheme why he never called in the aid of foreign missionaries to teach his followers the truth as it is in Christ Jesus, knowing full well that none of them would lend any countenance to such delusion. As early as April, 1849, when still in Kwei hien, he began to promulge his decrees in the form of revelations received from the Heavenly Father and Elder Brother, when one or the other came down into the world to tell him what course he should pursue. In March, 1853, just before capturing Nanking, he issued a book of "Celestial Decrees," containing a series of these revelations, from which the real nature of his character can be learned. Two extracts will be sufficient to quote:

The Heavenly Father addressed the multitude, saying, O my children! Do you know your Heavenly Father and your Celestial Elder Brother? To which they all replied, We know our Heavenly Father and Celestial Elder Brother. The Heavenly Father then said, Do you know your Lord, and truly? To which they all replied, We know our Lord right well. The Heavenly Father said, I have sent your Lord down into the world to become the Celestial King (*Tien-wang*); every word he utters is a celestial command; you must be obedient; you must truly assist your Lord and regard your King; you must not dare to act disorderly, nor to be disrespectful. If you do not regard your Lord and King, every one of you will be involved in difficulty.[1]

It is only from these official documents that we can learn the real political and religious tenets of the revolutionists now intrenched at Yung-ngan, and soon to burst forth in fury upon their country. It was in vain to expect gospel figs from such a bramble bush.

Another extract exhibits their jugglery still more clearly. It is dated December 9, 1851, and contains the proceedings and sentence in the case of Chau Sih-nang, who had been detected holding intercourse with General Saishangah at Taitsun. Four of the kings were that day consulting upon some weighty matters, when suddenly the Heavenly Father came down among them and secretly told them to instantly arrest Chau and two others and bring them to Yang, the Eastern King, while he returned to heaven. They did so, and reported the matter to the Tien-wang, but none of them had any evidence to proceed upon. "Happily, however, the Heavenly Father gave himself the trouble to appear once more," and ordered two of the royal cousins to go and inform the several princes of his presence. They all attended at court and entreated the Heavenly King to accompany them. Hereupon, his Majesty, guarded by the princes and body-guards, together with a host of officials, advanced into the presence of the Heavenly Father. They all kneeled down and asked, "Is the Heavenly Father come down?" He replied, addressing the Tien-wang, "Siu-tsuen, I am going to take this matter in hand to-day; a mere mortal would find it a hard task. One Chau has been holding collusive commu-

[1] This decree bears the date April 19, 1851, at Tung-hiang, a village near Wusiuen.

nication with the enemy yesterday, and has returned to court, intending to carry into effect a very serious revolt. Go and bring him here." The culprit soon came, and the examination is reported in full. In answer to the question, "Who is it that is now speaking to you?" he replied, "The Heavenly Father, the Supreme Lord and Great God (Shangtí) is addressing me." He said soon after, "I am aware that the Heavenly Father is omnipotent, omniscient, and omnipresent." By a series of questions his guilt was proved, and he and his accomplices, with his wife and son, were all put to death as a warning to traitors, in presence of a large concourse, to whom they confessed the justice of their fate.

When in possession of Nanking, Hung Siu-tsuen was formally proclaimed by his army to be Emperor of China, and assumed the style and insignia of royalty. Five leading chiefs were appointed to their several corps as South, East, West, North, and Assistant Kings; Fung Yun-shan was the Southern King. Who among them were the efficient disciplinarians and leading minds in carrying on their plan cannot be now ascertained, so complete was the secrecy which enveloped the whole movement from first to last as to the *personnel* of the force. Dr. Medhurst's translations of their orders, tenets, laws, revelations, and text-books furnish the most authentic sources for estimating its character, but they fail to describe its living agents. In so large an army, composed of the most heterogeneous elements, it cannot be expected that there would be at any time much knowledge of the sacred Scriptures, on which its leaders based their assumed powers derived from the 'Heavenly Father and Elder Brother;' but there certainly was a remarkable degree of sobriety and discipline among them during the first few years of their existence. A most perplexing question, which increased in its urgency and difficulty as soon as opposition drove the rebel general to intrench himself at Lienchu, was temporarily arranged by forming a separate encampment for the women, and placing over them officers of their own sex to see that discipline was maintained. In doing this he allowed the married people as great facilities for the care of their children as was possible under the conditions of army life; but during their progress through the land in 1852 and 1853, much suffering must have been endured.

In 1852 the state and size of the army in Yung-ngan fully authorized the leaders of the revolt to march northward. Several engagements had given their men confidence in each other as they saw the imperialists put to flight; defeats had furthermore shown that their persevering enemy entertained no idea of sparing even one of them if captured. The want of provisions during their five months' siege within its walls further trained them to a certain degree of patient endurance; when, therefore, they broke through the besieging force in three divisions on the night of April 7, 1852, they were animated by success and hope to possess themselves of the Empire. Marching north they now attacked Kweilin, the provincial capital, May 15th, but having no cannon fit to besiege a walled city of that size, crossed the border and captured Tau in Hunan, which gave them access to the River Siang and means of transportation. Their course was thenceforth an easy conquest of the towns along its valley. Kweiyang chau, Chin chau, Tunghing, Nganjin, and others were taken and evacuated, one after the other, until they reached the capital of this province, September 18th. Changsha and Siangtan together form one immense city, and its defenders fully understood their peril, and the probability of entire destruction if they allowed it to be captured. For eighty days the Tai-pings exerted themselves in vain to obtain possession, losing, however, very few men, and doing no great harm to their enemy, who kept beyond reach. December 1st they raised the siege, and by the 13th reached Yohchau on the Yangtsz', which was taken without a struggle. Ten days after, replenished and encouraged by the spoil found in Yohchau, they occupied Hanyang and Wuchang, the capital of Hupeh province, lying on the other side of the river. Its garrison was unable to escape, and many soldiers were destroyed. Hwangchau and Kiukiang, two prefect cities lower down, were captured January 12th and February 18th, while Nganking, the capital of Nganhwui, fell a week later. Nothing seemed able to resist the advance of the insurgents, and on March 8th they encamped before Nanking. It was garrisoned by

Manchus and Chinese, who, however, made no better defence than their comrades in other cities; in ten days its walls were breached, and all the defenders found inside put to death, including Luh, the governor-general of the province. Chinkiang and Yangchau soon were dragged to the same fate, thus depriving the imperialists of their control of the Grand Canal.

This rapid progress through the land since leaving Yung-ngan eleven months previously had spread consternation among the demoralized officers and soldiers of the Emperor, who, on his part, was as weak and ignorant as any of his subordinates. The march of the insurgents showed the utter hollowness of the imperial troops, the incapacity of their most trusted leaders, and the little interest taken by the great body of the nation in the conflict. Many causes which might adequately explain this extraordinary success cannot now be ascertained, but a national dislike of the Manchus on the part of the Chinese lay at the bottom of their coldness. They felt, too, that a government which could not protect them against a few thousand foreign troops might as well give place to a native one. The insurgents had perhaps not more than ten thousand adherents, including women and children, when they left Yung-ngan;[1] but these went forth in the full conviction of the heavenly commission of their leader to destroy idolatry, set up the worship of the true God, and inaugurate the kingdom of heaven in the person of the "Heavenly King." The term *Shangti* was known by every schoolboy to be the name of the God worshipped at Peking by the Emperor in his right as Son of Heaven, and the successor of the ancient sovereigns mentioned in the *Shu King;* accordingly, when the insurgents set up the worship of the true God as they had been able to learn it from Gutzlaff's revised version of the Bible, their countrymen immediately recognized the challenge. It was an attack on the religious as well as political position of Taukwang; whoever maintained his side in the gage of battle, with him were undoubtedly the powers above. The progress of the new banner

[1] Though one of their officers told Mr. Meadows, at Nanking, that the force was about three thousand.

from Yung-ngan to Nanking was like that of a fiery cross, and the sufferings of the people, except in a few large cities, were really more owing to the savage imperialists than to the Tai-pings. The latter grew in strength as they advanced, owing to indiscriminate slaughter on the part of their enemies of unoffending natives, and at last reached their goal with not much less than eighty thousand men.

Their position was now accessible to foreigners—who had been watching their rise and progress under great disadvantages in arriving at the truth—and they were soon visited by them in steamers. The first to do so was Governor Bonham in H. M. S. Hermes, accompanied by T. T. Meadows, one of the most competent linguists in China, who published the result of his inquiries. The visitors were at first received with incredulity, but this soon gave way to eager curiosity to learn the real nature of their religious views and practices. The insurgents themselves were even more ignorant of foreigners than were these of the rebels, so that the interest could not fail to be reciprocal, nor could either party desire to come into collision with the other.

About two months after the cities of Nanking, Chinkiang, and Yangchau had been taken, garrisoned, and put in a state of defence by their inhabitants, working under the direction of Tai-ping officers, the leaders felt so much confidence in their cause, their troops, and their ability, that they despatched a division to capture Peking. No particulars of its size or composition are given, but its course and achievements are recorded in the *Peking Gazette*. The force landed not far from Kwachau, where it defeated a body of Manchus, and then proceeded to Liuho and Fungyang fu without finding serious opposition. Crossing the province of Nganhwui, they entered that of Honan, and in one month from landing the troops laid siege to Kaifung, the provincial capital, June 19th. Three days later they were repulsed, and their leaders crossed the Yellow River to Hwaiking fu, about a hundred miles west of Kaifung. For two months they were baffled by an unusual resistance on the part of the imperialists, and were compelled to leave it and go west into Shansí, where they took Pingyang fu and flanked the enemy by turning east and north-east till they crossed the Liuming pass and got into Chihlí. It was their design to have gone down the River Wei to Lintsing chau on the Grand Canal, but they were compelled to make a detour of some hundreds of miles to reach this last place. In doing so they ascended the steep defiles leading from the basin of the Yellow River to the plateau in South Shansí. This march was accomplished in the month of September, and on October 9th the prefect city of Shinchau in Chihlí, only two hundred miles from Peking, was taken. Their army remained at Shinchau for a fortnight, when they marched across the plain northeasterly to Tsinghai hien, on the Grand Canal. Here they intrenched themselves on October 28th, but twenty miles south of Tientsin. A detachment sent to attack that city was repulsed, and the whole body were blockaded on November 3d by the Manchu force, which had followed it from Hwaiking, and other corps ordered from the north to intercept its progress toward the capital. In six months this insurgent force had traversed four provinces, taken twenty-six cities, subsisted themselves on the enemy, and defeated every body of imperialists sent against them. The men who performed this remarkable march of fully one thousand five hundred miles in the face of such odds, would have accomplished even greater deeds under better training. Considering all things, it is quite equal to General Sherman's march to the sea in 1864; yet so little is known of the details of this feat, that we are not even certain of its leader's name—whether Lin Fung-tsiang, spoken of by the *Gazette* as a 'Pretended Minister,' or some other general, was in command.

It is rather hard to understand why the Tai-pings intrenched themselves so near to Tientsin, but the officials of that city, in 1858, ascribed it to the fact that water covered the plain, preventing all operations against the town. Perhaps their want of siege guns, and the cavalry now brought from Mongolia, decided the leaders to intrench themselves at Tsinghai and send to Nanking for reinforcements. The Tai-ping Wang immediately despatched an auxiliary force, which also crossed Nganhwui to Funghien on the north bank of the Yellow River; this place was captured March 17, 1854, "after taking city after city," as the Emperor Hienfung expressed it. The ice was gone when the army reached Lintsing chau, April 12th, and that city was taken by a fierce assault against the combined resistance of its garrison and the imperialists outside, after the insurgent auxiliary was attacked in force. The other body had left Tsinghai in February, starved out rather than driven away, and gone to the district town of Hien, which they left March 10th for Fauching, and probably rejoined their comrades somewhere between that and Lintsing. They were about a hundred miles apart, and the intervening region was no doubt forcibly drained of its supplies. This joint army remained in possession of their depots as long as they saw fit, and treated the inhabitants reasonably well, among whom there were no Manchus. The inability to understand each other's speech kept the people of this district from mixing with the southerners, and, combined with the impossibility of keeping open the road to Nanking, decided the Tai-pings to return. This they did in March, 1855, by re-entering Nganhwui and rejoining the main body wherever ordered; but no details are known of their movements for nearly a year before that date. Peking and the Great Pure dynasty were saved, however; while the failure of Hung Siutsuen to risk all on such an enterprise proved his ignorance of the real point of this contest. He never was able to undertake a second campaign, and his followers soon degenerated into banditti.

The possession of Nanking, Chinkiang, and Kwachau, with the large flotilla along the Yangtsz' River west to Íchang in Hupeh, a distance of over six hundred miles, had entirely sundered the Emperor's authority over the seven south-eastern provinces. The country on each side for fifty or one hundred and fifty miles was visited by the insurgents' troops merely for supplies. Their boats penetrated to Nanchang in Kiangsí, went up the River Siang even beyond Changsha in Hunan, ravaged one town after another in quest of provisions and reinforcements, which were either taken to Nanking or used to support the crews; but nowhere did the leaders set up anything like a government, nowhere did they secure those who submitted or pursued their avocations quietly any protection against imperialist or other foes. As a revolution involving a reorganization of the Chinese nation on Christian principles, and a well-defined assertion of the rights and duties of rulers and subjects, it had failed entirely within a year after the possession of Nanking. There was no hope that any of the leaders in the movement would develop the ability to initiate the establishment of a consistent and suitable control, since not one of them was endowed either with the experience necessary to introduce provisional government over conquered communities, or with that tact calculated to impress their inhabitants with enduring confidence in them. All their prisoners were compelled to work or fight in their service, and were willing to earn their food and clothes; while in obeying such orders, and going through such religious ceremonies as were told them, they of course had not much to complain of; but this conduct did not imply hatred of the mandarins or an abjuration of Buddhism.

During the three years after Nanking had been occupied, the people in the Yangtsz' valley had suffered much from the conflict. Both armies lived on the land, and the danger of resisting the demands for food, clothes, and animals was nearly equalled by that of joining the contending forces; in either case beggary or loss of life was sure to be the end. As an instance of by no means unexampled suffering, the populous mart of Hankow and its environs was taken by assault six different times during the thirty months ending in May, 1855, and finally was left literally a heap of ruins. In country places the imperialists were, of the two parties, perhaps the more terrible scourge, but as the region became impoverished each side vied with the other in exhausting the people. The Tai-pings were gradually circumscribed to the region around Nanking and Nganking by the slow approaches of the government troops, and in 1860 seemed to be near their end. The interest which had been aroused at Shanghai in 1853, upon hearing of their Christian tenets and organization, had been satisfied in the various visits of foreign functionaries to Nanking, the intercourse with the leaders and men, perusal of their books, and observation of their policy.

One inherent defect in the enterprise, when viewed in its political bearing, ere long showed itself. Nothing could induce Hung Siu-tsuen to lead his men to the north and risk all in an attack on Peking. His own conviction of his divine mission had been most cordially received by his generals and the entire body of followers which left Yung-ngan in 1852; but their faith was not accepted by the enormous additions made to the Tai-pings as they advanced to Nanking, and gradually the original force became so diluted that it was inadequate to restrain and inspirit their auxiliaries. Moreover, the Tien-wang had never seriously worked out any conception of the radical changes in his system of government, which it would be absolutely necessary to inaugurate under a Christian code of laws. Having had no knowledge of any western kingdom, he probably regarded them all as conformed to the rules and examples given in the Bible; perhaps, too, he trusted that the "Heavenly Father and Elder Brother" would reveal the proper course of action when the time came. The great body of literati would naturally be indisposed to even examine the claims of a western religion which placed Shangtí above all other gods, and allowed no images in worship, no ritual in temples, and no adoration to ancestors, to Confucius, or to the heavenly bodies. But if this patriotic call to throw off the Manchu yoke had been fortified by a well-devised system of public examinations for office—modified to suit the new order of things by introducing more practical subjects than those found in the classics—and had been put into practice, it is hard to suppose that the intellectual classes would not gradually have ranged themselves on the side of this rising power. The unnecessary cruelty and slaughter practised toward the Manchu garrisons and troops carried more dread into the hearts of the population than stimulus to co-operate with such ruthless revolutionists. The latter had weakened their prospects by destroying confidence in their moderation, justice, and ability to carry out their aim to establish a new sway. There was a large foundation of national aspirations and real dislike to the present dynasty, on which the Tien-wang could have safely reckoned for help and sympathy. But he was far from equal to the exigency of his opportunity. The doubts of his countrymen as to his competency were proved by the satisfaction and relief felt when his movement collapsed.

When the remnants of the two corps which returned from the north in 1855 were incorporated into the forces holding the Grand Canal and the Liang Kiang province, their outposts hardly extended along the Great River beyond Chinkiang on the east and Nganking on the west. In that year dissensions sprung up among the leaders themselves inside of Nanking, which ended in the execution of Yang, the Eastern King, the next year; a fierce struggle maintained by Wei, the Northern King, on behalf of the Tien-wang, upheld his supremacy, but at a loss of his best general. Another man of note, Shih Ta-kai, the Assistant King, losing faith in the whole undertaking, managed to withdraw with a large following westward, and reached Sz'chuen. The early friend of Hung Siu-tsuen, Fung Yun-shan, known as the Southern King, disappeared about the same time. Rumors of these conflicts reached Shanghai in such a contradictory form that it was impossible to learn all their causes.

One source of strife arose by Yang assuming to be the Holy Ghost. Receiving communications from the Heavenly Father and Elder Brother, he thus placed himself above the Tien-wang, and, it is said by Wilson,[1] "required him to humble himself and receive forty lashes" for some misdemeanors complained of by the Comforter. The notices of this man which have reached us show that he early took a prominent part in the movement, and perhaps manipulated "descents of the Heavenly Father," like the one referred to above as mentioned in the "Book of Declarations" in the case of Chau Sih-nang.[2] Many proclamations were issued in his name on the progress to Nanking, which set forth the principles under which the Heavenly Dynasty were trying to conquer. Incentives addressed to the patriotic feelings of the Chinese were mixed up with their obligations to worship Shangtí, now made known to them as the Great God, our Heavenly Father, and security promised to all who submitted.

---

[1] *The "Ever-Victorious Army," Lt.-Col. Gordon's Chinese Campaign*, p. 43.

[2] J. Milton Mackie, *Life of Tai-ping-Wang, Chief of the Chinese Insurrection*, Chap. XXXIV., New York, 1857.

In one sent forth by him when nearing Nanking, he thus summarizes the rules which guided the Tai-pings:

I, the General, in obedience to the royal commands, have put in motion the troops for the punishment of the oppressor, and in every place to which I have come the enemy, at the first report, have dispersed like scattered rubbish. As soon as a city has been captured, I have put to death the rapacious mandarins and corrupt magistrates therein, but have not injured a single individual of the people, so that all of you may take care of your families and attend to your business without alarm and trepidation. I have heard, however, that numbers of lawless vagabonds are in the villages, who previous to the arrival of our troops take advantage of the disturbed state of the country to defile mens' wives and daughters, and burn or plunder the property of honest people. . . . I have therefore especially sent a great officer, named Yuen, with some hundreds of soldiers, to go through the villages, and as soon as he finds these vagabonds he is commissioned forthwith to decapitate them; while if the honest inhabitants stick up the word *shun* ['obedient'] over their doors, they will have nothing to fear.[1]

Such manifestoes could not reassure the timid population of the valley of the Yangtsz', and the carnage of the unresisting Manchus in Nanking, Chinkiang, and elsewhere indicated a ruthless license among the followers of the Tien-wang, which made them feel that their success carried with it no promise of melioration. In addition, as the vast spoil obtained from these cities and towns up to 1856 was consumed, the outlook of the rebels was most discouraging. Among their forces, the disheartened, the sick, and the wounded, with the captived and desperate, soon died, deserted, or skulked, and their places were filled by forced levies. Under these circumstances the dissensions within the court at Nanking imperilled the whole cause, and showed the incapacity of its leaders in face of their great aim. Yang had sunk into a sensual, unscrupulous faction leader who could no longer be endured; by October, 1856, he and all his adherents, to the number of twenty thousand, were utterly cut off by Wei. But this latter king speedily met with a like fate. Shih, the Assistant King, was at this time in the province of Kiangsí. It had become a life struggle with Siu-tsuen, and his removal of the four kings resulted in leaving him without any real military chief on whose loyalty he could depend. The rumors which

[1] Lindley, *Tai-ping Tien-kwoh*, Vol. I., p. 94.

reached Shanghai in 1856 of the fierce conflict in the city were probably exaggerated by the desire prevalent in that region that the parties would go on, like the Midianites in Gideon's time, beating down each other till they ended the matter.

The success of the Tai-pings had encouraged discontented leaders in other parts of China to set up their standards of revolt. The progress of Shih Ta-kai in Sz'chuen and Kweichau engaged the utmost efforts of the provincial rulers to restore peace. In Kwangtung a powerful band invested the city, but the operations of Governor Yeh, after the departure of Sü Kwang-tsun in 1854, were well supported by the gentry. By the middle of 1855 the rising was quenched in blood. The destruction of Fatshan, Shauking, and other large towns, had shown that the sole object of the rebels was plunder, though it was thought at first that they were Tai-pings. The executions in Canton during fourteen months up to August, 1856, were nearly a hundred thousand men; but the loss of life on both sides must be reckoned by millions. A band of Cantonese desperadoes seized the city of Shanghai in September, 1853, killing the district magistrate and some other officials. They retained possession till the Chinese New Year, January 27, 1854, leaving the city amid flames and carnage, when many of the leaders escaped in foreign vessels.[1] None of these men were affiliated with the Tai-pings.

In Formosa and Hainan, as well as in Yunnan and Kansuh, the provincial authorities had hard work with their local contingents to maintain the Emperor's authority. This wretched prince was himself fast bound under the sway of Suhshun and his miserable coterie, devising means to replenish his coffers by issuing iron and paper money, and proposing counters cut out of jade stone to take the place of bullion. The national history, however, had many notices of precisely such disastrous epochs in former times, and the nation's faith in itself was not really weakened.

By 1857 the imperialists had begun to draw close lines about

[1] No foreigners here or elsewhere in China were injured designedly during all this insurrection.

the rebels, when they were nearly restricted to the river banks between Nganking and Nanking, both of which cities were blockaded. Two years later the insurgent capital was beleaguered, but in its siege the loyalists trusted almost wholly to the effects of want and disease, which at last reached such an extreme degree (up to 1860) that it was said human flesh was sold on the butchers' stalls of Nanking. Their ammunition was nearly expended, their numbers were reduced, and their men apparently desirous to disperse; but the indomitable spirit of the leader never quailed. He had appointed eleven other *wang*, or generals, called *Chung Wang* ('Loyal King'), *Ying Wang* ('Heroic King'), *Kan Wang* ('Shield King'), *Ting Wang* ('Listening King'), etc., whose abilities were quite equal to the old ones. As the siege progressed events assumed daily a more threatening aspect. Chang Kwo-liang and Ho Chun, two imperialist generals, invested the city more and more closely, driving the insurgents to extremity in every direction. The efforts of these men were, however, not aggressive in consequence of the war then waging with the British and French on the Pei ho. This encouraged the beleaguered garrison to a desperate effort to free themselves, and on May 6, 1860, a well-concerted attack on the armies which had for years been intrenched behind outworks about the city scattered them in utter disorder. A small body of Tai-pings managed to get out toward the north of Kiangsu, near the Yellow River. Another body had already (in March) carried Hangchau by assault by springing a mine; as many as seventy thousand inhabitants, including the Manchu garrison, perished here during the week the city remained in possession of the rebels. On their return to Nanking the joint force carried all before it, and the needed guns and ammunition fell into their hands. The loyalist soldiers also turned against their old officers, but the larger part had been killed or dispersed. Chinkiang and Changchau were captured, and Ho Kwei-tsing, the governor-general, fled in the most dastardly manner to Suchau, without an effort to retrieve his overthrow. Some resistance was made at Wusih on the Grand Canal, but Ho Chun was so paralyzed by the onslaught that he killed himself, and Suchau fell into the hands of Chung Wang with no resistance whatever.

It was, nevertheless, burned and pillaged by the cowardly imperialists before they left it, Ho Kwei-tsing setting the large suburbs on fire to uncover the solid walls. This destruction was so unnecessary that the citizens welcomed the Tai-pings, for they would at least leave them their houses. With Suchau and Hangchau in their hands, the Kan Wang and Chung Wang had control of the great watercourses in the two provinces, and their desire now was to obtain foreign steamers to use in regaining mastery of the Yangtsz' River. The loss of their first leaders was by this time admirably supplied to the insurgents by these two men, who had had a wider experience than the Tien-wang himself, while their extraordinary success in dispersing their enemies had been to them all an assurance of divine protection and approval.

The populous and fertile region of Kiangnan and Chehkiang was wholly in their hands by June, 1860, so far as any organized Manchu force could resist them. The destruction of life, property, and industry within the three months since their sally from Nanking had been unparalleled probably since the Conquest, more than two centuries before, and revived the stories told of the ruthless acts of Attila and Tamerlane. Shanghai was threatened in August by a force of less than twenty thousand men led by the Chung Wang, and it would have been captured if it had not been protected by British and French troops. Many villages in the district were destroyed, but the flotilla approaching from Sungkiang recoiled from a collision with foreigners, and the insurgents all retired before September. They, however, could now be supplied with munitions of war, and even began to enlist foreigners to help them drill and fight. It was an anomalous condition of things, possible only in China, that while the allied force was marching upon Peking to extort a treaty, the same force was encircling the walls of Shanghai, burning its suburbs to destroy all cover, and aiding its rulers to preserve it to Hienfung—all in order to conquer a trade. It was then the moment for the Tai-pings to have moved rapidly upon Chihlí and tried the gage of battle before the metropolis, as soon as possible after Lord Elgin had withdrawn. But they had now very few left to them of the kind of troops which threatened the capital in 1853–54, and could not depend on recruits from Kiangnan in the hour of adversity.

At this juncture the imperialists began to look toward foreigners for aid in restoring their prestige and power by employing skill and weapons not to be found among themselves. An American adventurer, Frederick G. Ward, of Salem, Mass., proposed to the Intendant Wu to recapture Sungkiang from the Tai-pings; he was repulsed on his first attempt at the head of about a hundred foreigners, but succeeded on the second, and the imperialists straightway occupied the city. This success, added to the high pay, stimulated many others to join him, and General Ward ere long was able to organize a larger body of soldiers, to which the name of *Chang-shing kiun*, or 'Ever-victorious force,' was given by the Chinese; it ultimately proved to be well applied. Its composition was heterogeneous, but the energy, tact, and discipline of the leader, under the impulse of an actual struggle with a powerful foe, soon moulded it into something like a manageable corps, able to serve as a nucleus for training a native army. Foreigners generally looked down upon the undertaking, and many of the allied naval and military officers regarded it with doubt and dislike. It had to prove its character by works, but the successive defeats of the insurgents during the year 1862 in Kiangsu and Chehkiang, clearly demonstrated the might of its trained men over ten times their number of undisciplined braves.

But we must retrace our steps somewhat. In 1860 the possession of the best parts of Kiangsu and Chehkiang led the Tien Wang to plan the relief of Nganking by advancing on Hankow with four separate corps. They were under the leadership of the Chung Wang, and, so far as the details can be gathered, manifested a practical generalship hardly to be expected. The Ying Wang was to move through Nganhwui from Luchau westerly to Hwangchau; the Attendant King (Shih) was to leave Kiangsí and co-operate with the Chung Wang by reaching the Yangtsz' as near Hankow as possible, and a smaller force under the Tu Wang was to recover Hukau at the mouth of Poyang Lake and ascend the Great River in boats. The area through which this campaign was to be carried on may be understood when we learn that the Chung Wang's march of five hundred miles was over the two ranges of mountains on the frontiers of Kiangsí, and that of the Ying Wang two hundred miles through the plains of Nganhwui. This last king did act ually take his force of about eighty thousand men two hundred miles to Hwangchau (fifty miles below Hankow) in eleven days, but none of his colleagues came to his aid. The experience of eight years had quite changed the elements of the contest.

The people now generally realized that neither life, property, nor government was secured under the Tai-pings; the imperialists had learned how to obtain the co-operation of the patriotic gentry, and the rank and file of the Tai-pings were by this date mostly conquered natives of the same region, as no recruits had ever come from Kwangsí. Moreover, the region was impoverished, and this involved greater privations to all parties. Yet the Chung Wang went from Wuhu south-west to Kwangsin, crossed the water-shed into Kiangsí, defeated a force at Kienchang, crossed the River Kan near Linkiang, and marched north-west to Wuning hien on the River Siu. Here he heard of the defeat of Tu Wang, and the non-arrival of Shih's force; and, lest he should be hemmed in himself, as the failure of the campaign was evident, he led his army back across the province to Kwangsin by September, 1861. The particulars of this last great exploit of the Tai-pings are so imperfectly known, that it is impossible to judge of it as a military movement accomplished under enormous difficulties; but the Loyal King must have been a strategist of no mean rank.

In November, 1861, Nganking succumbed to the imperialists. Its defenders and the citizens endured untold sufferings at the last, while its victors had an empty shell; but the river was theirs down to Nanking. On his return east, Chung Wang moved into Chehkiang and overran all the northern half of that province, his men inflicting untold horrors upon the inhabitants, whom they killed, burned, and robbed as they listed. Ningpo was taken December 9th and held till May 10th, when it was recaptured by the allies; foreign trade had not been interrupted during this period, and the city suffered less than many others. In September the Tai-pings were driven out of the valley of the Yung River, but the death of General Ward at Tsz'kí deprived the imperialists of an able leader. The career of this man had been a strange one, but his success in training his men was endorsed by honorable dealing with the mandarins, who had reported well of him at Peking. He was buried at Sungkiang, where a shrine was erected to his memory, and incense is burned before him to this day.

It was difficult to find a successor, but the command rather devolved on his second, an American named Burgevine, who was confirmed by the Chinese, but proved to be incapable. He was superseded by Holland and Cooke, Englishmen, and in April, 1863, the entire command was placed under Colonel Peter Gordon, of the British army. During the interval between May, 1860, when Ward took Sungkiang, and April 6, 1863, when Gordon took Fushan, the best manner of combining native and foreign troops was gradually developed as they became more and more acquainted with each other and learned to respect discipline as an earnest of success. Such a motley force has seldom if ever been seen, and the enormous preponderance of Chinese troops would have perhaps been an element of danger had they been left idle for a long time.

The bravery of the Ever-victorious force in the presence of the enemy had gradually won the confidence of the allies, as well as the Chinese officials, in whose pay it was; and when it operated in connection with the French and British contingent in driving the Tai-pings out of Ningpo prefecture, the real worth of Ward's drill was made manifest. The recapture of that city by Captain Dew's skilful and brave attack in reply to their unprovoked firing at H. M. S. Encounter, brought out the bravery of all nationalities, as well as restored the safety of the port. An extract from Captain Dew's report will exhibit the dreadful results to the common people of this civil war:

I had known Ningpo in its palmy days, when it boasted itself one of the first commercial cities of the Empire; but now, on this 11th of May, one might have fancied that an angel of destruction had been at work in the city as in the suburbs. All the latter, with their wealthy hongs and thousands of houses, lay levelled; while in the city itself, once the home of half a million of people, no trace or vestige of an inhabitant could be seen. Truly it was a city of the dead. The rich and beautiful furniture of the houses had become firewood, or was removed to the walls for the use of soldiers. The canals were filled with dead bodies and stagnant filth. The stonework of bridges and pavements had been uplifted to strengthen walls and form barricades in the streets; and in temples once the pride of their Buddhist priests, the chaotic remains of gorgeous idols and war gods lay strewn about—their lopped limbs showing that they had become the sport of those Christian Tai-pings whose chief, the Tien-wang, eight years before at Nanking, had asked Sir George Bonham if the Virgin Mary had a pretty sister for him, the King of Heaven, to marry! It has been my good fortune since to assist at the wresting of many cities from these Tai-pings, and in them all I found, as at Ningpo, that the same devilish hands had been at work—the people expelled from their houses and their cities ruined.[1]

Yet so speedy was the revival from the ruins, that we are told that in one month houses had been refurnished and shops opened; their owners had mostly fled across the river into the foreign settlement. A larger force was now organized—MM. Le Brethon and Giquel being in charge of a Franco-Chinese regiment—and an advance made on Yüyau, which was retaken, and one thousand drilled Chinese left to defend it. Tsz'kí, Funghwa, and Shangyü were also cleared of rebels, and during the month of March they evacuated the prefect city of Shauhing, never again to return to this fertile valley. Their inroad had been an unmitigated scourge, for they had now given up all pretense of Christianity, and had not the least idea of instituting a regular government; to plunder, kill, and destroy was their only business. Their sense of danger from the hatred of the people whom they had so grievously maltreated led them at this time to defend the walled cities with a reckless bravery that made their capture more difficult and dangerous. This was shown in the siege of Shauhing fu, within whose walls about forty thousand Tai-pings were well led by the Shí Wang. The possession of cannon enabled them to reply to the balls thrown by Captain Dew's artillery, while despair lent energy to their resistance; so that the attack turned into a regular siege of a month's duration, when, food and ammunition being exhausted, they retreated *en masse* to Hangchau.

While this success relieved the greater part of Chehkiang from the scourge, the failure of the Ever-victorious force to

---

[1] A. Wilson, *The "Ever-Victorious Army,"* p. 102, London, 1868.

retake Taitsang and Fushan, under Holland and Brennan, had discouraged Governor Lí, who had now come into power. He applied to General Stavely, who, with a full appreciation of the exigencies of the case, and concurrence of Sir Frederick Bruce, aided in reorganizing Ward's force and placing Colonel Gordon over it with adequate powers. There were five or six infantry regiments of about five hundred men each, and a battery of artillery; at times it numbered five thousand men. The commissioned officers were all foreigners, and their national rivalries were sometimes a source of trouble; the non-commissioned officers were Chinese, many of them repentant rebels or seafaring men from Canton and Fuhkien, promoted for good conduct. The uniform was a mixture of native and foreign dress, which at first led to the men being ridiculed as 'Imitation Foreign Devils;' after victory, however, had elevated their *esprit du corps*, they became quite proud of the costume. In respect to camp equipage, arms, commissariat and ordnance departments, and means of transport, the natives soon made themselves familiar with all details; while necessity helped their foreign officers rapidly to pick up their language. It is recorded, to the credit of this motley force, that "there was very little crime and consequently very little punishment; . . . as drunkenness was unknown, the services of the provost-marshal rarely came into use, except after a capture, when the desire for loot was a temptation to absence from the ranks."[1]

In addition, the force had a flotilla of four small steamers, aided by a variety of native boats to the number of fifty to seventy-five. The plain is so intersected by canals that the troops could be easier moved by water than land, and these boats enabled it to carry out surprises which disconcerted the rebels. Wilson well remarks concerning Gordon's force: "Its success was owing to its compactness, its completeness, the quickness of its movements, its possession of steamers and good artillery, the bravery of its officers, the confidence of its men, the inability of the rebels to move large bodies of troops with

[1] Wilson, *ibid.*, p. 132.

rapidity, the nature of the country, the almost intuitive perception of the leader in adapting his operations to the nature of the country, and his untiring energy in carrying them out." [1]

The details of this singular troop are worth telling with more minuteness than space here allows, for its management will no doubt form a precedent in the future; but the good its remarkable chief effected in restoring peace to Kiangsu calls for that recognition which skill, tact, and high moral purpose ever deserve. Being formally put in command on March 24, 1863, he promptly reinstated the foreign officers belonging to the force, paid their dues, and within a few days was in readiness to march upon Fushan, a town on the Yangtsz' above Paushan. The fall of this place on April 6th led to the capture of Chanzu, when preparations were made for besieging Taitsang fu, where an army of ten thousand rebels, aided by foreign adventurers, presented a formidable undertaking for his force of two thousand eight hundred men, although supported by a large body of imperialists. In its capture (May 2d) the killed and wounded numbered one hundred and sixty-two officers and men; the booty obtained was so large that Colonel Gordon led his men back to Sungkiang, in order to reorganize them after this experience of their conduct. Finding that their former license in appropriating the loot thus obtained tended to demoralize them all, he accepted the resignations of some of the discontented officers, and adopted stringent measures to bring the others to render military obedience. Consequently, when he started for Kiunshan with about three thousand men, he had his force in a much better condition. This city occupied an important position between Shanghai, Chanzu, Taitsang, and other large towns on the east, and Suchau on the west. The rebels had set up a cannon foundry within its walls, and from it obtained supplies for the last-named city, with which it was connected by a causeway. By means of the armed steamer Hyson, Colonel Gordon was able to bring up through one of the canals a company of three hundred and fifty men and field artillery, cutting the causeway and pursuing its defenders, some

---

[1] *Ibid.*, p. 138.

into the town and some toward Suchau, almost to its very gates. On the return of the steamer in the night, the commander found the imperialists engaged with the garrison in a sharp contest, in which the foreigners then aided, and completely routed the rebel body of nearly eight thousand men. Fully four thousand of them were killed outright, and others were drowned or cut off by the exasperated peasantry before the day was over. This was on May 30th. The captured town was made headquarters by its victors, as a more eligible location than Sungkiang, though against the wishes of the native officers, who desired to go back there with their booty. The loss of men, material, and position to the rebels was very great, and Colonel Gordon could now safely turn his whole thoughts to the capture of Suchau.

This city is like Venice in its approaches by canals; owing to its location it was deemed best, before attempting its capture, to reduce certain towns in the vicinity, from which it derived supplies, so that the Chung Wang should not be able to co-operate with its garrison. The district towns of Wukiang and Kahpu were both taken in July with comparatively little loss. This rapid reduction of many strong stockades, stone forts, and walled towns, with the panic exhibited by the men, proved how useless to the rebels the foreigners in their service had been in rendering them really formidable enemies, and how incapable the wangs had been to appreciate the nature and need of discipline. After these places had been occupied, Colonel Gordon found his position beset with so many unexpected annoyances, both from his rather turbulent and incongruous troops as well as from the Chinese authorities, that he went to Shanghai on August 8th for the purpose of resigning the command. Arriving here, however, he ascertained that Burgevine had just gone over to the Tai-pings with about three hundred foreigners, and was then in Suchau. The power of moral principle, which guided the career of the one, was then seen in luminous contrast to its lack as shown in the other of these soldiers of fortune. To his lasting credit Colonel Gordon decided to return at once to Kiunshan, and, in face of the ingratitude of the Chinese and jealousy of his officers, to stand by the imperialist cause. He gradually restored his influence over officers and men, ascertained that Burgevine's position in the Tai-ping army did not allow him freedom enough to render his presence dangerous to their foes, and began to act aggressively against Suchau by taking Patachiau on its southern side in September.

Emissaries from the foreigners in the city now reported considerable dissatisfaction with their position, and Colonel Gordon was able to arrange in a short time their withdrawal without much danger to themselves. It is said that Burgevine even then proposed to him to join their forces, seize Suchau, and as soon as possible march on Peking with a large army, and do to the Manchus what the Manchus had done, two hundred and twenty years before, to the Mings. Colonel Gordon's own loyalty was somewhat suspected by the imperialist leaders, but his integrity carried him safely through all these temptations to swerve from his duty.

As soon as these mercenaries among the rebels were out of the way, operations against Suchau were prosecuted with vigor, so that by November 19th the entire city was invested and carefully cut off from communication with the north. The city being now hard pushed, the besieging force prepared for a night attack upon a breach previously made in the stockade near the north-east gate. It was well planned, but the Muh Wang, *facile princeps* among the Tai-ping chiefs in courage and devotion, having been informed of it, opened such a destructive fire that the Ever-victorious force was defeated with a loss of about two hundred officers and men killed and wounded. On the next morning, however (November 28th), it was reported that the cowardly leaders in the city were plotting against the Muh Wang—the only loyal one among their number—and were talking of capitulating, using the British chief as their intermediary.

This rumor proved, indeed, to be so far true, that after some further successful operations on the part of Gordon's division, the Wangs made overtures to General Ching, himself a former rebel commander, but long since returned to the imperial cause and now the chief over its forces in Kiangsu. The Muh Wang was publicly assassinated on December 2d by his comrades, and on the 5th the negotiations had proceeded so far that interviews were held. Colonel Gordon had withdrawn his troops a short distance to save the city from pillage, but did not succeed in obtaining a donation of two months' pay for their late bravery from the parsimonious Lí. He therefore proposed to lay down his command at three o'clock P.M., and meanwhile went into the city to interview the Na Wang, who told him that everything was proceeding in a satisfactory manner. Upon learning this he repaired to the house of the murdered Muh Wang in order to get his corpse decently buried, but failed, as no one in the place would lend him the smallest assistance. While he was thus occupied, the rebel wangs and officers had settled as to the terms they would accept; and on reaching his own force, Gordon found General Ching there with a donation of one month's pay, which his men refused.

The next morning he returned into the city and was told by Ching that the rebel leaders had all been pardoned, and would deliver up the city at noon; they were preparing then to go out. Colonel Gordon shortly after started to return to his own camp and met the imperialists coming into the east gate in a tumultuous manner, prepared for slaughter and pillage. He therefore went back to the Na Wang's house to guard it, but found the establishment already quite gutted; he, however, met the Wang's uncle and went with him to protect the females of the family at the latter's residence. Here he was detained by several hundred armed rebels, who would neither let him go nor send a message by his interpreter till the next morning (December 7th), when they permitted him to leave for his boat, then waiting at the south gate; narrowly escaping, on his way thither, an attack from the imperialists, he reached his bodyguard at daybreak, and with them was able to prevent any more soldiers entering the city. His preservation amid such conflicting forces was providential, but his indignation was great when he learned that Governor Lí had beheaded the eight rebel leaders the day before. It seems that they had demanded conditions quite inadmissible in respect to the control of the thirty thousand men under their orders, and were cut off for their insolent contumacy. Another account, published at

Shanghai in 1871, states that nearly twenty chiefs were executed, and about two thousand privates.

As Colonel Gordon felt that his good name was compromised by this cruelty, he threw up his command until he could confer with his superiors. On the 29th a reply came to Lí Hung-chang from Prince Kung, highly praising all who had been engaged in taking Suchau, and ordering him to send the leader of the Ever-victorious force a medal and ten thousand taels—both of which he declined. The posture of affairs soon became embarrassing to all parties. The rebellion was not suppressed; the cities in rebel hands would soon gather the desperate men escaped from Suchau; Colonel Gordon alone could lead his troops to victory; and all his past bravery and skill might be lost. He therefore resumed his command, and presently recommenced operations by leading his men against Íhing hien, west of Suchau.

Concerning this wretched business of the Suchau slaughter, much was said both in the foreign communities in China and later in England. Mr. Wilson, in his book compiled largely from Colonel Gordon's notes on this campaign, discusses the question with as great fairness as precision, and concludes—as must every well-wisher of China with him—that it was in every way fortunate, both for his reputation and the cause to which he had lent himself, that this heroic man returned to his thankless task. Summing up the arguments of the Chinese and the various attendant circumstances that brought about this execution, Mr. Wilson points to Lí's not unnatural desire after revenge for his brother's murder by the rebels before Taitsang; to the army still under control of the wangs; to the almost absolute certainty of massacre of those imperialists who had already entered the city should he refuse compliance with their demands; as also to the impossibility of arresting these chiefs without an alarm of treachery spreading among their troops within the walls, and thus giving them time to close the gates, cutting off the imperial soldiers inside the city from those who were without. "Lí was in a very difficult and critical position," he says, "which imperatively demanded sudden, unpremeditated action; and though, no doubt, it would have been more honorable for him to have made the wangs prisoners, he cannot in the circumstances be with justice severely censured for having ordered the Tai-ping chiefs who were in his power, but who defied his authority, to be immediately killed. It is also certain that Colonel Gordon need not have been in a hurry to consider himself as at all responsible for this almost necessary act, because in a letter to him (among his correspondence relating to these affairs) from the Futai [Lí], dated November 2, 1863, I find the following noteworthy passage, which shows that the governor did not wish Gordon to interfere at all in regard to the capitulation of the Suchau chiefs: 'With respect to Moh Wang and other rebel leaders' proposal, I am quite satisfied that you have determined in no way to interfere. Let Ching look after their treacherous and cunning management.'"[1]

On reaching Ihing, the dreadful effects of the struggle going on around Gordon's force were seen, and more than reconciled him to do all he could to bring it to an end. Utter destitution prevailed in and out of the town; people were feeding on dead bodies, and ready to perish from exposure while waiting for a comrade to die. The town of Liyang was surrendered on his approach, and its inhabitants, twenty thousand in number, supplied with a little food. From this place to Kintan proved to be a slow and irksome march, owing to the shallow water in the canal and the bad weather. On March 21st an attack was made on this strong post by breaching the walls; but it resulted in a defeat, the loss of more than a hundred officers and men, and a severe wound which Colonel Gordon received in his leg — oddly enough the only injury he sustained, though frequently compelled to lead his men in person to a charge. Next day he retired, in order, to Liyang, but hearing that the son of the Chung Wang had retaken Fushan he started with a thousand men and some artillery for Wusih, which the rebels had left. The operations in this region during the next few weeks conclusively proved the desperate condition of the rebels, but a hopeless cause seemed often but to increase their bravery in defending what strongholds were left them. At the same time a

[1] Wilson, *The "Ever-Victorious Army,"* p. 204.

body of Franco-Chinese was operating, in connection with General Ching on the south of Suchau, against Kiahing fu, a large city on the Grand Canal, held by the Ting Wang. This position was taken and its defenders put to the sword on March 20th, but with the very serious loss of General Ching, one of the ablest generals in the Chinese army. Hangchau, the capital of Chehkiang, capitulated the next day, and this was soon followed by the reduction of the entire province and dispersion of the rebels among the hills.

Colonel Gordon had recovered from his wound so as to lead an attack on Waisu April 6th, which town fell on the 11th, when most of its defenders were killed by the peasantry as they attempted to escape. His force was also much weakened, and needed to be recruited. With about three thousand in all, he now went to aid Governor Lí in reducing Changchau fu, and invested it on the 25th. The entire besieging force numbered over ten thousand; and as the rebels were twice as many, on the whole well provided, and knew that no mercy would be shown, their resistance was stubborn. Several attacks were repulsed with no small loss to Gordon's force, so that slower methods of approach were resorted to till a general assault was planned on May 11th, when it succumbed. Only fifteen hundred rebels were slain, and the greater part of the prisoners were allowed to go home, the Kwangsí men alone being executed. With this capture ended the operations of the Ever-victorious force and its brave leader. Nanking was now the only strong place held by the Tai-pings, and there was nothing for that army to do there, as Tsăng Kwoh-fan, the generalissimo of the imperial armies, had ample means for its capture. Colonel Gordon, therefore, in conjunction with Governor Lí, dissolved this notable division; the latter rewarded its officers and men with liberal gratuities, and sent the natives home. During its existence of about four years down to June 1, 1864, nearly fifty places had been taken (twenty-three of them by Gordon), and its higher discipline had served to elevate the *morale* of the imperialists who operated with them. It perhaps owed its greatest triumph to the high-toned uprightness of its Christian chief, which impressed all who served with him. The

Emperor conferred on him the highest military rank of *tí-tuh*, or 'Captain-General,' and a yellow jacket (*ma-kwa*) and other uniforms, to indicate the sense of his achievements. Sir Frederick Bruce admirably summed up his character in a letter to Earl Russell when sending the imperial rescript:

HONGKONG, July 12, 1864.

MY LORD,

I enclose a translation of a despatch from Prince Kung containing the decree published by the Emperor, acknowledging the services of Lieutenant-Colonel Gordon, R. E., and requesting that her Majesty's government be pleased to recognize them. This step has been spontaneously taken. Lieutenant-Colonel Gordon well deserves her Majesty's favor; for, independently of the skill and courage he has shown, his disinterestedness has elevated our national character in the eyes of the Chinese. Not only has he refused any pecuniary reward, but he has spent more than his pay in contributing to the comfort of the officers who served under him, and in assuaging the distress of the starving population whom he relieved from the yoke of their oppressors. Indeed, the feeling that impelled him to resume operations after the fall of Suchow was one of the purest humanity. He sought to save the people of the districts that had been recovered from a repetition of the misery entailed upon them by this cruel civil war. I have, etc.,

F. W. A. BRUCE.

The foreign merchants at Shanghai expressed their sense of his conduct in a letter dated November 24th, written on the eve of his return to England, in which they truly remark: "In a position of unequalled difficulty, and surrounded by complications of every possible nature, you have succeeded in offering to the eyes of the Chinese nation, no less by your loyal and disinterested line of action than by your conspicuous gallantry and talent for organization and command, the example of a foreign officer serving the government of this country with honorable fidelity and undeviating self-respect." [1]

Such men are not only the choice jewels of their own nation (and England may justly be proud to reckon this son among

[1] "The rapidity with which the long-descended hostility of the Chinese government became exchanged for relations of at least outward friendship, must be ascribed altogether to the existence of the Tai-ping Rebellion, without whose pressure as an auxiliary we might have crushed, but never conciliated the distrustful statesmen at Peking."—*Fraser's Magazine*, Vol. LXXI., p. 145, February, 1865.

her worthies), but leave behind them an example, as in the case of Colonel Gordon, which elevates Christianity itself in the eyes of the Chinese, and will remain a legacy for good to them through coming years.[1]

After the dissolution of the Ever-victorious force, its leader visited Nganking and Nanking to see the governor-general, Tsăng Kwoh-fan, and his brother, who were directing operations against the rebels, in order to propose some improvements in their future employment of foreign soldiers and military appliances. They listened with respect, and took notes of important suggestions—knowing at the same time that their subordinates were unable to comprehend or adopt many such innovations. The work before Nanking indicated the industry of its besiegers in the miles of walls connecting one hundred and forty mud forts in their circumvallations, and in various mines leading under the city walls. The Tai-pings at that date seldom appeared on the walls, and had recently sent out three thousand women and children to be fed by their enemies, proof enough of their distressed condition. The only general capable of relieving the Tien Wang was the Chung Wang, whose army remained on the southern districts of Kiangsu, while he himself was in the city with the Kan Wang (Hung Jin), now the trusted agent of his half-brother. All egress from the doomed city was stopped by June 1st, when the explosion of mines and bursting of shells forewarned its deluded defenders of their fate. Of the last days of their leader no authentic account has been given, and the declaration of the Chung Wang in his autobiography, that he poisoned himself on June 30th, "owing to his anxiety and trouble of mind," is probably true. His body was buried behind his palace by one of his wives, and afterward dug up by the imperialists.

On July 19, 1864, the wall was breached by the explosion of forty thousand pounds of powder in a mine, and the Chung Wang, faithful to the last, defended until midnight the Tien Wang's family from the imperialists. He and the Kan Wang

---

[1] Compare further Col. C. C. Chesney's *Essays on Modern Military Biography* (from the *Edinburgh Review*), pp. 163–213, London, 1874.

then escorted Hung Fu-tien—a lad of sixteen, who had succeeded to the throne of Great Peace three weeks before—with a thousand followers, a short distance beyond the city. The three leaders now became separated, but all were ultimately captured and executed. The Chung Wang, during his captivity before death, wrote an account of his own life, which fully maintains the high estimate previously formed of his character from his public acts.[1] He was the solitary ornament of the whole movement during the fourteen years of its independent existence, and his enemies would have done well to have spared him. More than seven thousand Tai-pings were put to death in Nanking, the total number found there being hardly over twenty thousand, of whom probably very few were southern Chinese—this element having gradually disappeared.

After the recapture of Nanking, two small bodies of rebels remained in Chehkiang. The largest of them, under the Tow Wang, held Huchau fu, and made a desperate resistance until a large force, provided with artillery, compelled them to evacuate. During this siege the sanguinary conduct of the Tai-pings showed the natural result of their reckless course since their last escape from Nanking; the narrative of an escaped Irishman, who had been compelled to serve them in Huchau for some months, is terrible enough: "All offences received one punishment—death. I saw one hundred and sixty men beheaded, as I understood, for absence from parade; two boys were beheaded for smoking; all prisoners of war were executed; spies, or people accused as such, were tied with their hands behind their backs to a stake, brushwood put around them, and they burned to death." The rebel force numbered nearly a hundred thousand men, and their vigorous defence was continued for a fortnight, till on August 14th their last stockade was carried by the imperialists, and about half their number made good their escape to the neighboring hills, leaving the usual scene of desolation behind them. This body undertook to march south through the hilly regions between Kiangsí and

[1] *The Autobiography of the Chung-Wang, translated from the Chinese by* W. T. Lay, Shanghai, 1865.

Chehkiang. The best disciplined portion was led by the Shí Wang, who had joined it with his men from the former province, and arranged an attack on Kwangsin, near which they were defeated. The remainder managed to march across the intervening districts south-westerly to the city of Changchau, near Amoy, where they intrenched themselves till the next spring, subsisting on the supplies found in it and the neighborhood. The Shí Wang and Kan Wang then left it April 16th, in two bodies, unable to resist the disciplined force of eight thousand men brought from the north. Feeling that their days were numbered, they seem to have scrupled at nothing to show their savagery—as, for example, when they slaughtered sixteen hundred imperialists who had surrendered on a promise of safe-conduct. No mercy was therefore shown them by the inhabitants; at Chănping in Kwangtung they even cut down their growing rice in order to prevent the rebels using it. The last straggling relics of the Tai-ping Heavenly King's adherents were thus gradually destroyed, and his ill-advised enterprise brought to an end.

Fifteen years had elapsed since he had set up his standard of revolt in Kwangsí, and now there was nothing to show as a return for the awful carnage and misery that had ensued from his efforts. No new ideas concerning God or his redemption for mankind had been set forth or illustrated by the teachings or practices of the Tai-ping leader or any of his followers, nor did they ever take any practical measures to call in foreign aid to assist in developing even the Christianity they professed. True the Kan Wang called Mr. Roberts to Nanking, but instead of consulting with him as to the establishment of schools, opening chapels, preparing books, or organizing any kind of religious or benevolent work to further the welfare of his adherents, the Tien Wang did not even grant an interview to the missionary, who, on his part, was glad to escape with his life to Shanghai.

If this rebellion practically exhibited no religious truth to the educated mind of China, it was not for lack of publications setting forth the beliefs its leaders had drawn from the Bible, or for laws sanctioned by severe penalties, both of which were scattered through the land. Dr. Medhurst's careful translations of these tracts has preserved them, so that the entire disregard manifested by the new sect of their plainest injunctions may be at once seen.[1] The strong expectations of the friends of China for its regeneration through the success of Hung Siu-tsuen, would not have been indulged if they had better known the inner workings of his own mind and the flagitious conduct of his lieutenants.

In his political aspirations the Tien Wang entertained no new principle of government, for he knew nothing of other lands, their jurisprudence or their polity, and wisely enough held his followers to such legislation as they were familiar with. They all probably expected to alter affairs to their liking when they had settled in Peking. But if this mysterious iconoclast had really any ideas above those of an enthusiast like Thomas Münzer and the Anabaptists in the early days of the Reformation—whose course and end offers many parallels to his own—he must have lamented his folly as he reviewed its results to his country. The once peaceful and populous parts of the nine great provinces through which his hordes passed have hardly yet begun to be restored to their previous condition. Ruined cities, desolated towns, and heaps of rubbish still mark their course from Kwangsí to Tientsin, a distance of two thousand miles, the efforts at restoration only making the contrast more apparent. Their presence was an unmitigated scourge, attended by nothing but disaster from beginning to end, without the least effort on their part to rebuild what had been destroyed, to protect what was left, or to repay what had been stolen. Wild beasts roamed at large over the land after their departure, and made their dens in the deserted towns; the pheasant's whirr resounded where the hum of busy populations had ceased, and weeds or jungle covered the ground once tilled with patient industry. Besides millions upon millions of taels irrecoverably lost and destroyed, and the misery, sickness, and starvation

[1] *Pamphlets issued by the Chinese Insurgents at Nan-King; to which is added a history of the Kwangsi Rebellion*, etc., etc., compiled by W. H. Medhurst, Senr., Shanghai, 1853. Compare R. J. Forrest in *Journal N. C. Br. R. A. Soc.*, No. IV., December, 1867, pp. 187 ff. *The China Mail* for February 2, 1854.

which were endured by the survivors, it has been estimated by foreigners living at Shanghai that, during the whole period from 1851 to 1865, fully twenty millions of human beings were destroyed in connection with the Tai-ping Rebellion.[1]

[1] The most complete authorities on this conflict are files of the *North China Herald* (Shanghai) and the *China Mail* (Hongkong) during the years from 1853 to 1869; a careful summary of these has been made by M. Cordier in his *Bibliotheca Sinica*, pp. 273–281, which will be useful alone to those who can gain access to these newspapers. The number of articles on various phases of the rebellion contained in English and American magazines is exceedingly numerous, and can be readily found by reference to Poole's *Index*. Among these compare especially the *London Quarterly*, Vol. 112, for October, 1862; *Fraser's Magazine*, Vol. 71, February, 1865; *Blackwood's*, Vol. 100, pp. 604 and 683; W. Sargent in the *North American Review*, Vol. 79, July, 1854, p. 158. See also the various *Blue Books* relating to China; Capt. Fishbourne, *Impressions of China and the Present Revolution*, London, 1855; Callery and Yvan, *L'Insurrection en Chine*, Paris, 1853—translated into English, London, 1853; Charles Macfarlane, *The Chinese Revolution*, London, 1853; T. T. Meadows, *The Chinese and their Rebellions*, London, 1856; J. M. Mackie, *Life of Tai-ping Wang*, N. Y., 1857; Commander Lindesay Brine, *Narrative of the Rise and Progress of the Taeping Rebellion in China*, London, 1862; "Lin-le," *Ti-Ping Tien-kwoh, the History of the Ti-Ping Revolution*, London, 1866—a rather untrustworthy record; Sir T. F. Wade in the *Shanghai Miscellany*, No. I.; Richthofen, *Letter on the Province of Shensi*.

CHAPTER XXV.

THE SECOND WAR BETWEEN GREAT BRITAIN AND CHINA.

The particulars given in the last chapter respecting the Tai-ping Rebellion did not include those details connected with foreign intercourse during the same period which have had such important results on the Chinese people and government. It is a notable index of the vigor and self-poise of both, that during those thirteen terrible years, the mass of inhabitants in the ten eastern provinces never lost confidence in their own government or its ability to subdue the rebels; while the leading officers at Peking and in all those provinces at no time expressed doubt as to the loyalty of their countrymen when left free to act. The narrative of foreign intercourse is now resumed from the year 1849, when the British authorities waived the right of insisting upon their admission into the city of Canton according to the terms of the convention with Kíying in 1847. The conduct of the Cantonese, in view of the forcible entrance of English troops into their city, is an interesting exhibition of their manner of arousing enthusiasm and raising funds and volunteers to cope with an emergency. The series of papers found in Vol. XVIII. of the *Chinese Repository* well illustrates the curious mixture of a sense of wrong and deep concern in public affairs, combined with profound ignorance and inaptitude as to the best means for attaining their object.

A candid examination of the real meaning of the Chinese texts of the four earlier treaties makes clear the fact that there were some grounds for their refusal; but more attractive than this appears the study of an address from the gentry of Canton, sent upon the same occasion, to Governor Bonham at Hongkong, dissuading him from attempting the entry. Their conduct was naturally regarded by the British as seditious, and of these many urged their authorities to vindicate the national honor and force a way over the walls into the city. The practice of an unwonted approach toward self-government which this popular movement in defence of their metropolis gave the citizens, was of real service to them in the year 1855, when it was beleaguered by the rebels, since they had learned how to use their powers and resources. One result of their fancied victory over the British at this time was the erection of six stone *pai-lau*, or honorary portals, in various parts of the city and suburbs, on each of which was engraved the sentence, "Reverently to commemorate glory conferred," together with a copy of the edict ordering their establishment, and a list of the wards and villages which furnished soldiers during their time of need.[1]

The outcome of the working of treaty provisions between foreigners and natives at the five opened ports during the ten years up to 1853, had been as satisfactory to both sides as could have been reasonably expected. The influx of foreigners had more than doubled their numbers; and as almost none of them could talk the Chinese language, it happened that natives of Canton became their brokers and compradores—rather more by reason of speaking *pigeon-English* than by their wealth or capacity. The vicious plan of marking off a separate plat of land for the residence of foreigners at each port was adopted, and their development tended to build up *concessions*, or settlements, which were to be governed by the various nationalities. In doing this the local authorities vacated their rights over their own territory, and these settlements have since become the germs of foreign cities, if not colonies. The British and French consuls at Shanghai claimed territorial jurisdiction over all who settled within the limits of their allotted districts, and carried this assumption so far as to exercise authority over the natives against their own rulers. The British ere long gave up this pernicious system, which had no legal basis by treaty or conquest, and yielded the entire internal management

[1] The one placed near the southern gate became a target for the British gunners in October, 1856, its demolition, most unfortunately, involving the destruction and burning of millions of Chinese books in the shops on that street.

of all consular communities to those foreigners which composed them. There were not enough residents elsewhere to raise this question of local government to any importance, but the progress of the Tai-pings and the rapid growth of Shanghai as a centre of trade for the Yangtsz' basin, compelled the preparation and adoption of a set of land regulations in order to institute some means of governing the thousands of foreigners who had flocked thither. George Balfour, the first British consul in that port, had sanctioned a series of rules in 1845, which purported to be drawn up by the *tautai*, or intendant of circuit, and which worked well enough in peaceful times.

In the year 1853, however, the civil war altered the conditions, when certain Cantonese rebels captured Shanghai and killed some of its magistrates, driving others into the British settlement, to which ground the custom-house was shortly afterward removed. The collector of the port, Wu Kien-chang, had formerly been a hong merchant at Canton, and he willingly entered into an arrangement for putting the collection of foreign duties into the hands of a commission until order was restored. The presence there of the British, American, and French ministers facilitated this arrangement. Their respective consuls, R. Alcock, R. C. Murphy, and B. Edan, accordingly met Wu on June 29, 1854, and agreed to a set of custom-house rules which in reality transferred the collection of duties into the hands of foreigners. The first rule contains the reason for this remarkable step in advance of all former positions, and has served to perpetuate the employment of foreigners at all the open ports, and maintain the foreign inspectorate:

RULE I.—The chief difficulty experienced by the superintendent of customs having consisted in the impossibility of obtaining custom-house officials with the necessary qualifications as to probity, vigilance, and knowledge of foreign languages, required for the enforcement of a close observance of treaty and custom-house regulations, the only adequate remedy appears to be in the introduction of a foreign element into the custom-house establishment, in the persons of foreigners carefully selected and appointed by the *tautai*, who shall supply the deficiency complained of, and give him efficient and trustworthy instruments wherewith to work.[1]

---

[1] *McLane's Correspondence*, 1858. *Senate Ex. Doc.*, No. 28, p. 154.

In carrying out the new arrangement, each consul nominated one man to the intendant, viz., T. F. Wade for the British, L. Carr for the American, and Arthur Smith for the French member of the board of inspectors, who together were to take charge of the new department. The chief responsibility for its organization fell on Mr. Wade, inasmuch as he alone of this number was familiar with the Chinese language, and possessed other qualifications fitting him for the post. He, however, resigned within a year, and the intendant appointed H. N. Lay, a clerk in the British consulate, who completed the service organization. This proceeding shows the readiness with which the Chinese will shirk their own duties and functions in government employ, and illustrates as well many peculiar traits in their character.

The city of Shanghai had been in possession of a Cantonese chief, Liu Tsz'-tsai, and his rabble since September 7, 1853, and the position of foreigners at that port in the presence of such a body of outlaws developed new points of international law. If the foreigners had all been of one nationality the consul would probably have assumed temporary control of the city and port to assure their safety; but in this case a naval force under each flag lying in the river guaranteed ample protection of life and property. As soon as the city was occupied the difficulty of restraining the disorderly elements, as well among foreigners as natives, became painfully apparent to their rulers. Foreign rowdies eagerly purchased the plunder brought to them and supplied arms and other things in return—a line of conduct very naturally irritating to the officials in charge of the siege and inclining them at once toward coercive measures.

The fact that the French settlement adjoined the moat on the north side of the city made its authorities desirous to dislodge the brigands, which they essayed to do January 6, 1855, by joining the imperialists in breaking the walls; they were repulsed, however, with a loss of fifteen men killed and thirty-seven wounded, out of a rank and file numbering two hundred and fifty. Another joint attack, undertaken a month later, was likewise unsuccessful, though the attempt seems to have frightened the force within the walls, since on the night of February

16th they retired, leaving the place in ruins. A like cordiality was nevertheless not always maintained between native and foreign soldiers, for in the previous year (April 4, 1854) occurred a collision with the imperialists, in consequence of their near approach to the foreign quarter, in which over three hundred Chinese soldiers were killed by the foreigners who landed to resist them. This untoward rencontre did not, however, interrupt amicable relations with the intendant, and was followed by consular notifications that whoever entered the service of the combatants in or out of the city would forfeit all protection. These notices were nevertheless soon disregarded as the struggle went on, for the temptation to enjoy a lawless life was too strong for hundreds of sailors then found in that port. It was an anomalous state of affairs, and the exigency led to some acts of violence by consuls in control of men-of-war.

The city of Amoy had been captured by insurgents on May 18, 1852, but no contravention occurred; the number of foreigners residing at this port was small, while the opposite island of Kulang su afforded a refuge beyond the range of missiles. The city was regained by the imperialists before a year had passed. The districts north of Canton, whence Hung Siu-tsuen and many of his adherents originated, began the same year to send forth their bands of robbers to pillage the province. These gangs had really no affinity with the Tai-pings, either in doctrine or plans, and none of them succeeded in gaining even a temporary success. When the booty was expended they usually quarrelled, and the imperialists destroyed them in detail. Every part of the province was at one time or another the scene of savage conflict between these contestants, and it was soon shown that no regenerating principle was involved on either side. The confidence of the educated and wealthy classes in the just cause and final success of their rulers was shown in raising men and money for the public service and organizing bodies of local police; but the want of a sagacious leader to plan and execute, so that all this material and action should not be frittered away, was painfully apparent.

In the capture of Nanking by Tai-pings, the restless leaders of sedition in Kwangtung saw their opportunity, and gathered their bands of freebooters in the southern prefectures. In June, 1854, the district town of Tungkwan near the Bogue was taken, the rich manufacturing mart of Fuhshan (or Fat-shan) near Canton fell a month later, followed by that of Shunteh, San-shui, and other lesser places, throwing the southern part of the province into a state of anarchy. The theory of the Chinese government, that if the capital is preserved the whole province is loyal, and its officers can use its revenue, enabled Governor-General Yeh to concert measures to repress these disorders. The City of Rams was environed during August by large bodies of insurgents, whose wants were supplied from Fuhshan. In this crisis about one thousand five hundred houses abutting outside the city walls were destroyed, and the ward police strengthened for the better protection of their neighborhoods against incendiaries. In all these proceedings the foreigners at Canton were never consulted or referred to by the officials, but their merchant steamers kept the Pearl River open to the sea, while their men-of-war lying off the factories proved a safeguard to the crowded city. The rebels had occupied a post near Whampoa, and their gunboats prowled through every creek in the delta, burning, destroying, capturing, and murdering without restraint. They would be followed by a band of imperialists, whose excesses were sometimes even more dreadful than those of their enemies. So terrible was the plight of the wretched countrymen that the headmen of ninety-six villages near Fuhshan formed a league and armed their people to keep soldiers from either side from entering their precincts.

In September, at a general meeting of the gentry of Canton, a proposal to save the city by asking foreign aid was approved by Yeh, but happily the project failed of fulfilment and only resulted in showing them how much better was a reliance upon their own resources. The news of this discussion led Chin Hien-liang, the rebel leader near Whampoa, to circulate proposals among the foreigners asking them to help him in capturing the city and promising as reward a portion of the island of Honan. The condition of the people at this time was sad and desperate indeed, and their only remedy was to arm in self-defence, in doing which they found out how small a proportion of the inhabitants was disloyal. No quarter was given on either side, and the carnage was appalling whenever victory remained with the imperialists. During this year the emigration to California and Australia became larger than ever before, while the coolie trade waxed flourishing, owing to the multitudes thrown out of employment who were eager in accepting the offers of the brokers to depart from the country and escape the evils they saw everywhere about them. The terrors of famine, fighting, and plundering paralyzed all industry and trade, and enabled one to better understand similar scenes described by ancient historians as occurring in Western Asia.

The exhaustion and desperation consequent on these events had almost demoralized society in and around Canton, which was overcrowded with refugees, raising food to famine prices. It was creditable to these poor and sickly people that their influx produced no other fear than that of a higher rate of living—none of pestilence or plunder, even in the extremity of their sufferings. In Fuhshan, fifteen miles away, no one was safe. The rebels had depleted its resources, killed its gentry, and oppressed the townsfolk until a quarrel broke out in their camp, and they departed about the season of Christmas, leaving the whole a smoking ruin. One of the insurgent practices consisted in driving great numbers of people into squares and there shooting them down by cannon placed in the approaching streets, while the houses around them were burning. The flames could be seen for two or three days from Canton, and it was estimated that during this conflict fully two hundred thousand human beings perished. The town was the manufacturing centre for the foreign trade, where silks, satins, shawls, paper, fire-crackers, pottery, and other staples were made, and their workmen resided. After this dreadful act the insurgents grew more and more desperate, feeling that they could not hold out much longer for want of booty and supplies to keep their men together. By March the force of fifteen thousand men inside the city was ready, and on the 6th it went quietly down to attack the fort below Whampoa. The onset and resistance were most determined; before the position succumbed, some twenty-five thousand men must have perished by battle or flood; the rebel leader escaped toward Hiangshan. The insurrection was, however, scotched, and its victors celebrated their triumph three days later in the city to a grateful and applauding concourse. When the city of Shauking, west of Canton, was retaken in May, its victors boasted that thirty thousand rebels were drowned or beheaded.

Notwithstanding these reverses the insurgents did not yet disappear, but maintained themselves along the watercourses in large flotillas during many months. The Portuguese and British also fitted out expeditions to pursue the pirates, as the same men were now called, destroying them and their haunts at Kulan Lantao, and elsewhere. In rooting out these land and sea brigands, the merciless character of the people was made manifest; every one convicted of rebellion was straightway executed by the authorities. At Canton, where prisoners were received from all such districts, the executions were on a terribly huge scale, as many as seven or eight hundred persons being beheaded in a single day. A count taken at the city gate whence they all issued on their way to the field of blood near the river, revealed the fact that fully eighty thousand were thus executed in the year 1855. This did not include thousands who committed suicide in places provided for them near their homes, from which their relatives could take their bodies to the family tomb. As might be expected, other thousands left the province for the north, or escaped into distant lands as coolies and emigrants.

Public attention abroad was at this time so engrossed with the greater rebellion going on along the Yangtsz' River that the horrors of that in Kwangtung were overlooked. There were many foreigners at Whampoa and Hongkong who sided with the leading brigands, reported their successes in the newspapers, and supplied them with munitions of war. The inefficiency of a foreign consul to restrain his countrymen thus flagrantly violating all their treaty obligations toward China, showed most conclusively how easy it is for the stronger party in such cases to demand their rights, and shirk their duties if it suits their convenience.

During the year 1856 affairs between the Chinese government and foreign powers became more and more hampered, while all attempts to arrange difficulties as they arose were defeated by the obstinate refusal of Yeh Ming-chin, the governor-general at Canton, to meet any foreign minister. He intrenched himself behind the city gates, and would do nothing. Sir John Bowring, the British plenipotentiary and governor of Hongkong, had most reason to be dissatisfied with this conduct, inasmuch as there were many questions which could have been easily arranged in a personal interview. It was ascertained from some documents[1] afterward found in Yeh's office that this seclusion was a part of the system devised at Peking to maintain a complete isolation and keep the dreaded foreigners at a distance. No course could be more likely to bring upon the government the evils it feared, and at the same time show more conclusively the ignorant and inapt character of those who carried it on. This state of things could not long continue when such powerful agencies were at work along the coast to disorganize legal trade and thwart the utmost efforts of all officials to restrain the reckless conduct of their subjects. The ten years now elapsed since the opening of the five ports had involved the Chinese in more complications, miseries, and disasters than had been known since the Manchu conquest; nevertheless, neither rebellion nor foreign complications seem to have impressed their lessons upon the proud bureaucracy in Peking, which was as unwilling to remedy as unable to appreciate the real nature of the difficulties that beset the country.

In the struggle between nations, as between individuals, the agony and weakness of one side becomes the opportunity of the other; and these conditions were now open to the British, who speedily found their excuse for further demands. In order to develop the trade of the free port of Hongkong, its laws encouraged all classes of shipping to resort thither, by removing all charges on vessels and granting licenses, with but few and unimportant restrictions, to Chinese craft to carry on trade under the British flag. This freedom had developed an enormous smuggling trade, especially in opium, which the Chinese revenue service was unable to restrain or unwilling to legalize.

---

[1] *Blue Book*, 1857.

These boats cruised wherever they might find a trade to invite or reward them, wholly indifferent to their own government, which could exercise no adequate control over them, and kept from the last excesses only on account of the risk of losing their cargoes. To the evils of smuggling were added the worse acts and dangers of kidnapping natives to supply baracoons at Macao. The Portuguese had many of these lorchas to carry on their commerce, and gradually a set of desperate men had so far engrossed them in acts of daring and pillage that honest native trade about any part of the coast south of Shanghai became almost impossible except under their convoy. The two free ports of Macao and Hongkong naturally became their resorts, where they all took on the aspect of legitimate traders, which, indeed, most of them were—save under great temptations.

It was not surprising that Chinese rulers should confound these two classes of vessels, nor, from the traders' side, was it a wonder that their crews should use the flag which gave them the greatest protection when beyond foreign inspection and jurisdiction. Few nations have ever been subjected to such continuous and prolonged irritation in respect to its commercial regulations as was the Canton government from those two alien communities during the ten years ending with 1856; few nations, on the other hand, have acted more unwisely in exertions toward peace and the removal of such difficulties than did the unspeakable Governor-General Yeh. That the inevitable collision between the Chinese and British was now at hand, follows almost as a matter of course, when to our knowledge of the commissioner's character we add Mr. Justin McCarthy's very appropriate estimate of the two Englishmen in whose hands well-nigh all British affairs in China were vested: "Mr. Consul Parkes," says he, "was fussy. Sir John Bowring was a man of considerable ability, but . . . full of self-conceit, and without any very clear idea of political principles on the large scale."[1]

Early in the morning of October 8th, two boat-loads of

[1] *A History of Our Own Times*, Chap. XXX.

Chinese sailors, with their officers, put off from a large war-junk, boarded the lorcha Arrow lying at anchor in the river before Canton, pinioned and carried away twelve of the fourteen natives who composed her crew, and added to this unexpected "act of violence," as Mr. Parkes stated it, "the significant insult of hauling down the British ensign." One Kennedy, a young Irishman who is described as a very respectable man of his class, was master of the lorcha, but chanced at the time to be on another boat lying in the immediate neighborhood of his own, and could in consequence offer no resistance. It is probable, judging from testimony given at the British consulate, that the hauling down of the flag was a mere bit of wantonness on the part of the junk's officer upon his finding that no foreigner was on board, and the offence might readily have been followed by an apology had the command of negotiations been in any other hands than those of Yeh. The Arrow was owned by a Chinese, Fong A-ming, her nominal master being engaged by Mr. Block, the Danish consul at Hongkong; his vessel was not, however, entitled to protection, inasmuch as her British register had expired by its own limitation eleven days before the episode in Canton River, and the lorcha was already forfeited to the crown.[1] Her papers were then at the consulate, and it was contended by Mr. Parkes that under Clause X. of the ordinance she retained a right to protection; a mere quibble, since the cause refers to the vessel when upon a voyage, and the Arrow had confessedly remained about the ports of Macao and Canton during a month.

Consul Parkes, after ascertaining the facts connected with this high-handed outrage, pushed off to the war-junk—which remained the while quietly at anchor—to claim the captured sailors and "explain to the officers, if it were possible that they had acted in error, the gross insult and violation of national

---

[1] Sir John Bowring indeed conceded that "the Arrow had no right to hoist the British flag," but alleged that the Chinese had no knowledge of the expiry of the license, and that this ignorance deprived them of the legal value of the truth. He quoted, moreover, Article IX. of the Supplementary Treaty, requiring that "all Chinese malfaisants in British ships shall be claimed through the British authorities."

rights which they had committed."[1] This was in vain. Among the men was a notorious pirate, he was told, and their orders were that the suspected crew should be sent to the governor for examination. Yeh stoutly upheld the act of his subordinate, and affirmed that the lorcha had no right to fly the British flag, disclaiming, however, any intention of molesting lawful traders under the emblem. Naturally enough, he would not yield the right of jurisdiction over his own subjects, and in doing this was asserting precisely what Great Britain and every other nation on the globe knew to be the first privilege of an independent government. The case was not unlike that much-discussed affair of the American Commodore Wilkes, who boarded the Trent in 1863 and captured Mason and Slidell—performing a right-enough action, but in a wrong and hasty fashion.

In his reply to Mr. Parkes, Yeh declares that he has held an examination of the sailors and finds that three of them were implicated in a piracy of the preceding month on St. John's Island, that the officers had good reasons for seizing these men, that the remaining nine shall be sent back to their vessel; which he straightway does, but they are as promptly returned by the consul because the entire crew is not given up. Sir John Bowring now demands, through his representative at Canton (1), "an apology for what has taken place, and an assurance that the British flag shall in future be respected;" (2) "that all proceedings against Chinese offenders on board British vessels must take place according to the conditions of the treaty;"[2] in case of refusal the consul is to concert with the naval authorities the measures necessary for enforcing redress. This threat extracted from the governor-general a promise that "hereafter Chinese officers will on no account, without reason, seize and take into custody the people belonging to foreign lorchas;" adding very properly, "but when Chinese subjects build for themselves vessels, foreigners should not sell registers to them, for if this be done, it will occasion confusion between native and foreign ships, and render it difficult to distinguish

[1] *Blue Book: Papers relating to the Proceedings of her Majesty's Naval Forces at Canton*, p. 1.

[2] *Blue Book, Ibid.*, p. 12.

between them."[1] Twelve days afterward (October 22d) the entire crew were returned, but once more refused by Mr. Parkes, ostensibly because the apology was not sent with them —and this the commissioner could not offer either in justice to his government or to the cause of truth.

Ensconced behind the walls of Canton city, Yeh resolved to stand firm on his rights as he understood them, even should the doing so involve the lives and property of thousands of his countrymen. To all foreigners in China this affair was intimately connected with most important possibilities and consequences: the inviolability of national flags, protection to every one whom they covered, personal intercourse with Chinese officers, maintenance of treaty rights. In upholding these the British drew to their side the good wishes of all intelligent observers for their success in arms, however unhappy their excuse for a resort to such means might be. One more word from Mr. McCarthy before leaving the initial episode of this war. "The truth is," he sums up, "that there has seldom been so flagrant and so inexcusable an example of high-handed lawlessness in the dealings of a strong with a weak nation,"[2] but like many another conflict where strength and justice have been ranged on opposite sides, the latter was speedily pushed to the wall. The incident of the Arrow appeared a trifling one; nevertheless on so slight a hinge turned the future welfare and progress of the Chinese people in their intercourse with other nations, a hinge which, opening outward, unclosed the door for all parties to learn the truth respecting the countries of each, and, in the end, agree upon the only grounds on which a beneficial and intelligent intercourse could be maintained.

It is hardly necessary to recount in detail the steps by which Governor Bowring and Admiral Seymour vainly attempted to bring Yeh to their terms. "Acknowledge that you are in the wrong," was their ultimatum, "by merely sending the three

---

[1] *Ibid.*, p. 15.

[2] *History of Our Own Times*, Vol. III., Chap. XXX. Lord Elgin in his journal refers frankly enough to "that wretched question of the Arrow, which is a scandal to us, and is so considered, I have reason to know, by all except the few who are personally compromised."—*Letters and Journals of Lord Elgin*, edited by T. Walrond, p. 209.

suspects to the consulate, and ask that they be returned on charge of piracy." The long-continued national policy of exclusion could not, however, be so easily overthrown; its reduction must be by force. The seizure of a military junk was the first act of the British, then the capture of the Barrier forts, followed by that of all others on the south of Canton, and lastly breaching the city wall opposite Yeh's yamun. This was entered by Admiral Seymour with a small party of marines.

Sir John Bowring had already made the demand that the city gates should be opened to them in accordance with the agreement entered into ten years before between Governor Davis and Kíying, and expresses his gratification to the consul that now one great object of hostile action had been satisfactorily accomplished—an object which Mr. Parkes declares was clearly based on treaty rights. However, they did not see Yeh, who resorted to all manner of petty annoyances, the evils of which mostly fell on his own people, without in the least advancing his cause.

On November 15th, to the complications with the English was added a quarrel with the Americans, whose boats had been twice fired into and one man killed by the Chinese officers in command of the Barrier forts. Commodore J. Armstrong had under his command the San Jacinto, Portsmouth, and Levant, then lying at Whampoa. He ordered the two latter to go as near to these forts as possible, and directed Captain A. H. Foote of the Portsmouth to destroy them all. Foote accordingly organized a large force and attacked them on the 16th, 20th, and 21st, till they were reduced and occupied. The resistance of the Chinese on this occasion was unusually brave and prolonged, the admirable position of the forts enabling each of them to lend assistance to the others. On the part of the Americans, seven were killed and twenty-two wounded; perhaps three hundred Chinese were put *hors de combat*; the guns in the forts (one hundred and seventy-six in all) were destroyed, and the sea-walls demolished with powder found in the magazines.[1] This skirmish is the only passage of arms ever

[1] One brass gun of eight-inch calibre was twenty-two feet five inches long; the entire armament of these forts was superior in equipment to anything before seen in China.

engaged in by American and Chinese forces—one which Yeh seemed to regard as of slight moment, and for which he cared neither to apologize nor sympathize. His unexampled indifference in referring to the affair less than two days after the demolishment of his forts[1] was met by an equal frankness on the part of Dr. Parker, who at once resumed correspondence with the commissioner, and, content with the practical lesson just administered, said no more about "apologies and guarantees." This episode is interesting chiefly as an example of the American course regarding an insult to the national flag, as contrasted with the English dealing with an injury not very different either in nature or degree.

Relations between Great Britain and China continued in this constrained position until the opening of another year, the conflict now being almost wholly restricted to unimportant collisions with village braves on land and voluminous discussions with the governor-general on paper. In November the French minister withdrew his legation from Canton, there being by that time neither French citizens nor interests to watch over. Principal among the events during this interval was the burning of the foreign factories by order of Yeh, December 14th. They were fired in the night and were entirely consumed with all their contents, as well, too, as the contiguous portion of the suburbs. The offer of thirty taels head-money for every Englishman killed or captured resulted in a few endeavors on the part of natives, whereby they kidnapped or slew two or three seamen when separated from their ships. These attempts at guerilla warfare were so promptly met and rewarded on the part of the English, by wholesale punishment of offending villages, as to cause little annoyance after the lesson of certain retribution had been taken to heart by the Chinese. More important than all these was a dastardly attempt, on January 11,

[1] "There is no matter of strife between our respective nations. Henceforth let the fashion of the flag which American ships employ be clearly defined, and inform me what it is beforehand. This will be the verification of the friendly relations which exist between the two countries."—Hoppin, *Life of Admiral Foote*, pp. 110–140. *Correspondence of McLane and Parker*, *Senate Document* No. 22, December 20, 1858, pp. 1019 ff. *Blue Book*, p. 137.

1857, to poison the foreigners at Hongkong, by putting arsenic in the bread supplied from a Chinese baker. This, it was afterward ascertained, was at the instigation of certain officials on the mainland, but fortunately even here their villany was foiled, owing to the overdose contained in the dough. It ought to be stated, in passing, that such acts are not common in China, and, in this case, that the baker's employers were proven entirely innocent.

During much of this time Canton had been reminded of the presence of the British force by intermittent bombarding of the city from guns in Dutch Folly Fort. Sir John Bowring had demanded an interview with Yeh in November, but received a prompt refusal, followed by a still more vigorous carrying on of the war in his peculiar fashion, and by raising the price on English heads. Admiral Seymour had now less reason for remaining within the Bogue, as all trade was at an end. Hundreds of foreigners had already been thrown out of employment, their property destroyed, their plans broken up, and in a few instances their lives lost in consequence of this quarrel. After holding an intrenched position around the church and barracks of the factories for the space of a month, the uselessness of this effort when sustained by so paltry a force seems to have moved the admiral (January 14, 1857) to retire from Canton, falling back upon Macao Fort until reinforcements should arrive from India. Before leaving the site of the factories, however, he burned down the warehouses of those native merchants in the vicinity, their inmates having previously been warned to leave them. These buildings and their contents were private property, and the intrenched position in the factory garden was not endangered by their remaining. The leaders of the British operations had hitherto professed to spare private property; and even if the performance was meant as a parting menace to the governor-general—"to show him," as Mr. Parkes remarked, "that we can burn too"—it was one of the few acts, on their side, which has left a stigma upon the English name in China. The hostile proceedings of the Chinese authorities had been both petty and useless, but as Admiral Seymour's force was inadequate to take and hold Canton, a more serious cannonading of the imperial quarters might have been a more honorable method of taking retribution for outrages, and better calculated than this counter-incendiarism to increase respect for British arms and civilization.

The news of these operations in China excited great interest and speculation in Europe, inasmuch as all its nations were more or less interested in the China trade. Parliament was the scene of animated argument as to the policy of Sir John Bowring and his colleagues; the moral, commercial, and political features of British intercourse with China were discussed most thoroughly in all their bearings, the arguments of both parties in the debate being drawn from the same despatches. One remarkable series of papers was presented to the House of Lords in February, 1857, entitled *Correspondence respecting Insults in China*, "containing the particulars of twenty-eight outrages committed by the Chinese upon British and other foreigners between the years 1842 and 1856." This publication was intended apparently to show how impracticable the Chinese authorities were in all their intercourse with foreigners, and its contents became to members of the House so many arguments for placing this intercourse on a better basis at the imperial court. To those who had watched since 1842 the results of treaty stipulations upon the people of China and their rulers, it was plain that no satisfactory political intercourse could be hoped for so long as the governor-general at Canton had the power of concealing and misrepresenting to his government everything that happened between foreign representatives and himself. Nevertheless such a series of papers was but one side of the insults endured. As long as the British government upheld the opium trade, and did nothing to restrain smuggling and the awful atrocities of the coolie traffic at Macao, which were filling the ears of all the world with their shocking tales, these few "outrages" seem very petty if put forward as a defence of Lord Palmerston's going to war on account of the lorcha Arrow.

In the vote upon the question of employing force in China, the better sense of Parliament protested against the policy which had directed recent events; but the Premier knew his countrymen, and in forty days from the dissolution (March 21st) England returned him a House of Commons strongly in his favor. He now decided to complete what had been wanting in the treaty of Nanking, and obtain a residence for a British minister at Peking. The governments of France, Russia, and the United States were invited to co-operate with England so far as they deemed proper, and their united interests were those of Christendom. No well-wisher to China could patiently look forward to a continuation of the past tantalizing semblance of official intercourse at Canton, and the varied experience of twelve years at other ports proved that the Chinese people did not sympathize in this policy. The French Emperor had a special grievance against H. I. M. Hienfung, on account of the judicial murder of Père Chapdelaine, a missionary in Kwangsí province, who had been tortured and beheaded at Sí-lin hien on February 29, 1856, by order of the district magistrate. This outrage was in direct violation of the rescript of 1844, and some atonement and apology were justly demanded. How totally unconscious of all these discussions and plans were Hienfung and his counsellors at Peking, may be guessed from their blind fright during subsequent events, while their inability to devise a course of action corresponded to their childish ignorance of their position and duties.

A powerful though unspoken reflection among these rulers must not here be overlooked as a secret motive in deciding many of their short-sighted counsels. Remembering the way in which their ancestors had captured the Empire over two centuries before, they felt that great risk was run in admitting the barbarians to the capital now, since the same game would probably be played over again. The visits of foreign ministers to the insurgents at Nanking, and their readiness at Canton to quarrel about so trifling a point as pulling down a flag and carrying off a few natives under its protection, all indicated, in their opinion, nothing short of conquest and spoliation. With such tremendous power arrayed against so weak an adversary, they knew well enough what would ensue. Their miserable policy of isolation had left them more helpless in their ignorance than diminished in their resources, and they had to pay dearly for their instruction.

The appointments of Lord Elgin and Baron Gros as plenipotentiaries for Great Britain and France were most fortunate as a selection of eminent diplomatists and clear-headed men. The two ambassadors entered into most cordial relations as soon as the land and sea forces placed at their disposal arrived on the Chinese coast. Lord Elgin reached Hongkong in July, but learning the state of affairs in that region, and that no advances had been made from Peking to settle the dispute, concluded to take the Shannon to Calcutta, to the assistance of Lord Canning against the mutineers; from this place he proposed to proceed in the cold weather, when the force detailed for China would all be ready. Returning to Hongkong by September 20th, he was obliged to tarry yet another month before the last of his reinforcements, or those of the French, had joined him. By the end of November the American minister, W. B. Reed, in the frigate Minnesota, and the Russian admiral, Count Poutiatine, in the gunboat Amerika, had likewise come.

Early in December, after a refusal on the part of Yeh of their ultimatum, the allied forces advanced up the Canton River. An extract from one of Lord Elgin's private letters illustrates admirably the spirit in which he entered upon the work he had been chosen to do. "December 22d.—On the afternoon of the 20th I got into a gunboat with Commodore Elliot, and went a short way up toward the Barrier forts, which were last winter destroyed by the Americans. When we reached this point, all was so quiet that we determined to go on, and we actually steamed past the city of Canton, along the whole front, within pistol-shot of the town. A line of English men-of-war are now anchored there in front of the town. I never felt so ashamed of myself in my life, and Elliot remarked that the trip seemed to have made me sad. There we were, accumulating the means of destruction under the very eyes and within the reach of a population of about one million people, against whom these means of destruction were to be employed! 'Yes,' I said to Elliot, 'I am sad, because, when I look at that town, I feel that I am earning for myself a place in the Litany, immediately after "plague, pestilence, and famine."' I believe, however, that, as far as I am concerned, it was impossible for me to do otherwise than as I have done. . . . When we steamed up to Canton and saw the rich alluvial banks covered with the luxurious evidences of unrivalled industry and natural fertility combined—beyond them barren uplands sprinkled with a soil of reddish tint which gave them the appearance of heather slopes in the Highlands, and beyond these again the White Cloud mountain range standing out bold and blue in the clear sunshine—I thought bitterly of those who, for the most selfish objects, are trampling under foot this ancient civilization."[1]

On the 27th the British and French, about six thousand in all, landed on the east bank a short distance below the walls. During the whole of the following day a furious bombardment was opened upon the city from the ships, driving thousands of the frightened natives into the western suburbs and destroying considerable portions of the town. By three o'clock of the 29th the city was in the hands of the foreigners—almost exactly the two hundred and seventh anniversary of its capture and entire reduction by the Manchus (November, 1650). The victory was not a brilliant one, since scarcely any one could be found with whom to fight; three or four forts to be entered, the wall scaled, a loss of one hundred and ten in killed and wounded to the victors, perhaps five times as many to the vanquished—this was all. Immediately upon their entry within the hitherto forbidden city the chiefs were forced to turn their energy upon their own troops and prevent them from bullying and looting the helpless Chinese.

Governor-General Yeh was, after some little search, found and captured while attempting an escape from his yamun,[2] and within twenty-four hours the lieutenant-governor, Tartar general, and all others in high authority came into possession of the invaders. Yeh was carried forthwith on board H. B. M. S. Inflexible, a wise step which deprived him of further power of

[1] *Letters and Journals*, p. 212.

[2] Some very curious documents were found among his archives illustrating the character both of the man and his government. See Oliphant, *Elgin's Mission to China*, Vol. I., Chap. VIII. Reed's *Correspondence*, 1858, pp. 443–488.

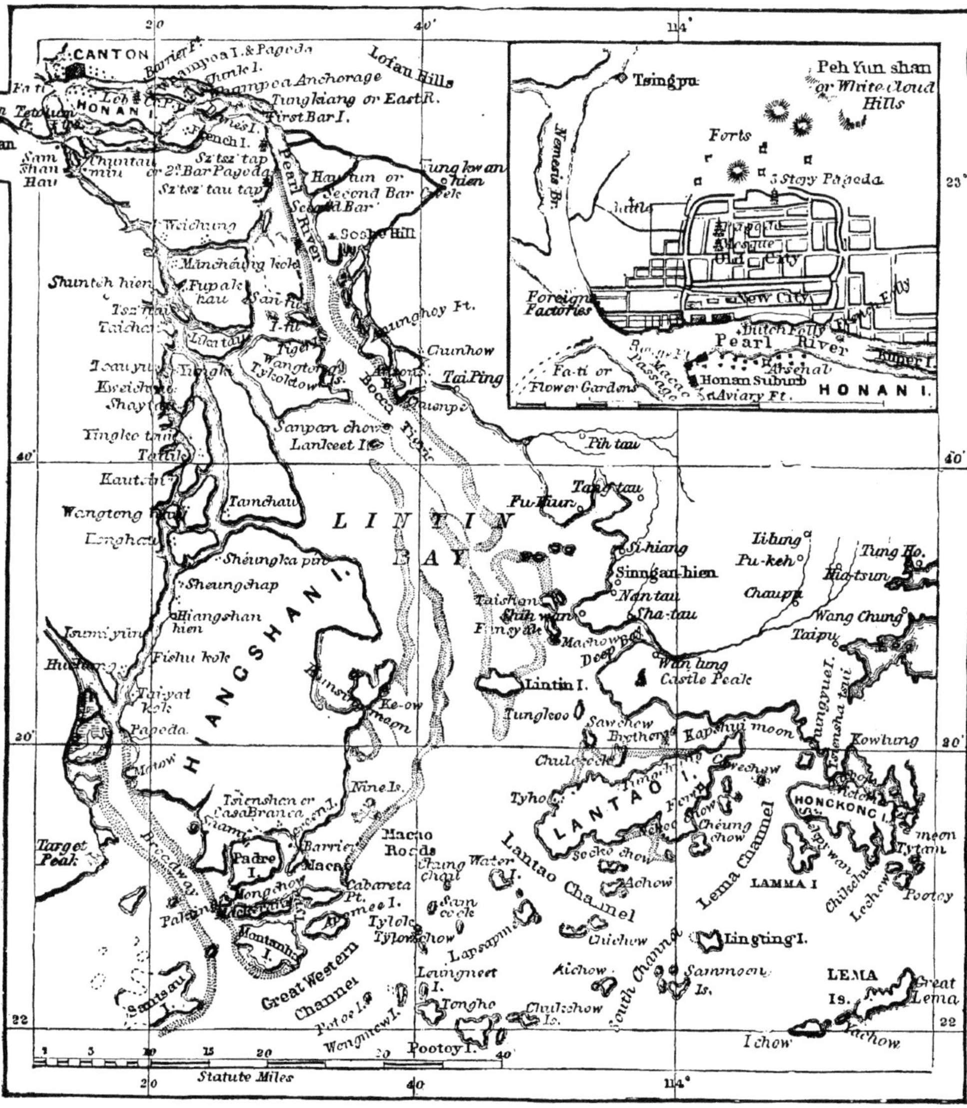

THE CITY OF CANTON AND ADJACENT ISLANDS.

resistance and misrepresentation, and left the plenipotentiaries free to arrange some method of temporary government for the city. This was a difficult problem, chiefly owing to the lack of competent interpreters, but rendered more so by the natural irritation of the conquered people at the losses they had sustained, the flight of the local officers, and the alarming extent of robbery by natives, somewhat countenanced by foreign soldiers. The skill and tact of Lord Elgin were never better shown than in the construction out of such incongruous materials of a mixed government whose subsequent easy working abundantly proved the master mind of the builder.[1] The two Manchus, Governor Pihkwei and the commandant of the garrison—called also the Tartar general—were now brought forward to assist in saving their capital from destruction and to form with the allies a joint tribunal. Pihkwei became legally (by Yeh's capture) the governor-general of the Liang Kwang, and his functions in that capacity were not interfered with; those of his colleague had always been restricted within the city walls. On January 9th they were installed by Lord Elgin and Baron Gros with all possible ceremony as rulers of the city, under the surveillance of three foreigners, Colonel Holloway and Consul Harry Parkes for the British, and Captain Martineau for the French. This commission had its headquarters in the same extensive yamun with Pihkwei, in whom happily were combined some estimable qualities for managing the difficult post he filled. The orderly habits of the literati and traders in and around Canton afforded a guaranty that no seditious proceedings would be countenanced against this joint authority if it gave them the security they had asked from the allies. A force of marines and the Fifty-ninth Regiment were quartered on Pagoda Hill, on the north side of the city, and ere long the commandant's yamun was cleared of its rubbish and put in order for the commission, leaving the other for Pihkwei. The allied chiefs deemed it wisest to attempt to govern as little in detail as possible, and their commissioners found enough to do in adjusting complaints brought by

[1] "You may imagine," he writes, "what it is to undertake to govern some millions of people when we have *in all* two or three people who understand the language! I never had so difficult a matter to arrange."

the Chinese against their own men. The Cantonese did not fail to contrast the considerate treatment they received from their foreign captors with the carnage and utter ruin which would have followed the occupation of the city by the Tai-pings or other insurgents, and during the whole period quietly submitted. The greater part of the responsible labor came upon Mr. Parkes, because of his ability to talk Chinese, but before many months he had taught many natives how to assist in carrying out the necessary details. He showed much skill in circumventing the designs of the discontented officials at Fuhshan, giving Pihkwei all the native criminals to judge, restraining the thievery or cruelty of the foreign police, and sending out proclamations for the guidance and admonition of the people.[1]

The kindness shown by Lord Elgin after the capture of Canton infused itself into the minds of those working with and under him, and the newly installed governor soon recovered his composure as he found himself in possession of his own dignities and power. The local and provincial officers under him kept themselves at Fuhshan, now recovering from its destruction of three years before. By the end of January affairs were put in order, the blockade was taken off the port, foreign merchants returned and settled in the warehouses still unharmed on Honam, while the native dealers reopened their shops in the vicinity.[2] Sixteen months had elapsed since the affair of the Arrow, and every one felt that a new day had begun to dawn on the relations of China with other lands.[3] Among the papers

---

[1] *Blue Book: Lord Elgin's Correspondence*, July 15, 1859, Despatches Nos. 88, 94, 108, and 128. Oliphant, *Elgin's Mission to China*, Vol. I., p. 170.

[2] Oddly enough, among the most earnest appeals for the restoration of commerce came one from Pihkwei himself, who wrote to Lord Elgin: "The eagerness with which merchants will devote themselves to gain, if the trade be now thrown well open, will increase manifold the good understanding between our nations, and the step will thus, at the same time, enhance your excellency's reputation."—*Blue Book*, January 24, 1858.

[3] The letters of G. W. Cooke, the *Times*' correspondent (London, Routledge, 1858), contain a fairly complete account of the proceedings of the allies at Canton; his conversations with Governor-General Yeh on the way to Calcutta are less valuable. Compare an article in the *Revue des Deux Mondes* (1e juillet, 1859), by C. Lavallée, *Un Historiographe de la Presse anglaise dans la guerre de Chine.*

taken in Yeh's yamun were the ratified copies of the treaties between China and Great Britain, France, and the United States, carefully preserved there, it was said, by directions from Peking, in order to serve for reference in case of dispute as to the text. It was, however, one of the indexes proving the desire of the Emperor to keep himself aloof from personal contact with foreigners.

The allied chiefs, early in the month of February, proposed to their American and Russian coadjutors to join them in laying their demands before the Peking Court, and affording it one more opportunity to amicably settle the pending difficulties by sending an officer to Shanghai with full powers for that end. Both Russians and Americans were cordially in unison with the allies, and their several despatches addressed to Yü, the first member of the *Nui Koh*, or 'Inner Council,' at Peking, were taken up to Shanghai and thence to Suchau, where Ho Kwei-tsing received and forwarded them before the end of February. These four letters simultaneously sent to the secluded court at Peking contained nothing which could alarm its members; but such was the ignorance of the highest officers there, that they knew not what to do—ostrich-like, hiding their heads from the approaching danger, simply declining to answer any unpleasant communication, hoping thereby to put far off the evil day. Their isolation would remain if left to themselves, and to have sent Kiying again to the south would only have cherished their stupid pride and worked their subjects ultimate injury. Their old-time policy of absolute non-intercourse lay like some great frigate sunk athwart the mouth of a river; the obstacle once removed, nothing remained to prevent the vast and populous regions beyond the barrier from an active and profitable communion with the whole world. They could no longer be left *in statu quo*, and few can find fault with the plan proposed to solve their difficulties—a plan which brought the four most powerful nations of Christendom in joint consent to set themselves on a fair and advantageous footing with the most ancient and populous nation of Asia. To those who admit the direct government of the Almighty Ruler in ordering the policy of nations in accord with His wise plans, this simultaneous approach to Peking will always be deemed as one of the waymarks of human progress.

The letters presented to the Emperor[1] form in their topics and tone a pleasant contrast to the communications in past years. That of the Russian minister was peculiar in bringing forward the desirableness of allowing the profession of Christianity to all natives desirous of embracing it; but this point was made the subject of an address by the British missionaries at Ningpo and Shanghai to Lord Elgin, whose reply was a happy exposition of the dangers and difficulties connected with the toleration of Christianity by a government ignorant of its precepts. The imperial replies to these advances were, as every one expected, in the strain of *non possumus.* Lord Elgin returned his copy to Ho Kwei-tsing at Suchau, and enclosed therewith another despatch to Yü, in which he announced his intention to proceed to Taku, where he would await the arrival of a commissioner qualified to treat upon the points in dispute.

The force designed to accompany the allied chiefs was gathering at Shanghai, and by the middle of April most of the ships and transports had anchored off the Pei ho, together with the American frigates Minnesota and Mississippi and the Russian gunboat Amerika, having the legations of those nations on board. Nothing could be more dreary than the aspect of the rendezvous at this season. The ships were obliged to anchor about eight miles from shore, which was level, and would have been invisible if it had not been for the forts at the entrance of the river. The dim, hazy horizon was lurid with the rays of the sun shining through the dust that came in clouds from the plains of Mongolia and Chihlí. The turbid waters were often lashed into foam by the conflicting forces of tides and winds which acted on it from every quarter, and kept the gulf in a turmoil. No native boats ventured out to traffic, as would have been the case in the south, and the only signs of life were the gunboats and launches running in and out of the river, or the barges passing from ship to ship. Added to other discommodi-

[1] These are all given in the correspondence of Mr. Reed, printed by the Senate—Despatch No. 9, *Ex. Document* No. 30, March 13, 1860, pp. 122–183.

ties, were occasional blasts of hot air which swept over the water, charged with fine dust that settled on the decks and rigging, and insinuated itself into the dress and faces in an uncomfortable manner.

As usual the Chinese had done nothing. The increasing number and size of the ships which were anchored off the Pei-ho had, however, been duly reported at Peking, and the Russian admiral had received a reply to his announcement of arrival. On April 23d communications were addressed by the four ministers to Yu-ching at Peking, and on the 26th replies came from Tan Ting-siang, governor-general of Chihlí, informing them that he, with Tsunglun and Wu, had been deputed to "receive their complaints and investigate and manage." The governor-general was not empowered to settle upon the terms of a treaty, but he desired to have a personal conference to learn what was demanded. Upon the day appointed the Russian and American ministers met Tan at the Taku forts (April 30th) at separate hours, when they learned that he had not been invested with "full powers," like those granted to Kíying and Ílipu in 1842, but had authority to discuss all matters preparatory to signing a treaty. The truth was that they were quite ignorant of the important questions raised at Canton; but while willing to discuss them, they were equally set on keeping the foreigners away from the capital. Here the allied chiefs and their two colleagues took issue. The former held out for commissioners to be sent with full powers; but the latter deeming that the governor-general had adequate authority, accordingly presented him with the main points of their demands and afterward with the drafts of their treaties. The negotiations were delayed by the difficulties of the entrance, but they afforded a needed instruction to these conceited and ignorant men, who were thus enabled at their leisure to prepare for the struggle. Not only were the officers themselves brought face to face with their dreaded visitors, and made to perceive the folly of resisting the armaments at their command, but with the democratic habits usual in Chinese courts, the hundreds of attendants present at the conferences heard all that passed.

Ere the non-belligerent powers had completed their negotiations, the allies turned over theirs into the hands of the two admirals, MM. Seymour and Rigault de Genouilly. These advanced up the river on May 20th, forcing the slight boom across the stream, and capturing all the forts on both banks, with all their stores. Comparatively few Chinese were killed, and their defence of the forts was creditable to their courage and skill. All the troops fled or were driven from their intrenched camps as far as Taku town, and the other defences, stockades, and fire-rafts having been destroyed, the gunboats proceeded to Tientsin. The losses by shot on the part of the Allies were unhappily doubled by the explosion of a powder magazine in a fort as a party of Frenchmen entered. The news that the foreigners had forced the defences at the mouth of the Pei ho was soon spread through the towns along its banks, and myriads of unarmed people flocked to the shore to see the gun-boats, whose smoke and masts towering above the low land indicated their presence to the amazed inhabitants.

A house having been prepared at Tientsin for the allied chiefs, Lord Elgin and Baron Gros reached the city at daylight on May 30th, followed by the other two ministers, all of them having come up during the night without mishap or opposition. The inhabitants of the city were highly excited at the presence of the vessels and those of whom they had heard such dreadful stories, but their curiosity and fear kept them quiet and civil, and they were content with lining the shores in dense crowds, to gaze and talk. The general ignorance of each other's language did not prevent a constant intercourse with the citizens, all the more agreeable after the confinement on board ship. One old man was found managing a ferry-boat, who remembered Lord Amherst's visit in 1816. After his inquiries as to the meaning of the flags on board the ships had been answered, he exclaimed, "How easily you and we could get along if you but understood our language"—to which the crowd around reëchoed their hearty assent.

Two higher commissioners now appeared on the scene of action, Kweiliang and Hwashana, who superseded the discomfited Tan, Tsunglun, and Wu, and presented their cards as having been invested with full powers to treat. Negotiations were opened with them, and thus, after months of delay, the plan which Yeh had so foolishly adhered to at Canton in October, to refuse all personal discussion, was accomplished at Tientsin under far more promising circumstances. The Chinese were obliged to accept almost any terms offered them, for negotiations carried on under such conditions were hardly those of free agents. The high commissioners were ignorant beyond conception of the gravity of their position and the results which were to flow from these treaties, whose provisions, linked into one compact by the favored nation clause, were, in fact, to form the future magna charta between almost the two halves of the human race. It was true that the Chinese commissioners were not altogether their own masters in making them, but owing to their perverse seclusion, they had foolishly shut themselves out from the opportunity of learning their rights. They had, of course, no desire to learn what they knew nothing about, and there was no alternative other than the display of force to break down the barriers which pride alone made strong. They had some grounds for fear, from their recent occupation of Canton, that the British wished for more territory than Hongkong; and the frequent visits of the national vessels of Great Britain, the United States, and France to the insurgents at Nanking indicated serious results in the future, for the latter owed all their religious fanaticism to foreign inspiration. To the persistent smuggling of opium along the whole coast since the treaties negotiated by Kíying sixteen years before, and the many social and financial evils entailed thereby, were now added the atrocities of the coolie trade in Kwangtung province. Yet the reserve of the officials upon these and other topics on which they might be expected to have expressed their views or remonstrances, was only equalled by the politeness and freedom with which they met their enemies in consultation. Never again in the history of nations can functionaries to whom were confided the settlement of questions of so great moment, be brought together in such honest ignorance of the other's intentions, fears, and wishes. It was high time for each of the five powers, now face to face, to have the way opened for the removal of this ignorance and a better understanding substituted.

The despatches of Lord Elgin and Mr. Reed contain translations of many reports and memorials which were found in Yeh's yamun at Canton, and give one a good idea of the sort of information furnished to the Emperor by his highest officers. It is a wrong view of these papers to regard their extraordinary misstatements as altogether designed to deceive the court and screen the ill-success of the writers, for they had had no more facilities to investigate the real condition of foreign lands and the policy of their rulers than had the poor boy Caspar Hauser to learn about his neighbors.

One untoward event occurred during the negotiations. This was the sudden arrival of Kíying (June 8th) and his effort to force himself into the company of the plenipotentiaries. Since his departure from Canton in 1847 he had filled the premiership before the death of the late Emperor Taukwang, after which he had been deprived of all power and most of his honors. He seemed to have tried to recover them by making large promises at court respecting his influence over the *barbarians*; but when he reached Tientsin he was without credentials enabling him to participate, and acted as if his misfortunes had in a measure unsettled his reason. The British minister was suspicious of his designs, and sent his two secretaries, on the 9th, to learn what they could of or from him. These gentlemen plainly pointed out to the old man the difficulties in the way of settling the present troubles in any other manner than by acceding to the demands of Lord Elgin. Kíying had, however, put himself in a serious dilemma. Finding very soon that he was powerless to change the course of events and get the steamers away from Tientsin (as he no doubt had promised to do, and thus prove his influence), he returned to Peking on the 12th, though he had announced the reception of his full powers only the day before. His colleagues were not sorry to have him depart, but nothing definite was learned of his fate until at the end of three weeks, when the Emperor's rescript ordering him to commit suicide was received. His case was deemed of sufficient importance to call for a summation of the principal features in order to prove the righteousness of his sentence, and manifest the Emperor's extreme desire to be at once just and gracious in his decree. Kíying's case is rather an unusual one among Chinese officials, but the real reasons for his fall are probably not all stated; his prominence abroad, arising from his connection with the Nanking treaty, was no criterion of his influence at home or of the loss to the government by his death.[1]

Soon after his departure the impertinence of a native crowd to a party of British officers while walking through the city, lent some strength to the belief that Kíying's counsel had been warlike, and that a *coup*, similar to the one made at Canton in 1841 by Yihshan, had been suggested, and the destruction of all the foreigners in Tientsin was hoped for as its result. Their relations with the citizens thus far had been amicable on the whole, and the interruption in this desirable state of things was very brief. Negotiations continued, therefore, but with an undercurrent of doubt as to details on some important points among the foreign envoys. Lord Elgin had the greatest responsibility, indeed, and the task before him was difficult and delicate, but he failed in drawing to himself his colleagues and learning their views. They hardly knew what to do, for none of them wished to thwart his desires for complete and honorable intercourse with the central government, though the manner of reaching this end might admit of discussion. This he never invited. The position of the American and Russian envoys, pledged to their instructions not to fight, and having the feeling that their nations were to obtain the advantages resulting from the hostilities of the allies, was not a pleasant one; but it could have been made so, and he himself relieved of his main anxiety as to the result, by an interview. In contrast

---

[1] Oliphant's *Mission of Lord Elgin to China and Japan*, pp. 238–253 (American edition), N. Y., 1860. It is interesting to note, before leaving this episode, a Frenchman's opinion of the character of this statesman: "Kíying a été de 1842 à 1844 le grand négociateur de la Chine. Les ministres étrangers ont vanté son habileté, sa finesse, ses façons aimables et courtoises. . . . Son nom symbolisait une politique nouvelle, bienveillante pour les étrangers, tolérante, libérale; il représentait une sorte de jeune Chine."—M. C. Lavallée in the *Revue des Deux Mondes*, 15 Déc. 1859, p. 602. The same article contains an interesting account of the first expedition up the Pei ho and its results.

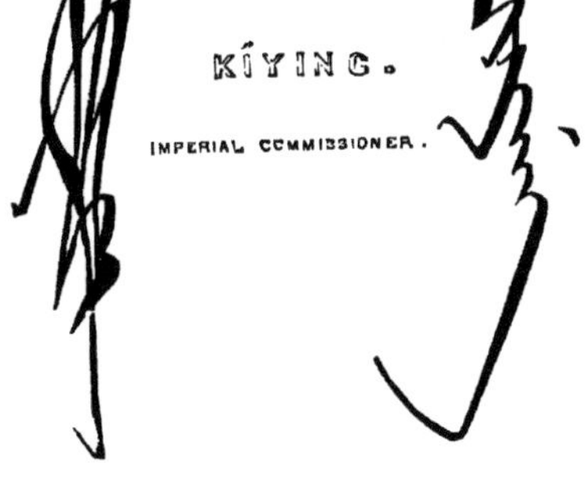

KÍYING.

IMPERIAL COMMISSIONER.

with Lord Elgin's general bearing toward those around him, as detailed in his correspondence, his biographer gives an extract from a private letter written the day after signing his treaty, which describes his perplexities:

June 29th.—I have not written for some days, but they have been busy ones. We went on fighting and bullying, and getting the poor commissioners to concede one point after another, till Friday the 25th, when we had reason to believe that all was settled, and that the signature was to take place the following day. On Friday afternoon, however, Baron Gros came to me with a message from the Russian and American ministers to induce me to recede from two of my demands—1, a resident minister at Peking, and, 2, permission to our people to trade in the interior of China; because, as they said, the Chinese plenipotentiaries had told them that they had received a decree from the Emperor stating that they should infallibly lose their heads if they gave way on these points.

The resident minister at Peking I consider far the most important matter gained by the treaty; the power to trade in the interior hardly less so. I had at stake not only these important points in my treaty, for which I had fought so hard, but I know not what behind. For the Chinese are such fools that it was impossible to tell, if we gave way on one point, whether they would not raise difficulties on every other. I sent for the admiral; gave him a hint that there was a great opportunity for England; that all the powers were deserting me on a point which they had *all*, in their original applications to Peking, demanded, and which they all intended to claim if I got it; that, therefore, we had it in our power to claim our place of priority in the East by obtaining this when others would not insist on it. Would he back me? This was the forenoon of Saturday, 26th, and the treaty was to be signed in the evening.

I may mention, as a proof of the state of people's minds, that Admiral Seymour told me that the French admiral had urged him to dine with him, assuring him that no treaty would be signed that day! I sent Frederick to the imperial commissioners to tell them that I was indignant beyond all expression at their having attempted to communicate with me through third parties; that I was ready to sign at once the treaty as it stood; but that if they delayed or retreated, I should consider negotiations at an end, go to Peking and demand a great deal more, etc. Frederick executed this most difficult task admirably, and at six P.M. I signed the treaty of Tientsin. I am now anxiously awaiting some communication from Peking. Till the Emperor accepts the treaty I shall hardly feel safe. Please God he may ratify without delay! I am sure that I express the wish just as much in the interest of China as in our own. Though I have been forced to act almost brutally, I am China's friend in all this.[1]

The importance of these two provisos was not exaggerated in his mind, but he might have seen that the difficulties with his colleagues were increased by his own reticence.

[1] Walrond's *Life and Letters of Lord Elgin*, p. 252.

However much a different course might have harmonized these discordant views, the pressure on the city of Tientsin was too near and severe upon the Chinese, and they yielded from fear of worse consequences when no other arguments could have induced them. It was not Lord Elgin alone who felt very sensibly, on that occasion, "the painfulness of the position of a negotiator who has to treat with persons who yield nothing to reason and everything to fear, and who are at the same time profoundly ignorant of the subjects under discussion and of their own real interests." Looked at in any point of view, this period of negotiation at Tientsin in 1858 was a remarkable epoch. The sole great power of paganism was being bound by the obligations of a treaty extorted from its monarch by a handful of men in possession of the entrance to its capital. As one of the British officers pithily stated it, two powers had China by the throat, while the other two stood by to egg them on, so that all could share the spoil. Yet the past sixteen years had proven most conclusively that, unless this pressure was exerted, the imperial government would make no advance, admit no opening for learning its real position among the nations of the world, but mulishly cherish its ignorance, its isolation, its conceit, and its folly, until these causes had worked out the ruin so fondly hoped to be avoided. Even the necessity of coming into personal official relations with the foreign consuls to promote the maintenance of good order between their subjects had been hampered or neutralized by the Chinese authorities at all the ports; and there was no hope of introducing a better state of things until foreign ministers were received at Peking. Happily, Lord Elgin then saw the question in all its bearings, and no one ever proved to be a truer friend to China than did he in forcing it upon her. He had little idea, probably, of one motive for their resistance, namely, the fear of the Manchu rulers, already referred to, that in admitting the enemy to the capital they would be as summarily ejected as had been their predecessors in 1644.

However, by the first week in July the four treaties had been signed and ratified by Hienfung, and all the vessels had left the Pei ho, which itself was no doubt the greatest proof to his Majesty that they were valid compacts; for if the tables had been turned he would not have let them off so easily, and perhaps wondered that Tientsin had not been ransomed at the same rate that Elliot had spared Canton in 1841. It is difficult to fully appreciate the crass ignorance and singular perversity of the men in whose hands the sway of the Chinese people were now lodged. He who is unwilling to acknowledge the overruling hand of God in this remarkable meeting of nations, would find it very difficult to acknowledge it anywhere in human history.

The revision of the tariff had been deferred for a future discussion among those qualified for the work. Five Chinese commissioners reached Shanghai early in October for this and other purposes, of whom Kweiliang and Hwashana were two. In this part of the negotiations the controlling power was properly left in the hands of the British, for their trade was worth more than all others combined. They used this power most selfishly, and fastened on the weak and distracted Empire a veritable remora, which has gone on sucking its resources without compunction or cessation. By making the tariff an integral part of the treaty, they theoretically made every infraction a *casus belli*, and as no provision was left for revision, it was virtually rendered impossible, since the original four powers could not again be brought to unite on its readjustment with a view to the rights of China. While particular provision was made in it for preventing the importation of salt and the implements and munitions of war, the trade in opium was legalized at a lower rate than was paid on tea and silk entering England, and the brand of immorality and smuggling was removed from its diffusion throughout China. The weakness and ignorance of the Chinese were such as laid them open to the power and craft of other nations, but the inherent wrong of the principle of ex-territoriality was never more unjustly applied than in breaking down the moral sense of a people by forcing them to legalize this drug. The evils of smuggling it were insufferable, but a heavy duty was desirable as a check and stigma upon the traffic. The solution to a statesman in Lord Elgin's position was exceedingly difficult in relation to this point, and he perhaps took the safest course under the existing circumstances, but it has proved to be fraught with evils to the Chinese. One who now reads his biography and learns his nice sense of right and equity in national affairs, will not be surprised to see his doubts as to the best course to take where all were so many moves in the dark.

The war which arose about the Arrow was now virtually closed, but many things remained to be enforced in carrying out the treaty stipulations or restraining the irritation they produced. The vastness of the Empire sundered its inhabitants so widely that each felt the troubles it endured only when they came near; but to all of them the obligations of treaty were of the most shadowy nature. It would require years of patient instruction to educate the mass of natives up to the idea that these obligations affected them as individuals. One means of this instruction, which subsequent years have shown to be both practical and profitable, was the extension and reorganization of the administration of the customs under foreign supervision. Its short service at Shanghai had proved it to be easy and safe of operation, and the increased fidelity everywhere in collecting the duties gratified the central and provincial governments exceedingly. It was a startling proof of the degrading effects of the opium and smuggling trade upon the honor of the foreign merchants that they generally resisted the transfer of collecting duties from native to foreign hands, and endeavored in a thousand ways to thwart and ridicule the altered system. This feeling, however, disappeared with the incoming of a new set of merchants, and the Chinese government has, since the first, found no difficulty in utilizing the skill, knowledge, and power of their employés, not only in fiscal departments, but whereever they felt the need of such qualifications. Beginning at Shanghai, when the local officers were helpless against their own subjects, mandarins and people alike desired the advantages of an honestly collected tariff to be extended to every port opened for foreign trade.

The changes formulated in the treaties of Tientsin could receive their accomplishment only after patient efforts on the part of ministers, consuls, and collectors to carry them into effect with due regard to the position of the native rulers. In order to open the way into the country, Lord Elgin visited Hankow in four ships in November, after he had signed the tariff. The rebels in possession of Nanking and other towns, being unapprised of his character, fired at him from some of their forts, for which "they were pounded pretty severely in return." But a few words afterward proved more effectual than many shots, and no further altercation occurred. The voyage to and return from Hankow occupied seven weeks, and inaugurated a commerce and intercourse which has resulted in much good to the natives by making them rapidly acquainted with foreigners. The right of China to the exclusive navigation of her internal waters was summarily set aside by making Hankow a seaport; on the other hand, the government derived many advantages in the moral assistance given her at the time against the rebels by having them restrained, and, up to the present day, in the stimulus given to internal trade and rapid intercourse between the peoples of remote districts.

The year 1858 was fraught with great events, involving the welfare of the people of China and Japan and their future position and progress. Much against their will they had been forced into political relations with Europe and America, and in a measure deprived of their independence under the guise of treaties which erected an *imperium in imperio* in their borders. Their rulers, ignorant of the real meaning of these principles of ex-territoriality, were tied down to observe them, and found themselves within a few years humbled before those of their own subjects who had begun to look to foreigners for protection. The perplexity of the Chinese commissioners at Shanghai in this new position was exhibited in a despatch addressed on November 1, 1858, to the three envoys. In it they discuss the right of foreigners who have no treaties to go into the interior, and insist upon the absolute necessity of restraining them, which their own mercantile consuls could not and would not do.

"Being unacquainted," they wrote, "with the usages of foreign nations in this respect, and unwilling of ourselves to lay down preventive regulations respecting issuing passports, we desire first to receive the result of your deliberations before we act in the premises." They then proceed to show how necessary it will be for the future peace between conflicting interests and nationalities that consuls should not be merchants, for "some of those of your respective nations have formerly and often acted in a manner calculated to impede and mar the harmony that existed between their nations and our own; wilfully disregarding everything but their own opinions, they have carried out their own high-handed measures to the ruin of all cordial feeling." The writers had no idea how this despatch was an argument and a proof of the need of strong measures to drag them out of their stupid ignorance and childish desires for isolation, and compel them to understand their duties. The education then begun was the only means through which to raise the Chinese rulers and people to a higher plane of civilization and liberty. One document like this carries in itself enough to show how ignorant were its writers and their colleagues of their own duties, and how hopeless was the prospect of their emerging voluntarily from their seclusion. The treaties bound them down to keep the peace, while they opened the channels through which the people could learn whatever was true and useful, without fear of punishment or reproach. The toleration of Christianity, the residence of foreign ministers at Peking, and the freedom to travel through the land were three avenues heretofore closed against the welfare and progress of China which the treaties opened, and through which she has already made more real advances than ever before in her history.[1]

---

[1] For full details on these important negotiations, see the Blue Book presented to Parliament July 15, 1859, containing Lord Elgin's correspondence; *U. S. Senate Executive Document* No. 30, read March 13, 1860, containing correspondence of Messrs. Reed, Williams, and Ward, from June, 1857, to September 17, 1859; Oliphant's *Mission of Lord Elgin to China and Japan*, London and New York, 1860; Lieutenant-Colonel Fisher, *Personal Narrative of Three Years' Service in China*, London, 1863; le Marquis de Moges, *Baron Gros's Embassy to China and Japan*, 1860; Walrond's *Letters and Journals of James, Earl of Elgin*, London, 1872; Lieut. J. D. Johnston, *China and Japan*, Philadelphia, 1860; *North American Review*, Vol. XC., p. 125; *Blackwood's Magazine*, Vols. LXXXVI., p. 647, LXXXVII., pp. 430, 535, and LXXXIX., p. 373.

By the end of December, 1858, the four envoys had left China, as well as most of the small force under their control. None of them had reached Peking, so that the Emperor was relieved of his fear that he would be carried off as was his commissioner, Yeh, from Canton; he had, moreover, another year of grace to learn what he ought to do to carry out the treaties. He was also relieved by the refusal of the allies to join their quarrel with the efforts of the Tai-pings and march together to the conquest of the Empire. In Canton the presence of the allies had been an irritation chiefly to the provincial officers, who busied themselves in stimulating large bodies of braves in its vicinity to assassinate and rob individual foreigners near or in the city, keeping up in this manner a lasting feeling of discontent. Several skirmishes took place, and a large district within the city near the British quarters on Kwanyin Shan was burned over to insure protection against sudden attacks. The new governor-general, Hwang, had formed a league of the gentry and braves, which chiefly exhibited their power in harassing their own countrymen. He was removed in disgrace at Lord Elgin's request, and all these puny and useless attacks brought to an end.

An incident which occurred near Canton about fifteen months after the city had been captured, strikingly shows the character of the people: "February 11th.—On the 8th a body of troops about one thousand strong started on an expedition which was to take three days. I accompanied, or rather preceded them on the first day's march, about twelve miles from Canton. We rode through a very pretty country, passing by the village of Shek-tsing, where there was a fight a fortnight ago. The people were very respectful, and apparently not alarmed by our visit. At the place where the troops were to encamp for the night a cattle fair was in progress, and our arrival did not seem to interrupt the proceedings. February 13th.—The military expedition was entirely successful. The troops were everywhere received as friends. Considering what has been of yore the state of feeling in this province toward us, I think this almost the most remarkable thing which has happened since I came here. Would it have happened if I had given way to those who wished me to carry fire and sword through all the country villages?" [1]

These same villages furnished thousands of volunteers in May, 1841, to attack Sir Hugh Gough's army, and had been engaged in a desperate struggle with their countrymen only three years before, so that this change was owing neither to cowardice nor sulkiness. It had been brought about chiefly through considerate treatment of the people by the British garrison in Canton, by honest payment for supplies, and by regard for the traffic and local government of the city; the citizens consequently had no complaint to make or revenge to satisfy. Those who from infancy had been brought up to call every foreigner a *fan-kwei*, or 'foreign devil,' now slowly appreciated the fact that they had been mistaken—nor were the misconceptions all on their side. During the three years the city was occupied, public opinion there underwent an entire change; and the Cantonese are now as courteous as they before were ill-mannered.

At this season of rebellion and foreign war under which China was now suffering, the province of Kwangtung had a special cause for just irritation against all foreigners in the coolie trade. The headquarters of this trade were at Macao, and by 1860 it had become nearly the only business carried on there. The population of the colony is perhaps seventy-odd thousand, of whom less than five thousand wear a foreign dress. Traffic and industry are mostly carried on by Chinese, who do all the work. When the trade of hiring Chinese as contract laborers to go to Cuba, Peru, and elsewhere began, there was no difficulty in obtaining men willing to try their fortunes abroad. As rumors of gold diggings open to their labors in California were spread abroad and confirmed by returning miners, the coolie ships were readily filled by men whose ignorance of outer lands made them easily believe that they were bound to El Dorado, whatever country they shipped for. The inducement for hiring them was the low rate of wages ($4 a month) at which they were willing to sell their labor, and the profits derived from introducing them into western tropical regions. The temptations

[1] Walrond's *Letters and Journals of Lord Elgin*, p. 308.

of this business became so great that within ten years the demand had far exceeded the supply. Seldom has the unscrupulous character of trade, where its operations are left free from the restraints either of competent authority or of morality, been more sadly exhibited than in the conduct of the agents who filled these coolie ships. The details of the manner in which natives of all classes, scholars, travellers, laborers, peddlers, and artisans, were kidnapped in town and country and sent to Macao, were seldom known, because the victims were unable to make themselves heard. When the rebels at Fuhshan were defeated in 1855, thousands of their followers were glad to save their lives by shipping as coolies, but this lasted only a short time.

The allied commissioners in charge of Canton took cognizance of these outrages, and upon the representations of Governor-General Lao took vigorous measures for breaking up the trade at Whampoa.[1] The United States minister, Hon. J. E. Ward, lent his aid in February, 1860, by allowing the Chinese authorities to take three hundred and seventeen men out of the American ship Messenger in order to ascertain whether any of them were detained on board against their will. Every one of them declined to go back to the ship, but it was not proved how many had been beguiled away on false pretences—the usual mode of kidnapping. The report of the commission sent to Cuba a dozen years later asserts, as the result of careful inquiries, that the majority of the coolies in Cuba "were decoyed abroad, not legitimately induced to emigrate."

The Portuguese rulers of Macao were unwilling to make thorough investigation into the facts about this business until after the return of the commission sent to Cuba in 1873, whose report disclosed the inevitable evils and wrongs inherent in the traffic. Urged by the British government, they finally (in 1875) closed the barracoons, and thus put an end to it. During the twenty-five years of its existence about five hundred thousand coolies were taken away.

---

[1] Compare Lieutenant-Colonel Fisher, *Personal Narrative of Three Years' Service in China*, pp. 260–342, where the matter is pretty thoroughly discussed and Lao's proclamations given in detail.

To return to the war: throughout the winter no event of note occurred in any part of China, but the imperial government was busily employed in fortifying the mouth of the Pei ho to prevent the entrance of the allies. They demolished the old forts to rebuild new ones of materials gathered on the spot, and constructed somewhat after the manner laid down in foreign authorities on fortification. These books had been translated for them by natives trained in mission schools. Notwithstanding all that Kweiliang and Hwashana may have assured them to the contrary, the Emperor and his officers could not divest themselves of their fears of serious reprisals, if not of conquest, should they permit the allied gunboats to anchor a second time at Tientsin and their embassies to enter the capital. The two commissioners awaited at Shanghai the arrival of the British, French, and American plenipotentiaries, for the purpose of urging them to exchange the ratifications in that city. Nevertheless, since Peking was expressly appointed in the first two treaties as the place for signing them, Mr. Bruce and M. Bourboulon, the English and French ministers, determined to insist upon this detail. The poor commissioners, on the other hand, knowing more than they dared to tell of the hostile preparations going on, steadily declined the offer of a passage to Taku. Mr. Ward was not tied down to any place or time for exchanging the American treaty, but decided to do so at the same place with his colleagues. The three ministers remained in the south to exchange views and allow the British gunboats to collect off Taku before their arrival, when they all joined them on June 20th. The appearance of the forts was entirely different from last year, and confirmed the reports of the great efforts making to prevent foreigners reaching the capital in large numbers. The river was found to be barred by an elaborate boom of timber and chains; but though no soldiers were in sight on the battlements, it was evident that a collision was intended. The reconnoissance had been carefully made from the 17th to the 24th, and the Chinese general, Săng-ko-lin-sin, felt confident of his ability to hold his own against the ships inside of the bar. All official intercourse was refused with Admiral Hope, though he had stated his purpose clearly, because, as was alleged, these forts and men were merely gathered by the common people to defend themselves against pirates.

In order to discover the real state of feeling toward a neutral, Commodore Tatnall took Mr. Ward, in the United States chartered steamer Toeywan, into the river on the 24th, and proceeded toward a jetty near the fort. The steamer ran aground when about half a mile short of it; the minister then sent his interpreters to the jetty, where they were met by a dozen or more miserably dressed fellows who had come from the fort for that purpose. On learning the errand of the foreigners, one or two of the men spoke up in a way which showed that they were officers—probably disguised as coolies—telling the deputation that the passage to Tientsin by the Pei ho had been barred, but that the governor-general, Hăngfuh, was then at Pehtang, a place about ten miles up the coast, where he was ready to receive the American minister. They added that they had no authority to take any letter or card for him; that they knew very well the nationality of the Toeywan, which would not be harmed if she did not attempt to break through the boom laid just above the jetty; and, lastly, that they were not at all empowered to aid or advise the Americans in getting up to Pehtang. The whole episode was a ridiculous ruse on the part of the Chinese to hide their design of forcibly preventing the ministers from ascending the river; but by so undignified a behavior the general commanding the works forfeited whatever moral advantage might otherwise have remained on his side. After Admiral Hope had commenced his operations against the barriers, Hăngfuh did indeed send a letter to the British minister—then lying nine miles off the shore—informing him of the arrangements made at Pehtang to take the allied envoys from thence to the capital. These arrangements certainly violated no article of the treaties, nor any promise made to the foreigners, though they neutralized entirely the journey to Peking upon which the British government had determined to send its plenipotentiary.

One may learn from the letters of Mr. Bruce to Lord Malmesbury (of July 5th and 13th) many details of the impertinent reception accorded to Admiral Hope's messengers by the rabble and soldiers near the Taku forts, all proving plainly enough their hostile intentions. But the minister overlooks what we, in retracing the history of these years, cannot too attentively keep in mind, namely, the ever-present fear of trickery and foul play with their unknown engines of war which the Emperor's counsellors momentarily dreaded from their foreign adversaries. On the other hand, what could be done with a government which would never condescend to appreciate its own weakness, would never speak or act the truth, would never treat any other nation as an equal? These and other despatches from the Blue Book afford a key to the policies of both parties in this remarkable contest, and convince the impartial student of the necessity of personal contact and acquaintance before it was possible to reach a lasting understanding between the holders of so widely separated views.

During the night of the 23d, after the Toeywan had floated at high water, the British advanced and blew up the first boom, leaving, however, the second and stronger obstruction untouched. The attempt to ascend the river in force was commenced by the allies in the following afternoon, when the forts opened fire upon them and by evening had sunk or silenced almost every vessel. In this fleet thirteen small gunboats were engaged, one of the largest among them, a French craft, carrying six hundred men; besides these were some six hundred marines and engineers designed to serve as an escort upon the journey to the capital. This guard was now landed in the mud before the forts and an attempt made to carry the works by escalade, but the effort failed, and by daylight the men were all once more afloat. From the gunboats twenty-five men were killed and ninety-three wounded; the loss among the marines was naturally heavier—sixty-four killed and two hundred and fifty-two wounded, while of the boats four were sunk.[1]

Throughout this action the American vessel Toeywan remained inside of the bar, being a non-combatant. The gallant energy of Commodore Tatnall, who in the thick of the fight passed through the fleet to visit the British admiral lying

---

[1] One of these afterward floated of itself and was preserved.

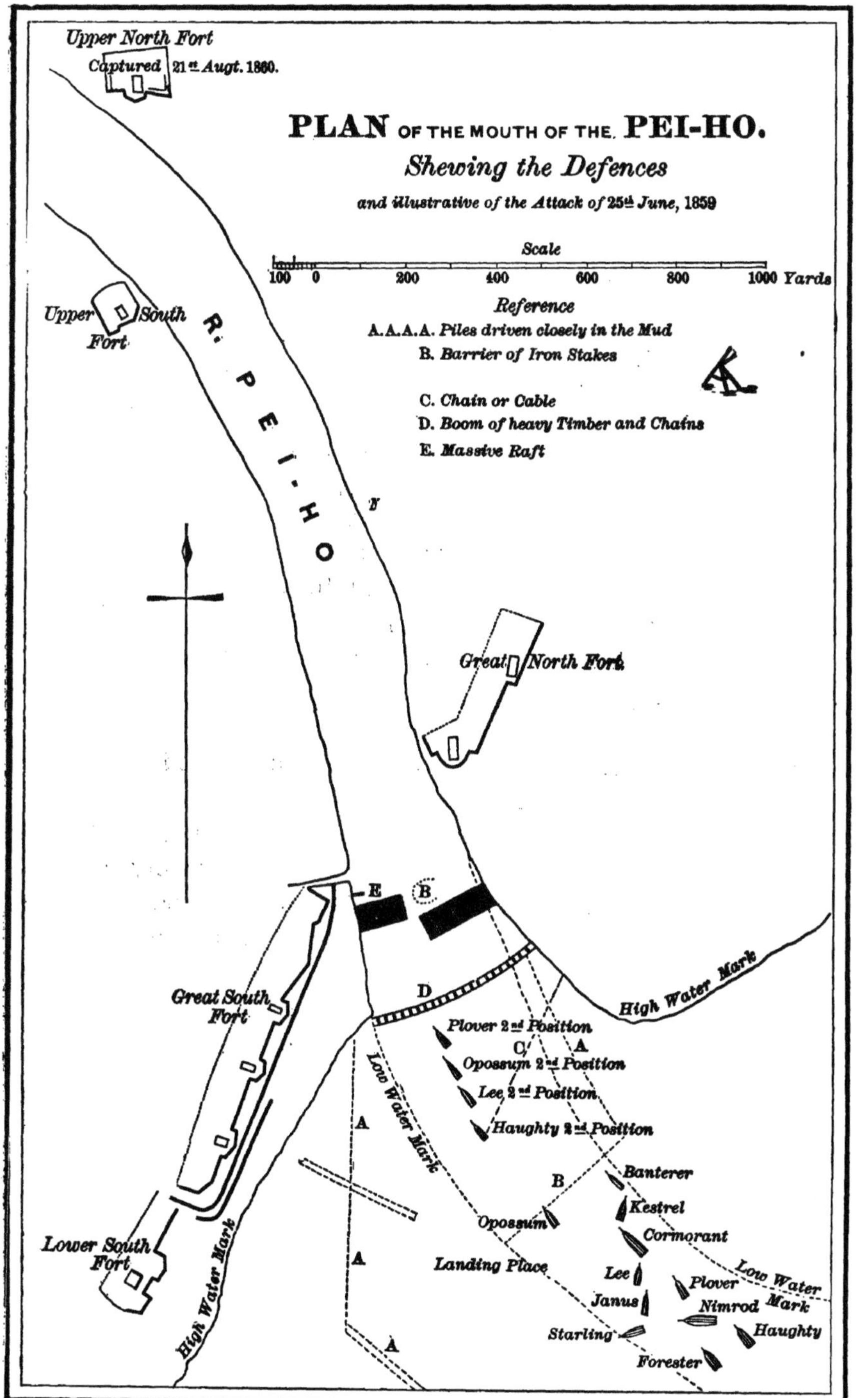

STRUTHERS, SERVOSS & CO., ENGS. N.Y.

wounded in the Plover, well-nigh cost him his life; a shot from the Chinese guns tore into the stern of his barge, killing the coxswain, and narrowly missed sinking the boat with all on board. Tatnall's declaration, in extenuation of his technical violation of international law by towing boat-loads of British marines into action, that "blood is thicker than water," has indissolubly associated his name with this battle of the Pei ho.[1]

The American minister was present as a spectator at this repulse before the Taku forts, but this could not be properly considered as a reason for not making further attempts to reach Peking. He accordingly, though not without some difficulty, notified the governor-general at Pehtang of his arrival, and four days later a pilot was sent off and the Toeywan taken up to Pehtang. Mr. Ward, in his report to Washington, expresses his belief that he would not be allowed to reach Peking, while the Chinese had no other intention than to escort him there and bring him safely back. On July 8th boats were sent to conduct his party to the place of meeting, which they reached through a line of soldiers in uniform placed along the sides of the streets, and were ushered into a large hall amid a crowd of officials. The recent encounter at Taku was discussed in a sensible manner, without apparent anxiety or bravado, and then the arrangements for taking the whole party of twenty to Peking were made known. Among other topics of inquiry brought forward was the cost of such vessels as had been sunk in the Pei ho by their guns—as if the officials had been estimating the probable expense of their victory when the English brought in their usual bill of damages. But the offer of Commodore Tatnall to place his surgeons at the disposal of the Chinese, to aid in treating the wounded men at the forts, was declined.

Everything being made ready by July 20th, the American minister set out under the escort of Chunghow, now first brought into contact with foreigners. About forty miles of flat, saltish plain was crossed, until the party reached Pehtsang, on the Pei ho, where were lying the boats prepared for

[1] Lieutenant-Colonel Fisher's *Personal Narrative of Three Years' Service in China*, Chaps. XIII. and XIV.

their reception. As they proceeded up the river the inhabitants flocked to the banks to behold the dreaded foreigners, but no expressions of vaunting or hostility were heard among the myriads who now gazed for the first time upon them. The vast crowd at Tungchau, when the twenty Americans landed, comprised apparently the whole population of that city; clad in white summer garments, and preserving a most remarkable stillness and decorum as they lined the river banks and highway, this silent, gazing multitude produced upon the strangers an effect incomparably weird. The day was oppressively hot, and many preferred the carts to the mules provided for the trip to Peking, where they all arrived on the 27th. A ridiculous rumor, illustrated by appropriate pictures, respecting this journey was circulated in Paris about a fortnight afterward, stating that Mr. Ward and his party were conducted from the coast in an immense "box or travelling chamber, drawn overland by oxen," and then put "on a raft to be towed up the river and Imperial Canal as far as the gate of the capital. They were well treated, and were taken back to the coast in the same manner." This *jeux d'esprit* probably expressed the popular sentiment in France of what was expected from the Chinese, and has ever since been associated with it.

On announcing his arrival, a meeting was arranged for the 30th between Mr. Ward and Kweiliang and Hwashana, at which all the time was occupied in discussing the question of the manner of audience. The minister had the advantage in this interesting colloquy, for he had come up at the invitation of the governor-general, had no directions from the President upon the matter, was quite indifferent as to the result of the conference, and had no presents to be rejected as Lord Amherst's were in 1816. The nature of the *kotow* and the reasons for requiring it of all who had audience of the Emperor were fully discussed at several interviews in the most amicable and courteous manner. The Chinese were anxious to bring about an audience, and went so far as to waive the *kotow*, or knocking head, from the first, and proposed instead that the envoy should bend one knee as he approached the sovereign. This was even less of an obeisance than English courtiers paid their Queen, and might have been accepted without difficulty—if any compromise were possible—had not one of the party previously declared the religious nature of the ceremony by saying, "If we do not kneel before the Emperor, we do not show him any respect; it is that or nothing, and is the same reverence which we pay the gods." Kweiliang further said that he himself would willingly burn incense before the President of the United States if asked to do so.[1]

During their whole national history the Chinese rulers and people had accepted this ceremony as the inseparable prerogative of the Son of Heaven; and as this discussion in their capital was in the hearing of a great crowd of officials, who, doubtless, were prompt enough in circulating among the populace a report of the disagreement, one may appreciate the feelings of the latter when the American embassy was allowed quietly to leave the city without entering into the "Great Interior" to behold the Dragon's Face. Foreigners have been so ready in China to ridicule or depreciate whatever partakes of resistance to their notions (unless it be backed up by force to make it respected), that this remarkable discussion on a vital point in Chinese etiquette and theology was generally regarded as silly verbiage on their part or ascribed to the effect of fear on the part of the Americans. As the time and place for exchanging ratifications were not mentioned in the treaty, there was no insuperable difficulty in adjourning the ceremony to another place; yet it seemed a grotesque ending to the four days' discussion for Kweiliang to seriously ask the minister for what purpose he had come to Peking, he himself being quite at a loss to understand the reason. Mr. Ward replied that it was to deliver the letter from the President, and to exchange the ratifications. It would have been better if he had held him to the promise made by the governor-general at Pehtang to do so in Peking. However, the return trip was concluded by the exchange of ratifications on August 15th at Pehtang, and the departure of the frigate for Shanghai soon after.

---

[1] See Ward's despatches, pp. 594–617, *U. S. Senate Executive Document* No. 30, read March 13, 1860; *American Eclectic Magazine*, New York, Vol. 51, April and May, 1861; *North China Br. R. A. Society*, Vol. I., No. 3, 1859.

The mortification of having been repulsed at Taku was not concealed by the British public or press, when they ascribed it to the too hasty landing at sunset on a mud flat over which there was no pathway or footing. There certainly was no treachery on the part of the Chinese, as Mr. Swinhoe declares in his *North China Campaign*, for they plainly told what they would do if the passage were attempted.[1] Yet it was a grievous disappointment to find that the exchange of ratifications had been interrupted from any cause; and though it will probably always be a debatable point whether it was right for the allied envoys to refuse the offered means of reaching Peking by way of Pehtang, there was no debate now as to the necessity of hastening to the capital at once.

The British and French governments moved immediately in the matter, and wisely decided to place the settlement of the question in the same hands that had carried it thus far. In April, 1860, Earl Russell wrote to Lord Elgin that "Her Majesty resolved to employ every means calculated to establish peace with the Emperor of China, and had determined to call upon him again to give his valuable services to promote this important object." The indispensable conditions were three, viz., an apology for the attack on the allied forces at the Pei ho; the ratification and execution of the treaty; and payment for the expenses incurred by the allies. Lord Elgin's colleague was Baron Gros, and the two were ready to leave Europe in April. They were supported in making their demands by an army of about ten thousand British troops of all arms, gathered from England, Cape Colony, and India, and nearly seven thousand French sent from France. Their respective naval forces were not largely added to, but the requisite transports increased the fleets to more than two hundred vessels in all, of which thirty-three

---

[1] Though they told many lies as well. These charges against the Chinese were reiterated until they were believed by all the world; but in the effort to find a good reason for proceeding to Peking in order to exchange the ratifications, it was not needful to say that the forts fired upon the British ships without notice. Mr. Bruce's despatches to Lord Malmesbury (of July 13th), together with the enclosures and translations of native documents, discuss this question with much good sense.

were French. The latter had small iron gunboats, fitted to carry one gun, brought from home in fifteen pieces each; when screwed together each boat had three compartments, made water-tight with layers of vulcanized rubber at the joinings. The British forces gathered at Talien-wan Bay on the south-eastern side of Prince Regent's Sword, and the French at Chifu on the coast of Shantung. The plenipotentiaries had arrived in July of this year and found the imperial government maintaining its old attitude of conciliation and undue assumption. On March 8th the foreigners' terms had been made known by Mr. Bruce, and a reply shortly afterward transmitted to him through Ho Kwei-tsing at Shanghai. In it the lurking fear of reprisals, so largely actuating its conduct, appears from the conclusion, when the council says: "If Mr. Bruce will come north without vessels of war and with but a moderate retinue, and will wait at Pehtang to exchange the treaties, China will not take him to task for what has gone by. But if he be resolved to bring up a number of war-vessels, and if he persist in proceeding by way of Taku, this will show that his true purpose is not the exchange of treaties."[1] After such a declaration there was but one way left by which to prove to the Emperor how thoroughly in earnest were the allies in their intention of exchanging the treaties. The last bulwark of Chinese seclusion was now to be broken down—never more, we may hope, to be erected against the advancing influences of a more enlightened civilization.

After the usual delays incident to moving large bodies of troops with their various equipages, the combined forces left their anchorages on July 26th, presenting with their long lines of ships a grand sight as they went up the smooth waters of the Gulf of Pechele toward the mouth of the Pehtang River. This assemblage was many times larger than the armaments sent to the same region in the two previous years, and the experiences of those years had prepared both parties to regard this third attempt to reach the Court of Cambaluc as decisive of their future relations. The forces found much inconvenience in ef-

---

[1] Wolseley's *Narrative*, p. 14. Fisher's *China*, Chap. XXIII.

fecting a landing at Pehtang, where the beach at low tide extends over miles of ooze and sticky mud, but met no forcible opposition. The towns in this region are among the most repulsive-looking on the whole Chinese coast. In consequence of the saline soil no trees or grass are to be seen on the wide plain; the only green things being a few fruit trees near the houses, or scattering patches of salsola and similar plants. The houses are built of mud and chopped straw; their walls rest on layers of sorghum stalks spread on the foundation to intercept the saline influences, while the thatched roofs also contain much mud. These soon present a scanty covering of grass, which, speedily withering in the hot sun, imparts to the dwelling a still more forlorn aspect. Cheerless enough on a bright day, the appearance of one of these hamlets in wet weather—with mud streaming from the roofs, the streets reeking with noisome filth, through which loaded carts and half-naked men wend dolefully their way—is certainly melancholy beyond any description.

The allies were on shore by the evening of August 2d, and in a most pitiable plight in their own eyes. The men had been obliged to wade through the mud left by the retiring tide to reach solid ground, and then cross a moat that received the drainings of the town, a reeking mass much worse, of course, than the other. No fresh water was to be had, and the time which elapsed before the men could be supplied from the boats was spent in putting themselves up for the night, wet, dirty, and hungry as they were. In the morning it was found that the few forts which they were to attack were merely for show, and soon the town was occupied by the troops, their generals taking the temples for quarters. In less than three days every house in it had been pillaged, and whatever was worthless for plunder was destroyed as useless, "the few natives that still lingered by their unusurped domiciles," adds Mr. Swinhoe, "quietly watching with the eye of despair the destruction of all the property they possessed in the world, and the ruin of their hopes perhaps forever." Even the poor wretches who were trying to carry off their goods in packs were stopped and stripped by the prowling soldiers.

In less than a fortnight the entire force had been brought ashore without accident or opposition. There were men, tents, guns, horses, provisions, animals, stores, ammunition, baggage, —everything, in short, which an army now needs and which steam easily brings to it. Besides these, two thousand five hundred Cantonese coolies, each of whom is estimated by Colonel Wolseley, with supreme candor, to have been of more general value than any three baggage animals. They were working constantly for ten days, carrying water, landing stores, and performing the toil devolving on camp followers, for which this author magnanimously praises them by saying: "They were easily fed, and when properly treated most manageable."

On August 12th the forces were ready to move on the Taku forts lying about five miles distant across the plain, now rendered miry by the constant rains. A single causeway three miles long, flanked by deep ditches, traversed it, and along this progress, especially for the heavy artillery, was exceedingly slow. Upon their passage of this road the Chinese general, Săngkolinsin, yielded the only vantage-ground where he could have encountered his enemy with hope of success. This ignorant blunder on the part of so energetic a commander seems all the more unaccountable, since a week previously the Chinese cavalry had been much emboldened by some slight successes over a reconnoitring party of the allies, and "approached our outposts with wonderful courage, a few even advancing to within a few hundred yards, brandishing the swords and making grotesque gesticulations."

At last the allies were ready to advance to the attack of the Chinese. The Mongol horsemen commenced the engagement by rushing fearlessly forward in several irregular lines of skirmishers, and bravely received the shot from the Armstrong guns, until they charged with a loud, wild yell the Sikh cavalry, with whom they engaged in close conflict. But "in less than a minute the Tartars had turned and were flying for their lives before our well-armed irregulars supported by two squadrons of the finest dragoons in the British army; the pursuit lasted for five miles, and was then only ended by our horses being pumped out. Had they been in good working order the results would have been far more satisfactory, and the worthy tax-payers at home would have had the pleasure of gloating over the account of an immense list of slain enemies."[1]

The allied infantry had already reached the intrenched camp, near the village of Sinho, and the "beautifully precise practice" of the Armstrongs, together with the accurate rifled guns of the French, were brilliantly successful in knocking over the Chinese who served their gingalls at the ranges of fourteen hundred or a thousand yards.

The reader cannot desire further particulars of this unequal contest as described by Colonel (now Lord) Garnet Wolseley. The various forces of the Chinese were entirely routed by the allies; the plain was speckled for miles by native corpses, while the care of wounded men called out the sympathies and skill of their conquerors. The village of Sinho was plundered, and its inhabitants fled, glad to escape with their lives.[2] The next morning an advance was made by the entire force upon the five forts and intrenched camps at Tangku, three miles off, from which the imperialists were dislodged with considerable loss on their part, the rest retreating across the Pei ho toward Taku. Tangku town was occupied by the foreigners, who took under their care everybody left in it, and relieved the wounded and starving while preparing for the intended attack on the forts. This kindness, and the consequent increased acquaintance arising between the contending parties in obtaining supplies, did much to remove their ignorance and contempt of each other—a result far more desirable and useful than the capture of forts and prisoners.

The French having already encamped on the further bank of the Pei ho, each army commenced the building of a bridge[3] across the stream, completing the structure so speedily that by the morning of August 21st the whole attacking force was in position. The twenty-three pieces of artillery now began to fire upon the north fort, from which the Chinese replied with

[1] Wolseley, *Narrative*, p. 103.

[2] A great collection of official documents disclosing the views of the court upon the struggle was found in the *yamun*.

[3] Lieutenant-Colonel Fisher, *Personal Narrative*, pp. 404–409.

all the alacrity they could, although taken thus in rear. About six o'clock, when the fire waxed hotter and hotter, and the troops were anxiously looking for the signal to advance, "a tall black pillar, as if by magic, shot up from the midst of the nearest fort, and then bursting like a rocket after it had obtained a great height, was soon lost in the vast shower of earth and wood into which it resolved itself—a loud, bursting, booming sound marking the moment of its short existence." But the fire from the fort only ceased for a minute or two, and the gunners served their pieces most manfully, though sometimes unprotected in any way from the crushing shell fire opposed to them. The attack began about seven o'clock, nearly four thousand men all told forming the advance. A gallant defence was made to a still braver onset, but the victory naturally fell to the disciplined forces of the allies, who had possessed themselves of all the defences before noon. A few guns taken from the ships destroyed June 25, 1859, were now recovered by the British, but otherwise the fort contained nothing of value. The loss of life on both sides was comparatively slight. The British had seventeen killed and one hundred and eighty-three wounded; the French, one hundred and thirty casualties in all; the Chinese lay dead in heaps in the fort, and their total loss probably exceeded two thousand. The interior testified in every part the noble manner in which it had been defended, even after the disastrous explosion had crippled the resources and discouraged the enthusiasm of its garrison. From this position the allies moved on the other northern fort with their artillery, under a continual fire from its walls; but before the guns could open upon it, many white flags appeared on the parapets; messengers were ere long seen to leave the great southern fort. They were all given up before sunset, and the famous Taku forts, which had last year witnessed the discomfiture of the allies, now saw them enter as conquerors[1]—"the tarnished honor of our arms was gloriously vindicated."

---

[1] When the allied generals came to carefully examine the construction of the walls, casemates, and internal arrangements, with the preparation made outside to hinder the enemy, they declared them to be absolutely impregnable from seaward if defended as well as the north fort had been.

Lord Elgin was quietly resting in Tangku, and refused to receive their surrender, or even to hold intercourse with Hangfuh, the governor-general of Chihlí, then in command, but turned him over to the commander of the forces. The path being now open for the troops to march upon Tientsin, the gunboats were sent forward to see that the river was clear. On the 25th the two plenipotentiaries were again housed at Tientsin, accompanied by naval and land forces amply strong to take them to Peking. No opposition was, however, experienced in reaching that city, while the pleasing contrast in the surface of this country with that of the dreary flats near Pehtang and Taku refreshed the men as much as the abundant supplies and peacefulness of the people aided them. Such remarkable contrasts in China illustrate the inert character of this extraordinary people; and further, also lead one to inquire what is the reason for their loyalty to a government which fails so completely in protecting them from their enemies. Mr. Swinhoe records[1] a conversation held with a well-to-do Chinese, in which this inquiry receives a partial answer in the peaceful education of a race which has no alternative.

His intrenchments at Sinho and Tangku being demolished, his vaunted defences upon the river razed, his enemies' ships in possession of Tientsin, nothing now remained for Săngkolinsin save to move his entire army nearer Peking, and there again meeting the invaders, endeavor to preserve the capital from capture. He would not there be able to shift the odium of defeat on the difficulties of the river defences, while the moral effect would be incomparably greater if he were vanquished near the palace.

The aged Kweiliang, the father-in-law of Prince Kung, was again directed to repair to Tientsin, where he arrived about August 28th. He and two others (all of them Manchus) endeavored to negotiate a peace so as to prevent the allies from advancing on Peking with their armies. Finding that they were trifling, Lord Elgin stopped the palaver, and started for Tungchau on September 8th, the British taking the left bank and

---

[1] *North China Campaign*, pp. 158–161.

the French keeping the southern. Near Yangtsun a new commission of higher rank reported itself, but it was rejected, and the army continued on its way. Further on, at Hosí-wu and Matau, signs of serious strife began to appear, but the commissioners assured their negotiators, Messrs. Wade and Parkes, that everything was or would be ready at Tungchau to conclude the convention. Affairs were becoming critical in the matter of supplies and transport, for Săngkolinsin's army prevented the people from safely bringing animals and making sales. The commissariat, therefore, was obliged to seize what could be found to feed the advancing force, and this involved ransacking most of the towns and hamlets lying near the river between Hosí-wu and Tungchau. The progress of the force was, therefore, much slower than below Tientsin, though the possession of sixty or eighty small boats helped to bring on the ammunition and other supplies.

On September 14th the interpreters, Messrs. Wade and Parkes, reached Tungchau, in order to meet Prince Ĭ and his colleague to discuss the terms for stopping the army and exchanging the ratifications. This interview was marked with apparent sincerity, and resulted in an order for the army to move forward to a place designated near the town of Changkia-wan, about three leagues from Tungchau, where the troops were to encamp. The camp broke up from Hosí-wu early on the 17th to carry this arrangement into effect. Mr. Parkes was again sent forward to Tungchau (twenty-five miles), accompanied by an escort of twenty-six Sikh and other soldiers, to inform the imperial commissioners, and finally arrange terms. The ground pointed out was reached, and seemed to be well suited for the purpose. At Changkia-wan the party met an officer at the head of some cavalry, who challenged them, but allowed all to go on to Tungchau. Mr. Parkes soon met another high official in charge of a guard, who treated them with marked courtesy, informing them that he had been the general at Sinho, and let them proceed. They were received at Tungchau and conducted through the town to a temple by a messenger sent from the prince. At one o'clock the discussions began, but instead of entering into the details of carrying out the agreement, difficulties were made about Lord Elgin's delivering his letter of credence to the Emperor. The whole afternoon was consumed in this debate, which probably was grounded not a little on the recent decision of Hienfung to leave the capital for his summer palace at Jeh-ho while the way was yet clear. At eventide the commissioners waived the settlement of the audience, and soon agreed to all the other points relating to the encampment near Changkia-wan. In the morning Mr. Parkes, Colonel Walker, and eleven others, leaving the rest of their party in the temple to await the arrival of the plenipotentiaries the next day, departed to view the designated encampment. Their journey was somewhat eventful. As they reached Changkia-wan they met bodies of Chinese infantry going south, but no notice was taken of them, and the foreigners rode on to reach the appointed spot. In doing so they came across a body of a thousand dismounted horsemen concealed in a dry watercourse, or *nullah*, evidently placed there in ambush; while riding along in front no interruption was made to their progress. Further on, in a small village, they detected a large force hidden behind the houses and in gardens, but still no hindrance to their advance was interposed by these men. A short distance ahead they came upon a masked battery of twelve guns just placed in position, from which they were driven away. It was now plain that Săngkolinsin was preparing an ambushment for the allied forces to enter, feeling confident, no doubt, of his success.

Mr. Loch, who accompained Mr. Parkes thus far, was now designated to force his way through the Chinese troops, so as to meet the allied generals and tell them the state of things. Sir Hope Grant had already noticed some bodies of men on his flanks, and was preparing for them when he learned the truth; but in order to give Mr. Parkes and the others a chance to escape from Tungchau, he agreed to delay two hours before opening upon the enemy. Mr. Loch accordingly started, in company with Captain Brabazon and two horsemen, to return to Tungchau. They reached it in a few hours and found their friends, unconscious of the danger, wandering through the town. Mr. Parkes had learned something of it, and called on Prince Ĭ at his quarters to claim protection; this dignitary was in a state of much excitement, and said that "until the question of delivering the letter of credence was settled there could be no peace; there must be war." On returning to their temple the foreigners immediately started off in a body, but some of their horses were jaded, and the country was filled with moving bodies of troops.

When about five miles were gone over they came on a brigade of matchlock men, and ere long an officer of rank stopped them from going further, but offered to accompany two of them to obtain from the general a pass allowing the whole party to ride around the Chinese army on their way back. Mr. Parkes and Mr. Loch and a Sikh accordingly went with him, and he bravely looked after their safety. Meanwhile the battle had alreadybegun, as the booming cannon intimated. They had advanced only a few rods when the trio found themselves in the midst of a large body of infantry, some of whom seized their bridles, but their guide rushed in, striking right and left, and thus cleared the way. Ten rods in the rear they met the Chinese general, to whom Mr. Parkes addressed himself, pointing to the flag of truce and asking for a pass for the whole party to return to the British army. Săngkolinsin "gave a derisive laugh, and broke out into a torrent of abuse. He accused Parkes of being the cause of all the troubles and difficulties that had arisen. Not content with attempting to impose conditions which would have been derogatory to the dignity of the Emperor to accept, he had now brought the allied armies down to attack the imperial forces." This is only a part of his excited conversation with Mr. Parkes, as reported by Mr. Loch. They were now imprisoned, and ordered to be taken in an open cart with two French prisoners to Tungchau, and delivered over to Prince Î. The others, twenty-three in all, had also been made prisoners where they were waiting, and ere long conducted to Tungchau in charge of a guard.

The five in the cart reached Tungchau after Prince Î had left his temple, and were therefore hurried on to Peking after him, but on the way were turned off near Pa-lí-kiau (*i.e.*, 'Eight *Lí* Bridge') and taken to the quarters of Jinlin, a general then in command of the Peking gendarmerie. He questioned Mr. Parkes upon the strength of the allied forces, until the latter ended this catechising under the torture of kneeling with the arms twisted behind him, by pretending to faint. In the afternoon, while again undergoing examination by some officials formerly with Prince I, they were suddenly interrupted by a commotion, and everybody ran off, leaving them alone. Soon a number of soldiers rushed in and bound their arms, while they were led away to be beheaded in an outer court. But just as they crossed the yard a mandarin hurried forward, and seizing hold of the soldier, then waving his sword over Mr. Loch, rescued them both and hurried them into a cart, where the other three prisoners lay, upon which they immediately started for Peking by the great stone road. The torture and jolting of this ride over the rough causeway were increased by their weariness, hunger, and cramped position, and when they got out of the cart at the *Hing Pu*, in Peking, they were utterly prostrated. Nevertheless, their misery during the ride of ten miles was transient and light compared with what awaited them inside of the Board of Punishments. They were there separated, heavily pinioned, and put with the native prisoners. Mr. Loch justly commends these wretched men for their sympathy, and mentions many little acts of kindness to him in dividing their cakes and giving him a special bench to sit on during the ten days he was quartered with them. He was then taken to the room with Mr. Parkes, and they were soon driven away to a temple in the northern part of the city, where rooms had been fitted up for them. As to the party of twenty-three English and thirteen Frenchmen left by Parkes at his capture, they had been taken to Yuen-ming Yuen under a strong guard.

Meanwhile the allied army had come up to the Chinese forces. These, about twenty thousand men in all, had been posted with considerable skill between Changkia-wan and the Pei ho, showing a front of nearly four miles, much of which was intrenched and presenting a succession of batteries. The battle on the 18th died away as the allies reached that town, having driven Săngkolinsin's troops toward Peking, captured eighty guns, and burned all his camps. The loss of life was much less among his men than at the Taku fort, for here none of them were chained to their guns, and were able to escape when their position was untenable. Changkia-wan was thoroughly pillaged that night by those who could get at it, especially the poor natives who followed the army.

On the 21st the Chinese forces made another stand near the Eight Lí Bridge over the Canal, from which the French dislodged them without much difficulty. The British came up on their flanks and drove them in upon their centre, which of course soon resulted in a general dispersion. The artillery opened up at long range; the cavalry riding in upon the Chinese horsemen, easily scattered them, often burning the separate camps before returning. The contest at the bridge was the most serious, and their loss here was estimated at three hundred; on the whole field it probably did not exceed five hundred, for neither their cavalry nor infantry often presented a solid front. The entire losses of the allies were less than fifty killed and wounded. Nothing interposed now between them and Peking, but they delayed to move until October 3d, when their entire force had come up, siege guns and commissary stores included. Full knowledge had been obtained of the environs of Peking, and negotiations had been going on respecting the return of the prisoners as a preliminary to the close of hostilities. These were now conducted with Prince Kung, the next younger brother of the Emperor, who was himself by this time safe at Jeh-ho.

On October 6th Lord Elgin and the generals were settled in the spacious quarters of the Hwang sz', a lamasary near the northwest gate of Peking, and their army occupied much of the open spaces between it and the city. On that day, the outposts of the French army and some of the British cavalry reached the great cantonment of Hai-tien (where the Manchu garrison of Peking was quartered) and the palace of Yuen-ming Yuen near by. This was soon pillaged under circumstances and in a barbarously wasteful manner which will reflect lasting obloquy upon General Montaubon, who, more than any other person, could have interposed to save the immense and precious collection of objects illustrating Chinese art, architecture, and literature. Lord Elgin's journal gives his view of this act in a few words:

October 7th, 5 o'clock P.M.—I have just returned from the Summer Palace. It is really a fine thing, like an English park—numberless buildings with handsome rooms, filled with Chinese *curios*, handsome clocks, bronzes, etc. But alas! such a scene of desolation. The French general came up, full of protestations. He had prevented looting in order that all the plunder might be divided between the armies, etc. There was not a room that I saw in which half the things had not been taken away or broken to pieces. I tried to get a regiment of ours sent to guard the place, and then sell the things by auction; but it is difficult to get things done by system in such a case, so some of the officers are left [there], who are to fill two or three carts with treasures, which are to be sold. Plundering and devastating a place like this is bad enough, but the waste and breakage are much worse. Out of a million pounds' worth of property, I daresay fifty thousand pounds will not be realized. French soldiers were destroying in every way the most beautiful silks, breaking the jade ornaments and porcelain, etc. War is a hateful business. The more one sees of it the more one detests it.[1]

Mr. Swinhoe's account of one room in this palace has now a historical interest—but his description must be condensed:

Facing the gate (he says) stood the grand reception hall, well adorned outside, and netted with copper wire under the fretted eaves to keep off the birds. Entering it we found ourselves on a marble floor in front of the Emperor's ebony throne; this was adorned with carved dragons in various attitudes; its floor was covered with light red cloth, and three low series of steps led up to it, on the central and widest of which his subjects made the kotow. The left side of the hall was adorned with a picture representing the grounds of the palace, and the side tables contained books in yellow binding and ornaments. There was somehow an air of reverence throughout this simple but neat hall. On an audience day the Emperor here seated himself attired in a yellow robe wrought with dragons in gold thread, his head surmounted with a spherical crown of gold and precious stones with pearl drops suspended around by light gold chains. Eunuchs and ministers in court costume kneel on each side in long lines, and the guard and musicians are arranged in the outer court. The name of the person to be introduced is called out, and as he approaches the band strikes up. He draws near the "Dragon's Seat" and kneels before the central step, removes his hat, placing it on the throne floor with the peacock's feather toward the imperial donor. His Majesty moves his hand and down goes the head, striking on the step three times three. The head is then raised, but with downcast eyes the man hears the behests of his great master. When

---

[1] *Elgin's Letters*, p. 361.

the voice ceases, again the head makes the nine knocks, thus acknowledging the sovereign right, and the man withdraws. How different the scene now, adds Mr. Swinhoe. The hall filled with crowds of a foreign soldiery, and the throne floor covered with the Celestial Emperor's choicest curios, destined as gifts for two far more worthy monarchs. "See here," said General Montaubon, pointing to them, "I have had a few of the most brilliant things selected to be divided between the Queen of Great Britain and the Emperor of the French."[1]

On the following day—October 8th—the commanders were greatly relieved by the return of Parkes, Loch, d'Escayrac de Lauture, and five soldiers; the first two of these gentlemen had been comparatively well treated after their terrible experiences within the Hing Pu. A few days later both armies were horrified by the appearance in camp of eleven wretched men—all who had survived from the party of French and English made prisoners near Tungchau; Anderson, Bowlby, de Norman, and others had succumbed to the dreadful tortures caused by the cords which bound them. The coffined bodies were all brought to camp within a few days, hardly recognizable from the effects of lime thrown upon them. On the 16th occurred the impressive ceremony of their interment in the Russian cemetery near Peking, Lord Elgin, Sir Hope Grant, Parkes, and Loch being chief mourners, while a deputation from every regiment in the allied armies followed in the train.

Two days after this Lord Elgin ordered the destruction of the palace of Yuen-ming Yuen; a sudden though deliberate act. Feeling probably that such a decision would be closely criticised by those who were far removed in time and place from the exciting scenes around him, he took occasion to review his position in a long despatch. It was impossible in his situation to learn whether the responsibility for the capture and savage treatment of these men rested with the same Chinese officials.[2] This

[1] Swinhoe, *North China Campaign*, pp. 294 ff.—the most detailed and interesting account of this palace and its destruction. Compare M. C. Lavallée in the *Revue des Deux Mondes* for August 1, 1865. Other French writers on this war are Lieutenant de vaisseau Pallu, *Relation de l'expédition de Chine*, Paris, 1863; le Comte d'Escayrac de Lauture, *Mémoires sur la Chine*, Paris, 1864; Sinnebaldo de Mas, *La Chine et les puissances chrétiennes*, 1861.

[2] Probably not. The prisoners were in the hands of lictors whose habit it was to torture in the hope of extorting money on their own account. The

much, nevertheless, was plain—that the Chinese were fully aware of the obligations of a flag of truce, inasmuch as they had already often availed themselves of its privileges. Lord Elgin makes the Emperor personally responsible for the crimes which had been committed, but specifies Săngkolinsin as the real culprit. He then says:

> I had reason to believe that it was an act which was calculated to produce a greater effect in China and on the Emperor than persons who look on from a distance may suppose. It was the Emperor's favorite residence, and its destruction could not fail to be a blow to his pride as well as to his feelings. To this place he brought our hapless countrymen, in order that they might undergo their severest tortures within its precincts. Here have been found the horses and accoutrements of the troopers seized, the decorations torn from the breast of a gallant French officer, and other effects belonging to the prisoners. As almost all the valuables had already been taken from the palace, the army would go there, not to pillage, but to mark, by a solemn act of retribution, the horror and indignation with which we were inspired by the perpetration of a great crime. The punishment was one which would fall, not on the people, who may be comparatively innocent, but exclusively on the Emperor, whose direct personal responsibility for the crime committed is established, not only by the treatment of the prisoners at Yuen-ming Yuen, but also by the edict in which he offered a pecuniary reward for the heads of the foreigners.[1]

The work of destruction left hardly a trace of the palace of the "Round-bright Garden;" indeed, the provocation for this act was great. The despatch refers only to the palace where Hienfung spent most of his time, and it is probable that Lord Elgin intended to burn that alone. He gave no orders for the destruction of the buildings on Wan-shao shan, Yuh-tsien shan, the Imperial Park near Pih-yun sz', and other places five to ten miles distant. All of these residences or villas had been erected or enlarged by former Emperors of the present dynasty; none have since been rebuilt. It is, nevertheless, easy to gather from Colonel Wolseley's record that his lordship's satisfaction in this

candid spirit of Loch's narrative is wanting in the more colored accounts of Wolseley and Swinhoe, written in the flush of victory. The charges they make against Prince Ĭ of treachery toward Mr. Parkes are not borne out; the deaths of Captain Brabazon and the Abbé de Luc seem to have been by order of Pao, and not from Săngkolinsin. Compare an article in the *Revue des Deux Mondes* (15 juillet, 1865) by C. Lavallée, *L'Expedition anglo-française en Chine*

[1] *Elgin's Letters and Journals*, p. 366.

"retribution" was not greatly impaired by its over-zealous performance on the part of the troops. In addition to the loss of the palaces, the Chinese had to pay £100,000 as indemnity to be given to the prisoners and their families, before the victors would consent to sign the convocation.

On the 13th the ultimatum had been accepted by Prince Kung, who about two hours before noon opened the An-ting or northeast gate of Peking, which commanded the whole city. Arrangements were gradually completed for the grand entry of the plenipotentiaries into Peking. The *Lí Pu*, or Board of Rites, was selected as the place for exchanging the ratifications of the treaty of Tientsin and signing the convention, while the *fu*, or palace of Prince Î, had been chosen for Lord Elgin's residence in the city. On October 24th the latter was escorted to both these places by many officers, together with a body of four hundred infantry and one hundred cavalry, while in all the streets leading to them were guards placed. The whole city was out to witness the unusual parade. The procession passed slowly through the wide avenues, the music of the band heralding its approach to the dignitaries anxiously awaiting the arrival. The utmost care had been taken that no excuse should be ever after brought forward that the Emperor had not assented to the two documents signed that day; but much besides was done to show Prince Kung and his officers that they were in the presence of their conquerors.[1]

The following day Baron Gros signed his convention and exchanged the ratifications of the French treaty under similar formalities. The principal points in the British convention of nine articles were—the payment of eight million taels; the permission given by imperial sanction for the emigration at will of Chinese subjects as contract laborers or otherwise; the cession of Kowlung to the crown as part of the colony of Hongkong.

Without delaying for additional comment, the insertion here of a portion of Lord John Russell's despatch to Lord Elgin will

[1] The frontispiece of this volume is intended to represent this ceremony. Its interest lies chiefly in the fact that it is from the work of one of the ablest painters in the capital, and represents from a native's stand-point one of the most remarkable and important events in the history of modern China.

not be uninteresting in connection with these treaties. His lordship's document reads like the balance-sheet of a London merchant at the termination of some successful adventure: "The Convention is entirely satisfactory to Her Majesty's Government. It records the reparation made by the Emperor of China for his disregard in the previous year of his treaty engagements; it sets Her Majesty's government free from an implied engagement not to insist in all particulars on the fulfilment of those engagements; it imposes upon China a fine in the shape of an augmented rate of indemnity; it affords an additional opening for British trade; it places on a recognized footing the emigration of Chinese coolies, whose services are so important to Her Majesty's colonial possessions; it relieves Her Majesty's colony of Hongkong from a source of previous annoyance."[1]

The French convention of ten articles contained like demands and rewards, but instead of a slice of territory, the sixth provided that Roman Catholic Christians should be indemnified for "all such churches, schools, cemeteries, lands, and buildings as were owned on former occasions by persecuted Christians, and the money handed to the French representative at Peking for transmission to the Christians in the localities concerned." The fulfilment of this article required over ten years; and as the injuries had been done in some cases as far back as the reign of Louis XIII., great irritation was aroused in the minds of the natives who had for generations been quietly in possession of lands which they had purchased.[2]

---

[1] "The practical result was not very great," concludes Mr. McCarthy. "Perhaps the most important gain to Europe was the knowledge that Peking was by no means so large a city as we had all imagined it to be. . . . There is some comfort in knowing that so much blood was not spilt wholly in vain." —*A History of Our Own Times*, Chap. XLII., Vol. III.

[2] An instance is mentioned in No. IV. of the *Journal of the N. C. Br. R. A. Soc.*, 1867, pp. 21–33, where a Roman Catholic church at Hangchau, which had been confiscated by the Emperor Yungching (about 1730), was changed into a temple dedicated to *Tien Hao*, the Queen of Heaven, "to serve the double purpose of extirpating a religion of false gossip and obduracy, and of making an offering to a spirit who really has a beneficial influence over human destinies."

The great objects of the expedition were now attained, and foreign nations could congratulate themselves upon having settled their representatives in the Chinese capital on terms of equality. Two *fu*, or palaces, were immediately occupied by those from Great Britain and France. Subsequently, the ministers from other countries have grouped themselves around these, and a foreign quarter has gradually grown up in the south-eastern part of the city. The chief agents in this important opening, Lord Elgin and Baron Gros, were well fitted by their urbanity, philanthropy, and moderation for the delicate task assigned them. The terrified officials and citizens in Peking had expected the worst consequences on the capture of their city, but besides the destruction of Yuen-ming Yuen, their capital and national unity escaped uninjured.

It was probably a great aid to the policy adopted by Prince Kung and his colleagues that the Emperor and his court had fled to Jeh-ho, for their influence, as the sequel proved, would have opposed any pacification. It was still more important for all future co-operation that he never came back at all, and thus the real guidance of affairs fell into better hands.

The 24th day of October saw the ending of the seclusion of the Chinese from their fellow-men; the contest honestly enough begun in 1839 by Lin, to rescue his country from the curse of opium, was in a manner completed on that day by the admission of those regenerating influences which could alone effectually remove that evil. The intermediate twenty years had done much to prepare the Chinese for this concluding act; and the honorable manner in which they fulfilled their promises and payments will stand as a lasting monument to their national credit.

The retirement of the allies from Peking was accomplished without impediment from the Chinese army under Săngkolinsin; the money disbursed for boats, carts, supplies, fuel, etc., as the troops went down the river, compensating many natives for their losses. By the end of November all had embarked except the garrisons left at Tientsin and Taku, which latter were removed as soon as the portion of the indemnity involving their occupation was paid up. The effectual and salutary working of the treaty stipulations for the mutual welfare of all parties depended on the diplomatic and consular officers left in the capital and open ports. The British government alone was adequately supplied in this respect, and their consulates became the expositors to the local rulers of the manner in which the treaties were to be interpreted and enforced. The great mass of natives knew almost nothing of their provisions, and looked upon the struggle chiefly as one between their sovereign and the foreigners. The defeat of the latter was in remoter districts declared proven by their retirement from Peking; but along the coasts and up the Yangtsz' the actual sight of steamers and contact with foreigners who could talk with them and explain the new state of things, really did more than anything else to show them that these strangers were by no means overcome. What was thus achieved to enlighten the people near the trading marts only required time and contact to spread into distant regions of the interior. As for the citizens of Peking, they met only those foreigners who could talk with them, for that city was not open to trade; and thus one prolific source of misunderstanding was removed. The death of the Emperor Hienfung (August 17, 1861) relieved them, too, from any attempt he might have made, in his irritation on returning to the Forbidden City and seeing his ruined palaces, to vent his wrath on the few foreigners then living near him. Christian missionaries also began their work in 1861, and thus thousands, who had had only vague ideas about the "barbarians," could easily learn the truth concerning them. Most fortunately, then, circumstances were from the first favorable for forming an intelligent public opinion in the capital.

CHAPTER XXVI.

NARRATIVES OF RECENT EVENTS IN CHINA.

TWELVE months elapsed before the political atmosphere of China was disturbed by any break or change in its condition—a period of quiet which the government sorely needed for an appreciation of its relations with the foreigners who had forced their way into the capital. His Majesty Hienfung having ascended the Dragon Throne on high, left the Empire in the hands of his only son, a child six years old; whether through incapacity or disease, the debauched sovereign had long before his death allowed his courtiers to engross the reins of government, and these now formed a coterie which at Jeh-ho was all-powerful. At his death the administration rested in the hands of a council of eight, whose nominal head was Tsai-yuen, Prince Í, a member of the imperial family belonging to the same generation with the infant Emperor. The design of this cabal was to at once assume the absolute power of a regency, to retain possession of the young Emperor's person at Jeh-ho, to make way in secret with his mother and the Empress-dowager, and lastly to arrest and destroy his father's three brothers; these initiatory steps to sovereignty being accomplished, nothing would interrupt their complete mastery of the government.

But in Prince Kung,[1] the Emperor's oldest surviving brother.

[1] Kung Tsin-wang, 'Prince Respect'—called by the people Wu-ako, 'Fifth Elder Brother'—is the sixth son of Taukwang, and was born about 1831. Three older brothers died young; Hienfung, the fourth, succeeded his father, while the fifth, being adopted into a branch of the Emperor Kiaking's family, was dropped out of Taukwang's household, leaving Prince Kung in 1861 to be the first prince during the minority of Tungchí. His personal name, Yih-hü, is never employed by those outside his immediate family. He has a commendable record for an Asiatic statesman trained in habits of autocratic command. The background in the portrait on the opposite page is a bit of roofwork in the Foreign Office at Peking.

PRINCE KUNG

the conspirators found an opponent of no ordinary ability, to whose astuteness in outwitting their machinations (as may be safely affirmed in view of events which followed) is doubtless owing the continuance of the present reigning family. The prince was in concealment during the autumn of 1860, when his brother fled to Jeh-ho, but appearing when the capital was surrendered to the allies, he bore the brunt of that unpleasant task, signing the treaties, and undertook almost alone the management of affairs with foreigners while the government was recovering from its paralysis of defeat. It was a happy augury for the continuance of peace and friendly intercourse that to a man so well fitted by temperament for his difficult position should be joined the able and experienced statesman Kweiliang; though too old to take an active part in the settlement of the succession, this skilful diplomatist lent the greatest aid to his son-in-law by giving advice and a much needed support to the Empresses-dowager at this critical period.

Hastily quitting Jeh-ho with the boy—who had been proclaimed Emperor under the reign-name of Kí-tsiang, 'Lucky Omen'—the two Empresses availed themselves of their right to join the first prince, and repaired to Peking. Once settled in the Forbidden City they were able to impart to Prince Kung the magnitude of the plot against them, and concert measures with leading members of the imperial clan for the general safety. The arrest and trial of the traitors was promptly carried out; by a decree of December 2, 1861, Prince Ĩ and his principal coadjutor, Prince Chin, were allowed to commit suicide, while their powerful and clever colleague, Suhshun, was executed in the market-place, to the unfeigned delight of the populace. This conspirator in his machinations and gross assumptions had acted like a veritable Tigellinus, and earned for himself a hatred and contempt which even members of the war party could not conceal. Others of this unsuccessful clique were disgraced or banished, but the punishments were not numerous or barbarous. The reign-name was now changed from Kí-tsiang to *Tung-chí*, or 'Union Rule,' to mark the successful demolition of this conspiracy, while Prince Kung (now but thirty years old), the shrewd perpetrator of the *coup d'état*, was proclaimed *I-ching-wang*, or 'Regent Prince,' and with the Empresses constituted the regency during the minority.[1]

Considering all the circumstances of this palace intrigue, the rank of its leading members, and its successful suppression by the operation of legal methods alone, it may well deserve the attention of those interested in the political and historical development of China as an admirable instance of both the strength and weakness of her paternal government. To the ordinary outlays of the Empire were superadded the immense burdens of a foreign invasion just concluded and a terrible struggle with domestic enemies; yet neither the Regent nor his colleagues appear during this period of stress to have lost a particle of their confidence in the loyalty of the people; through loss and gain, failure of material or resource, treachery in palace or camp, abuse or assistance from foreigners, this faith in one another failed not. The face of China in 1865 was perhaps as wretched as that of Central Europe after the peace of Westphalia; indeed a more general desolation could hardly be imagined. Nevertheless the rapidity with which its inhabitants not only resumed their occupations as best they could but rebuilt dwellings and reorganized trade, startled even their habitual disparagers into praise and testified to the marvellous recuperative powers of this much-despised civilization.

Pleased with the excellent results of the introduction of western drill and arms into their military service, as against the Tai-pings, certain of the mandarins at the south proposed utilizing foreign war-vessels to the same end. To this scheme as at first suggested there was not, perhaps, much to say either in its behalf or otherwise. Their purpose was to purchase three or four gun and despatch boats, man them with as many scores of native seamen, and impart to these the necessary instruction by placing them under foreign officers. Mr. Horatio N. Lay had in 1856 proposed the use of armed revenue vessels in the customs service, a very similar suggestion. But innocent as were these conceptions, they assumed the gravest proportions

[1] *Journal N. C. Br. R. A. S.*, December, 1864, pp. 110–114. Dr. Rennie, *Peking and the Pekingese*, Vol. II., passim—an interesting contemporary record of this event.

when in 1861 Mr. Lay was allowed to visit England and there contract for the construction of a steam fleet and secure a number of British naval officers for three years' service.[1] The Peking authorities were still laboring under the disadvantages of their ignorance, and nothing can illustrate better than this remarkable enterprise the good influence which Sir Frederick Bruce had acquired in their counsels, and their willingness to follow his suggestions. Their secluded life in Peking had prevented them from learning many things in respect to the conduct of affairs in their new relations, but they could hardly have had a better counsellor than he. The instructions from Prince Kung sent to Mr. Lay in England described the kind of officers and hands which the vessels were to carry; they were to be men able and willing to teach ignorant sailors the practice of navigation, the management of machinery, and the use of guns of every kind. Instead of these he contracted for eight gunboats of different sizes, one or two of them powerful vessels, able to carry two hundred and more men; they arrived in China early in 1863 under the command of Capt. Sherard Osborne, R. N. Mr. Lay's disappointment was great and undisguised when, on reaching Peking in June, he found that Prince Kung and his advisers were totally unprepared for such a fleet, and unwilling to endorse the engagements he had entered into with the Queen's officers; nor were the funds for their current expenses provided. His ideas of his own position were soon modified, for he found that the vessels must necessarily be placed under the direction of the provincial authorities in operations against the rebels. One of the articles in the agreement with Captain Osborne stipulated that he should receive all his orders on those matters from the Foreign Office through Mr. Lay, and would follow his own choice in obeying others. Mr. Lay says himself that he was "ambitious of obtaining the position of middle-man between China and the foreign powers, because I thought I saw a way of solving the problem of placing pacific relations with China upon a sure footing. . . . My position was that of a foreigner engaged by the Chinese government to perform certain work *for*

[1] *Blue Book*, China, No. 2 (1864), p. 7.

them, not *under* them. I need scarcely observe, in passing, that the notion of a gentleman acting *under* an Asiatic barbarian is preposterous."[1] Ideas like these quite unfitted him for working with the Chinese, either *under* or *for* them. He could not understand that the former days of coercion and bullying had passed away, and that time must be allowed for them to gradually learn in their own way how to rise in the scale of nations, and adopt such improvements as they pleased.

In his perplexity and chagrin, he began to blame the British minister for lukewarmness in supporting his schemes, and to weary the members of the Tsung-lí Yamun by his demands. The controversy continued to grow warmer after Captain Osborne's arrival at Peking in September, where he first learned its real nature. Finally, in October, Prince Kung refused to ratify Mr. Lay's agreement made in England, very properly remarking upon the obnoxious article which required the commander of the flotilla to act only under orders from Peking. Happily for China, the dissolution of the force was decided on. The ships were to be sent back, for it was impossible to prevent the native officials from selling them after they had full control, and persons were already looking at them for their own lawless designs. At this juncture Sir F. Bruce came to the relief of the Chinese, and took the ships off their hands on account of the British government, paying back from the indemnity fund due to England all claims for wages, salary, and other expenses to officers and men till their arrival in London. This settlement involved an outlay of about $525,000, but the total cost of the vessels, crews, and outfit from first to last was not much less than a million sterling. The Peking government had, therefore, by this arrangement escaped a serious imbroglio with the provincial governors and generals—one which would have soon neutralized all responsibility, and perchance, even at that late date, entailed the success of the Tai-pings.

Mr. Lay, blinded by his own egotism and ambition, ascribes his failure to the negligence, treachery, ignorance, and ill-will

---

[1] *Our Interests in China: A Letter to Earl Russell*, p. 19.

of Sir F. Bruce, whose performances in these lines are fully detailed in his *Letter to Earl Russell*[1] of November 26, 1864. This statement of what occurred in relation to the Lay-Osborne flotilla exhibits the difficulties in the progress of Asiatic nations in the path of what we call *civilization*, and the ideas which such men have as to the way in which they are to be forced into this desirable condition. This extraordinary paper is an instructive exhibition of British interference in the administration of Asiatic countries, and how totally alien "the spirit of trade and progress" is to the independence and elevation of a pagan people when it alone is the chief agency depended on. In no case, nor under the best control, could Mr. Lay's plan have worked real benefit to China; but carried out under the domineering leadership of such a man, the scheme would have not only been humiliating in the last degree to those whom it was designed to assist, but would have inevitably resulted in the restoration of the conservative party to power and another profitless struggle with the foreigners.

Upon the dismissal of Mr. Lay the management of the Imperial Maritime Customs was placed in the hands of Robert Hart, Esq., who for a period of two years had given proof of his discretion in this position, and (in the words of Mr. Burlingame) had "by his tact and ability won the regard of every one." Already the imperial officers began to appreciate the immense material advantages of a regular income from the open ports, especially in the practical help it furnished toward the expenses of the dying rebellion. The contact of native and foreign rule in the same territory necessarily involved much assumption of power and friction of authority growing out of the undefined limits of the laws of ex-territoriality; but the legitimate working of treaty provisions—the prompt reference of grievances from complainant to consul, from the consul to his minister at Peking—served to enlighten court and country as to the gen-

[1] *Our Interests in China*, by H. N. Lay, C.B., London, 1864, pp. 66. See also correspondence in *Blue Book*, and letter of Sir F. Bruce, of November 19, 1863. *U. S. Diplomatic Correspondence* for 1864, Part III., pp. 348–378; and for 1865, Part I., p. 670. A. Wilson, *The "Ever-Victorious Army,"* pp. 260-266. *Fraser's Magazine*, February, 1865, p. 147.

eral honesty of their quondam enemies, in a fashion which neither preaching nor fighting could ever have accomplished.[1] In the year 1866 the arsenals at Fuhchau, Nanking, and Shanghai were reorganized and made to include schools for naval and military instruction as well as engine and gun works; the value of such works was promptly understood by the Chinese, and has been already the source of a creditable navy.[2]

The retirement of the Hon. Anson Burlingame from the position of United States minister in November, 1867, furnished to the Chinese government both an admirable agent and opportunity for an initial step in establishing diplomatic intercourse with the treaty powers. Into the hands of this gentleman was placed the charge of a general mission to those governments, there being added two co-ordinate Chinese ministers, an English and French secretary, and six students from the Tung-wăn Kwan at Peking. The three ministers were appointed Imperial Envoys and furnished with a letter of credence to eleven governments. The party left Shanghai February 25, 1868, for San Francisco, which port they reached about a month later. Few persons can now appreciate the excitement and discussion in China and elsewhere caused by this first diplomatic effort of the imperial government to take its place among the family of nations. Mr. Burlingame, naturally hopeful and enthusiastic, described his mission as an earnest of future peaceful relations with the Middle Kingdom. Wherever he went he elevated the estimate held of that ancient land by his hearers, and urged the European courts to but wait in patience until its backward people might be prepared for the changes it wished to adopt. Those changes and improvements were only to be

---

[1] The trial and condemnation of an American, who was hung at Shanghai in 1864 for the murder of two Chinese, tended to repress lawlessness on the part of foreigners and assure the native rulers of their earnest co-operation in bringing the guilty to punishment. The enlightened and friendly action of Prince Kung in issuing a proclamation, at request of Mr. Burlingame, against allowing any American Confederate cruisers to enter Chinese waters, was warmly appreciated by this and the other treaty powers as an interesting testimonial of the genuine friendship which was already disarming fear.

[2] Compare Captain Bridge, *The Warlike Power of China*, in *Fraser's Magazine*, Vol. 99, pp. 778 ff.

adopted when China had become convinced of their need and practicability; but many of Mr. Burlingame's hearers were both more eager and more ambitious than he, regarding the introduction of railroads, telegraphs, and steamers as opening an enormous field for their own immediate activity and gain. The consequent indignation among foreign merchants in China and at home upon learning the extent of his exaggeration was universal; the British merchants especially representing in strong terms the evil consequences of such "baseless expectations." The different points of view of the two parties will account for their opposite opinions. On the one side, the merchants were vexed that their hopes of a general trade arising all over China, as a result of the treaties of Tientsin, were likely to be disappointed, owing to the increasing attention of native traders in their own internal and external commerce to the exclusion of foreigners; while on the other, Mr. Burlingame laid great stress on those things which the Chinese government desired and intended to do as they became more and more qualified to act for themselves, through the agencies and institutions which they were inaugurating. The merchants seemed to think that nothing had as yet been accomplished in the direction of "progress," inasmuch as their personal expectations of an instant and lucrative trade were not realized; in reply to Mr. Burlingame's "enthusiastic fictions," they called for "tangible evidence of the existence of this spirit which he celebrates so loudly—some tittle of proof to support his sweeping theory."[1]

Without dwelling further upon these discussions, it pertains to the present narrative to briefly point out the two salient features of China's initial attempt to knock at the doors of

---

[1] See the letters to the *Daily News* of J. Barr Robertson, of Shanghai, which have been taken as a fairly characteristic specimen of the mercantile and political view. An article by the same gentleman in the *Westminster Review* for January, 1870, is rather calmer in language. Other data and opinions may be gathered from a work filling 890 pages, by the late J. von Gumpach, entitled *The Burlingame Mission: A Political Disclosure*, etc., 1872. Compare also the English newspapers issued in Shanghai and Hongkong in 1867–70; *British Parliamentay Papers; U. S. Ex. Doc., Foreign Relations*, 1868–71; *Harper's Monthly Magazine*, Vol. XXXVII., p. 592; *The Galaxy*, Vol. VI., p. 613.

other nations. Of these the first may be described as wholly sentimental; but it was the healthy sentiment of justice and good feeling toward a distant and unknown community, which Mr. Burlingame's tact and ability called forth in behalf of his clients' cause from their recent conquerors. During the years 1868 and 1869 he spoke for the right and privilege of the Chinese to manage their own affairs, and in America, England, France, Prussia, and other countries had already created a more healthy feeling of forbearance toward them, when his sudden death at St. Petersburg (February, 1870) cut short the complete achievement of his mission.[1]

In the United States the passage of this embassy might have made but a transient impression had it not negotiated a treaty of eight articles (July 28, 1868), regarded as an integral part of the Reed treaty of ten years previous. This, the second feature of the mission, has been attended with consequences whose influence does not yet appear to have ceased. Owing to the surprise of the Chinese government, which had given no express instructions as to treaty-making, the Foreign Office was somewhat tardy in ratifying this compact. This was, however, done in the following year. Its fifth article provides that the contracting powers "cordially recognize the inherent and inalienable right of man to change his home and allegiance, and also the mutual advantage of the free migration and emigration of their citizens and subjects respectively from the one country to the other for the purposes of curiosity, or trade, or as permanent residents. The high contracting parties therefore join in reprobating any other than an entirely voluntary emigration for these purposes." At this time the British and French ministers had recently agreed to a convention with Prince Kung respecting the conduct of the coolie trade in accordance with the stipulations made at Peking in October, 1860. The draft of those regulations had been submitted to the American as well as all other foreign legations, but only the Spanish treaty contained

[1] His colleagues, Chí-kang and Sun Kia-kü, afterward visited Italy, Spain, and other countries, returning to China within the same year. Neither of them was, however, brought forward at the capital as an adviser in relation to foreign affairs.

an article allowing the engagement of Chinese laborers in their own country for service abroad. This traffic had become so infamous from the cruelties and wrongs perpetrated on the coolies, both in China before they embarked and in Cuba and Peru after they had landed, that the American Congress had already passed laws against it; and this article was drawn up almost wholly with reference to that trade, and to show the abhorrence with which it was regarded. Chinese immigrants had come to San Francisco to the number of fifty-three thousand since 1855, and had been harshly treated by the miners and others in their common struggle for gold; the Burlingame treaty simply acknowledged their right to immigrate like other foreigners.[1]

Meantime at Peking the foreign ambassadors were in the way of learning that in their relations with the government to which they were accredited they had to deal with men of acute minds, whose prejudices and conservatism only needed enlightening to bring them quite upon a level with any other body of intelligent diplomatists. It was indeed a crucial period with Prince Kung and his coadjutors of the Tsung-lí Yamun—Wănsiang, Tung Siun, Tan Ting-siang, Hăng-kí—who were placed between the two great pressures of a warped and bigoted multitude of literati wedded to the old régime and the ministers of the outside powers, themselves dwelling complacently in the imperial city and representing armies and navies which had been found invincible. The pride of the "Celestial" was necessarily brought low, but the situation was accepted, on the whole, both wisely and cautiously; the good fortune of having men of the kindness and honor of Bruce, Vlangali, Berthémy, and Burlingame as heads of the four chief legations, can hardly be exaggerated in its encouraging and healthful effects upon the impression taking root in the minds of Chinese officers.

At this juncture occurred the massacre at Tientsin of twenty

---

[1] But notwithstanding its acceptance of their "inalienable right" to freely change their residence, the clamor against this admission was afterward so great among the people on the Pacific coast that a special embassy of three commissioners was sent to Peking in 1880, which relegated the right of admitting Chinese as immigrants into American territory entirely to Congress.

French and Russians and destruction of the French consulate, cathedral, and orphanage, by a mob on June 21, 1870, attended by circumstances of great atrocity. The event was a severe blow as well to the anxious mandarins at the capital as to every honest friend of the new order of things throughout the Empire. The Peking authorities were slow at first in opening an investigation, but testified to their earnestness and righteous indignation at the enormity in disposing troops about the capital and summarily examining the criminals, so that by the end of a month every fear of a general *émeute* had vanished.

The causes which led to this outbreak appear to have been almost wholly local, taking their rise in the year 1861, when the French occupied as their consulate a temple in Tientsin, where in former times the citizens used to promenade; this and other unpopular acts kept the natives at enmity with them. A more especial account of the most important of these is contained in Mr. Low's despatch of June 27th: "At many of the principal places in China open to foreign residence, the Sisters of Charity have established institutions, each of which appears to combine in itself a foundling hospital and orphan asylum. Finding that the Chinese were averse to placing children in their charge, the managers of these institutions offered a certain sum per head for all the children placed under their control given to them, it being understood that a child once in their asylum no parent, relative, or guardian could claim or exercise any control over it. It has been for some time asserted by the Chinese, and believed by most of the non-Catholic foreigners residing here, that the system of paying bounties induced the kidnapping of children for these institutions for the sake of the reward. It is also asserted that the priests or Sisters, or both, have been in the habit of holding out inducements to have children brought to them in the last stages of illness, for the purpose of being baptized *in articulo mortis*. In this way many children have been taken to these establishments in the last stages of disease, baptized there, and soon after taken away dead. All these acts, together with the secrecy and seclusion which appear to be a part and parcel of the regulations which govern institutions of this character everywhere, have created suspicions in the minds of the Chinese, and these suspicions have engendered an intense hatred against the Sisters on the part of all the common people who live anywhere near a mission; and any rumor concerning the Sisters or their acts, however improbable or absurd, found thousands of willing and honest believers among the ignorant and superstitious people. Some time about the end of May or beginning of June an epidemic prevailed at the Sisters' institution at Tientsin, and a considerable number of the children died. In some way the report got abroad that the Sisters were killing the children to get their eyes and hearts for the purpose of manufacturing some sort of a medical specific much sought after in Europe and commanding a fabulous price. This report spread from one to another, and soon the belief became general. Crowds of people assembled from time to time near the mission buildings, demanding the liberation of the children, and on one occasion they became so noisy that the Sisters, fearing violence from the mob, consented that an examination should be made by a committee of five. The consul, hearing of the disturbance, made his appearance about this time, and although the committee had been selected and were then in the building, he stopped the whole proceeding and drove away the committee with angry words. Subsequently the district magistrate took a man who had been industriously spreading the reports, who said he could point out the persons who were guilty of acts of sorcery and other crimes, to question him in the presence of the Sisters, and when confronted by them admitted that all his stories were without foundation and false. The day prior to the outbreak the district magistrate (*chihien*) called upon the French consul, and stated that unless permission be given for a thorough examination of the Sisters' establishment, it was difficult to foretell the result. The consul, construing the language into a threat, replied that the magistrate being inferior in rank to the consul, no negotiation could take place between them for the purpose indicated or any other."[1]

---

[1] *Foreign Relations of the United States*, 1870, p. 355. A private letter quoted in the *Westminster Review* for April, 1871, says: "Even then (on the 19th) I think the riot could have been prevented if the consul had earnestly joined

This very unwise answer turned the popular rage against the French consulate as well as the cathedral and orphanage, and the 21st saw a surging multitude assembled in their vicinity ready for any violence. M. Fontanier, the French consul, now thoroughly alarmed, hurried off to the yamun of Chunghow (the superintendent of customs), while stones flew about the building he was quitting. For the rest, this poor man's fate is involved in uncertainty. Reaching Chunghow's office in a "state of excitement bordering upon insanity," he failed, either by persuasion or menace, in getting that dignitary to promise the impossible—to quell at once the angry mob. The officials, indeed, by this time were as helpless as he, and could only urge his remaining in the compound until the streets were clear. But the Frenchman and his clerk heeded nothing; how they were cut down in the way, after firing into the angry mob, how the rampant populace now attacked and pillaged the three or four French buildings, how the defenceless Sisters were butchered in their orphanage after suffering nameless barbarities, and how the frenzied host left the burning ruins to glut their passions upon the neighboring houses, has come to the world solely on Chinese authority, and must remain always in the obscurity resulting from greatly conflicting testimony. The children of the orphanage, however, were taken off, and though attempts upon some of the Protestant buildings were made, nothing serious resulted. Among the saddest casualties of this bloody day was the death of a Russian, his young bride, and a friend, who in escaping toward the foreign settlement of Tsz'-chuh-lin, two miles away, were mistaken for Frenchmen and promptly hacked to pieces on the road. The total number of victims in the massacre amounted to twenty foreigners and as many more Chinese servants, acolytes, and others.

To the joint note of the seven foreign ministers in Peking, calling for immediate and vigorous measures in the face of this terrible news, Prince Kung replied (on the 25th) that in vindication of the honor and justice of the imperial government toward

with the local authorities in making a full inquiry, with a number of the gentry, inside of the infirmary and church, to show them again that the rumors of foul deeds therein were groundless."

foreigners, Tsăng Kwoh-fan (governor-general of the province) and Chunghow had already been directed to do everything in their power to suppress the spirit of riot and arrest lawless men. An imperial edict was issued for the apprehension of Chau, Chang, and Lin, the intendant, prefect, and magistrate of Tientsin, for their remissness and complicity in the riot. The fact that no foreign armed vessel was there on the 21st doubtless had its weight with these officials in carrying out their plans at the moment. They now saw that they had pursued their ill-will too far, and that retribution was sure to follow for their atrocities. Exaggerated reports of their doings had rapidly gone over the world, and as the extent and strength of the disaffection in other provinces could not be ascertained, the inference was made that all foreigners in China were in imminent jeopardy, and that the people had at last risen in their strength to aid their sovereign to drive them out of the land. When the storm had passed over, and those in authority had examined the criminals and given such justice as they could, the opinions of the best informed observers as to the immediate causes were found to be sustained.

In a few weeks the naval forces of the leading powers had assembled at Tientsin. The French chargé d'affairs, Count Rochechouart, took the lead and demanded the execution of the prefect and magistrate for having instigated the riot. The Chinese refused to do this until a trial had proved their guilt—having, perhaps, in some measure recovered their composure upon learning of the commencement of hostilities between France and Germany. The imperial government was unable itself to coerce the turbulent populace of Tientsin, for it had no troops who could be depended on to punish the rioters, with whom the soldiers sympathized. The extravagant statements and demands continually put forth in the Shanghai and Hongkong newspapers tended to irritate and disconcert those high officials, who were already at their wits' end and were anxious to prevent a worse disaster. The foreigners seemed to think that they could utter hard charges indiscriminately against the Chinese rulers and people, who on their part were not to say a word. Minister Low, in his despatch of August 24th, when speaking of the thousands of fans sold at Tientsin containing pictures of the riot and murdering of foreigners, says: "These fans are made to suit the taste of the people, and the fact that such engravings will cause a better sale for the fans is a conclusive argument that there is no sentiment of regret or sorrow among the people over the result of the riot. There is, undoubtedly, greater unanimity of opinion in Tientsin in favor of the rioters than in Ireland among the peasantry in favor of one of their number who shoots his landlord. If this feeling in Ireland is strong enough to baffle all attempts of the English government to bring to justice by the ordinary forms of law a peasant accused of injuring the person or property of his landlord, is it surprising that this feeble central government should find it difficult to ascertain and punish the rioters in a city of four hundred thousand inhabitants, all of whom either aided in the massacre or sympathized with the rioters?"[1]

The judicial investigations in Tientsin were conducted in a dilatory manner, but the above indicates some of the difficulties in the way of the presiding judges. However, on October 5th and 10th H. I. Majesty's decrees were made known to the foreign ministers, stating that the prefect and magistrate had been banished to Manchuria, twenty criminals who had killed the foreigners sentenced to death, and twenty-one others actively aiding in the riot banished. On the morning of October 18th sixteen were decapitated in the presence of the foreign consuls and others assembled as witnesses. This closing act of the tragedy, as a condign punishment of guilt, was, however, unfortunate; it was made rather an occasion of showing to the people that the sufferers had the sympathy of their rulers, while many foreigners looked upon the execution as a ghastly farce—"a cold-blooded murder." Many believed that the sixteen men were purchased victims; the proofs were ample, however, of the complicity of all; indeed, some of them gloried in what they had done, and were escorted by admiring friends to the block.[2]

---

[1] *Foreign Relations of the United States—China*, 1871, p. 380.

[2] As an instance of some of the bitter sentiment rampant upon this occasion, may be quoted the open proposition of a British missionary, who insisted that one-half of the city of Tientsin be razed by a detachment of foreign troops of

It is a palpable exaggeration of the power or desires of a Chinese official to affirm that he is capable of buying up candidates for immediate execution.

As to the remaining four condemned culprits, M. Vlangali, the Russian minister, judiciously refused to accept their deaths as a proper satisfaction for the murder of the three Russians until satisfied personally of their direct complicity in the deed. A careful examination of their case having been made before the consul-general of the Czar at Tientsin, revealed the fact that only two were guilty of the actual crime; the minister consented then that the punishment of the other two should be commuted to banishment. The sum of Tls. 400,000 was paid to the French for loss of life and property; in addition to this the loss done to Protestant mission premises was also made good. Chunghow was appointed imperial commissioner to proceed to France and present to that government a formal apology for the affair. This mission left Peking early in 1871 and returned the following year. The American missionaries who had in August been frightened away from their post in Tăngchau[1] by the warnings and threats of certain evil disposed persons, were taken back from their asylum in Chifu two months later in the U. S. S. Benicia, and publicly received by the prefect. This was the only instance throughout the Empire, connected with the riot of June, in which foreigners were interfered with, and here grave doubts exist as to the reality of danger and need of flight from Tăngchau.

In estimating the conduct of the Chinese in dealing with this eruption, the foreign press habitually spoke of them as if they were unwilling to grant any redress or take any measures for the future safety of those living among their subjects. Little consideration was made for the enormous difficulties of their position. They had been reared in ignorance of the multiplied questions and responsibilities involved in the recent treaties with other nations; and though the foreign ministers were

---

various nationalities, and that a pillar be erected upon the open space thus made, with a suitable inscription as to the occasion and authors of the monument.

[1] On the promontory of Shantung.

really acting most kindly toward them in forcing them to carry out every plain treaty obligation, the fair-minded observer can find small excuse for the harsh criticism, not to add abuse, which was hurled at everything said or done by Prince Kung and his colleagues in their peril and perplexity. The writers in newspapers seemed to look upon China as an appanage of Europe—one Englishman even going so far as to urge the most reckless employment of force to compel her rulers to give up the three odious officials to be dealt with and publicly executed. Another says that the execution of the sixteen criminals could "hardly be viewed as other than cold-blooded murder while those men are shielded from the demands of justice." Yet these writers forgot that all the treaties required that "Chinese subjects guilty of criminal acts toward foreigners shall be arrested and punished by the Chinese authorities according to the laws of China;" and each nation obliged itself to try and punish its own criminals. Chunghow was the object of much abuse because he had not prevented or put down the mob, though he was merely a revenue officer and had neither territorial nor military jurisdiction at Tientsin. Even the members of the Tsung-lí Yamun were freely charged with complicity in the tragedy, if not knowledge or approval. In short, the whole history of the riot—its causes, growth, culmination, results, and repression—combine as many of the serious obstacles in the way of harmonizing Chinese and European civilizations as anything which ever occurred.[1]

As a natural sequence to the judicial proceedings which ter-

[1] The records of this event are widely scattered in the local papers published in China and in diplomatic correspondence. See the *Missionary Recorder*, November, 1870, and January, 1871: *Journal of N. C. Branch of R. A. Soc.*, No. VI., pp. 186–196; *Edinburgh Review*, January, 1871; *Westminster Review*, April, 1871, Art. VI.; *The Tientsin Massacre*, &c., by Geo. Thin, M.D., Edinburgh, 1870; *Foreign Relations of the United States* for 1870 and 1871; *Legation to China; Parliamentary Blue Book*, 1871; H. Blerzy, *Les affaires de Chine en* 1871, *Revue des Deux Mondes*, 1 juillet, 1871; *North China Daily News* and *North China Herald* for 1870. One of the most carefully prepared and interesting accounts of the massacre is contained in Baron Hübner's *Ramble Round the World*, translated by Lady Herbert, New York, 1875, pp. 526–573.

minated the Tientsin tragedy, came the inquiry of the imperial counsel into what was briefly summed up as the "missionary question." More than ten years had now elapsed since the general repeal of all pre-existing edicts against Christianity in the Empire, and the officials were already concerned as to the movements and rumors respecting the new sect which had come to their ears since that time. Accordingly in February, 1871, after an earnest study of the matter from their stand-point, the Foreign Office sent to the various legations the following note and memorandum:

TUNGCHÍ, 9th year, 12th moon, 24th day.

SIR: In relation to the missionary question, the members of the Foreign Office are apprehensive lest in their efforts to manage the various points connected with it they shall interrupt the good relations existing between this and other governments, and have therefore drawn up several rules upon the subject. These are now enclosed, with an explanatory minute, for your examination, and we hope that you will take them into careful consideration.

With compliments, cards of WĂNSIANG.
SHĂN KWEI-FĂN.

The rules proposed (1) that only the children of native Christians be received into Romish asylums; (2) that "in order to exhibit the reserve and strict propriety of Christianity," no Chinese females should enter the chapels nor foreign women propagate the doctrines; (3) that missionaries should confine themselves to their proper calling, and that they "ought not to be permitted to set up an independent style and authority;" (4) that they should not interfere in trials of their native converts when brought into criminal courts; (5) that passports given to missionaries should not be transferred, but returned to the Chinese authorities when no longer required, "nor should they avail themselves of the passport to secretly go elsewhere," as the French ofttimes did; (6) that the missionaries should never receive men of bad character into the church, nor retain those of notoriously evil characters; moreover that quarterly reports of the converts be handed in to the provincial officers, as did the Buddhist and Taoist houses; (7) that missionaries should not use official seals, nor write official despatches to the local authorities, nor otherwise act as if they were officials instead of commoners. The last rule complained of the unreasonable demands of the Romish missionaries for lands and houses to be restored to them in accordance with the Peking convention; it proposed that no more be restored, and that lands bought for erecting churches be held in the name of the native church members.

This state paper was remarkable as being the first in which the Chinese government had expressed its desire for a satisfactory discussion and decision of the difficult questions involved in Christian missions, and the quasi independence allowed their foreign agents by the treaties. The public sentiment among foreigners in China was that these good people had a right to do everything not expressly prohibited by treaty until their own consular officers notified them to the contrary. The unauthorized conduct of Romish missionaries in two western provinces had already given rise to riots, in which Frenchmen had been killed. In such judicial proceedings as that described by Abbé Huc in his interesting travels are seen the high-handed perversion of justice denounced in the seventh section of this paper.[1] The writers of these rules were hardly aware of the serious import of the questions they had grappled, still less of the ignorance they exhibited in their handling of them. All the strictures referred exclusively to the Roman Catholics, for Protestant missionaries were hardly known to the Chinese magistrates, no complaints having been entered against them.

Most of the foreign ministers long delayed their answers to this minute, so that no personal discussion ever took place between the parties most interested. The straightforward and earnest reply of Mr. Low, the United States envoy (dated March 20th), carefully went over all the main points, and gave Wănsiang and Shăn Kwei-făn a clear idea of what they might expect from other ministers, together with many good suggestions as to their own duties. Nothing practical ever came of the paper, but the discussions it caused throughout the country showed the interest felt in the whole matter.[2] A few Protestant missionaries themselves indulged in harsh strictures on the native officials,

[1] *Travels in the Chinese Empire*, Vol. I., Chap. VI.

[2] *Foreign Relations of the United States*, 1871, pp. 99–111; also for 1872, pp. 118–130 and 137–138. *Missionary Recorder*, Vols. III. and IV. passim.

one going the length of saying that he "looked upon the document rather as an excuse offered beforehand for premeditated outrages than as an indication of measures being taken to prevent them." However, no evil results ever came to the converts or their teachers from the discussion of the minute, and its diffusion gave many readers their first information on the whole subject. Differences of opinion led to a comparison of facts, and the small number of grievances reported upheld the conclusion that the Chinese officials and literati had been, on the whole, extremely moderate, considering their limited opportunities to examine the question and the irritation aroused by the demands and hauteur of the Romish missionaries. The unjust manner in which they possessed themselves of the ground within the city of Canton on which the governor-general's yamun once stood had made a deep impression on the citizens; and when their cathedral, towering above all the temples and offices of the metropolis, was located upon this site, their indignation knew no bounds.

The year 1873 saw the conclusion of the Mohammedan insurrection in the north-western provinces, the exact extent of which has never been perfectly made known. The capture of Suhchau (near the Kiayü Pass in Kansuh) by the imperial troops under General Tso Tsung-tang brought to an end all organized rebellion in China Proper.[1] As is customary, the central government threw the responsibility of promoting the peace of the provinces upon their governors, and the well-disposed among the people were usually sure of protection. The foreign administration of the import customs turned a large and certain revenue into the hands of the Peking officials, and their development of the defences of the coast in building forts, launching war steamers, and making war material at the new arsenals, indicated their fears of foreign reprisals and their unwisdom in deeming such outlays effectual. The same money spent in making good wagon roads, working iron, coal, and other mines, deepening navigable watercourses, and intro-

[1] *Foreign Relations of the United States*, 1874, p. 250. *Peking Gazette*, December 28, 1873.

ducing small steamers on them, would have brought more substantial returns. But these were achievements which the future alone could accomplish, and the people must be somewhat taught and prepared for them before any permanent advances would ensue.[1]

On October 16, 1872, occurred the marriage of the Emperor Tungchí to Aluteh, a Manchu lady. The ceremonies attending her selection, betrothal, and espousal were elaborate and complete in every particular. Such an event had only once before taken place during the Manchu dynasty—when Kanghí was a minor, in 1674—all the other emperors having been married during their fathers' reigns. The occasion, therefore, excited great attention, while the attendant expenses were enormous; but all passed off without the least disturbance and apparently to general satisfaction. The two Empresses-dowager controlled the details, the most important of which were announced to the Empire in a series of edicts prepared by members of the *Lí Pu*, or Board of Rites, containing directions for every motion of the two principal actors, as well as for those who joined the ceremonies during the occasion till the 21st of the month.[2]

The young Emperor entered into the spirit of the preparations with great interest, and on the day before sending the bride her phœnix robes and diadem he ordered three princes to offer sacrifice and burn incense on the altar to heaven, "these informing heaven that he was about to marry Aluteh, the wise, virtuous, and accomplished daughter of Chung, duke and member of the Hanlin." Another prince informed mother earth, and a third announced it to the imperial ancestors, in their special temple. During the weeks preceding and following the happy day, all courts throughout the land were closed and a general jail delivery promulgated.

Many of the ceremonies and processions in Peking were not

[1] Compare a rather enthusiastic article by Captain A. G. Bridge, *The Revival of the Warlike Power of China*, *Fraser's Magazine* for June, 1879, p. 778.

[2] A translation of these papers was made at Shanghai, not long after, by Miss L. M. Fay, an American lady, and furnishes an interesting and authentic account of the whole wedding.

public, for considerations of state and security demanded great care.[1] On the 19th the wedding was thus announced to the foreign ministers by H. I. Majesty, through Prince Kung: "We having with pious veneration succeeded to the vast dominion founded by Our ancestors, and enjoying in its fulness the glorious lot to which We have been destined, have chosen one virtuous and modest to be the mistress of Our imperial home. Upon October 15th, We, by patent, installed Aluteh, daughter of Chung Chí, a *shí-tsiang* in the Hanlin College, as Empress. This from the Emperor." The court had not as yet outgrown its exclusiveness further than this step of announcing the marriage and its completion; and to those best acquainted with the etiquette observed for centuries, even this seemed to be a good deal in advance of former times. The great counsellors of state soon arranged for closing the regency which had existed since 1861. The Emperor Tungchí, though born on April 27, 1856, was called seventeen at his marriage. The Empresses-dowager accordingly announced on October 22d that he would attain his majority at the next Chinese new year, and be inaugurated with all the usual ceremonies. One of his special imperial functions, that of offering sacrifices to heaven at the winter solstice, would be performed by him in person—a ceremony which had been intermitted since December, 1859. Accordingly, on February 23, 1873, he issued a decree through the Board of Rites, as follows: "We are the humble recipient of a decree from their Majesties the two Empresses, declaring it to be their pleasure that We, being now of full age, should in person assume the superintendence of business, and in concert with Our officers in the capital and in the provinces, attend to the work of good government. In respectful obedience to the commands of their Majesties, We do in person enter upon the

---

[1] For a report of what could be watched of this ceremony, see William Simpson, *Meeting the Sun*, Chap. XV. The bridal procession came off during the night, when a bright moonlight enabled him to see it pass, without molestation, from the shop where he was hidden. This chiaroscuro sort of panorama rather suited the ideas of the people, and was submitted to by the Pekingese crowd without a murmur. Compare K. Bismark in the *Galaxy*, Vol. XIX., p. 182; *Cornhill Magazine*, Vol. XXVII., p. 82.

important duty assigned to Us on the 26th day of the 1st moon of the 12th year of the reign Tungchí."

This announcement was on the same day communicated to the ministers of Russia, Germany, the United States, Great Britain, and France. They returned a collective note the following morning, and asked Prince Kung to "take his Imperial Majesty's orders with reference to their reception." This intimation could not have been unexpected to him and his colleagues, but with their usual habit of putting off the inevitable, they began to make excuses. After deferring the consultation with the envoys a fortnight on the plea of Wănsiang's illness, they met at the Russian legation on March 11th. The question of the *kotow* was the crucial point, as it had been in 1859 between Kweiliang and Mr. Ward. Then the court was willing to accept a sort of curtsey instead of a prostration when the American minister approached the throne. Now the court had put the strongest argument into the hands of foreign ministers by sending the Burlingame mission to their courts, and the rights of independent nations could not be waived or implicated by the least sign of inferiority. The conference was amicable and the matter fully ventilated. The demands upon the Chinese were summarized by the ministers: That a personal audience with the Emperor was proper and needful; that it should not be unnecessarily delayed; and that they would not kneel before him, nor perform any other ceremony derogatory to their own dignity or that of their nationalities. These points were maintained as their united decision in the weary series of conferences, correspondence, and delays which ensued during the next four months in Peking. The prince and his colleagues, by their discussion of the point, had aroused the resistance of the great body of literati and conservative officials in the Empire, who had grown up in the belief that its unity and prosperity were involved in the performance of the kotow. The discussion in July, 1859, when the Emperor Hienfung could safely decline to admit Mr. Ward to an audience without it, had exhausted their arguments; but his son had come to the throne under the new influences, which were rapidly breaking down all those old ideas and safeguards. The prince had, moreover, learned that the foreign ministers were not very strongly supported by their own governments, none of whom intended to make the audience question a *casus belli*, or even a reason for withdrawing their legations from Peking. Perhaps the Yamun thought that the departure of the Russian and German ministers would leave the other three less inclined to persist in their demand, if serious consequences were likely to result.

The American minister clearly states the pith of the matter in his despatch of March 24th in his closing words: "I attach importance to the proper settlement of the audience question at the earliest time possible. To demand it, and urge compliance with the demand, is a duty every western nation owes to its own dignity and to the welfare of its citizens and subjects residing here; it is also a kindness to this government to try through this means to improve relations, and thus prevent, or at least postpone, what are now likely at any time to occur—hostile collisions, with their dreadful consequences."[1] This alternative was not a fanciful one, and this cause of chronic dispute and irritation between China and other nations during many centuries was removed chiefly through the patient persistance of Mr. Low in this discussion. His despatches contain every fact and argument of importance in perhaps the most serious controversy ever brought before China. One cannot but sympathize with Prince Kung and his colleagues in their dilemma, and to this embarrassment Mr. Low gives due weight.

The Chinese officials took a month to discuss the points among themselves, and signs of yielding were apparent both in the note of Prince Kung of April 16th and the memorandum of the 29th brought forward at an interview with the legations. Much of the same ground was gone over again; a vacation ensued, then another protocol on May 15th appeared, followed by notes on the 20th and 29th from both sides, all tending to the desired conclusion. At last the audience question was settled on June 29th by the Emperor first

[1] *Foreign Relations of the United States*, 1873, p. 169. See also the despatches of that year, and compare Pauthier's *Histoire des Relations Politique de la Chine*, Paris, 1858. Narrative of the American Embassy's visit to Peking, *N. C. Br. R. As. So.*, Vol. I, 1859.

receiving Soyeshima, the ambassador from Japan, by himself; and immediately afterward the five ministers of Russia, the United States, Great Britain, France, and Holland, accompanied only by Mr. Carl Bismarck, the German secretary, who interpreted for them.[1] Mr. Low's despatch of July 10th, giving the details of the ceremonies and the previous discussion in settling them, with the difficulty the prince and others had in swallowing the bitter pill, is very valuable as a description of the finale of this last struggle of Chinese seclusion to resist the incoming wave of western power. The wall of their separation was at last broken down. They were really stronger and wiser than ever, and every nation interested felt a relief that the days of proud assumption were ended. The young Emperor held only three more audiences during his short reign of nineteen months; and in all these discussions he seems to have taken no active part, nor did he oppose the conclusion. His ignorance of the whole question made his opinion a matter of small moment.

Among other advantages resulting to all parties by the settlement of this question was the right adjustment of the Chinese government in its relations with other courts. This acknowledgment of their equality as independent nations did not in anywise interfere with the obeisance of native officials when approaching their sovereign; but it smoothed the way for future diplomatic relations. No western power could maintain an envoy near the *Hwangtí* at Peking with the least self-respect if he were not allowed to see this potentate unless by prostrating himself. While none of the great nations would deem a mere matter of ceremony a sufficient pretext for resorting to war—since war itself often fails to convince—a long continuance of this state of affairs must inevitably have led to complications the more unpleasant to diplomatists because sure to be oft-recurring. It was probably owing to the personal influence of Prince Kung and Wănsiang, the two most enlightened statesmen of this period, that a further insistance upon the kotow was not made, and preparations thus arranged for reciprocal courtesies when Chinese ambassadors appeared at foreign courts.

---

[1] Compare the *Illustrated London News* for June 23, 1873.

WÂNSIANG.

But against what tremendous odds of superstition and national prejudice these two officials were pitted in this curious contest those who have never lived in the Empire can hardly appreciate.[1]

The years 1873 and 1874 were marked by the abolition of the coolie trade at Macao, which since its rise in 1848 had been attended with many atrocities on land and sea. During these twenty-five years attempts had been made to conduct the trade with some regard for the rights of the laborers, but experience had shown that to do this was practically impossible if the business were to be made remunerative. Driven from Hongkong and Whampoa, the agents of this traffic had long found shelter in the Portuguese harbor of Macao, from which semi-independent port they could despatch Chinese crimps on kidnapping excursions for their nefarious trade. When at last the governor closed this haven to its continuance, the Spaniards and Peruvians were the only nationalities whom the action affected; but Spain, falling back on her treaty of 1864, insisted that the coolie trade be allowed. The Yamun was advised not to admit this privilege until the harsh treatment of the laborers in Cuba had been inquired into. This was done in 1873, by means of a commission composed of three foreigners and two Chinese, who made as thorough an inquiry as the Cuban authorities would permit and reported the results in 1874. Since the dreadful disclosures which transpired in their report the trade has never revived. Peru, indeed, sent M. Garcia as its envoy to Peking to negotiate a treaty and obtain the right of engaging laborers,

---

[1] Of Wănsiang's personal history little is known. He was a Manchu, and a man of uncommonly prepossessing manner, being perhaps most highly esteemed of all the officials who came in contact with the foreign legations. At the termination of hostilities and the organization of the Tsung-lĭ Yamun in 1861, he came prominently forward as a most efficient and sagacious adviser of the government. We have already in this narrative had occasion to note the influence of his name in the settlement of the Lay-Osborne flotilla and in the missionary question, the satisfactory conclusion of which was a meet tribute to his talents and judgment. He died at an advanced age in 1875, at the head of the administration. In his death the Chinese government lost an unselfish patriot and a keen observer of those things which were for the best interests of his country.

but this gentleman met with no success whatever. The Chinese negotiations on this occasion showed the good results of their freer intercourse with foreigners in the improved character of their arguments for maintaining their rights.[1] The lamentable condition of Chinese laborers in Peru was fully enough proved, inasmuch as their appeal for relief to their home government had been before the Yamun since 1868, but it could do nothing effectual to help them.

The Japanese government undertook in this year to try the issue of war with the Chinese in order to settle its demand of redress for the murder, in 1871, of some fifty-four Lewchewan sailors by savages on the eastern coast of Formosa. Japan had recently deposed the native authorities in Shudi, and being hard pressed for some employment of the feudal retainers of the retired daimios, undertook to redress Lewchewan grievances by occupying the southern part of Formosa, asserting that it did not belong to China because she either would not or could not govern its savage inhabitants. This view of the divided ownership of the island was promptly rejected by the foreign ministers resident at Tokio, but the officials were persuaded that all they had to do was to occupy the whole southern district, and the Chinese could not drive them out when once their intrenchments were completed.

The Mikado accordingly gathered his forces in Kiusiu during the years 1873–74, placing them under the command of General Saigo, and engaging qualified foreign military men to assist. The expedition was called a High Commission, accompanied by a force sufficient for its protection, sent to aboriginal Formosa to inquire into the murder of fifty-four Japanese subjects, and take steps to prevent the recurrence of such atrocities. A proclamation was issued April 17, 1874, and another May 19th, stating that General Saigo was directed to call to an account the persons guilty of outrages on Japanese subjects. As he knew that China was not prepared to resist his landing at Liang-kiao, his chief business was to provide means to house

---

[1] *Foreign Relations of the United States*, 1874, pp. 198–232. *Westminster Review*, Vol. 100, p. 75. *Customs Report on Cuban Coolie Trade*, 1876.

and feed the soldiers under his command. The Japanese authorities do not appear very creditably in this affair. No sooner did they discover the wild and barren nature of this unknown region than they seemed fain to beat an incontinent and hasty retreat, nor did the troops landed there stand upon the order of their going. They had in some measure been misled by the fallacious arguments of Gen. Charles Le Gendre, formerly United States consul at Amoy, who had travelled through these districts in 1865; the enormous cost which they had already incurred made them hesitate about proceeding further, though they had announced their intention of retaining possession of the territory. The aborigines having fled south after the first rencontre, the Japanese leader employed his men as best he could in opening roads through the jungle and erecting houses.

Meanwhile the Peking authorities were making preparations for the coming struggle, and though they moved slowly they were much in earnest to protect their territory. General Shin Pao-chin having been invested with full powers to direct operations against the Japanese forces, began at once to draw together men and vessels in Fuhchau and Amoy. The Japanese consuls at Amoy and Shanghai were allowed to remain at their posts; and during the year two envoys arrived at Peking to treat with the Court. Their discussions soon narrowed down to a demand on the Japanese ministers, Yanagiwara and Okubo, to withdraw from Formosa before treating with them upon the outrages there; which was met by a refusal on the ground that the Emperor had voided his sovereignty by having for three years taken no steps to punish his subjects, notwithstanding the repeated requests made to this end. The Chinese proved that the Japanese had violated their treaty, and acted in an underhand manner in certain negotiations with their envoy, Soyeshima, the preceding year; but this continued sparring was mere child's play. The probabilities were strong against any settlement, when the parties were induced to arrange their quarrel by the intervention and wise counsel of Sir T. F. Wade, the British minister. The Japanese accepted five hundred thousand taels for their outlays in Formosa for roads, houses, and defences; agreeing thereupon to retire and leave the further punishment of the aborigines to the Chinese authorities. The two envoys left Peking, and this attempt at war was happily frustrated.[1]

The history of this affair was exceedingly instructive to those who saw the risks to their best interests which both these nations were running in an unnecessary appeal to force. Never, perhaps, has the resort to arbitration been more happy, when to the difficulty of keeping out of a quarrel which so many fortune-seekers were ready to encourage was added the fact that both nations had been eagerly developing their land and marine forces by adopting foreign arms, drill, ships, and defences; every friend felt the uselessness of a disastrous conflict at this time and willingly strove to prevent any such result. The civilization of all parts of Formosa has since rapidly advanced by the extension of tea and sugar culture, the establishment of Christian missions, and the better treatment of the native tribes. A single incident at this time illustrated the undefined position of the parties in this dispute. This was the arrival in Peking, after Okubo's departure, of a large embassy of Lewchewans to make their homage to the Emperor Tungchí. The Japanese chargé d'affaires was denied admittance to the Lewchewan hotel, and the Yamun refused to dismiss the embassy, but gave it an audience, as was the usage in former days—probably the last in their history. The experience acquired by these three nations in their quarrel concerning Formosa has not prevented considerable bitterness about their rights to Lewchew.

No sooner had the Chinese government escaped from the Japanese imbroglio by the payment of half a million taels than it found itself involved in another and more troublesome question with the British. This arose from the persistent attempts of the latter to open a trade through Burmah, along the Irrawadi River, with Yunnan and other south-western parts of China. The Indian government had sent or encouraged explorers to go through the little known regions lying between

---

[1] *Is Aboriginal Formosa a part of the Chinese Empire?* with eight maps, folio, Shanghai, 1874, pp. 20. *Foreign Relations of the United States* for 1873 and 1874—China and Japan, passim. *The Japan Herald* and *North China Herald* for those years record all the leading events.

the Brahmaputra and Lantsang rivers, but no trade could be developed in so wild and thinly settled a region. During the Tai-ping Rebellion the Emperor's authority in Yunnan had been practically in abeyance, and over the western half of the province it had been superseded by a revolt of the Panthays, a Mohammedan tribe long settled in that region. These sectaries date their origin from the Tang dynasty, and had been generally unmolested by the Chinese so long as they obeyed the laws. During the Mongol sway their numbers increased so that they began to participate in the government, while ever since they have enjoyed more or less the control of affairs.[1] The differences in faith and practice, however, aided in keeping them distinct; and in Yunnan their numbers were recruited by settlers from Kansuh and Koko-nor, so that they were led to throw off the Chinese rule altogether.

They began about the year 1855 to defend themselves against the imperialists, captured Talí in 1857, pushing their arms as far eastward as the provincial capital Yunnan fu, which was seized and held for a brief period; but in 1867 they proclaimed Tu Win-siu as their Imam, and located their capital in Talí. With affairs in this condition law and order speedily vanished, life and property were sacrificed, and general misrule furnished the lawless with an opportunity to burn, kill, and destroy until the land became a desert. The Panthays, as the Burmese called the insurrectionists, turned their hopes westward for succor, and to this end endeavored to keep open the trade with Burmah and India, but under the circumstances it could not flourish. The British in those countries were, however, quite ready to countenance, if not aid, the new ruler at Talí, as soon as his power was sufficiently consolidated to keep open the roads and protect traders.

In 1868 a party was ordered to proceed to this city and "discover the cause of the cessation of trade formerly existing by these routes, the exact position held by the Kakhyens, Shans, and Panthays with reference to that traffic, and their disposition or

[1] Compare Dr. Anderson, *From Mandalay to Momien*, p. 223. Du Halde, *Histoire*, Tome I., p. 199. Grosier, *China*, Vol. IV., p. 270. Garnier, *Voyage d'Exploration*, Tome I. Cooper, *Travels of a Pioneer of Commerce.*

otherwise to resuscitate it." This party, numbering a hundred in all, was in charge of Major Sladen, assisted by five qualified men, and guarded by an escort of fifty armed police; its object embraced diplomacy, engineering, natural science, and commerce. Their steamer reached Bhamo January 22, 1868, and the party began their travels early in March, arriving after much delay at Momein (or Tăng-yueh chau), a town on the Taping River, one hundred and thirty-five miles from Bhamo and about five thousand feet above the sea. Another forced delay of nearly two months convinced them of the impossibility of their getting to Talí (nearly as far again); in face of the determined opposition, therefore, both of the hill tribes and Chinese traders, Major Sladen was fain to retire in safety to Bhamo. The retreat of this anomalous expedition could be officially ascribed to the weakness of the Panthay rulers, the wild region traversed, and its yet wilder inhabitants. But to what principles of justice or equity can we attribute the action of the British in retaining their minister at the capital of an Empire while sending a peaceful mission to a rebel in arms at its boundaries? This impertinence seems thinly veiled by dubbing the expedition one of inquiry concerning trade; no trade did or could exist with an ill-assorted rabble of wild mountaineers; when these had been duly subjected an expedition for purposes of science would meet with as ready assistance from the authorities as did that of the Frenchman, Lieutenant Garnier, then exploring eastern Yunnan. This disregard of the courtesies and rights of independent nations reflects as little credit upon the powerful nation which used her strength thus unfairly as does her similar attempt of negotiating with another rebel, Yakub Beg in Ílí.

Major Sladen's mission, owing to the admirable qualities of its leader, made so fair an impression upon the natives along his route that upon his return in 1873 his progress was materially assisted, instead of retarded, by them as far as Momein. In the years intervening the Imam at Talí, with about forty thousand of his followers, had been hemmed in by the Chinese forces under the leadership of Lí Sieh-tai, or Brigadier Lí. The Mohammedans felt their weakness against such odds, and the so-called Sultan Suleiman sent his son Hassan to London to implore recognition and aid from the British government; but before he returned his father had killed himself and the victorious Chinese had massacred most of their opponents and regained possession of the whole province in 1873. Its western half had been virtually independent since 1855, during which period the wretchedness of the inhabitants had greatly reduced their numbers and resources.

Trade soon revived. The British appointed an agent to reside at Bhamo and learn its amount and character. In 1874 an expedition—this time provided with Chinese passports—was planned to make the trip across China from Burmah to Hankow, as Lieutenant Garnier had done from Saigon. The Chinese traders in Burmah set themselves to circumvent it, for its success boded disaster to them, as they better knew the resources of their competitors. The British plan was to send an accredited agent across the country from Hankow to Bhamo, there to meet a party under charge of Col. Horace Browne, which was to "thoroughly examine the capabilities of the country beyond Momein." As only six years had passed since Sladen's party had reached that town on its way to the Panthays at Talí, there had perhaps been hardly time to remove all suspicion among the local officials about the objects of this new move. One of the consular clerks, Augustus R. Margary, was furnished with necessary passports and instructions from her Majesty's legation to go to Bhamo and act as Colonel Browne's guide and interpreter. His journals testify that no better choice could have been made, and all who knew him were hopeful of the success of this young man.[1] He left Hankow September 2d and reached Bhamo January 17th without molestation or accident, having been received with respect by all Chinese officials, whom the governor-general of Yunnan had required thus to act. While the party in Bhamo prepared the equipment for its journey, Dr. Anderson observes that the Chinese "watched its movements with a secret feeling that the objects contemplated were somewhat beyond the peaceful pursuits of commerce and scientific inquiry."[2]

[1] *Journals of A. R. Margary*, edited by Sir R. Alcock, London, 1877.

[2] The report was also circulated that the party was going to lay down a railroad.

Mr. Margary intimated that he thought there were intrigues going on at Manwyne adverse to the advance of the mission ; but Brigadier Lí, who treated him there with great honor, did every thing to promote his journey to Bhamo.

The arrangements as to routes and escorts were at last completed so far as to allow the party finally to leave Bhamo February 3, 1875; it numbered nearly fifty persons in all, together with a Burmese guard of one hundred and fifty. The rivalries and deceptions of the Kakhyen tribes proved to be worse than in 1868, and progress was slower from the difficulty of providing animals for transport. By the 18th it had crossed the frontier, and the next morning Mr. Margary left, with five Chinese, for Manwyne, to arrange there for its reception by Brigadier Lí. Increased dissensions among the tribes as to escort, transport, and pay led Colonel Browne to push on after him with a guard so as to reach that town and find some competent authority to aid his expedition. Many signs of serious opposition had by this time manifested themselves; and when he was preparing to start from Seray on the 23d, large bodies of armed men were seen on the opposite hills coming to attack the British. A Burmese messenger also arrived from Manwyne with letters giving an account of the horrid murder of Mr. Margary and his attendants by the treacherous officials there on the 20th. The Chinese soldiers or robbers were in a manner repulsed by the bravery of Browne's escort and by firing the jungle, but the expedition was in face of too powerful an opposition to contemplate advancing after such disasters. The return to Bhamo was soon made, and the earnest efforts of the Burmese officers there to recover everything belonging to the British proved their honesty.

The disappointment at this rebuff was exceeded by the general indignation at the treachery which marked the murder. It was soon known that Lí Sieh-tai was not at Manwyne at the time, though the real actors in the tragedy belonged to his army, and must have made him cognizant of the deed.[1]

---

[1] *Mandalay to Momien: A Narrative of Two Expeditions to Western China*, by Dr John Anderson, contains a most satisfactory narrative of these attempts; the writer's opinion is of the highest value.

When news of this disaster reached London and Peking, the British minister was directed to demand an investigation of the facts connected with the outrage in presence of a British officer in Yunnan, the issue by the Yamun of fresh passports for a new mission, and an indemnity. After months of delay and correspondence with the Yamun Sir Thomas Wade, the British minister, was able to make up his commission and despatch it from Hankow, November 5th, for Yunnan fu. It consisted of the Hon. T. G. Grosvenor, second secretary of the legation, and Messrs. Davenport and Baber of the consular service, all of them well fitted by previous training for attaining the objects of their expedition. The journey was performed in company with a Chinese escort, without danger or interference, the city of Yunnan being reached in March. The gentlemen found the provinces through which they travelled perfectly at peace, and the Emperor's authority everywhere acknowledged—a fact extremely creditable to the Chinese after more than twenty years of civil war.

The Chinese appointed to conduct the inquiry into the murder, in connection with Mr. Grosvenor, was Lí Han-chang, governor-general at Wuchang and brother of Lí Hung-chang. He was long in making the journey, but the two began their proceedings, having Sieh Hwan, an old member of the Yamun in 1864, as aid. Those who had any experience or acquaintance with similar joint commissions in China anticipated but one result from it—an entire failure in proving or punishing the guilty parties; while those who wish to see their character should read Mr. Grosvenor's various reports [1] to learn how slow are the advances of the Chinese in truth-telling. Nevertheless, such an investigation had some prospective benefit in that the trouble which the British made on account of the taking of one life warned the officials to exercise the greatest caution in future. In this preventive aspect, the mission doubtless accomplished more than can be estimated. Mr. Baber is sure that Margary was killed (and his opinion is entitled to great respect) by the discontented Chinese train bands then around Manwyne—

[1] *Blue Book—China*, No. 1 (1876) and No. 3 (1877).

a lawless set, who were afterward hunted to death.[1] The weight of evidence obtained at Yunnan fu went to prove that the repulse of the British party was countenanced, if not planned, by the governor-general, and carried into effect with the cognizance of Brigadier Lí. Amid so much irreconcilable evidence, the inference that the officers, chiefly by so doing, intended to prevent the extension of trade by the British, offers the most adequate explanation. When the impoverished condition of Southwestern China is remembered, the question arises, Why should the Indian government strive to open a trade where industry and population have been so destroyed? But the expectation that thereby a greater market would be found for its opium in all Western China is a sufficient reason, perhaps, for undertaking so costly an experiment.

No sooner had Sir Thomas Wade learned of Margary's death than he impressed upon the Chinese government the necessity for unremitting and vigorous measures toward the arrest and punishment of the guilty. In addition to what has been already stated concerning this reparation, he brought forward some other matters affecting the intercourse between the two countries. They were long and painfully debated, and those agreed on were embodied in a convention which was signed by himself and Lí Hung-chang, on the part of Great Britain and China, September 13, 1876. The correspondence relating to this convention is given, with its text, in the Parliamentary Blue Books,[2] and is worth perusal by all who wish to learn the workings of the Chinese government.

The Yunnan case was settled by immediate payment of two hundred thousand taels ($280,000), which included all claims of British merchants on the Chinese government; by posting an imperial proclamation in the cities and towns throughout the Empire; by sending an envoy bearing a letter of regret to Queen Victoria for what had occurred in Yunnan; and by

---

[1] *Blue Book—China*, No. 3, 1878. *Report of Mr. Baber on the route followed by Mr. Grosvenor's mission between Talí fu and Momein.* Reprinted, with his other interesting travels and researches in Western China, in *Supplementary Papers*, Vol. I., Part 1, 1882, of *Roy. Geog. Soc.*, London.

[2] *Blue Book—China*, No. 1 (1876) and No. 3 (1877).

stationing British officers at Talí or elsewhere in that province to "observe the conditions of trade." The proclamation[1] was posted very widely (three thousand copies in Kiangsu province alone), and through it the people learned that the safety of all foreigners travelling through their country was guaranteed by the Emperor. Other matters agreed upon in this convention were the manner of official intercourse between native and foreign officers at Peking and the ports, so that perfect equality might be shown; the better administration of justice in criminal cases between their respective subjects, every such case being tried by the official of the defendant's nationality, while the plaintiff's official could always be present to watch proceedings; the extension of trade by opening four new ports as consular stations, and six on the Yangtsz' River for landing goods, with other regulations as to opium, transit, and *lí-kin* taxes on goods; and lastly, the appointment of a joint commission to establish some system that should enable the Chinese government to protect its revenue without prejudice to the junk trade of Hongkong.

This final article might well have been omitted. The concessions and advantages in it accrued to the British, and through them also measurably to other nationalities. But while the Chinese under the circumstances had no right to complain of paying heavily for Margary's life, it was manifestly unfair to cripple their commerce by sheltering Hongkong smugglers under promise of a commission which could never honestly agree. In order to better understand the British minister's views regarding the political and commercial bearing of his convention, the reader is referred to his labored minute of July 14, 1877,[2] in which the fruits of thirty-five years of official experience in China impart much value to his opinions. The singular mixture of advice, patronizing decisions, and varied knowledge running through the whole render the paper extremely interesting. The Chinese historian of the next century will read with wonder the implied responsibility of the British minister for the conduct of the Empire in its foreign manage-

---

[1] *Blue Book—China*, No. 3 (1877). [2] *Ibid*., pp. 111–147.

ment, and the enormous development of the principle of ex-territoriality so as to cover almost every action of every British subject. He may also be instructed by this proof of the ignorance and fears of the former rulers, as well as their conceit and hesitation in view of their wants and backwardness to cope with the advancing age. He must acknowledge, too, that the sharp and prolonged discussion of eighteen months between Sir Thomas and the Yamun was one of the most profitable exercises in political science the high officers of Peking ever had allowed them.

Since the convention of Chifu the progress of China at home and abroad has been the best evidence of an improved administration. The reign of Hienfung ended in 1861, with the prestige, resources, and peace of the realm he had so miserably governed reduced to their lowest ebb. During the twelve years of his son's nominal régime, the face of affairs had quite changed for the better. Peace and regular government had been for the most part resumed throughout the Eighteen Provinces, and even to the extreme western frontier of Kashgar and Kuldja. The people were returning to their desolated villages, while their rulers did what they could to promote agriculture and trade. The young Emperor gave small promise of becoming a wise or efficient ruler; and when he died (January 12, 1875) it was felt that an effigy only had passed away, and no change would ensue in the administration. In the question of selecting his inheritor were involved some curious features of Chinese customs. It is a rule that the succession to the *Lung-wei*, or 'Dragon's Seat,' cannot pass to the preceding generation, since this would involve the worship of a lower or younger generation by an older one. The line of Hienfung died out in his childless son; the eldest of his brothers had, as we have seen, been made posthumous heir of an uncle in 1854, consequently his son, Pu-lun, was ineligible. The elevation of Prince Kung's son Tsai-ching to be Emperor was in the highest degree inexpedient, as this would necessitate the retirement of his father from active participation in the government, arising from their relationship of father and son. The next eligible candidate, Tsai-tien, a child of Prince Chun—the seventh son of Taukwang—born August 15,

1871, was unanimously chosen by the Empresses dowager and assembled princes of the Manchu Imperial Clan. His parents were brother and sister of those of his predecessors, while the same regency had been reappointed, so that his tender age involved neither difficulty nor alteration during the minority. He took the reign-name of *Kwang-sü*, or 'Illustrious Succession,' having reference to the disturbance in the regular descent. By this arrangement the same general set of officials was continued on the government, and the risk to its peaceful working from the freaks of Tungchí avoided.[1]

A most notable event during the last decade has been the recovery of the vast regions of the Tarim Valley to the imperial sway. Their loss took place during the early part of the Tai-ping Rebellion, beginning in Kansuh, where the discontented Moslem population, aided by the reckless and seditious of all clans, arose and drove out the governmental minions even to the eastern side of Shensí. Of this extended revolt little is known in the west save the name of its figure-head and leading character under whose mastery it culminated and succumbed.

The famous Yakub Beg, whom the jealous attentions of both England and Russia had united in raising to the rank of a hero, commenced his military career as lieutenant of Buzurg khan, a son of the notable Jehangír, kojeh of Kokand. By the year 1866 the energetic lieutenant had made way with his licentious and cowardly chief, and possessed himself of a large part of Western Kashgaria; then, turning his attention to the rebellious Dunganis north of him, a series of vigorous campaigns ended in leaving him undisputed ruler of all Tien-Shan Nan Lu. These conquests over, hordes of neighboring rebels must now be recognized as fatal errors in the policy of Yakub. The Atalik Ghazi, or 'Champion Father' as he was now called, had not only attracted the distrust of Russia—manifested in their taking of Kuldja from the Dunganis before his approach was possible—but in annihilating other Moslem insurrectionists,

[1] The Eastern Empress-dowager, the legal widow of Hienfung, whose only child, a daughter, died early in 1875, followed her to the grave in 1881, leaving the regency with her coadjutor, the Empress An, aided by Prince Kung.

had constituted himself an avenger of Chinese wrongs, and prepared the way of his own enemies whenever the terrible day of reckoning should come.

The attempt on the part of China to restore its prestige in a territory where every hand was turned against her seemed indeed hopeless. Her exhausted resources, her constant fear of the foreigners within her gates, her suspicions of Russia, the immense distances to be traversed, seemed to unite every factor against her success. Nevertheless, by 1871 symptoms of disorganization began already to appear among the rebels, while in the wishes of the common people for a strong power to insure order and encourage trade Tso Tsung-tang, the Chinese general, found both assistance and men.

A moment's attention to the relations between the Chinese and Mohammedans of this region will throw much light on their contest. Since their conquest by Kienlung, the inhabitants of Eastern Turkestan had enjoyed an unexampled period of tranquillity and prosperous trade. The Chinese, known as Kitai, settled in their cities and brought a degree of wealth and civilization far ahead of anything previously known, while the rulers, or ambans, joined to their duties as administrators of justice a fostering care of trade routes and methods for developing the country. They have at all times been celebrated for irrigating their provinces, and now reproduced their wonderful canals (says Boulger) "even in this outlying dependency. Eastern Turkestan is one of the worst-watered regions in the world. In fact there is only a belt of fertile country around the Yarkand River, stretching away eastward along the slopes of the Tien Shan as far as Hami. The few small rivers which are traced here and there across the map are during many months of the year dried up, and even the Yarkand then becomes an insignificant stream. To remedy this, and to husband the supply as much as possible, the Chinese sunk dikes in all directions. By this means the cultivated country was slowly but surely spread over a great extent of territory, and the vicinity of the three cities of Kashgar, Yangi Hissar, and Yarkand became known as the garden of Asia. Corn and fruit grew in abundance, and from Yarkand to the south of the Tien

Shan the traveller could pass through one endless orchard. On all sides he saw nothing but plenty and content, peaceful hamlets and smiling inhabitants. These were the outcome of a Chinese domination."[1]

In addition to the fields and rivers, mines were worked, mountain passes cut and kept in repair, and the internal government of tribes placed on an equable basis. As to the precise manner in which discontent and rebellion crept into this apparently happy territory, it must always remain a matter of conjecture. The customs of its inhabitants have for ages been based on the tribal principle to such an extent that they found it impossible to assimilate with the Chinese and their methodical government, even though for their advantage to do so. The repeated failures of the United States to introduce a certaindegree of civilization among the Indians present an analogous case. Uneasiness among the natives caused by agents from Kokand and Tashkend was speedily followed by larger demands from turbulent Mussulmans, who saw in Chinese moderation an evidence of weakness and decline. Jehangír's rebellion not unjustly incensed a government which had devoted more than half a century to the building up of a shattered State, and was punished with merciless rigor. Oppression from the Chinese met by resistance, equitable rule alternating with weakness and injustice, trade impeded by illegal imports, ambitious Usbeck chiefs exciting their tribes to rise against their conquerors—these and similar causes had been at work to prevent all permanent progress in Turkestan.

During the lowest ebb of Manchu authority in the Empire, when foreigners and Tai-pings were straining the utmost resources of the government in the East, a small village of Kansuh was the scene of a sudden riot. When after two days couriers brought word that the disturbance was quelled with some loss of life, the authorities began to suppose that the affair had already been forgotten; but it proved to be the fuse that lighted an outbreak scarcely smaller than the other civil war

[1] *Life of Yakoob Beg*, London, 1878, p. 59. See also R. B. Shaw, *Visits to High Tartary, Yarkand, and Kashgar*, London, 1871, Chaps. II. and III.

within the provinces.[1] The Dunganis had arisen and spread the infection of revolt wherever they existed—over large districts of Shensí, but principally toward the west, to Turfan, Kuche, and Aksu—continuing the weary story of surprise, slaughter, and barbarity even to the city of Kuldja.[2] Allying with themselves the Tarantchi, a sort of fellah class which the Chinese had imported into the regions from Kashgar, the victorious rebels established one of those ephemeral governments over the Tien Shan and its adjoining valleys that have so frequently arisen in the history of Central Asia. Under their rule travel beyond the Kiayü Pass was of course impossible, while trade diminished throughout the country, and Russia, as we have seen, wrested Kuldja from Abul Oghlan in order to secure her own borders. The first serious check received by this confederation was its virtual overthrow, when Yakub advanced upon Aksu and from thence cleared the great road eastward to Turfan.

Tso's first labor, then, was to clear Shensí and Kansuh of the rebels, in which his progress was marked by admirable foresight and energy in disposition of men, arrangement of courier service, and use of modern arms. Establishing himself by 1876 in Barkul and Hami as headquarters, by the following spring he was prepared for a concerted movement from the north (Gutchen and Urumtsi) and east (Pidshan) upon Yakub Beg at Turfan. The redoubtable chieftain was finally caught by the tardy but certain power which he had long despised with impunity, and driven backward through the towns of Toksun and Harashar to Korla, where he died or was murdered, May, 1877. During this and the following years the governor-general succeeded in reinstating the authority which had been in abeyance nearly a score of years. His army under two able generals advanced along the parallel roads north and south of the Tien Shan, punishing the rebels without mercy, while "the Moham-

[1] "It is impossible not to connect this event in some degree with that unaccountable revival among Mohammedans, which has produced so many important events during the last thirty years, and of which we are now witnessing some of the most striking results."—Boulger, *Life of Yakoob Beg*, p. 95.

[2] Which fell in January, 1866, after the Chinese governor had destroyed himself and his citadel by gunpowder.

medans who submitted themselves were permitted to revert to their peaceful avocations."[1] When upon the desert the troops were provisioned from Russian territory, but during the early years of the campaign it appears that the soldiers were made to till the ground as well as construct fortifications. The history of the advance of this "agricultural army" would, if thoroughly known, constitute one of the most remarkable military achievements in the annals of any modern country.[2]

With the fall of Kashgar (December 17, 1877) the reconquest was practically completed, though Yarkand and the neighboring towns held out some months longer, at the end of which the chiefs of the Moslem movement had either fled to Ferghana or succumbed in the fight. The Chinese now turned their attention to the occupation of Kuldja, and sent Chunghow in December, 1878, to St. Petersburg upon a mission relating to its restoration. The envoy needed, indeed, but to remind the Czar of Russian promises made in Peking in 1871 concerning the prompt retrocession of the occupied territory when China should have reasserted her authority in those regions; but neither European nor Oriental diplomats seemed to regard the city "held in trust for China by the Russian government" as in the least likely to return to the dominion of the Hwangtí, while many were persuaded that Russia would resort to arms before surrendering one of the most prosperous of her possessions in order to keep a rash promise.[3]

Chunghow—whose capacity had been in some degree tested in the Tientsin riot—was hardly the best choice for envoy even among the still ignorant officers at Peking, inasmuch as to the seemingly apparent defect of an unusually Bœotian temperament was added a profound ignorance of any European language, of modern methods of diplomacy, and of the topography of the territory in question. It is almost needless to add that

---

[1] *Peking Gazette.*

[2] *The Spectator*, April 13, 1878, *Pall Mall Gazette*, June, 1878, and *London Times*, November, 1878. Boulger, *Life of Yakoob Beg*, Chaps. XII.-XIV.

[3] For an excellent illustration of the prevailing sentiment on this question, even after Chunghow's embassy, see Mr. D. C. Boulger in *Fraser's Magazine* for August, 1880, p. 164.

such an embassy was ill-prepared to cope with the astute diplomatists of an eager court, or that it speedily fell a prey to the designs upon it. A treaty of eighteen articles was signed at Livadia yielding a portion of the Kuldja district to China, Russia retaining, however, the fruitful valley of the Tekes River, all the more important strategic strongholds and passes in the Tien Shan, and the city of Yarkand; China, moreover, to pay as indemnity five million rubles for the cost of occupying Kuldja. Other important concessions, such as a trade route from Hankow through Suhchau to Kuldja and Siberia, the opening to Russian caravans of thirty-six frontier stations, the modification of the Kashgarian frontier, the arming of Muscovite merchants, and the navigation of the Songari River, were apparently added to this compact according as the Russians increased their experience of the "gullability" of these remarkable ambassadors.

Even officers of the Czar's army, in referring afterward to this treaty, were prone to add to their remarks some measure of apology. When in January, 1880, Chunghow returned home with the unwise and humiliating document in his possession, he could not have felt wholly certain of a triumphant reception. Nevertheless it is not likely that the luckless ambassador contemplated being at once deprived by imperial edict of all his offices and turned over to a board for trial and punishment. Statesmen of both parties joined in denouncing him, Lí Hung-chang and Tso alike presenting memorials to the same effect, while a flood of petitions more or less fierce poured upon the government from mandarins of all ranks. On the 28th the returned envoy was cashiered for having signed away territory and promised indemnity without special authorization, and in punishment was sentenced to decapitation. The actors in this movement, which upon the manifestation of such prompt and furious measures assumed the phase of an intrigue of the war party, were Tso and Prince Chung, who seized upon the popular wrath as an opportune moment for a master stroke against Prince Kung.

With the appearance of danger such as this the party in power recoiled at once from its angry position, depreciated the highly bellicose tone of court officials, and accepted the good offices of the foreign ministers who joined in protesting against the unworthy treatment of Chunghow and the monstrous barbarity of his sentence. Possibly the temperance of Russia's attitude in demanding the unconditional pardon of Chunghow before consenting to receive a second ambassador—the Marquis Tsăng, minister to England, already appointed—materially aided in quieting the storm. Fortunately, too, amid the rumors of a resort to arms and manifest preparations of the palace discontents to force an issue, Colonel Gordon visited the capital, and in a communication to Governor Lí pointed out the folly of attempting a foreign conflict and the peculiar dangers in overwhelming, by courting a certain defeat, the great benefits which must come to the Chinese army by its gradual reorganization upon modern methods. "Potentially," said this unpalatable but honest critic, "you are perhaps invincible, but the outcome of this premature war will show you to be vulnerable at a thousand points." Counsels such as these carried unusual weight as coming from a man whom all parties in China respected and admired; there can be little doubt that it sensibly decreased the war feeling, and possibly prevented the country from rushing to certain disaster.

Chunghow was accordingly reprieved, and in June of this year set free. The intelligence and experience of Tsăng[1] proved an acceptable contrast to his predecessor's unguarded conduct, and resulted in an agreement (May 15th) on the part of the Czar's negotiators to recede nearly the whole of the contested district, excepting a narrow strip upon its western edge for purposes of colonization or retreat for those inhabitants of Ílí who preferred to remain under Russian control.[2] In return

[1] Upon his return to China the marquis published his diary, some portions of which have found their way into the *China Review* (Vol. XI., p. 135) and are extremely interesting as the outspoken opinion of an appreciative and enlightened Chinese gentleman.

[2] Precisely the extent of this strip depends upon the exact definition of the boundary here under Taukwang. The present line is laid down in that portion of the new treaty quoted in Volume I., p. 218; the territory forms approximately a wedge whose apex is in the Ala Tau Mountains, and whose base, about three degrees south of this point, lies against the crest of the Tien Shan. It meets the old boundary at the Muzart (or Muz-daban) Pass. Since the treaty

"for military expenses incurred by Russia in holding and protecting Ílí on behalf of China since the year 1871, and in satisfaction of all claims by Russian merchants for losses previously suffered by pillage within Chinese territory, and by Russians who have suffered outrage," the Chinese agreed to pay nine million roubles. This appears to have been less repugnant to oriental diplomacy than five millions in acknowledgment of getting back their borrowed property. As for the other points, the treaty does not seem to have been greatly altered, save in the Songari River and other more vexatious clauses. This treaty was ratified August 19, 1881.

From domestic wars and political complications, the influences of which have hardly as yet disappeared from our morning newspapers, our attention must be turned to the yet sadder spectacle of famine and pestilence. The occasional notices of a great scarcity of food in Northwestern China which drifted into the news items of western countries may still remain within the memory of many; those, however, who live under the ascendancy of occidental institutions can with difficulty appreciate, from any mere description of this scourge, its immense influence as a factor in removing somewhat the suspicions of the ignorant and apathetic Chinese against their fellow-men in other lands. The sympathies and charities of the Christian world, as called forth by this terrible visitation, were more effectual in making acceptable the distasteful presence of foreigners within their cities than had been the united influence of two wars and a half-century of trade, diplomacy, and social intercourse.

The Great Famine of 1878 was in some measure foretold over Shansí and Shensí by the decreasing rainfall of the four previous years. The peculiar nature of this loess-covered region, and its absolute dependence for fertility upon a sufficient supply of moisture, has been pointed out in another chapter of this work. Here, then, and in Shantung the missionaries of all denominations were called upon to organize methods

---

strenuous efforts have been made by the officers of both nationalities stationed there to entice the Usbeck, Kirghis, and Dunganis of the region to settle permanently on their side of the boundary.

of relief as early as the summer of 1877. By the opening of the following spring a central committee in Shanghai and their agents in Chifu and Tientsin—all Protestant and Roman Catholic missionaries—had put forth so great energy in their well-directed efforts as to gain the zealous co-operation of Lí Hung-chang, governor-general of Chihlí, and active countenance of the rulers and gentry in other provinces. "At the beginning of their labors," writes the secretary of the committee, "the distributors were received with a degree of prejudice and suspicion which utterly frustrated any attempt to prosecute the work. They were supposed to have sinister objects in view, and not only was their charity refused, but they were even in imminent danger of their lives. It required the utmost carefulness on their part to carry on their operations with any degree of success. They were urged to act in a way that contemplated the speedy exhaustion of their funds and their evacuation of the place. So far as we can ascertain, however, the distributors conducted themselves in a most commendable manner, and after a time at least bore down the ill-will and aspersions of all classes, changing their sentiments and feelings of doubt and distrust into those of the deepest gratitude and respect, so that they are now regarded as the very saviours of the people." [1]

After the experience of some weeks in the destitute regions, it was found that only the strictest adherence to a business system of distribution could be attended with any mitigation of the evil. Tickets representing certain amounts of money were given to the houses of each community which appeared on the catalogues of needy families furnished by village elders. Food being plenty in the south, the means of transportation and storage during distribution constituted the chief labor of those concerned in this work. When brought to the starving settlements, grain was promptly doled out in exchange for the tickets, and to the lasting credit of the Chinese character it must here be noticed that not a single raid upon the provisions or resort to force in any way has been recorded of these famished multitudes.

---

[1] Rev. W. Muirhead, in *Report of the China Famine Relief Fund*, Shanghai 1879, p. 4.

That good-will, affection, and gratitude should take the place of the old mistrust under these conditions was most natural.[1] Nevertheless the terrors of their experiences in this awful time were hardly lightened by this cheering aspect of the curse. Misery and desolation such as this overwhelmed every other sentiment save that of compassion. The visitor was often met by the solitary remnant of a large household, to hear from him a harrowing recital of suffering and death, fitted to shock the most callous of humanity. Again, he would come upon the corpse of one recently fallen in the vain effort to walk to a neighboring town, and about it a lazy pack of wolves squatting—gorged and stupid from the fulness of many ghastly meals. At other times a silent dwelling might be found giving shelter only to the cadaverous bodies of its former inmates; or anon a ruined house would tell where the timbers had been plucked out and sold for a little bread. Of the last extreme of famine, cannibalism, which cropped out here and there, but which in most cases met with instant punishment when discovered, it is hardly necessary to add notice or description. The remarkable patience under suffering exhibited by the people made their relief comparatively easy, though the despair which had rendered them insensible to excitement or violence often prevented their recuperation from the fever and plague which laid hold upon their weakened bodies even after plenty had returned to the land.

In their report the committee at Shanghai acknowledge Tls. 204,560 as having passed through their hands, while about as much more may safely be said to have been otherwise expended by foreigners for the relief of the sufferers.[2] The Chinese government furnished food and supplies amounting to

[1] A notable exception to this universal sentiment of kindliness was exhibited among the officials and gentry of Kaifung, the capital of Honan, in which city foreigners were to the last forbidden to remain, or even to carry on their work in the environs.

[2] About $22,670 were subscribed in the United States—which does not include, however, the donation from the Pacific slope. An effort was made to induce Congress to return on this occasion the surplus of the Chinese indemnity fund, amounting to nearly $600,000, but upon this the Committee on Foreign Affairs reported adversely, alleging among other reasons that all the starving people would be dead before the machinery of both nations would admit of this money being exchanged for food!

more than Tls. 2,000,000, while rich natives contributed very largely in their own districts. Sixty-nine foreigners were personally engaged upon the work of distribution in the four afflicted provinces, of whom Messrs. Hall, Hodge, Barradale, and Whiting died in consequence of exposure and overwork.[1] Upon the mortality connected with this frightful visitation there exist but the vaguest figures. "The destruction as a whole is stated to be from nine and a half to thirteen millions," observes the *Report*[2] already quoted, and its proofs in support of this statement are as trustworthy as any that can be compiled. No famine is recorded in the history of any land which equalled this in death-rate. The area at the base of the Tibetan and Mongolian highlands will always be subject to great vicissitudes of heat and moisture,[3] and the future, like the past, cannot but suffer from these frightful droughts unless a careful attention to the climatic influence of trees and irrigation mitigate in some degree the dreadful comings of these plagues.

The Chinese plenipotentiary in London, Kwoh Sung-tao, gave utterance to the sincere sentiments of his government in saying:

> The noble philanthropy which heard, in a far-distant country, the cry of suffering and hastened to its assistance, is too signal a recognition of the common brotherhood of humanity ever to be forgotten, and is all the more worthy to be remembered because it is not a passing response to a generous emotion, but a continued effort, persevered in until, in sending the welcome rain, Heaven gave the assuring promise of returning plenty, and the sign that the brotherly succor was no longer required. Coming from Englishmen residing in all parts of the world, this spontaneous act of generosity made a deep impression on the government and people of China, which cannot but have the effect of more closely cementing the friendly relations which now so happily exist between China and Great Britain. But the hands that gave also assumed the arduous duty of administering the relief; and here I would not forget to offer my grateful thanks and condolence to the families of those, and they are not a few, who nobly fell in distributing the fund.[4]

---

[1] Mr. Whiting was honored by the governor of Shansi with a public funeral in Taiyuen, the provincial capital.

[2] P. 7.

[3] Mr. A. Hosie in the *N. C. Br. R. A. S. Journal*, Vol. XIII., 1878, has translated the native lists of more than eight hundred famines and droughts occurring in the Yangtsz' basin and northward on the Plateau during a thousand years ending A.D. 1643.

[4] Letter of October 14, 1878, to Lord Salisbury.

One who has been acquainted with Chinese affairs for the last fifty years can better than younger persons appreciate from this letter the vast stride which has been made by China since the withdrawal of the East India Company's factory in 1834. The Empire had then been closed for more than a century, and its inhabitants had been taught to believe that all mankind outside of its boundaries were little better than ignorant savages. Their rulers had maintained that "barbarians could only be ruled by misrule," and in their honest efforts to keep them from entering the gates of the Celestial Empire in order that the people might not become contaminated, had faithfully though ineffectually endeavored to fulfil the first duty of every government. We have seen how small was their success when dealing with the iniquitous opium traffic; no amount of moral or ethical principle in the cause which he represented could make up to Commissioner Lin for his ignorance and stiff-neckedness in pushing his injudicious methods of reforming this abuse. Had he succeeded as he and his imperial master had planned, they would have sealed their country against the only possible remedies for those evils they were striving to remove—free intercourse, commercial, intellectual, and political, with their fellow-men.

The story of China's rapid progress from semi-barbarism toward her appropriate position among nations is now fully known to any whose interests have directed their attention thither. It cannot be denied that the advance has been hampered by the mass of superstitions, assumptions, and weaknesses through which every such stride to reformation must push forward; nor is it strange that interested foreigners from their vantage-ground of a more perfect civilization should at times bemoan the wearisome course and manifold errors of this regeneration. Nevertheless, hopeful signs abound on every side; against a few errors may be balanced a multitude of genuine successes, and the fact that these latter have come about deliberately assures us that they are permanent. In the hands of statesmen as far-sighted and patriotic as those who now control the government, there is little cause to apprehend retrograde steps or a return to the exclusive policy of Commissioners Lin and Yeh. As for the conservative spirit which yet characterizes the present régime, in this will be found the safeguard against extravagant and premature adoption of western machines, institutions, methods, dress, and the thousand adjuncts of modern European life which, if too rapidly applied to an effete and backward civilization, push it rather into bankruptcy and overthrow than out into a new existence.

Before closing these volumes, and as an illustration of these observations, it remains to notice the so-called Chinese Education Commission—a highly lauded project which is still fresh in the minds of many Americans. Soon after the Tientsin riot and Chunghow's mission of apology, Yung Wing, a Chinese graduate of Yale College, proposed to Lí Hung-chang and others in authority a plan of utilizing certain surplus moneys remaining from the fund for military stores, to defray the expenses of educating a number of Chinese boys in the United States. The scheme found such favor with the governor-general and members of the Foreign Office, that early in the year 1872 thirty boys were selected by competitive examination at Shanghai, and took passage for San Francisco July 12th, Yung Wing having preceded them to make the necessary arrangements. This gentleman's acquaintance with the social life and educational methods in New England was so complete as to enable him readily to place the students—usually in pairs—in comfortable households, where they might learn English and become initiated into the manner of life among western peoples as agreeably as possible.

The commission established its headquarters in Hartford and easily disposed their boys in adjoining towns of Connecticut and Massachusetts, where numbers of families welcomed them with open arms. Prince Kung's satisfaction upon learning of this friendly reception was expressed in a personal note of thanks to Mr. Low at Peking, while the fair prospects of the scheme now tended to hasten other parties of students to these shores until their number was swelled to one hundred and twenty.[1] These lads proved themselves almost without excep-

[1] The original plan included the sending of one hundred and fifty boys, but the fund laid aside for the purpose was found to be insufficient to cover the cost of the full number.

tion capable and active in the studies set before them, and as their hold upon the language increased, began to outrank all but the brightest of their American classmates. As they advanced into the higher scientific schools or colleges, greater liberty was allowed them, each boy pursuing his inclination as to a special course or institution. With the appointment of Yung Wing to the Chinese legation at Washington and the arrival of one Wu Tsz'-tăng (who knew no English) as commissioner in his place at Hartford, the complexion of this enterprise seems to have changed. In the spring of 1881 a formal memorial, endorsed by Chin Lan-pin, the minister at Washington, was addressed to the home government, complaining of the course of study pursued by these youths as including Latin and Greek and other unnecessary subjects; of the disrespectful behavior of the boys when brought before their chiefs; of their deplorable lack of patriotism; of their forgetting their mother tongue, and other sins of omission and commission. The memorial seems to have fallen in with the desires of those momentarily in power at Peking; the commission and students were all recalled by the return mail, and arrived at Shanghai in the fall of the same year.

Although this action may have been in some degree prompted by a spirit of conservatism and distrust, the leading motive of the Chinese government cannot be far to seek. Had these boys of a dozen years each received his fifteen years' instruction in our common-school, classical, and professional courses, it is impossible to believe that they would not at the end of this time have been more American than Chinese. Their speedy recall was a matter of regret to the many friends these interesting lads had made in New England, but from a truly Chinese stand-point this foreign popularity would become as the flesh-pots of Egypt to them after their return to the arid intellectual life in China—and the event in one or two instances appears to have proved the shrewdness of this surmise. However, this experiment can in no wise be considered a failure, even if we consider only the knowledge of English and elements of a western education obtained by each student; how considerable has been its success will be seen when the young men—now engaged by their government in telegraph posts, arsenals, schools, etc.—shall have achieved sufficient distinction in their various professions to prove their fitness for the pains bestowed upon them. The organization of schools for other than Chinese methods of education is already begun in China—as, for example, the Tung-wăn Kwan, under charge of Dr. Martin, at Peking—and from these a much more rational advance to their proper position in scientific knowledge may be expected, than by hazardous schemes of foreign tuition.

The pages of this brief compendium of our present knowledge of the Chinese Empire were not written in the first place, nor have they been revised, with any intent to laud that people beyond their just deserts. What there is of weakness, vice, narrowness, bigotry, in the national character has been pointed out with great frankness, while their blindness and folly after the lessons of two warlike visitations from foreign nations have not passed unnoticed. The experiences of the last three decades will probably prove more momentous for the Chinese than those of any previous century in their history, and these have not come about without much bitterness and the surly traces of misunderstanding and misrepresentation. But the great fact must have become apparent, even to the cursory reader, that in the Chinese character are elements which in due time must lift her out of the terribly backward position into which she had fallen and raise her to a rank among the foremost of nations. There is a basis of encouragement when we keep in mind the literary institutions of the country and their early attention to obtaining a corps of scientific men of their own nationality, as in the effort just mentioned.[1]

[1] The reserved force in the Chinese character was very strikingly brought out in a new-year's call at Peking, which the writer remembers, in 1870. The topic came up as to how to diminish the expense of getting coal from the mines to the city (which up to that time was carried on camels and mules), so as to put it within the reach of the poor people. I suggested a tram road as the best plan for the fifty miles distance from the mines, and involving trifling expense. After listening to the plan, Tan Ting-siang, one of the members of the Board of Revenue, and Prince Kung, together exclaimed, "*Tieh-lu lai liao! Tieh-lu lai liao!*" ('Railroads are coming in time'). The ex-

Another ground of hope—and these words are as pertinent to-day as when written thirty-five years ago—lies in the matter-of-fact habits of the Chinese, their want of enthusiasm and dislike of change, which are rather favorable than otherwise to their development as a great community. The presentation and reception of the highest truths and motives the human mind can realize always excites thought and action ; the chiefest fear must be that of going too fast in schemes of reform and correction, and demolishing the fabric before its elements are ready for reconstruction. The non-existence of caste, the weakness of a priesthood which cannot nerve its persecuting arm with the power of the State, the scanty influence religion has over the popular mind, the simplicity of ancestral worship, the absence of the allurements of gorgeous temples, splendid ritual, seductive music, gay processions, and above all, sanctified licentiousness, to uphold and render it enticing to depraved human nature, the popular origin of all government holidays, and lastly, the degree of industry, loyalty, and respect for life and property—these are characteristics which furnish some grounds for trusting that the regeneration of China will be accomplished, like the operation of leaven in meal, without shivering the vessel.

---

istence of the treaty principle of ex-territoriality and its consequences is constantly before the Chinese high officers, though they appreciate as well the fact that their country is preparing and will be the better for such improvements.

INDEX.

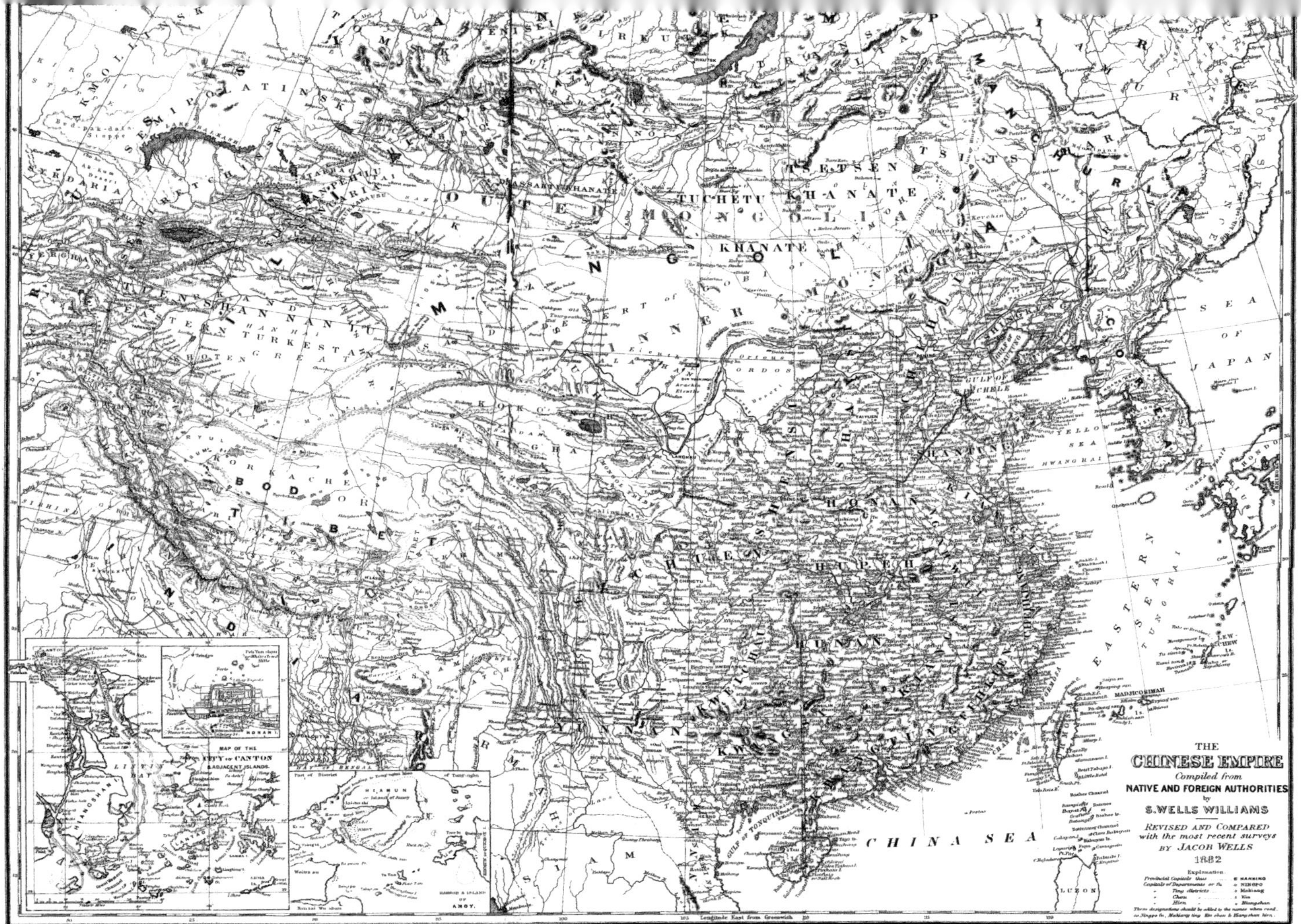

Copyright 1883. By Charles Scribner's Sons.

G. Stern, Engraver

For Product Safety Concerns and Information please contact our EU representative GPSR@taylorandfrancis.com Taylor & Francis Verlag GmbH, Kaufingerstraße 24, 80331 München, Germany

Batch number: 10726515

Printed by Printforce, the Netherlands